W9-AHJ-684

JOURNEY MIDDLE SCHOOL		
YEAR	STUDENT NAME	DIV.
~~	~~~~~~~~~~ Cody M 5th 03	
	Bobby Gunderson	7
	Kyle Brian Murphy	7
	TRAMPUS CHOOPMAN	7

29 - 34
Chapters
Read.

WORLD HISTORY

Title Page: With the invention of writing, it became possible to record history and thereby share in the events of the past

WORLD HISTORY

Jerome R. Reich/Mark M. Krug
Edward L. Biller

HOLT, RINEHART AND WINSTON
AUSTIN NEW YORK SAN DIEGO CHICAGO TORONTO MONTREAL

About the Authors

Jerome R. Reich is Professor of History at Chicago State College. Dr. Reich received his Ph.D. in history from the University of Chicago. He has written a study of Leisler's Rebellion and has contributed articles to numerous publications. He is co-author of a number of textbooks, including the American history textbook *Building the American Nation*.

Mark M. Krug is Professor of Education in History at the Department of Education of the University of Chicago, where he directs the training of history and social studies teachers. Dr. Krug received his Ph.D. in history at the University of Chicago. Dr. Krug was chairman of the study project on teaching U.S. History, of the Organization of American Historians. His writings include many articles in a variety of scholarly publication, biographies of Aneurin Bevan and Lyman Trumbull, the studies *History and the Social Studies* and *Teaching World History—A Global Perspective*.

Edward L. Biller is retired from the Baltimore City Public Schools, where he was a Specialist in Curriculum and Staff Development. He also served as Supervisor of Social Studies, Coordinator of Curriculum, and Supervisor of Geography. Mr. Biller is co-author of several social studies textbooks, including *Story of the American Nation, The World Around Us, America: Its People and Values* and, with Dr. Reich, *Building the American Nation* and *United States History*.

Acknowledgments

The quotations that appear on the following pages were taken from the sources listed: p. 87, "Twenty-fourth Psalm," *Holy Bible*, Revised Standard Version (New York: Thomas Nelson and Sons, 1952); p. 124, *The Wisdom of Confucius*, edited and translated by Lin Yutang (New York: Random House, 1938); p. 145, Plato, *The Republic*, Book 2 (Chicago: Great Books Foundation, 1948); p. 215, Geoffrey Chaucer, *The Canterbury Tales*, translated by Nevill Coghill (New York: Penguin Books, 1977); p. 405, J. H. Robinson and M. Whitcomb, eds., *Translations and Reprints from Original Sources of European History*, vol. 2, no. 6 (Philadelphia: University of Pennsylvania, 1975); p. 348, Thomas Aquinas, "Treatise on Law," *Summa Theologica* (Chicago: Great Books Foundation, 1948); p. 463, Thomas Paine, *The Crisis*, no. 1 (December 23, 1776); p. 623, Nikolai Lenin, *Religion* and *State and Revolution*, in George Seldes, *The Great Quotations* (New York: Lyle Stuart, 1960); p. 646, Mohandas Gandhi, in Louis Fischer, *The Essential Gandhi* (New York: Random House, 1962); p. 744, "Thatcher Sees Benefits for West If Gorbachev Reshapes U.S.S.R.," *The New York Times*, September 28, 1988; p. 751, Mikhail Gorbachev, excerpt from speech to Communist Party conference, *The New York Times*, June 29, 1988; p. 778, James Joyce, *A Portrait of the Artist as a Young Man* (New York: Viking, 1982).

Copyright © 1990, 1984 by Holt, Rinehart and Winston, Inc.

All rights reserved. No part of this publication may be reproduced or transmitted in any form or by any means, electronic or mechanical, including photocopy, recording, or any information storage and retrieval system, without permission in writing from the publisher.

Requests for permission to make copies of any part of the work should be mailed to: Copyrights and Permissions Department, Holt, Rinehart and Winston, Inc., 1627 Woodland Avenue, Austin, Texas 78741.

Printed in the United States of America

5 069 98765

ISBN 0-03-028898-3

CONTENTS

Maps

Special Features

Introduction to World History

The world you live in today is an exciting and fast-moving place. You can watch television and see things as they are happening in other lands thousands of miles away. You could even fly to these faraway lands in a few hours on a jet plane. It is easy to see why the world today certainly is an interesting place. But the world always has seemed interesting and exciting to the people who lived in it. As you will discover, the story of the world's people is as exciting as any adventure story you ever read.

World history is the true story, or the record, of the people who lived on the earth during past years. World history tells you about the lives of men and women in all parts of the world. It tells the story of the peoples who lived in Europe, Africa, Asia, and in North America and South America. World history tells you about each of these peoples' ways of living. It tells you the kinds of work these peoples did, how they dressed, and what their family life was like. World history tells you about the religion, the art, and the writings of these peoples.

World history also tells you about the great nations and great empires that these peoples built in their lands. It tells you about the famous men and women who were the leaders of these peoples. It tells you about wars that peoples fought to conquer other lands or to protect their own land.

World history tells you about many important events, or things that happened to the peoples of the world. As you read about these events in history, you will also find out why these events happened, when they happened, and how they affected the peoples' lives.

Grand Canyon, Arizona

Unit 1
The Story of Early People

THE CHAPTERS IN UNIT 1 ARE

1 The Earliest People
2 People in the Old Stone Age
3 People in the New Stone Age

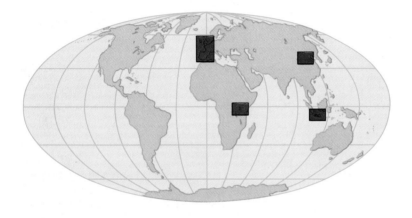

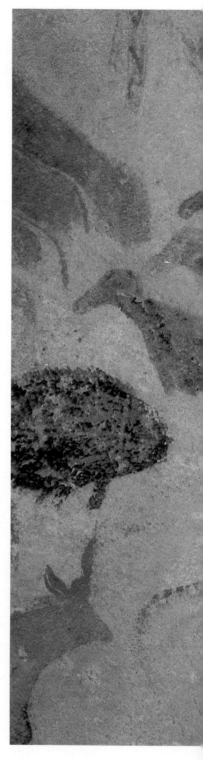

Many scientists believe that the earliest people lived on earth over one million years ago. During these early years, people slowly learned how to improve their lives. They learned to use stone tools and to hunt animals. Later, they began to farm, to settle down in groups, and to live in villages. In this unit, you will learn about these early people.

Prehistoric cave painting showing animals being herded

Chapter 1
The Earliest People

GETTING STARTED

1   The events that you will be reading about in this chapter do not tell about important persons whose names are known. This chapter tells something about what is thought to be the earliest humanlike people who lived a very long time ago.

Scientists have to make various guesses about these early people. But clues show that they lived on earth more than 1 million years ago. The early people you will read about in this chapter lived from about 1 million B.C. to about 40,000 B.C.

2   Before you begin reading the chapter lesson, "survey" the lesson, or look over the lesson, to find out what it is about. First, read the beginning of the lesson. Then look through the lesson and read the headings. The headings are the words in larger black letters that tell what the different parts of the lesson are about. Next, study the pictures to learn what they show. Read the captions, or the words that describe each picture. Then study the map on page 20, which shows where the earliest people lived. Finally, read the review section called "Summing Up" at the end of the lesson. This survey will help you to discover the important ideas in this chapter.

Know the Main Idea

As you read the chapter lesson, try to remember the following important MAIN IDEA of the chapter.

The earliest people appeared over 1 million years ago. The first type of modern people did not appear until about 40,000 B.C.

The following questions will help you to understand the MAIN IDEA. Try to answer these questions as you read the lesson.

1. Where did scientists find the remains of the earliest known people?
2. In what three ways were early people different from animals?
3. Which men and women were the first type of modern people?

Know These Important Terms

prehistoric people	Homo sapiens
Neanderthal	Cro-Magnon

Know the Years of This Chapter

Look at the time line below. It shows the years of this chapter, about 1 million B.C. to about 40,000 B.C.

1 million B.C.	40,000 B.C.	4000 B.C.

Prehistoric cave painting showing people, cattle, and a hut.
What does this painting reveal about the way prehistoric
people lived?

EXPLORING THE TIME

Who were the earliest people on earth?
What were they like? How did these early
people live? How are modern men and
women different from these early people?
In this chapter, you will learn some interesting things about the first people who lived
on earth.

Some Very Early People Lived in East Africa

The earliest people on earth are known as
prehistoric (PREE-hiss-TOR-ik) **people.** "Prehistoric" means "before written history." In
recent years, scientists in East Africa have
discovered what they think are the remains
ot the earliest prehistoric people. These
"East Africa humans" lived over 1 million

19

THE EARLIEST PEOPLE

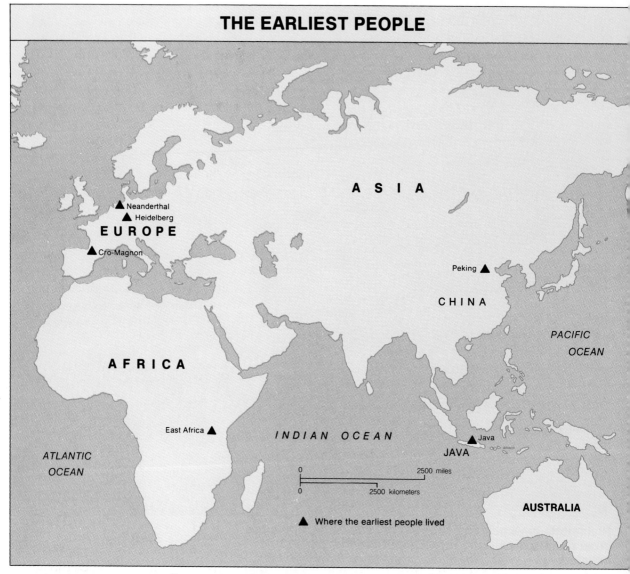

On which continents did the earliest people live?

years ago. Some scientists believe these early people appeared over 2 million years ago. Remains of these early East Africa humans were discovered only recently. Scientists are trying to learn more about them. But they believe East Africa humans were the first type of early people.

Other Early People Lived in Europe and Asia

Another type of early person was "Java human," who appeared over ½ million years ago. These early Java humans lived on the island of Java, off the coast of southeastern Asia. "Peking human," who lived in China, and "Heidelberg (HY-del-BURG) human," who lived in Europe, were other types of early people. However, they appeared after Java people. The humans found in Peking and Heidelberg had larger brains than the one found in Java. What were these early people like, and how did they live?

Early People Learned to Improve Their Lives

The earliest people probably lived much like animals. They ate small animals or fish that they caught with their hands, and they lived in caves or trees. But even these very early men and women were "human beings" and not animals. What was it about early people that made them "human"?

Human beings' better and larger brains were the most important things that made them "human." People were able to use their brains to remember and to plan ahead. People learned how to do things, and they used what they learned to improve their ways of living. In this way, human beings were very different from animals.

People used their larger and better brains to learn more and more about the world around them. After many thousands of years of development, people were able to overcome many dangers and to win control of the world they lived in.

Early People Made Tools and Developed Ideas

Another thing that made people "human" was their ability to use their hands. Slowly, early people learned to use their hands to make tools and weapons. And these tools and weapons helped early men and women to protect themselves and to stay alive.

The ability to speak was also very important. Early people slowly were able to develop a language, or way of expressing their ideas. In this way, early men and women began to exchange ideas with each other. These ideas helped them to find food and shelter and to warn each other of danger.

Early People Slowly Developed into Modern Men and Women

Long after East Africa humans and Peking humans lived, another type of early person appeared, called **Neanderthal** (nee-AN-dur-THAL). Neanderthal humans lived in Europe and in other parts of the world from about 70,000 B.C. to 40,000 B.C. Anthropologists have found that Neanderthal humans

Famous anthropologist Mary Leakey and a colleague study human remains in Africa

This site containing the bones of bison tells scientists that people once hunted there

had broad, short bodies and heavy shoulders. Their heads were large, and they walked fully erect. But Neanderthal humans were different from earlier people in one important way. The brain was almost as large as the brain of a modern person.

Neanderthal humans are considered to belong to a group of people that appeared about 40,000 B.C. called **Homo sapiens** (HOH-moh SAY-pih-ENZ), or "thinking person." **Cro-Magnon** (kro-MAG-nun) **humans** were also Homo sapiens. They appeared in Europe, Africa, and Asia. Cro-Magnon humans were tall, stood straight, and were strong. They had a much larger brain and were better at using tools and weapons than were cave people.

SUMMING UP

The earliest people on earth lived over 1 million—or perhaps 2 million—years ago in East Africa. But East Africa humans and all other early people were very different from people of today. The first type of modern person was Homo sapiens, or "thinking person," who appeared about 40,000 B.C. In the next chapter, you will find out how early prehistoric people lived.

UNDERSTANDING THE LESSON

Do You Know These Important Terms?

For each sentence below, choose the term that best completes the sentence.

1. The earliest people who lived on earth are called **(ancient people/prehistoric people)**.
2. A group of people that appeared about 40,000 B.C. are called **(Homo sapiens/ Java humans)** or "thinking person."
3. The **(Neanderthal human/Cro-Magnon human)** appeared in Europe, Africa, and Asia.
4. **(Neanderthal humans/prehistoric people)** had broad, short bodies and heavy shoulders.

Do You Remember These People and Events?

1. Tell something about each of the following prehistoric people.

East Africa	Neanderthal
Java	Homo sapiens
Peking	Cro-Magnon
Heidelberg	

2. Many important things happened during the long period of years in prehistoric times. Try to explain how each of the following developments of prehistoric times may have happened.

   a. People learned to think.
   b. People learned to walk on two feet.
   c. People learned to speak.

Can You Locate These Places?

Use the map on page 20 to do the following map work.

1. Find the following places on the map.

Africa	Asia
China	Europe
Java	

2. Tell how each location is related to the developments in this chapter.

Do You Know When It Happened?

About what year did Homo sapiens, or "thinking person," appear on earth?

Do You Remember the Main Idea?

Which one of the following ideas is the MAIN IDEA of this chapter?

1. Early people learned how to think, how to plan, how to make tools, and how to speak about 30,000 B.C.
2. Modern people developed from the most advanced type of early prehistoric people.
3. The earliest human appeared over 1 million years ago. The first type of modern humans did not appear until about 40,000 B.C.

What Do You Think?

From what you have read in this chapter, try to answer the following thought questions.

1. What do you imagine prehistoric people were like?
2. Why is it difficult to know about early prehistoric people?
3. Why do you think prehistoric people lived together in small groups?

Chapter 2
People in the Old Stone Age

GETTING STARTED

1   Life was very difficult for the earliest people! They faced many dangers and hardships in hunting animals for food. They did not have fire for heating or clothing for warmth. If the climate changed from warm to cold, they were forced to move to a warmer place. But, in time, the early people slowly learned how to change their ways of living in order to meet their needs.

During the long period of years from about 1 million B.C., early people were beginning to develop their first simple tools. And by 8000 B.C., some early people were beginning to develop better tools and so better ways of living.

2   Before you being reading the chapter lesson, survey the lesson. Begin your survey by reading the beginning of the lesson. Then look through the lesson and read the headings. Next, study the pictures and read the picture captions—the words that tell about each picture. Then study the map showing the Ice Age on page 26. Finally, read the review section called "Summing Up" at the end of the lesson. This survey will help you to discover the important ideas in this chapter.

Know the Main Idea

As you read the chapter lesson, try to remember the following important MAIN IDEA of the chapter.

During the Old Stone Age, people learned to make tools and weapons. They developed simple, but successful, ways to live.

The following questions will help you to understand the MAIN IDEA. Try to answer these questions as you read the lesson.

1. What kinds of tools and weapons did prehistoric men and women have?
2. What great changes took place in early people's ways of living?
3. What was prehistoric people's main supply of food?

Know These Important Terms

culture	Old Stone Age
archeology	glaciers
archeologists	hand ax
Stone Age	cave paintings

Know the Years of This Chapter

Look at the time line. It shows the years of this chapter, 1 million B.C. to 8000 B.C.

1 million B.C.	8000 B.C.	4000 B.C.

Rock painting showing a hunter with a camel

EXPLORING THE TIME

All peoples develop a certain way of life, or ways of living, called a **culture.** The culture, or ways of living, developed by a people includes their way of behaving, their knowledge, their tools, and their beliefs. Prehistoric people, or early people, also developed a culture, as you will learn in this chapter.

How We Learn About Early People's Past

In recent years, we have begun to learn more about the culture of prehistoric people. Most of the things they used disappeared long ago. But we now are able to learn many things about early people through **archeology** (ARR-kee-AWL-uh-gee). Archeology is the study of people's past from the objects, or things, that they left

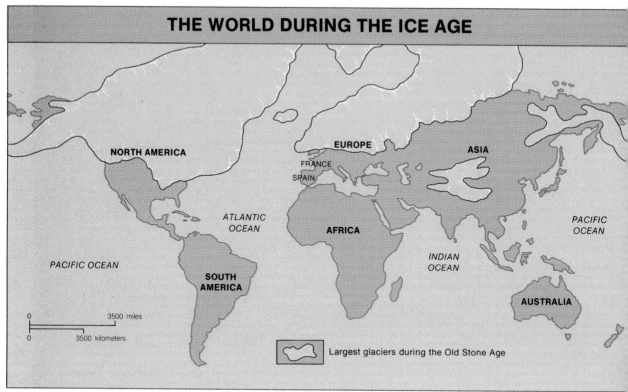

THE WORLD DURING THE ICE AGE

NORTH AMERICA

EUROPE

ASIA

FRANCE

SPAIN

ATLANTIC
OCEAN

AFRICA

PACIFIC
OCEAN

PACIFIC OCEAN

INDIAN
OCEAN

SOUTH
AMERICA

AUSTRALIA

0   3500 miles

0   3500 kilometers

Largest glaciers during the Old Stone Age

Which continents were untouched by the Ice Age glaciers?

behind—such as tools, weapons, and pottery.

Perhaps you have seen pictures of **archeologists,** or people who study archeology, digging up remains of old buildings or searching in caves. From time to time, archeologists find things that help us to learn important facts about prehistoric life.

Early People Made Their Tools of Stone

Archeologists have discovered that prehistoric people used many stone tools. For this reason, the long period of years when prehistoric men and women lived on earth is called the **Stone Age.** Archeologists sometimes divide this long period into two parts. The first part, called the **Old Stone Age,** began when early men and women first appeared about 1 million years ago. The second part, the New Stone Age, began about 8000 B.C. and lasted to about 4000 B.C.

The Ice Age Changed Early People's Lives

The Old Stone Age occurred during what is called the "Ice Age." During much of the Ice Age, the northern parts of North America, Europe, and Asia were very cold. These lands were covered with huge, thick sheets of ice called **glaciers** (GLAY-shurs). Many prehistoric animals and plants died from the cold. Some early people were forced to move to warmer places. But other early people found ways to live in the cold north.

Early People Began to Wear Clothing

To protect themselves from the cold, prehistoric people learned to wear clothing. The first clothes were made from skins of animals. Archeologists have not found any of these skins, but they have found bone "buttons" and bone "needles" used by early men and women to sew their clothing.

Early People Discovered the Use of Fire

Fire also was very important in the lives of early people. When and how did early people first learn to use fire? No one really knows. Perhaps early people learned to use fire when they saw a tree burn after it was struck by lightning. At first, they knew only how to keep such a natural fire going. Later, they learned how to make their own fire by rubbing sticks of dry wood or hitting stones together. Prehistoric people then learned to use fire for heat, for cooking, for light, and to frighten away dangerous animals.

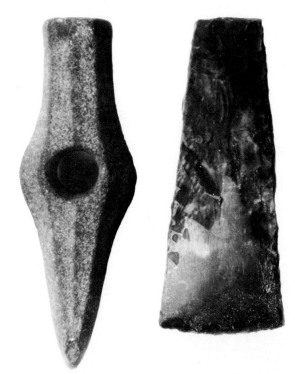

Stone axes were made by people during the Old Stone Age

Early People Learned to Make Better Tools

Early people also needed better tools and weapons. The first tools and weapons probably were stones. Early people simply picked up a stone when they wanted to hit or to scrape something. When they were finished, they threw the stone away.

Slowly, prehistoric people began to make stones into more useful tools. They did this by chipping the stone until it became very sharp. One of the tools they produced by chipping a stone was the **hand ax.** Hand axes were probably used for cutting and chopping, and also as weapons. Sometimes Old Stone Age people tied handles to the axes to make them into better weapons.

Men and women of the Old Stone Age used stone as drills, chisels, daggers, and tips for their spears. They also carved bones to make fishhooks, fish spears, needles, and buttons. By the end of the Old Stone Age, people also learned how to build canoes and sleds for moving from place to place.

Early People Hunted for Their Food

The Old Stone Age people were mainly hunters, and meat was their most important food. These people knew nothing about raising animals or farming. They ate whatever animals they killed, whatever fish

During the Old Stone Age, huge ice sheets called glaciers covered much of the earth

they caught, and whatever wild fruits and plants they found growing. Early people moved from place to place to find food. And a good hunting catch often decided whether they lived or died of hunger.

By the end of the Old Stone Age, animals became so important to prehistoric people that they painted pictures of animals on their cave walls. Some of these **cave paintings** in bright, beautiful colors can be seen today in caves in France and in Spain. Why did people paint these pictures? Was it to bring themselves luck on their hunts for animals? Was it to exchange hunting ideas with other hunters? We do not know. Whatever the reason, these beautiful, colorful cave paintings tell us how important animals were to early people.

SUMMING UP

The long period of years when early people lived on earth is called the Stone Age. We are now beginning to learn more about what happened in these years. We know that early people made stone tools and weapons. And we know that early people used these tools and weapons to hunt animals for food. In the next chapter, you will find out more about how early people lived.

UNDERSTANDING THE LESSON

Do You Know These Important Terms?

For each sentence below, choose the term that best completes the sentence.

1. The ways of living developed by a people are called their (nation/culture).
2. (Surveying/Archeology) is the study of people's past from the objects they left behind, such as tools, weapons, and pottery.
3. (Surveyors/Archeologists) study the objects left from prehistoric times.
4. The long period of years when prehistoric people lived on earth is called the (Stone Age/Glacier Age).
5. The first part of the Stone Age is sometimes called the (First Stone Age/Old Stone Age).
6. Huge, thick sheets of ice that cover land are called (glaciers/icebergs).
7. One of the tools produced by chipping stone was the (fire maker/hand ax).
8. Paintings made by prehistoric men and women on cave walls are called (cave paintings/prehistoric magic).

Do You Remember These People and Events?

1. Tell something about each of the following subjects.

   a. Archeologists.
   b. Ice Age.
   c. Early tools.
   d. Early clothing.
   e. Early use of animals.
   f. The discovery of fire.

Can You Locate These Places?

Use the map showing the Ice Age on page 26 to find the following places. Tell how each place is related to the developments in this chapter.

North America	**France**	**Asia**
Europe	**Spain**	

Do You Know When It Happened?

The Old Stone Age began about 1 million years ago. About what year did it end?

Do You Remember the Main idea?

Which one of the following ideas is the MAIN IDEA of this chapter?

1. Archeologists know very little about the life of prehistoric people. But they have discovered a few tools of early people.
2. During the Old Stone Age, people learned to make tools and weapons. They developed simple, but successful, ways to live.
3. Prehistoric people painted pictures of animals on cave walls because they believed in magic.

What Do You Think?

From what you have read in this chapter, try to answer the following thought questions.

1. Explain how prehistoric people may have discovered that a handle made it easier to use an ax.
2. After prehistoric people discovered fire, how do you suppose they learned to cook their food?
3. Give several reasons to explain why prehistoric men and women wished to paint pictures of animals on cave walls.

Chapter 3
People in the New Stone Age

GETTING STARTED

1   Today, people try to improve their lives, or to make their lives better, in every way that they can. Prehistoric people also tried to improve their lives. As a result, they slowly developed better ways of doing things. For example, prehistoric people wanted and needed better tools. They needed better tools in order to perform more difficult tasks. Therefore, they set to work inventing better tools.

During the years from 8000 B.C. to 4000 B.C., early people made so many improvements in their tools and ways of doing things that new ways of living began to take shape. And these improved ways of living led to the beginning of modern history.

2   Before you begin reading the chapter lesson, survey the lesson. Begin your survey by reading the beginning of the lesson. Then look through the lesson and read the headings. Next, study the pictures and read the captions—the words that tell about each picture. Finally, read the review section called "Summing Up" at the end of the lesson. This survey of the lesson will help you to discover the important ideas in this chapter.

Know the Main Idea

As you read the chapter lesson, try to remember the following important MAIN IDEA of the chapter.

During the New Stone Age, prehistoric people greatly improved their ways of living.

The following questions will help you to understand the MAIN IDEA. Try to answer these questions as you read the lesson.

1. How did a change in climate affect people living in the New Stone Age?
2. What were some of the important changes during the New Stone Age?
3. How did New Stone Age people develop government and religion?

Know These Important Terms

New Stone Age	temples
domesticate	government
artisans	

Know the Years of This Chapter

Look at the time line below. It shows the years of this chapter, 8000 B.C. to 4000 B.C.

1 million B.C.   **8000 B.C.   4000 B.C.**

Prehistoric millstone used for grinding. How do you think these stones were used for grinding grain?

EXPLORING THE TIME

About 8000 B.C., many important changes began to take place in early people's lives. In this chapter you will read about these important changes. You will learn how early people's ways of living improved during the years of the New Stone Age.

A New Age Began as the Ice Age Ended

If you remember, much of the northern part of the world was covered with glaciers during the Old Stone Age. About 8000 B.C., however, the glaciers began to melt, and the climate grew warmer. As this happened, a new period began in early human development. This period is called the **New**

Stone Age. The New Stone Age lasted from about 8000 B.C. to about 4000 B.C. During the New Stone Age, prehistoric people improved many of their ways of living.

New Stone Age People Began Farming

The New Stone Age people began to change their ways of getting a food supply. For thousands of years, prehistoric people had depended mainly on hunting animals to get food. However, as the climate grew warmer, many animals were not able to live in this climate, and they moved away or died. People now had to find new ways of getting food.

One new way of getting food was by farming. As the climate became warmer, new plants appeared. The New Stone Age men and women learned how to supply their own food by growing wheat and barley, and fruit and vegetables. Before long, New Stone Age people began to use a hoe to soften the earth for planting and watering. They learned to make a sickle to cut the wheat and barley that they grew.

New animals also appeared during the New Stone Age. Some of these animals were easy to **domesticate,** or tame. The New Stone Age people domesticated dogs, sheep, goats, cattle, and pigs, which supplied both food and clothing skins for their owners.

Reconstruction of a New Stone Age site, 6000 B.C. Which building was probably the temple? Why?

32

New Stone Age People Began to Settle Down

The change from hunting food to growing food led to very important changes in New Stone Age people's ways of living. As long as people were mainly food hunters, they were always forced to move from place to place to find food. But as people turned to farming and to taming animals, they now had a more dependable food supply. People were able to settle down, build huts, live in larger groups, and form villages.

New Stone Age People Became Artisans

The change to farming led to other changes in living, too. Sometimes farmers grew more food than they needed. Sometimes they were not able to grow enough food. Toward the end of the New Stone Age, people began making pottery, or pots of baked clay, which they used for storing extra food for the times when food was scarce.

Some people began to specialize, or to do special jobs, such as making pottery. These people then traded some of their pottery for food. Other people specialized in making tools. They traded their extra tools for food. People who specialize in making a product are called artisans. These artisans also were able to improve their products all during the New Stone Age.

New Stone Age People Worshiped Many Gods

Prehistoric people believed that powerful gods of nature controlled their lives. They believed that these gods controlled the rainfall, the rising and the setting of the sun, the moon, and the food supply. Prehistoric

Prehistoric drawing of an animal

people may have believed that they needed to please these gods in order to have their crops grow and their animal herds increase. These beliefs may have been the beginning of religious practices.

During the New Stone Age, the village people built **temples,** or places to worship their gods. Some people became priests, or leaders of religion. The priest's main duty was to watch over the temple to see that the gods were kept happy. This duty was so important that the priest was often the most powerful person in the village.

New Stone Age Governments

In the Old Stone Age, the main job of the leader of a small group of people was to decide when to go hunting and how to divide up the food. But in a New Stone Age village, new and difficult problems arose.

For example, where did one person's farm end and another's farm begin? What

Prehistoric rock painting showing a hunter. What are the hunter's weapons?

happened when two people said that they owned the same goat? To settle these problems, some kind of **government** was needed. A government is a group of people who make the rules, or laws, that people must obey. In a New Stone Age village, the government was usually headed by the priest. The priest ruled the village with the help of a council, or group of wise people.

Modern Human History Began About 4000 B.C.

These important changes in early people's ways of living during the New Stone Age led to the beginning of modern people's history about 4000 B.C. You will begin to study this history in the next chapter.

SUMMING UP

During the New Stone Age, early people made better tools and weapons and settled down in farming villages. Religion became important, and village governments were set up. These important changes in early people's ways of living led to the beginning of modern history. In the next chapter, which begins Unit 2, you will read about Mesopotamia, one of the earliest nations in history.

UNDERSTANDING THE LESSON

Do You Know These Important Terms?

For each sentence below, choose the term that best completes the sentence.

1. The period from about 8000 B.C. to 4000 B.C. is usually called the (**New Stone Age/Age of Invention**).
2. Early people learned to (**corral/domesticate**), or tame, animals such as dogs, sheep, goats, cattle, and pigs.
3. People who are skilled at making certain products are called (**artisans/workers**).
4. Early men and women built places to worship their gods, and these places are called (**monuments/temples**).
5. A group of people who make the laws that people must obey is called a (**government/corral**).

Do You Remember These Events?

1. Tell something about each of the following subjects.

   a. Prehistoric farming.
   b. Better weapons and tools.
   c. New use of animals.
   d. Prehistoric religion.
   e. Prehistoric government.

2. The following developments in prehistoric times were very important. Try to explain how each of these developments might have happened.

   a. Prehistoric people learned to domesticate, or tame, animals.
   b. Prehistoric men and women began to worship many gods.

   c. Prehistoric people set up governments.

Do You Know When It Happened?

Tell why the following years are important.

   about 8000 B.C.   **about 4000** B.C.

Do You Remember the Main Idea?

Which one of the following ideas is the MAIN IDEA of this chapter?

1. During the New Stone Age, prehistoric people greatly improved their ways of living.
2. After the Ice Age ended, prehistoric people settled in villages and towns.
3. Prehistoric people provided a better food supply for themselves by farming and by domesticating animals.

What Do You Think?

From what you have read in this chapter, try to answer the following thought questions.

1. Which prehistoric development was the most important? Explain why you think so.
2. What kinds of problems do you think developed in an early prehistoric village?
3. Give some reasons why prehistoric men and women might have developed ideas about religion.

Unit 2
The Peoples of Mesopotamia

THE CHAPTERS IN UNIT 2 ARE

4 Mesopotamia—the "Land Between the Rivers"
5 Life in Mesopotamia
6 Mesopotamian Culture

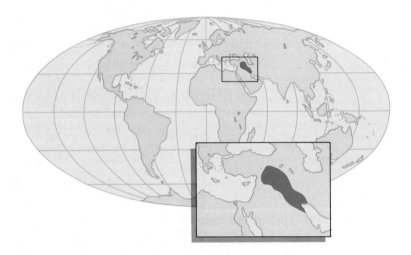

Many early nations were located in the lands of the Near East. Mesopotamia was one of the most important of these nations. The land of Mesopotamia was settled and ruled by several different peoples during its long history. In this unit, you will find out about the peoples of Mesopotamia.

Relief showing Assyrian warriors

Chapter 4

Mesopotamia—the "Land Between the Rivers"

GETTING STARTED

1 Many early peoples were wanderers who moved from place to place looking for a good location, or place, to settle down. Some of these early peoples traveled over very great distances.

From their travels, these early peoples learned that all locations were not alike. Some locations were better than other locations for building settlements. This chapter tells about several groups of people who discovered and settled in good locations between the years 4000 B.C. and 538 B.C.

2 Before you begin reading the chapter lesson, survey the lesson. Begin your survey by reading the beginning of the lesson. Then look through the lesson and read the headings. Next, study the pictures and read the picture captions. Then study the map of the Near East and Mesopotamia on page 41. Finally, read the review section called "Summing Up" at the end of the lesson. This survey will help you to discover the important ideas in this chapter.

Know the Main Idea

As you read the chapter lesson, try to remember the following important MAIN IDEA of the chapter.

Mesopotamia developed one of the great cultures of early history. However, Mesopotamia was overrun and ruled by different peoples many times.

The following questions will help you to understand the MAIN IDEA. Try to answer these questions as you read the lesson.

1. What people developed the first great culture in Mesopotamia?
2. Why was it easy for invading peoples to overrun Mesopotamia?
3. Who were some of the invading peoples who conquered Mesopotamia?

Know These Important Terms

Near East	city-states
Sumerians	Code of Laws
irrigation	empire

Know the Years of This Chapter

Look at the time line below. It shows the years of this chapter, 4000 B.C. to 538 B.C.

4000 B.C.	538 B.C.	100 B.C.

Relief showing Assyrian archers from the capital city of Nineveh. What protective gear are they wearing?

EXPLORING THE TIME

The people of early history soon discovered that warm river valleys were good places to live. One of these places was a land called Mesopotamia (MES-uh-puh-TAY-mee-uh) in the **Near East.** The Near East includes the lands at the eastern end of the Mediterranean Sea and the lands of southwestern Asia. In this chapter, you will learn about the early peoples who settled in the river valleys of Mesopotamia, a name that means the "land between the rivers."

Mesopotamia's River Valleys Provided Good Farming Land

Mesopotamia was located in the valley of the Tigris (TY-gris) River and the Euphrates (you-FRAY-teez) River. These two rivers flow from the mountains of Asia Minor southward to the Persian (PURR-zhun) Gulf. Mesopotamia's climate was hot and dry, but its soil was rich. As a result, many peoples settled in Mesopotamia and became farmers.

However, Mesopotamia did not have any high mountains or wide, hard-to-cross

Every summer, the Tigris River and Euphrates River flowed over their banks and flooded the nearby land

deserts to protect it from attack by outsiders. As a result, all during its long history, Mesopotamia was overrun by one group of people after another.

The Sumerians Settled in Mesopotamia

The first settlers of Mesopotamia probably wandered into Mesopotamia during the New Stone Age. These people learned how to tame animals and how to farm the land. They then settled down in villages in the northern part of Mesopotamia.

About the year 4000 B.C., another group of people settled in Mesopotamia, near the Persian Gulf. These people were called the **Sumerians** (soo-MER-ee-unz). The Sumerians developed skills that later were also learned by all the peoples in lands around the Near East.

The Sumerians Developed a Way of Watering the Soil

One important skill developed by the Sumerians was **irrigation,** or a means of watering the land with river water. Every summer, the Tigris River and Euphrates

THE NEAR EAST AND MESOPOTAMIA

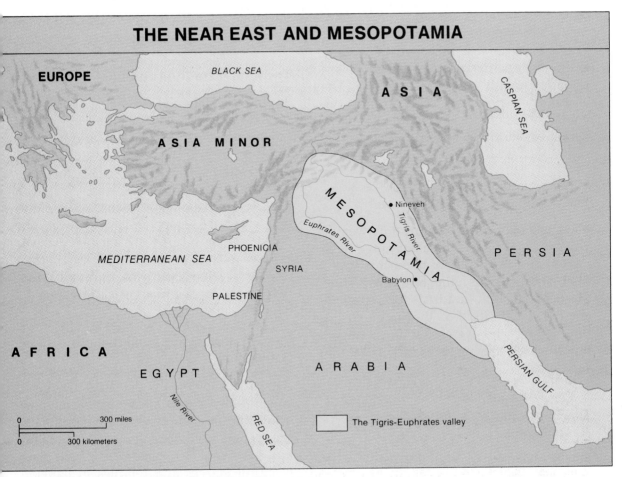

EUROPE

BLACK SEA

ASIA

CASPIAN SEA

ASIA MINOR

MESOPOTAMIA

• Nineveh

Tigris River

Euphrates River

PERSIA

PHOENICIA

MEDITERRANEAN SEA

SYRIA

Babylon •

PALESTINE

AFRICA

EGYPT

ARABIA

PERSIAN GULF

Nile River

RED SEA

0   300 miles
0   300 kilometers

The Tigris-Euphrates valley

Into which body of water do the Tigris River and the Euphrates River flow?

River flowed over their banks and flooded the nearby land. Sometimes these floods brought too much water. Sometimes the floods did not bring enough water to keep the crops growing during the rest of the year.

To provide water all year long, the Sumerians dug large ditches. During flood times, river water flowed through the ditches into pools, where it was stored for future use. This irrigation system helped the Sumerians water their crops and grow enough food to feed many people.

Mesopotamian Cities Became One Nation

By 3000 B.C., the Sumerians lived in many cities. Each city had its own god and a chief priest for that god. The people believed that the god ruled the city by giving orders to the priest. They believed that the priest then carried out the god's orders. In this way, the chief priest really ruled the city.

These early cities of Mesopotamia were really small countries, or **city-states**. Often, these city-states fought wars with each other to conquer more lands or to gain a new water supply. However, the city-states began to learn that they had to work together to build irrigation ditches in order to provide enough water for everyone. They also needed a stronger army to fight their enemies. Therefore, these cities joined together and formed one nation under one ruler called a king.

The Sumerians Lost Their Power

Mesopotamia's king had great power. He was the chief priest, the chief judge of the nation, and the leader of the army. Led by their strong kings, the Sumerians ruled Mesopotamia for hundreds of years. But about the year 2500 B.C., the Sumerians lost their power and were conquered. Again, the cities of Mesopotamia began to fight each other.

The Babylonians Conquered Mesopotamia

Finally, Babylon (BAB-uh-lon) became the most powerful city in Mesopotamia, and it conquered most of Mesopotamia. The most important early ruler of the Babylonians (BAB-uh-LOH-nee-unz) was Hammurabi (HAM-muh-RAH-bee).

Hammurabi is remembered today for his famous **Code of Laws,** or collection of laws, which was written down in 1700 B.C. This Code of Laws was one of the first collections, or sets, of laws used to rule a whole nation.

Babylon remained the most powerful city in Mesopotamia for a long time. The only other important city in these years was Nineveh (NIN-uh-vuh), the capital city of the Assyrians (uh-SEER-ee-unz). The Assyr-

ians were a warlike people who lived in the northern part of Mesopotamia.

The Assyrians Built and Lost an Empire

During the 700's and 600's B.C., the powerful Assyrian army conquered all of Mesopotamia and Egypt, and all the land between these countries. The Assyrian kings built a great **empire,** or a strong nation that conquered and ruled many lands. Nineveh then replaced Babylon as the most important city in Mesopotamia. However, the Assyrian kings ruled so harshly that the peoples in their empire fought to win their freedom. After about one hundred years, the Assyrian Empire was defeated by Babylon's armies.

The Persians Conquered the Babylonians

After the Babylonians defeated the Assyrians, the city of Babylon again became powerful. The best known Babylonian king of this period was Nebuchadnezzar (NEB-uh-kud-NEHZ-ur). Nebuchadnezzar built many beautiful palaces and temples in Babylon. But Babylon did not remain powerful. In the year 538 B.C., the Persians conquered the Babylonians.

SUMMING UP

The Sumerians built one of the first great cultures of the world in Mesopotamia. However, Mesopotamia was ruled by many peoples during its long history. The Sumerians, the Assyrians, the Babylonians, and finally the Persians ruled Mesopotamia. As you will learn in the next chapter, however, the Sumerian culture continued in Mesopotamia.

UNDERSTANDING THE LESSON

Do You Know These Important Terms?

For each sentence below, choose the term that best completes the sentence.

1. The lands at the eastern end of the Mediterranean Sea and the lands of southwestern Asia are called the (**Far East/Near East**).
2. The people who settled in Mesopotamia and who developed many skills were the (**Euphrates/Sumerians**).
3. A system of watering the land with river water is called (**aqueduct/irrigation**).
4. A (**municipality/city-state**) is a city that is like a small country.
5. A collection of Babylonian laws was called a (**Code of Laws/Legal Document**).
6. A strong nation that conquers and rules many lands is called an (**empire/invader**).

Do You Remember These People and Events?

1. Tell something about each of the following subjects.

Sumerians	Hammurabi
city-states	Nebuchadnezzar
Babylonians	Persians

Can You Locate These Places?

1. Use the map on page 41 to locate the following places. Tell how each place is related to the developments in this chapter.

Tigris River	Nineveh
Euphrates River	Egypt
Babylon	Persia

Do You Know When It Happened?

What important events happened in the following years?

   1700 B.C.   **538 B.C.**

Do You Remember the Main Idea?

Which one of the following ideas is the MAIN IDEA of this chapter?

1. The lands of Mesopotamia changed hands many times during the early years of its history.
2. The Sumerians developed a system of irrigation and a government which lasted for many years.
3. Mesopotamia developed one of the great cultures of early history. However, Mesopotamia was overrun and ruled by different peoples many times.

What Do You Think?

From what you have read in this chapter, try to answer the following thought questions.

1. What problems do you think the Assyrians faced in governing their large empire?
2. Why do you think a Code of Laws was needed in Mesopotamia? Explain your answer.
3. The Near East has been called one of the most important crossroad locations in the world. How do you think that this location helped Mesopotamia to develop?

Chapter 5
Life in Mesopotamia

GETTING STARTED

1 So far, archeologists have been able to learn only a few things about the lives of prehistoric people. But archeologists have discovered a great deal about the lives of the people of Mesopotamia. Archeological ruins show that the people of Mesopotamia built great cities. The ruins left from these cities tell us many facts about everyday life in Mesopotamia.

As the time line at the bottom of this page shows, Mesopotamia's history lasted from about 3000 B.C. to 538 B.C. During this period, the Mesopotamians lived and worked in their cities, never knowing that peoples who lived long after them might be interested in learning about their everyday lives.

2 Before you begin reading the chapter lesson, survey the lesson. Begin your survey by reading the beginning of the lesson. Then look through the lesson and read the headings. Next, study the pictures and read the picture captions. Finally, read the review section called "Summing Up" at the end of the lesson. This survey of the whole lesson will help you to discover the important ideas in this chapter.

Know the Main Idea

As you read the chapter lesson, try to remember the following important MAIN IDEA of the chapter.

Mesopotamia became a great trading nation. Its people were divided into classes according to their importance.

The following questions will help you to understand the MAIN IDEA. Try to answer these questions as you read the lesson.

1. What were the classes of people in Mesopotamia?
2. How did the laws of Mesopotamia favor the upper classes?
3. Where did Mesopotamians travel to trade their products?

Know These Important Terms

    classes   tablet houses

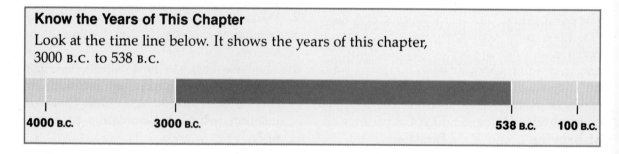

Know the Years of This Chapter

Look at the time line below. It shows the years of this chapter, 3000 B.C. to 538 B.C.

4000 B.C.   3000 B.C.   538 B.C.   100 B.C.

A Babylonian glazed brick wall picture of a mythical animal.
What features of real animals can you find on this mythical
beast?

EXPLORING THE TIME

The Mesopotamians lived so long ago that
you may think that their way of life was
very different from yours. And it was different, in many important ways. But you may
be surprised to learn that some of their
ways of living were like yours. In this
chapter, you will read about the peoples of
Mesopotamia and learn how they lived.

Three Classes of People Lived in Mesopotamia

The people of Mesopotamia belonged to
three **classes,** or groups. These classes included the upper class, the common people, and the slaves. The king, the nobles,
the priests, and the rich landowners belonged to the upper class. The class of
common people included traders, soldiers,
farmers, and workers. The slaves, who

were the lowest class, included people captured in wars and poor people who owed money.

The laws of Mesopotamia favored the upper-class people. If a slave hit an upper-class person, the slave was punished by having an ear cut off. But an upper-class person who hit someone only had to pay the doctor's bill. If a worker or farmer put out the eye of a rich landowner, the worker or farmer was punished by having an eye removed. But an upper-class person who put out someone's eye only had to pay a fine.

However, nobody in Mesopotamia was forced to remain in a lower class just because he or she was born in that class. Even a slave was able to rise and become a member of a higher class. And slaves were allowed to carry on some business dealings.

Men Ruled the Family in Mesopotamia

Women in Mesopotamia had more rights than the women of many other lands at that time. They were allowed to own land and property and even to set up their own businesses. But they were not believed to be equal to men. In upper-class families, for example, women stayed in a separate part of the house.

Marriages in Mesopotamia usually were arranged by the parents of the couple to be married. If the father was rich enough, he usually gave the bride a gift of gold, silver, furniture, or slaves. The bride was allowed to use this gift in any way that she wished. She was even allowed to set up her own business.

But in other ways, women in Mesopotamia had little freedom. A husband even had the right to sell his wife into slavery if he needed money to pay his debts.

Only Upper-Class Boys Attended School in Mesopotamia

Mesopotamia had schools, but the schools were only for upper-class boys. The boys

Warriors with spears, grouped together for an attack

from lower-class families learned a skill from their fathers, such as boatbuilding or brickmaking. The girls were trained to become wives.

The schools in Mesopotamia were called **tablet houses**—probably because Mesopotamian school books were written on clay tablets. Pupils learned writing, arithmetic, grammar, history, and geography.

Boys started school at the age of eight or nine. They began their school day at sunrise, and they stayed in school until sunset. If the pupils did not do good work, they often were given a beating.

The Mesopotamians Had Enough Food

Most Mesopotamians ate fairly well. The food of the lower classes was mainly fish, cheese, vegetables, and bread made from dates and barley. Rich people ate beef, mutton (sheep), and duck. Rich people also ate four meals a day, and they often enjoyed music with their meals.

Beer and date wine were the most popular drinks in Mesopotamia. Rich Mesopotamians also drank grape wine, a more costly drink that was brought from other countries.

The Mesopotamians Dressed According to Their Class

Most of the common people in Mesopotamia wore a simple woolen tunic, or shirt, that reached half-way down to their knees. Upper-class people wore finer clothes. Over their tunics, they wore a sleeveless robe that reached down to their ankles. They also wore a belt either under or over the robe. Their shoes were sandals.

The wealthy Mesopotamian women dressed carefully. They wore bracelets,

GEOGRAPHY AND HISTORY

Sumerian city of Ur

It is generally believed that cities first developed in Mesopotamia in the fertile valley of the Tigris and Euphrates rivers. The Sumerians who lived in this valley were farmers, and they built dams and dikes to keep water out of the fields.

As the population increased, some of the farmers moved north along the rivers. The land there was drier, so the farmers built irrigation canals to bring water to their fields. After a while, the land between the Tigris and Euphrates rivers was crisscrossed with canals. All the people depended on the irrigation system. Because the system was so important, the farming villages had to work together to keep it in good working order and to regulate the water supply. This was one reason that city-states developed. Each city included a number of villages and had its own laws.

The Sumerian cities traded with each other and with other lands. They used their canals and rivers to transport goods. In time, the cities became important centers of trade.

Question: Why did Sumerian farming villages grow into cities?

Stone carving of an Assyrian ruler (left) and a servant. What differences can you see in their appearances?

necklaces, and rings, and often they colored their lips and eyelids.

Wealthy men and women arranged their hair in stylish ways. The Babylonians and Assyrians wore their hair and beards long. The Sumerian men shaved their hair and did not have beards. Only upper-class men wore hats. The lower-class men tied their hair back with a string.

Mesopotamia Was a Great Trading Nation

Mesopotamia was a rich nation, and much of its wealth came from trade. Large amounts of Mesopotamian grain, dates, pottery, and woolen cloth were traded to other nations in return for metal, stone, wood, and other products that were scarce in Mesopotamia. Mesopotamian traders traveled to Egypt, Phoenicia, Asia Minor, and even faraway India and China.

SUMMING UP

Mesopotamia became a great trading nation. In Mesopotamia, people were divided into three classes. The upper classes were treated much better than the lower classes, and the men had more rights than the women. Most people in Mesopotamia ate well. Rich people dressed well, and only the sons of rich families attended schools. In the next chapter, you will find out about the culture of Mesopotamia and its peoples.

UNDERSTANDING THE LESSON

Do You Know These Important Terms?

For each sentence below, choose the term that best completes the sentence.

1. Mesopotamians divided into (**classes/ rows**) according to their importance.
2. Mesopotamian schools were called (**tablet factories/tablet houses**).

Do You Remember These Events?

1. Tell something about each of the following subjects.

   a. The classes of people in Mesopotamia.
   b. The role of men and women in Mesopotamia.
   c. Mesopotamian schools.
   d. The food of the Mesopotamians.
   e. The trade of Mesopotamia.

2. Ways of living differed a great deal among the three classes of Mesopotamian people. Describe some of the differences among these three classes in the following matters.

   laws   food
   education   dress

Can You Locate These Places?

Use the map on page 41 in Chapter 4 and the map on page 268 in Chapter 39 to do the following map work.

1. Locate the land that was called Mesopotamia.
2. Locate each of the following places.

   Egypt   India
   Asia Minor   China

3. The places just listed are places where Mesopotamian traders were active. Which location is closest to Mesopotamia? Which location is farthest from Mesopotamia? Which places are located to the east of Mesopotamia?

Do You Know When It Happened?

What are the years of this chapter?

Do You Remember the Main Idea?

Which one of the following ideas is the MAIN IDEA of this chapter?

1. Mesopotamians belonged to one of three classes of people.
2. Mesopotamian laws were applied to each of the different classes of people in different ways.
3. Mesopotamia became a great trading nation. Its people were divided into classes according to their importance.

What Do You Think?

From what you have read in this chapter, try to answer the following thought questions.

1. Can you describe what you imagine a typical day was like in the life of a Mesopotamian teen-ager of the upper class? of the middle class? of the slave class?
2. What do you think the study of history was like in a Mesopotamian school?
3. Do Mesopotamian women seem different from women of today, or do they seem like women of today? Explain your answer.

Chapter 6
Mesopotamian Culture

GETTING STARTED

1   How important are law and order? Are laws, or rules, necessary to keep a nation strong? The answer is yes. One important reason that the peoples of Mesopotamia were able to develop and continue their great culture for thousands of years was that they had a strong system of laws. In fact, many historians believe that the Mesopotamians were the first people to set up a code of laws. But laws were only one of the great contributions of the Mesopotamians. Throughout their long history, they contributed many ideas that became important to other peoples and nations.

2   Before you begin reading the chapter lesson, survey the lesson. Begin your survey by reading the beginning of the lesson. Then look through the lesson and read the headings. Next, study the pictures and read the picture captions. Finally, read the review section called "Summing Up" at the end of the lesson. This survey of the whole lesson will help you to discover the important ideas in this chapter.

Know the Main Idea

As you read the chapter lesson, try to remember the following important MAIN IDEA of the chapter.

The peoples of Mesopotamia developed a great culture. They contributed many skills and ideas that helped other peoples and nations to develop.

The following questions will help you to understand the MAIN IDEA. Try to answer these questions as you read the lesson.

1. What was the Sumerian way of writing? Why was the Sumerian method of writing important?
2. What contributions did the peoples of Mesopotamia make in transportation? in astronomy? in buildings?
3. Why were the Babylonian laws important?

Know These Important Terms

cuneiform
ziggurats

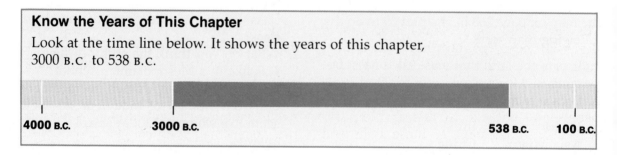

Know the Years of This Chapter
Look at the time line below. It shows the years of this chapter, 3000 B.C. to 538 B.C.

4000 B.C.   3000 B.C.   538 B.C.   100 B.C.

An Assyrian ruler standing in a chariot

EXPLORING THE TIME

The peoples of Mesopotamia lived several thousand years ago, but they built a great culture that is still remembered today. The peoples of Mesopotamia contributed skills and ideas which were used later by other people and nations. In this chapter, you will learn about some of these skills and ideas of the peoples of Mesopotamia.

The Sumerians Invented a New Way of Writing

Nobody really knows who invented writing. But we know that the Sumerians probably were the first people to invent a new way of writing.

The first kind of Sumerian writing was made up of groups of pictures. To write that two houses had been bought, a picture of two houses was drawn. A picture of an arm and someone else would show that the person in the picture had been hit by the arm.

But such picture writing was hard to write and hard to read. Therefore, the Sumerians improved their writing in two ways. First, they made each picture stand for a short sound, such as "sar" or "dag." Second, the Sumerians turned each picture into a combination of lines and wedges shaped like triangles. This kind of writing is called **cuneiform** (kyoo-NEE-uh-FORM), which means "wedge-shaped writing." Cuneiform writing was taken over and used by all the peoples of Mesopotamia.

The Sumerians Wrote on Clay Tablets

The Sumerians did not have paper. Instead, they wrote upon soft clay tablets and used a sharp piece of wood as a pen. After the writing was done, the tablet was baked to harden it.

The baked clay tablets were heavy and hard to move around. For this reason, the Sumerians made their writing small in order to use fewer tablets.

Most of the Sumerian tablets were records of history, laws, treaties, business dealings, or religious stories and poems. The Mesopotamian palaces and temples had many of these tablets. Some of these clay tablets are shown in museums today, and they tell us important information about the Sumerians.

Wheels and Ships Were Sumerian Inventions

The Sumerians were probably the first people to make another very important invention that we still use today—the wheel.

Sumerians did not have paper. Instead, they wrote upon soft clay tablets using sharp pieces of wood.

Prehistoric people had to pull their wagons along the ground without wheels. But Sumerian wagons had solid wooden wheels. You can imagine how much faster a wagon with wheels traveled than did a wagon without wheels.

The Sumerians also invented some of the earliest sailing ships. On these ships, Sumerian traders traveled to many far-off lands.

The Sumerians and Babylonians Studied the Sky

Astronomy—or the study of the stars and planets—was also important to the Sumerians and the Babylonians. They believed that by studying the sky they might learn when the yearly floods were going to take place and also learn the wishes of their gods.

The Sumerians and Babylonians learned a great deal about the moon, the planets, and the stars by watching the sky. They also learned to keep records of time. They learned that the time from sunrise to sunset was about 12 hours and that night lasted for about 12 hours—or that one whole day was 24 hours.

The Sumerians also divided each hour into 60 minutes. Today, we still measure time based on the 60-minute hour.

The Sumerians Built Tall Temples for Their Gods

The Sumerians believed in many gods. They worshiped their gods from the tops of high temples called **ziggurats** (ZIG-uh-RATZ). A ziggurat usually was seven stories high, and each story was a little narrower than the one below it. Long stairways, or ramps, led to the top. The ziggurats looked something like our modern office build-

King Hammurabi wrote the Babylonian Code of Laws. These laws were carved into stone tablets.

ings. These high temples were the centers of Mesopotamian life.

Mesopotamia had very little stone. Therefore, all buildings in Mesopotamia were made from dried clay bricks. However, clay bricks do not last as long as stone. This helps to explain why so few remains of Mesopotamian buildings have lasted until today.

Sumerians worshiped their gods in high temples called ziggurats. What material was used to build this ziggurat?

Hammurabi's Laws Were Hard but Fair

The Babylonian Code of Laws written by King Hammurabi in 1700 B.C. tells us a great deal about Mesopotamian culture. Many of these laws were cruel. For example, a person was put to death if he or she accused another person of murder but was not able to prove it. If a person tried to steal something from a burning house, he or she was thrown into the fire. However, many of the laws were fair. For example, workers had to be paid at least a certain amount of money for their work. Also, when farmers' crops were poor, the farmers were not expected to pay any of the money they owed during that year.

Everything from getting married to selling a farm was covered in Hammurabi's laws. Whether the Mesopotamian people liked these laws or not, they at least knew what their rights and duties were. Every nation must have laws if it is to become great. Hammurabi's Code of Laws shows that Mesopotamia developed a great culture for its time.

SUMMING UP

The peoples of Mesopotamia were among the first to develop a great culture. The most important parts of Mesopotamian culture were cuneiform writing, the use of wheels, the invention of sailing ships, a way of measuring time, and Hammurabi's Code of Laws. In the next chapter, which begins Unit 3, you will find out about the history of Egypt, a country near Mesopotamia.

UNDERSTANDING THE LESSON

Do You Know These Important Terms?

For each sentence below, choose the term that best completes the sentence.

1. Sumerian writing is called (**cuneiform/ picture**) writing.
2. The tall temples used by the Sumerians in worshiping their gods are called (**ziggurats/monuments**).

Do You Remember These Events?

1. Tell something about each of the following subjects.

    a. Sumerian clay tablets.
    b. Sumerian astronomy.
    c. Hammurabi's Code of Laws.
    d. Sumerian religion.

2. Tell which Mesopotamian skills and ideas are still used today.

    a. A system of writing.
    b. The idea of democracy.
    c. A system of laws.
    d. The wheel.
    e. Sailing ships.

Can You Locate These Places?

Use the map of Mesopotamia in Chapter 4 (page 41) to find the following places.

Babylon	Mesopotamia
Tigris River	Euphrates River
Egypt	Persian Gulf

1. Compare the kind of letters used for the labels for "Mesopotamia" and "Egypt" with the letters used for the "Babylon" label. How are they different?

2. Notice also the kind of letters used to label rivers and other bodies of water. How are these water labels different from each other and the other labels for a country and for a city?

Do You Know When It Happened?

In about what year was Hammurabi's Code of Laws written down?

Do You Remember the Main Idea?

Which one of the following ideas is the MAIN IDEA of this chapter?

1. Mesopotamians had the most advanced culture of their time because they invented the wheel and the sailing ship.
2. We know little about Mesopotamian culture because Mesopotamians built with mud bricks that later fell apart and left behind few remains.
3. The peoples of Mesopotamia developed a great culture. They contributed many skills and ideas that helped other peoples and nations to develop.

What Do You Think?

From what you have read in this chapter, try to answer these thought questions.

1. What were the three most helpful skills or ideas of the Mesopotamians? Give reasons for your answer.
2. Do you think that all of Hammurabi's Code of Laws might be useful today? Why or why not?
3. What type of writing might have developed if Mesopotamians had used other things besides clay tablets to write on?

Unit 3
The People of Egypt

THE CHAPTERS IN UNIT 3 ARE

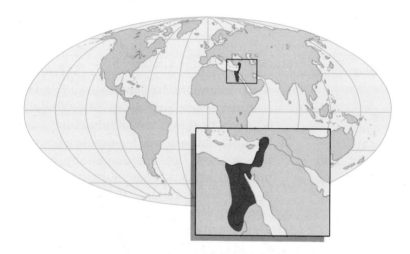

Egypt was one of the most powerful nations of early times. The Egyptians built a great kingdom in Africa, and they developed one of the most important cultures of early times. Today, the tall pyramids and Egyptian statues remind us of Egypt's great past. In this unit, you will find out how the people of Egypt built their great nation.

Egyptian pyramids were huge, four-sided buildings built as tombs for the dead pharaohs

Chapter 7
Egypt—the "Gift of the Nile"

GETTING STARTED

1   You have already learned that people during the New Stone Age found the fertile river valleys of Mesopotamia a good place in which to settle. Not too far away, another fertile river valley in northeast Africa also favored settlement of another land—Egypt. And like Mesopotamia, Egypt, too, was first settled during the years of the New Stone Age.

Look at the time line at the bottom of this page to see the years of this chapter—4000 B.C. to 332 B.C. During this period, people in both Egypt and Mesopotamia were developing great cultures. However, the people of Egypt also built up a great empire during this period.

2   Before you begin reading the chapter lesson, survey the lesson. Begin your survey by reading the beginning of the lesson. Then look through the lesson and read the headings. Next, study the pictures and read the picture captions. Then study the map of Egypt on page 60. Finally, read the review section called "Summing Up" at the end of the lesson. This survey of the whole lesson will help you to discover the important ideas in this chapter.

Know the Main Idea

As you read the chapter lesson, try to remember the following important MAIN IDEA of the chapter.

For almost three thousand years, Egypt developed as a great nation along the Nile River.

The following questions will help you to understand the MAIN IDEA. Try to answer these questions as you read the lesson.

1. How did the Nile River help Egypt?
2. How did Egypt become united as one nation?
3. What were the three periods of Egyptian history?

Know These Important Terms

delta	Middle Kingdom
pharaoh	Hyksos
Old Kingdom	New Kingdom

Know the Years of This Chapter

Look at the time line below. It shows the years of this chapter, 4000 B.C. to 332 B.C.

4000 B.C.   332 B.C.   100 B.C.

The Nile River flows from central Africa northward through
Egypt before it empties into the Mediterranean Sea

EXPLORING THE TIME

Long ago, Egypt was called the "gift of the Nile." No better name for Egypt has ever been found. That is because life in Egypt, even more than life in Mesopotamia, was shaped by a river. In this chapter, you will learn how the Nile River helped Egypt to develop.

The Nile River Shaped the Life of Egypt

The Nile River is one of the longest rivers in the world. It flows from central Africa northward through Egypt before it empties into the Mediterranean Sea. About 100 miles from the sea, the Nile River divides into several streams that flow through a triangle of land called a **delta**. Most of the Egyptian people lived along the Nile River and its delta.

Egypt has a hot, dry climate. Only the land along the Nile River has enough water for farming. The rest of Egypt is a desert. This desert was so difficult to cross that Egypt was not as easy to invade as was

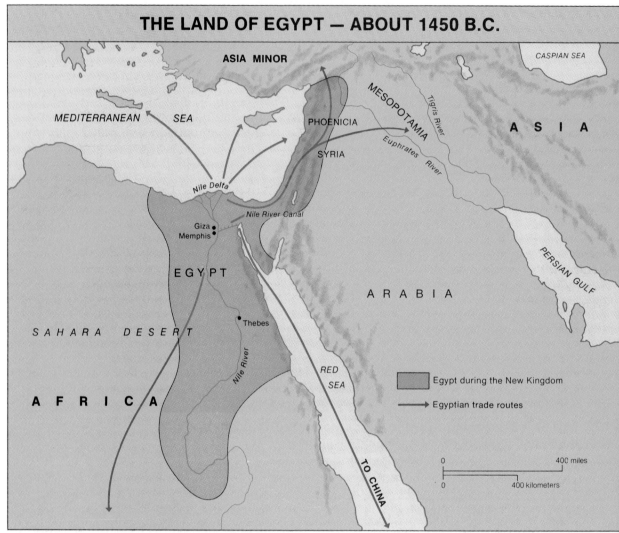

THE LAND OF EGYPT — ABOUT 1450 B.C.

CASPIAN SEA

ASIA MINOR

MEDITERRANEAN   SEA

PHOENICIA

MESOPOTAMIA

Tigris River

A S I A

SYRIA

Euphrates River

Nile Delta

Nile River Canal

Giza
Memphis

E G Y P T

A R A B I A

PERSIAN GULF

SAHARA   DESERT   •Thebes

Nile River

A F R I C A

RED
SEA

Egypt during the New Kingdom

Egyptian trade routes

TO CHINA

0   400 miles

0   400 kilometers

On which two seas did Egyptian traders travel?

Mesopotamia. As a result, Egypt was able to develop into a stronger nation than Mesopotamia.

Settlers Came to Egypt from Many Lands

Settlers wandered into the Nile River valley during the New Stone Age. Some people came from western Africa, some came from Asia, and some moved northward along the Nile River from central Africa. These settlers formed many small farming villages along the Nile River, and these settlers slowly became the Egyptian people.

The Nile River Helped Farming in Egypt

Each year about the middle of June, the Nile River flowed over its banks. Mud and water spread over the land on each side of the river. The rich layer of earth left by the flood waters made it possible for Egyptian farmers to grow two good crops a year.

But, like the farmers of Mesopotamia, Egyptian farmers also faced the problem of having either too much water or too little water at flood time. How did the Egyptians solve this problem? They built walls along the river banks to hold back the flood waters. Then they dug irrigation ditches to bring the water from the river to their fields.

Egypt Became United as One Nation

As Egypt became settled, each Egyptian village and town had its own chief, or leader. Some of these villages fought with each other over the water supply. Soon some villages became more powerful than others and conquered other villages. Before long, all of northern and all of southern Egypt were each ruled by a different king. But Egyptians were able to travel and trade in both the northern and southern parts of Egypt. This trade helped to unite, or bring together, the two parts of Egypt. About 2900 B.C., Egypt became one nation under one strong ruler, Menes (MEE-neez).

The Pharaoh Ruled the Egyptian People

From the time of Menes, Egypt's ruler was called **pharaoh** (FAIR-oh), which means "the great house," or "great family." The pharaohs were very powerful rulers. They not only made Egypt's laws, they were Egypt's chief judges, highest priests, and leaders of the army. Of course, Mesopotamia's king also had these powers. But the Egyptian pharaoh was even more powerful than Mesopotamia's king. The Egyptian people also worshiped their pharaoh as a god.

The pharaoh's officials were the nobles and priests. The nobles helped the pharaoh to run the irrigation works, collect the taxes, train the army, run the courts, and carry on the pharaoh's many building projects. The priests looked after religious matters. But all of these officials took their orders from the pharaoh.

Tablet showing an Egyptian pharaoh (center)

Early Egyptian History Had Three Periods

Egyptian history covered so many years that it is divided into three main periods. The period from 2800 B.C. to 2250 B.C. is called the **Old Kingdom.** The capital city during this time was Memphis, which was near the Nile River delta. During the Old Kingdom, many great tombs, or burial places, were built.

**Early painting showing how Egyptian farmers worked.
Describe the tools the farmers are using.**

The Old Kingdom came to an end when Egypt began to split up as wars broke out between different parts of the nation. About 2000 B.C., however, a strong pharaoh united the country again. The period from 2000 B.C. to 1780 B.C. is called the **Middle Kingdom.** The capital city during this time was Thebes. During the Middle Kingdom, the Egyptians produced fine art and writing.

Egypt Became an Empire During the New Kingdom

About the 1730's B.C., a people from Asia called the **Hyksos** (HICK-sohz) attacked Egypt. The Hyksos ruled most of Egypt until about 1580 B.C., when they were finally forced out. Then a new period began in Egypt from about 1580 B.C. to 1085 B.C. called the **New Kingdom.** During the New Kingdom, Egypt became an empire, or a strong nation that conquered and ruled many other lands. Thebes remained the capital, and many temples and palaces were built there.

But after 1085 B.C., Egypt slowly lost its power, and Egypt was conquered by one nation after another. Finally, in 332 B.C., Alexander the Great of Greece conquered Egypt. You will read more about Alexander in Chapter 22.

SUMMING UP

For almost three thousand years (2900 B.C. to 332 B.C.), Egypt was an independent nation. During this time, Egyptian life along the Nile River prospered. Egypt grew strong during the Old and Middle Kingdom periods. And under the New Kingdom, Egypt built a great empire. In the next chapter, you will read about life in Egypt.

UNDERSTANDING THE LESSON

Do You Know These Important Terms?

For each sentence below, choose the term that best completes the sentence.

1. The Nile divides into several streams that form a triangle of land called a **(fan/delta)**.
2. The ruler of Egypt was called the **(sphinx/pharaoh)**.
3. The period from 2800 B.C. to 2250 B.C. is called the **(Old Kingdom/Old Country)**.
4. The period from 2000 B.C. to 1780 B.C. is called the **(Middle Road/Middle Kingdom)**.
5. The **(Assyrians/Hyksos)** were a people from Asia who ruled Egypt between the Middle Kingdom and the New Kingdom.
6. The period from 1580 B.C. to 1085 B.C. is called the **(New Kingdom/Final Period)**.

Do You Remember These People and Events?

1. Tell something about each of the following subjects.

Menes	Middle Kingdom
pharaoh	Hyksos
Old Kingdom	New Kingdom

Can You Locate These Places?

Use the map of Egypt on page 60 to do the following map work.

1. Locate the following places. Tell how each location is related to the developments in this chapter.

Nile River	Memphis
Nile delta	Thebes

2. Trace the route of the Nile River. Into what body of water does it empty?

Do You Know When It Happened?

Why are the following years important in Egyptian history?

   about 2900 B.C.   332 B.C.

Do You Remember the Main Idea?

Which one of the following ideas is the MAIN IDEA of this chapter?

1. For almost three thousand years, Egypt developed as a great nation along the Nile River.
2. The history of Egypt is divided into three periods because it covers almost three thousand years.
3. Settlers moved into Egypt because the floods of the Nile River made the soil rich.

What Do You Think?

From what you have read in this chapter, try to answer the following thought questions.

1. Explain how the Nile River helped to shape the history of Egypt from earliest times.
2. Why do you think the Nile River valley is one of the most important river valleys in the world?
3. What might have happened if northern Egypt and southern Egypt had not become united?

Chapter 8
Life Among the Egyptians

GETTING STARTED

1   Today, ways of life change very rapidly. People today dress, eat, and live differently from the way people did one hundred or two hundred years ago. In the last hundred years, dozens of major changes have taken place in the way people live. But centuries ago, life in Egypt did not change that rapidly. In fact, the Egyptian ways of living changed very little in one hundred or two hundred years.

The Egyptian people developed their ways of living during the years of early Egyptian history. These ways of life did not allow most Egyptians to have much freedom. But these Egyptian ways of living are still interesting to us today.

2   Before you begin reading the chapter lesson, survey the lesson. Begin your survey by reading the beginning of the lesson. Then look through the lesson and read the headings. Next, study the pictures and read the picture captions. Finally, read the review section called "Summing Up" at the end of the lesson. This survey of the whole lesson will help you to discover the important ideas in this chapter.

Know the Main Idea

As you read the chapter lesson, try to remember the following important MAIN IDEA of the chapter.

The Egyptians developed their own special ways of life. Trade, art, education, and family life were important to Egyptians.

The following questions will help you to understand the MAIN IDEA. Try to answer these questions as you read the lesson.

1. Into what three classes were the Egyptian people divided?
2. What did Egypt do to improve trade with nations in Asia and Africa?
3. Why is the art produced by the Egyptians important to us today?

Know This Important Term

scribes

Know the Years of This Chapter

Look at the time line below. It shows the years of this chapter, 3500 B.C. to 332 B.C.

| 4000 B.C. | 3500 B.C. | | 332 B.C. | 100 B.C. |

Egyptian tomb painting showing grapes being picked

EXPLORING THE TIME

You have already read about how the people of Mesopotamia lived. What was life in Egypt like? Was it like life in Mesopotamia in any way? In this chapter, you will learn about Egyptian ways of living.

Three Classes of People Lived in Egypt

The people of Egypt were divided into three classes. The upper class included the pharaoh and his family, the nobles, and the priests. The people of the upper class lived in fine houses and had servants.

The middle class included writers called **scribes,** government clerks, traders, and craftspeople. The scribes wrote down most Egyptian records because few Egyptians knew how to read or write.

Most Egyptians, however, belonged to the lower class. This class included the workers and captured slaves. These people worked long, hard hours on farms, irrigation works, and road and building projects. The free workers had to pay high taxes to the pharaoh, and most workers were very poor. However, as in Mesopotamia, a few free workers and slaves in Egypt were able to become members of a higher class.

Egypt Produced a Large Food Supply

Most Egyptians ate well, whether they were rich or poor. Egyptian farms raised plenty of wheat, barley, fruits, and vegetables for everyone. Upper-class Egyptians also had meat and fish to eat. The lower-class Egyptians drank beer, but the upper-class Egyptians drank wine.

Egypt Traded with Many Nations

If you study the map of Egypt in Chapter 7, on page 60, you can see that Egypt was well located for trade—at the place where Africa and Asia meet. And Egypt traded with many nations. From central Africa, Egyptian traders received ivory and gold. From Phoenicia (fuh-NEE-shuh), a country north of Egypt on the Mediterranean coast, the Egyptians received wood. Egypt also traded with Mesopotamia, the Mediterranean islands, and even China.

Trade with Asia and Africa was increased after the Egyptians dug a canal from the delta of the Nile River across to the Red Sea. This canal made it possible for Egyptian traders to sail through the Red Sea and go directly eastward to China.

Egyptian Family Life Was Pleasant

Egyptian women were treated with respect. They were not "hidden away" in a separate part of the house, as were women in Mesopotamia. Egyptian women owned their own property, as did women in Mesopotamia. But the Egyptian women also were able to pass their property on to their daughters. A few women—usually the wives

Stone carving showing Egyptian traders

of dead pharaohs—even became rulers of Egypt.

Egyptian children were also treated well. Their parents gave them many toys and games, and the children were encouraged to enjoy themselves.

Egyptian Schools Were Important

Egyptian schools were located in the cities and were directed by the priests. At first, only upper-class boys attended school. However, later some boys from lower-class Egyptian families were allowed to attend school, too.

However, most lower-class boys did not remain in school for many years. After a few years, they left in order to learn a skill from their fathers. Upper-class boys who continued their education went to special schools. In these schools, the boys were trained to serve in the government or to become priests or doctors.

The Egyptians Liked to Dress Up

The everyday clothes of most Egyptians were simple. The men wore short skirts and shaved their faces. The women wore slim dresses down to their ankles. Sometimes they also wore sandals.

In the upper class, dressing was fancier. The men sometimes wore a coat of light cloth and put on false beards. The women wore beautiful jewelry and painted around their eyes with color. They also colored their lips and fingernails. Both the men and women of the upper class wore black wigs.

Egyptians of the upper class wore fancy things on their heads. The pharaoh wore a double crown—a red helmet over a white helmet. This double crown showed that he ruled both the northern part and the southern part of Egypt.

Egyptian sculpture of Queen Nefertiti. Queen Nefertiti and her husband, Pharaoh Ikhnaton, ruled Egypt from 1375 to 1358 B.C.

The Egyptians Liked Sports and Games

Outdoor sports, such as hunting, fishing, and trapping birds, were very popular with Egyptians. Chariot races became popular among the Egyptian people after horses were brought into Egypt. In their free time the people of the lower classes also enjoyed wrestling and dancing.

Painting showing Egyptian worship. What animal is used to decorate these headdresses?

The Egyptians Recorded Their Life in Art

Artists were very important in Egypt. Many artists carved statues and painted the walls of tombs, temples, and homes. Many of the Egyptian wall paintings and statues were preserved, and you can see some of them in museums all over the world today. These works of art tell a great deal about Egyptian life because they show how the Egyptian people lived.

SUMMING UP

Egyptians were divided into three classes, or groups. The upper-class Egyptians lived the best life, but most Egyptians had enough food and clothing. Egyptian family life was pleasant. Women shared some of the rights of men. Egyptians enjoyed sports and games, too. Art was also important to Egyptians. In the next chapter, you will find out about the culture of the Egyptians.

UNDERSTANDING THE LESSON

Do You Know This Important Term?

For the sentence below, choose the term that best completes the sentence.

1. Egyptians who wrote official records were called **(scribes/secretaries).**

Do You Remember These Events?

1. Tell something about each of the following subjects.

   **Egyptian trade   Egyptian art
   pharaoh's double crown**

2. Describe the differences in the ways of life among Egypt's upper, middle, and lower classes in relation to the following topics.

   a. work
   b. food and drink
   c. clothing
   d. family life
   e. education

Can You Locate These Places?

On the map in Chapter 7 (page 60), locate the following places. Tell how each is related to developments in this chapter.

Mesopotamia	Mediterranean Sea
Egypt	Red Sea
Africa	Nile River canal
Phoenicia	

Do You Know When It Happened?

What are the years of this chapter?

Do You Remember the Main Idea?

Which one of the following ideas is the MAIN IDEA of this chapter?

1. The ways of life that developed among the three classes of people of Egypt were like those that developed in Mesopotamia.
2. Egyptian ways of life were very similar in trade, art, and education among the three classes of people.
3. The Egyptians developed their own special ways of life. Trade, art, education, and family life were important to Egyptians.

What Do You Think?

From what you have read in this chapter, try to answer the following thought questions.

1. Which Egyptians do you think had the most power—the nobles or the priests? Give reasons for your answer.
2. Select one of the three classes of Egyptians and explain what a typical day was like for a member of that class.
3. Compare the family life of the Egyptians with the family life of the Mesopotamians. Which is the most like our modern kind of family life?
4. Why do you think that Egyptian art was important to the Egyptian people?

Chapter 9
Egyptian Culture

GETTING STARTED

1   The pictures of Egyptian buildings and Egyptian ways of life in these chapters on Egypt show that life in Egypt was not like life in the modern world. The Egyptians did things very differently from us. Yet, the Egyptians made many contributions to other peoples and nations. Many Egyptian ideas were taken over by other peoples who used and improved them. In this way, the Egyptians helped other cultures to develop. For this reason, it is important for us to know about the culture and contributions of the Egyptians. As a reminder, the time line at the bottom of this page shows that the Egyptians developed their culture between 3500 B.C. and 332 B.C. This chapter will discuss that culture.

2   Before you begin reading the chapter lesson, survey the lesson. Begin your survey by reading the beginning of the lesson. Then look through the lesson and read the headings. Next, study the pictures and read the picture captions. Finally, read the review section called "Summing Up" at the end of the lesson. This survey of the whole lesson will help you to discover the important ideas in this chapter.

Know the Main Idea

As you read the chapter lesson, try to remember the following important MAIN IDEA of the chapter.

The Egyptians produced a great culture. And many Egyptian ideas were used by other peoples and nations.

The following questions will help you to understand the MAIN IDEA. Try to answer these questions as you read the lesson.

1. Describe the Egyptian contributions in buildings.
2. Why was the Egyptian calendar an important contribution?
3. What invention of the Egyptians helped them to write books that lasted?

Know These Important Terms

pyramids	hieroglyphics
mummies	papyrus
Great Pyramid	

Know the Years of This Chapter

Look at the time line below. It shows the years of this chapter, 3500 B.C. to 332 B.C.

4000 B.C.	3500 B.C.		332 B.C.	100 B.C.

The Great Sphinx immortalized the Fourth Dynasty ruler Khafre

EXPLORING THE TIME

You may remember that the Sumerian culture of Mesopotamia developed skills and ideas that are still important today. Egyptian culture also produced some great and lasting ideas. In this chapter, you will find out what the culture of Egypt was like.

The Egyptians Built Great Tombs

The Egyptians built great temples, tombs, and treasure houses. Many of these build-

ings still stand today. The most famous Egyptian buildings are the **pyramids** (PEER-uh-MIDZ). These huge, four-sided buildings were built as tombs for the dead pharaohs. Why did the pharaohs need these huge tombs? The reason can be found in the beliefs that Egyptians had about the dead.

The Egyptians believed that after a person died, he or she lived a second life through the spirit in his or her body. They believed that it was possible to preserve this spirit in the person's dead body. The Egyptians treated a dead body with certain chemicals, wrapped the body in linen cloth, and placed it in a tomb to protect it. These dead bodies are called **mummies.**

The Egyptians placed food, clothing, tools, and weapons in the tomb, because they believed that the dead person used these things in his or her second life. The pharaohs built the pyramids in order to protect their mummies and the things buried with them from robbers.

The largest pyramid, called the **Great Pyramid** at Giza (GHEE-zuh), was built by Khufu (KOO-FOO), a pharaoh of the Old Kingdom. This pyramid is almost 800 feet wide on each side and was almost 500 feet high (about 50 stories) when it was built.

Several million blocks of stone—each weighing over 2 tons—were used in building it!

How did the Egyptians lift these heavy stones to the top of the pyramid? Probably the stones were pulled and pushed up ramps, or human-made slopes, by thousands of slaves. After the pyramids were completed, the ramps were removed.

The Egyptians Believed in Many Gods

During most of their history, the Egyptians worshiped many gods. However, one pharaoh, Ikhnaton (ik-NAY-tun), did not accept

An Egyptian temple near the Nile River

all these gods. Ikhnaton, who ruled from 1375 B.C. to 1358 B.C., believed that only one god, Aten (AH-tun), ruled the whole world. Ikhnaton closed the temples of all the other gods. Most Egyptians, however, did not accept the new idea of one god above all others. After Ikhnaton died, most Egyptians again went back to the old idea of worshiping many gods.

The Egyptians Developed Their Own Calendar

The Egyptians divided their calendar into 12 months. Each month included 30 days. Five extra days were added at the end of the year to make the year 365 days long. Our own calendar of today was developed from the Egyptian calendar.

The Egyptians developed their calendar by watching the changing locations of the sun, moon, and stars at different times of the day and year. In this way, they learned a great deal about astronomy, or the study of the stars and planets.

The Egyptians Were Interested in Science and Mathematics

The Egyptian writings show that the Egyptian doctors knew something about the human body and about treating sicknesses with medicines made from plants. And our modern word "chemistry" comes from an Egyptian word that meant "Egyptian science."

The Egyptians also helped to develop geometry (gee-OM-uh-TREE), in order to measure land. Each year when the Nile River overflowed, the waters washed away the boundary marks that showed where one field began and another field ended. The Egyptians used geometry in order to set up these field boundary marks every

PEOPLE IN HISTORY

Pharaoh Ikhnaton

Pharaoh Amenhotep the Fourth, who ruled Egypt from 1375 B.C. to 1358 B.C., changed his name to Ikhnaton (ik-NAY-tun). Ikhnaton means "servant of Aten." Ikhnaton changed his name to show that he believed Aten, the Egyptian sun god, was the only true god. For this reason, Ikhnaton also tried to make the Egyptian people end their worship of all other Egyptian gods.

To help the people forget the old gods, Ikhnaton moved the capital of Egypt from Thebes to Akhetaton. Many new buildings were built, and Egyptian artists made statues for the new capital city. Many statues and picture drawings were made of Ikhnaton and his lovely wife Nefertiti. And some of these Egyptian statues and drawings can be seen in museums today.

However, Egypt's worship of one god did not last long. When Ikhnaton died, his new religion and his new capital city also ended. Later, the Hebrew people again began the idea of one god.

Question: What was Ikhnaton's new idea about Egyptian gods?

73

year. The Egyptians also used geometry to plan and build the pyramids and temples.

The Egyptians Developed Picture Writing

The Egyptians used a form of writing called **hieroglyphics** (HY-ruh-GLIF-iks). The word "hieroglyphic" means "holy signal."

In hieroglyphic writing, words were written as pictures. For example, the word "forest" was a drawing of two trees. The word "eye" was a drawing of an eye. However, these drawings later came to stand for ideas as well as things. The picture of an eye meant not only an eye but also the idea of "seeing."

However, when these signs with different meanings were put together in sentences, they were very difficult to read. As a result, few Egyptians were able to read or write. This helps to explain why scribes, who wrote down most records, were so important in Egypt.

The Egyptian Books Were Written on Paper

At first, the Egyptians carved their books on stone. Later, they wrote on a kind of paper produced from the stem of a plant, the **papyrus** (puh-PY-rus). Our word "paper" comes from the Egyptian word "papyrus." The Egyptians made paper sheets from the stem of the papyrus plant. They wrote on these sheets with a sharp reed, or plant stem. Their ink was a mixture of dirt, plant juice, and water.

Egyptian books were made up of rolls of papyrus sheets. As a result of the hot, dry climate of Egypt, many of these books have been preserved.

Sculpture with Egyptian writing. What is this type of writing called?

SUMMING UP

The Egyptians produced a great culture that was never forgotten. The Egyptians built many great pyramids. They started the idea of a supreme god for the world. They developed the 365-day calendar. And they made important beginnings in science, medicine, and mathematics. In the next chapter, which begins Unit 4, you will find out about another early nation that was forgotten for a long time—the Hittites.

UNDERSTANDING THE LESSON

Do You Know These Important Terms?

For each sentence below, choose the term that best completes the sentence.

1. **(Sphinxes/Pyramids)** were huge four-sided buildings that the Egyptians built as tombs for dead rulers.
2. **(Zombies/Mummies)** were dead bodies which Egyptians treated with chemicals and wrapped in linen cloth.
3. The **(Great Pyramid/Karnak Temple)** was built during the Old Kingdom.
4. The Egyptian writing was called **(cuneiform/hieroglyphics)**.
5. The Egyptians made a kind of paper from the stems of a plant called **(barley/ papyrus)**.

Do You Remember These People and Events?

1. Tell something about each of the following subjects.

Khufu	**Egyptian geometry**
Ikhnaton	**Egyptian hieroglyphics**

Can You Locate These Places?

Use the map of Egypt in Chapter 7 (page 60) to do the following map work.

1. Locate the following places.

Egypt	**Mesopotamia**
Nile River	**Mediterranean Sea**
Red Sea	**Sahara Desert**

2. Seas, rivers, and deserts are natural features on the earth's surface. Nations, such as Egypt and Mesopotamia, are developed by humans. Therefore, they might be called "human-made features." How is the difference between natural features and human-made features shown in the lettering of names on this map?

Do You Know When It Happened?

Which pharaoh ruled in the following years? Why was this pharaoh important?

   1375 B.C.-1358 B.C.

Do You Remember the Main Idea?

Which one of the following ideas is the MAIN IDEA of this chapter?

1. The Egyptians developed many ideas which were useful to the people of Mesopotamia.
2. The Egyptians produced a great culture. And many Egyptian ideas were used by other peoples and nations.
3. Egyptian culture is remembered because it lasted for about three thousand years, and because the Egyptians left many ruins and remains.

What Do You Think?

From what you have read in this chapter, try to answer the following thought questions.

1. Which idea of the Egyptians do you consider the most valuable for us today?
2. How do you think that Egyptian doctors tried to cure diseases?
3. How do you think archeologists are able to translate, or read, the writing of the Egyptians?

Unit 4
The Peoples of the Near East

THE CHAPTERS IN UNIT 4 ARE

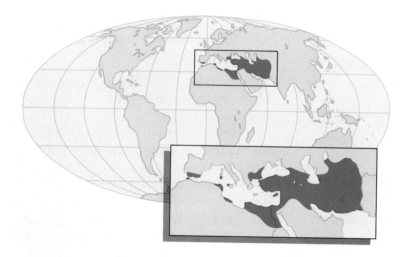

Most of the early nations of the Near East were small nations. But these nations made important contributions to our lives. You read about Mesopotamia in Unit 2. In this unit, you will learn about other important nations of the Near East and discover how their peoples lived.

A surviving staircase in the ancient Persian capital, Persepolis. Persepolis was partially damaged by Alexander the Great in 330 B.C.

76

Chapter 10
The Hittites and Their Empire

GETTING STARTED

1   The culture of Egypt and Mesopotamia lasted for thousands of years. Many of the ideas from Egypt and Mesopotamia were taken over by other peoples in the Near East. Some of these peoples used and improved the older ideas. And some peoples added new ideas of their own to the old ideas.

In this chapter, you will read about the Hittites, a group of people who lived in the Near East from 2000 B.C. to about 1200 B.C. These people borrowed many ideas from Egypt and Mesopotamia, but they also produced many new ideas of their own. They built a powerful nation.

2   Before you begin reading the chapter lesson, survey the lesson. Begin your survey by reading the beginning of the lesson. Then look through the lesson and read the headings. Next, study the pictures and read the picture captions. Then study the map of the Hittite Empire on page 80. Finally, read the review section called "Summing Up" at the end of the lesson. This survey of the whole lesson will help you to discover the important ideas in this chapter.

Know the Main Idea

As you read the chapter lesson, try to remember the following important MAIN IDEA of the chapter.

The Hittites built a large empire because they developed new and better weapons. The Hittites also borrowed many ideas from other nations.

The following questions will help you to understand the MAIN IDEA. Try to answer these questions as you read the lesson.

1. What were the important contributions of the Hittites?
2. What ideas did the Hittites borrow from other nations?
3. Why did the Hittite Empire finally end?

Know These Important Terms

    iron weapons   horse-drawn chariots

Know the Years of This Chapter

Look at the time line below. It shows the years of this chapter, 2000 B.C. to 1200 B.C.

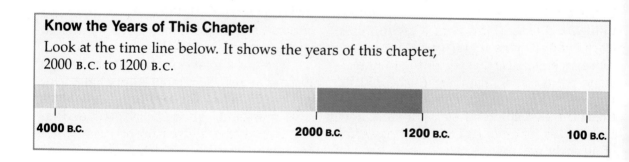

| 4000 B.C. | | 2000 B.C. | 1200 B.C. | 100 B.C. |

Hittite archer hunting a boar

EXPLORING THE TIME

Did you ever hear of the Hittites (HIT-tytz)? If your answer is "no," you are not alone. Many people never heard of the Hittites, because the Hittites were nearly forgotten until recent times. Now we are beginning to learn many things about the Hittites, because archeologists are beginning to understand better the meaning of the Hittite writing. In this chapter, you will learn how the Hittites conquered Asia Minor and how the Hittites set up one of the most powerful of all early nations.

Asia Minor Was a Land Bridge Between Europe and Asia

Asia Minor is a large piece of land between Europe and southwestern Asia. Today, Asia Minor is the land where the nation of Turkey is located. But in early history, Asia Minor was the homeland of many different peoples, including the Hittites.

Most of the land in Asia Minor is high and rocky, and the rainfall is very light. This land is not good for farming, but it does have grasslands good for animals to feed on. The northeastern part of Asia Minor has mountains that are rich in iron ore. As

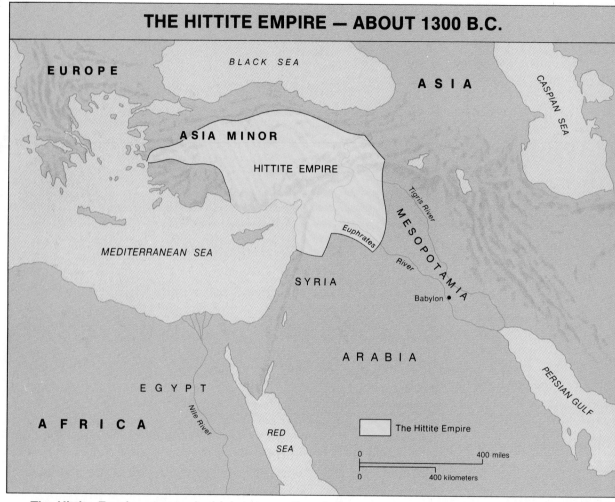

THE HITTITE EMPIRE — ABOUT 1300 B.C.

EUROPE

BLACK SEA

ASIA

CASPIAN SEA

ASIA MINOR

HITTITE EMPIRE

Tigris River

MESOPOTAMIA

Euphrates River

MEDITERRANEAN SEA

SYRIA

Babylon •

ARABIA

EGYPT

Nile River

AFRICA

RED SEA

PERSIAN GULF

The Hittite Empire

0   400 miles
0   400 kilometers

The Hittite Empire spanned which two continents?

you will see, the use of iron was very important to the Hittites.

The Hittites Settled in Asia Minor

The Hittites arrived in Asia Minor some time before the year 2000 B.C. They came from the grasslands north of the Black Sea and the Caspian Sea, where they kept large herds of cattle, sheep, and horses.

The Hittites were one of the first people to tame horses and to use them for pulling wagons. Before long, the Hittites spread over most of Asia Minor and settled down with their herds of animals.

The Hittites Used Many Ideas from Mesopotamia and Egypt

The Hittites borrowed many ideas from other nations. From Mesopotamian traders who visited Asia Minor, the Hittites learned the Sumerian way of writing by using cuneiform letters on clay tablets. The

Hittites also began to worship many of the Mesopotamian gods as a part of their own religion.

From Egypt, the Hittites borrowed Egyptian styles of art and Egyptian writing. They also worshiped some Egyptian gods. But although the Hittites borrowed many ideas from other nations, they also developed their own ways of doing things.

The Hittite Laws Were Fair

A great development by the Hittites was their system of laws. Many of these laws were based on the Mesopotamian Code of Laws of Hammurabi, but the Hittite laws were not as cruel. For example, the Hittites seldom punished a person by death. A person who hurt another person only had to pay money to the person who was hurt. Under the Hittite laws, persons were punished less if they were able to prove that their crime was done by accident.

The Hittite King Had Limited Powers

The Hittite king had many of the same powers held by the rulers of Egypt and Mesopotamia. However, he was not worshiped as a god, as was the Egyptian pharaoh. And the Hittite king did not make the laws of the nation. If the king broke a law, he might be called before a group of nobles and punished. This never happened to the rulers of Egypt or Mesopotamia.

The Hittites Used Iron Weapons to Build Their Empire

By 1900 B.C., many Hittite groups joined to form one nation. The capital city of the Hittites was located near Ankara, which is today the capital of Turkey. The new Hittite nation slowly grew very powerful.

Stone carving showing a Hittite warrior with iron weapons

The use of **iron weapons** helped the Hittite nation to become powerful. The Hittites learned how to use the iron ore from the mountains of northeastern Asia Minor to make iron weapons. These iron weapons were stronger and harder than the softer copper or bronze weapons used by most other nations at that time.

The Hittites Used Horse-drawn Chariots to Defeat Their Enemies

Another reason for the Hittites' success was their use of light, **horse-drawn chariots** in battles against enemy soldiers. Using these swift chariots, the Hittites were able to surround and destroy enemy soldiers who were on foot or in slow chariots pulled by donkeys. This use of horse-drawn chariots helped the Hittites to conquer other peoples and to build an empire.

One reason for the Hittite army's success in battle was its use of light, horse-drawn chariots. What weapon was being used?

The Hittite Empire Was Finally Destroyed

For many years, no nation was able to defend itself against the Hittites. The Hittites even captured the mighty city of Babylon, the capital of Mesopotamia. In time, some nearby nations also began to make iron weapons and to use horse-drawn chariots. These nations later attacked the Hittites and forced them to return to Asia Minor.

But the Hittites soon built another empire. This empire included most of Mesopotamia and the Near East, as well as Asia Minor. However, the second Hittite Empire began to fall apart about the year 1200 B.C. as new groups of people moved into Asia Minor. The Hittites tried to fight back, but they were defeated. Other nations now knew how to use iron weapons and horse-drawn chariots against the Hittites. As a result, the Hittite Empire was soon destroyed.

SUMMING UP

The Hittites were the first nation to use iron weapons and horse-drawn chariots. With these weapons, the Hittites built up a large empire. However, other nations also learned how to use these weapons, and they slowly defeated the Hittites. The Hittites developed their own system of laws, but they borrowed many ideas about religion, art, and writing from other nations. In the next chapter, you will read about another early people of the Near East, the Hebrews.

UNDERSTANDING THE LESSON

Do You Know These Important Terms?

For each sentence below, choose the term that best completes the sentence.

1. The strong weapons developed by the Hittites were called **(copper weapons/ iron weapons).**
2. The Hittites' success against their enemies was partly a result of using **(horse-drawn chariots/bows and arrows).**

Do You Remember These People and Events?

1. Tell something about each of the following subjects.

   Hittite weapons   **Hittite kings**
   Hittite system of laws

2. Explain how each of the following events probably took place.

   a. The Hittites began to use ideas from Mesopotamia and Egypt.
   b. The Hittite Empire finally ended.

Can You Locate These Places?

Use the map on page 80 to do the following map work.

1. Locate each of the following places. Tell how each place is connected to the developments in this chapter.

   Hittite Empire   **Egypt**
   Asia Minor   **Mesopotamia**

2. Locate these places.

   Black Sea   **Mediterranean Sea**
   Caspian Sea

3. How is the lettering of these names different from the names of countries and continents?

Do You Know When It Happened?

Why are the following years important in Hittite history?

   about 1900 B.C.   **about 1200 B.C.**

Do You Remember the Main Idea?

Which one of the following ideas is the MAIN IDEA of this chapter?

1. The Hittites built a large empire because they developed new and better weapons. The Hittites also borrowed many ideas from other nations.
2. The Hittites were a warlike people who built a powerful empire in the Near East.
3. The Hittites had little to do with their neighbors. They developed their own system of art, writing, and religion.

What Do You Think?

From what you have read in this chapter, try to answer the following thought questions.

1. How do you think that enemies of the Hittites felt when they first saw the Hittites' iron weapons and horse-drawn chariots?
2. Explain how the daily life of a Hittite was different from the daily life of a person living in Mesopotamia or in Egypt.
3. What Hittite contribution or idea do you consider the most valuable for us today? Explain your answer.

Chapter 11
The Hebrews and Their God

GETTING STARTED

1   You may have heard many stories from the Bible. Today, you can even see movies based on the Bible. The first part of the Bible tells the story of the Hebrew people, another of the peoples who lived in the Near East. During the period from about 2000 B.C. to about 586 B.C., the Hebrews ruled themselves for only a short time. But during this time, the Hebrews made two very important contributions to the world. One was the idea of monotheism, or the belief in one God. The other contribution was the Old Testament. In this chapter, you will find out about these contributions.

2   Before you begin reading the chapter lesson, survey the lesson. Begin your survey by reading the beginning of the lesson. Then look through the lesson and read the headings. Next, study the pictures and read the picture captions. Then study the map of Palestine on page 86. Finally, read the review section called "Summing Up" at the end of the lesson. This survey of the whole lesson will help you to discover the important ideas in this chapter.

Know the Main Idea

As you read the chapter lesson, try to remember the following important MAIN IDEA of the chapter.

The Hebrews gave the world two great contributions—the idea of a belief in one God and the Old Testament.

The following questions will help you to understand the MAIN IDEA. Try to answer these questions as you read the lesson.

1. What great leader helped the Hebrew people to escape from slavery in Egypt?
2. Who was leader of the Hebrew people in the years of their greatest power?
3. What idea kept the Hebrew people together and united?

Know These Important Terms

Ten Commandments	monotheism
Old Testament	Bible

Know the Years of This Chapter

Look at the time line below. It shows the years of this chapter, 2000 B.C. to 586 B.C.

4000 B.C.	2000 B.C.	586 B.C.	100 B.C.

View from the top of Mount Sinai, a peak in the peninsula between Egypt and Israel

EXPLORING THE TIME

The Hebrews were never a large nation. They ruled the small land of Palestine in the Near East for only a few hundred years. Yet, the ideas developed by the early Hebrew people have lasted until today. In this chapter, you will find out about the contributions that the Hebrews made to the world.

Palestine Was a Small Country

Palestine was a narrow desert land at the eastern end of the Mediterranean Sea —about as large as the state of New Jersey.

Palestine was located on a trade route between Egypt and Mesopotamia, and the cultures of both nations were well known in Palestine. In fact, Palestine was ruled by Egypt and Mesopotamia during most of its history.

The Hebrews Won Control of Palestine

The earliest Hebrews were shepherds who moved into Palestine from Mesopotamia about 2000 B.C. Some of the early Hebrews stayed in Palestine, but others moved southward into Egypt. However, the

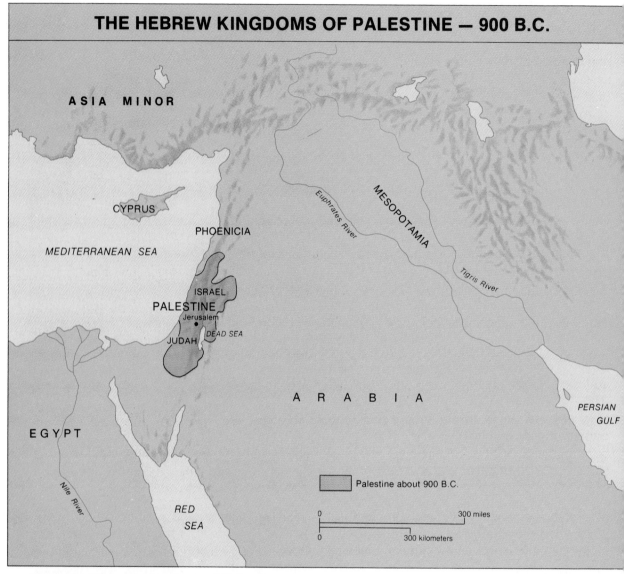

THE HEBREW KINGDOMS OF PALESTINE — 900 B.C.

ASIA MINOR

CYPRUS

PHOENICIA

MEDITERRANEAN SEA

Euphrates River

MESOPOTAMIA

Tigris River

ISRAEL

PALESTINE

Jerusalem

DEAD SEA

JUDAH

A R A B I A

PERSIAN GULF

EGYPT

Nile River

RED SEA

Palestine about 900 B.C.

0   300 miles

0   300 kilometers

Name the Hebrew kingdoms of Palestine.

Hebrews were not happy in Egypt. They were treated badly, and they were forced to work as slaves. But a great leader named Moses helped the Hebrews to escape from slavery. About 1275 B.C., Moses led the Hebrews out of Egypt to freedom.

When the Hebrews returned, Palestine was not ruled by Egypt or Mesopotamia.

But it was not a united country, either. Each city ruled itself and the land around it. The Hebrews fought for many years to win control of all the land of Palestine.

The Hebrews Formed a Kingdom

Saul, David, and Solomon were the three

rulers who helped the Hebrews to become one nation. Saul became the first king of the Hebrews about 1025 B.C. Saul led the Hebrews against the warlike Philistines (FILL-uh-STEENZ), who lived near Palestine. But Saul was killed, and the Philistines were not defeated. King David, who ruled after Saul, did defeat the Philistines. David formed the Hebrew kingdom, and he made Jerusalem (juh-ROO-suh-LUM) its capital city.

The Hebrew kingdom reached its greatest power under Solomon, who was David's son. Solomon traded with many nations and built many fine buildings in Jerusalem. These buildings included beautiful palaces for himself and a great Hebrew temple.

The Hebrew Kingdom Became Divided

King Solomon's costly building program required the Hebrews to pay heavy taxes and to work very hard. After Solomon died (about 930 B.C.), the unhappy Hebrews revolted, and the Hebrew kingdom became divided into two parts. The northern part became the kingdom of Israel (IZ-ree-UL), and the southern part became the kingdom of Judah (JOO-duh).

However, neither of the two Hebrew kingdoms was very strong. Israel was destroyed by the Assyrians in 722 B.C. And Judah was finally conquered in 586 B.C. by Mesopotamia.

The Hebrews Remained One People

Although both Hebrew kingdoms were conquered, the Hebrews did not disappear as a people. What was it that kept the Hebrew people together and united?

The Hebrew religion kept the Hebrews together and united. The Hebrews worshiped one great, all-powerful God. They

DOCUMENTS IN HISTORY

David—King of Judah and Israel

Much of Hebrew history is recorded in the Old Testament of the Bible. The Old Testament tells the story of the kingdom of Israel and of the Hebrew kings. David, the second king of Israel, united his people and ruled for about forty years.

The Old Testament contains many stories about King David the great warrior and leader, who was also a poet and musician. Many of David's poems and songs are preserved in the book of Psalms (SAHMZ). The following excerpt is from one of the Psalms, or sacred songs, of David.

Who shall ascend the hill of the Lord?
And who shall stand in his holy place?
He who has clean hands and a pure
   heart,
Who does not lift up his soul to what
   is false,
And does not swear deceitfully.
He will received blessing from the
   Lord....

Question: What is a Psalm?

The Hebrews in Egypt were forced to work as slaves

believed that God loved them, protected them, and required them to obey God's laws. The Hebrews believed that God had given a set of laws to Moses when the Hebrew people left Egypt. These laws were known as the **Ten Commandments.**

The Hebrews Believed in One God for All Peoples

At first, the Hebrews believed that other nations had gods of their own. But later, the leaders of the Hebrew religion declared the Hebrew God was the one and only God for all peoples. This belief in one God is called **monotheism** (muh-NOH-thee-iz-um).

Monotheism, or the belief in one God, became the basis of the Hebrew religion. The Hebrews came to believe that God loved justice and truth and demanded good deeds from all peoples. Therefore, if the Hebrews were to be good human beings, they must obey God's laws, the Ten Commandments. If they did not obey the Ten Commandments, God punished them. This strong God—who gave them great laws to live by—also gave the Hebrews a reason for remaining together as one people.

The Old Testament Gave the Hebrews a Guide for Living

The teachings of the Hebrew religious leaders, the history of the Hebrew people, and the laws to be followed by the Hebrews were written down in the **Old Testament,** a collection of books about the Hebrew people and their God. These books contain the ideas and beliefs of the Hebrew people. With these books to guide them, the Hebrews were able to remain Hebrews wherever they lived—in Mesopotamia, in Egypt, or anywhere else.

Today, the Hebrew religion is called the Jewish religion and the people who follow the Jewish religion are known as Jews. Books of the Jewish religion later became part of the Christian **Bible,** the religious book of the Christian religion. You will read more about the beginning of the Christian religion in Chapter 28.

SUMMING UP

The Hebrew people made two very important contributions to the world. One was the idea of monotheism, or the belief in one God. The other contribution was the Old Testament. Both monotheism and the Old Testament helped the Hebrews to remain together as a people. In the next chapter, you will learn about the Phoenicians, who developed a new writing system.

UNDERSTANDING THE LESSON

Do You Know These Important Terms?

For each sentence below, choose the term that best completes the sentence.

1. The **(Code of Laws/Ten Commandments)** were laws that the Hebrews believed were given to them by God.
2. A belief in one God is called **(worship/monotheism)**.
3. The book that contains the history, the ideas, and the beliefs of the Hebrew people is **(the Old Testament/papyrus)**.
4. The **(Bible/Koran)** became the religious book of the Christian religion.

Do You Remember These People and Events?

1. Tell something about each person.

Moses	**David**
Saul	**Solomon**

2. Explain how or why each of the following events happened.

   a. The Hebrew nation split into two parts.
   b. The Hebrews remained one group of people, although they were conquered many times.

Can You Locate These Places?

Use the map on page 86 to do the following map work.

1. Locate the following places and tell how each place is related to the chapter.

Palestine	**Judah**
Egypt	**Jerusalem**
Israel	**Mesopotamia**

2. How does the crossroad location of Palestine (between Egypt, Mesopotamia, and Asia Minor) help to explain why the Hebrew people were conquered many times?

Do You Know When It Happened?

Why are the following years important in Hebrew history?

   1275 B.C.   586 B.C.

Do You Remember the Main Idea?

Which one of the following ideas is the MAIN IDEA of this chapter?

1. The Hebrews were a large group of people in the Near East who were able to conquer both Egypt and Mesopotamia.
2. The Hebrews made a contribution to our culture of today through their number system and code of laws.
3. The Hebrews gave the world two great contributions—the idea of a belief in one God and the Old Testament.

What Do You Think?

From what you have read in this chapter, try to answer the following thought questions.

1. How did the Hebrews' belief in one God differ from most early beliefs?
2. Why do you think the Hebrews chose Palestine as a place to settle and build a nation?
3. Why do you think that the Hebrews were shepherds rather than farmers? What kinds of conditions are needed for farming?

Chapter 12
Phoenicia—a Land of Traders

GETTING STARTED

1 You have already read how the Egyptians, the Mesopotamians, and the Hittites conquered and ruled great empires during early history. These peoples were successful conquerors because they had strong armies and good weapons. Between 1500 B.C. and 700 B.C., a smaller group of people called Phoenicians built an empire that was very different from the older empires. The Phoenicians became famous as the greatest sea traders in early history. This chapter tells about this new kind of empire—an empire that began on the sea and was spread across the sea to other lands.

2 Before you begin reading the chapter lesson, survey the lesson. Begin your survey by reading the beginning of the lesson. Then look through the lesson and read the headings. Next, study the pictures and read the picture captions. Then study the map of Phoenicia and its colonies on page 92. Finally, read the review section called "Summing Up" at the end of the lesson.

This survey of the whole lesson will help you to discover the important ideas in this chapter.

Know the Main Idea

As you read the chapter lesson, try to remember the following important MAIN IDEA of the chapter.

The Phoenicians became great traders. As traders, they spread their culture and ideas to many nations.

The following questions will help you to understand the MAIN IDEA. Try to answer these questions as you read the lesson.

1. What conditions helped the Phoenicians to become a trading nation?
2. What products did the Phoenicians trade to other nations?
3. What important idea did the Phoenicians develop that we use today?

Know These Important Terms

colonies   alphabet

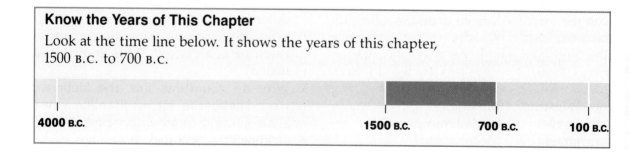

Know the Years of This Chapter

Look at the time line below. It shows the years of this chapter, 1500 B.C. to 700 B.C.

4000 B.C.   1500 B.C.   700 B.C.   100 B.C.

The Phoenician sea traders spread important ideas across the sea to other lands. What powered the Phoenician ships?

EXPLORING THE TIME

The Phoenicians (foh-NISH-unz) were not conquerors like the Hittites. The Phoenicians did not develop a great religion like the Hebrews. The Phoenicians became famous as the greatest sea traders in early history. In this chapter, you will find out how the Phoenician traders spread important ideas to the lands around the Mediterranean Sea.

Phoenicia Became a Trading Nation

The country of Phoenicia was located south of Asia Minor along the eastern shore of the Mediterranean Sea. Phoenicia was a long, narrow country about 200 miles from north to south and only about 12 miles from east to west.

Phoenicia did not have enough good farming land for all its people. But it had many cedar and fir trees for shipbuilding. And Phoenicia also had deep harbors for

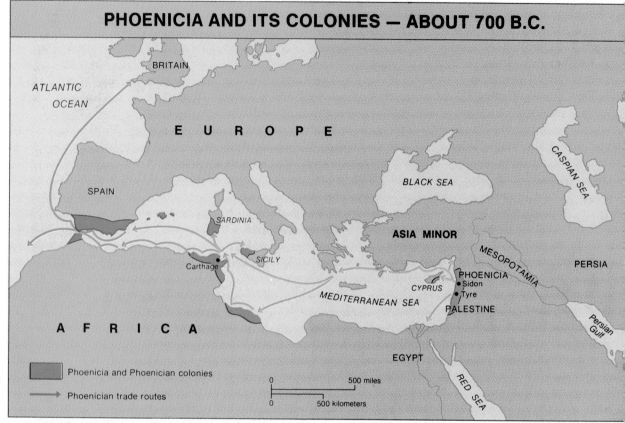

PHOENICIA AND ITS COLONIES — ABOUT 700 B.C.

ATLANTIC
OCEAN

BRITAIN

E U R O P E

SPAIN

BLACK SEA

CASPIAN SEA

SARDINIA

ASIA MINOR

MESOPOTAMIA

PERSIA

Carthage

SICILY

CYPRUS

PHOENICIA
Sidon
Tyre

MEDITERRANEAN SEA

PALESTINE

Persian Gulf

A F R I C A

EGYPT

RED SEA

Phoenicia and Phoenician colonies

Phoenician trade routes

0   500 miles

0   500 kilometers

How far did the northernmost Phoenician trade route reach?

seagoing ships. Very early in their history, the Phoenicians began to build wooden ships and to trade with nations around the Mediterranean Sea.

Many Phoenician cities grew up along the coast of Phoenicia. The three most important Phoenician cities were Tyre (TIRE), Sidon (SY-dun), and Byblos (BIBB-luss).

The Phoenicians Were Ruled by Many Nations

The people who first settled Phoenicia about 1500 B.C. came from the lands around the Persian Gulf and the islands of the eastern Mediterranean Sea. But the Phoenicians never built a strong nation. At dif-

ferent times, the Phoenicians were ruled by the Egyptians, the Mesopotamians, the Hittites, the Assyrians, and the Persians.

However, from about 1200 B.C. to about 700 B.C., most of the Phoenician cities ruled themselves. After this period, the Phoenicians were ruled by Mesopotamia. During the period when they ruled themselves, the Phoenicians became the chief traders of the Mediterranean Sea.

The Phoenicians Made Colorful Glassware

The Phoenicians produced many fine products for trade. One of their most valuable products was glassware. The Phoenician skill of glassmaking came from Egypt, but the Phoenicians improved the Egyptian glassmaking method. And they produced more glassware than any other nation.

The Phoenicians shaped glass into beautiful jugs, mirrors, vases, perfume bottles, and beads. Some Phoenician glassware was clear and white. But other Phoenician glassware was blue, green, yellow, brown, or a mixture of these colors. Phoenician glass was very popular, and it was sold to peoples of many nations around the Mediterranean Sea.

The Phoenicians Made Colorful Cloth and Many Other Products

Another fine Phoenician product was cloth. Phoenician wool, linen, and silk cloth were famous for their bright colors, particularly purple. The rare purple dye of Phoenicia came from a tiny shellfish that lived in the waters off the Phoenician coast. A purple Phoenician cloak cost so much that it was worn mainly by kings and nobles.

Phoenicia had many skilled craftspeople as well as sailors and traders. In fact, the Phoenician carpenters were so famous that King Solomon asked them to come to Palestine to help build his great Hebrew temple. Phoenician artisans made fine furniture, jewelry, pottery, tools, and weapons—all products that were desired by the peoples of other nations.

Phoenician Traders Traveled to Many Lands

Phoenicia traded a great deal with Egypt, Mesopotamia, Asia Minor, and Persia. However, Phoenician traders had so many products to sell that they were always searching for new customers. The first

Phoenician sculpture

place visited by Phoenician trading ships was the island of Cyprus (SY-prus), about 100 miles west of Phoenicia. Later, Phoenician traders visited other lands around the Mediterranean Sea.

The Phoenician sailors were even brave enough to sail to the western end of the Mediterranean Sea and then sail down the unexplored western coast of Africa. The Phoenicians traded for gold, ivory, and animal skins in these places. Other groups of Phoenician traders sailed as far north as Britain (today Great Britain), where they obtained tin.

The Phoenicians Formed Settlements Around the Mediterranean Sea

Before long, the Phoenician traders began to set up trading centers in the lands around the Mediterranean Sea. These trading centers became Phoenician **colonies,** or

Phoenician Writing

The alphabet you use today came from the Greeks by way of the Romans. But the Greeks did not begin the alphabet. They learned it from the Phoenicians.

By looking at the names of the letters, you can find clues about how the alphabet may have started. The first letter of the Phoenician alphabet was written like this ∀ , and it was called "aleph." To the Phoenicians, "aleph" meant ox. Now look again at how the Phoenicians wrote this letter. If you look carefully, you can see that the letter is really a picture showing the head of an ox.

Other Phoenician letters were based on the same idea. For example, the letter "mem," written as ∿ , meant water. The letter "ayin," written as ○ , meant eye. The letter "shin," written as ɯ , meant tooth. These clues of the Phoenician alphabet show you that our alphabet probably began as pictures. Later, these pictures were made simpler in order to make our reading and writing easier.

Question: Where did our alphabet begin?

settlements, and had their own governments. Some Phoenician colonies were located in the land that today is called Spain. Phoenician colonies also were formed on many Mediterranean islands, including Cyprus (SY-prus), Sicily (SISS-uh-LEE), and Sardinia (sar-DIN-ee-uh). These colonies helped to spread the ideas of the eastern Mediterranean nations to other lands.

The most important Phoenician colony was Carthage (KARR-thij), which was located on the northern African coast. Carthage grew into an important city and later became a powerful Mediterranean empire, as you will learn in Chapter 23.

The Phoenicians Developed the Alphabet

The Phoenicians borrowed most of their ideas from other nations. However, they developed their own **alphabet**, or a system of letters used for writing words and sentences. This system proved so easy to use that it was borrowed by other peoples around the Mediterranean Sea. The Phoenician alphabet became the basis of the alphabet that we still use today.

SUMMING UP

The Phoenicians were great sailors, traders, and artisans. Phoenician workers built fine seagoing ships and produced excellent glassware, cloth, and other products. Phoenician traders traveled to many lands, and they spread the eastern Mediterranean culture and ideas to many nations. The Phoenicians developed their own alphabet, which was used by other peoples. In the next chapter, you will find out about Persia, another great empire of the Near East.

UNDERSTANDING THE LESSON

Do You Know These Important Terms?

For each sentence below, choose the term that best completes the sentence.

1. Settlements made by people in lands away from their own nation are called **(centers/colonies)**.
2. A system of letters used for writing words and sentences is called an **(outline/alphabet)**.

Do You Remember These Events?

1. Tell something about each of the following subjects.

   Phoenician glassmaking
   Phoenician alphabet
   Phoenician cloth

2. Explain how each of the following events took place.

   a. The Phoenicians became sailors and traders.
   b. The Phoenicians spread their culture and ideas to the lands around the Mediterranean Sea.

Can You Locate These Places?

Use the map on page 92 to do the following map work.

1. Locate the following places. Tell how each place is related to developments in this chapter.

Phoenicia	Mesopotamia
Tyre	Asia Minor
Sidon	Egypt
Carthage	Spain
Persia	Sicily
Cyprus	Sardinia

Do You Know When It Happened?

Tell what happened during the following years in Phoenicia's history.

about 1200 B.C. to about 700 B.C.

Do You Remember the Main Idea?

Which one of the following ideas is the MAIN IDEA of this chapter?

1. The Phoenicians were ruled by many nations, but they were able to keep their own culture.
2. The Phoenicians developed the skills of glassmaking and coloring cloth.
3. The Phoenicians became great traders. As traders, they spread their culture and ideas to many nations.

What Do You Think?

From what you have read in this chapter, try to answer the following thought questions.

1. How was the empire built up by the Phoenicians different from the empires of the Egyptians, Hittites, and Mesopotamians?
2. What problems do you suppose the Phoenician sailors faced on their trips to Britain that they did not have on trips in the Mediterranean Sea?
3. What conditions are necessary before trade can take place between people or nations? How did these conditions help the Phoenicians to becoming a trading nation?

Chapter 13
The Persian Empire

GETTING STARTED

1   As you have already read, the lands of the Near East were great culture centers in early history. In the Near East, many empires developed in different ways. This chapter tells about the Persian Empire, which conquered all the other peoples in the Near East. An important part of Persian culture was the Persian belief in life after death. This belief was also a part of the Hebrew, Christian, and Muslim religions. The Persians ruled the Near East between 550 B.C. and 330 B.C. After the Persian Empire ended, however, the Near East became less important as a great center of world culture.

2   Before you begin reading the chapter lesson, survey the lesson. Begin your survey by reading the beginning of the lesson. Then look through the lesson and read the headings. Next, study the pictures and read the picture captions. Then study the map of the Persian Empire on page 99. Finally, read the review section called "Summing Up" at the end of the lesson. This survey of the whole lesson will help you to discover the important ideas in this chapter.

Know the Main Idea

As you read the chapter lesson, try to remember the following important MAIN IDEA of the chapter.

The Persians built up and ruled the largest empire in the Near East. The Persians borrowed many ideas, but they also contributed important ideas to other peoples.

The following questions will help you to understand the MAIN IDEA. Try to answer these questions as you read the lesson.

1. How did the Persians succeed in building their huge empire?
2. Why did many nations accept rule by the Persians?
3. What religious idea of the Persians was taken over by many other religions?

Know These Important Terms

satrap   Ahura Mazda

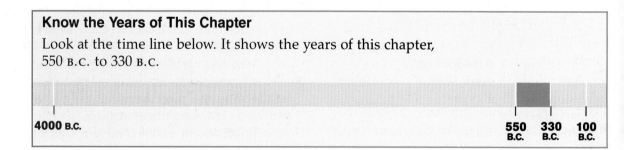

Know the Years of This Chapter
Look at the time line below. It shows the years of this chapter, 550 B.C. to 330 B.C.

4000 B.C.   550   330   100
                                                   B.C.   B.C.   B.C.

Bas-relief at the Treasury in Persepolis showing King Darius of Persia (seated)

EXPLORING THE TIME

The last and largest of the empires in the Near East was the Persian Empire. This empire lasted from about 550 B.C. to about 330 B.C.—a period of over two hundred years. In this chapter, you will learn how the Persian Empire was formed, how it was organized, and how it finally came to an end.

Persia Was a Dry Land with Many Mountains

Persia was located between the Caspian Sea and the Persian Gulf. Most of Persia was made up of high land and mountains. In addition, Persia had very little rainfall. For these reasons, farming was difficult. As a result, most Persians were shepherds who moved from place to place to find good grassland for their animal herds.

GEOGRAPHY AND HISTORY

Cyrus the Great

Roads helped the Persian kings to unify their empire. Cyrus the Great, who ruled from about 550 B.C. to 529 B.C., built a road that reached from the Persian capital of Susa to the shores of Asia Minor. This Royal Road, paved with stones, was about 1,200 miles long.

Government messengers carried mail, news, and official papers along the road. Horses were kept at numerous stations on the road so that the messengers could change horses and continue their journeys without delay. Ordinary people traveled freely on the road. Some drove carts or wagons, some rode horses, others walked. Merchants used the road to carry goods to distant markets.

The Royal Road had branches into every province. This meant that the Persian kings could receive payments of tribute quickly. They could also respond rapidly to trouble in remote parts of the empire. The roads strengthened Persian rule and helped to unify the empire's many peoples.

Question: Why were horses stationed on the Royal Road?

The Persians Built a Great Empire

Two important groups of people moved into Persia—the Medes (MEEDZ) and the Persians. Both groups came from between the Caspian Sea and the Black Sea. The Medes soon became the strongest group in Persia. Before the 600's B.C., the Medes helped to destroy the Assyrian Empire.

After the defeat of the Assyrians, the Medes ruled all of Persia. But about 550 B.C., a mighty Persian leader named Cyrus (SY-russ) the Great united the Persians and conquered the Medes. After this victory, King Cyrus led the Persian armies westward into Mesopotamia and Asia Minor, and then eastward into India. This was the beginning of the Persian Empire.

About 525 B.C., Cyrus' son, Cambyses (kam-BY-seez), conquered Egypt. The Persian Empire now stretched from northern Africa to India—nearly three thousand miles! How were the Persians able to rule this huge empire for two hundred years?

The Persians Learned How to Govern a Large Empire

A part of the success of the Persian Empire was the way it was governed. King Darius (duh-RY-us), one of the rulers who followed Cyrus, was a great organizer. Darius divided Persia into twenty districts and appointed a **satrap** (SAY-trap), or governor, for each district. Darius also sent other officials to all parts of the empire to see that his orders were obeyed.

Roads Helped to Unite the Persian Empire

Another reason for the success of the Persian Empire was that the Persians built many good roads. These roads made it

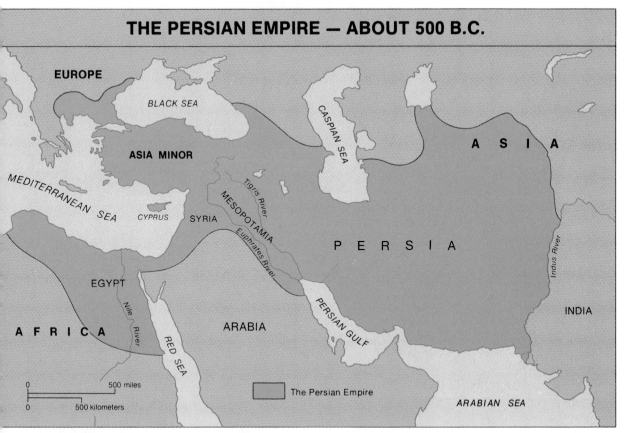

THE PERSIAN EMPIRE — ABOUT 500 B.C.

EUROPE

BLACK SEA

ASIA MINOR

CASPIAN SEA

A S I A

MEDITERRANEAN SEA

CYPRUS

SYRIA

MESOPOTAMIA

Tigris River

Euphrates River

P E R S I A

Indus River

EGYPT

Nile River

RED SEA

ARABIA

PERSIAN GULF

AFRICA

INDIA

0   500 miles
0   500 kilometers

The Persian Empire

ARABIAN SEA

Name the seas that bordered the Persian Empire.

possible for royal officials, messengers, and armies to reach faraway parts of the empire. Every few miles along the roads, messengers were able to change to fresh horses as they swiftly carried messages back and forth between the king and a satrap. By this means, the king's messages were able to travel over a thousand miles in a week.

The Persians Treated Their Conquered Nations Well

The Persians were not cruel to the nations that they conquered, as were the Assyrians. Instead, the Persian kings tried to please the conquered peoples by allowing them to keep their own ways of doing things.

As long as the nations in the Persian Empire obeyed the king and paid taxes, they were allowed to do what they wished and to worship their own gods. Thus, most of them accepted Persian rule.

The Persians Borrowed Many Ideas from Other Peoples

The Persians also borrowed many ideas from the nations that they conquered. Persian buildings, for example, were copied from Mesopotamian and Egyptian buildings. The Persians learned much about astronomy from Mesopotamia, and they got some ideas about medicine from Egypt. Many of the laws used by the Persians came

99

King Darius III, the last King of Persia, in a battle with Alexander the Great, the conqueror of the Persian Empire

from the Mesopotamian Code of Laws of Hammurabi. And the Persians learned how to use coins for money from the people in Asia Minor.

The Persians Developed Their Own Religion

One idea which the Persians did not borrow was their religion. The early Persians, like the Mesopotamians and Egyptians, worshiped many gods. But just before the rise of the Persian Empire, a great Persian religious leader named Zoroaster (ZOR-oh-ASS-tur) began a new religion.

Zoroaster taught that a god of good and truth named **Ahura Mazda** (AH-hoo-rah MAHZ-duh) watched over the world. However, Ahura Mazda was carrying on a great struggle with a god of evil, who caused people to suffer. The Persians believed that in the end Ahura Mazda must finally defeat the power of evil.

The Persians also believed in life after death. If a person lived a good life, he or she was to be rewarded in the next life. This belief was important. It was a part of the Hebrew religion, and later it also became part of the Christian religion and Muslim religion.

The Persian Empire Ended About 330 B.C.

During the 400's B.C., times were good in most of the Persian Empire, and farmers and traders lived well. But later, the government of the Persian Empire began to fall apart. Satraps began to collect very high taxes from the conquered peoples. As a result, many of the conquered nations revolted. The Persian armies stopped most of these revolts, but this fighting weakened the empire. As you will learn, the Persian Empire was conquered by Alexander the Great about 330 B.C.

SUMMING UP

The Persian Empire included a huge area of land from Egypt to India. This empire lasted from 550 B.C. to 330 B.C., and it was well governed. An important part of Persian culture was the Persian religious belief in life after death. This belief was also a part of the Hebrew, Christian, and Muslim religions. In the next chapter, which begins Unit 5, you will read about the land of India.

UNDERSTANDING THE LESSON

Do You Know These Important Terms?

For each sentence below, choose the term that best completes the sentence.

1. The governor of a district in the Persian Empire was called a **(colonial/satrap)**.
2. The Persian god of good and truth was named **(Hammurabi/Ahura Mazda)**.

Do You Remember These People and Events?

1. Tell something about each of the following subjects.

   Medes   Cambyses
   Persians   King Darius
   Cyrus the Great   Zoroaster

2. Tell how each of the following events happened.

   a. Most Persians became shepherds.
   b. Conquered nations of the Persian Empire accepted Persian rule.

Can You Locate These Places?

Use the map on page 99 to do the following map work.

1. Locate the following places. Tell how each place is related to the developments in this chapter.

   Caspian Sea   Persian Gulf
   Persia   India
   Egypt   Mesopotamia

2. Give the names of some of the lands that were part of the Persian Empire.
3. In which direction did the Persian army march to conquer India? to conquer Egypt?

4. Compare this map with a map of the Near East today. (See Chapter 106, page 692.) What present-day nations occupy the land where Persia was once located?

Do You Know When It Happened?

Why are the following years important in Persian history?

   about 550 B.C.   about 330 B.C.

Do You Remember the Main Idea?

Which one of the following ideas is the MAIN IDEA of this chapter?

1. The Persians conquered a huge empire in the Near East. They ruled it for many years until they finally were conquered.
2. The Persians built up and ruled the largest empire in the Near East. The Persians borrowed many ideas, but they also contributed important ideas to other peoples.
3. The Persians borrowed all their ideas from other nations in the Near East. Their empire was taken over by the Egyptians.

What Do You Think?

From what you have read in this chapter, try to answer the following thought questions.

1. In which of the empires in the early Near East would you want to have lived? Explain your choice.
2. Why do you think a people such as the Persians wanted to build a great empire?
3. How important is it for an empire to govern its conquered peoples well?

Unit 5
The Peoples of India and China

THE CHAPTERS IN UNIT 5 ARE

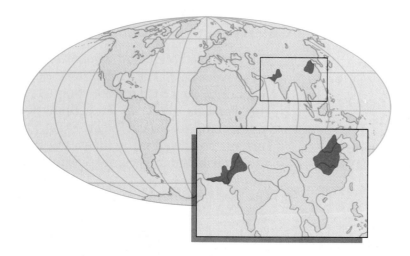

In Asia, two great nations—India and China —developed in early times. The peoples of these two nations developed ways of living, or cultures, that were different from the nations of the Near East. In this unit, you will find out about life in early India and China.

The Shore Temple in India

Chapter 14
India—Land of the Indus River

GETTING STARTED

1   About the same time that great cultures were developing in the Near East, other great cultures were developing in lands far away from the Near East. Between 3000 B.C. and 1500 B.C., a great river valley culture was growing up along the Indus River in southern Asia. This part of Asia is today called Pakistan and northern India.

2   Before you begin reading the chapter lesson, survey the lesson. Begin your survey by reading the beginning of the lesson. Then look through the lesson and read the headings. Next, study the pictures and read the picture captions. Then study the map of early India on page 106. Finally, read the review section called "Summing Up" at the end of the lesson. This survey of the whole lesson will help you to discover the important ideas in this chapter.

Know the Main Idea

As you read the chapter lesson, try to remember the following important MAIN IDEA of the chapter.

The culture of early India was as great as the cultures of Egypt and Mesopotamia. The culture of early India developed along the Indus River.

The following questions will help you to understand the MAIN IDEA. Try to answer these questions as you read the lesson.

1. Why did farming become the main occupation of the early people of India?
2. How have archeologists learned about the Indus culture?
3. What finally happened to the Indus culture?

Know This Important Term

    Aryans

Know the Years of This Chapter

Look at the time line below. It shows the years of this chapter, 3000 B.C. to 1500 B.C.

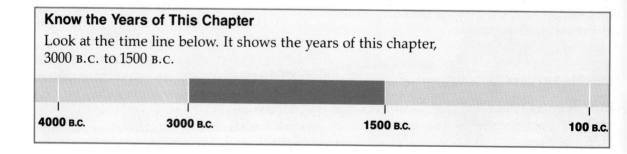

4000 B.C.   3000 B.C.   1500 B.C.   100 B.C.

Early sewer drainage ditch for carrying used water away from houses

EXPLORING THE TIME

In earlier chapters, you learned that the nations of Egypt and Mesopotamia grew up around rivers. India was another nation that grew up around a river—the Indus (IN-duss) River. In this chapter, you will find out about the early people who settled in the Indus River valley.

India Is Located in Southern Asia

India is a large land which is located in the southern part of Asia. As you can see on the map on page 106, India looks something like a large triangle. The widest part of this triangle is northern India, where the highest mountains in the world, the Himalaya (HIM-uh-LAY-uh) Mountains, are located. These mountains divide India from the rest of Asia.

South of the Himalaya Mountains is a great plain that includes the valleys of two important rivers—the Indus River and the Ganges (GAN-jeez) River. The Indus River flows from the Himalaya Mountains southwest to its delta on the western coast of India. (Today, this area is the nation of Pakistan.) The Ganges River flows from the Himalaya Mountains southeast to its delta on the eastern coast of India.

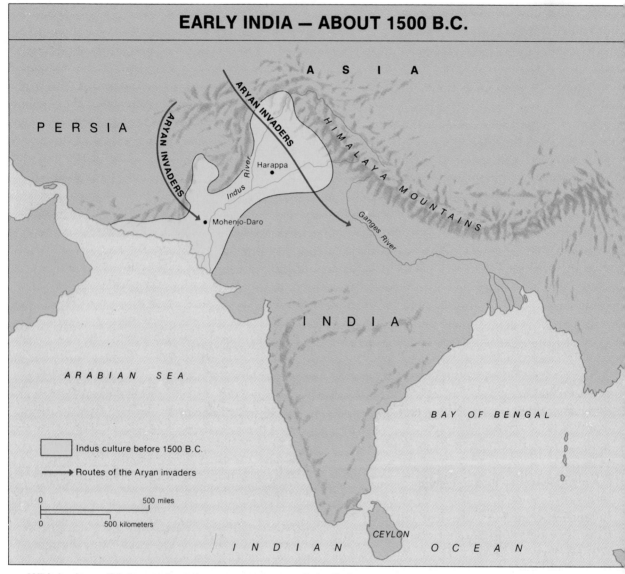

EARLY INDIA — ABOUT 1500 B.C.

ASIA

PERSIA

ARYAN INVADERS

ARYAN INVADERS

HIMALAYA MOUNTAINS

Harappa

Indus River

Mohenjo-Daro

Ganges River

INDIA

ARABIAN SEA

BAY OF BENGAL

Indus culture before 1500 B.C.

Routes of the Aryan invaders

0   500 miles

0   500 kilometers

CEYLON

INDIAN OCEAN

Which river did Aryan invaders cross to reach India?

The rest of India reaches southward into the Indian Ocean. This part includes a central upland section and the tip of India.

In most of India, March, April, and May are hot and dry. From June to November, winds from the Indian Ocean bring heavy rains to India. Then there is a cool season from December to February.

However, not all of India receives heavy rainfall during the wet season. Some parts remain dry. Most people in India settled in the northern plain. This northern plain is very warm, and this part of India has a great deal of rich farming land.

Life in India Grew Up Along the Indus River Valley

India, like Egypt and Mesopotamia, had people living in it before the period of written history began. By the year 3000 B.C., these people learned how to farm, and they were beginning to use copper tools. The villages of these early people were in the hilly country just west of the Indus River.

Within the next five hundred years, many of these people moved eastward to the banks of the Indus River, where life proved to be much easier. If too little rain fell to grow crops, the people were able to get water for their crops from the Indus River. Soon, towns and cities grew up along the Indus River valley.

An Important Culture Developed in the Indus River Valley

The people of the Indus River valley built a thriving culture. Their settlements stretched a thousand miles from north to south and covered an amount of land almost as large as the present-day state of Alaska.

Although the Indus culture lasted about a thousand years, we know less about it than we do about the cultures of Mesopotamia and Egypt. That is because we cannot read the Indus writing. However, archeologists have learned enough from studying the Indus towns to tell us a great deal about the people who lived in them.

The Indus Valley Had Important Cities

The two largest cities along the Indus River were Harappa (hah-RAHP-uh) and Mohenjo-Daro (moh-HEN-joh-DAH-roh). These two cities had a high level of culture.

Indian sculpture of an Indus god

They both had temples, meeting halls, storehouses for grain, and bathhouses. Both cities had wide streets and were laid out with city blocks of houses and stores. Many people—including craftspeople and traders—must have lived in these two cities. These cities were probably the centers of the Indus River valley farming settlement.

The Indus Culture Was Well Developed

The people of the Indus River valley were probably as advanced in some ways as the peoples of Mesopotamia and Egypt. The Indus people, for example, used fire-baked bricks for building. Only sun-dried bricks were used in Mesopotamia. The Indus tools, weapons, jewelry, and cotton cloth were all well made. These goods were traded among the many towns along the Indus River and even carried to faraway Mesopotamia.

Early soft stone carved seals from Mohenjo-Daro in the Indus Valley. What animals can you identify?

Cotton was an important crop grown in the Indus River valley, but barley and wheat were the main food crops. The farmers kept herds of cattle, sheep, and goats, which supplied the people with food and clothing. The Indus people also tamed camels and buffaloes.

Very little is known about the Indus government. Perhaps each town was ruled by a priest, in the same way that the early Sumerian city-states were ruled.

The Indus Culture Was Destroyed by the Aryans

About 2000 B.C., the Indus culture began to weaken. A new people began to attack India from the northwest. These people came from the highlands of Persia. They were called **Aryans** (AIR-ee-UNZ). By 1500 B.C., the Aryans conquered the Indus cities and destroyed the Indus culture.

Very little is known about the next thousand years of India's history. But we do know that the Aryans settled down and became farmers. Slowly, they spread from the valley of the Indus River eastward to the valley of the Ganges River.

SUMMING UP

Life in India first grew up in the Indus River valley between the years 3000 B.C. and 1500 B.C. In some ways, the Indus culture was as well developed as the cultures of Mesopotamia and Egypt. However, about 1500 B.C., the Indus culture was destroyed by the Aryans, who conquered the Indus people and moved into the valley of the Ganges River. In the next chapter, you will read about the culture developed by the Aryans in the valley of the Ganges River.

UNDERSTANDING THE LESSON

Do You Know This Important Term?

For the sentence below, choose the term that best completes the sentence.

1. People who invaded the Indus River valley from the highlands of Persia were called **(Aryans/Assyrians)**.

Do You Remember These People and Events?

1. Tell something about each of the following subjects.

   a. The size of the Indus settlements.
   b. The trade of the Indus people.
   c. The occupations of the Indus people.

2. Explain how each of the following events took place.

   a. Prehistoric people moved into the Indus River valley.
   b. Archeologists can study and learn things about the Indus culture even though they cannot read the Indus writing.
   c. The Aryans destroyed the Indus Valley culture.

Can You Locate These Places?

Use the map on page 106 to do the following map work.

1. Locate each of the following places. Tell how each place is related to the developments in this chapter.

Indus River	Mohenjo-Daro
Persia	Ganges River
Harappa	India

2. Locate the Himalaya Mountains, which separate southern Asia from the rest of Asia.

3. Find where the Indus River and the Ganges River begin. What body of water does each of these rivers finally empty into?

Do You Know When It Happened?

By what year did the Aryans conquer the Indus cities and destroy the Indus culture?

Do You Remember the Main Idea?

Which one of the following ideas is the MAIN IDEA of this chapter?

1. The earliest settlements in India grew up along the Ganges River.
2. The culture of early India was as great as the cultures of Egypt and Mesopotamia. The culture of early India developed along the Indus River.
3. The first culture in India grew up along the Indus River, but it soon ended.

What Do You Think?

From what you have read in this chapter, try to answer the following thought questions.

1. How do you think that the people of the Indus River valley learned about the people in Egypt and Mesopotamia?
2. What clues do you think are used by archeologists to find out how early people lived when archeologists cannot read the writing of these early people?
3. What do you think happened to the Indus people after they were conquered by the Aryans?

Chapter 15
Hinduism and Buddhism in India

GETTING STARTED

1 Today, the Ganges River of India is regarded as a holy river by many people in India. Thousands of India's people bathe in its water every day.

The Ganges River has been important to the people of India since very early times. People settled in the Ganges valley between 1500 B.C. and 300 B.C. These are the years of this chapter. These early settlers developed many ideas that helped to form the cultures of other peoples in southern Asia as well as to form the culture of the people in India. Two great religions grew up in India—Hinduism and Buddhism. Hinduism had many gods, priests, and a caste system. Buddhism did not have a caste system.

2 Before you begin reading the chapter lesson, survey the lesson. Begin your survey by reading the beginning of the lesson. Then look through the lesson and read the headings. Next, study the pictures and read the picture captions. Finally, read the review section called "Summing Up" at the end of the lesson. This survey of the whole lesson will help you to discover the important ideas in this chapter.

Know the Main Idea

As you read the chapter lesson, try to remember the following important MAIN IDEA of the chapter.

A great culture in India grew up along the Ganges River. This culture produced two important religions, and it united the people of India in the Maurya Empire.

The following questions will help you to understand the MAIN IDEA. Try to answer these questions as you read the lesson.

1. What religion did the Aryans develop?
2. What religion was started by people who did not like the Hindu religion?
3. How did the emperor control the government in the Maurya Empire?

Know These Important Terms

Vedas	untouchables
Hinduism	Buddhism
caste system	

Know the Years of This Chapter

Look at the time line below. It shows the years of this chapter, 1500 B.C. to 300 B.C.

4000 B.C.　　　　　　　　　1500 B.C.　　　　　　300 B.C.　100 B.C.

An Indian painting of a seated Buddha

EXPLORING THE TIME

The people of India call the Ganges River "the mother Ganges." The Ganges River was the center of a new culture in India. This new culture was developed by the Aryans. In this chapter, you will find out about the culture of the Aryans.

The Aryans Developed a New Religion

Between the years 1500 B.C. and 500 B.C., the Aryans composed, or put together, several holy books. The earliest of these holy books were called the **Vedas** (VAY-duz). "Veda" is an Aryan word that means "knowledge."

The Vedas were the holy books of a great new religion that developed in India called **Hinduism.** The Vedas contained prayers, ideas about religion, and religious songs and ceremonies. Most of what we know about Aryan life and religion in India during this thousand-year period comes from these holy books.

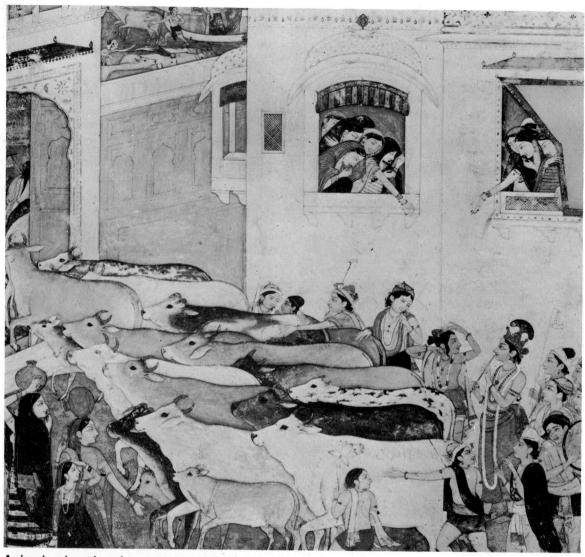

Animals played an important part in the Hindu religion. How can you tell that the animals were well treated?

The Aryans Worshiped Many Gods

The Vedas books tell that the early Aryans worshiped nature. They believed that the sun, stars, sky, thunder, and fire were all gods. These beliefs were the beginning of Hinduism, or the Hindu religion. The three most important Hindu gods were Brahma (BRAH-muh) the "creator," Vishnu (VISH-noo) the "preserver," and Siva (SEE-vuh) the "destroyer."

As time went on, Hinduism added hundreds of other gods. The Hindus came to believe that all horned animals —particularly cows—were sacred, or holy. Some Hindus refused to eat any meat at all.

The Hindus Were Divided into Many Groups

One important development in Hinduism was the **caste** (KAST) **system.** The caste system began about 1500 B.C.

In the Hindu caste system, people were divided into four main castes, or groups. In the order of their importance, these groups were (1) priests, (2) rulers and soldiers, (3) farmers and traders, (4) workers and servants. At first, people were able to move from a lower caste to a higher caste. Later, the caste system became fixed, and people remained in the caste they were born in.

The people of the first two castes had more rights than the people of the two lower castes. Some people were not even allowed to belong to any caste—even the lowest caste. Those people were known as **untouchables.** A Hindu was not allowed to have anything to do with an untouchable. The untouchables received the worst treatment of any people in India.

Hindus Believed in Life After Death

Hindus, like other peoples, believed in life after death. But the Hindus did not share the Egyptian belief that people lived the same lives again. The Hindus believed that when a person died, the soul was born again in a different body.

If a person lived a bad life, the soul was reborn in the body of an untouchable, or even in a dog or a pig. Only good people were reborn as members of a higher caste. The Hindus believed that only the priests (the highest caste) lived perfect lives. Only if a person led a perfect life did the soul go to the Hindu heaven. Therefore, all Hindus hoped to be reborn as priests in order to be able to enter the Hindu heaven.

Sculpture of the Hindu god Brahma, "the creator"

Another New Religion Began in India

The Hindu religion did not please everyone in India. Some religious leaders believed that the Hindus worshiped too many gods and had too many priests. And many religious leaders did not like the caste system. These religious leaders felt that the caste system allowed only certain people (the priests and rulers) to enjoy a good life.

Sculpture of the Hindu god Siva, "the destroyer"

About 530 B.C. a great religious leader, Gautama Buddha (GOW-tuh-muh BOO-duh), began a new religion called **Buddhism** (BOO-dizz-UM). Buddha was against the Hindu caste system. He believed that all people deserved to be rewarded for living good lives no matter what caste of people they belonged to.

Buddha preached all over northern India. He taught that the way to be good was to live a simple life and to be kind, truthful, and unselfish. He taught that this way of living was the way to find peace and happiness.

Buddhism slowly gained many followers. Some of these followers lived together and obeyed Buddha's rules completely. These followers spread Buddhism all over India. Later, you will learn how Buddhism spread to other nations in Asia.

The Ayrans Set Up a Strong Government for India

While Buddhism was developing in India, the government of India also was developing. At first, the Aryans were divided into many tribes, or groups. Later, many of the tribes joined together and formed small kingdoms ruled by kings.

The kingdoms often fought each other. Before 300 B.C., however, the Maurya (MORR-yuh) kingdom took over all of northern India and became an empire.

The Maurya Empire was well organized. The government controlled all business, mining, and farming in the empire. However, the Maurya emperor had the power to do whatever he wished. This meant that he had the power to force people to obey any rule that he made. This harsh kind of government was used in India by many later rulers, too. (You will read more about the Maurya Empire in Chapter 38.)

SUMMING UP

Two great religions grew up in India —Hinduism and Buddhism. Hinduism had many gods, priests, and a caste system. Buddhism did not have a caste system. It taught that people might find peace and happiness by living simple, good lives. A new government also ruled India when by 300 B.C., India was united under the Maurya Empire. In the next chapter, you will read about the beginning of China.

UNDERSTANDING THE LESSON

Do You Know These Important Terms?

For each sentence below, choose the term that best completes the sentence.

1. The holy books of the Hindu religion are called the (**Siva/Vedas**).
2. Another name for the Hindu religion is (**Hinduism/Hindustan**).
3. The (**Vishnu system/caste system**) was a development of the Hindu religion which divided the people into four main groups.
4. People who were not included in one of the four main groups of Hindus were called (**Aryans/untouchables**).
5. A religion of India that taught people to "live a good life" was (**Buddhism/the caste system**).

Do You Remember These People and Events?

1. Tell something about each of the following subjects.

   Brahma   Siva
   Vishnu   Gautama Buddha

2. Tell how each of the following developments took place.

   a. All Hindus wanted to be reborn into a higher caste.
   b. Buddhism appealed to those who did not like Hinduism.
   c. The Maurya emperor controlled the Maurya Empire.

Can You Locate These Places?

Use the map on page 106 (in Chapter 14) to do the following map work.

1. Locate each of the following places. Tell how each place is related to the developments in this chapter.

   Ganges River   Asia

2. Locate the delta of the Ganges River. What other river delta did you read about in an earlier chapter?

Do You Know When It Happened?

Why are the following years important in the history of India?

   about 530 B.C.   about 300 B.C.

Do You Remember the Main Idea?

Which one of the following ideas is the MAIN IDEA of this chapter?

1. Most of the people in India joined the Buddhist religion because they disliked the Hindu caste system.
2. The people of India were united for the first time when the Maurya Empire was formed in northern India.
3. A great culture in India grew up along the Ganges River. This culture produced two important religions and united the people of India in the Maurya Empire.

What Do You Think?

From what you have read in this chapter, try to answer the following thought questions.

1. What beliefs might a Hindu and a Buddhist share?
2. Why do you think it was easier for the people of northern India to form an empire than those of southern India?

Chapter 16
The Beginning of China

GETTING STARTED

1   You have read about the cultures of three great river valleys. These were the Egyptian culture along the Nile River, the Mesopotamian culture in the valley of the Tigris River and Euphrates River, and the culture along the Indus River valley.

East of the Indus River valley, another great river valley culture also developed. This river was in China. During the years from 2000 B.C. to 221 B.C., the early people of China developed a somewhat different way of life from the other great cultures you have been reading about. One reason for these differences, as you will see, was that the early Chinese people lived in a different kind of land and had different problems.

2   Before you begin reading the chapter lesson, survey the lesson. Begin your survey by reading the beginning of the lesson. Then look through the lesson and read the headings. Next, study the pictures and read the picture captions. Then study the map of early China on page 118. Finally, read the review section called "Summing Up" at the end of the lesson. This survey of the whole lesson will help you to discover the important ideas in this chapter.

Know the Main Idea

As you read the chapter lesson, try to remember the following important MAIN IDEA of the chapter.

The earliest culture of China developed along the Huang He valley. The early Chinese people developed their writing, their religion, and their calendar.

The following questions will help you to understand the MAIN IDEA. Try to answer these questions as you read the lesson.

1. What natural feature helped early China to become a strong nation?
2. How was early Chinese writing like the writing in Egypt and in Mesopotamia?
3. What ruling family was able to unite the people in two important river valleys of China?

Know These Important Terms

dynasties	ancestor worship
Shang dynasty	Chou dynasty

Know the Years of This Chapter

Look at the time line below. It shows the years of this chapter, 2000 B.C. to 221 B.C.

4000 B.C.   2000 B.C.   221 B.C.   100 B.C.

116

Part of the 7,500 life-size pottery soldiers being excavated near the tomb of China's first emperor, Qin Shih Huang Ti. The emperor, who also had the Great Wall of China built, had this huge Imperial Bodyguard made of pottery so that it might be buried with him and protect him after death.

EXPLORING THE TIME

Early China, like early India, Egypt, and Mesopotamia, developed along a river. The first Chinese culture grew up along the Huang He, a river of eastern Asia. Along this river was rich farming land used by the first Chinese settlers. Yet this river's terrible floods have given it another name —"China's sorrow." In this chapter, you will read about China's early growth along the Huang He.

The Chinese People Settled in Three River Valleys

China is a large land in Asia. In northern China, people settled along the Huang He. In central China, life grew up around the Chang Jiang (CHAHNG JYAHNG). In southern China, life developed around the Xi (SHEE) River, or West River.

Western China has many mountains. This helps to explain why most of the Chinese people settled in the river valleys in eastern China. The western mountains

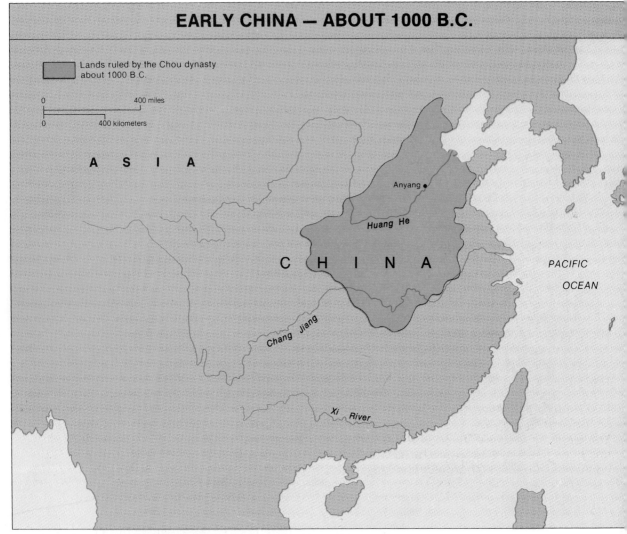

EARLY CHINA — ABOUT 1000 B.C.

Lands ruled by the Chou dynasty about 1000 B.C.

0   400 miles

0   400 kilometers

ASIA

Anyang

Huang He

CHINA

PACIFIC OCEAN

Chang Jiang

Xi River

What rivers were in the lands ruled by the Chou dynasty?

protected China from attacks, and helped China to become a strong nation very early.

China Began in the Huang He Valley

The earliest people in China lived by hunting, fishing, and farming. They also domesticated, or tamed, horses, sheep, and cattle. About the year 2000 B.C., they settled in the Huang He valley, in northern China.

As the years went by, the Chinese people came to be governed by ruling families called **dynasties** (DY-nuhs-TEEZ). These dynasties provided strong governments that helped China to become a united country. From 2000 B.C. to 1500 B.C., the Chinese people developed rapidly under the dynasty rule. They built irrigation ditches and dams. They began to make bronze tools and weapons. They learned how to use the silk from silkworms to make silk cloth. They also began to develop a writing system.

The Shang Dynasty Ruled China for Five Hundred Years

About 1500 B.C., the **Shang dynasty** took over China and ruled for five hundred years. During this period, the capital city was moved many times, probably because of floods from the Huang He. The most important city was located near the modern city of Anyang (AN-yang).

From the many tools, weapons, and ornaments found around Anyang, we know a great deal about life during the Shang period. We know that the Chinese people produced fine bronze work during this time. They also carved ivory and jade, and they made marble statues.

We know, too, that the Shang government was led by a king, who was also a war leader and a priest. The king ruled with the help of officials from his own family. Other government officials, or nobles, were chosen for their skills or education. They collected taxes, controlled the repair of public buildings, and directed the digging of irrigation canals.

Chinese Writing Developed During the Shang Period

Chinese writing, like the early Egyptian and Mesopotamian writing, was based on pictures. But the Chinese writing developed differently. The Chinese people used signs instead of pictures. These signs were combined, or put together, to make words.

Several thousand signs were used in the Shang period. And the number of signs increased during China's long history. As a

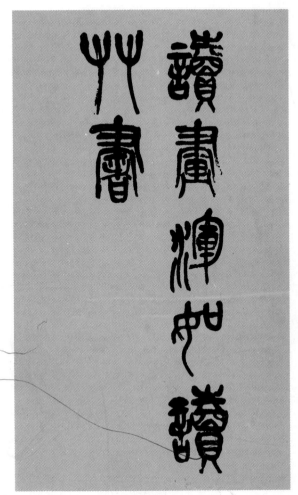

Chinese writing is based on signs

result, modern Chinese writing has over fifty thousand signs!

The Chinese people always wrote from top to bottom, rather than from left to right as we do. They carved their writing on metal, bone, turtle shells, and wood. The Chinese people also used silk cloth to write on, using a brush dipped in ink.

The Chinese Calendar Developed During the Shang Period

In the Chinese calendar, a Chinese "week" was 10 days long. Three weeks made a

A dish from the time of the Shang Dynasty

By the Shang period, the Chinese also worshiped their ancestors, or dead relatives. The Chinese believed that a dead person's soul lived on as a powerful spirit. This spirit either helped or hurt one's living relatives, depending on whether or not the spirit was kept happy. The Chinese people tried to please their ancestors' spirits by taking food and offerings to their graves. **Ancestor worship** became important in Chinese life.

The Chou Dynasty Replaced the Shang Dynasty

Shortly before 1000 B.C., the Shang dynasty was overthrown by a new ruling family, the **Chou** (JOH) **dynasty.** The Chou dynasty lasted for almost eight hundred years. It ruled a large empire that included the Huang He valley in the north and the Chang Jiang valley in the south.

But after 800 B.C., the Chou king lost much of his power, and the Chou Empire split into several states, or separate parts. Toward the end of the Chou dynasty, these states fought for control of all China. Then in 221 B.C., the state of Chin (JIN) conquered all of China. It was from the name "Chin" that China received its name.

month, and six 60-day periods made a year. Every few years, an extra 10, 20, or 30 days were added to the calendar to even it out. The Chinese calendar developed during the Shang period and was used in China (with some changes) for almost three thousand years.

The Chinese People Worshiped Their Ancestors

The early Chinese people, like other early peoples, worshiped many gods. And like other early peoples, the Chinese people also sacrificed, or killed, animals and even human beings because they believed that such actions pleased their gods.

SUMMING UP

Chinese life began in the valley of the Huang He. From 2000 B.C. to 1000 B.C., the Chinese people developed their writing, their calendar, and their religion. In the next chapter, you will read about the history of China during the next eight hundred years.

UNDERSTANDING THE LESSON

Do You Know These Important Terms?

For each sentence below, choose the term that best completes the sentence.

1. Ruling families in China were called (**dynasties/emperors**).
2. The (**Shang dynasty/Chou dynasty**) ruled nothern China from about 1500 B.C. to 1000 B.C.
3. The worship of dead relatives is called (**monotheism/ancestor worship**).
4. The (**Shang dynasty/Chou dynasty**) ruled the Huang He and Chang Jiang valleys of China for eight hundred years.

Do You Remember These People and Events?

1. Tell something about each of the following subjects.

   **Chinese officials   Chinese calendar
   Chinese writing**

2. Tell how each of the following developments probably took place.

   a. The Chinese worshiped their dead relatives.
   b. Archeologists and historians learned about the earliest dynasties in China.

Can You Locate These Places?

Use the map on page 118 to do the following map work.

1. Locate the following places. Tell how each place is related to the developments in this chapter.

   **Huang He   Xi River
   Chang Jiang   Anyang**

2. The highest lands of China are located in western China. Therefore, in which direction do the three main rivers of China flow? Into what body of water do these rivers empty? Which of the three rivers is located farthest north? On this map of early China, which of the three rivers shown is the shortest?

Do You Know When It Happened?

In what year did the state of Chin conquer all of China?

Do You Remember the Main Idea?

Which one of the following ideas is the MAIN IDEA of this chapter?

1. The earliest culture of China developed along the Huang He valley. The early Chinese people developed their writing, their religion, and their calendar.
2. The Huang He was called "China's sorrow" because of its many floods, which destroyed villages, people, and crops.
3. The earliest culture of China developed along the Chang Jiang valley.

What Do You Think?

From what you have read in this chapter, try to answer the following thought questions.

1. Do you think that the Chinese method of choosing government officials, or nobles, was a good method?
2. Why might ancestor worship have kept the Chinese people from moving from one place to another?

Chapter 17
China's Classical Age

GETTING STARTED

1   Almost every nation and empire has had a period when its culture reaches a high point of development. The period of the Chou dynasty, which you read about in the last chapter, was such a period in China's history. During the eight-hundred-year period from 1028 B.C. to 256 B.C. (see the time line below), many important ideas were developed in China. These ideas had lasting effects both on China and on other peoples in eastern Asia. You can see by the chapter title that this important period of early Chinese history is called China's "Classical Age."

2   Before you begin reading the chapter lesson, survey the lesson. Begin your survey by reading the beginning of the lesson. Then look through the lesson and read the headings. Next, study the pictures and read the picture captions. Finally, read the review section called "Summing Up" at the end of the lesson. This survey of the whole lesson will help you to discover the important ideas in this chapter.

Know the Main Idea

As you read the chapter lesson, try to remember the following important MAIN IDEA of the chapter.

During the Chou dynasty, great Chinese writers and thinkers developed ideas that helped to shape Chinese life.

The following questions will help you to understand the MAIN IDEA. Try to answer these questions as you read the lesson.

1. Who was the Chinese writer and thinker who put together important rules that shaped Chinese life and behavior?
2. What ideas about government did the Chinese people develop?
3. What important changes were made in Chinese ways of living during the Chou dynasty?

Know These Important Terms

Confucianism	Legalists
Taoism	Chin dynasty

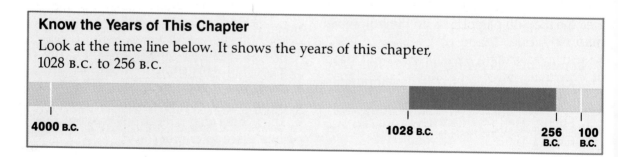

Know the Years of This Chapter
Look at the time line below. It shows the years of this chapter, 1028 B.C. to 256 B.C.

4000 B.C.   1028 B.C.   256 B.C.   100 B.C.

Early Chinese bronze vessel in the shape of a stag

EXPLORING THE TIME

The Chou dynasty ruled China from 1028 B.C. to 256 B.C., a period of nearly eight hundred years. Many of China's greatest writers lived during these years. And some of the most important ideas in Chinese culture were developed then. In this chapter, you will read how Chinese life and culture developed during the years of the Chou dynasty.

Many Books Were Written in China

One of the most interesting books produced during the Chou dynasty was a book of poetry that contains over three hundred poems. These poems tell how the Chinese nobles of this period felt about their lives and about love and war.

Another book of this period had rules to teach people how to behave at weddings, funerals, and other important occasions. Other books described the important

DOCUMENTS IN HISTORY

Confucius

The great Chinese thinker Confucius hoped to bring peace and good government back to China. He believed that good government depended on people living together in a well-ordered way. That meant following certain rules.

Confucius spoke of two basic laws. One was to do your duty, and the other was to respect others. Rulers should respect and care for their people and should obey moral laws. Parents should respect and care for their children and should obey their ruler. Children should respect, care for, and obey their parents. Confucius wrote:

> These three things—the relationship toward one's wife, toward one's children and toward one's self—are a symbol of the relationships among the people.

When asked if there was a single rule that could serve as a general guide in life, Confucius replied:

> Do not do to others what you do not want others to do to you.

Question: According to Confucius, what was the basis of good government?

events during the Chou period. All these books were written or put together by the great Chinese thinker Confucius (kun-FYOO-shuss). Confucius was born about 551 B.C.

Confucius Wanted People to Live Good Lives

Confucius lived during the later years of the Chou dynasty, when many wars took place in China. These wars divided China into many states, or separate parts. This made China weak and worried many Chinese thinkers. Confucius, the most famous of these thinkers, believed that China must return to earlier ways of living in order to rebuild peace and unity.

Confucius believed that, in earlier years, China was stronger because the king ruled for the good of the people and the nobles tried to treat the common people well. As a result, the common people supported the king and the nobles. In Chinese families, wives had respected their husbands, and children had obeyed their parents. Confucius taught that these things were necessary in order to make China a strong country again.

Confucius' Teachings Helped to Shape Chinese Life

Confucius believed that his rules were the correct way for people to lead their lives. These ideas are called **Confucianism** (kun-FYOO-shun-IZ-um), and millions of Chinese people try to live by these rules today. But Confucius' teachings were not accepted by the Chinese rulers until later. Then, books of Confucius were studied in schools, and Confucius was worshiped almost as a god.

Confucius' teachings helped the Chinese people to develop a close family life, a

Set of bronze sacrificial vessels made by 11th century B.C. artisans in China

belief in correct behavior, and a respect for learning. These ideas are still important in China today.

The Chinese People Developed Different Ideas About Government

Another belief that developed during the Chou period was **Taoism** (TOW-iz-UM). "Tao" means "the way," or "the path." The followers of Taoism believed that the "pathway" to a good life was to live simply and close to nature. They did not like rules or governments. They felt that people who lived properly did not need governments. Therefore, the weaker a government was, the better it was. Taoism's ideas about government were never accepted, but Taoism as a belief had many followers in China.

A group that did not agree with Taoism were the **Legalists** (LEE-gul-ISTZ). The Legalists believed that all people needed to be controlled by a strong ruler and strict laws. The Legalists' main interest in laws was to have a strong government. They were not interested in having laws to help the people. The Legalists also believed that if the common people were not educated they were more easily ruled by the government.

The **Chin dynasty,** the rulers who followed the Chou dynasty, took over the Legalists' ideas. The ideas of Confucious did not become official all over China until the end of the Chin dynasty. Even then, the Chinese government followed a policy based on the Legalists' belief in strict laws.

The Chinese Rulers Were Expected to Rule Wisely

The Chinese rulers had great power. The Chinese people even believed that their rulers were appointed by the gods. However, these rulers were supposed to rule for

Chinese artists and artisans produced beautiful works of art

the good of their people. If a ruler did not rule well, the Chinese people expected their gods to send another ruler.

Therefore, the Chinese ruler knew that he must rule well. Most Chinese rulers chose trained government officials to help them rule China. Many of these officials were educated according to the ideas of Confucius. But Chinese rulers did not allow the common people to share in making the laws of China.

Chinese Ways of Living Were Improved

During the eight-hundred-year rule of the Chou dynasty, the Chinese people greatly improved their ways of farming. They increased the size of their crops by building new irrigation canals, by making the soil richer, and by using the ox-drawn plow in place of the hoe. As a result, Chinese farmers were able to produce larger crops of rice and wheat to feed a growing population.

Chinese towns also increased in size and number during this period. And important trade grew up among these towns and also with other nations. Some of the goods traded were leather, silk, jade jewelry, and fine furniture. This growing trade also was helped when the Chinese people began to use coins for money.

SUMMING UP

During the years of the Chou dynasty, great Chinese writers and thinkers developed ideas that helped to shape Chinese life. The ideas of Confucius and of Taoism became widely accepted by the Chinese people. In these years, many important features of Chinese life were developed, including a government headed by strong rulers, farming based on large crops, and a growing trade. In the next chapter, which begins Unit 6, you will learn about the beginning of Greece.

UNDERSTANDING THE LESSON

Do You Know These Important Terms?

For each sentence below, choose the term that best completes the sentence.

1. Many Chinese people believed that people must live by a set of rules or ideas developed by a great Chinese thinker named Confucius. These ideas are called **(Confucianism/etiquette)**.
2. The belief that the "pathway" to a good life was to live close to nature was called **(nature study/Taoism)**.
3. The **(Legalists/Taoists)** believed that people needed to be controlled by a strong ruler and a strict set of laws.
4. The **(Shang dynasty/Chin dynasty)** followed the Chou dynasty as the rulers of China.

Do You Remember These People and Events?

1. Tell something about each of the following subjects.

   Confucius   **Taoism**
   Confucianism   **Legalists**
   Chin dynasty

2. Explain how each of the following developments took place.

   a. Many Chinese people accepted Confucianism.
   b. Important changes were made in the Chinese ways of living during the Chou dynasty.

Can You Locate These Places?

Use the map on page 118 (in Chapter 16) to do the following map work.

1. Locate each of the following places.

   Yellow River valley   Si River valley
   Yangtze River valley

Do You Know When It Happened?

Which dynasty ruled China during the following years?

   1028 B.C. to 256 B.C.

Do You Remember the Main Idea?

Which one of the following ideas is the MAIN IDEA of this chapter?

1. The Chinese people became followers of Confucius and developed a way of life based on his rules.
2. The Chou dynasty ruled China for eight hundred years, but it was not able to build a great empire.
3. During the Chou dynasty, great Chinese writers and thinkers developed ideas that helped to shape Chinese life.

What Do You Think?

From what you have read in this chapter, try to answer the following thought questions.

1. Do you think that someone could be both a sincere Legalist and Taoist at the same time? Explain.
2. How do you think that Chinese farmers were able to produce larger crops?
3. Why do you think other people might have been interested in trading with the Chinese?

Unit 6
The Development of Greek Culture

THE CHAPTERS IN UNIT 6 ARE

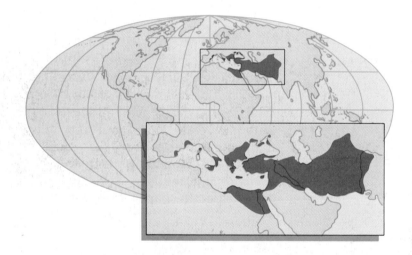

The Greek nation made many lasting contributions to the modern world. The Greeks developed many ideas in art, government, and ways of thinking that are still important today. In this unit, you will learn about Greek life and find out how Greek ideas spread to other lands.

The island of Delos, in Greece, was a sacred religious center

128

Chapter 18
The Cultures of Crete and Greece

GETTING STARTED

1 You have already read about the great cultures that developed in Egypt, Mesopotamia, India, and China. These cultures took thousands of years to develop. And these cultures are important today because their ideas helped other peoples to improve their ways of living and thinking.

The chapters in this unit tell about another great culture, the culture of early Greece. Greece reached its peak of greatness later in history than did the cultures you have already studied. But the beginnings of Greece go back to very early years—to about 3000 B.C. From 3000 B.C. to 1000 B.C., the Greek culture slowly developed, as you will learn in this chapter.

2 Before you begin reading the chapter lesson, survey the lesson. Begin your survey by reading the beginning of the lesson. Then look through the lesson and read the headings. Next, study the pictures and read the picture captions. Then study the map of early Crete and Greece on page 132. Finally, read the review section called "Summing Up" at the end of the lesson. This survey of the whole lesson will help you to discover the important ideas in this chapter.

Know the Main Idea

As you read the chapter lesson, try to remember the following important MAIN IDEA of the chapter.

The culture of the Near East spread to Crete and then to Greece. This early Greek culture was the basis of the great Greek culture that developed later.

The following questions will help you to understand the MAIN IDEA. Try to answer these questions as you read the lesson.

1. How did the people of Crete find out about many of the Egyptian and Mesopotamian ideas?
2. What city in Greece conquered Crete and took over its culture?
3. What finally happened to most of the culture from Crete which the Greeks took over?

Know This Important Term

Minoan culture

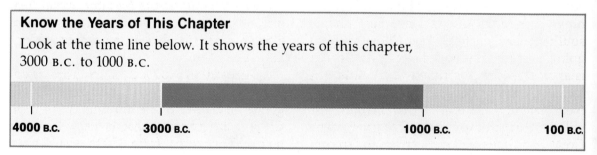

Know the Years of This Chapter

Look at the time line below. It shows the years of this chapter, 3000 B.C. to 1000 B.C.

| 4000 B.C. | 3000 B.C. | 1000 B.C. | 100 B.C. |

Painting on a late Minoan tomb. What do the men and women appear to be doing?

EXPLORING THE TIME

You have been reading about the beginnings of nations in the Near East and in southern and eastern Asia. Now you are going to study a nation that grew up on an island. The island is called Crete, and it is located halfway between the lands of the Near East and Greece. In this chapter, you will learn about the culture that grew up on Crete and that was later carried to Greece.

Crete's Location Was Good for Trade

Crete (KREET) is a small island located near the eastern end of the Mediterranean Sea, only sixty miles from the southern tip of Greece. Crete is also near northern Africa and Asia Minor.

As early as 3000 B.C., ships from Egypt and Mesopotamia were carrying trading goods to Crete. Soon, trading ships from Crete were carrying goods back to these lands. The ships from Crete also began

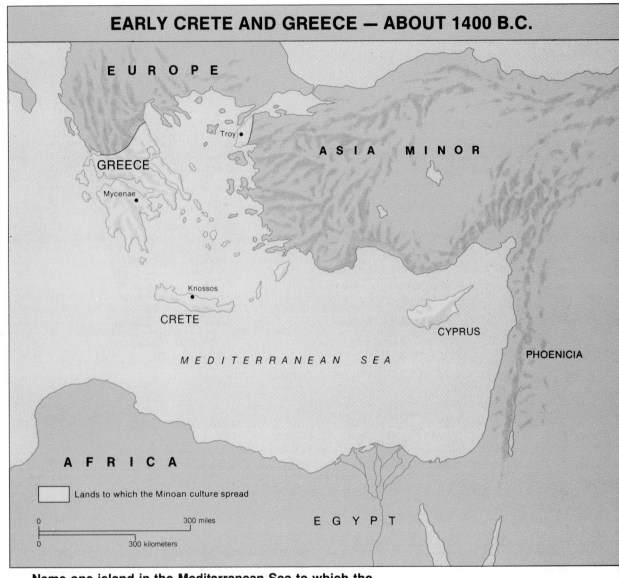

EARLY CRETE AND GREECE — ABOUT 1400 B.C.

EUROPE

Troy •

ASIA MINOR

GREECE

Mycenae •

Knossos •

CRETE

CYPRUS

PHOENICIA

MEDITERRANEAN SEA

AFRICA

Lands to which the Minoan culture spread

0   300 miles

0   300 kilometers

EGYPT

Name one island in the Mediterranean Sea to which the Minoan culture spread.

trading with other islands in the Mediterranean Sea.

Crete Developed an Important Culture

The Cretans (KREET-uhnz), or people of Crete, learned many things from trading with other nations. They learned how to make tools and weapons of copper and bronze. They learned how to make better pottery. And they learned how to build stone buildings. They also learned about Egyptian art and the religions of Asia Minor.

The Cretans made many changes in the ideas they borrowed. Cretan art was very different from Egyptian art. And Cretan writing was so different from Egyptian and Mesopotamian writing that we have just begun to learn to read it. The culture of Crete, therefore, has a name of its own. It is called **Minoan** (min-NOH-un) **culture.** The word "Minoan" comes from the name of a Cretan king, Minos (mih-NOHS).

Crete Spread Its Culture to Other Lands Around the Mediterranean Sea

By the year 2000 B.C., Crete was a great trading nation. Cretan ships carried olive oil, wine, jewelry, fine pottery, and tools to many lands around the Mediterranean Sea. From these places, the Cretan traders carried back grain, tin, ivory, and gold. The Cretan traders started their own colonies in Greece, Asia Minor, and on many Mediterranean islands. The Minoan culture of Crete also spread to these lands.

Crete Had a Famous Capital City Called Knossos

During its early history, Crete was divided into many city-states. A city-state, if you remember, was a city that ruled itself and the land around it. Shortly after 2000 B.C., earthquakes destroyed most of the Cretan cities. After that time, Knossos (kuh-NOSS-sus) became the strongest city and was the capital city of the whole island of Crete.

The ruins of the royal palace at Knossos show that the Cretan king was rich and powerful. This palace at Knossos had several chapels, a throne room, meeting rooms, and rooms where the king lived. The royal palace also had many storerooms—and metal pipes to carry fresh running water!

What sea animal is painted on this early Cretan vase?

What Life Was Like in Crete

Life for most Cretans was easier than life was for most Egyptians or Mesopotamians. Crete did not need large armies, because the Cretan navy provided Crete with protection from enemies. And the people of Crete had enough food, because Crete had plenty of rainfall for growing crops. Most of the Cretans enjoyed some of the riches that came from Crete's trade with other nations.

Mycenae Conquered Crete

About the year 1400 B.C., Knossos and other Cretan cities were destroyed by enemy ships from the city of Mycenae (my-SEE-nee). Mycenae was a city in southern Greece that began about 3000 B.C. By 1400

Mycenae Was Conquered by the Dorian Greeks

The Achaeans of Mycenae were a very warlike people. The Achaeans attacked Egypt and Asia Minor. The story of Mycenae's attack on the city of Troy in Asia Minor is told in the famous long poem written by Homer, the *Iliad* (IL-ee-UD).

Mycenae finally conquered Troy. But soon, Mycenae and its neighboring cities were attacked by new Greek invaders from the north. These new Greek invaders were called the Dorians (DOR-ee-unz). The Dorians used strong weapons made of iron. And by about 1000 B.C., the Dorians conquered most of Greece.

The Dorian invaders destroyed much of the culture of Mycenae. Reading and writing now became less important in Greece. And pottery and tools were not as well made as they were before the Dorians conquered Greece. However, not all of Mycenae's culture was destroyed. The idea of the city-state and certain ideas about religion were taken over by the Dorians when they became the new rulers of Greece.

Soldiers of Mycenae used a hollow, wooden horse to trick and conquer the people of Troy

B.C., Mycenae was ruled by a group of Greeks called Achaeans (uh-KEE-unz).

After Mycenae conquered Crete, the Achaeans took over Crete's Mediterranean trade. The Achaeans of Mycenae also took over much of the Cretan way of life. The Achaeans made fine jewelry, pottery, and metal ware. And Achaean builders were able to build walls that were from 10 to 20 feet thick. But the city of Mycenae never became as rich or as powerful as Crete had been. As a result, the Minoan culture of Crete did not develop further during the years after Mycenae conquered Crete.

SUMMING UP

The Minoan culture developed on the island of Crete. After Mycenae conquered Crete, the Minoan culture spread to Greece. About 1000 B.C., Mycenae was conquered by the Dorians, a warlike people who invaded Greece from the north. The Dorians conquered most of Greece and destroyed much of Mycenae's culture. But the idea of the city-state and certain religious beliefs continued. In the next chapter, you will read how the Greek city-states developed.

UNDERSTANDING THE LESSON

Do You Know This Important Term?

For the sentence below, choose the term that best completes the sentence.

1. The culture of early Crete is called (**Minoan culture/Mycenaean culture**).

Do You Remember These People and Events?

1. Tell something about each of the following subjects.

   Minos   **Homer**
   Achaeans   **Dorians**

2. Explain how each of the following developments took place.

   a. Life was easier for most Cretans than for most Egyptians and Mesopotamians.
   b. The Minoan culture was carried to Greece.
   c. The Dorian invaders destroyed much of the culture of Mycenae.

Can You Locate These Places?

Use the map on page 132 to do the following map work.

1. Locate each of the following places. Tell how each place is related to the developments in this chapter.

   Greece   Troy
   Crete   Mediterranean Sea
   Asia Minor   Knossos
   Egypt   Mycenae

2. In what way was Crete's location good for carrying on trade?

3. Locate and name another island in the Mediterranean Sea.
4. Use the scale of miles on this map to measure the distance from Crete to Greece; from Crete to Egypt.

Do You Know When It Happened?

By what year did the Dorians conquer most of Greece?

Do You Remember the Main Idea?

Which one of the following ideas is the MAIN IDEA of this chapter?

1. The people of Mycenae often fought wars. They attacked many cities in Egypt and in Asia Minor.
2. The culture of the Near East spread to Crete and then to Greece. This early Greek culture was the basis of the great Greek culture that developed later.
3. The Cretans took ideas from Egypt and Mesopotamia, and they changed these ideas to create a culture of their own.

What Do You Think?

From what you have read in this chapter, try to answer the following thought questions.

1. How do archeologists know that Cretan traders started their own colonies in Greece, Asia Minor, and on other Mediterranean islands?
2. Why was piped water seldom found even in a king's palace in early history?
3. Describe an imaginary trip taken by a Cretan trader. Which land do you think would be most interesting to visit?

Chapter 19
The Greek City-States

GETTING STARTED

1   You probably have heard the word "democracy" many times. Have you ever wondered how some of our ideas about democracy and freedom began? In the cultures you have studied so far, people did not have democratic ideas—ideas about having the people run their own government. In most cases, a king, emperor, or pharaoh was the ruler. Such a ruler was always powerful, and he often ruled his people harshly. The common people did not have many rights or freedoms. However, in this chapter, you will read about Athens, a city-state of Greece, where the first democratic ideas developed in the years from 1000 B.C. to 500 B.C.

2   Before you begin reading the chapter lesson, survey the lesson. Begin your survey by reading the beginning of the lesson. Then look through the lesson and read the headings. Next, study the pictures and read the picture captions. Then study the map of Greece and its colonies on page 138. Finally, read the review section called "Summing Up" at the end of the lesson. This survey of the lesson will help you to discover the important ideas in this chapter.

Know the Main Idea

As you read the chapter lesson, try to remember the following important MAIN IDEA of the chapter.

Greece was made up of many small city-states. Democratic ideas developed in Athens, one of the most important of the Greek city-states.

The following questions will help you to understand the MAIN IDEA. Try to answer these questions as you read the lesson.

1. Why were the Greek cities called "city-states"?
2. How did the Greeks fight for better government?
3. How was the city of Athens different from the city of Sparta?

Know These Important Terms

    peninsula   democracy
    tyrants

Know the Years of This Chapter

Look at the time line below. It shows the years of this chapter, 1000 B.C. to 500 B.C.

| 4000 B.C. | | | 1000 B.C. | 500 B.C. | 100 B.C. |

The Acropolis was a hill that was the religious center of early Athens.

EXPLORING THE TIME

In early times, Greece was not one great nation. Greece was divided into many very small nations, or city-states. In earlier chapters, you read about the city-states in Mesopotamia. In this chapter, you will learn what the Greek city-states were like and how the Greek city-states developed.

The Land of Greece Was Divided by Mountains

Greece is a **peninsula** (puh-NIN-suh-LUH), or a body of land surrounded by water on all but one side. Greece is a small land about as large as the state of Pennsylvania. Most of Greece is covered with rugged mountains. These mountains divide Greece into many small sections. They also make it

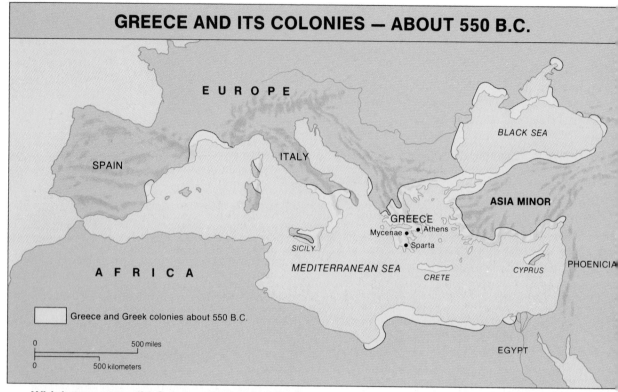

GREECE AND ITS COLONIES — ABOUT 550 B.C.

EUROPE

BLACK SEA

SPAIN

ITALY

ASIA MINOR

GREECE
Mycenae ● ● Athens
● Sparta

SICILY

AFRICA

MEDITERRANEAN SEA

CRETE

CYPRUS

PHOENICIA

☐ Greece and Greek colonies about 550 B.C.

0   500 miles
0   500 kilometers

EGYPT

Which two seas did Greek colonies border?

difficult for people to travel from one part of Greece to another. This explains why the early Greeks settled in small cities that were separated from each other by mountains. This also helps to explain why early Greece did not become a united nation as did Egypt and Mesopotamia.

The Greeks Lived in City-States

After the Dorians conquered Mycenae and the rest of Greece, they settled down around the Greek cities and became farmers. Slowly, the Dorians mixed with the peoples that they conquered. The Greek people were formed from this mixing.

Slowly, the Greek cities became the centers of life in Greece. Each city was like a

small nation. Each city-state had its own king, its own laws, and its own army of free citizens. The Greeks who lived in these city-states thought of themselves as citizens of their own city, not as citizens of Greece.

The Greek city-states were small. Each city-state included the city itself and the land around it. Most cities had less than ten thousand people. Yet these small cities were well organized and had strong governments. They fought wars, made treaties, and collected taxes from their citizens.

The Greek Nobles Grew Powerful

In each Greek city-state, the king ruled with the help of his nobles. By the year 750 B.C., however, the nobles became so powerful that they took away most of the king's powers. Often the nobles used these powers to tax the people. Most of the people were small farmers who were not able to pay high taxes. The nobles took away the land of many of these small farmers and sold the farmers into slavery.

The Idea of Democracy Began in Greece

Some of the Greek farmers tried to improve their lives by leaving Greece and forming colonies, or settlements, along the coast of Asia Minor, in Italy, in northern Africa, and on many of the Mediterranean islands. But other Greeks fought against the nobles and tried to replace them with rulers who were called **tyrants** (TY-runtz).

Today, the word "tyrant" means a cruel dictator. To the Greeks, however, a tyrant was simply a ruler who took control of the government. Many of the Greek tyrants were really wise rulers who cut down the power of the nobles and allowed the people to help make their own laws. These years of tyrant rule were the beginning of **democracy** (duh-MOCK-ruh-SEE) in Greece. A democracy is a government that is ruled by its people. In fact, the word "democracy" comes from the Greek word that means "rule by the people."

Athens Began to Develop Democracy

The city of Athens was the leading Greek city-state that developed democracy. During the 600's B.C., the Athenian nobles made all the laws of Athens. But these laws were not written down, and few of the common people knew what these laws were. About 620 B.C., however, a noble named Draco (DRAY-koh) wrote down these laws in order to help the common people know what their rights were.

GEOGRAPHY AND HISTORY

Ancient Piraeus

Greece is a land of mountains and sea. This has affected its history in many ways. The rugged mountains and narrow valleys have made transportation over land difficult. Because of this, the early Greeks turned outward and used the sea as their route to other cities and lands. Most of the early Greek cities developed along the coast.

The port of Athens was Piraeus (pi-RAY-us), a natural harbor about 5 miles west of the city. Piraeus was well protected from invaders. To reach Piraeus by sea, ships had to travel through a narrow strait that was defended by Athenian ships. To protect the land route to their port, the Athenians built high stone walls. These walls extended all the way from Piraeus to Athens. As long as the walls stood, the city could receive food and supplies from the port.

In 404 B.C., the Spartans broke through the long stone walls protecting the route to Athens. Cut off from its port, Athens was forced to surrender to the Spartans.

Question: What made Piraeus a safe port?

Solon was one of the nobles who helped Athens to become a democracy

In 594 B.C., Solon (SOH-lun), another noble, also tried to help the common people. Times were then bad for many Greek farmers. Many of them owed money to the nobles, who owned most of the land and wealth. Solon ordered that this money did not have to be paid. He also made it unlawful for anyone to be sold into slavery if the person was not able to pay the money he or she owed. Solon also limited the amount of land that anyone might own. And he allowed the common people to share in making the laws of Athens.

When the Athenian nobles tried to fight against these changes, the common people supported the tyrants, or strong rulers, who defeated the nobles.

By 500 B.C., Athens was ruled by an Assembly, or meeting, of all citizens over eighteen years of age. The Assembly soon became so large that it finally selected a Council of five hundred and a group of ten generals to carry on the city's government. However, all of the Council's actions had to be approved by the Assembly. In this way, Athens became a democracy, or a city-state that was ruled by its citizens.

Sparta Began to Develop Its Army

Not every Greek city-state became a democracy. Sparta was a city-state that did not develop democracy. Sparta was ruled by two kings and a Council of nobles. One king was the leader of the Spartan religion. And all laws for Sparta were passed by the Council of nobles.

In Sparta, the needs of the city-state were considered more important than the needs of the people. Boys had to serve in the Spartan army from the age of seven to the age of thirty. Girls were trained to be wives and mothers of soldiers. In this way, Sparta became a strong, warlike city-state.

SUMMING UP

Greece was made up of many city-states. Athens was a city-state that became a democracy, or a city-state ruled by its people. Sparta was a city-state that built a strong army but did not become a democracy. In the next chapter, you will read about the great culture that developed in Greece.

UNDERSTANDING THE LESSON

Do You Know These Important Terms?

For each sentence below, choose the term that best completes the sentence.

1. A body of land surrounded by water on all but one side is called a **(point/ peninsula)**.
2. The Greeks called rulers who took control of the government **(tyrants/nobles)**.
3. **(Democracy/Tyranny)** is a government ruled by the people.

Do You Remember These People and Events?

1. Tell something about each of the following persons.

   Draco   Solon

2. Tell how each of the following developments took place.

   a. Greece did not become a united nation as did Egypt or Mesopotamia.
   b. Greek city-states were formed.
   c. Democracy developed in Athens.

Can You Locate These Places?

Use the map on page 138 to do the following map work.

1. Locate each of the following places. Tell how each place is related to developments in this chapter.

   Mycenae   Athens
   Greece   Sparta

2. You have already learned that a peninsula is a body of land surrounded by water on all but one side. What body of water surrounds the peninsula of Greece? Use this map to locate and name other peninsulas in the Mediterranean Sea.

Do You Know When It Happened?

Why are the following years important in the development of democracy in Greece?

   about 620 B.C.   594 B.C.

Do You Remember the Main Idea?

Which one of the following ideas is the MAIN IDEA of this chapter?

1. Greece became a united nation and developed some ideas of democracy that we use today.
2. Greece was made up of many small city-states. Democratic ideas developed in Athens, one of the most important of the Greek city-states.
3. The Dorian invaders of Greece settled in Sparta, and they developed a city-state based on army rule and military power.

What Do You Think?

From what you have read in this chapter, try to answer the following thought questions.

1. Why do you think that the word "tyrant" has a different meaning today from its meaning in early Greece?
2. Which Greek city-state do you think was the most pleasant place to live in? Give reasons for your answer.
3. In what ways was the government of Athens like the government of your own city? different from your own city?

Chapter 20
The Golden Age of Greece

GETTING STARTED

1 In China, you may recall, the period when Chinese culture was greatest is called the "Classical Age." The greatest period in the development of Greek culture took place between 500 B.C. and 404 B.C. This period of years in Greece is called the "Golden Age" of Greece.

Great ideas, great writing, and great art were produced during the Golden Age of Greek history. The Golden Age had its center in Athens. And during the Golden Age, Athens became a powerful city-state. As you will see, the Golden Age of Greece lasted as long as Athens was powerful. The Golden Age was ended by a war between Athens and Sparta.

2 Before you begin reading the chapter lesson, survey the lesson. Begin your survey by reading the beginning of the lesson. Then look through the lesson and read the headings. Next, study the pictures and read the picture captions. Then study the map of the Greek city-states on page 144. Finally, read the review section called "Summing Up" at the end of the lesson. This survey of the whole lesson will help you to discover the important ideas in this chapter.

Know the Main Idea

As you read the chapter lesson, try to remember the following important MAIN IDEA of the chapter.

During the Golden Age of Greece, Athens produced some of the world's greatest thinkers, artists, and writers.

The following questions will help you to understand the MAIN IDEA. Try to answer these questions as you read the lesson.

1. What conditions in Greece led to the beginning of the Golden Age?
2. Who helped to make the government of Athens more democratic?
3. What war ended the Golden Age of Greece?

Know These Important Terms

Golden Age	tragedies
Acropolis	philosophers
comedies	

Know the Years of This Chapter

Look at the time line below. It shows the years of this chapter, 500 B.C. to 404 B.C.

500 B.C. 404 B.C.		B.C. 0 A.D.	500 A.D.

The Parthenon, the temple of the Greek goddess Athena, was the most famous temple on the Acropolis. Why do you think it was placed high on the hill?

EXPLORING THE TIME

Sometimes everything seems to work out well for a person or a nation. During the years of the 400's B.C., the land of Greece enjoyed a wonderful period called the **Golden Age.** In this chapter, you will learn about the great culture that developed in Athens and in Greece during the Golden Age.

The Greeks Defeated Persia

From the years 499 B.C. to 479 B.C., Athens and other Greek city-states fought a long war against the Persians. The Persian Empire included the Greek colonies located on the coast of Asia Minor.

About 500 B.C., the Greek colonies revolted against Persia. When Athens sent ships to help these colonies, Persia went to war against Athens. In 480 B.C., the Greeks

THE GREEK CITY-STATES — ABOUT 450 B.C.

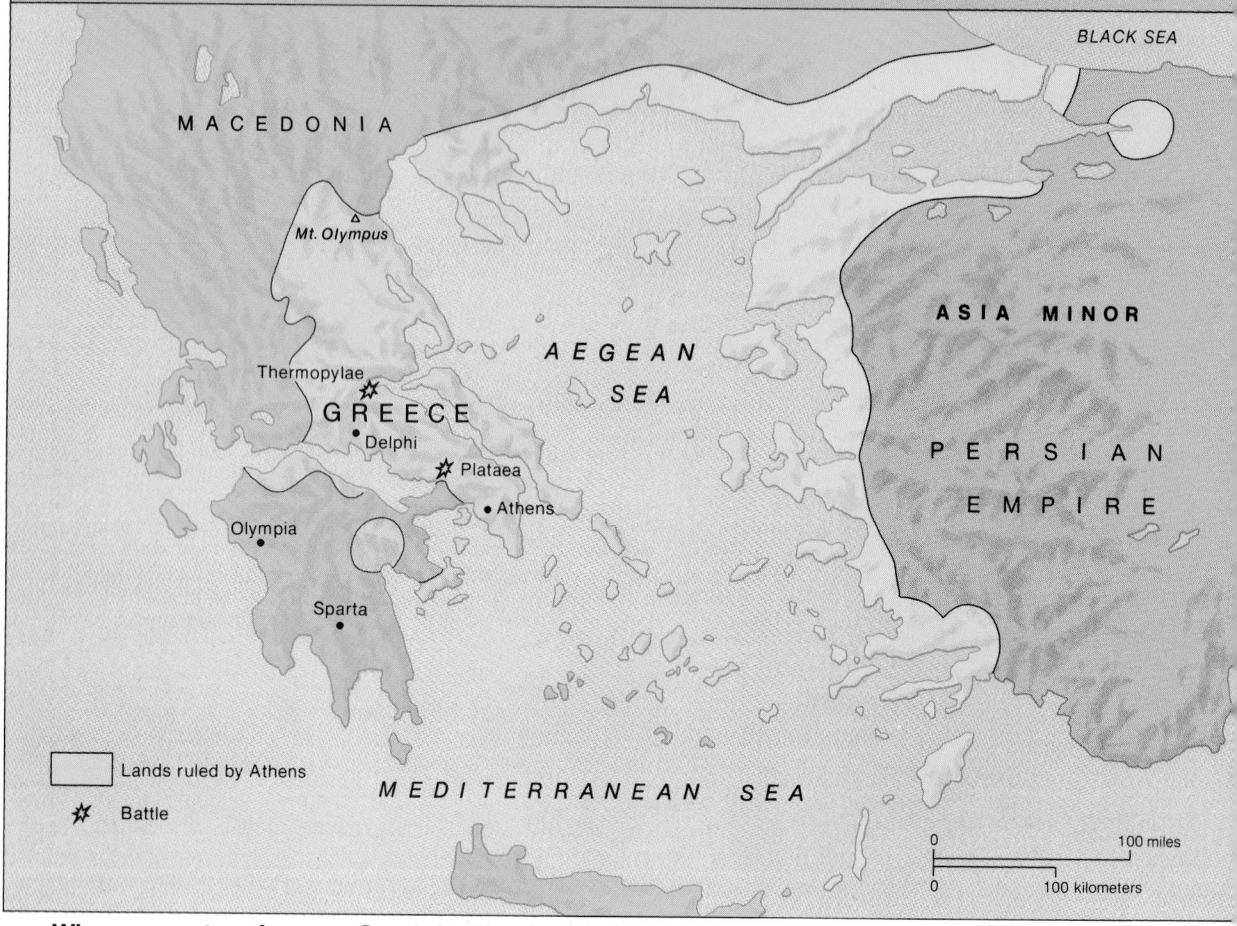
BLACK SEA
MACEDONIA
Mt. Olympus
ASIA MINOR
AEGEAN SEA
Thermopylae
GREECE
Delphi
Plataea
Athens
PERSIAN EMPIRE
Olympia
Sparta
Lands ruled by Athens
Battle
MEDITERRANEAN SEA
0
100 miles
0
100 kilometers

Where were two famous Greek battles fought?

lost a battle at a mountain pass at Thermopylae (thur-MOP-uh-LEE). But in 479 B.C., the Greeks won the war when they defeated the Persians at Plataea (plah-TEE-uh).

The Golden Age Began in Athens

During the war with the Persians, much of Athens was destroyed. The Athenians began to rebuild their homes and the city walls. They also rebuilt the temples on the **Acropolis** (uh-KROP-uh-LUS), a hill that was the religious center of Athens. The most famous temple on the Acropolis was the Parthenon (PAR-thuh-NAHN), the temple of the Greek goddess Athena.

The Parthenon and other Greek temples were built of marble and were among the most beautiful buildings in the world. The Greek temples on the Acropolis had wonderful statues made by the greatest sculptors, or statue carvers, of the period.

Athens Became More Democratic—but Not for All Athenians

Between 460 B.C. and 429 B.C., Athens' government became more democratic. The Assembly gained more power, and all Athenian citizens gained the right to serve as government officials. The man who helped to bring about these changes was Pericles (PAIR-uh-KLEEZ). Pericles was the greatest government leader in the history of Athens.

However, only men whose fathers were Athenian citizens and whose mothers were Athenians were allowed to be citizens. Women, slaves, and persons from other city-states were not allowed to become citizens. Most Greek city-states had such rules. As a result, democracy in Greece was a limited democracy. Even so, the Greeks were the first people to develop democracy, and they spread the idea of democracy to other peoples.

The Golden Age Produced Great Play Writers

The Athenians enjoyed attending plays. These plays were presented in large outdoor theaters. If an Athenian citizen was too poor to pay to see a play, the Athenian government paid the price of admission for the citizen.

The Greek plays were either comedies or tragedies. The **comedies** were plays that made fun of leading Greek citizens. The **tragedies** were plays that dealt with serious matters, such as the meaning of life and the struggle between good and evil. These Greek plays are among the greatest plays ever written. Even today, many people enjoy reading or seeing these plays.

DOCUMENTS IN HISTORY

Greek bronze sculpture

The Greek philosopher Plato was interested in why states (nations) came into being. In his book *The Republic*, Plato explained that states were created because they were needed. Plato wrote the book in the form of a conversation between his teacher, Socrates, and some friends.

Socrates is speaking:

A State ... arises out of the needs of mankind ....

Then, as we have many wants, and many persons are needed to supply them, one takes a helper for one purpose and another for another; and when these partners and helpers are gathered together in one habitation the body of inhabitants is termed a State ....

And they exchange with one another, and one gives and another receives, under the idea that the exchange will be for their good ....

Question: According to Plato, what is the origin of the state?

Pericles was Athens' great government leader of the Golden Age

The Golden Age Produced Great Thinkers

Athens was the home of the three most famous Greek **philosophers,** or thinkers—Socrates (SOCK-ruh-teez), Plato (PLAY-toh), and Aristotle (AIR-iss-TOT-ul). Socrates is remembered as a philosopher who searched for the truth by asking many questions. Plato is remembered for his book *The Republic,* which set up a plan for the perfect nation. Aristotle is remembered for his ideas about science and government. As you will learn in later chapters, the ideas of these three great thinkers became very important to the whole world.

Other famous Greeks began the study of many other subjects. Hippocrates (hih-POCK-ruh-TEEZ) was the "father of medicine." All medical doctors today still take the oath of Hippocrates, as Hippocrates wanted his pupils to do.

Herodotus (huh-ROD-uh-TUSS), another great Athenian, was the "father of history."

Most of what we know about the Greek war against Persia comes from the writings of Herodotus.

Athens Became More Powerful

Even after the Greeks defeated the Persians, Athens and the Greek colonies around the Mediterranean Sea still feared Persia. As a result, the Greeks formed a large navy to provide protection against a Persian attack. With this navy, Athens built up its sea trade and became more powerful. Later, Athens became the leader of a strong group of more than two hundred Greek city-states.

The Golden Age of Greece Was Ended by War

Sparta and some other Greek city-states wished to stop Athens' growing power. In 431 B.C., a war broke out between Athens and Sparta. This long and costly war lasted until 404 B.C., when Athens finally was defeated by Sparta. But the war weakened both Athens and Sparta, and these Greek city-states were no longer powerful. The Golden Age of Greece now came to an end.

SUMMING UP

After the Greeks defeated Persia, the Greek city-states began a great Golden Age. During this time, Athens produced some of the world's greatest thinkers, artists, and writers. Athens' great government leader of the Golden Age was Pericles, who helped to make Athenian democracy stronger. But the Golden Age was ended by a war between Athens and Sparta. In the next chapter, you will read about everyday life among the Greeks in peace and war.

UNDERSTANDING THE LESSON

Do You Know These Important Terms?

For each sentence below, choose the term that best completes the sentence.

1. The greatest period of Greek culture is called the (**Golden Age/Classical Age**).
2. The (**Acropolis/Republic**) was the hill which was the religious center of Athens.
3. (**Comedies/Sculptors**) were plays that made fun of leading Greek citizens.
4. Greek plays that dealt with serious matters were called (**Socrates/tragedies**).
5. Greek (**philosophers/traders**) were great Greek thinkers.

Do You Remember These People and Events?

1. Tell something about each of the following subjects.

Acropolis	**Aristotle**
Pericles	**Hippocrates**
Socrates	**Herodotus**
Plato	

2. Explain how each of the following events took place.

   a. Athens became more democratic.
   b. Athens became famous for its great play writers.
   c. The Golden Age of Greece came to an end.

Can You Locate These Places?

Use the map on page 144 to do the following map work.

1. Locate each of the following places. Tell how each place is related to the developments in this chapter.

Persian Empire	**Athens**
Plataea	**Sparta**

2. Study Athens' location. Why do you think a navy was as important to Athens as its army?

Do You Know When It Happened?

Which of the following years were the years of the Golden Age of Greece?

   200's B.C.   400's B.C.

Do You Remember the Main Idea?

Which one of the following ideas is the MAIN IDEA of this chapter?

1. The Golden Age of Greece was ended by wars with Sparta. Little remains of the old Greek culture.
2. The city-state of Athens became the center of Greek life, but war with Persia weakened Athens.
3. During the Golden Age of Greece, Athens produced some of the world's greatest thinkers, artists, and writers.

What Do You Think?

From what you have read in this chapter, try to answer the following thought questions.

1. Democracy in Athens was not perfect. What are some of the ways that democracy in Athens might have been improved?
2. Do you think that the war against the Persians helped the Golden Age of Greece to begin? Explain your answer.

Chapter 21
Life in Greece

GETTING STARTED

1   Relay races, pole vaulting, discus throwing—you probably know these sports from school track and field events. But did you know that these sports began long ago, in the time of the Greeks? It was the Greeks who invented the Olympic games, which today are held every four years. In these games, men and women of all nations take part in many track and field events.

   As you can guess, sports were very important to the Greeks. Notice on the time line at the bottom of this page that the years of this chapter are 500 B.C. to 404 B.C. During this period, sports, education, government, and religion played an important part in the everyday life of the people who lived in Greece.

2   Before you begin reading the chapter lesson, survey the lesson. Begin your survey by reading the beginning of the lesson. Then look through the lesson and read the headings. Next, study the pictures and read the picture captions. Finally, read the review section called "Summing Up" at the end of the lesson. This survey of the whole lesson will help you to discover the important ideas in this chapter.

Know the Main Idea

As you read the chapter lesson, try to remember the following important MAIN IDEA of the chapter.

Good government, education, religion, and sports were important parts of Greek life.

   The following questions will help you to understand the MAIN IDEA. Try to answer these important questions as you read the lesson.

1. What kind of schools did the Greeks have?
2. What duties were expected of a Greek woman?
3. What place did slaves have in Greek life?

Know These Important Terms

   gymnasia   Olympic games

Know the Years of This Chapter

Look at the time line below. It shows the years of this chapter, 500 B.C. to 404 B.C.

| 500 B.C. | 404 B.C. | | B.C. | 0 | A.D. | | 500 A.D. |

Early Greek vase showing women at a water fountain. How are the women carrying their water jars?

EXPLORING THE TIME

A very important part of Greek culture was the way that the Greeks lived. Education, government, religion, and sports were important to the Greeks in their everyday lives, in both peacetime and wartime. In this chapter, you will learn many interesting things about how the people of Greece lived.

The Greeks Worshiped Many Gods

The Greeks believed that their gods belonged to a great family of gods. Zeus (ZOOS) was the king and father of the gods. Athena (uh-THEE-nuh) was the goddess of wisdom. Aphrodite (AF-ruh-DYE-tee) was the goddess of love and beauty. The Greeks believed that these gods and many other Greek gods lived on Mount Olympus (oh-LIMM-puss), in northern Greece.

HIGHLIGHTS IN HISTORY

A Greek painting of the Oracle

Today, some people go to fortune-tellers to learn about the future. In early Greece, people went to oracles. Oracles were men and women who the Greeks believed were able to receive messages from the Greek gods. The most famous oracle in Greece was the oracle of the god Apollo at Delphi.

When someone went to the oracle at Delphi to ask the gods a question, the priestess of Apollo heard the question, then she left. She went alone into an underground part of the temple by herself. There she went into a trance, or a deep sleep, and began to speak. The priests of Apollo were nearby. They then told the question-asker what the priestess was saying.

These priests were wise men of great learning. They worded the priestess' message from the gods very wisely. When the oracle's answers turned out to be wrong, the priests said that the question-asker had not understood the words correctly. As a result, the Greeks believed that the Oracle of Delphi was very wise and was able to help them.

Question: Who received messages from the Greek gods?

The Greeks believed that their gods controlled people's actions. But the Greeks also believed that their gods acted like human men and women in many ways. The Greeks told many beautiful stories about how their gods quarreled with each other and played tricks on one another.

The Greeks worshiped their gods in their own homes and in temples. But no one was forced to worship the Greek gods. And the Greeks did not have priests to help them worship their gods.

Greek Schools Trained Young Men to Be Good Citizens

The Greeks believed that educated people made good citizens. But only Greek men were allowed to be citizens. Therefore, education in Greece was mainly for boys.

The Greek schools were private, and families had to pay to have their sons attend school. Boys attended school from age six to age fourteen. They learned reading, writing, arithmetic, poetry, music, and athletics.

If a boy's family was rich, he continued his studies with a private teacher and learned geometry, astronomy, grammar, and public speaking. After finishing these studies, a young Greek was ready to become a useful and active citizen of his city-state.

The Greeks Enjoyed Many Sports

The Greeks believed that building up their bodies through sports was an important part of their education for citizenship. Greek sports included running, jumping, boxing, wrestling, and discus throwing. Greek men and boys spent much of their time practicing sports in large sports grounds called **gymnasia** (jim-NAY-zee-UH).

Cloth was made by spinning wool and weaving it

Today, we call a practice room for sports a "gym."

Every four years—even during a war—athletes from all the Greek city-states gathered at the city-state of Olympia for the **Olympic games.** These games were sports contests. It was a great honor for an athlete and his city-state to win an Olympic game.

Greek Women Had Very Few Rights

Democracy in Greece was only for men, not for women. Women were not allowed to vote or to own property. Girls were ruled by their fathers until they were married at fifteen or sixteen. After marriage, they were ruled by their husbands.

Women were allowed to see a play and to take part in a religious ceremony. But they were not allowed to go to parties or to other social gatherings with men. A wife's main duty was to look after her home and to teach her daughters how to cook and to

make clothing. When wealthy Greek women went out to shop at the market place, a slave always went along to protect them.

However, women of poor Greek families led a more active life than women of rich Greek families. The poorer women worked at all kinds of jobs, including the selling of goods in the market place.

The Greeks Used Slaves to Do Their Work

Like other early peoples, the Greeks used many slaves to do their work for them. Wealthy Greeks owned several slaves. Sometimes a rich person owned as many as fifty slaves. The use of slaves allowed many Greek citizens to serve in the government and to take part in sports contests. Slave owners were supposed to treat all of their slaves well. But in general, slaves with special skills were treated much better than

A Greek carving showing actors in a play

unskilled slaves. Sometimes slaves were able to save enough money to buy their own freedom.

The Greeks Made Their Living as Farmers, Traders, and Artisans

The farms of Greece were small farms which grew grain, olives, grapes, and vegetables. Farmers also raised goats, sheep, and chickens. But these small farms did not produce enough food for the Greek people. Therefore, the Greeks had to get much of their food by trading. Greek traders traveled to all parts of the Mediterranean Sea and traded pottery, olive oil, and honey for food and other products.

Greece also had artisans who made many products, such as pottery, jewelry, and metal ware. These products were made in the workers' homes or in small shops. Often the artisan who made the product also sold it. But shop workers usually did not earn much money, because slaves often did the same work more cheaply.

SUMMING UP

The Greeks worshiped many gods, but they did not force anyone to worship these gods. Education and sports were important to the Greeks for training good citizens. However, only Greek men were allowed to be citizens. Greek women had few rights. And the Greeks used many slaves. The Greeks made their living as farmers, artisans, and traders, but Greece depended upon trade to supply its people with much of their food. In the next chapter, you will read how Greece was conquered by a new nation to the north.

UNDERSTANDING THE LESSON

Do You Know These Important Terms?

For each sentence below, choose the term that best completes the sentence.

1. The **(discus/gymnasia)** were large sports grounds where Greek men and boys spent much of their time practicing sports.
2. Sports contests held every four years, even during a war, were called **(city-state games/Olympic games)**.

Do You Remember These People and Events?

1. Tell something about each of the following subjects.

   Zeus   **Aphrodite**
   Athena

2. Explain how or why each of the following developments took place.

   a. The Greek gods acted like human men and women in many ways.
   b. Education was important for Greek citizenship.
   c. Wealthy Greeks owned several slaves.

Can You Locate These Places?

Use the map in Chapter 20 (page 144) to locate the following places. Tell how these places are connected with developments in this chapter.

   Mount Olympus
   Mediterranean Sea

Do You Know When It Happened?

What are the years of this chapter on Greek life?

Do You Remember the Main Idea?

Which one of the following ideas is the MAIN IDEA of this chapter?

1. The Greeks lived a good life. They were able to produce almost everything they needed in their own city-states.
2. The Greeks wanted all their people to have an education for citizenship.
3. Good government, education, religion, and sports were important parts of Greek life.

What Do You Think?

From what you have read in this chapter, try to answer the following thought questions.

1. How were the Greek schools like your school? How were they different from your school?
2. Why do you suppose that the Greeks did not allow women to become citizens? Do you think that women of today have more freedom than did the women of Greece?
3. If you were an athlete in the Olympic games, which sport would you want to take part in? Why might you want to be in the Olympics besides wanting to be a winner?

Chapter 22
The Hellenistic World

GETTING STARTED

1   The Greeks never built a large empire. However, many of the ideas of Greece spread to other peoples and helped to shape their lives. Some of the Greek ideas became mixed with the ideas of other peoples, such as the Persian and Hindu peoples. This mixing of ideas resulted in the development of a great new Greek culture that produced important art, writing, and scientific progress.

2   Before you begin reading the chapter lesson, survey the lesson. Begin your survey by reading the beginning of the lesson. Then look through the lesson and read the headings. Next, study the pictures and read the picture captions. Then study the map of the empire of Alexander the Great on page 156. Finally, read the review section called "Summing Up" at the end of the lesson. This survey of the whole lesson will help you to discover the important ideas in this chapter.

Know the Main Idea

As you read the chapter lesson, try to remember the following important MAIN IDEA of the chapter.

Alexander the Great ruled Greece and many other lands. Alexander built up a great world empire that developed an important new culture.

The following questions will help you to understand the MAIN IDEA. Try to answer these questions as you read the lesson.

1. What nation conquered and united the city-states of Greece?
2. What new culture developed from Alexander's conquest?
3. What were some of the lasting contributions of Alexander's new culture?

Know This Important Term

Hellenistic culture

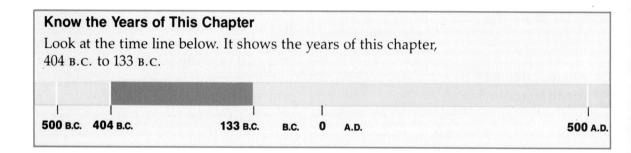

Know the Years of This Chapter

Look at the time line below. It shows the years of this chapter, 404 B.C. to 133 B.C.

| 500 B.C. | 404 B.C. | 133 B.C. | B.C. | 0 | A.D. | 500 A.D. |

An ancient Greek amphitheater at the base of the Acropolis that is still in use today

EXPLORING THE TIME

The Greek city-states never were able to form one nation. As a result, they were too weak to prevent a stronger nation from conquering them. In this chapter, you will learn how the wars among the Greek city-states made it possible for Macedonia (MASS-uh-DOH-nee-uh) to conquer Greece.

The Macedonians Conquered and United the Greeks

After the war between Athens and Sparta ended in 404 B.C., some of the Greek city-states continued to fight for the control of Greece. Meanwhile, Macedonia, a new nation that was located just north of Greece, was growing stronger.

The Macedonians were very much like the Greeks—particularly in their language and religion. Philip, the Macedonian king, built a strong army and began to conquer the Greek city-states. In the year 338 B.C., Philip finally won complete control of Greece.

Philip allowed the Greek city-states to run their own affairs. However, he became the leader of all the Greek armies and navies. Greece was united at last, but it took the Macedonians to do it.

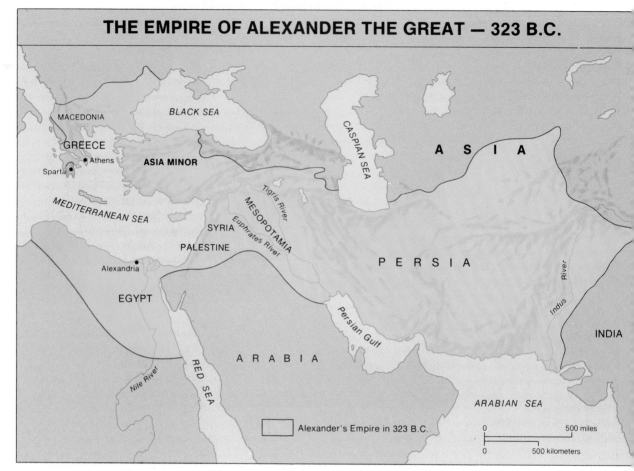

THE EMPIRE OF ALEXANDER THE GREAT — 323 B.C.

MACEDONIA

BLACK SEA

CASPIAN SEA

GREECE

Athens

ASIA MINOR

A S I A

Sparta

MEDITERRANEAN SEA

Tigris River

MESOPOTAMIA

Euphrates River

SYRIA

PALESTINE

P E R S I A

Indus River

Alexandria

EGYPT

Persian Gulf

INDIA

A R A B I A

Nile River

RED SEA

ARABIAN SEA

Alexander's Empire in 323 B.C.

0   500 miles

0   500 kilometers

What city in Alexander's empire was named for him?

Alexander Became the Ruler of Greece

Philip now planned to lead the combined Macedonian and Greek armies against the Persian Empire. But Philip was murdered, and his twenty-year-old son, Alexander (AL-ug-ZAN-dur), became king.

Alexander of Macedonia had received a good education. His teacher was the great Greek philosopher Aristotle. Alexander also became a fine soldier and an athlete. Therefore, he was well prepared to be a great leader. In fact, later he was called "Alexander the Great."

When one Greek city-state rebelled, or revolted, against Alexander, he easily conquered it. And he soon stopped rebellions, or revolts, in other Greek city-states. Alexander was one of the greatest generals of all time. Before long, he ruled all of Greece.

Alexander Conquered the Persian Empire

Alexander next decided to attack Persia. The Persian army was large but not as well trained as Alexander's armies. Between 334 B.C. and 331 B.C., he conquered Asia Minor,

156

Egypt, Syria, Palestine, Mesopotamia, and all the rest of the Persian Empire.

But Alexander had still greater plans. He wanted to add India to his empire. From Persia, he marched his soldiers eastward to India. Alexander might have conquered India, too. But his soldiers now were tired of fighting, and they forced him to turn back.

Alexander Tried to Build a Great World Empire

Alexander's wish was to spread Greek culture wherever he went. He also hoped to start a new "world culture," based on the best ideas of the Greek, Persian, and Hindu cultures. Greek laws and the Greek language were to be the basis of this new "world culture," which came to be called **Hellenistic** (HELL-uh-NISS-tick) **culture.** The Greek name for Greece was "Hellas." "Hellenistic" means "like Greece." The Hellenistic period lasted for nearly two hundred years—from 323 B.C. to 133 B.C.

Alexander started new Greek colonies all over his empire. The Greeks who settled in these colonies introduced the Greek language and culture to the conquered people around them. And the Greek settlers also learned a great deal from the peoples of the conquered nations.

Alexander tried to spread the Hellenistic culture by building new cities and rebuilding old cities as culture centers. He also tried to make all the people in his empire feel that they were a united people. He encouraged people of different nations to marry each other. He took people of all religions into the army and the government. And he set up the same money system in all of his empire in order to make trading easier.

PEOPLE IN HISTORY

Alexander the Great

Alexander the Great was one of the greatest army leaders and rulers in history. In a few years, he ruled one of the largest empires in the world. In the spring of 334 B.C., Alexander set out to conquer the Persian Empire. His army of Macedonians and Greeks only had about 35,000 soldiers. Within a few years, Alexander conquered all of the lands of the Near East. He defeated the Persian king, Darius the Third, and he became ruler of the Tigris River and Euphrates River valleys. Then, he led his armies to the east and invaded northern India.

Alexander wanted all the different peoples in his empire to live together in peace. He worked hard to mix Greek ways of living with the cultures of the Near East. Alexander himself married a Persian princess, and he wore Persian robes. However, Alexander did not live to see his dream of a great and peaceful world empire. In June of 323 B.C., Alexander died of a fever. After his death, his great empire was divided up and ruled by three of Alexander's generals.

Question: What was Alexander's dream for his empire?

The Hellenistic sculpture, "Winged Victory"

Alexander's Empire Split into Three Parts

But Alexander did not live long enough to complete his plans for a world empire. He died in the year 323 B.C. at the age of thirty-two. The empire that he left was divided into three sections, each ruled by an army general. Macedonia and Greece were ruled by Antigonus (an-TIG-uh-NUSS). Egypt and Palestine were ruled by Ptolemy (TAHL-uh-MEE). And the rest of the empire was ruled by Seleucus (suh-LOO-kuss).

Each general tried to become a strong ruler of his part of the empire. But this plan did not succeed in Greece and Macedonia. Instead, the Greeks and Macedonians continued to help make the laws that governed them.

The Hellenistic Culture Produced Important Ideas and Discoveries

The Hellenistic period produced great art, great writing, and advances in science. These Hellenistic contributions were a result of mixing the best ideas of Greek culture and the cultures of the Near East nations. The center of the Hellenistic culture was in Alexandria, Egypt. Alexandria was named after Alexander the Great, and it was the largest city of the Hellenistic world.

During the Hellenistic period, important discoveries were made in science. A Greek scientist discovered that the earth was round, and learned how to measure the earth's size. Another Greek scientist discovered that the earth moves around the sun. A Greek mathematician in Alexandria named Euclid (YOO-klid) developed geometry further. And a Greek scientist named Archimedes (AR-kuh-MEE-deez) discovered how to weigh matter.

SUMMING UP

Philip of Macedonia conquered Greece in 338 B.C., and his son, Alexander the Great, conquered the Persian Empire. Alexander built his own empire and spread the Hellenistic culture of Greece to the lands of the Near East. The great contributions of Hellenistic culture in art, writing, and science had lasting results for the world. In the next chapter, which begins Unit 7, you will read about Rome, a city-state in Italy.

UNDERSTANDING THE LESSON

Do You Know This Important Term?

For the sentence below, choose the term that best completes the sentence.

1. The "world culture" started by Alexander was a mixture of Greek ideas and the ideas of other nations, and it is called **(Alexandria culture/Hellenistic culture).**

Do You Remember These People and Events?

1. Tell something about each of the following persons.

Philip	Seleucus
Alexander the Great	Euclid
Antigonus	Archimedes
Ptolemy	

2. Explain how each of the following events took place.

   a. Alexander the Great conquered a great empire.
   b. Alexander the Great encouraged the development and spread of Hellenistic culture.
   c. The Hellenistic culture produced important ideas and discoveries.

Can You Locate These Places?

Use the map on page 156 to do the following map work.

1. Locate the following places. Tell how each place is related to the developments in this chapter.

Athens	Mesopotamia
Macedonia	Alexandria
Asia Minor	Sparta
Persia	Palestine
Egypt	India

2. Use the scale of miles on the map to find out how far it was from Alexandria to Athens.

Do You Know When It Happened?

What great new world culture developed in the following years?

   323 B.C. to 133 B.C.

Do You Remember the Main Idea?

Which one of the following ideas is the MAIN IDEA of this chapter?

1. Alexander the Great ruled Greece and many other lands. Alexander built up a great world empire that developed an important new culture.
2. Alexander the Great ruled a great empire. He was interested in conquering India and the lands of Asia.
3. During the Hellenistic period, great Greek thinkers developed many important ideas in science, engineering, and mathematics.

What Do You Think?

From what you have read in this chapter, try to answer the following thought questions.

1. Do you think that Alexander the Great was a good ruler? Explain your answer.
2. How might world history have been different if Alexander had lived for another twenty years?

Unit 7

The Development of Roman Culture

THE CHAPTERS IN UNIT 7 ARE

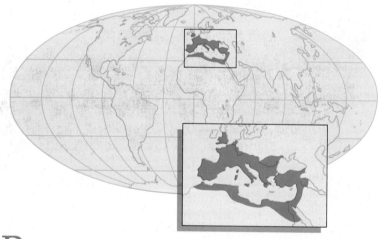

Rome began as a small city, but it soon conquered a large empire in the lands along the Mediterranean Sea. In this unit, you will learn how the Romans ruled this large empire. You also will find out how the Christian religion began and how it spread in the Roman Empire.

The original cobblestone "Appian Way" leading to Rome, Italy. The many roads that were built helped to unify the Roman Empire.

Chapter 23
The Rise of the Roman Republic

GETTING STARTED

1   A great culture also developed in Italy, a peninsula in the Mediterranean Sea not far from Greece. This great culture was developed by the Romans. Roman culture began about the year 1000 B.C. As you will learn, the Roman people soon built a very strong nation. You will learn some of the reasons for the strength of the Roman Republic as you read the chapter lesson.

2   Before you begin reading the chapter lesson, survey the lesson. Begin your survey by reading the beginning of the lesson. Then look through the lesson and read the headings. Next, study the pictures and read the picture captions. Then study the map of the early Roman Republic and Carthage on page 164. Finally, read the review section called "Summing Up" at the end of the lesson. This survey of the lesson will help you to discover the important ideas in this chapter.

Know the Main Idea

As you read the chapter lesson, try to remember the following important MAIN IDEA of the chapter.

The people of Rome set up a republic. The Roman Republic grew very powerful after it conquered all of Italy and Carthage.

The following questions will help you to understand the MAIN IDEA. Try to answer these questions as you read the lesson.

1. What three groups of people moved into Italy very early in history?
2. What type of government was set up in the city-state of Rome?
3. How were the common people of Rome able to gain more rights for themselves?

Know These Important Terms

Latins	consuls
Etruscans	Senate
patricians	plebeians
republic	tribunes

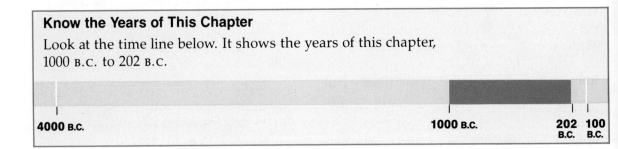

Know the Years of This Chapter

Look at the time line below. It shows the years of this chapter, 1000 B.C. to 202 B.C.

4000 B.C.   1000 B.C.   202 B.C.   100 B.C.

Painting of mourning Etruscan women gathered together as a funeral chorus

EXPLORING THE TIME

Just before Alexander the Great died, he was planning to lead his armies westward to conquer Italy. But as it turned out, Italy was conquered instead by one of its own cities—Rome. In this chapter, you will read about the rise of the Roman Republic.

Italy Had Many Mountains but Good Soil

Italy is a long and narrow land that stretches into the Mediterranean Sea. It is about twice the size of Greece. In the north, high mountains called the Alps divide Italy from the rest of Europe. Mountains also are found in other parts of Italy. However, Italy had rich land, a warm climate, and plenty of rainfall for good farming. Therefore, many settlers in Italy became farmers.

Three Main Groups of People Settled Italy

About the year 1000 B.C., several groups of people wandered into Italy. One group of people came from the north across the Alps mountains into Italy. This group of people

THE EARLY ROMAN REPUBLIC AND CARTHAGE

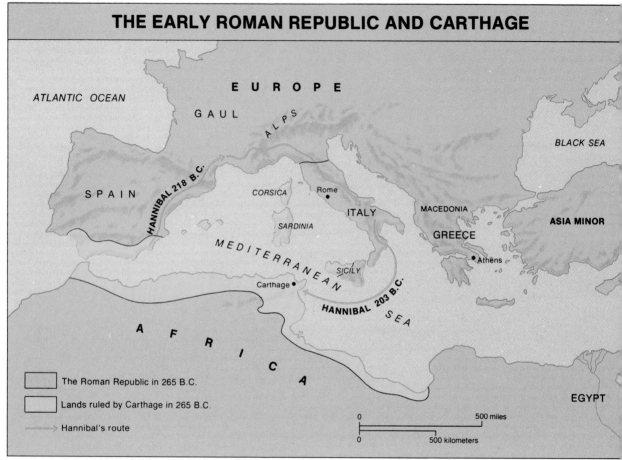

Trace Hannibal's route from Spain to Carthage.

was called the **Latins** (LAT-unz). The Latins started a settlement at Rome. Another group was the **Etruscans** (ih-TRUSS-kunz), a people from Asia Minor, who settled in western Italy. Another group came from Greece and settled in southern Italy.

The Latins learned a great deal from the Etruscans and the Greeks. The Etruscans taught them about building roads and about planting crops. The Greeks taught them the Greek alphabet and the Greek religion. And like the Greeks, the Latins and the Etruscans who came into Italy and settled there lived in city-states.

Rome Became the Strongest City-State in Italy

Rome was settled about 750 B.C., and it became the most powerful Italian city-state. It was built on seven hills along the Tiber River in central Italy. These hills protected Rome from the attacks of enemies. But Rome was able to attack and conquer the other Italian cities that were north and south of it. Rome became a trading center because it was located near several trade routes, or trading paths. In this way, Rome's location helped it grow rapidly.

The Roman Nobles Set Up the Roman Republic

Between 750 B.C. and about 500 B.C., Rome was ruled by the Etruscans. The Etruscan king ruled with the help of rich landowners called **patricians** (puh-TRISH-unz), or nobles. The patricians slowly gained more power. About 500 B.C., they overthrew the Etruscan king and set up a **republic,** or a government with officials who were elected by the citizens. The Roman Republic, however, was really controlled by the patricians.

At the head of the Roman Republic were two elected **consuls.** The consuls were the leaders of the Roman army, the government, and religious affairs. But the consuls' power was limited because they served only one year. The real power of the Roman government was in the **Senate.** The Senate was made up of three hundred patrician Romans who were appointed by the consuls to serve for life. The Senate passed the laws and chose the citizens who were to be voted upon for consul. Only patricians were allowed to serve as consuls, sit in the Roman Senate, or hold most other government offices.

The common people of Rome were the **plebeians** (plih-BEE-unz). The plebeians included Roman soldiers, farmers, workers, and traders. The plebeians elected an Assembly, but this Assembly had little power in the Roman government.

The Roman Plebeians Won More Rights

The plebeians, or common Roman citizens, finally won more power by using a clever plan. They simply moved out of Rome! The patricians were helpless without soldiers, farmers, workers, and traders to keep Roman life going. In this way, the plebeians

The Roman Senate was the center of real power in the Roman Republic after 500 B.C.

won the right to elect two **tribunes** (TRIB-yoonz) to represent them in the government. The tribunes had the power to veto, or turn down, laws the plebeians did not like.

The plebeians also won more power for their Assembly. And the plebeians won the right to have the Roman laws written down so that the common people knew what the laws were. Later the plebeians also won the right to sit in the Senate and to hold all government jobs. But the patricians still held the most important government offices.

HIGHLIGHTS IN HISTORY

Roman Plebeians

Twenty-five hundred years ago, the Romans saw a March out of Rome. As you know, the common people of Rome, or plebeians, disliked some of the things the patricians did. However, the patricians refused to stop or to change these things.

In the year 494 B.C., therefore, the plebeians decided to move out of the city of Rome and set up camp a few miles outside Rome. The patricians now were greatly worried. What if an enemy attacked Rome? Or what if the plebeians themselves attacked Rome? The patricians soon decided to send someone to ask the plebeians to return to Rome.

After much discussion, an agreement was made. The plebeians agreed to return to Rome, but only after the patricians promised to agree to their demands. The March out of Rome showed how important the plebeians were.

Question: Who were the plebeians?

Rome Conquered Carthage and Its Empire

By 270 B.C., Rome ruled most of Italy. The Romans allowed the conquered cities to rule their own city affairs. In return, the conquered cities were required to pay taxes and supply soldiers for the Roman army.

Rome soon needed a large army because it feared an attack from the powerful city of Carthage in northern Africa. Carthage ruled a large empire that included part of Spain, part of northern Africa, and some western Mediterranean islands. In 264 B.C., a war broke out between Rome and Carthage.

Rome won the first part of the war, but Carthage soon tried to defeat Rome again. Hannibal (HAN-uh-BULL), a great general of Carthage's army, decided to attack Rome by surprise. Hannibal marched through Spain, crossed the Alps into Italy, and then marched southward toward Rome. Hannibal surprised the Roman armies, and he was able to conquer them.

Hannibal remained in Italy for fifteen years. But in 202 B.C., a large Roman army conquered Carthage. Rome took over the empire that belonged to Carthage, and later Rome destroyed Carthage completely.

SUMMING UP

Rome began as a small city-state ruled by its patricians, who set up the Roman Republic about 500 B.C. By 270 B.C., Rome conquered most of Italy. By 202 B.C., the Roman Republic grew even more powerful after it conquered Carthage. In the next chapter, you will read how the Roman Republic ended and the Roman Empire began.

UNDERSTANDING THE LESSON

Do You Know These Important Terms?

For each sentence below, choose the term that best completes the sentence.

1. The group of people who started the settlement at Rome were called (**Latins/ Hellenists**).
2. The (**Italians/Etruscans**) were people from Asia Minor who settled in Italy.
3. Rich landowners who slowly gained power in the government of Rome were called (**landlords/patricians**).
4. A (**republic/kingdom**) is a form of government in which officials are elected by the citizens.
5. Two elected (**congressmen/consuls**) headed the Roman Republic.
6. The group of Romans who passed the laws and who chose the citizens to be voted on for consul was the (**Consul/ Senate**).
7. The (**patricians/plebeians**) were the common people of Rome.
8. The common people elected (**masters/ tribunes**) to represent them in the government.

Do You Remember These People and Events?

1. Tell something about each of the following subjects.

   Etruscans   Hannibal   Latins

2. Explain how or why each of the following developments occurred.

   a. Greek ideas were used by the people of Rome.
   b. The common people of Rome gained some rights in the Roman government.

Can You Locate These Places?

Use the map on page 164 to locate the following places. Tell how each place was related to developments in this chapter.

Alps   Italy
Carthage   Rome

Do You Know When It Happened?

Why are the following years important?

500 B.C.   202 B.C.

Do You Remember the Main Idea?

Which one of the following ideas is the MAIN IDEA of this chapter?

1. The Romans were one of the first peoples to develop a form of government in which the people elected their leaders.
2. The people of Rome set up a republic. The Roman Republic grew very powerful after it conquered all of Italy and defeated Carthage.
3. Rome developed as the most powerful city-state in Italy because it had the best location.

What Do You Think?

From what you have read in this chapter, try to answer the following thought questions.

1. What might have happened if Alexander the Great had conquered Italy?
2. Explain how the government of the Roman Republic used some democratic ideas.
3. Why was Hannibal's invasion of Italy a surprise to the Romans?

Chapter 24
The End of the Roman Republic

GETTING STARTED

1   Where was the Roman Republic heading? Rome had conquered Carthage in 202 B.C., and it was now a powerful nation. But were the Roman people and government prepared to govern conquered lands? As you will see, during the period between 202 B.C. to 27 B.C., important changes took place in Roman life and in the Roman government. These changes led to the end of the Roman Republic. But these changes also led to the beginning of the Roman Empire.

2   Before you begin reading the chapter lesson, survey the lesson. Begin your survey by reading the beginning of the lesson. Then look through the lesson and read the headings. Next, study the pictures and read the picture captions. Then study the map of the Roman Republic on page 170. Finally, read the review section called "Summing Up" at the end of the lesson. This survey of the whole lesson will help you to discover the important ideas in this chapter.

Know the Main Idea

As you read the chapter lesson, try to remember the following important MAIN IDEA of the chapter.

After the Roman Republic began to conquer new lands, many important changes took place in Roman life and in the Roman government.

The following questions will help you to understand the MAIN IDEA. Try to answer these questions as you read the lesson.

1. What lands did Roman armies conquer after the war with Carthage?
2. How did the new class of very rich Romans change life in the Roman Republic?
3. How did a fight for power among Roman leaders help lead to the end of the Roman Republic?

Know These Important Terms

province   emperor
Julian calendar

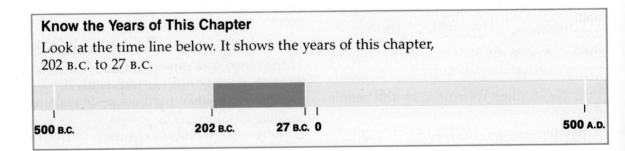

Know the Years of This Chapter
Look at the time line below. It shows the years of this chapter, 202 B.C. to 27 B.C.

500 B.C.   202 B.C.   27 B.C. 0   500 A.D.

The Roman Forum was once a marketplace and a gathering spot for political discussions. Note that the architectural style is similar to that of many government buildings in Washington, D.C.

EXPLORING THE TIME

After Rome defeated Carthage in 202 B.C., the Roman Republic became the strongest nation in the world on both land and sea. Soon the mighty Roman armies conquered many new lands. In this chapter, you will learn how these conquests changed the Roman Republic into the Roman Empire.

Rome Won Control of the Mediterranean Sea

After the war with Carthage, the Roman armies conquered Macedonia, Spain, and Greece. Later, part of Asia Minor also was ruled by Rome. Egypt became an ally of Rome, but it was allowed to remain independent. By 133 B.C., Rome controlled nearly the whole Mediterranean region.

Some Romans Grew Rich from the Wars

Before the wars with Carthage, most Romans—whether rich or poor—lived fairly simply and without many luxuries. After the wars with Carthage, however, a new class of rich Romans appeared. This new class changed Roman life.

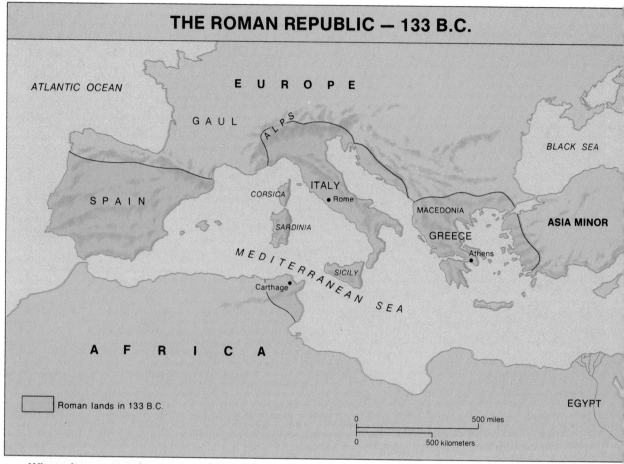

THE ROMAN REPUBLIC — 133 B.C.

ATLANTIC OCEAN

E U R O P E

G A U L

ALPS

SPAIN

ITALY

CORSICA

● Rome

SARDINIA

MACEDONIA

GREECE

● Athens

BLACK SEA

ASIA MINOR

M E D I T E R R A N E A N   S E A

SICILY

Carthage ●

A   F   R   I   C   A

Roman lands in 133 B.C.

EGYPT

0 ——————— 500 miles

0 ——————— 500 kilometers

What city was at the center of the Roman Republic?

The new class of rich Romans grew up in the following way. When the Romans conquered a nation, they usually organized it as a Roman **province**, or a conquered land ruled by Roman officials. But often these Roman officials ruled their provinces badly. They forced the conquered peoples to pay heavy taxes, and then the Roman officials used the tax money to make themselves rich. And some Romans grew rich by selling food and supplies to the Roman armies in the provinces. In this way, some Romans built up large fortunes and lived in great luxury.

Some Romans Suffered from the Wars

But not all Romans became rich from the wars. During the wars, taxes in Italy were so high that many small farmers had to sell their farms to pay their debts. Some of the rich Romans bought up these farms and formed them into very large farms that were worked by slaves. The small farmers who sold their farms were no longer able to make a living as farmers. Many farmers tried to find work in Rome, but Rome did not have jobs for them either. Many of these jobless, or unemployed, workers formed street mobs in Rome and often became beggars.

Trouble Began to Develop in the Roman Republic

The newly rich Romans gained power over the Roman Senate. Their main interest in the government was to protect their own riches. But the growing class of poor, jobless Romans had little power in the government. Yet this group was forced to depend on the government to feed them.

This growing class of unemployed Romans worried some Roman leaders. They feared that these jobless Romans might revolt against the government.

Two Brothers Tried to Help the Common People

In 133 B.C., Tiberius Gracchus (ty-BEER-ee-us GRACK-us), a rich Roman plebeian, was elected tribune. Tiberius wished to help the poor people of Rome. He tried to limit the amount of land that any Roman might own. All land over this limit was to be divided up and given to Romans who did not own land. However, many of the Roman Senators were landowners, and they did not want to give up any land. In order to stop Tiberius' plan, they had him murdered.

In 123 B.C., Tiberius' younger brother, Gaius (GAY-us) Gracchus, became a tribune. Gaius tried to pass several laws to help the poor. One of these laws gave poor people some land. Another law provided that new colonies were to be started where poor people might lead better lives. Gaius also had the government sell food to poor people at low prices. However, the Senate did not favor these changes. In 121 B.C., Gaius killed himself when he learned that his enemies were planning to murder him.

PEOPLE IN HISTORY

The Death of Spartacus

Slavery caused trouble in Roman times. Roman slaves hated slavery and took part in many revolts. The most famous slave revolt began in the year 73 B.C. This revolt was led by a slave named Spartacus (SPAHR-tuh-KUS).

Spartacus was a gladiator. He was able to lead about seventy gladiators in an escape from Rome to southern Italy. There, Spartacus and his group were soon joined by many other runaway slaves. The Roman army attacked Spartacus' group several times, but the slaves won every battle. Soon Spartacus had an army of thousands of soldiers, and he controlled most of southern Italy.

For three years, Spartacus' army won victories. However, the former slaves did not stick together. Although Spartacus fought bravely, a Roman army finally defeated Spartacus and killed him and most of his followers. In this way, the slave revolt finally was put down, but the Romans had been frightened by this slave revolt.

Question: What part of Italy did Spartacus and his group control?

Roman carving showing soldiers of the Roman Empire

War Broke Out in Rome

After Gaius' death, conditions in Rome grew worse. Army leaders fought for control of the government. Some of the generals were supported by the common people, and some generals were supported by the Senate. These army leaders fought each other for many years.

Meanwhile, the Roman government grew weaker. Two more generals, Pompey (POM-pee) and Julius Caesar (JOOL-yus SEEZ-ur), soon fought for control of the government. Caesar was a famous general who had conquered Gaul (GAWL), a large land in western Europe. In 49 B.C., Caesar returned to Italy and was strong enough now to make himself the ruler of the whole Roman Republic.

Julius Caesar Ruled the Roman Republic Well

Caesar took over complete power in the Roman Republic. However, he used his power to help the common people. He gave Roman citizenship to the people of some of the Roman provinces. He had laws passed to help the poor people pay their debts. He tied the Roman provinces closer together by improving Roman roads. And he improved the Roman calendar. The **Julian calendar,** started by Caesar, was used in Europe for more than a thousand years.

Caesar planned other changes, but his enemies stopped him from carrying them out. A group of Roman Senators feared that Caesar intended to make himself king and take away the Romans' rights. In March of 44 B.C., they killed Caesar.

The Roman Empire Was Set Up in 27 B.C.

Caesar's death caused new fighting, which led to the end of the Roman Republic. In 27 B.C., Caesar's grandnephew, Octavian (ock-TAY-VEE-UN), became the first **emperor,** or ruler, of the new Roman Empire.

SUMMING UP

After Rome conquered new lands, many changes took place in Roman life. Rich landowners bought up many small farms. Those who lost their farms became unemployed workers. The government of the Roman Republic did not help these unemployed Romans or govern its provinces wisely. After many years of fighting, Rome became an empire in 27 B.C. In the next chapter, you will read about Roman life during the years of the Roman Republic.

UNDERSTANDING THE LESSON

Do You Know These Important Terms?

For each sentence below, choose the term that best completes the sentence.

1. When the Romans conquered a nation, they organized it into a Roman territory called a **(province/state)**.
2. The **(Gregorian calendar/Julian calendar)** was started by Caesar and was used in Europe for more than a thousand years.
3. The leader or ruler of the Roman Empire was called **(a king/an emperor)**.

Do You Remember These People and Events?

1. Tell something about each of the following persons.

   Tiberius Gracchus   **Julius Caesar**
   Gaius Gracchus   **Octavian**
   Pompey

2. Explain how or why each of the following developments took place.

   a. Poor Romans often were jobless and had to depend on the government.
   b. The Gracchus brothers were killed.
   c. Powerful generals tried to take control of the Roman Republic.
   d. Julius Caesar ruled the Roman Republic well.

Can You Locate These Places?

Use the map on page 170 to do the following map work.

1. Locate the following places. Tell how each is related to the events in this chapter.

Macedonia   Asia Minor
Greece   Egypt
Gaul

Do You Know When It Happened?

Why are the following years important in Roman history?

   44 B.C.   27 B.C.

Do You Remember the Main Idea?

Which one of the following ideas is the MAIN IDEA of this chapter?

1. The unemployed workers in Rome became so angry that they revolted against the Roman Republic.
2. Powerful generals took control of the Roman Republic and built a powerful empire that was strong on land and sea.
3. After the Roman Republic began to conquer new lands, many important changes took place in Roman life and in the Roman government.

What Do You Think?

From what you have read in this chapter, try to answer the following thought questions.

1. Why were powerful generals able to take over the government of the Roman Republic? Do powerful generals still take over governments today?
2. What changes do you think might be made in a nation's government when it changes from a republic to an empire?

Chapter 25
Life in Rome

GETTING STARTED

1   If you had a time machine to travel back in time, would you want to watch a battle scene or a scene showing people in their everyday lives? Of course, battle scenes would be exciting, but the everyday lives of the people in early times also would be interesting. It would be interesting to compare the things that happen in your own life with the things that happened in people's lives long ago.

For example, how did the Romans live? What were the Romans' ideas about family life, religion, education, and sports? In this chapter, you will learn about Roman life during the years of the Roman Republic— from about 202 B.C. to 27 B.C.

2   Before you begin reading the chapter lesson, survey the lesson. Begin your survey by reading the beginning of the lesson. Then look through the lesson and read the headings. Next, study the pictures and read the picture captions. Finally, read the review section called "Summing Up" at the end of the lesson. This survey of the whole lesson will help you to discover the important ideas in this chapter.

Know the Main Idea

As you read the chapter lesson, try to remember the following important MAIN IDEA of the chapter.

Religion, family life, education, and sports were important in Roman life. Roman schools trained citizens to become lawyers and government officials.

The following questions will help you to understand the MAIN IDEA. Try to answer these questions as you read the lesson.

1. Who was the most important member of a Roman family?
2. What were the problems caused by the Romans' use of many slaves?
3. In what ways did the Romans spend their free time?

Know These Important Terms

gladiator fights   arena

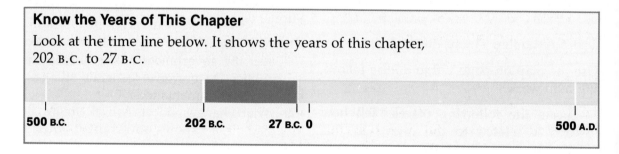

Know the Years of This Chapter

Look at the time line below. It shows the years of this chapter, 202 B.C. to 27 B.C.

| 500 B.C. | 202 B.C. | 27 B.C. 0 | 500 A.D. |

The Pantheon is the finest example of circular Roman temples. It has been in use, as a place of worship, for two thousand years.

EXPLORING THE TIME

In earlier chapters, you read how Rome became one of the greatest nations of early times. But how did the Romans live their daily lives during the Roman Republic? In this chapter, you will read about the life of the Roman people in these years.

The Romans Worshiped Many Gods

The Romans worshiped most of the same gods as the Greeks. But the Romans changed the Greek gods' names to Roman names. Jupiter (JOO-pih-TUR) was the Roman name for Zeus. And Minerva (mih-NUR-vuh) was the Roman name for Athena. The Romans had many other gods. And each Roman family also had a household god that was worshiped in the home.

Religion was an important part of Roman life. Rome had many priests and temples, and the Romans celebrated many religious holidays. Some priests, called augurs (AW-gurz), advised government officials about how the gods felt about important matters. No important government business was carried on unless the augurs approved of it.

Early Roman mosaic showing cargo being moved from one ship to another. Trade was very important to Rome's development.

The Father Controlled the Roman Family

During the period of the Roman Republic, the Roman father ruled his family. He ruled his wife, children, and grandchildren as long as he lived. The father also controlled his wife's property. And he selected wives for his sons and husbands for his daughters.

Roman women had few legal rights during the Republic. They were not allowed to vote or to serve in the government. But Roman women had more freedom than Greek women. In the homes, Roman women directed the household work, trained the children, and greeted and took care of visitors. Roman women also visited other homes with their husbands.

The Romans usually married at very young ages. Sons often were married as young as the age of fourteen, and daughters often were married as young as the age of twelve. In most Roman families, members treated each other with respect.

Schools Trained Romans for Important Jobs

Roman education, like Roman religion, was shaped by Greek ideas. But the Roman schools trained citizens mainly to do important work, rather than to be good citizens, as the Greek schools trained their citizens.

All Roman schools were private schools. In the early school years, both boys and girls learned to read, write, and solve arithmetic problems. Then, after that, only the sons of rich Romans attended school. These boys studied the Latin (Roman) and Greek languages, the books of great writers, and public speaking. Some Roman students even went to the city of Athens, in Greece, to complete their studies. They were then prepared to become lawyers or government officials.

Slavery Was an Important Part of Roman Life

The Romans depended on the use of many slaves. Most slaves in Rome were captured in war. Some of these slaves—especially Greek slaves—were doctors, teachers, or engineers. Other slaves were skilled artisans or were used as household servants. Most slaves were used to do the hard work on farms, in artisans' shops, or in the mines. Most of these slaves were treated badly.

Slavery was not only hard on the slaves, it caused thousands of free Romans to become unemployed. As more and more slaves were used, fewer free workers were able to find work. And the increasing number of slaves caused many Romans to become lazy and to depend on slaves for everything. As a result, the Romans no longer worked hard to find ways to improve their lives.

Romans Enjoyed Attending Their Bath Houses

The Roman bath houses were as important to the Romans as sports and athletics were to the Greeks. The bath houses provided more than just pools to bathe in. They had libraries, gardens, and rooms to exercise in. The cost of going to the bath houses was very low. Some bath houses held more than three thousand bathers at a time.

Carving showing young Roman students at school. From what you have read, how did Roman and Greek schools differ?

177

A gladiator was a slave trained to be a powerful fighter. Gladiators fought against other gladiators and wild animals. What animals are they fighting here?

The Romans greatly enjoyed their bath houses. Before or after their bath, they exercised, read books, or just talked with their fellow bathers. The Roman bath houses were the social centers of Rome.

The Romans Enjoyed Chariot Races and Gladiator Fights

The Romans amused themselves in many other ways, too. They went to theaters to see plays, as did the Greeks. But among the Romans, chariot races were more popular than were plays.

Among the sports that Romans enjoyed were the **gladiator** (GLAD-ee-AY-tur) **fights,** which were held in a large **arena,** or stadium. A gladiator was a slave trained to be a powerful fighter. Sometimes the gladiators fought wild animals. Sometimes the gladiators fought against each other.

Usually, the defeated gladiator was killed by the winning gladiator. But if the loser fought well, the people in the arena sometimes held their thumbs up to tell the winning gladiator not to kill him. If the crowd did not like the losing gladiator, they pointed their thumbs downward. This meant the loser was to be killed. Our saying of "thumbs down" to mean "no" came from this Roman practice.

SUMMING UP

In the daily life of the Roman people, religion and a family life were very important matters. Education also was important, since schools trained Romans to do important work. Slaves were increasingly used by the Romans. The use of many slaves made life easier for many Romans, but it also caused free workers to become unemployed. In the next chapter, you will read about the contributions of Roman culture to the world.

UNDERSTANDING THE LESSON

Do You Know These Important Terms?

For each sentence below, choose the term that best completes the sentence.

1. **(Gladiator fights/Nubian fights)** were sports in which slaves fought against each other or against wild animals.
2. A Roman stadium used for sports events was called an **(arena/open-air theater)**.

Do You Remember These People and Events?

1. Tell something about each of the following subjects.

   Jupiter   Minerva

2. Explain how or why each of the following developments took place.

   a. Roman boys and girls received their education.
   b. Women had a higher position in Rome than did women in Greece.
   c. Slavery had a bad effect on the lives of the Romans.
   d. Bath houses were very popular.

Can You Locate These Places?

Use the map in Chapter 24 (on page 170) to do the following map work.

1. Locate the following places. Tell how each place is related to the events in this chapter.

Greece	Rome
Athens	Italy

2. The everyday life of the Romans described in this chapter was the life led by the people who lived in Rome and in other Italian cities. This kind of life was also that of the Romans who lived in lands ruled by Rome. Name some of these lands ruled by Rome.

Do You Know When It Happened?

What are the years of this chapter?

Do You Remember the Main Idea?

Which one of the following ideas is the MAIN IDEA of this chapter?

1. Religion, family life, education, and sports were important in Roman life. Roman schools trained citizens to become lawyers and government officials.
2. The use of an increasing number of slaves in Rome made all the Romans lazy.
3. Many ideas used by the Romans in their everyday lives were really Greek ideas.

What Do You Think?

From what you have read in this chapter, try to answer the following thought questions.

1. What do you think life was like for boys and girls in a Roman family? Explain your answer.
2. What sports are played today in large arenas similar to those used by the Romans?
3. Which do you consider more important, the purpose of Greek education or the purpose of Roman education? Explain your answer.

GETTING STARTED

1   As you can imagine, the Roman army was a powerful, well-trained group of soldiers. Think of how these soldiers looked marching into battle. They marched in straight, proud rows. Their shields and armor gleamed. It was this powerful army that fought to win a large empire for Rome.

But we do not remember the Romans only for their conquests. Instead, we remember them mainly for their great culture, which contributed so much to the development of other peoples and nations. During the years of the Roman Empire, from 27 B.C. to 476 A.D., the Romans developed a great culture that still affects our lives today.

2   Before you begin reading the chapter lesson, survey the lesson. Begin your survey by reading the beginning of the lesson. Then look through the lesson and read the headings. Next, study the pictures and read the picture captions. Then look at the map of the Roman Empire on page 182. Finally, read the review section called "Summing Up" at the end of the lesson. This survey of the whole lesson will help you to discover the important ideas in this chapter.

Know the Main Idea

As you read the chapter lesson, try to remember the following important MAIN IDEA of the chapter.

The Romans made lasting contributions in laws, government, building, and writing. These contributions helped to shape the lives of many peoples and nations.

The following questions will help you to understand the MAIN IDEA. Try to answer these questions as you read the lesson.

1. Which of the Roman contributions was probably the greatest?
2. What modern languages are based on the Latin (Roman) language?
3. What new building method did the Romans develop to support bridges and buildings?

Know These Important Terms

Colosseum   aqueducts
Justinian's Code of Laws

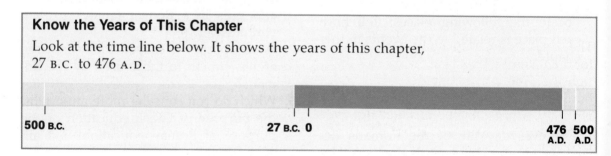

Know the Years of This Chapter
Look at the time line below. It shows the years of this chapter, 27 B.C. to 476 A.D.

500 B.C.   27 B.C. 0   476   500
                                                         A.D.   A.D.

A reconstruction of ancient Rome

EXPLORING THE TIME

The Romans are remembered today more for their culture, or way of life, than for their fighting. The Romans made lasting contributions in laws, government, building, and writing that have helped to shape our lives. In this chapter, you will learn what these lasting Roman contributions were.

The Romans Carried on Greek Culture

One of the most important Roman contributions was to preserve the great culture of Greece. Without the Romans, Greece might have been forgotten. But the Roman people accepted Greek art, Greek writing and ideas, and Greek science. And just as important, the Romans spread Greek ideas to other nations—particularly the nations of

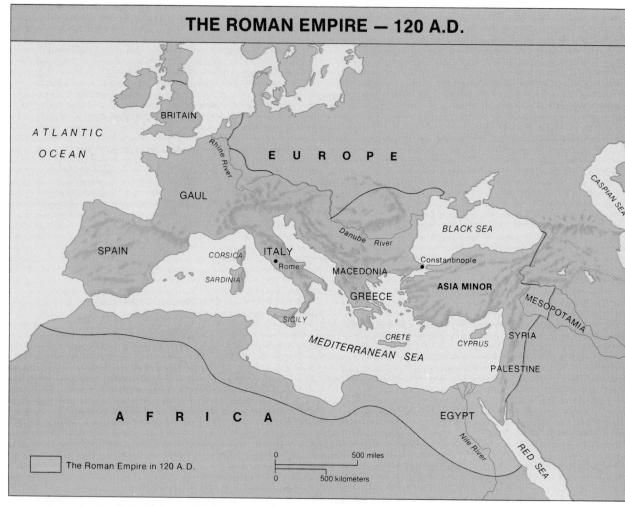

THE ROMAN EMPIRE — 120 A.D.

The Roman Empire in 120 A.D.

0   500 miles

0   500 kilometers

Describe the extent (boundaries) of the Roman Empire.

Europe. It is from the culture of Greece that the idea of democracy, or rule by the people, developed.

The Romans Governed Their Empire Well

The Roman Empire lasted for nearly five hundred years—from 27 B.C. to 476 A.D. At its largest, it included all of western and southeastern Europe, northern Africa, Asia Minor, Syria, Palestine, and part of Mesopotamia. It was not easy to govern this huge empire, but the Romans did it well.

The most important powers of the Roman Empire government were held by the central, or main, government at Rome. Other powers were given to the governments of each province in the empire. The main Roman government did not try to run the governments of the provinces. Rome simply required that the conquered peoples obey the Roman laws, keep the peace, and pay taxes. In this way, Rome was able to govern its empire successfully.

In some ways, the Roman Empire government was like the federal government that we have in the United States. We, too, have a central, or main, government, and also a government for each state, or part of the nation. But, in the United States, the people have freedom and have an important part in their government. In the Roman Empire, the people had few freedoms, and they did not have an important part in their government.

The Roman Language Helped to Shape Many Other Languages

Latin, the language spoken by the Romans, was another great Roman contribution. Latin became the basis of such modern languages as Spanish, French, Portuguese, and Italian. Even our English language has many Latin words. For example, some English words that come from Latin are "art," "culture," "government," and "language."

After the Roman Empire ended, Latin was still written and spoken by educated people all over Europe. Today, the Roman Catholic Church still uses Latin as its official language. And lawyers and doctors still study Latin as students in order to understand certain words used in medicine and law.

Roman Law Spread All over the World

Probably the greatest contribution of the Romans was Roman law. You may remember that the Roman plebeians forced the patricians to write down the laws to help all Romans to understand what the laws were. Later, as the Roman Empire grew, the Roman laws grew more difficult to understand, but the laws also became more fair.

During the Roman Republic, a special group of lawyers organized the Roman laws and explained the meaning of the laws. The most famous code, or collection, of Roman laws was made later, in the 500's A.D., by the Emperor Justinian (jus-TIN-ee-UN).

Justinian's Code of Laws contained all of the Roman laws. It also explained the meaning of these laws. This Code of Laws later became the basis of the laws used by many nations all over the world.

The Romans Were Great Builders

The Roman buildings were not as beautiful as the Greek buildings. But the Roman buildings were larger and stronger than the Greek buildings because the Romans used concrete and cement as building materials. The **Colosseum** (KOLL-uh-SEE-um), a huge Roman arena that still stands in Rome, is an example of how strong Roman buildings were.

The Romans used many arches in their buildings. The arches were used to support bridges and **aqueducts** (AK-wuh-DUCKTS), or the pipes that carried water to cities. The Romans also built special arches as monuments. The arches built to honor the emperors Titus and Constantine (KON-stun-TEEN) nearly two thousand years ago still stand in Rome today.

The Romans also built many paved roads. Thousands of miles of Roman roads tied the empire together. Many of the European roads of today are built over the old Roman roads. The most famous of these roads is the Appian Way, which extends from Rome to a seaport in southwestern Italy.

The Roman Colosseum, an amphitheater, opened in 80 A.D. and became the center of early Christian martyrdom. Thousands of Christians died while up to ninety thousand spectators at a time watched.

The Romans Wrote Plays, Poems, and History

Although the Roman writers liked the Greek writers, many Roman writers developed their own writing style. Roman writers wrote many interesting comedies about Roman life.

The most famous Roman poet was Vergil (VUR-jul). His poem the *Aeneid* (ih-NEE-id) tells the story of Rome's beginning. Much of what we know about Roman history comes from the writings of two Roman historians, Livy (LIV-ee) and Tacitus (TASS-uh-TUS). And the speeches and writings of the famous Roman leader Cicero (SISS-uh-ROH) tell a great deal about Roman life.

SUMMING UP

The Romans made great contributions that helped to shape our lives. The Romans preserved and passed on Greek culture. They also made their own great contributions in government, laws, buildings and roads, language (Latin), and writing. In the next chapter, you will read about the events that led to the end of the Roman Empire.

UNDERSTANDING THE LESSON

Do You Know These Important Terms?

For each sentence below, choose the term that best completes the sentence.

1. The Roman collection of laws which later became the basis of laws used by many nations of the world was (**Justinian's Code of Laws/Hammurabi's Code of Laws**).
2. The huge Roman arena that still stands in Rome is called the (**Parthenon/Colosseum**).
3. (**Water mains/Aqueducts**) were pipes supported by arches and were used to carry water to Roman cities.

Do You Remember These People and Events?

1. Tell something about each of the following persons.

    Justinian   **Vergil**   **Cicero**
    Livy   **Tacitus**

2. Explain how each of the following developments took place.

    a. The Romans helped to preserve Greek culture.
    b. Roman law became one of the greatest contributions of the Romans.
    c. The Romans left many records of their own history.

Can You Locate These Places?

Use the map on page 182 to do the following map work.

1. Locate each of the following places. Tell how each place is related to the developments in this chapter.

Greece   Palestine
Rome   Syria
Asia Minor   Mesopotamia

2. On this map, how are you able to tell that a location such as Rome is a city, while a location such as Palestine is a Roman province?

Do You Know When It Happened?

The Roman Empire lasted for 500 years. What were the years of the Roman Empire?

Do You Remember the Main Idea?

Which one of the following ideas is the MAIN IDEA of this chapter?

1. The Romans destroyed most Greek culture. Therefore, many of our ideas of today came from Rome rather than from Greece.
2. The Romans made outstanding contributions in almost all fields except government. They did not succeed in governing their own empire.
3. The Romans made lasting contributions in laws, government, building, and writing. These contributions helped to shape the lives of many peoples and nations.

What Do You Think?

From what you have read in this chapter, try to answer the following thought questions.

1. In what ways do you think that the Romans made good use of the Greek culture?
2. Is Latin still important today? Why?

Chapter 27
The End of the Roman Empire

GETTING STARTED

1 You have already read about many early empires. And you have learned that sooner or later these great empires ended. The same thing happened to the Roman Empire. Between the years 27 B.C. and 476 A.D., the Roman Empire reached its peak of power and then it began to grow weaker. Finally, parts of it were conquered by other peoples. The developments that weakened the Roman Empire and that led to its downfall are described in this chapter.

2 Before you begin reading the chapter lesson, survey the lesson. Begin your survey by reading the beginning of the lesson. They look through the lesson and read the headings. Next, study the pictures and read the picture captions. Then study the map showing the end of the Roman Empire on page 188. Finally, read the review section called "Summing Up" at the end of the lesson. This survey of the whole lesson will help you to discover the important ideas in this chapter.

Know the Main Idea

As you read the chapter lesson, try to remember the following important MAIN IDEA of the chapter.

The Roman Empire enjoyed peace for a long time. But the Roman Empire slowly weakened, and German tribes conquered parts of the empire.

The following questions will help you to understand the MAIN IDEA. Try to answer these questions as you read the lesson.

1. What caused the Roman Empire to grow weaker after 180 A.D.?
2. Who divided the Roman Empire into two parts?
3. What German tribe was first to capture the city of Rome?

Know These Important Terms

Pax Romana   vandalism
German tribes

Know the Years of This Chapter

Look at the time line below. It shows the years of this chapter, 27 B.C. to 476 A.D.

| 500 B.C. | 27 B.C. 0 | 476 500 A.D. A.D. |

An aqueduct, built in one of Rome's provinces in 19 B.C. Aqueducts were built throughout the Roman Empire as a means of providing water where it was needed. Water traveled in a conduit along the tops of the arches.

EXPLORING THE TIME

The first Roman emperor was called Augustus, a name that means "the great and noble one." The last Roman emperor was called Augustulus (aw-GUS-tuh-LUS) or "little Augustus." In some ways, this tells you the story of the Roman Empire. In the early years, the Romans were very proud of their empire. But later, they cared very little about their empire. In this chapter, you will read about the great days of the Roman Empire and learn how it ended.

Augustus Was Given More Power by the Senate

Octavian became the ruler of Rome in the year 27 B.C. Octavian wisely remembered that Julius Caesar was murdered because the Roman Senators feared that Caesar wanted to take away their power. Therefore, Octavian allowed the Senate to keep some of its power. In return, the Senate rewarded Octavian by giving him all the powers he needed and by calling him "Augustus." Today, we remember Octavian as the Emperor Augustus.

THE END OF THE ROMAN EMPIRE

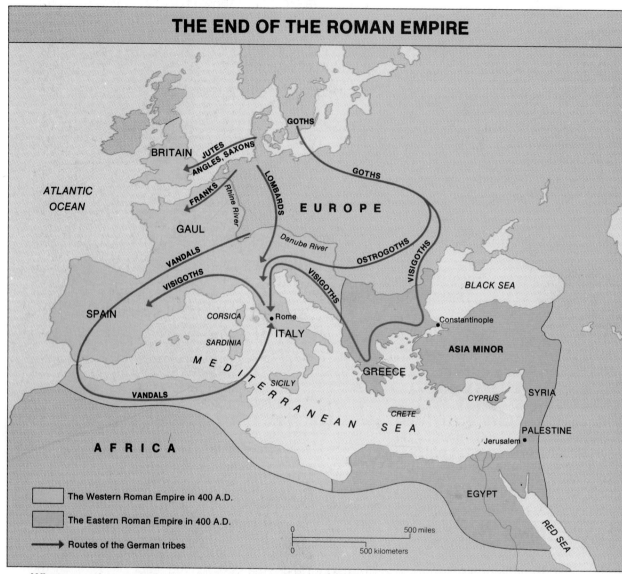

GOTHS

BRITAIN
JUTES
ANGLES, SAXONS

ATLANTIC
OCEAN

FRANKS

GAUL

VANDALS

VISIGOTHS

SPAIN

GOTHS

LOMBARDS

Rhine River

E U R O P E

Danube River

OSTROGOTHS

VISIGOTHS

VISIGOTHS

BLACK SEA

CORSICA

SARDINIA

Rome

ITALY

GREECE

Constantinople

ASIA MINOR

M E D I T E R R A N E A N   S E A

SICILY

CRETE

CYPRUS

SYRIA

PALESTINE
Jerusalem

VANDALS

A F R I C A

EGYPT

RED SEA

	The Western Roman Empire in 400 A.D.
	The Eastern Roman Empire in 400 A.D.
→	Routes of the German tribes

0 ———— 500 miles

0 ———— 500 kilometers

What was the capital city of the Western Roman Empire?

Augustus Worked for Peace in the Roman Empire

Augustus did not try to conquer new territory. Instead, he worked to improve the governments of the provinces already ruled by Rome. He tried to make them more honest. In this way, he hoped to prevent revolts. Augustus was so successful in improving the governments of the provinces that the Roman Empire enjoyed peace for almost two hundred years. This peace was known as the **Pax Romana** (PAKS roh-MAHN-uh), or Roman peace.

The Emperors Who Came After Augustus Were Good Rulers

Augustus died in 14 A.D. For the next two hundred years, Rome was ruled by many emperors. Until the year 180 A.D., most of the men who became emperor ruled Rome wisely and well. But in the hundred years following 180 A.D., Rome had fewer good emperors, and the Roman government did not rule well. Many revolts and wars took place within the Roman Empire.

Diocletian Made the Roman Empire Stronger

In 284 A.D., a general named Diocletian (DY-uh-KLEE-shun) became emperor. Diocletian became a strong ruler in order to keep the Roman Empire together. Diocletian made all government officials report directly to him. As a result, the Senate lost its power, and the Roman people lost most of their rights.

Diocletian divided the empire into two parts—an eastern half and a western half. He himself ruled the eastern half. But he chose another emperor to rule the western half of the empire. Diocletian's changes saved the Roman Empire, but the Roman people lost much of their freedom as a result of his changes.

The Roman Empire Became Two Separate Empires

After Diocletian's time, the eastern and western parts of the Roman Empire became separate empires. Rome remained the capital city of the western Roman Empire. Constantinople (KON-stan-tuh-NOH-pul) became the capital city of the eastern Roman Empire.

Emperor Augustus was so successful in improving the governments of the provinces that the Roman Empire enjoyed peace for almost two hundred years

The Western Roman Empire Was Too Weak to Defend Itself

The eastern Roman Empire lasted until 1453 A.D. But the western Roman Empire was destroyed by 476 A.D. What caused the end of the western Roman Empire?

One reason for the end of the western Roman Empire was the high taxes demanded by the Roman government. High taxes made many Romans turn against the Roman government.

Another reason for the end of the western Roman Empire was that many Romans died of diseases during this period. As a result of the smaller population, the Roman government had to hire soldiers from other nations to fight in its armies. Many of these

Many slaves worked for rich Roman families

soldiers were not loyal to Rome. Sometimes they deserted the Roman armies or even fought against Rome.

Slavery also helped to cause the end of the western Roman Empire. The use of slaves made many Romans lazy and less interested in improving Roman ways of living. The use of slaves also meant fewer jobs for Roman workers. And the jobless Romans gave less and less support to the government.

Many other reasons have been given for the fall of the western Roman Empire. But they all add up to one main reason. The Roman people and the armies no longer supported the western Roman Empire.

The Western Roman Empire Came to an End in 476 A.D.

The western Roman Empire faced the danger of attack from invading **German tribes** from the north. When the empire was strong, the German tribes were kept out of the empire. But as the empire weakened, German tribes entered and settled within its borders.

In 378 A.D., the Romans fought a battle against the Visigoth (VIZ-uh-GOTH) tribe, and the Visigoths won. This victory showed the German tribes that the western Roman Empire was too weak to defend itself.

The German tribes soon attacked the city of Rome itself. In 410 A.D., Alaric (AL-uh-RICK), the king of the Visigoths, captured Rome. In 455 A.D., another German tribe, the Vandals, also captured Rome. The Vandals nearly destroyed the city of Rome, and this attack added a new word to our language—**vandalism.** Then, in 476 A.D., a German general named Odoacer (OH-doh-A-ser) conquered Rome. The western Roman Empire now came to an end.

SUMMING UP

The Emperor Augustus' changes in government gave the Roman Empire almost two hundred years of peace. When wars and revolts broke out, Diocletian saved the empire by dividing it into two parts. The eastern Roman Empire lasted until 1453 A.D. But German tribes overthrew the western Roman Empire by 476 A.D. In the next chapter, you will learn about a new religion that developed during the early years of the Roman Empire.

UNDERSTANDING THE LESSON

Do You Know These Important Terms?

For each sentence below, choose the term that best completes the sentence.

1. The peace enjoyed by the Roman Empire for nearly two hundred years was the (**Pax Romana/Roman Holiday**).
2. The (**Swedish tribes/German tribes**) were groups of invading tribes who entered into the Roman Empire from the north.
3. (**Vandalism/Barbarianism**) is a word that means to destroy property.

Do You Remember These People and Events?

1. Tell something about each of the following subjects.

Augustus	**Odoacer**
Diocletian	**Visigoths**
Alaric	**Vandals**

2. Explain how or why each of the following events took place.

   a. The Roman Empire was able to enjoy peace for two hundred years.
   b. The western Roman Empire grew too weak to defend itself.
   c. The western Roman Empire ended.

Can You Locate These Places?

Use the map on page 188 to do the following map work.

1. Locate each of the following places. Tell how each place is related to the events in this chapter.

   Rome   Constantinople

2. Name some of the lands of the eastern Roman Empire. Name some lands of the western Roman Empire.
3. What rivers divided the western Roman Empire from the lands of the German tribes?

Do You Know When It Happened?

Why are the following years important?

   284 A.D.   476 A.D.

Do You Remember the Main Idea?

Which one of the following ideas is the MAIN IDEA of this chapter?

1. The Roman Empire enjoyed peace for a long time. But the Roman Empire slowly weakened, and German tribes conquered parts of the empire.
2. The Roman Empire became weak when Roman citizens lost interest in their government. The empire was finally captured by Roman tribes.
3. After the Roman Empire was conquered by German tribes, it continued to prosper under German rule.

What Do You Think?

From what you have read, try to answer the following thought questions.

1. Why do you think Diocletian believed that dividing the Roman Empire into two parts might make the empire stronger?
2. Why might the things that weakened the Roman Empire weaken any nation?
3. Suppose you were a member of an attacking German tribe. What might you have thought when you first saw Rome?

Chapter 28
The Rise of the Christian Religion

GETTING STARTED

1   During the time when Emperor Augustus ruled the Roman Empire, important events were happening in a faraway part of that empire. These events were to have a lasting effect on all of world history. This faraway part of the empire was Palestine. And the events concerned the beginning of a new religion in the world—a religion that was closely related to the history of the Jewish (Hebrew) people in Palestine.

You will recall that you read about Palestine and the Jewish people in Chapter 11, which described their history up to about 586 B.C. In 64 B.C., Palestine became part of the Roman Empire. Shortly after this time, a new religion began that spread to all parts of the Roman Empire by 380 A.D.

2   Before you begin reading the chapter lesson, survey the lesson. Begin your survey by reading the beginning of the lesson. Then look through the lesson and read the headings. Next, study the pictures and read the picture captions. Finally, read the review section called "Summing Up" at the end of the lesson. This survey of the whole lesson will help you to discover the important ideas in this chapter.

Know the Main Idea

As you read the chapter lesson, try to remember the following important MAIN IDEA of the chapter.

The Jewish religion and the teachings of Jesus Christ formed the basis of the Christian religion, which slowly spread throughout the Roman Empire.

The following questions will help you to understand the MAIN IDEA. Try to answer these questions as you read the lesson.

1. Describe the beginnings of the Christian religion in Palestine.
2. How did the Christian religion gain many followers?
3. When did the Christian religion become lawful in the Roman Empire?

Know These Important Terms

Messiah	missionaries
apostles	Pope

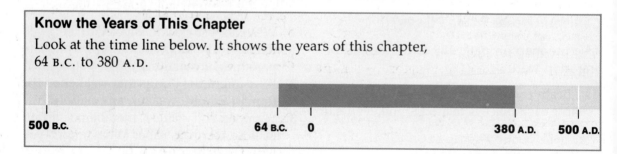

Know the Years of This Chapter
Look at the time line below. It shows the years of this chapter, 64 B.C. to 380 A.D.

| 500 B.C. | 64 B.C. | 0 | 380 A.D. | 500 A.D. |

Catacombs were built underground by Christians afraid of being martyred. They would meet in catacombs to worship. Some Christians who died were buried in catacombs.

EXPLORING THE TIME

During the early years of the Roman Empire, a very important event took place that helped to shape the history of the world. That event was the rise of the Christian religion. The Christian religion began in Palestine, a faraway part of the Roman Empire. Soon this new religion spread to many parts of the world. In this chapter, you will read of the beginnings of the Christian religion.

The Jewish People Hoped for a Leader to Free Them

To understand how the Christian religion began, you need to know about the history of the Jews in Palestine. After the Jews were conquered by Mesopotamia in 586 B.C., they were forced to live in the city of Babylon. Later, the Persians conquered Babylon and allowed the Jews to return to Palestine again. During these years, the Old Testament became the basic Jewish law. One of the teachings in the Old Testament

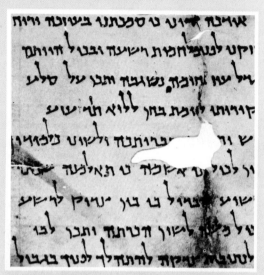

Part of a Dead Sea Scroll

In 1947, a young Arab boy was looking for some goats near the shores of the Dead Sea. The boy did not find his goats. Instead he made one of the most important discoveries of recent times. He found some early writings which we now call the Dead Sea Scrolls.

The largest of the Dead Sea Scrolls contains the complete Bible book of the prophet Isaiah. Most scholars believe that this scroll is about two thousand years old. Yet in nearly every way it is like the book of Isaiah in the Bible today. This shows how carefully the words of the Bible have been kept.

Other Dead Sea Scrolls tell about the life and beliefs of a group of people who lived long ago near the Dead Sea. Some of their teachings seem to be like the teachings of Jesus. Some scholars believe that this group of people was a link between the Jewish religion and the Christian religion.

Question: What book of the Bible is in one of the Dead Sea Scrolls?

was that someday a **Messiah** (muh-SY-uh), or leader, was to appear to help the Jews build a new nation.

This belief in a Messiah became important after the Roman Empire took over Palestine in 64 B.C. The Jewish people were very unhappy under Roman rule. Many of them hoped for the Messiah to appear and to free them from Roman rule.

However, not all Jews waited for a Messiah to save them. Instead, many Jews tried to fight for their freedom from the Roman Empire, but the Roman armies defeated them. To punish the Jews, the Romans destroyed Jerusalem.

A New Religious Leader Appeared in Palestine

It was during this bloody period in Palestine's history that Jesus Christ was born near Jerusalem in southern Palestine. We know very little about Jesus' life. However, Jesus' followers wrote that Jesus earned a living as a carpenter and that Jesus studied the teachings of the Old Testament.

Jesus accepted many of the teachings of the Old Testament. He began to preach to the Jews and soon gathered a group of followers. Jesus chose twelve **apostles** (uh-POSS-ulz), or followers, as special helpers.

No one really knows how long Jesus preached, but it was probably only a few years. Yet in this short period of time, Jesus' teachings formed a new religion that helped to shape the history of the world.

The Romans Feared Jesus and Had Him Killed

Jesus' main teaching was that God loved all people and that all men and women were brothers and sisters. Some people in Palestine believed that Jesus was the long-awaited Messiah. Other people did not accept Jesus as the Messiah. Meanwhile, the Romans feared that Jesus might become too powerful and cause a revolt against the Roman Empire. Therefore, the Roman governor ordered that Jesus be killed after Jesus was accused of being a traitor by some of the people.

The Christian Religion Gained Many Followers

After Jesus' death, some of the followers declared that Jesus was the Messiah. They began to spread Jesus' teachings to many other peoples. The most famous of these Christian **missionaries,** or teachers, was a Jew from Asia Minor named Paul.

Most of the early Christians were Jews, and they followed the old Jewish laws as well as the new Christian teachings. But Paul won many new followers for the Christian religion among other peoples in the Near East.

The Christian Religion Spread for Many Reasons

The Christian religion appeared at a time when many people in the Roman Empire were unhappy under the rule of Rome and when they no longer believed in their old gods or the old religions. The Christian religion gained many followers because it preached love and the familyhood of all people. The new religion also gained many followers because it taught a belief in life after death.

The Roman Empire itself made it easy to spread the Christian religion. The excellent Roman roads allowed Christian missionaries to reach all parts of the empire to spread their religion. And the missionaries used Latin (the Roman language) to spread

the Christian religion because all peoples of the empire understood Latin.

The Christian Religion Became the Religion of the Roman Empire

The early Roman emperors hated the Christians because Christians refused to worship the Roman gods, refused to support the Roman officials, and refused to serve in the Roman army. The Roman emperors made

Sculpture of St. Peter, an early follower of Jesus Christ and the first pope of the Church of Rome

195

Wall painting showing Emperor Constantine (with crown) greeting the Pope (on horse)

being a Christian a crime, and they punished Christians by putting them to death.

Thousands of Christians were killed, but the Christian religion grew. Slowly, the Christians built up a strong religion. The bishop of Rome became the head of the Christian religion, or the **Pope.** In 313 A.D., the emperor Constantine ruled that the Christian religion was lawful. In 380 A.D., it became the official religion of the Roman Empire.

SUMMING UP

The life and the teachings of Jesus Christ became the basis of the Christian religion. Many people in the Roman Empire who were unhappy under Roman rule became followers of the Christian religion. The Christian religion spread rapidly, and by the year 380 A.D. it became the official religion of the Roman Empire. In the next chapter, which begins Unit 8, you will read about the rise of the German kingdoms after the western Roman Empire ended.

UNDERSTANDING THE LESSON

Do You Know These Important Terms?

For each sentence below, choose the term that best completes the sentence.

1. The leader who the Jewish people hoped might someday build a new nation for them was called the (**Baptist/Messiah**).
2. The (**apostles/bishops**) were twelve followers chosen by Jesus to help spread the new religious ideas.
3. Teachers who spread the Christian religion among other peoples were called (**bishops/missionaries**).
4. The bishop of Rome became the head of the Christian religion, and he was called the (**apostle/Pope**).

Do You Remember These People and Events?

1. Tell something about each of the following subjects.

   Jesus Christ
   Paul

2. Explain how each of the following events took place.

   a. The Jewish people hoped for a Messiah to appear.
   b. Christian ideas spread throughout the Roman Empire.
   c. At first, the Romans hated the Christians.

Can You Locate These Places?

Use the map in Chapter 27 (page 188) to locate each of the following places. Tell how each place is related to the events in this chapter.

Palestine	**Jerusalem**
Asia Minor	**Rome**

Do You Know When It Happened?

Tell why the following year is important.

313 A.D.

Do You Remember the Main Idea?

Which one of the following ideas is the MAIN IDEA of this chapter?

1. The Christian religion began in Palestine, but it was not accepted by other people in the Roman Empire.
2. The Christian religion is based on the teachings of Jesus. Paul helped to spread these teachings to all parts of the Roman Empire.
3. The Jewish religion and the teachings of Jesus Christ formed the basis of the Christian religion, which slowly spread throughout the Roman Empire.

What Do You Think?

From what you have read in this chapter, answer the following thought questions.

1. Why do you think that the Christian religion spread to many lands?
2. If you were a Roman, do you think you would have accepted the Christians? Explain your answer.
3. Why do you think that Rome became the center of the Christian religion? Explain your answer.

Unit 8
Europe During the Early Middle Ages

THE CHAPTERS IN UNIT 8 ARE

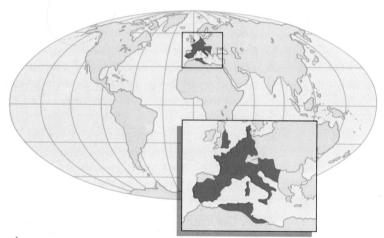

After the Roman Empire ended, a period began in Europe's history called the Middle Ages. During the early years of the Middle Ages, a whole new way of life called feudalism developed in western Europe. In this unit, you will find out why feudalism developed and how it affected the people's lives in western Europe.

A French castle, built in the Middle Ages

Chapter 29
The German Kingdoms

GETTING STARTED

1   For many years, the Roman Empire helped to bring law and order to all the lands around the Mediterranean Sea. But then the western Roman Empire grew weaker and was invaded by German tribes. From 476 A.D. to 814 A.D. (see the time line below), many leaders tried to rebuild the Roman Empire. But none of these leaders was able to rebuild the Roman Empire. Finally, the German tribes were able to take over parts of the Roman Empire and to form their own kingdoms there.

2   Before you begin reading the chapter lesson, survey the lesson. Begin your survey by reading the beginning of the lesson. Then look through the lesson and read the headings. Next, study the pictures and read the picture captions. Then study the map of the German kingdoms on pages 202 and 203. Finally, read the review section called "Summing Up" at the end of the lesson. This survey of the whole lesson will help you to discover the important ideas in this chapter.

Know the Main Idea

As you read the chapter lesson, try to remember the following important MAIN IDEA of the chapter.

The German tribes formed many kingdoms. The Frankish kingdom became the most important of these German kingdoms.

The following questions will help you to understand the MAIN IDEA. Try to answer these important questions as you read the lesson.

1. After the German tribes moved into the western Roman Empire, how did their ways of living change?
2. Who was the first important leader of the Franks?
3. What title was given to Charlemagne by the Pope?

Know These Important Terms

> war bands
> Franks

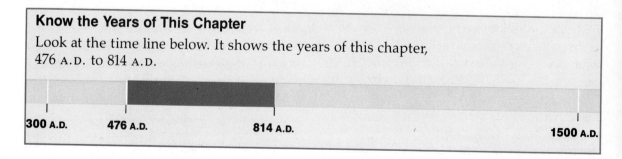

Know the Years of This Chapter
Look at the time line below. It shows the years of this chapter, 476 A.D. to 814 A.D.

| 300 A.D. | 476 A.D. | 814 A.D. | 1500 A.D. |

A church in the Kingdom of the Visigoths

EXPLORING THE TIME

Did you ever hear someone say, "There is nothing left to do but pick up the pieces"? That is what the German tribes did after the end of the western Roman Empire. Each German tribe tried to build a kingdom for itself in the lands where the Roman Empire had ruled. In this chapter, you will read about some of the new German kingdoms.

The Germans Learned New Ways of Living

Before they entered the Roman Empire, the Germans were wanderers. They raised small crops of grain, they hunted, and they kept herds of cattle, sheep, and horses. They were also skilled metal workers.

The Germans were strong, fierce fighters. They formed **war bands**, or groups under the leadership of a strong chief.

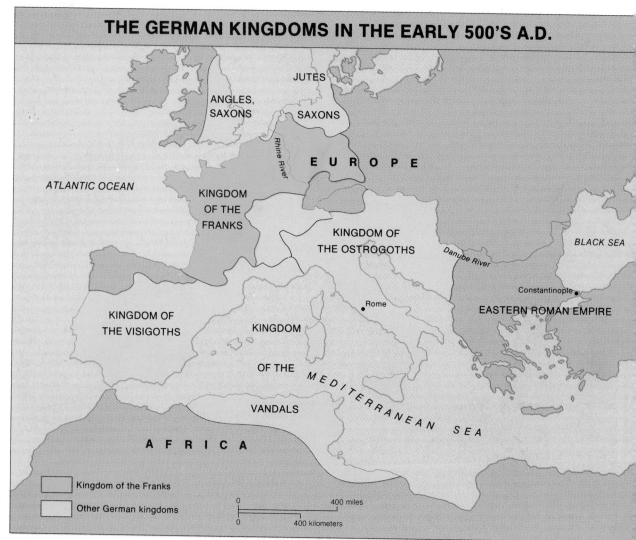

THE GERMAN KINGDOMS IN THE EARLY 500'S A.D.

JUTES

ANGLES,
SAXONS

SAXONS

Rhine River

E U R O P E

ATLANTIC OCEAN

KINGDOM
OF THE
FRANKS

KINGDOM OF
THE OSTROGOTHS

Danube River

BLACK SEA

Constantinople

Rome

EASTERN ROMAN EMPIRE

KINGDOM OF
THE VISIGOTHS

KINGDOM

OF THE

M E D I T E R R A N E A N   S E A

VANDALS

A F R I C A

Kingdom of the Franks

Other German kingdoms

0   400 miles

0   400 kilometers

What river marked the eastern edge of the Germanic kingdoms?

When the Germans invaded the western Roman Empire, their ways of living changed. Many of the Germans settled down and became farmers. And by living in or near the Roman Empire, the Germans learned many Roman ways of doing things. As a result, the Germans preserved some of the Roman culture in the new nations that they built.

The Germans Formed Many Kingdoms

In 476 A.D., the German general Odoacer (OH-doh-A-ser) conquered Rome. But in 493 A.D., Odoacer was defeated by the Ostrogoths led by Theodoric (thee-ODD-uh-RICK). Theodoric ruled Italy well for about thirty years. He upheld the Roman laws, and he had roads and aqueducts rebuilt. But after

Theodoric died, northern Italy was taken over by another group of Germans, the Lombards (LOM-bardz), who were less interested in preserving the Roman culture.

Other German tribes also set up kingdoms. The Visigoths, who were the first Germans to capture Rome, formed a kingdom in Spain. The Vandals formed a kingdom in northern Africa. And three German tribes—the Angles (ANG-ulz), the Saxons (SACK-sunz), and the Jutes (JOOTZ) —conquered the island of Britain, off the northwestern mainland of Europe.

The Franks Built Western Europe's Strongest Kingdom

The most important German kingdom belonged to a people called the **Franks.** The leader of the Franks was Clovis (KLOH-vus). When Clovis married a Christian, he, too, became a Christian and won the support of the Roman Catholic Church. By the early years of the 500's A.D., Clovis ruled a large kingdom that included most of the land of present-day France, Belgium, and western Germany.

The Frankish Kingdom Was Divided into Many Local Districts

The Frankish kings and their officials used Roman titles. But in other ways, the Frankish government was different from the old Roman government. Instead of paying taxes in money, the Franks paid their taxes in farm products. However, Frankish farmers found it difficult to carry farm products from one place to another. Therefore, the Frankish kings traveled around their kingdom to collect the taxes owed to them.

The Frankish kingdom was divided into many districts, or parts. Each district was ruled by a count, who commanded the

CHARLEMAGNE'S EMPIRE

Frankish kingdom before Charlemagne

Lands Charlemagne conquered by 814 A.D.

Charlemagne's empire stretched between which two seas?

district's troops. The count was also the judge and the tax collector for the district. The count had great powers and sometimes was even more powerful than the king.

A New Family Ruled the Frankish Kingdom

Clovis was followed by weaker kings. These kings allowed the Frankish kingdom to be ruled by a government official called the

In 800 A.D., Pope Leo the Third made Charlemagne the Protector of the Church and crowned him "Emperor of the Romans"

"mayor of the palace." The counts who ruled the districts often did not obey these kings. During the late 600's A.D., the Frankish kingdom was in danger of splitting up because the kings were so weak. However, a strong mayor of the palace named Pepin (PEP-in) ended this danger.

Pepin and his son, Charles Martel (mahr-TELL), forced the counts to obey the king. About 751 A.D., Charles Martel's son, Pepin the Short, became ruler of the Franks.

When Pepin the Short became ruler, the Pope, who was head of the Roman Catholic Church, supported Pepin. In return, Pepin's army captured some Italian territory from the Lombards for the Pope. When Pepin's son became ruler, he and the Pope continued to work together.

Charlemagne Set Up a New Western Roman Empire

Pepin's son was called Charlemagne (SHARR-luh-MAIN), or Charles the Great.

Charlemagne spent most of his life adding more land to the Frankish kingdom. Charlemagne conquered northern Spain, the land south of the Danube River, and northern Italy. Charlemagne also conquered the Saxons of northern Germany and made them become Christians.

Pope Leo the Third realized that Charlemagne was now so powerful that the Church needed Charlemagne's support. In 800 A.D., the Pope made Charlemagne the protector of the Church and crowned him the "Emperor of the Romans." In this way, the German kingdom carried on the idea of a western Roman Empire. In fact, the German kingdom later was called the Holy Roman Empire. And the eastern Roman emperor at Constantinople accepted Charlemagne as the western Roman emperor.

Charlemagne Ruled His Empire Well

Charlemagne divided his empire into districts ruled by counts. But Charlemagne sent out two officials to see that the counts carried out their duties as Charlemagne wished. Until he died in 814 A.D., Charlemagne gave the people of western Europe the wisest government they had had since the days of the Roman Empire.

SUMMING UP

The German tribes formed many kingdoms after the fall of the western Roman Empire. The Frankish kingdom was the most important of these kingdoms. The greatest Frankish ruler, Charlemagne, became emperor in 800 A.D., and he ruled his empire well. In the next chapter, you will read about life in western Europe during the period of the new German kingdoms.

UNDERSTANDING THE LESSON

Do You Know These Important Terms?

For each sentence below, choose the term that best completes the sentence.

1. The Germans formed many (war bands/outposts), or groups under the leadership of a strong chief.
2. The most important German kingdom was formed by a people called the (Franks/Saxons).

Do You Remember These People and Events?

1. Tell something about each of the following persons.

   Odoacer   Charles Martel
   Theodoric   Pepin the Short
   Clovis   Charlemagne
   Pepin   Pope Leo the Third

2. Explain how or why each of the following developments took place.

   a. Some German tribes tried to save the Roman culture.
   b. The Franks built the strongest and most important kingdom.
   c. The Pope wished to work together with Frankish kings.

Can You Locate These Places?

Use the maps in this chapter to do the following map work.

1. Use the map on page 202 to locate the kingdoms formed by the following German tribes.

   Ostrogoths   Vandals   Franks
   Visigoths   Saxons   Angles

2. Use the map of Charlemagne's empire on page 203 to locate the following places.

   Britain   Spain

3. Compare the map on page 202 with the map of Europe on page 722. What present-day nations are located where Charlemagne's empire used to be?

Do You Know When It Happened?

What are the years of this chapter?

Do You Remember the Main Idea?

Which one of the following ideas is the MAIN IDEA of this chapter?

1. The German tribes formed many kingdoms. The Frankish kingdom became the most important of these German kingdoms.
2. German tribes completely destroyed the western Roman Empire, and they were not able to build new kingdoms.
3. Some German tribes moved to northern Africa and Britain, but they did not build kingdoms in western Europe.

What Do You Think?

From what you have read in this chapter, answer the following thought questions.

1. Do you think that the German tribes had a good effect or bad effect on the western Roman Empire? Explain your answer.
2. Why do you think that Charlemagne was a great ruler?
3. Why did the Popes want to be on good terms with the Frankish kings?

Chapter 30
Europe in the Early Middle Ages

GETTING STARTED

1   When German tribes began to invade the western Roman Empire, they brought their own culture with them. In many ways, German culture was not as advanced as Roman culture. But the Germans lived so closely to the Romans for so many years that many Roman ideas became part of the German culture. At the same time, the Germans also were developing their own new ways of living as each tribe tried to build a kingdom. The German tribes developed their kingdoms between 476 A.D. and 1000 A.D., which are the years of this chapter. Check these years on the time line at the bottom of this page.

2   Before you begin reading the chapter lesson, survey the lesson. Begin your survey by reading the beginning of the lesson. Then look through the lesson and read the headings. Next, study the pictures and read the picture captions. Finally, read the review section called "Summing Up." This survey will help you to discover the important ideas in this chapter.

Know the Main Idea

As you read the chapter lesson, try to remember the following important MAIN IDEA of the chapter.

Life in Europe changed and became more difficult for most people during the Early Middle Ages. European ways of life during this period were a mixture of Roman ideas and German ideas.

The following questions will help you understand the MAIN IDEA. Try to answer these questions as you read the lesson.

1. Where did Roman culture remain strong during the Early Middle Ages?
2. Where did more and more people live during the Early Middle Ages?
3. What German ruler helped to preserve learning in Europe during the Early Middle Ages?

Know These Important Terms

Middle Ages   villa
Early Middle Ages   ordeal

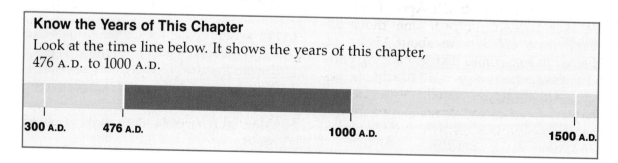

Know the Years of This Chapter
Look at the time line below. It shows the years of this chapter, 476 A.D. to 1000 A.D.

| 300 A.D. | 476 A.D. | | 1000 A.D. | 1500 A.D. |

In this painting from the Middle Ages, what familiar tools are being used by the farmers?

EXPLORING THE TIME

As the Roman Empire was fading away, a new period was beginning in Europe. This period is called the **Middle Ages**. The Middle Ages lasted for over one thousand years, from 476 A.D. to about 1500 A.D. Historians sometimes divide this long period of years into two parts, the Early Middle Ages and the Later Middle Ages. In this chapter, you will read about Europe during the **Early Middle Ages**, which lasted from 476 A.D. to about 1000 A.D.

Roman Culture Remained in Some Parts of Europe

The Early Middle Ages, from 476 A.D. to about 1000 A.D., used to be called the "Dark Ages." This meant that it was a period of little learning and little progress. Yet the "Dark Ages" were not really as dark as many people thought. During this time, the people of Europe were slowly developing new ideas, new farming and trading methods, and new ways of living. Besides, the Roman culture continued in some parts of Europe.

In Germany and Britain, Roman culture was known because Roman soldiers had been stationed there. And in France (the Frankish kingdom) the Franks used the Latin (Roman) language and Roman laws. Of course, in Italy, the home of the Romans, the Roman culture remained strongest of all.

Cities Became Less Important During the Early Middle Ages

During the period of the Roman Empire, Europe had many large cities. These cities were the centers of busy trade. But many of these cities were destroyed during the wars that took place in the Roman Empire in the 400's A.D. As a result, less trade was carried on as the empire split up. After the Germans invaded the western Roman Empire, trade became even less important. The cities of Europe were no longer busy and important centers of life.

Most People of Europe Became Farmers

As cities became less important, more and more people lived on farms. Many of these farms were very large. During Roman times, a large farm was called a **villa** (VILL-uh). Villas were worked mainly by tenant farmers, or farmers who had to pay a large part of their crop to the landowner.

During the years when armies were fighting all over the Roman Empire, life was dangerous. Only the owners of villas were able to hire soldiers to protect their land. In order to be protected, many small farmers gave up their farms and became tenant farmers on the large villas.

When the German tribes conquered the western Roman Empire, they took over many of the villas and small farms there. Some German leaders became large land-

The Germans used "the ordeal" to decide if a person was guilty of a crime

owners in this way, and they forced other Germans to farm their land for them.

German Law and Roman Law Were Mixed to Form a New Legal System

The German kingdoms used Roman laws, but they also used many of their own laws. For example, the Germans set up their own system of fines. The Germans used fines to punish almost every kind of crime. Even murder was punished by a fine. Only a few crimes, such as the murder of a king, were punished by death.

Another kind of German law was the **ordeal**. The ordeal was a test to determine if a person was guilty or innocent. Sometimes the ordeal required a person to carry a hot

The Roman Catholic Church helped to preserve books and learning in Europe during the Middle Ages

piece of iron or to place a hand in boiling water. If the person's hand healed in a short time, the person was judged innocent. But if the hand did not heal, the person was judged guilty!

The Catholic Church Helped to Preserve Learning

During the Early Middle Ages, learning was not important to most people. Making a living was so difficult that most people had little time for education. However, the leaders of the Roman Catholic Church tried to preserve learning in Europe.

Latin (Roman) was the language used by the Catholic Church, and the Catholic leaders studied the works of the great Ro-

man writers and poets. The Catholic Church did not use Greek at all. Therefore, the Greek language and many Greek ideas were almost completely forgotten in western Europe.

Charlemagne Encouraged Learning

Charlemagne, the Frankish king, also helped to preserve learning. During the first years of the Early Middle Ages, most of the educated people lived in Italy, Spain, Britain, or Ireland. France (the kingdom of the Franks) had few educated people. But Charlemagne changed this when he started a school at his palace. The head of Charlemagne's school was the finest teacher of that time. Charlemagne also required the

During the Middle Ages, most people in Europe were farmers. What crop is being harvested here?

SUMMING UP

Catholic Church to open schools to help educate Frankish children.

Charlemagne had good copies made of the old Latin books in order to preserve them and their ideas. This work was so successful that Charlemagne's schools were able to train many fine thinkers and teachers. These educated people helped to preserve Latin writing, and they also wrote many new books.

During the Early Middle Ages, cities became less important as less trade was carried on and more people lived on farms. The Early Middle Ages were difficult years for the peoples of Europe. But Roman culture and learning were preserved in the Frankish kingdom by the Roman Catholic Church and by Charlemagne. In the next chapter, you will read about life in Europe during the years of the Early Middle Ages.

UNDERSTANDING THE LESSON

Do You Know These Important Terms?

For each sentence below, choose the term that best completes the sentence.

1. The period that began in Europe in 476 A.D. and lasted until 1500 A.D. is called the **(Early Ages/Middle Ages)**.
2. The first part of the Middle Ages, from 476 A.D. to about 1000 A.D., is called the **(Early Ages/ Early Middle Ages)**.
3. During Roman times, a large farm was called a **(plantation/villa)**.
4. The **(trial/ordeal)** was a test used to determine whether a person was guilty or innocent of some crime.

Do You Remember These People and Events?

1. Tell how each of the following encouraged learning in the Early Middle Ages.

   Charlemagne   Catholic Church

2. Explain how each of the following developments took place.

   a. Cities became less important during the Middle Ages.
   b. Life for most people in Europe became dangerous and difficult.

Can You Locate These Places?

Use the map of Charlemagne's empire on page 203 to do the following map work.

1. Locate the following places. Tell how each place is related to this chapter.

   Britain   Ireland
   Frankish kingdom   Italy
   Spain

2. Name a city in the Frankish kingdom. Name two large rivers that flowed through the Frankish kingdom. By the kind of letters used, how can you tell the name of a kingdom? the names of cities? the names of rivers?

Do You Know When It Happened?

The Early Middle Ages lasted for over 500 years. What years were they?

Do You Remember the Main Idea?

Which one of the following ideas is the MAIN IDEA of this chapter?

1. During the Early Middle Ages, life for most people in Europe did not change very much from what it had been before.
2. During the Early Middle Ages, little progress was made because education and learning almost ended.
3. Life in Europe changed and became more difficult for most people during the Early Middle Ages. European ways of living during this period were a mixture of Roman ideas and German ideas.

What Do You Think?

From what you have read in this chapter, answer the following thought questions.

1. Did the lack of interest in learning during the Early Middle Ages affect people's ways of living? Explain.
2. What do you suppose European cities were like during the Early Middle Ages?
3. Do you think that the ordeal was a fair way to determine if a person was guilty or innocent of a crime?

Chapter 31
The Growth of Feudalism

GETTING STARTED

1   During the Early Middle Ages, life in Europe developed a new and different pattern. Governments were weak, and wars broke out frequently. Armed bandits roamed across the land, robbing and killing. Therefore, life in Europe became difficult and dangerous for most people.

The main problem for most people during the Early Middle Ages was the need for protection against attack. As a result, a new system of government and way of life developed in the years between 476 A.D. and 1000 A.D. The time line at the bottom of this page shows this period. This new system of government and way of life developed in most European lands during the Early Middle Ages.

2   Before you begin reading the chapter lesson, survey the lesson. Begin your survey by reading the beginning of the lesson. Then look through the lesson and read the headings. Next, study the pictures and read the picture captions. Finally, read the review section called "Summing Up" at the end of the lesson. This survey of the whole lesson will help you to discover the important ideas in this chapter.

Know the Main Idea

As you read the chapter lesson, try to remember the following important MAIN IDEA of the chapter.

Feudalism was the way of life and the system of government that grew up in Europe during the Early Middle Ages.

The following questions will help you to understand the MAIN IDEA. Try to answer these questions as you read the lesson.

1. Why did many small farmers in Europe give up their land to the large landowners?
2. Who were the most important persons in the feudal system?
3. What three things was a vassal expected to provide for his lord?

Know These Important Terms

feudalism	lord	vassals
nobles	fief	

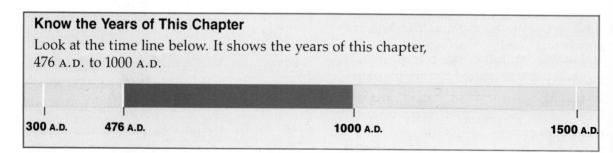

Know the Years of This Chapter

Look at the time line below. It shows the years of this chapter, 476 A.D. to 1000 A.D.

| 300 A.D. | 476 A.D. | 1000 A.D. | 1500 A.D. |

The armor carried into battle by lords and knights was awkward and heavy

EXPLORING THE TIME

Have you ever read about the knights in armor who rode their horses into battle during the Middle Ages? These knights fought for their master and were ruled by a system of government called **feudalism** (FEWD-ul-IZ-um). What was feudalism? You will discover the answer when you read this chapter.

Feudalism Began in the German Kingdoms of Western Europe

Feudalism was the kind of government and the way of life that developed in Europe during the Early Middle Ages. Feudalism began in western Europe in the years after the western Roman Empire ended.

In the years from 476 A.D. to 1000 A.D., most of the German kingdoms were weak. The rulers who ruled these kingdoms did

213

not have strong armies to protect their people. As a result, those who were large landowners began to form their own local armies to defend themselves.

Many small farmers gave up their lands to these large landowners and agreed to work for the landowner if the landowner protected them. Some landowners soon received more land than they were able to use. Often they gave some of this land to people who owned no land if they agreed to stay on the land and farm it. These large landowners became known as **nobles**.

The German tribes helped feudalism to grow. Each German chief, or leader, had followers who helped fight in wars. In return, the German chief gave the followers food, shelter, weapons, and a share of the goods or money that they captured. As the German tribes attacked the Roman Empire and settled down in the Roman lands, the chiefs rewarded their followers by giving them conquered Roman land. In return, these followers promised to fight for their chief whenever war broke out.

The Need for Horse Soldiers Helped Feudalism to Develop

The need to have cavalry, or horse soldiers,

European nobles often used their armies to fight other nobles or the ruler during the Middle Ages

for fighting wars was a very important part of feudalism. By the middle 800's A.D., only armies with many horse soldiers were able to win wars. In order to build strong armies with cavalry, most rulers needed help from the large landowners—the nobles. These nobles had their own cavalry who protected their lands. During a war, these nobles joined the ruler's army and brought with them many knights, or horse soldiers in armor.

Weak Rulers Helped Feudalism to Develop in Europe

When the rulers were strong, they needed less help from the nobles. Both Clovis, the first Frankish king, and Charlemagne were strong kings. But the kings who came after Charlemagne were weaker rulers. Under these kings, feudalism spread more rapidly.

The weak rulers spent much of their time fighting each other. As a result, they needed help from the nobles. To get the help of the nobles, these kings were forced to give them more power to rule their own lands.

In the years after 830 A.D., the Frankish kingdom was attacked by peoples from Spain, northern Africa, Hungary, and northern Europe. The Frankish rulers were now forced to give more and more power to the nobles in order to get the support of their armies. As a result, the nobles then became even stronger than before. By the 900's A.D., the feudal system had spread throughout most of western Europe.

Under Feudalism, Vassals Had to Serve Their Lords

The feudal system was like a huge pyramid, with the ruler at the top. The ruler was

DOCUMENTS IN HISTORY

A Knighting Ceremony

During the Middle Ages, the knights of Europe followed a code of conduct called chivalry. The knights were supposed to be honorable, courteous, generous, brave, loyal, skillful in battle, respectful to women, and helpful to the weak.

Much of what we know about chivalry comes from the literature of the Middle Ages. In the 1300's, the English poet Geoffrey Chaucer wrote a long poem called *The Canterbury Tales.* In this poem, Chaucer described what it meant to follow the ideals of chivalry:

> There was a knight, a most distinguished man,
> Who from the day on which he first began
> To ride abroad had followed Chivalry.
> Truth, honor, generousness and courtesy.
> He had done nobly in his sovereign's King's war
> And ridden into battle, no man more.
> As well as Christian as in heathen places,
> And ever honored for his noble graces.

Question: What ideals of chivalry did Chaucer describe?

The ruler (right) gave nobles the right to own their lands as vassals of the crown

vassals promised to obey the noble and to bring an army of knights to the noble in time of war. But you must remember that the noble was, in turn, the vassal, or servant, of the ruler, and the ruler was the noble's lord.

The noble's vassals often had vassals of their own. The noble gave fiefs, or land, to several vassals, and these vassals were expected to supply armies of knights when needed. Under the feudal system, the same person might be both a lord and a vassal and might even be a vassal of several lords.

Both Lords and Vassals Had Duties Toward Each Other

The lord's main duty was to protect the vassals. In return, the vassal was expected to provide an army of knights to help the lord in battles. The vassal was also expected to pay money or goods to the lord in return for a fief. And the vassal also was expected to feed and entertain the lord whenever the lord came to visit. Sometimes, these visits cost the vassal much of the harvest!

supposed to own all the land in the country. But most of the land was really controlled by powerful nobles. These nobles were **vassals** (VASS-ulz), or "servants" of the crown. They promised to obey the ruler as their **lord**, or master, and to fight for the ruler when necessary. The land that the ruler gave to a noble was called a **fief** (FEEF).

These great nobles had their own armies. How did a noble get an army? The nobles gave fiefs, or land, to each of those who became followers, or vassals. These

SUMMING UP

Feudalism was the way of life and the system of government that grew up in Europe during the Early Middle Ages, from 476 A.D. to 1000 A.D. Feudalism developed when most of the rulers were weak and when the nobles gained more power. Under the feudal system, both lords and vassals had certain duties toward each other. In the next chapter, you will learn what life was like in the feudal castle in Europe.

UNDERSTANDING THE LESSON

Do You Know These Important Terms?

For each sentence below, choose the term that best completes the sentence.

1. The system of government and way of life that grew up during the Early Middle Ages was called **(knighthood/feudalism)**.
2. **(Nobles/Squires)** were large landowners who had their own armies.
3. "Servants" to the king or to nobles were called **(peons/vassals)**.
4. A person who had "servants" who were pledged to fight for him was a **(lord/governor)**.
5. The land given by a lord to the vassal was called a **(fief/farm)**.

Do You Remember These People and Events?

1. Tell how each of the following persons was related to the growth of feudalism.

    Clovis   Charlemagne

2. Explain how or why each of the following developments took place.

    a. The Germans helped feudalism to develop.
    b. The nobles gained more power when the king was weak.
    c. The same person might be both a lord and a vassal. One might also be a vassal of several lords.

Can You Locate These Places?

Use the map in Chapter 29 (page 202) to locate the following places.

    Europe   Africa

1. In which European lands did feudalism become very strong in the 800's A.D.?
2. In which part of Europe was feudalism widespread by the 900's A.D.?

Do You Know When It Happened?

The years of this chapter are the years when feudalism developed in Europe. What are the years of this chapter?

Do You Remember the Main Idea?

Which one of the following ideas is the MAIN IDEA of this chapter?

1. The German tribes had a feudal system of government. They developed feudalism when they conquered the western Roman Empire.
2. Feudalism was the way of life and the system of government that grew up in Europe during the Early Middle Ages.
3. Feudalism developed in Europe in the Early Middle Ages because the nobles were afraid of the ruler.

What Do You Think?

From what you have read, try to answer the following thought questions.

1. What might make you guess that the feudal system of government had some weaknesses? Give your reasons.
2. If you had lived in the Early Middle Ages, would you have wanted to be a knight or a farmer? Why?
3. Why do you think a cavalry, or armored knights on horseback, was so important in winning wars during the Early Middle Ages?

Chapter 32
Feudal Life in the Castle

GETTING STARTED

1   As you have learned, the feudal system developed because it helped people to protect themselves. A lord, whether a king or a noble, needed the help of vassals in order to build a strong army and to obtain money and supplies. The lord also needed a strong castle to protect everyone from attacks by enemies.

During the Early Middle Ages, nobles began to live in feudal castles for protection. Just as a reminder, the Early Middle Ages began about 476 A.D. and lasted until about 1000 A.D. Check the time line below to see this period of years.

2   Before you begin reading the chapter lesson, survey the lesson. Begin your survey by reading the beginning of the lesson. Then look through the lesson and read the headings. Next, study the pictures and read the picture captions. Finally, read the review section called "Summing Up." This survey will help you to discover the important ideas in this chapter.

Know the Main Idea

As you read the chapter lesson, try to remember the following important MAIN IDEA of the chapter.

The feudal noble's main business was fighting. He had well-trained knights, and he lived in a strong, well-defended castle.

The following questions will help you to understand the MAIN IDEA. Try to answer these questions as you read the lesson.

1. Who was allowed to become a knight during the feudal period?
2. What were some of the rules of chivalry that a knight was required to follow?
3. What sport was the favorite of most nobles?

Know These Important Terms

page	drawbridge
squire	donjon
chivalry	tournaments
moat	

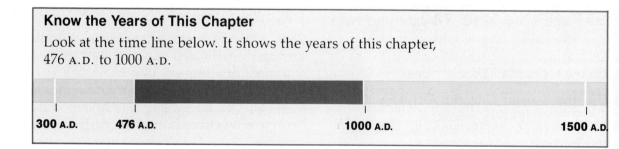

Know the Years of This Chapter

Look at the time line below. It shows the years of this chapter, 476 A.D. to 1000 A.D.

| 300 A.D. | 476 A.D. | 1000 A.D. | 1500 A.D. |

Painting of a scene at a feudal castle

EXPLORING THE TIME

During the years of the Middle Ages, many of the nobles in Europe lived in strong castles for protection. In this chapter, you will read about the nobles of Europe and the kind of life that these nobles lived in the feudal castles.

The Knights Had a Long Training Period

One of the most important kinds of work during the feudal period, or the years of feudalism in Europe, was the work performed by a knight. Only a noble's son was allowed to become a knight. And the child became a knight only after a long period of training.

Knights required the help of their squires when putting on the awkward armor used in battle

At the age of seven, a noble's son was sent to the castle of his parents' lord, where he served as a **page**, or helper, until the age of fourteen. During these years, the page was taught religion, good manners, and sometimes reading and music.

At the age of fourteen or fifteen, the page became a **squire**, or an assistant to a knight. The young squire's real training to become a knight now began. Squires learned how to ride a horse, to hunt, to wear armor, and to use weapons.

When the squire finished the training, a special ceremony was held. The squire kneeled and the noble he was to serve made the squire a knight by touching a sword across the shoulders.

The Knights Followed Certain Rules

All knights were supposed to follow a special code, or way of life, called **chivalry** (SHIV-ul-REE). The rules of chivalry required that the knight be brave and loyal. The knight was required to fight for the lord. The knight was expected to treat people politely, and to fight to defend the Christian religion. And knights were expected to protect the farmers who lived on the land. The knight's code of chivalry was the beginning of our modern idea of good manners.

The Knights Fought Many Wars

When we think about knights, we often think of them fighting battles. And a great deal of fighting did go on during the feudal period. But the feudal wars were very different from wars of today. Feudal armies were much smaller, and they had fewer weapons. Fewer people died in battle because the knights were well protected by their armor. Also, the knights tried to capture their enemies rather than to kill them. The knight then was paid "ransom money" for allowing the captured enemy to go free.

The people who were hurt the most by the feudal wars were the common people. These people often lost their homes and even their lives during the fighting. To protect the common people, the Popes of the Roman Catholic Church started the "Peace of God" and the "Truce of God." The Peace of God made it unlawful for soldiers to attack farmers, traders, or religious leaders. The Truce of God made it unlawful to fight between Wednesday evening and Monday morning and during certain times of the year. In these ways, the Church helped to cut down some of the fighting in the feudal wars.

The Feudal Castles Were Very Strong

To defend themselves against attack, the feudal nobles lived in castles, or fort-palaces. The first castles were simple wooden forts. By the later years of the Middle Ages, however, castles were large stone buildings with high towers and thick walls.

Most castles were built on top of a hill. The castle often was surrounded by a **moat,** or ditch filled with water. They only way to cross this moat was over a **drawbridge,** or bridge that was lowered from inside the castle wall. In case of attack, the drawbridge was pulled up to keep an enemy from crossing the moat. The gate to the castle was covered with heavy iron for extra protection.

The **donjon** (DUN-jun) was the strongest part of the castle. It contained storerooms and the rooms where the lord and the lord's family lived. The donjon also had cells, or rooms, for prisoners. The word "dungeon" comes from the feudal word "donjon."

The castles were built so strongly that they were difficult to capture. Not until gunpowder and guns were used later on in the 1300's A.D. and 1400's A.D. did it become easier for enemies to attack and destroy castles.

Life in a Castle Was Not Very Comfortable

The feudal castles were strong but they were not very comfortable. The rooms were dark because the window openings were small. The rooms also were cold and damp. Heat came only from fireplaces, which were also used for cooking. Floors were made of stone and covered with straw. Often, the only water was a well in the courtyard.

HIGHLIGHTS IN HISTORY

Fighting a Tournament

In the Middle Ages, people watched tournaments the way modern people watch baseball games or football games. Tournaments were "play" battles in which knights showed off their skill. Knights and ladies often traveled a long way to attend tournaments. No one dared to try to stop a knight on the way to a tournament.

Sometimes the knights fought in groups. Other times, one knight fought another knight. In tournaments, knights had special tips on their swords and lances so that no one would be seriously hurt. Still, knights were sometimes wounded at a tournament.

Tournaments sometimes lasted for several days. Then they might end with a grand ball. The noble lady who had been chosen "queen" of the tournament awarded prizes to the knights who had proved their fighting skill. It was a great honor to win these prizes. The knights who won always were very proud to be a part of these tournaments.

Question: What kind of weapons were used at tournaments?

European castles were designed to be strong fortresses

The castle rooms were furnished very simply. Large boards were used as tables, and stools and benches were used for chairs. Wooden chests held clothing and bedding. Beds were built on platforms and covered with curtains in order to keep cold air out.

The Nobles Enjoyed Games of Fighting

The nobles were heavy eaters and drinkers. When they were not fighting, they amused themselves by hunting, listening to singers, and playing chess games or dice games. But the favorite sport of nobles was fighting.

In peacetime, nobles and their friends held "battle games" called **tournaments**. Sometimes these tournaments seemed more like real battles. Sometimes a knight killed or seriously injured another knight. But tournaments were exciting events and were watched by many people.

SUMMING UP

Feudal knights were well trained, and followed a special way of life called chivalry. The knights spent much time fighting. The Roman Catholic Church tried to cut down warfare, but fighting still remained the nobles' main business and main sport. Nobles lived in strong castles that protected them against enemy attacks. In the next chapter, you will read about the life of the common people in the Early Middle Ages.

UNDERSTANDING THE LESSON

Do You Know These Important Terms?

For each sentence below, choose the term that best completes the sentence.

1. The young child of a noble who was sent to the castle of its parents' lord for training was called a **(pupil/page)**.
2. A young page who, at the age of fourteen or fifteen, became an assistant to a knight was a **(feudal army/squire)**.
3. **(Gentle Code/Chivalry)** was the required way of life for a knight.
4. The **(canal/moat)** was a ditch filled with water that surrounded a castle.
5. A **(drawbridge/portbridge)** was a bridge that was lowered from the castle wall to allow people to enter the castle.
6. The strongest part of the castle was called the **(donjon/tower)**.
7. "Battle games" held by nobles were called **(tournaments/matches)**.

Do You Remember These People and Events?

1. Tell something about each of the following subjects.

   page   **knight**
   squire

2. Explain how or why each of the following developments took place.

   a. Feudal wars were very different from the wars of today.

   b. The Roman Catholic Church helped to cut down some of the destruction of feudal wars.
   c. Life in a castle was not comfortable.

Do You Know When It Happened?

What are the years of this chapter?

Do You Remember the Main Idea?

Which one of the following ideas is the MAIN IDEA of this chapter?

1. All nobles received training to teach them to become knights.
2. All nobles built strong forts called castles.
3. The feudal noble's main business was fighting. A noble had well-trained knights, and lived in a strong, well-defended castle.

What Do You Think?

From what you have read in this chapter, try to answer the following thought questions.

1. In what way do you think that the rules of chivalry were the beginning of our ideas of a well-mannered person?
2. Why was it very difficult to capture a castle in the years before guns and gunpowder were used?
3. What might have happened to a knight who did not follow the rules of chivalry?

Chapter 33
Feudal Life on the Manor

GETTING STARTED

1   Sometimes, the nobles in the feudal castles led exciting lives. But most people who lived during the Early Middle Ages were not nobles. They did not live in castles or become knights on horseback. And their lives were not adventurous.

Most people in Europe, as you might guess, were poor farmers who lived on the land of the nobles. The farmers were the common people of Europe—the people who were at the bottom of the feudal system. As feudalism spread in Europe, farmers had few freedoms, and their lives were difficult. But even so, in some ways, the farmers' lives did improve. For example, farmers made some important changes in their ways of growing crops, as you will discover in this chapter.

2   Before you begin reading this chapter lesson, survey the lesson. Begin your survey by reading the beginning of the lesson. Then look through the lesson and read the headings. Next, study the pictures and read the picture captions. Finally, read the review section called "Summing Up" at the end of the lesson. This survey of the whole lesson will help you to discover the important ideas in this chapter.

Know the Main Idea

As you read the chapter lesson, try to remember the following important MAIN IDEA of the chapter.

During the Early Middle Ages, most people were farmers who had no freedom and who worked hard on the farmlands owned by nobles.

The following questions will help you to understand the MAIN IDEA. Try to answer these questions as you read the lesson.

1. How was the manor house of each village used?
2. What two inventions made the horse a valuable farm animal?
3. How much land on a large estate was owned by the lord?

Know These Important Terms

manor   three-field system
serfs

Know the Years of This Chapter

Look at the time line below. It shows the years of this chapter, 476 A.D. to 1000 A.D.

| 300 A.D. | 476 A.D. | 1000 A.D. | 1500 A.D. |

Describe some of the musical instruments in this painting of a garden scene at a feudal castle.

EXPLORING THE TIME

The nobles of the Middle Ages lived in the feudal castles, and they had some comforts and enjoyments. But most of the common people did not live in the feudal castles, and their lives were very difficult. In this chapter, you will learn how the common people lived during the period of the Early Middle Ages. And you will learn why life was so difficult for the common people.

Farmers Lived on Their Lord's Estate

During the Early Middle Ages, most people in Europe were farmers. They lived on land owned by the noble who was their lord, and they farmed this land. This land was called a **manor**.

Most feudal manors covered a large amount of land. Most manors included a village. Each manor village had a manor house, a church, many farmers' huts, barns, and a mill to grind grain. The lord lived in a castle, but stayed in the manor house when he visited the village.

Most People on the Manors Were Serfs

Two main groups of people lived on the manor. A small group of the people on the manor were free people. The free people owned or rented their land from the lord, but they were free to leave the manor.

The largest group of people on the manor were the **serfs**. The serfs had no freedom. They were not allowed to leave the manor without their lord's permission. They were required to pay for the use of the lord's grain mill. These payments were made in farm products, not in money. And the serf was required to work three or more days a week doing work for the lord of the manor.

In return, the serf was given a hut to live in and some land to farm. Serfs were allowed to use the manor's pasture land to feed the cows and pigs, and the serf was allowed to gather some wood in the lord's forest. And by living on the manor, the serf was protected by the lord from enemy attacks.

Improvements Were Made in Farming

New farming tools were developed during the feudal period. One of these tools was the heavy plow. The heavy plow made it easier to cut through hard soil. Another farming improvement was the use of horses, rather than cattle, to pull the plows. Two inventions made this change possible. One invention was iron shoes to protect the horse's feet. The other invention was the wooden horse collar to protect the horse's neck. The wooden collar made it possible for a horse to pull much heavier loads. Both these inventions were in use by the year 1000 A.D.

Painting of serfs cutting wheat on the fields of a feudal manor

Painting of a harvest scene outside a feudal castle. What are the men doing? What are the women doing?

A New Way of Using Farmland Developed

One important farming improvement was the use of the **three-field system** of farming instead of the old two-field system of farming. In the two-field system, the farmland was divided into two parts. Each year, one field was planted with grain. But nothing was planted in the other field in order to allow the soil to get back its richness.

In the three-field system, farmland was divided into three parts. One field was planted with wheat or rye in the winter. The second field was planted with oats, barley, beans, or peas in the spring. And the third field was not planted. By about 1000 A.D., the three-field system was the lord's own land. Each serf was given several small strips of land located in different parts of the three main fields. This meant that each serf had some good land, and each serf had some poor land. Some of the serf's land was close to the village, and some of the serf's land was farther away.

Much of the farm work was done by the serfs working together to plow each other's strips or to harvest the crop.

The Serfs' Lives Were Difficult

Serfs lived in small huts without windows. A hole in the roof let in light and air, and let out smoke. A bed, a table, a few stools, and perhaps a chest were about all the furniture most serfs owned. Serfs ate whatever food they raised. If the crop was bad—as often happened—the serfs might go hungry.

Did serfs ever enjoy themselves? Sometimes they did. Serfs did not work on Sundays or on the many holidays (holy days) that were celebrated in Europe during the feudal period. On these days, serfs were able to enjoy themselves by singing, dancing, wrestling, and playing games.

Feudal serfs enjoyed occasional holidays in what were otherwise very difficult lives

most popular farming system used. It increased the amount of crops grown, and many different crops were now grown.

The Serfs Farmed the Manor Fields

The fields of the manor were divided into strips. At least one-third of the land was the

SUMMING UP

During the Early Middle Ages, most of the common people in Europe lived on feudal manors owned by a lord. Most of the people on the manor were serfs. The serfs on the manor farmland had no freedom, and their lives were difficult. However, by living on the feudal manor, they were protected by their lord from enemy attacks. In the next chapter, you will read how the Roman Catholic Church developed in Europe during the Early Middle Ages.

UNDERSTANDING THE LESSON

Do You Know These Important Terms?

For each sentence below, choose the term that best completes the sentence.

1. The land owned by a noble and farmed by serfs was a **(manor/farm)**.
2. The largest group of people on a noble's manor and the group that farmed the manor was the **(peons/serfs)**.
3. The **(three-field system/two-field system)** was a new farming method that increased the number and kinds of crops grown in Europe.

Do You Remember These People and Events?

1. Tell something about each of the following subjects.

   serfs
   lord of a manor
   free people of a manor

2. Explain how or why each of the following developments took place.

   a. The lord of a manor depended upon the serfs, and the serfs depended on the lord of the manor.
   b. Improvements were made in methods of farming.
   c. A new farming method increased the amount and the kinds of crops that were grown.
   d. The lives of the serfs were difficult.

Do You Know When It Happened?

What are the years of this chapter?

Do You Remember the Main Idea?

Which one of the following ideas is the MAIN IDEA of this chapter?

1. During the Early Middle Ages, most people were farmers who had no freedom and who worked hard on the farmlands owned by nobles.
2. The manor was the center of life during the Early Middle Ages. Both serfs and free people lived on the manor.
3. The noble on a manor controlled the lives of the serfs, who found living very difficult.

What Do You Think?

From what you have read in this chapter, try to answer the following thought questions.

1. Would you rather have lived in a castle or in a manor village? Give reasons for your answer.
2. What do you think a typical day might have been like for a serf who lived on a feudal manor?
3. Do you think that religion was important in the life of the common people during the Early Middle Ages? Give reasons for your answer.

Chapter 34

The Roman Catholic Church in the Early Middle Ages

GETTING STARTED

1   Religion was very important during the Middle Ages. Life was so difficult that many people found hope for a better life only through their religious faith. Most people in Europe during the Middle Ages were followers of the Roman Catholic Church. The Roman Catholic Church was very important in these years. It not only guided the religious life of most people, it also played an important part in government. In fact, the Roman Catholic Church was the strongest power in Europe during most of the Middle Ages.

2   Before you begin reading the chapter lesson, survey the lesson. Begin your survey by reading the beginning of the lesson. Then look through the lesson and read the headings. Next, study the pictures and read the picture captions. Finally, read the review section called "Summing Up" at the end of the lesson. This survey of the whole lesson will help you to discover the important ideas in this chapter.

Know the Main Idea

As you read the chapter lesson, try to remember the following important MAIN IDEA of the chapter.

During the Middle Ages, the Roman Catholic Church grew more important. The Church played an important part in government as well as in religion.

The following questions will help you to understand the MAIN IDEA. Try to answer these questions as you read the lesson.

1. What territory did the Pope govern?
2. How did Catholic monks perform important work for the Church?
3. Which Pope took steps to correct the weaknesses in the Church?

Know These Important Terms

Papal States	Concordat of Worms
hermits	sacraments
monks	excommunicated
monasteries	

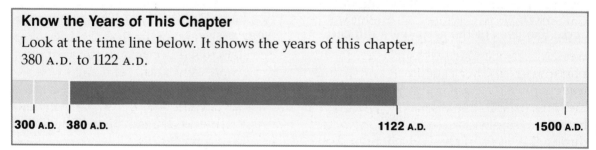

Know the Years of This Chapter

Look at the time line below. It shows the years of this chapter, 380 A.D. to 1122 A.D.

| 300 A.D. | 380 A.D. | 1122 A.D. | 1500 A.D. |

The Norman Chapel of St. John

EXPLORING THE TIME

During the Early Middle Ages, the Roman Catholic Church became as important in ruling the people's lives as the monarchs of western Europe. Monarchs played an important part in Church matters, and Church leaders played an important part in government matters. In this chapter, you will learn how the Catholic Church became important during the years of the Early Middle Ages.

The Catholic Church Grew More Powerful

The western Roman Empire became weaker during the period of the Early Middle Ages. The rulers of the Roman kingdoms of western Europe were weak, and the nobles in these kingdoms controlled and ruled much of the land. More and more, the people of Europe came to depend upon the Church for help and protection.

Soon, the Pope, or leader of the Roman Catholic Church, became the ruler of the papal kingdom as well as the leader of the Roman Catholic Church. The Pope ruled a large territory in Italy that included the city of Rome. This territory in Italy ruled by the Pope was called the **Papal States**.

Some Religious People Tried to Turn Away from the World

While some religious people became interested in government affairs, others turned away from the everyday world. These people, called **hermits**, went off by themselves in order to worship God in peace.

In time, such men joined together and became **monks**. The word "monk" comes from a Greek word meaning "alone." Groups of monks lived in settlements called **monasteries** (MAHN-uh-STAIR-eez).

Part of an illuminated manuscript of the early Middle Ages

Later, religious women who wanted to live apart from the everyday world were called nuns. They lived in nunneries. Monks and nuns had to give up everything they owned. They had to spend part of their time in prayer and part of their time at work. Monks and nuns were not allowed to marry.

The Monks Performed Very Important Work

The monks helped to spread the Christian religion to most parts of Europe. Monks and nuns did many other important things. Some nursed sick people and took care of the poor. Some monks started schools. Some monks copied old Latin and Greek books in order to preserve the learning in these books. Some monks also turned forests and useless swamps into good farmland. And some monks learned to carry on such skills as glassmaking, stonecarving, woodcarving, and weaving. Nuns sometimes made very fine lace and embroidery.

Nobles Gained More Power over the Church

As feudalism grew, however, the nobles became more powerful. By the years of the 900's A.D., the rulers no longer were able to protect Church property. Some nobles took over the Church land in their area. Other nobles forced the Pope to allow them to choose the Church leader for their territory. This Church leader, called a bishop or an abbot, then became the noble's vassal.

But the rulers and nobles who chose Church leaders often chose people who were more interested in land and money than in religion. In fact, some of the bishops and abbots even paid money to be chosen.

Groups of monks performed different services for the Roman Catholic Church. Some monks raised crops. What was the job of the man holding the stick in the air?

The Church also grew weaker because many Church leaders did not obey the Church's rules.

The Popes Tried to Help the Church Improve Itself

During the 900's A.D. and the 1000's A.D., the Popes were not able to improve conditions in the Church. Then, in the 1070's A.D., Pope Gregory the Seventh took an important step to make the Church stronger. He decided that only the Pope had the right to appoint bishops and abbots. But the German king, Henry the Fourth, refused to obey the Pope.

Pope Gregory then asked the German nobles to choose a new king to replace Henry unless he agreed to obey the Pope's order. The nobles disliked Henry, so they ordered him to make peace with the Pope. Henry decided to give in. Henry the Fourth went all the way to Italy and stood barefoot in the snow outside the Pope's castle for three days before Pope Gregory forgave him.

But the fight between the emperors and the Church was not over. Henry the Fourth later returned to Italy with an army and forced Pope Gregory to leave Rome. However, in 1122 A.D., an agreement was worked out called the **Concordat** (kon-KORR-dat) **of Worms**. The Concordat, or agreement, provided that the Pope was allowed to select all bishops, but the king had to approve the bishops who were selected by the Pope.

Pope Gregory the Seventh with the Abbot of St. Sophia. In the 1070's A.D., Pope Gregory helped the Church regain some of its power from the German rulers.

Most People in Western Europe Belonged to the Roman Catholic Church

By the year 1070 A.D., most people in western Europe belonged to the Roman Catholic Church. The Roman Catholic Church required all Catholics to obey certain rules and to take part in religious ceremonies called **sacraments.**

Church members who did not follow the Church's rules or did not take part in the sacraments might be **excommunicated** (EKS-kuh-MYOON-uh-KAY-tud), or forced to leave the Roman Catholic Church.

SUMMING UP

During the Early Middle Ages, the Catholic Church grew more important in western Europe. But as feudalism spread, the nobles gained more power over the Church. By the 1070's A.D., Pope Gregory the Seventh helped the Church to regain some of the power from the nobles and German rulers. In the next chapter, which begins Unit 9, you will read about what was happening in eastern Europe and the Near East in the Early Middle Ages.

UNDERSTANDING THE LESSON

Do You Know These Important Terms?

For each sentence below, choose the term that best completes the sentence.

1. The territory in Italy that was ruled by the Pope was called the (Vatican/Papal States).
2. (Hermits/Bishops) were religious men who went away by themselves in order to worship God in peace.
3. Religious leaders who lived in groups apart from other people were called (wanderers/monks).
4. Groups of monks lived in small settlements called (vestments/monasteries).
5. The (Council of Rome/Concordat of Worms) was an agreement between the Pope and the German king about choosing Catholic Church leaders.
6. (Sacraments/Holidays) are religious ceremonies of the Catholic Church.
7. Church members who did not follow the Church's rules were (sent away/excommunicated) from the Catholic Church.

Do You Remember These People and Events?

1. Tell something about each of the following persons.

    Pope Gregory the Seventh
    Henry the Fourth

2. Explain how or why each of the following developments took place.

    a. Monks performed very important work during the Middle Ages.
    b. Nobles began to gain power over the Catholic Church.

    c. The Roman Catholic Church was very important in people's lives during the Middle Ages.

Do You Know When It Happened?

Why are the following years important in the Roman Catholic Church's history?

   1070's A.D.   1122 A.D.

Do You Remember the Main Idea?

Which one of the following ideas is the MAIN IDEA of this chapter?

1. Nobles gained control of the Roman Catholic Church during the early part of the Middle Ages.
2. Religious leaders called monks spread the Roman Catholic religion across Europe. They also did other important work.
3. During the Middle Ages, the Roman Catholic Church grew more important. The Church played an important part in government as well as in religion.

What Do You Think?

From what you have read in this chapter, try to answer the following thought questions.

1. What do you think a typical day was like for a monk who lived in a monastery during the Middle Ages?
2. Why do you think nobles wanted to appoint the Church leaders in their area?
3. Do you think that any church or religion today has the power to take part in government matters in a nation? Explain your answer.

Unit 9
The Byzantine and Muslim Empires

THE CHAPTERS IN UNIT 9 ARE

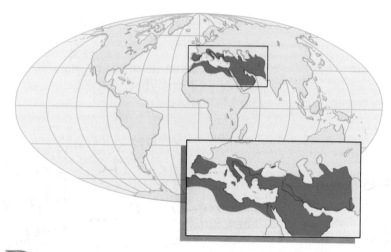

During the years of the Early Middle Ages in western Europe, important events were taking place in other lands. In eastern Europe, the Byzantine Empire continued to be a great nation for a thousand years after the Roman Empire ended. In the Near East and northern Africa, the Muslims built a great new empire. In this unit, you will study the Byzantine Empire and the Muslim Empire.

The Byzantine church, Hagia Sophia, in Constantinople

Chapter 35
The Byzantine Empire

GETTING STARTED

1   What was happening in the eastern part of the old Roman Empire as feudalism was developing in the western part? The eastern part of the old Roman empire also was attacked by German tribes. But these tribes were not able to conquer the eastern empire as they had conquered the western empire. In fact, between 330 A.D. and 1050 A.D., the eastern empire continued to grow more powerful. Check this period on the time line below. You may recall that these years also were the years of the Early Middle Ages in western Europe.

2   Before you begin reading the chapter lesson, survey the lesson. Begin your survey by reading the beginning of the lesson. Then look through the lesson and read the headings. Next, study the pictures and read the picture captions. Then study the map of the Byzantine Empire on page 240. Finally, read the review section called "Summing Up." This survey will help you to discover the important ideas in this chapter.

Know the Main Idea

As you read the chapter lesson, try to remember the following important MAIN IDEA of the chapter.

The eastern part of the Roman Empire became a powerful land called the Byzantine Empire. It preserved Greek culture and it spread the Christian religion.

The following questions will help you to understand the MAIN IDEA. Try to answer these questions as you read the lesson.

1. What city was built on the ruins of the city of Byzantium?
2. Which emperor made the Byzantine Empire stronger?
3. How did the Greek language help to tie the Byzantine Empire together?

Know These Important Terms

Patriarch
Greek Orthodox Church
Slavic languages

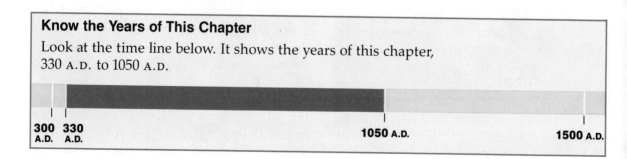

Know the Years of This Chapter

Look at the time line below. It shows the years of this chapter, 330 A.D. to 1050 A.D.

| 300 A.D. | 330 A.D. | 1050 A.D. | 1500 A.D. |

Theodora, Empress of the Eastern Roman Empire, with her court

EXPLORING THE TIME

As you remember, the Roman Empire was divided into an eastern and a western part by Diocletian. Then in the year 476 A.D., the western part of the empire was conquered by German tribes. But the eastern part of the empire continued, and it became powerful and rich. In this chapter, you will learn what happened to the people of the eastern Roman Empire.

The Eastern Roman Empire Became the Byzantine Empire

The eastern Roman Empire was called the Byzantine (BIZZ-un-TEEN) Empire. Constantinople was the capital city of the Byzantine Empire. As you may recall, the city of Constantinople was built by the Emperor Constantine in the year 330 A.D. Constantinople was built on the ruins of an older city, Byzantium (bih-ZAN-shum), and the Byzantine Empire took its name from this

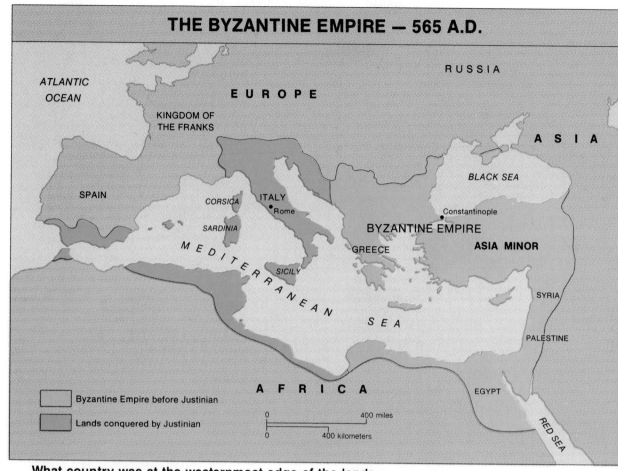

THE BYZANTINE EMPIRE — 565 A.D.

ATLANTIC OCEAN

EUROPE

RUSSIA

ASIA

KINGDOM OF THE FRANKS

BLACK SEA

SPAIN

CORSICA

ITALY
•Rome

Constantinople•

SARDINIA

BYZANTINE EMPIRE

ASIA MINOR

GREECE

MEDITERRANEAN SEA

SICILY

SYRIA

PALESTINE

AFRICA

EGYPT

RED SEA

☐ Byzantine Empire before Justinian

▨ Lands conquered by Justinian

0 ___ 400 miles
0 ___ 400 kilometers

What country was at the westernmost edge of the lands conquered by Justinian?

city. Constantinople was well located for trade between Europe and Asia. It was also well located to protect itself from attack.

The Emperor Constantine himself became a Christian. And he knew that more and more people in the eastern Roman Empire were becoming Christians. To gain their support, Constantine decided to give Christians religious freedom. Later, in 395 A.D., the Christian religion became the official religion of the Byzantine Empire.

The Byzantine emperors were strong rulers who controlled their governments and were powerful in religious affairs. They selected the **Patriarch** (PAY-tree-ARK) of Constantinople—the leader of the Byzantine Church.

The Byzantine Empire Won Back a Part of the Western Empire

The Byzantine Empire was strong enough to defend itself from the German tribes and other enemies. When Justinian became the Byzantine emperor in 527 A.D., the Byzantine Empire tried to reconquer the western empire. Justinian soon won back most of Italy, northern Africa, and part of Spain.

Justinian ruled the empire well until he died in 565 A.D. As you read earlier, Justinian put together all Roman laws into the famous Code of Laws. Justinian also rebuilt roads, bridges, and churches. The most famous of Justinian's buildings was the Church of Santa Sophia, or "Holy Wisdom," in Constantinople. This beautiful Byzantine church is still one of the finest buildings in the world.

The Byzantine Empire Fought the Persians and Arabs

But the Byzantine Empire was not strong enough to keep its western territory. The emperors who followed Justinian fought to protect this territory from the Byzantine Empire's two main enemies, the Persians and the Arabs.

The Byzantine emperors were able to defeat the Persians. But the Arabs conquered northern Africa, Egypt, Syria, and Palestine from the Byzantine Empire. However, by 750 A.D., the Arab conquests were stopped. The Byzantine Empire was now much smaller, but it remained the largest empire in Europe.

The Byzantine Empire Developed a Stronger Government

The hundred years of fighting caused several important changes in the Byzantine Empire's government. The emperor became a stronger ruler than ever before. He took over all government affairs. Another change was that the empire was divided into provinces. Each province was ruled by a general. All generals had to be approved by the emperor and report directly.

Ivory carving showing two Byzantine soldiers with their weapons

Another change was that Greek replaced Latin as the official language in the Byzantine Empire. Greek was used in all government records. Greek was also used in the Byzantine churches. The Greek language helped to tie the Byzantine Empire together.

The Byzantine Empire Regained Its Power

As its government became stronger, the Byzantine Empire again tried to conquer more land. During the 900's A.D. and early 1000's A.D., the Byzantine Empire conquered Greece and Macedonia, Asia Minor, and southern Italy.

Times were good in the Byzantine Empire during these years. The Byzantine

Inside a Byzantine church in northern Italy

of the Balkan Peninsula and southeastern Europe to spread its ideas.

The **Slavic languages** were spoken by all these peoples, and Byzantine priests rewrote the Bible into Slavic languages. The Byzantine priests developed a new alphabet for Slavic words. The alphabet developed by these Byzantine priests is still used in Slavic-speaking countries today.

The most important nation to accept the Greek Orthodox religion was Kiev (KEY-ev)—the name of early Russia. A little before 1000 A.D., the ruler of Russia and many of the people became Christians. After Russia accepted the Greek Orthodox Church, Byzantine art, writing, alphabet, and building styles also spread to Russia.

The Byzantine Empire Preserved Greek Culture

The Greek language was forgotten in western Europe. But in eastern Europe, Greek was the official language of the Byzantine Empire, and educated people were required to learn Greek. These people read the works of the great Greek philosophers and writers. Without these Byzantine scholars, Greek culture might have been lost forever.

SUMMING UP

The eastern part of the Roman Empire continued as the Byzantine Empire. The Byzantine Empire was strong during the 500's A.D. But later, it lost a great deal of land to the Arabs. However, by the 900's A.D., the empire became stronger. It spread the Greek Orthodox religion and helped to preserve Greek culture. In the next chapter, you will read how a new religion began in Arabia.

merchants traded with India, China, Persia, and Arabia, as well as with the nations of Europe. Byzantine silks, jewels, ivory, metalware, and glassware became world famous. Both the Byzantine traders and the Byzantine government became rich.

The Byzantine Church Spread the Christian Religion

Meanwhile, the Byzantine Church slowly split away from the Church of Rome. The Byzantine Church became known as the **Greek Orthodox Church.** It sent missionaries, or teachers of religion, to the peoples

UNDERSTANDING THE LESSON

Do You Know These Important Terms?

For each sentence below, choose the term that best completes the sentence.

1. The leader of the Byzantine Church was called the (**Patriarch/Pope**).
2. The Byzantine Church became known as the (**Holy Muslim Church/Greek Orthodox Church**).
3. The (**German languages/Slavic languages**) were spoken in the Balkan Peninsula and in southeastern Europe.

Do You Remember These People and Events?

1. Tell something about each of the following persons.

     Constantine   **Justinian**

2. Explain how each of the following developments took place.

   a. The Byzantine Empire developed from the eastern Roman Empire.
   b. The emperor of the Byzantine Empire was a very strong ruler.
   c. The Byzantine Church spread the Christian religion.
   d. Ideas from the Byzantine Empire spread to early Russia.

Can You Locate These Places?

Use the map on page 240 to do the following map work.

1. Locate each of the following places. Tell how each place is related to the events in this chapter.

     Constantinople   **Italy**
     Russia   **Asia Minor**

2. Merchants of the Byzantine Empire traded with many nations. In what way was Constantinople well located to carry on trade?

Do You Know When It Happened?

Why are the following years important in Byzantine history?

     300 A.D.   527 A.D.

Do You Remember the Main Idea?

Which one of the following ideas is the MAIN IDEA of this chapter?

1. The Greek Orthodox Church, a development of the Byzantine Empire, spread over the Balkan peninsula, southeastern Europe, and Russia.
2. The eastern part of the Roman Empire became a powerful land called the Byzantine Empire. It preserved Greek culture, and it spread the Christian religion.
3. The Byzantine Empire grew strong and traded with the rulers and nobles of western Europe.

What Do You Think?

From what you have read in this chapter, try to answer the following thought questions.

1. How was the government of the Byzantine Empire different from those in the kingdoms of western Europe?
2. What Byzantine contribution do you think was the most important? Give reasons for your answer.
3. In what main way was the Greek Orthodox Church different from the Roman Catholic Church?

Chapter 36
The Rise of the Muslim Empire

GETTING STARTED

1   Sometimes today in the Arabian Desert, you can still see Arab tribespeople in flowing robes and mounted on horses which they ride swiftly across the desert. These Arab equestrians appear suddenly at the top of sand dunes. Then just as suddenly they disappear.

In the years from 570 A.D. to 750 A.D., Arab tribes from Arabia swept from their homeland across northern Africa and into Europe. These Arabs were determined to spread a new religion to other parts of the world. While spreading this new religion, the Arabs succeeded in building a great empire that controlled the Mediterranean trade routes and became powerful enough to attack western Europe and the Byzantine Empire.

2   Before you begin reading the chapter lesson, survey the lesson. Begin your survey by reading the beginning of the lesson. Then look through the lesson and read the headings. Next, study the pictures and read the picture captions. Then study the map of the Muslim Empire on page 246. Finally, read the review section called "Summing Up" at the end of the lesson. This survey of the whole lesson will help you to discover the important ideas in this chapter.

Know the Main Idea

As you read the chapter lesson, try to remember the following important MAIN IDEA of the chapter.

The Muslim religion began in Arabia. The Muslims conquered and controlled a great empire in northern Africa, Spain, and southwestern Asia.

The following questions will help you to understand the MAIN IDEA. Try to answer these questions as you read the lesson.

1. Who began the Muslim religion?
2. By what name did the Muslims call their god?
3. What belief helped to make the Muslims brave fighters?

Know These Important Terms

Muslim religion	Hegira
Bedouins	Koran
Islam	Moors

Know the Years of This Chapter

Look at the time line below. It shows the years of this chapter, 570 A.D. to 750 AD.

300 A.D.	570 A.D.	750 A.D.	1500 A.D.

The Koran is the source of Islamic Law

EXPLORING THE TIME

"There is no God but Allah, and Muhammad is his Prophet!" This cry was shouted by bands of people on horseback who rode out of Arabia in the early years of the 600's A.D. to spread a new religion—the **Muslim religion**. In this chapter, you will learn how the Arabs spread this new religion and how they built up a great and powerful empire.

The Arabs Lived in the Deserts of Arabia

Arabia was a hot, dry land in the southwestern part of Asia. It was surrounded on three sides by water—the Red Sea on the west, the Arabian Sea on the southeast, and the Persian Gulf on the northeast.

The Arabs, or the people of Arabia, moved from place to place as **Bedouins** (BED-oo-INZ), or desert wanderers. They were

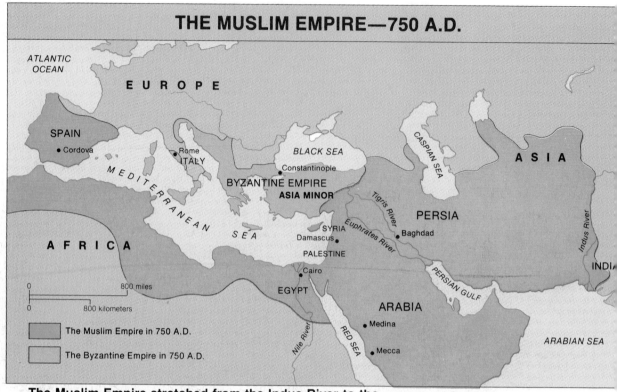

THE MUSLIM EMPIRE—750 A.D.

ATLANTIC OCEAN

EUROPE

SPAIN
• Cordova

• Rome
ITALY

MEDITERRANEAN SEA

AFRICA

BLACK SEA
Constantinople

BYZANTINE EMPIRE
ASIA MINOR

CASPIAN SEA

ASIA

PERSIA

Tigris River
Euphrates River
• Baghdad

Indus River

SYRIA
Damascus •

PALESTINE

• Cairo

EGYPT

PERSIAN GULF

INDIA

0   800 miles
0   800 kilometers

ARABIA
• Medina

• Mecca

Nile River

RED SEA

ARABIAN SEA

■ The Muslim Empire in 750 A.D.

□ The Byzantine Empire in 750 A.D.

The Muslim Empire stretched from the Indus River to the Atlantic Ocean. About how many miles was this?

divided into tribes, or groups. These tribes frequently fought each other.

Most Arabs worshiped many gods. They believed that these gods lived in trees and stones. Their holy city was Mecca (MEK-uh). An old temple called the Kaaba (KAH-buh) stood in Mecca. In the Kaaba was a sacred black stone, in honor of one of the most important Arabian gods.

The Muslim Religion Developed in Arabia

About 570 A.D., a boy named Muhammad (moh-HAHM-ud) was born in Mecca. Muhammad was very poor and had little education. Later, he earned a living as a leader of camel caravans, or trading groups.

During trips across the desert, Muhammad met both Christians and Jews, and spent much of this time thinking about religion. Then, when he was forty years old, Muhammad began to preach a new religion to the Arabs. This new religion was called **Islam** (is-LAHM), or the Muslim religion. The people who accepted this religion were called Muslims.

At first, Muhammad's preaching made him so disliked in his own town of Mecca that he was forced to escape to the town of Medina (muh-DEE-nuh), two hundred miles away. Muhammad's escape to Medina is called the **Hegira** (hih-JY-ruh), and it took place in 622 A.D. The year 622 A.D., therefore, became the first year of the Muslim calendar.

The Muslim Religion Was Based on Five Rules

What was this new religion that Muhammad preached? The answer can be found in the Muslim holy book, the **Koran** (koh-RAHN). The Koran was written a few years after Muhammad died. It provides the religious rules that all Muslims must follow.

All Muslims were required to follow five important rules. First, Muslims were required to worship only one God, Allah, and they were required to accept Muhammad as Allah's Prophet, or messenger. Second, all Muslims were required to pray five times a day, facing toward Mecca. Third, all Muslims were required to fast, or not eat, from sunrise to sunset during the one holy month of the year. Fourth, all Muslims were to treat other Muslims as brothers and sisters. Fifth, all Muslims were to visit Mecca at least one time in their lives.

Islam Tried to Help Muslims Lead Better Lives

The Muslim religion, or Islam, also had many other rules. Muslims were not allowed to eat pork or to drink liquor. Muslims were not allowed to gamble, or to bet. And Muslims who had slaves were supposed to treat their slaves well.

Many people were attracted to the Muslim religion because it taught family-hood among people. But Muslims also believed that they must make people of other religions become Muslims. They believed that any Muslim who died fighting for his religion entered the Muslim heaven—which the Koran described as a very pleasant and wonderful place.

A prayer niche

The Muslims Conquered Many Nations and Built a Great Empire

When Muhammad was forced to leave Mecca, his followers began a holy war

247

This painting of the 1400's shows Muslims visiting the Kaaba in Mecca

were at war. These wars weakened both empires at just the same time that the Muslim armies began to spread the Muslim religion. The Muslims easily conquered Syria, Mesopotamia, Persia, Egypt, Palestine, northern Africa, and the Mediterranean islands. Later, the Muslim armies even conquered a part of India.

In the early 700's A.D., a group of Muslims called **Moors** crossed from northern Africa into Europe and soon conquered most of Spain. The Muslims now had a huge empire that reached from Spain to India.

The Muslims Divided Western Europe from the Byzantine Empire

The Muslim victories greatly weakened the Byzantine Empire. And the Muslim victories also weakened the European nations. The Muslims gained control of the Mediterranean trade routes and cut down the trade between western Europe and the Byzantine Empire. As a result, the western part of the old Roman empire was almost completely cut off from the eastern part.

against the city. By 630 A.D., Mecca was conquered and it became the holy city of Islam. The Kaaba temple in Mecca and the sacred black stone were taken over by Islam.

By the time that Muhammad died in 632 A.D., most Arabians were Muslims. After Muhammad died, one of his closest friends became the leader of the Muslims.

In the last half of the 600's A.D., the Persian empire and the Byzantine Empire

SUMMING UP

Islam, or the Muslim religion, developed in Arabia. The great leader who began the Muslim religion was Muhammad. After Muhammad's death, Muslim armies spread the Muslim religion to many lands, and they built a great empire. By the early 700's A.D., the Muslim Empire controlled the Mediterranean trade routes and divided the Byzantine Empire from the nations of western Europe. In the next chapter, you will read about the great culture that was developed by the Muslims.

UNDERSTANDING THE LESSON

Do You Know These Important Terms?

For each sentence below, choose the term that best completes the sentence.

1. Muhammad started a religion called the **(Mogul religion/Muslim religion)**.
2. Arab tribes who moved from place to place were called **(Bedouins/Muhammadans)**.
3. **(Kaaba/Islam)** is another name for the Muslim religion.
4. The escape of Muhammad from Mecca is called the **(Medina/Hegira)**.
5. The **(Koran/Casbah)** is the holy book of the Muslim religion.
6. The **(Moors/Ashanti)** were a group of Muslims who conquered most of Spain.

Do You Remember These People and Events?

1. Tell something about each of the following subjects.

   Muhammad   **Moors**

2. Explain how each of the following developments took place.

   a. Islam tried to help Muslims lead better lives.
   b. The Muslims were able to conquer a great empire in northern Africa and in southwestern Asia.
   c. The Muslim victories weakened the Byzantine Empire.

Can You Locate These Places?

Use the map on page 246 to locate the following places. Tell how each place is related to the events in this chapter.

Arabia   Byzantine Empire
Syria   Palestine
Medina   Persia
Egypt   northern Africa
India   Spain
Mecca   western Europe

Do You Know When It Happened?

Why are the following years important in Muslim history?

   570 A.D.   622 A.D.

Do You Remember the Main Idea?

Which one of the following ideas is the MAIN IDEA of this chapter?

1. The Muslim religion began in Europe, and it quickly spread over southwestern Asia and northern Africa.
2. The Muslim Empire stretched from Spain to India.
3. The Muslim religion began in Arabia. The Muslims conquered and controlled a great empire in northern Africa, Spain, and southwestern Asia.

What Do You Think?

From what you have read in this chapter, try to answer the following thought questions.

1. Do you think that the rules of the Muslim religion were easy to follow?
2. How do you think the Muslims' conquest of Spain affected the other peoples of western Europe?
3. How do you think the Arabs felt toward Muhammad when he first began to preach the Muslim religion to them?

Chapter 37
The Culture of the Muslims

GETTING STARTED

1   While the peoples of western Europe were facing difficult times under the feudal system, the people in the Muslim lands were living in a well-organized empire. The Muslims traded widely with other parts of the world. Great thinkers and teachers lived in the Muslim Empire, discovering new facts and ideas in many different areas.

The time line at the bottom of this page shows the years of this chapter—570 A.D. to 1100 A.D. During this period, people in the Muslim lands developed many ideas that we still use today.

2   Before you begin reading the chapter lesson, survey the lesson. Begin your survey by reading the beginning of the lesson. Then look through the lesson and read the headings. Next, study the pictures and read the picture captions. Finally, read the review section called "Summing Up" at the end of the lesson. This survey of the whole lesson will help you to discover the important ideas in this chapter.

Know the Main Idea

As you read the chapter lesson, try to remember the following important MAIN IDEA of the chapter.

Trade and learning helped to unite the Muslim lands. The people of the Muslim lands made great contributions in art, science, mathematics, and writing.

The following questions will help you to understand the MAIN IDEA. Try to answer these questions as you read the lesson.

1. What language became the official language of the Muslim Empire?
2. How did the Muslims preserve the learning of the Greeks?
3. What contributions did the Muslims make in art, science, mathematics, and writing?

Know These Important Terms

caliph   minaret
mosques

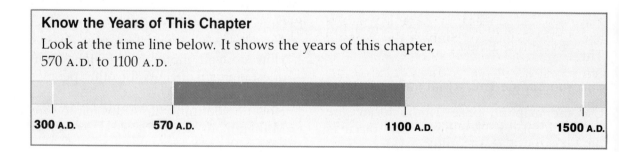

Know the Years of This Chapter

Look at the time line below. It shows the years of this chapter,
570 A.D. to 1100 A.D.

| 300 A.D. | 570 A.D. | 1100 A.D. | 1500 A.D. |

A Muslim mosque in Fez, Morocco

EXPLORING THE TIME

Have you ever heard the Arabian stories about "Aladdin" or "Sinbad the Sailor"? These exciting adventure stories were written to tell about life in the Muslim lands. However, these adventure stories tell only a little about what Muslim life was like. In this chapter, you will learn more about the life and culture of the Muslims.

The Muslim Empire Was Well Organized

As the Muslim Empire grew, its capital city was moved to Damascus (duh-MASS-kus). Then, about 760 A.D., Baghdad (BAG-dad) became the Muslim capital city. The Muslim ruler was called the **caliph** (KAY-lif). The first caliphs appointed only Arabs as important government officials. But later, Syrians, Persians, and Egyptians also served as government officials.

Muslim traders brought goods by camel from Asia and then shipped the goods to Europe

Arabic (AIR-uh-BICK), the Arabian language, was the official language in the Muslim Empire. The caliphs had new Arabic coins made to replace the old Byzantine and Persian coins that were used before. The caliphs also set up a postal system that carried mail to all parts of their empire. And they built roads, irrigation ditches, and canals to unite their empire.

The Muslim Empire Split into Several Parts

The Muslim Empire was well organized, but it was much too large for one ruler to rule. By the 800's A.D., the Muslim Empire split into several parts. Spain, Egypt, and Persia each had its own ruler. However, all of these lands remained Muslim lands.

Trade Increased in the Muslim Lands

The Muslim rulers encouraged trade. Muslim traders carried their goods all the way from India to Spain without having to pay a tax each time they entered a new country. As a result, Muslim traders were able to move their goods easily in all of the Muslim lands.

Fine cloth, metalware, rugs, leather goods, and spices were found in all large Muslim cities. And a rich Muslim was able to buy a great many products that were almost completely unknown in Europe at that time.

Learning Increased in the Muslim Lands

The easy travel in the Muslim lands and the use of Arabic by educated Muslims helped to spread learning among Arabs. The practice of visiting the holy city of Mecca also helped to spread learning. Muslims from all over the empire met at Mecca, exchanged ideas, and took new knowledge back home with them.

Much of Muslim science, writing, art, and thinking was borrowed from the peoples conquered by the Muslims. The Muslim rulers respected the learning of other peoples. And they encouraged educated people of all nations and all religions to increase their learning and knowledge.

Many of the educated people in the Muslim Empire were Christians and Jews. Both were allowed to worship as they wished as long as they paid special taxes to the Muslim government. These Christians and Jews, along with educated Muslims, rewrote many of the books by Greek and Roman thinkers into Arabic books.

A drawing from a Muslim book showing a doctor making medicine. Who was the most famous Muslim doctor of this period?

Educated Muslims Preserved Greek Ideas

The Muslims greatly respected the writings of the Greek philosophers, or thinkers, Plato and Aristotle. Their favorite Greek philosopher was Aristotle. Averroes (uh-VERR-oh-EEZ) and other Muslim philosophers tried to prove that the beliefs of Aristotle and of Islam were alike. These Muslim philosophers helped to preserve the Greek ideas. In later years, educated Europeans learned about Plato and Aristotle from the works of Averroes and other Muslims.

Muslims Did Important Work in Science and Mathematics

The Muslims had the greatest scientists of their time. Muslim doctors rediscovered the Greek medical knowledge. The most famous Muslim doctor was Avicenna (AV-ih-SENN-uh). Avicenna's medical books were studied in Europe for hundreds of years.

Muslim experts in mathematics borrowed their written number symbols from India. These symbols became the Arabic numerals we use today. The Muslims also improved on Hindu and Greek discoveries

Avicenna (seated) taught science and medicine to many Muslim students

in mathematics, astronomy, and geography.

The Muslims Had Great Writers

Muslim writers produced many wonderful books. Among their most famous stories are the *Arabian Nights* adventure stories. The Muslims also were fond of poetry. And many important Muslim books were written about history. The leading Muslim history writer, Ibn Khaldun (IB-un kal-DOON), was one of the world's greatest historians.

Muslim Temples Were Works of Art

The Muslim religion did not allow the drawing of human and animal figures.

Therefore, painting and sculpture did not develop in the Muslim lands. However, Muslim **mosques** (MAHSKS), or temples, were works of art in themselves. Every mosque had a tall, graceful **minaret** (MIN-uh-RET), or tower. Many mosques had beautiful decorations inside and outside. Some features of Muslim buildings were used later in European buildings.

The Muslims Had Good Schools

Good schools helped the Muslims make progress in learning. The Muslim schools often were held in a mosque. Children went to school at age five or six. They learned reading, writing, and arithmetic, and they studied the teachings of the Koran. The children from rich families continued their educations by studying science and great writings.

The Muslims also had advanced schools that were like colleges. Religion, law, medicine, mathematics, and science were studied in these colleges. The famous House of Wisdom in Baghdad was an education center that included a library, an astronomy section, and a language department.

SUMMING UP

The Muslim Empire split into several parts. However, religion, trade, and learning helped to unite the Muslim lands. The Muslims borrowed the best of the science, mathematics, art, and writings of the peoples they conquered. However, the Muslims also made great contributions of their own in these fields. In the next chapter, which begins Unit 10, you will read how the Muslim religion spread to India.

UNDERSTANDING THE LESSON

Do You Know These Important Terms?

For each sentence below, choose the term that best completes the sentence.

1. A Muslim ruler was called a (power/caliph).
2. (Mosques/Casa Blancas) were Muslim temples or churches.
3. The tall tower on a Muslim temple is called a (minaret/ziggurat).

Do You Remember These People and Events?

1. Tell something about each of the following subjects.

Plato	Avicenna
Aristotle	*Arabian Nights*
Averroes	Ibn Khaldun

2. Explain how each of the following developments took place.

   a. The Muslim lands continued to be well organized after the Muslim Empire was split into several parts.
   b. The Muslims encouraged learning and the spread of learning.
   c. Many scholars from other nations were able to study and work in Muslim lands.

Can You Locate These Places?

Use the map in Chapter 36 (page 246) to do the following map work.

1. Compare the size of the lands controlled by the Muslim Empire with the lands controlled by the Byzantine Empire. Which empire was larger?
2. What city was the capital of the Muslim Empire?
3. Near what body of water is Damascus located? is Baghdad located?

Do You Know When It Happened?

Why is the following year important in Muslim history?

   760 A.D.

Do You Remember the Main Idea?

Which one of the following ideas is the MAIN IDEA of this chapter?

1. Trade and learning helped to unite the Muslim lands. The people of the Muslim lands made great contributions in art, science, mathematics, and writing.
2. The Muslim Empire became a great center for trade and learning. But it became weak after it was divided.
3. The Muslims are remembered because they used and passed along to others the best ideas of the people they conquered.

What Do You Think?

From what you have read in this chapter, try to answer the following thought questions.

1. How do a postal system, good roads, the same language, and the same money help to keep a people united?
2. What do you consider to be the greatest contribution of the Muslims?
3. Muslims traded a great many products that were almost unknown in Europe during the Middle Ages. What were some of these products?

Unit 10

The Peoples of Asia and the Americas

THE CHAPTERS IN UNIT 10 ARE

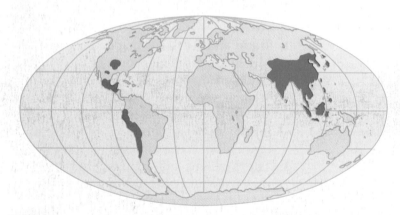

During the years of the Middle Ages in western Europe, nations in other parts of the world developed great cultures. In these years, India and China enjoyed a "Golden Age" of culture, and many ideas from these nations helped to shape life in other lands of Asia. In this unit, you will read about developments in India and China. You also will study the Indian peoples of the Americas.

An eighth century Brahman temple in India

Chapter 38
Buddhist, Hindu, and Muslim India

GETTING STARTED

1 India was located to the east of the great Muslim Empire. In the mid-700's A.D., the Muslims conquered part of the Indus River valley in northwestern India. But important developments were taking place in India before this conquest. These developments were concerned mainly with the different religious groups that ruled India. This chapter describes developments in India from about 300 B.C. to 1500 A.D. Check this period of years on the time line below before you read the lesson.

2 Before you begin reading the chapter lesson, survey the lesson. Begin your survey by reading the beginning of the lesson. Then look through the lesson and read the headings. Next, study the pictures and read the picture captions. Then study the map of the Maurya Empire on page 260 and the map of the Gupta Empire on page 261. Finally, read the review section called "Summing Up" at the end of the lesson. This survey will help you to discover the important ideas in this chapter.

Know the Main Idea

As you read the chapter lesson, try to remember the following important MAIN IDEA of the chapter.

The Maurya, Gupta, and Turkish empires each controlled India at different times. India made its most important progress under the Gupta Empire.

The following questions will help you to understand the MAIN IDEA. Try to answer these questions as you read the lesson.

1. In what way was Emperor Asoka a great ruler?
2. During what period did art, science, and writing make important progress in India?
3. What were some of the Muslim ideas that the Hindus borrowed when they were ruled by the Turks?

Know These Important Terms

Gupta rulers   Urdu
Puranas

Know the Years of This Chapter

Look at the time line below. It shows the years of this chapter, 300 B.C. to 1500 A.D.

500 B.C.	300 B.C.	B.C.	0	A.D.		1500 A.D.

Exterior of a South Indian Hindu temple showing figures of various Hindu deities

EXPLORING THE TIME

When you last read about India in Chapter 15, the Maurya emperors were ruling northern India. The Maurya emperors began to rule India shortly before the year 322 B.C. In this chapter, you will learn more about the Maurya Empire and the Gupta and Turkish empires in India that came after the Maurya Empire.

Emperor Asoka Became a Buddhist

The most famous of the Maurya emperors was Asoka (uh-SOH-kuh), who ruled India from 270 to 230 B.C. Asoka conquered most of India. The Maurya Empire soon included all of India except the very southern part. But then Asoka turned against the idea of war. He became a Buddhist, and he tried to rule by following the teachings of Buddha, who preached against fighting.

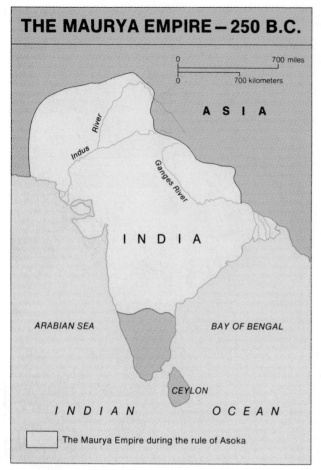

THE MAURYA EMPIRE — 250 B.C.

0 — 700 miles
0 — 700 kilometers

A S I A

Indus River

Ganges River

I N D I A

ARABIAN SEA

BAY OF BENGAL

CEYLON

I N D I A N   O C E A N

☐ The Maurya Empire during the rule of Asoka

What two rivers were part of the Maurya Empire?

Asoka proved to be a great and noble ruler. He did not fight any more wars. He allowed all his people to worship as they wished. He made sure that servants, slaves, and even animals were treated fairly. And he helped to spread the beliefs of Buddhism.

India Traded with Greece and Rome

But after Asoka died, the Maurya Empire slowly split up. By about 185 B.C., India again was divided into many small states.

Many of the states of India traded with Greece, and some Greek ideas were carried back to India. Some statues of Buddha now looked much like statues of the Greek god Apollo. Greek wines also became popular in India.

The states of India also later traded with the Roman Empire, and they made coins that were like Roman coins. And the Romans bought pearls, spices, drugs, ivory, and fine cloth from India's traders.

India's Greatest Period Was Under the Gupta Rulers

During the years of the 300's A.D. and 400's A.D., the **Gupta** (GOOP-tah) **rulers** ruled northern and central India. The Gupta Empire was the largest empire in India since the time of Asoka. During the Gupta Empire, art, science, and writing made great progress in India.

Many of India's most famous poems, plays, and books were written in these years. And the paintings and statues of this period are among the best ever produced in India. It was under the Gupta Empire that India began to use the zero and the decimal system in writing numbers.

Hinduism Grew Stronger During the Gupta Empire

Buddhists and followers of other religions were allowed to worship as they wished during the Gupta Empire. However, Hinduism again became the official religion of India. An important group of Hindu religious books, the **Puranas** (poo-RAH-nuz), were written at this time. As Hinduism grew stronger, the caste system of India also grew stronger.

After the Gupta Empire Ended, India Again Became Divided

Under the Gupta rulers, India enjoyed peace and good times. However, the Guptas were not powerful enough to protect their empire. About 600 A.D., invading peoples conquered northern India and the Gupta Empire split up.

For the next six hundred years, India was divided into many warring states. Art, writing, and science made very little progress. And few changes took place in India's ways of thinking and living.

The Turks Slowly Conquered India

India was now too weak to prevent attacks by foreign invaders. People from central Asia called the Turks moved into northwestern India. And by the early 1200's A.D., the Turks controlled all of northern India. The Turks made Delhi (DELL-ee) their capital city, and by 1320 A.D. they conquered and ruled all of India except southern India.

Under the Turks, Many Hindus Became Muslims

The Turks were Muslims and believed in only one God, Allah. When the Turks conquered India, they destroyed many Hindu and Buddhist temples and statues. The Turks later allowed the people of India to worship as they wished. Even so, many people in India became Muslims. Some Hindus became Muslims in order to become high government officials. Some lower-caste Hindus became Muslims in order to escape the harsh treatment that they received from higher-caste Hindus. In northern India especially, where Turkish rule was strongest, many Hindus became Muslims.

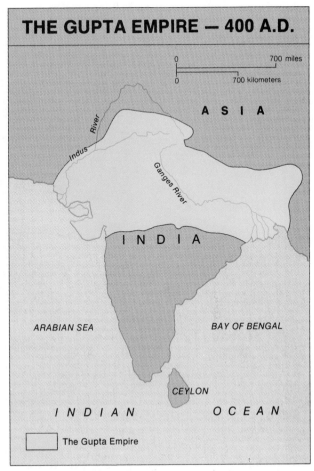

THE GUPTA EMPIRE — 400 A.D.

On which continent was the Gupta Empire?

The Turks Changed Life in India

The Muslims and the Hindus looked down on each other. And the Hindu caste rules prevented Hindus from eating or drinking with Muslims. But the two groups did work together. And a new language called **Urdu** (OOR-doo), made up of both Hindu and Turkish words, soon developed.

Hindu life was changed by the Turks in other ways as well. Turkish clothing styles became popular. The arch, the dome, and the minaret tower were added to Indian

261

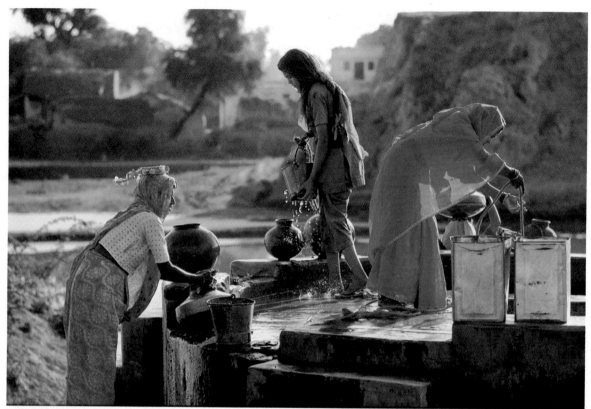

Women at a well in an Indian village. What kinds of containers are they using to carry water?

buildings. And upper-caste Hindu men began to keep women hidden in a separate part of the house as did Muslim men.

After Turkish Rule Ended, India Became Divided Again

The Turkish rule in India lasted until about 1500 A.D. At the time Delhi, the Turkish capital, was captured by fierce Mongol (MONG-gul) invaders from central Asia. As the Turks lost power, India again split into many small states. Some of these states were controlled by Hindus. Other states were controlled by Muslims. These religious differences led to terrible religious wars between the states of India. These wars kept India weak and later allowed European nations to conquer India.

SUMMING UP

Asoka built the Maurya Empire in the 200's B.C., and spread Buddhist ideas in India. Under the Gupta Empire in the 300's A.D. and 400's A.D., India's art, science, and writing developed greatly. Later, in the 1200's A.D., the Turks ruled India. But between these periods, India was divided into small, warring states. In the next chapter, you will read how the Chinese Empire developed.

UNDERSTANDING THE LESSON

Do You Know These Important Terms?

For each sentence below, choose the term that best completes the sentence.

1. The ruling family in India during the years of the 300's A.D. and 400's A.D. was the **(Gupta rulers/Hindu family)**.
2. An important group of Hindu religious books is called the **(Koran/Puranas)**.
3. **(Urdu/Bengalese)** was a mixture of Hindu and Turkish words which became a new language in India.

Do You Remember These People and Events?

1. Tell something about each of the following subjects.

   Asoka   Gupta rulers

2. Explain how each of the following developments took place.

   a. India's greatest period was under the Gupta rulers.
   b. Under the rule of the Turks, many Hindus became Muslims.
   c. India became divided again after the Turks' rule ended.

Can You Locate These Places?

Use the maps on pages 260 and 261 to do the following map work.

1. Locate the following places. Tell how each place is connected to developments in this chapter.

India	**Indus River**
central Asia	**Ganges River**

2. What map symbol is used to show the Maurya Empire? the Gupta Empire?
3. Which was larger, the Maurya Empire or the Gupta Empire?
4. What part of present-day India was not a part of either the Maurya Empire or the Gupta Empire?

Do You Know When It Happened?

During what years did the Gupta rulers rule India? By what year did the Turks conquer all of India?

Do You Remember the Main Idea?

Which one of the following ideas is the MAIN IDEA of this chapter?

1. The Maurya, Gupta, and Turkish empires each controlled India at different times. India made its most important progress under the Gupta Empire.
2. The greatest period of Indian history took place under the Gupta rulers. But this great period lasted only a short time.
3. The Maurya Empire grew weak because most of the people of India became Buddhists, and they did not believe in war.

What Do You Think?

From what you have read in this chapter, try to answer the following thought questions.

1. Why do you think that India became divided into many small states each time one of its great empires weakened?
2. Why do you think the southern part of India was the most difficult part to conquer and to control?

Chapter 39
China as an Empire

GETTING STARTED

1 In Chapters 16 and 17 you read about the early history of China. You may remember that China began to develop about as early as Egypt, Mesopotamia, and India. And many dynasties, or ruling families, governed China from a very early period. Between the years 221 B.C. and 590 A.D. (see the time line at the bottom of the page), the Chinese people built a great empire—an empire as large as the Roman Empire. You will read about the development of the Chinese Empire in this chapter.

2 Before you begin reading the chapter lesson, survey the lesson. Begin your survey by reading the beginning of the lesson. Then look through the lesson and read the headings. Next, study the pictures and read the picture captions. Then study the map of the Chinese Empire on page 268. Finally, read the review section called "Summing Up" at the end of the lesson. This survey of the whole lesson will help you to discover the important ideas in this chapter.

Know the Main Idea

As you read the chapter lesson, try to remember the following important MAIN IDEA of the chapter.

The Chinese people built a great empire during the Chin and Han dynasties. Even when this empire was overthrown, the Chinese people continued to make progress.

The following questions will help you to understand the MAIN IDEA. Try to answer these questions as you read the lesson.

1. What kind of government did Emperor Cheng set up in China?
2. Why was the Great Wall of China built?
3. Who was able to conquer China while the Chinese were fighting among themselves?

Know These Important Terms

Great Wall of China   war lords
Han dynasty

Know the Years of This Chapter

Look at the time line below. It shows the years of this chapter, 221 B.C. to 590 A.D.

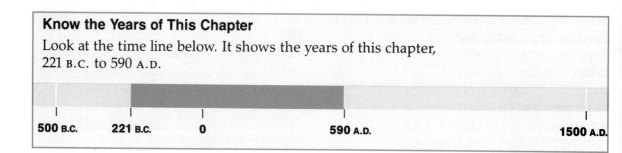

| 500 B.C. | 221 B.C. | 0 | 590 A.D. | 1500 A.D. |

Emperor Cheng had the Great Wall of China built along the northwestern part of China. It was 1,500 miles long, 25 feet high, and 15 feet thick. It was built of stone, brick, and earth.

EXPLORING THE TIME

What was happening in China while new empires were being formed in India? Perhaps you recall that in 221 B.C. China was taken over by the state of Chin. By that time, the teachings of Confucius were an important part of Chinese life. In this chapter, you will learn how China developed into a great and powerful empire.

Emperor Cheng Became China's Ruler

Cheng (JUNG) was the Chin ruler who became the first emperor of China. Cheng formed an empire by conquering all of the Chinese states. Cheng then took strong control over these states. First, he destroyed the power of the Chinese nobles by forcing the nobles to live in the capital city. Then he collected all weapons except those of his own army and melted them down.

265

Emperor Cheng ordered the Chinese people to burn all books on Confucius' teachings

Then he ordered all the books on Confucius' teachings to be burned. Cheng believed that Confucius' ideas did not encourage the Chinese people to support a strong emperor.

Cheng United China into a Strong Nation

To make his government stronger, Cheng divided China into many provinces, or parts, each governed by three officials. One official was the leader of the province's army. Another official was the leader of the province's government. The third official reported to Cheng on the work of the other two officials.

Cheng united China in other ways, too. The same money system was used all over China, and trade increased as a result. The Chin laws became the main laws used in China. Only one style of writing Chinese letters was used. The same taxes were used all over China. And wide roads were built to connect all parts of the empire.

Cheng also tried to protect China against attack. The armies marched into southern China and conquered the Xi River valley. For further protection, Cheng had the **Great Wall of China** built along the northwestern part of China. This wall was 1500 miles long, 25 feet high, and 15 feet thick! It was built of stone, brick, and earth. The Great Wall kept many enemies out of China.

The Han Dynasty Took Over China

Cheng was a strong ruler, but he was never popular. Many Chinese people disliked Cheng because they had to pay high taxes to the government and because they had to help build roads and the Great Wall. The Chinese nobles did not like Cheng because he did not allow the provinces to govern themselves. After Cheng died in 207 B.C., a revolt broke out against the Chin dynasty. The revolt was successful, and a new dynasty—the **Han dynasty**—came to power about 202 B.C.

The Han Rulers Governed China Well

The Han dynasty ruled China for the next four hundred years. The Han rulers learned a great deal from the mistakes of Cheng. The Han rulers allowed the Chinese provinces to have more freedom. The Han rulers again chose the followers of Confucius to serve in the government. And these people usually were excellent government officials.

The Han Rulers Made the Chinese Empire Larger

Under the Han rulers, the Chinese Empire gained more territory. One Chinese army conquered some Mongolian land northwest of the Great Wall. Another Chinese army conquered Korea. And a third Chinese army conquered new lands to the south of China. The Chinese Empire now stretched from the Pacific Ocean all the way to eastern Europe, as far as the Caspian Sea. This empire was almost as large as the Roman Empire was at its greatest!

China Made Great Progress During the Han Dynasty

The Han rulers encouraged learning, art, science, writing, and trade. Many important books of poetry and history were written during the Han dynasty. The first paper used in China was made during the Han dynasty. And the Chinese people carried on a busy trade with most of Asia as well as with the Roman Empire. So much progress took place during the Han dynasty that Chinese people today still call themselves "Children of Han."

After the Han Dynasty Ended, China Split into Several Parts

In the years before 200 A.D., high taxes and bad government caused the Chinese people to revolt against the Han dynasty. Chinese

A Chinese clay figure from the Han Dynasty

war lords, or bandit leaders, began to conquer many parts of China. About 220 A.D., the Han dynasty lost its power and came to an end.

Until about 590 A.D., China remained split into several parts, which fought each other for control of China. During these

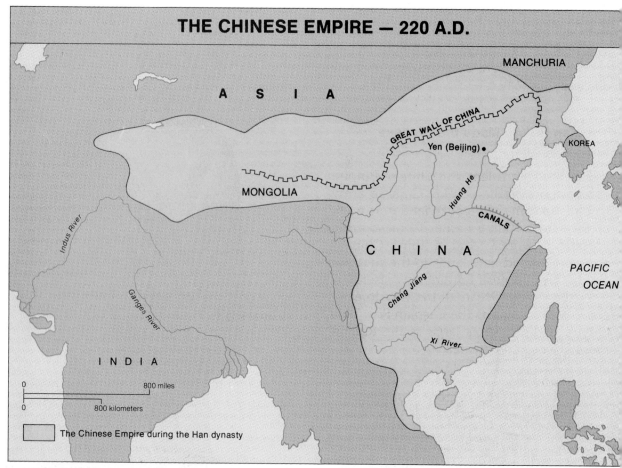

THE CHINESE EMPIRE — 220 A.D.

MANCHURIA

A S I A

GREAT WALL OF CHINA

Yen (Beijing)•

KOREA

MONGOLIA

Huang He

CANALS

Indus River

C H I N A

PACIFIC
OCEAN

Ganges River

Chang Jiang

Xi River

I N D I A

| 0 | | 800 miles |

| 0 | | 800 kilometers |

The Chinese Empire during the Han dynasty

Which rivers were connected by canals to the Pacific Ocean?

wars, schools, libraries, and temples were destroyed. While the Chinese were fighting among themselves, Mongol invaders from central Asia took over most of northern China.

This period was called China's "Dark Age." However, China's Dark Age was not completely "dark." The Mongol invaders soon learned the Chinese ways of living. Chinese schools continued to teach students the ideas of Confucius. And Buddhism spread to China during this time. The ideas of Buddhism soon were accepted by millions of Chinese people.

SUMMING UP

Emperor Cheng of the Chin dynasty formed the Chinese Empire. The Han dynasty ruled China for the next four hundred years. During the Han period, China became a larger empire. A "Dark Age" followed the overthrow of the Han dynasty in 220 A.D. But even during the Dark Age, the Chinese people made great progress in art, science, and writing. In the next chapter, you will learn how China became a great nation again.

UNDERSTANDING THE LESSON

Do You Know These Important Terms?

For each sentence below, choose the term that best completes the sentence.

1. The wall built to protect the northwestern part of China's empire was the **(Wall of Mongolia/Great Wall of China)**.
2. The **(Han dynasty/Mongolian dynasty)** replaced the Chin dynasty.
3. Chinese **(dynasty leaders/war lords)** were bandit leaders who conquered different parts of China.

Do You Remember These People and Events?

1. Tell something about each of the following subjects.

     Cheng   Han dynasty

2. Explain how each of the following developments took place.

   a. Cheng, the first emperor of China, began to build a strong empire.
   b. The rulers during the Han dynasty made the Chinese Empire larger.
   c. The Chinese people continued to make progress even after they were conquered by the Mongols.

Can You Locate These Places?

Use the map on page 268 to do the following map work.

1. Locate the following places. Tell something about each place.

     Xi River valley   Korea
     Mongolia   central Asia

2. Perhaps you have noticed how important directions are. Name the four main directions on a map. Then name the directions "in between" them.
3. Which is farther north, the Huang He or the Xi River? In what part of China is the Great Wall of China located?

Do You Know When It Happened?

What are the years of this chapter?

Do You Remember the Main Idea?

Which one of the following ideas is the MAIN IDEA of this chapter?

1. China was overrun by Mongol invaders, who took over the Chinese culture and built a great empire.
2. The Chinese people were able to build a great empire because they wrote and spoke the same language and because the same laws were used everywhere in China.
3. The Chinese people built a great empire during the Chin and Han dynasties. Even when this empire was overthrown, the Chinese people continued to make great progress.

What Do You Think?

From what you have read in this chapter, answer the following thought questions.

1. Do you think that the three-official system used by Emperor Cheng to govern his provinces was a good idea?
2. What lessons about government might you learn from the mistakes of the Chin dynasty and the success of the Han dynasty?

Chapter 40
China's Golden Age

GETTING STARTED

1   Does it seem to you that the story of the Chinese Empire is a story of "ups" and "downs"? In a way it was. Periods of greatness and progress in China were followed by periods when invaders attacked China or when fighting broke out within China itself. During the period from 590 A.D. to 1280 A.D. (see the time line at the bottom of this page), this same story continued in China. However, during these years the Chinese people rebuilt China into a greater nation than it was before.

2   Before you begin reading the chapter lesson, survey the lesson. Begin your survey by reading the beginning of the lesson. Then look through the lesson and read the headings. Next, study the pictures and read the picture captions. Finally, read the review section called "Summing Up" at the end of the lesson. This survey of the whole lesson will help you to discover the important ideas in this chapter.

Know the Main Idea

As you read the chapter, try to remember the following important MAIN IDEA of the chapter.

During the Tang and Sung dynasties, China developed a "Golden Age" of culture. At other times, wars broke out within China.

The following questions will help you to understand the MAIN IDEA. Try to answer these questions as you read the lesson.

1. What Chinese dynasty was able to unite China again after the Mongol conquest?
2. Which religious group in China was most favored when government appointments were made?
3. What were three reasons for the overthrow of the Tang dynasty in 906 A.D.?

Know These Important Terms

Sui dynasty   block printing
Tang dynasty   Sung dynasty
written exam system

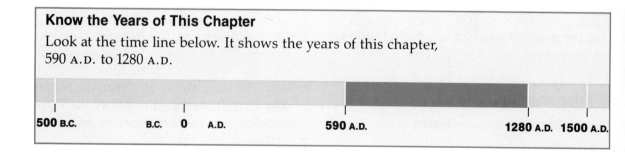

Know the Years of This Chapter

Look at the time line below. It shows the years of this chapter, 590 A.D. to 1280 A.D.

| 500 B.C. | B.C.   0   A.D. | 590 A.D. | 1280 A.D.   1500 A.D. |

Chinese women caring for children. What are some of the women's tasks?

EXPLORING THE TIME

Although China had its "Dark Age" and was divided for nearly four hundred years, China became a greater nation than it was before. In this chapter, you will read about China's "Golden Age." This "Golden Age" began about 618 A.D. with the Tang Dynasty and lasted for more than six hundred years.

The Sui Dynasty Built Up China Again

About the year 590 A.D., China was united again by the **Sui** (SWIH) **dynasty.** Though the Sui dynasty ruled harshly, it also repaired the Great Wall, improved the canals connecting northern China and southern China, and rebuilt several cities. This work helped to build up China. However, after about thirty years the Sui dynasty was replaced by the **Tang dynasty.**

Stone sculpture from the Tang Dynasty of the head of Bodhisattva

The Tang Dynasty Ruled China Well

The Tang dynasty came to power in 618 A.D. and ruled for almost three hundred years. Under the Tang dynasty, China began to enjoy a "Golden Age." The first Tang emperor, Tai Tsung (TY TSOONG), was one of China's greatest rulers. Tai Tsung was both a good general and a kind ruler who greatly improved Chinese government.

Under the Tang dynasty, land was given to poor farmers who owned no land.

And the harsh laws of the Sui dynasty were replaced by better laws. During its early years, the Tang Empire was larger than the Han Empire. But the later Tang rulers lost most of this land.

The Tang Dynasty Did Not Allow Freedom of Religion

During most of Chinese history, every Chinese person was allowed to worship as he or she wished. By the Tang period, the Buddhist beliefs and the beliefs of Confucius were the most popular religions among Chinese people. During the 800's A.D., however, Tang emperors became afraid of the growing wealth and power of the Buddhist church. Therefore, in 845 A.D. the Tang government took over the Buddhist churches and Buddhist-owned lands. As a result, the Buddhists became weaker and Buddhism lost much of its power in China.

Chinese Government Officials Were Chosen by Exams

As you read in Chapter 39, the Han rulers chose followers of Confucius as officials to help govern China. Many later Chinese rulers also chose followers of Confucius as government officials. At first, these men were selected by the ruler. But slowly, government officials were chosen on the basis of how well they did on written exams, or tests.

The **written exam system** became a part of Chinese life during the Tang period. These exams were tests based on the writings of Confucius and his followers, and they were very difficult. People had to study for many years before they were able to take these exams.

However, the written exam system provided China with many good, well-trained government officials. These officials also were trained to support the Tang government.

China Progressed Under the Tang Dynasty

Times were good for many Chinese people during the Tang dynasty. Painters, musicians, and writers produced many great works. Fine history books, books of facts (encyclopedias), and poetry were written during these years.

The art of **block printing** was invented in China during the 800's A.D. In block printing, the words for an entire page of a book were carved on a single block, or piece, of wood. This block then was printed on paper. Block printing made it possible to produce books faster and more cheaply than before. When more books were printed and they became cheaper, more Chinese people were able to read many of the fine books written during earlier periods of Chinese history.

The Tang Dynasty Was Overthrown

But the Tang dynasty was overthrown in 906 A.D. The reasons were the same reasons that caused the overthrow of earlier dynasties—high taxes, dishonest government officials, and attacks by enemies.

During much of the 900's A.D., wars took place in many parts of China. Bandits roamed across the country and made trade difficult. Roads and canals were not repaired. But about 960 A.D., the **Sung** (SOONG) **dynasty** took over China and restored order.

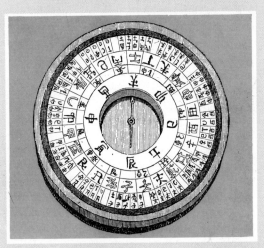

A Chinese Compass

The Chinese people have made many great inventions in the past. China was the first nation to invent printing, paper, and gunpowder. It also was the first nation to invent a compass.

The story of the magnetic compass is one of the most interesting of these Chinese inventions. The compass was first invented by the Chinese fortune-tellers. Their "needles" were sometimes shaped like spoons and sometimes shaped like fishes. The Chinese compass was invented in the 500's A.D. However, this compass was not used by Chinese ships until about five hundred years later.

By the 1100's A.D., the Muslims learned about the Chinese compass. Muslim traders brought the compass back to Europe just as Europeans were becoming interested in trading by sea with other parts of the world. European sailors improved the compass in many ways. And this Chinese invention soon helped Europe to explore other parts of the world.

Question: What group of traders brought the Chinese compass to Europe?

Painting of Chinese nobles from the Sung Dynasty

The Sung Dynasty Rebuilt China

The Sung dynasty ruled China for about three hundred years. Much of northern China was still occupied by enemy tribes during the later Sung period, but the parts of China under Sung control were well governed.

The Sung rulers repaired canals, rebuilt old cities, and started new cities. Trade within China and with other nations increased. China again enjoyed a Golden Age of culture and peaceful times.

The increase in the number of books helped to improve education during the Sung period. Public schools were opened to train government officials. New exams for government officials were made easier, and exams were now based more on a knowledge of government than on a knowledge of the great Chinese writings.

SUMMING UP

Between the Tang and Sung dynasties, China was greatly weakened by wars in many parts of the nation. But during the Tang and Sung dynasties, China had a "Golden Age." One great Chinese invention in the Tang dynasty was block printing, which helped to produce more books and improved Chinese education. In the next chapter, you will find out what was happening in the lands of Asia located to the east and to the south of China.

UNDERSTANDING THE LESSON

Do You Know These Important Terms?

For each sentence below, choose the term that best completes the sentence.

1. The **(Sui dynasty/Tang dynasty)** ruled China harshly.
2. China enjoyed a "Golden Age" under the **(Sui dynasty/Tang dynasty)**.
3. The **(Confucian system/written exam system)** was started as a basis for choosing government officials during the Tang dynasty.
4. Carving an entire page of a book on a block of wood and then printing it on paper was called **(stamp printing/block printing)**.

Do You Remember These People and Events?

1. Tell something about each of the following subjects.

   Sui dynasty   **Tang dynasty**
   Tai Tsung   **Sung dynasty**

2. Explain how or why each of the following developments took place.

   a. The Tang and Sung dynasties produced a "Golden Age" in China.
   b. The government officials were chosen by a written exam system.
   c. Books became cheaper and more widely read by the Chinese people.

Can You Locate These Places?

Use the map in Chapter 39 (page 268) to do the following map work.

1. Locate the following places. What developments took place in each?

northern China   southern China

2. What map symbol is used to show canals? What two rivers did the canals in China connect? In which direction do these two rivers flow?

Do You Know When It Happened?

Block printing was invented in China during the 800's A.D. Which dynasty ruled China in these years?

Do You Remember the Main Idea?

Which one of the following ideas is the MAIN IDEA of this chapter?

1. During the Tang and Sung dynasties, China developed a "Golden Age" of culture. At other times, wars broke out within China.
2. The Tang dynasty was able to develop high levels of culture because it almost completely ended the Buddhist religion.
3. The period of the Tang and Sung dynasties is called China's "Golden Age" because the written exam system began at this time.

What Do You Think?

From what you have read in this chapter, answer the following thought questions.

1. Do you think that the written exam system was a good method of choosing government officials? Explain your answer.
2. Which idea that developed during the "Golden Age" of China do you think was most valuable? Why do you think so?

GETTING STARTED

1 The Chinese culture was like a great fountain. Many of the ideas from this "culture fountain" flowed to other parts of Asia, particularly to Japan and Southeast Asia.

Southeast Asia, the area between China and India, was a "crossroad"; that is, many ideas, people, and trade passed through Southeast Asia constantly. And not only China but India as well had an important effect in this area. This chapter describes how China and India helped to shape the cultures of Japan and Southeast Asia between 200 B.C. and 1500 A.D. These years are shown on the time line at the bottom of this page.

2 Before you begin reading the chapter lesson, survey the lesson. Begin your survey by reading the beginning of the lesson. Then look through the lesson and read the headings. Next, study the pictures and read the picture captions. Then study the map of Japan and Southeast Asia on page 280. Finally, read the review section called "Summing Up" at the end of the lesson.

This survey will help you to discover the important ideas in this chapter.

Know the Main Idea

As you read the chapter lesson, try to remember the following important MAIN IDEA of the chapter.

In many ways, Japan was shaped by Chinese culture. The nations of Southeast Asia were shaped by ideas from both China and India.

The following questions will help you to understand the MAIN IDEA. Try to answer these questions as you read the lesson.

1. In what way did Japan's location affect its growth as a nation?
2. What Chinese ideas were adopted by the Japanese people?
3. In what ways were the people of Southeast Asia shaped by the culture of India?

Know These Important Terms

frontier	Shinto
Ainu	bushi
Yamato tribe	shogun

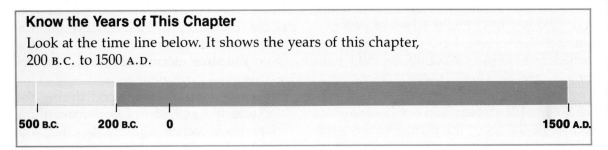

Know the Years of This Chapter

Look at the time line below. It shows the years of this chapter, 200 B.C. to 1500 A.D.

| 500 B.C. | 200 B.C. | 0 | 1500 A.D. |

A Japanese priest outside the Meiji Shrine in winter

EXPLORING THE TIME

You have probably heard about the American **frontier**, or the land just beyond the settled parts of early America. In Asia, too, there were frontiers beyond India and China. These frontier lands were Japan and the lands of Southeast Asia. In this chapter, you will read about these frontier lands of Asia.

The Islands of Japan Were near China

The islands of Japan are located off the eastern mainland of Asia. These islands stretch three thousand miles from north to south. But these islands are small, and so Japan is not a large nation.

The Japanese islands were far enough from Asia to be protected from attack. Yet Japan was close enough to Asia for the cultures of Asia to reach Japan. Beginning

The Great Buddha of Kamakura in Japan

Japan Became United into One Nation

One of the Japanese groups—the **Yamato** (yah-MAH-toh) **tribe**—lived on the Yamato plain on the largest Japanese island, the island of Honshu. The Yamato tribe learned how to make iron weapons. They used these weapons to conquer other Japanese tribes. By the year 200 B.C., the Yamato chief, or leader, became the emperor of Japan. But the Yamato emperor had little power. The other Japanese chiefs, or nobles, really ruled their own people.

Japan Took Over Many Chinese Ideas

The Japanese people had many contacts with China. The teachings of Confucius, the teachings of other Chinese philosophers, and even the Chinese way of writing were taken over by the Japanese people. After Buddhism spread from India to China, the Japanese people began to build their buildings in the Chinese style. They used the Chinese calendar, wore Chinese-style clothes, and studied Chinese books.

The Japanese people also modeled their government after the Chinese government. As a result, the Japanese emperor became more important than he was before. Japan was divided into many parts, as was China. Each part of Japan was ruled by government officials selected by the Japanese emperor. These officials had to pass exams that were like those taken by Chinese officials.

Japan Changed Many Ideas That It Borrowed from China

However, the Japanese people changed many Chinese ideas to meet their own needs. For example, the Japanese nobles were too strong to be destroyed by the Japanese emperor. Therefore, the emperor

in the early part of Japanese history, China became very important in shaping Japanese life.

The Early Japanese People Led Simple Lives

The first people who settled in Japan probably were the **Ainu** (AY-noo), who lived on the most northern Japanese island. The later groups that entered Japan came from central Asia and from islands south of Japan. These people mixed together and formed the Japanese people.

The early Japanese people lived together in tribes. These early people of Japan were hunters and fishers, as well as farmers who planted rice and vegetables.

gave the nobles the most important government jobs. The Japanese people also had their own religion, called **Shinto** (SHIN-toh), or the "way of the gods." And the Japanese people also changed the Chinese way of writing to fit the needs of the Japanese language.

Japan Was Ruled by an Army Government After 1200 A.D.

About 800 A.D., the Japanese emperors began to lose their power to the Japanese nobles, or feudal lords. The Japanese feudal lords were called **bushi** (BOO-shee).

About 1200 A.D., Yoritomo (YORR-ih-TOH-moh) became the most powerful feudal lord. Yoritomo allowed the Japanese emperor to keep his title, but Yoritomo held all the power. Yoritomo's own title was **shogun** (SHOH-gun), or general. As shogun, Yoritomo controlled the army and the treasury. For the next six hundred years, Japan was ruled by the shogun and the army.

Southeast Asia Was Shaped by the Cultures of China and India

The territory between China and India is called Southeast Asia. Today, Southeast Asia includes a great many important nations—Vietnam (VEE-et-NAHM), Thailand (TY-land), Burma, Laos, Kampuchea (Kam-poo-CHEE-uh) (formerly Cambodia), Malaysia, and Indonesia. Like Japan, these nations were made up of many different peoples. These nations of Southeast Asia were shaped by the culture of China and by the culture of India.

At one time or another, China ruled many of the lands of Southeast Asia. Even those nations not ruled by China modeled their governments after the Chinese government. Most of these nations of Southeast Asia were ruled by emperors.

Drawing of a powerful Japanese shogun of the 1500's A.D.

The religious beliefs of the people of Southeast Asia came from India. Some peoples in Southeast Asia became Hindus, some became Buddhists, and some became Muslims.

Southeast Asia Became a Rich Trading Area

Southeast Asia had many seaports. Ships sailing back and forth between Europe and Asia usually stopped at one of these seaports. Many merchants from China, India, and the Muslim lands west of India settled in these seaports, bringing their ways of life and their products with them.

Southeast Asia also produced many fine products of its own. The gold, tin, ivory, spices, and jewels of Southeast Asia were popular among wealthy people in Europe and Asia. As you will read later, Southeast Asia became very important to Europe in the 1400's A.D. and 1500's A.D.

279

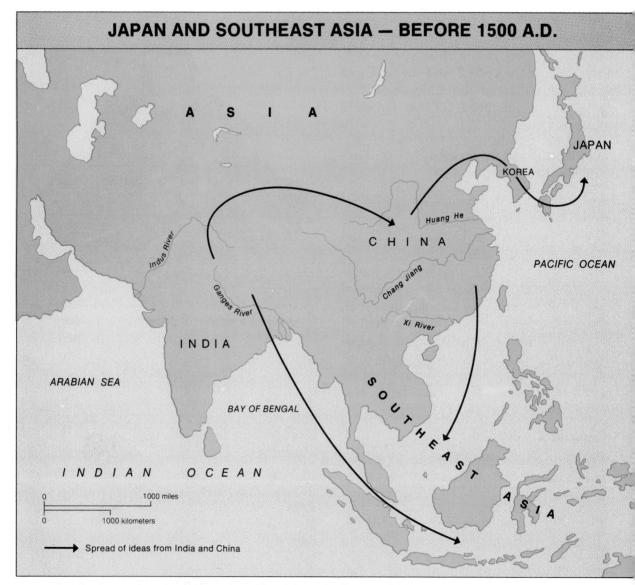

JAPAN AND SOUTHEAST ASIA — BEFORE 1500 A.D.

ASIA

JAPAN

KOREA

Huang He

CHINA

PACIFIC OCEAN

Chang Jiang

Xi River

Indus River

Ganges River

INDIA

ARABIAN SEA

BAY OF BENGAL

SOUTHEAST ASIA

INDIAN OCEAN

0   1000 miles

0   1000 kilometers

→ Spread of ideas from India and China

Name two countries influenced by ideas from India and China.

SUMMING UP

Two important frontier lands of Asia were Japan and Southeast Asia. Japan was ruled first by an emperor, later by a shogun and the army. In many ways, Japan was shaped by the Chinese culture. Southeast Asia also was shaped by Chinese ideas, but it accepted the religious beliefs of India. In the next chapter, you will read how groups of people moved from the continent of Asia and settled in the Americas.

UNDERSTANDING THE LESSON

Do You Know These Important Terms?

For each sentence below, choose the term that best completes the sentence.

1. Japan and Southeast Asia were **(frontier/ faraway)** lands that were beyond the more settled parts of Asia.
2. The first people who settled in Japan were probably the **(Ainu/Thais).**
3. The **(Yamato tribe/Quanto tribe)** grew to be the strongest Japanese tribe, and it conquered other Japanese tribes.
4. The Japanese religion was called **(Judo/ Shinto),** or the "way of the gods."
5. The Japanese feudal lords were called **(bushi/samurai).**
6. The Japanese noble who held most of the power and controlled the Japanese army was called the **(emperor/shogun).**

Do You Remember These People and Events?

1. Tell something about each of the following subjects.

    Ainu   Yoritomo

Can You Locate These Places?

Use the map on page 280 to do the following map work.

1. Locate the following places. Tell how each place is related to developments in this chapter.

    Japan   Southeast Asia
    China   India

2. Explain in what way Southeast Asia is located at a "crossroad."

3. Compare this map with the map of Southeast Asia today on page 686. What countries are located in Southeast Asia today? Name them.

Do You Know When It Happened?

What are the years of this chapter on Japan and Southeast Asia?

Do You Remember the Main Idea?

Which one of the following ideas is the MAIN IDEA of this chapter?

1. The people of Japan and Southeast Asia used ideas from the Chinese culture.
2. In many ways, Japan was shaped by Chinese culture. The nations of Southeast Asia were shaped by ideas from both China and India.
3. Japan and the nations of Southeast Asia developed rich cultures of their own and became rich trading areas.

What Do You Think?

From what you have read in this chapter, try to answer the following thought questions.

1. In what ways do you think that the feudal system of Japan was like the feudal system in Europe?
2. How important do you think that location was in the development of culture in Japan? in Southeast Asia?
3. The people of Southeast Asia today speak many languages and have formed many nations. Why did Southeast Asia develop into many nations instead of one united nation, such as Japan?

Chapter 42
The Indian Peoples of the Americas

GETTING STARTED

1   Most of North America and South America is located far to the east of Asia. Yet, many historians believe that the first settlers of the Americas probably came from Asia. These historians believe that settlers from Asia reached North America by crossing the Bering Strait, the water passage that now separates Alaska from Asia. This was possible because thousands of years ago the Bering Strait was land, not water.

    This chapter tells about the early settlers of the Americas and about the remarkable cultures that some of them developed between 100 A.D. and 1500 A.D. Check this period of years on the time line below.

2   Before you begin reading the chapter lesson, survey the lesson. Begin your survey by reading the beginning of the lesson. Then look through the lesson and read the headings. Next, study the pictures and read the picture captions. Then study the map of the early Indian nations of the Americas on page 284. Finally, read the review section called "Summing Up" at the end of the lesson. This survey of the whole lesson will help you to discover the important ideas in this chapter.

Know the Main Idea

As you read the chapter lesson, try to remember the following important MAIN IDEA of the chapter.

The Americas were settled by people from Asia. Later, some of these people built great Indian nations in Mexico, Central America, and South America.

    The following questions will help you to understand the MAIN IDEA. Try to answer these questions as you read the lesson.

1. Who gave the peoples of America the name "Indians"?
2. Where did the Maya Indians develop the first great Indian culture?
3. Which Indian nation developed in the western part of South America?

Know These Important Terms

American Indians	Aztec Indians
Maya Indians	Inca Indians

Know the Years of This Chapter

Look at the time line below. It shows the years of this chapter, 100 A.D. to 1500 A.D.

500 B.C.	0 100 A.D.	1500 A.D.

Temple of the Warriors atop a pyramid in Mexico. In what ways is this structure similar to the pyramids in Egypt?

EXPLORING THE TIME

Long before China, India, or the other lands of Asia became nations, some groups of people from Asia settled in North America and South America. These groups were the first to settle in the Americas. In this chapter, you will learn about these people and about the great nations they built.

The First Settlers in the Americas Arrived During the Old Stone Age

The first settlers in the Americas probably came from Asia some time during the Old Stone Age. These people who came from Asia probably reached North America by crossing over the Bering Strait.

These people from Asia gradually moved into the land of North America.

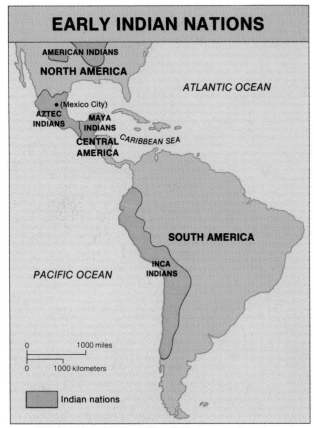

EARLY INDIAN NATIONS

AMERICAN INDIANS
NORTH AMERICA

ATLANTIC OCEAN

• (Mexico City)
AZTEC INDIANS
MAYA INDIANS
CENTRAL AMERICA
CARIBBEAN SEA

SOUTH AMERICA

PACIFIC OCEAN
INCA INDIANS

0   1000 miles

0   1000 kilometers

Indian nations

Name four early Indian nations. Where was each found?

After many years, some of these people wandered into Mexico, Central America, and South America.

Peoples of the Americas Learned How to Farm and to Tame Animals

The peoples of the Americas were able to settle down after they learned to grow their own food in the New Stone Age. The first important crops were corn, beans, and squash. Later, they learned how to grow fruits and other vegetables.

These people did not have horses, sheep, or cattle. They domesticated, or tamed, only a few animals. Among the animals that they tamed were the dog, the turkey, and the llama (LAH-muh)—a type of camel found in South America.

Columbus Named the People of the Americas "Indians"

Today, these people who came from Asia are called Indians. Are you wondering why? In 1492 A.D., Christopher Columbus, an Italian sea captain, discovered North America while sailing westward across the Atlantic Ocean. Columbus believed that he had reached some islands south of India. Therefore, he called the people he found there "Indians."

The American Indians' Culture Remained a Stone Age Culture

The **American Indians** of North America had few metal tools and weapons. Most of their tools and weapons were stone. Also, they never learned to use the wheel. Therefore, they did not develop great nations as were developed elsewhere. But three great Indian nations did develop in Mexico, Central America, and South America.

The Maya Indians Were Great Builders

The **Maya** (MY-yuh) **Indians** of Central America developed the earliest Indian culture. About the year 100 A.D., the Maya Indians began to live in city-states ruled by priests and nobles.

In Maya city-states, the most important buildings were the temples. Most Maya temples were built at the top of large pyramid-like buildings. Some of these buildings were more than 200 feet high and were covered with carvings.

The Maya Indians Worshiped Many Gods

Like other early peoples, the Maya Indians worshiped many gods. When things did not go well, the Mayas believed that the gods were angry with them. The Mayas believed that the only way to please the gods was by a human sacrifice, or by killing a human being.

The Maya Indians Were Skilled in Mathematics and Astronomy

The Maya Indians used a number system very much like ours, except that it was based on units of 20 instead of 10. The Mayas also learned to use the zero in their number system.

The Maya Indians also learned a great deal about astronomy by studying how the planets moved. This study helped them to make a calendar. In the Maya calendar, the year was 365¼ days long. It was not until the 1500's A.D. that European astronomers learned to make a calendar more accurate than the Maya calendar.

The Aztec Indians Carried on Maya Culture

Between about 900 A.D. and 1200 A.D., the Maya Indians were conquered by other Indians. Then during the early 1200's A.D., the **Aztec** (AZ-teck) **Indians** built a great nation. The capital city of the Aztec Indians was located where Mexico City is today.

The Aztecs built a major empire which exhibited outstanding accomplishments in the development of architecture, agriculture, education, and the arts. Like the Maya Indians, the Aztecs also sacrificed human beings in order to please their gods.

GEOGRAPHY AND HISTORY

Suspension Bridge. Part of the Inca Highway.

The Inca Empire included what is now Peru and extended along the high Andes (AN-deez) Mountains. To unify the empire, the Inca rulers built thousands of miles of roads through the Andes and along the Pacific coast.

The mountain highway was about 3,250 miles long. This is longer than the eastern seacoast of the United States from Maine to Florida. Road building in the mountains was a challenge. In places, the Inca Indians had to cut steps into the steep mountainsides. To help shorten routes, they built bridges to cross rivers and gorges. Some of these were hanging bridges made of ropes.

To make highway travel easier, the Inca Indians placed distance markers, supply houses, and resting places along the way. Messengers and soldiers could travel two hundred miles on foot in a single day.

Question: Through what mountains did the Inca Highway pass?

Aztec calendar carved in stone

The large Inca Empire was divided into districts, or parts. Good roads and bridges tied the Inca Empire together. Inca runners carried messages along these roads to all parts of the Inca Empire. Inns and forts were located along these Inca roads. By building good roads and bridges, and by using runners to carry messages throughout the empire, the Inca rulers met the communication and transportation challenges they faced.

The Inca Indians Were Farmers, Builders, and Artisans

Most of the Inca Indians were farmers on government-owned land. Other people took care of llama herds, were artisans, or worked in gold and silver mines. Each year, all workers had to give some of their earnings to the Inca government.

The Inca Indians were fine artisans. Their pottery, woven cloth, and metal work were very beautiful. The Inca Indians were also good builders. Some of their buildings were as large as the Egyptian pyramids.

SUMMING UP

The peoples who first settled the Americas came from Asia. Some of these people later started the great Indian nations of Mexico, Central America, and South America—the Maya, Aztec, and Inca nations. Most of the people in these nations were farmers. But these great Indian nations developed rich cultures. In the next chapter, which begins Unit 11, you will return to Europe and Asia and read about a long war that was fought between many of the Christian nations and the Muslim lands.

The Aztec Indians Were Fighters and Traders

The Aztec Indians successfully conquered many other Indian groups and forced them to pay taxes to the Aztec government in gold, cotton, and other valuable products. The Aztecs used these products to make jewelry, cloth, and tools. Then Aztec traders sold these finished goods all over Central America.

The Inca Indians Built a Strong Nation

In the western part of South America, another great Indian nation developed—the **Inca** (INK-uh) **Indians.** The Inca ruler had great power and was also worshiped as a god. The ruler owned all the land in the Inca Empire. Two challenges the Inca rulers faced were to provide for good communication and transportation throughout the Inca empire.

UNDERSTANDING THE LESSON

Do You Know These Important Terms?

For each sentence below, choose the term that best completes the sentence.

1. The early people from Asia who settled in the Americas were called (**Malaysians/ American Indians**).
2. The (**Maya Indians/Inca Indians**) of Central America developed the earliest Indian culture.
3. The (**Aztec Indians/Pueblo Indians**) built a great nation in Mexico.
4. The (**Inca Indians/Sioux Indians**) developed a great Indian nation in western South America.

Do You Remember These People and Events?

1. Tell something about each of the following subjects.

American Indians   **Aztec Indians**
Maya Indians   **Inca Indians**

2. Explain how or why each of the following developments took place.

   a. The people who came from Asia and settled in the Americas were called Indians.
   b. The Maya Indians were skilled in mathematics and astronomy.
   c. The Inca Indians developed a well-organized empire.

Can You Locate These Places?

Use the map on page 284 to locate the following places. Tell how each place is related to developments in this chapter.

Central America   **South America**
Mexico City   **North America**

Do You Know When It Happened?

About what year did the Maya Indian nation begin to develop?

Do You Remember the Main Idea?

Which one of the following ideas is the MAIN IDEA of this chapter?

1. The Americas were settled by people from Asia. Later, some of these people built great Indian nations in Mexico, Central America, and South America.
2. The American Indians were not important, because most of them did not develop beyond their Stone Age cultures. The Maya Indians were the most important of these peoples.
3. The Inca Indians of South America built a well-organized nation.

What Do You Think?

From what you have read in this chapter, try to answer the following thought questions.

1. How do you think that the earliest settlement of the Americas by the Indians took place?
2. Why do you think that the American Indians in North America were not able to build a great empire?
3. What present-day people of the Americas do you think have been most affected by the early Indian cultures? Give reasons for your answer.

Unit 11
The Development of the Near East, Asia, and Africa

THE CHAPTERS IN UNIT 11 ARE

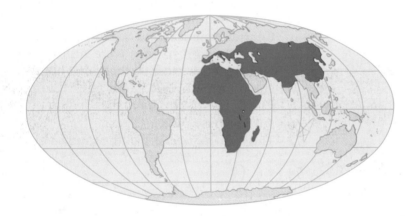

Wars always have been an important part of history. In the later years of the Middle Ages, the Christian nations of Europe fought against the Muslims to try to win the Near East. The Muslims also won control of many lands in Asia during these same years. In this unit, you will learn about these developments. You also will study some of the early kingdoms of Africa.

Warfare in the Middle Ages

288

Chapter 43
The Wars of the Crusades

GETTING STARTED

1 You have already read about the growing importance of the Roman Catholic Church in Europe during the Middle Ages. You have also read about the spread of the Muslim religion and the growth of the Muslim Empire in the Near East, in northern Africa, and even in Spain. And in 640 A.D., the Muslim Empire also conquered the Holy Land in Palestine, which was the birthplace of the Christian religion.

Between 1095 A.D. and 1300 A.D., the Christians of Europe fought wars to try to win back the Holy Land from the Muslims. These wars between the Christians and Muslims helped to bring an end to the Middle Ages in Europe.

2 Before you begin reading the chapter lesson, survey the lesson. Begin your survey by reading the beginning of the lesson. Then look through the lesson and read the headings. Next, study the pictures and read the picture captions. Then study the map of the routes of the Crusaders on page 292. Finally, read the review section called "Summing Up" at the end of the lesson. This survey will help you to discover the important ideas in this chapter.

Know the Main Idea

As you read the chapter lesson, try to remember the following important MAIN IDEA of the chapter.

The wars of the Crusades were fought to free the Holy Land from the Muslims. Most of the Crusades failed, but they had many important results for Europe.

The following questions will help you to understand the MAIN IDEA. Try to answer these questions as you read the lesson.

1. Who organized the First Crusade against the Muslims?
2. Why was it necessary to have more than one Crusade?
3. What Italian cities grew rich from the trade that developed as a result of the Crusades?

Know These Important Terms

Holy Land   Council of Clermont
Crusades

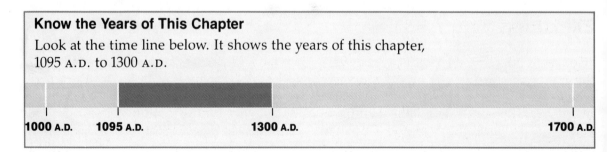

Know the Years of This Chapter

Look at the time line below. It shows the years of this chapter, 1095 A.D. to 1300 A.D.

| 1000 A.D. | 1095 A.D. | 1300 A.D. | 1700 A.D. |

A castle in Syria used by Christian Crusaders during their fight to free the Holy Land from the Muslims. What do you think the castle's windows were used for?

EXPLORING THE TIME

"God wills it!" These exciting words were the cry of thousands of Christian soldiers who set out from Europe for the **Holy Land** in the year 1095 A.D. The Holy Land was Palestine, the birthplace of the Christian religion. But the Holy Land was now ruled by the Muslims, who had conquered it in 640 A.D. Beginning in 1095 A.D., the Christians fought **Crusades,** or religious wars, to try to win back the Holy Land from the Muslims. In this chapter, you will read how the Crusades began and how they ended.

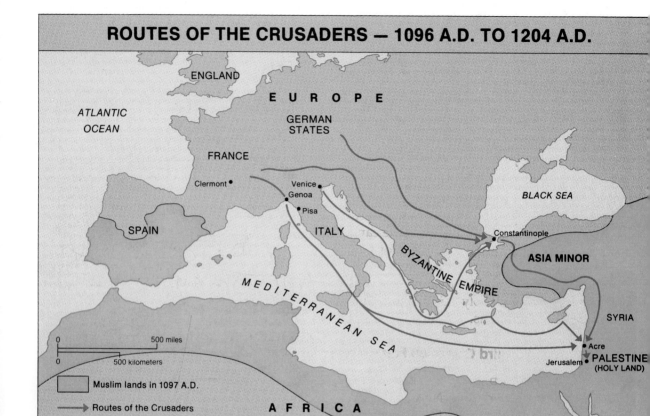

ROUTES OF THE CRUSADERS — 1096 A.D. TO 1204 A.D.

Which cities did the Crusaders who were traveling overland from Europe pass through on their way to the Holy Land?

The Muslim Lands and Christian Lands Were at War

Fighting between Christians and Muslims had gone on for hundreds of years in Spain, the Mediterranean islands, and the Byzantine Empire. During the 1000's A.D., the Christians were winning in Spain and the western Mediterranean islands. However, the Byzantine Empire faced danger from the Turks, a group of Muslims who had conquered Syria, Palestine, and most of Asia Minor. This led the Byzantine emperor to ask Pope Urban the Second for help.

The Pope Asked for a Crusade Against the Muslims

Pope Urban the Second was the leader of the Roman Catholic Church. He believed that all Europe must fight the Turks to win back the Holy Land. Therefore, he called a meeting—the **Council of Clermont**—in France in 1095 A.D. At the Council of Clermont, the Pope asked for a Crusade, or a holy war, against the Muslims. The name "crusade" came from the cross worn on the Christian soldiers' uniforms in these wars.

The Pope told the Council of Clermont that Christians in the Holy Land were being persecuted, or treated cruelly, by the Turks. The Pope promised to forgive the sins of Europeans who went to fight in this Crusade against the Turks. He also urged that the feudal knights stop fighting among themselves and instead fight together in a war against the Muslims.

The First Crusade Was Successful

About fifteen thousand fighting men left Europe in 1095 A.D. to fight in the First Crusade. By 1096 A.D., the Crusaders reached Constantinople, the Byzantine capital city. From there, they marched toward the Holy Land. By 1099 A.D., Syria and Palestine (the Holy Land) were conquered and Jerusalem (the Holy City) again belonged to the Christians.

The Second and Third Crusades Failed

However, by 1147 A.D., the Muslims recaptured some of the land of the Near East held by the Christians. This led to the Second Crusade, which was fought to defend Jerusalem. But the Second Crusade failed.

In 1187 A.D., Saladin (SAL-uh-DIN), a great Muslim ruler, reconquered Jerusalem. Two years later, three European kings— Frederick Barbarossa (BAR-buh-ROSS-uh) of Germany, Philip Augustus of France, and Richard the Lion-Hearted of England—led the Third Crusade. But this Crusade failed, too. However, King Richard of England did succeed in getting the Muslim ruler, Saladin, to allow Christians to visit Jerusalem to worship.

Later Crusades Also Failed

A Fourth Crusade took place from 1202 A.D. to 1204 A.D. But in this Crusade, the city of Venice (VENN-us), Italy, led the Crusaders to

PEOPLE IN HISTORY

Eleanor of Aquitaine

Eleanor of Aquitaine was an important person in the politics of Europe during the 12th century. She was married first to the King of France, and later to the King of England. She also lived to see two of her sons reign as kings of England.

When Eleanor was 15, her father died and she inherited Aquitaine, a large and powerful part of France. Within a month of her father's death, Eleanor married the heir to the throne of France, who soon became King Louis VII. After they were divorced, Eleanor married Henry Plantagenet who would soon become Henry II, King of England. This very strong-willed husband did not allow Eleanor to have the kind of political power she had had in France. As a result, she worked through her children, setting them against their father. Their plot to overthrow Henry failed and Henry imprisoned Eleanor. She remained in prison for 15 years, until Henry's death.

Eleanor regained her political influence when her son Richard and, later, John became King of England.

Question: How did Eleanor of Aquitaine regain her power?

293

A drawing of the way Venice, Italy, looked in the Middle Ages

attack Constantinople instead of the Holy Land! The Crusaders captured Constantinople and divided the Byzantine Empire among themselves. And the city of Venice now replaced Constantinople as the leading trading city in the Mediterranean area.

Several other Crusades were fought later to reconquer the Holy Land, but all of them failed. In 1291 A.D., the Muslims recaptured the last part of the Holy Land still held by the Christians. The Muslims now controlled most of the lands in the Near East and northern Africa.

The Crusades Had Important Results

The Crusades failed to win back the Holy Land for the Christians, but the Crusades were important for other reasons. The Crusades made the Pope and the Roman Catholic Church stronger. The Crusades also cut down the power of feudal nobles in Europe and helped to build up the power of Europe's rulers. This happened because many nobles lost their lands and their lives during the Crusades. The Crusades also helped to make European trading cities and towns more important. Some of these towns grew rich from selling supplies and lending money to the Crusaders.

But probably the most important result of the Crusades was the increase in trade and in the exchange of ideas between Europe and Asia. During the Crusades, ships from the Italian seaports of Venice, Genoa (JENN-oh-UH), and Pisa (PEE-zuh) carried spices, drugs, carpets, fine cloth, and many other products from Asia back to Europe. Europeans now learned about these products for the first time. And some Europeans also learned many Muslim ideas during the Crusades. These Muslim ideas were important in spreading learning in Europe.

SUMMING UP

The Crusades began as wars to win back the Holy Land for the Christians. At first the Crusaders were successful. But later, most of the land in the Near East conquered by European Christians was recaptured by the Muslims.

However, the Crusades had many important results. The Crusades helped the Roman Catholic Church and the rulers of Europe to become more powerful. The Crusades also resulted in greater trade and in the exchange of ideas between Europe and Asia. In the next chapter, you will read more about the history of China.

UNDERSTANDING THE LESSON

Do You Know These Important Terms?

1. The birthplace of the Christian religion was the (**Byzantine Empire/Holy Land**).
2. Religious wars fought between Christians and Muslims were called (**Campaigns/Crusades**).
3. The meeting at which the Pope organized the first holy war against the Muslims was called the (**Council of Clermont/Council of Constantinople**).

Do You Remember These People and Events?

1. Tell something about each of the following persons.

   Pope Urban the Second   Saladin
   Frederick Barbarossa
   Richard the Lion-Hearted
   Philip Augustus

2. Explain how or why each of the following developments took place.

   a. The First Crusade was organized.
   b. The Crusades cut down the power of the feudal nobles in Europe.
   c. The Crusades led to an increase in trade and the exchange of ideas between Europe and Asia.

Can You Locate These Places?

Use the map on page 292 to do the following map work.

1. Locate each of the places in the following list. Tell how each place is related to the developments in this chapter.

   Palestine   Jerusalem

   Genoa   Venice
   Constantinople   Pisa

2. Notice the water routes used by the Crusaders to reach the Holy Land. How did the location of the Italian cities help them to take control of the water trade routes to Asia during the Crusades?

Do You Know When It Happened?

In what year did the fighting in the First Crusade begin? In what year did the Muslims win back all of the Holy Land?

Do You Remember the Main Idea?

Which one of the following ideas is the MAIN IDEA of this chapter?

1. The Crusades were successful for the most part because they succeeded in freeing the Holy Land from the Muslims.
2. The Crusades were not successful for the most part because the Muslims kept control of the Holy Land.
3. The wars of the Crusades were fought to free the Holy Land from the Muslims. Most of the Crusades failed, but they had many important results for Europe.

What Do You Think?

From what you have read in this chapter, answer the following thought questions.

1. What were some of the reasons why Europeans joined the Crusades?
2. Which results of the Crusades do you think were the most important? Explain.
3. Do you feel that the Fourth Crusade was really a "holy war"? Why or why not?

Chapter 44
The Mongols and Mings in China

GETTING STARTED

1   About the same time that the Crusaders were trying to free the Holy Land from the Muslims, invaders from central Asia were attacking China. You may recall that the Chinese people built the Great Wall of China to keep out invaders. But in the late 1100's A.D. and early 1200's A.D., people from central Asia called Mongols invaded China. These Mongol invaders caused important changes in China.

2   Before you begin reading the chapter lesson, survey the lesson. Begin your survey by reading the beginning of the lesson. Then look through the lesson and read the headings. Next, study the pictures and read the picture captions. Then study the map of the Mongol Empire on page 298. Finally, read the review section called "Summing Up" at the end of the lesson. This survey of the whole lesson will help you to discover the important ideas in this chapter.

Know the Main Idea

As you read the chapter lesson, try to remember the following important MAIN IDEA of the chapter.

During the 1200's A.D., China became part of the Mongol Empire. But later, the Ming dynasty overthrew the Mongols, and China ruled itself again.

The following questions will help you to understand the MAIN IDEA. Try to answer these questions as you read the lesson.

1. Who was the leader of the Mongols who conquered a great empire?
2. What were some of the things that Europeans learned from the Chinese people during the period when the Mongols ruled China?
3. What changes were made in Chinese trade when the Ming dynasty regained control of China?

Know These Important Terms

Mongols   Ming dynasty

Know the Years of This Chapter
Look at the time line below. It shows the years of this chapter, 1200 A.D. to 1644 A.D.

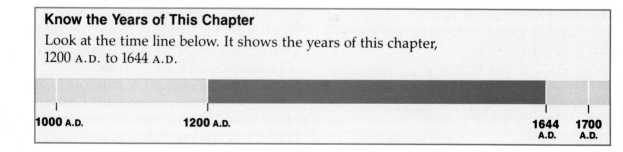

| 1000 A.D. | 1200 A.D. | 1644 A.D. | 1700 A.D. |

Mongols from central Asia invaded and conquered China

EXPLORING THE TIME

You read in Chapters 39 and 40 how China was attacked by many peoples from Asia during its long history. Some of these people succeeded in conquering parts of China, but only for a short time. In this chapter, however, you will read about a group of invading people from Mongolia called the **Mongols**, who conquered China and who then ruled China for almost a hundred years.

Invading Tribes Conquered Northern China

Perhaps you recall that China enjoyed peaceful times under the rule of the Sung dynasty, which began in about 960 A.D. However, even during these peaceful times, northern China was attacked by invading tribes. The Sung rulers tried to make these tribes leave China by offering them large amounts of money and goods. But the tribes did not leave. Slowly, northern China was taken over by the invaders.

THE MONGOL EMPIRE — ABOUT 1300 A.D.

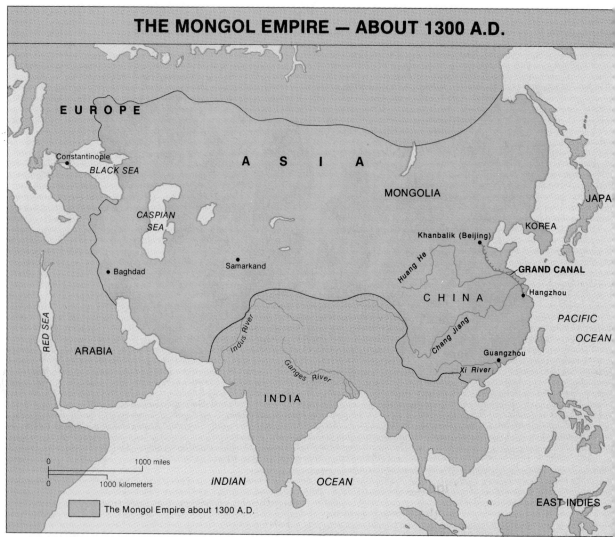

Describe the extent of the Mongol Empire.

The Mongols Built Up a Great Empire

During the late 1100's A.D. and the early 1200's A.D., the Mongols invaded China. The Mongols were tribes from Mongolia, a land in central Asia. Their leader was Genghis Khan (JENN-ghiz KAHN). Led by Genghis Khan, the Mongols built up a great empire that stretched from the eastern coast of China across Asia to eastern Europe.

China Became a Part of the Mongol Empire

By the 1220's A.D., the Mongols took over most of northern China and Korea. How did the Mongols conquer so much land in so short a time? The Mongols were so successful because they were excellent horse soldiers. They moved swiftly and attacked without warning. The Mongals were also trained to fight under great hardships, such as hunger and thirst. By the year 1279 A.D., Kublai Khan (KOO-bluh KAHN), the grandson of Genghis Khan, defeated the last Sung ruler and soon after became the emperor of China.

China Made Great Progress Under Kublai Khan

Kublai Khan was a great and wise ruler. He rebuilt Chinese cities, repaired the canals, and finished building the Grand Canal, a thousand-mile-long waterway that connected northern and southern China. Under Kublai Khan, officials were again chosen by the exam system. However, the most important government jobs were held by the Mongols.

The Mongol rulers greatly increased Chinese trade with other nations. Chinese ships traded with India, Japan, and the East Indies (the islands off southeastern Asia). China also traded by land with western Asia and Europe.

China Was Part of a Huge Empire

The Mongol Empire was the largest empire ever built in the world! And China was one of the most important nations in the Mongol Empire. Roads were built to connect China with all parts of the Mongol Empire. Chinese paper money was used all over Asia. Chinese traders settled in the important cities of the Mongol Empire. And Arab and European merchants and traders settled in China. From China, the people of Europe learned about the use of gunpowder, about the magnetic compass to show sailing directions, and about block printing.

Kublai Khan's Mongol Empire included China and most of Asia

The Mongols Were Forced to Leave China

The Mongols were not harsh rulers, but the later Mongol rulers did not rule as wisely as did Kublai Khan. The later rulers raised taxes, but they cut down important government services, such as repair of the irrigation ditches and canals. Soon, revolts against the Mongols broke out all over China. By 1368 A.D., a new Chinese dynasty, the **Ming dynasty,** forced the Mongols to leave China. The Ming dynasty then ruled China for almost three hundred years until 1644 A.D.

Chinese painting from the Ming Dynasty

The Ming Rulers Helped to Rebuild China

The Ming dynasty found China in bad condition. The Ming rulers repaired the irrigation and canal systems, rebuilt city walls, and rebuilt highways. The Ming capital city became Beijing (BAY-jying), which is still China's capital city today.

The Ming rulers brought back the Chinese system of government and ended all the Mongol laws. But the Ming dynasty favored the followers of Confucius. Therefore, the exams to fill government jobs became much more difficult than they were before. Only people who had studied the writings of Confucius were able to pass the exams.

The Ming Rulers Did Not Like Foreigners

The Ming rulers disliked foreigners, or people living in other lands, because many foreigners had helped the Mongols rule China. Therefore, the Ming rulers tried to keep all foreigners out of China. The Ming rulers forbade Chinese ships to sail to other countries. The Chinese people themselves were forbidden to leave China. Some foreign traders were allowed to enter China, but they were allowed to settle only in certain seaport cities. However, foreign products were very welcome in China. Corn, peanuts, sweet potatoes, and tobacco were all first brought to China during the Ming period.

SUMMING UP

For about one hundred years (from 1279 A.D. to 1368 A.D.), China was part of the Mongol Empire. During this time, China traded more and exchanged more ideas with the rest of the world than it ever had before. In 1368 A.D., the Ming dynasty overthrew the Mongols. During the Ming dynasty, China's government followed Confucius' ideas, and foreigners were not welcome. However, many foreign products were brought to China in this period. In the next chapter, you will learn about a great Muslim empire that grew up and developed in India.

UNDERSTANDING THE LESSON

Do You Know These Important Terms?

For each sentence below, choose the term that best completes the sentence.

1. Invaders from Mongolia, a land in central Asia, were called (**Mongols/Khans**).
2. The (**Chin dynasty/Ming dynasty**) succeeded in regaining control of China from the Mongols.

Do You Remember These People and Events?

1. Tell something about each of the following subjects.

   Genghis Khan   **Ming dynasty**
   Kublai Khan

2. Explain how or why each of the following developments took place.

   a. China became part of the huge Mongol Empire.
   b. The Mongol rulers greatly increased Chinese trade with other nations.
   c. The Ming rulers tried to keep foreigners out of China.

Can You Locate These Places?

Use the map on page 298 to do the following map work.

1. Locate each of the following places. Tell how each place is related to the developments in this chapter.

   Mongolia   **China**
   Korea   **Europe**
   India   **Japan**

2. Notice how much land was controlled by the Mongol Empire. About how many miles was the Mongol Empire from east to west? from north to south? (Use the scale of miles on the map to answer these questions.)
3. Why do you think that Japan did not become part of the Mongol Empire?

Do You Know When It Happened?

Why is the following year important in Chinese history?

   1368 A.D.

Do You Remember the Main Idea?

Which one of the following ideas is the MAIN IDEA of the chapter?

1. China became a part of the huge Mongol Empire and built up trade with many parts of the world.
2. During the 1200's A.D., China became part of the Mongol Empire. But later, the Ming dynasty overthrew the Mongols, and China ruled itself again.
3. During the Ming dynasty, people in Europe learned many things from the Chinese because trade flowed freely.

What Do You Think?

From what you have read in this chapter, try to answer the following questions.

1. What kind of ruler was Kublai Khan? Explain your answer.
2. Which Chinese products or ideas do you think that Europeans found most valuable? Why?
3. How do you think that the strict Ming rules to keep foreigners out of China affected the Chinese people?

Chapter 45
The Mogul Empire in India

GETTING STARTED

1   Did you ever hear the word "mogul" used to describe anyone? A "mogul" is a person who is great and powerful. This term came from the period in India's history when it was ruled by a people from Asia called the Moguls.

The Moguls entered India in the 1500's. The Moguls were related to the Mongols, who had ruled a great empire in Asia shortly before. The Moguls succeeded in uniting the warring states of India, and they built an empire that lasted from the early 1500's A.D. to 1707 A.D. These years are shown on the time line below.

2   Before you begin reading the chapter lesson, survey the lesson. Begin your survey by reading the beginning of the lesson. Then look through the lesson and read the headings. Next, study the pictures and read the picture captions. Then study the map of Mogul Empire in India on page 304. Finally, read the review section called "Summing Up" at the end of the lesson. This survey of the whole lesson will help you to discover the important ideas in this chapter.

Know the Main Idea

As you read the chapter lesson, try to remember the following important MAIN IDEA of the chapter.

The Moguls united all the people of India. They set up a well-organized system of government, and they produced skilled artists and builders.

The following questions will help you to understand the MAIN IDEA. Try to answer these questions as you read the lesson.

1. Who was the most famous ruler of the Moguls?
2. How was the Mogul Empire organized?
3. In what ways did the Mogul Empire become weaker after Akbar?

Know These Important Terms

Moguls	**illuminated manuscripts**
Din Illahi	**Taj Mahal**

Know the Years of This Chapter

Look at the time line below. It shows the years of this chapter, 1500 A.D. to 1707 A.D.

```
1000 A.D.                        1500 A.D.        1707 A.D.  1800 A.D.
```

The Taj Mahal in India is a tomb built by the Mogul ruler, Shah Jahan, for his wife. She died trying to give birth to their fourteenth child.

EXPLORING THE TIME

The Turkish rule of India came to an end by the early 1400's A.D. But some parts of India were still controlled by Muslim rulers. It was not until about one hundred years later that a new empire took control of India. In this chapter, you will read about the great empire that the **Moguls** (MOH-gulz) built in India during the early 1500's A.D.

The Moguls Conquered Northern India in the Early 1500's A.D.

The Turkish rule of India ended in the early 1400's A.D., and then India became divided into many states, or parts, that fought each other. In the early years of the 1500's A.D., another people from central Asia called Moguls entered northern India. Their leader was a young man named Baber (BAH-bur).

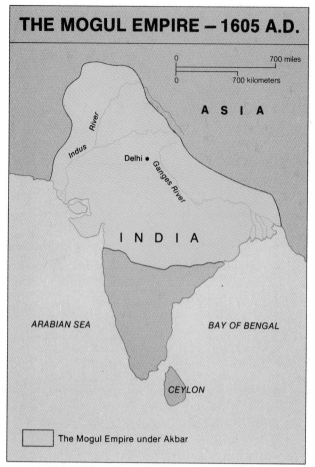

THE MOGUL EMPIRE — 1605 A.D.

0   700 miles
0   700 kilometers

ASIA

Indus River

Delhi

Ganges River

INDIA

ARABIAN SEA

BAY OF BENGAL

CEYLON

The Mogul Empire under Akbar

Into which body of water does the Ganges River flow? the Indus River?

The Moguls were related to the Mongols, and Baber himself believed that he was related to Genghis Khan, the first Mongol emperor of China. Within a few years, Baber conquered most of the states in northern India, and Delhi (DELL-EE) again became the capital city of northern India.

Akbar the Great Built the Mogul Empire

The most famous Mogul ruler was Akbar (ACK-bahr) the Great, the grandson of Baber. Akbar ruled from 1556 A.D. to 1605 A.D. During these years, Akbar conquered all of northern and most of central India.

Under Akbar, the Mogul Empire in India reached its greatest power. Akbar set up special departments to take charge of the law courts and public buildings, and also to take care of other government matters. Akbar himself was the leader of the Mogul army, and he kept it powerful and well trained.

Akbar's empire was governed well. The Mogul Empire was divided into states, and these states were divided into districts. Governors ruled the states, and other government officials ruled the districts, the large cities, and the villages. All these officials were paid by the emperor, and they took orders from the emperor.

Akbar also set up fair taxes. Farmers had to pay a tax that was equal to one-third of the value of their crops. Under later rulers, each village was taxed a certain amount, and each farmer in the village had to pay a share of this amount.

Akbar's government worked well as long as he was emperor. But the later Mogul rulers who followed him were less interested in honest and fair government. However, Akbar's government system continued to operate in India long after he died.

Akbar Tried to Unite All the People of India

Akbar was a Muslim, but he won the support of the Hindus in India because he allowed them to worship as they wished. Akbar also ended the special taxes that Hindus had to pay. And he chose Hindus to serve in high offices in the government.

Akbar became interested in many religions. He even encouraged people of all religions in India to explain their beliefs to him. Then, in 1582 A.D., Akbar began a new religion, the **Din Illahi** (DINN uh-LAH-hee), or "divine faith." Akbar's "divine faith" was a mixture of all of India's religions. He hoped to unite, or bring together, all the people of India with this new religion. But few people in India were interested in Akbar's new religion, and it soon disappeared.

The Mogul Empire Was a Great Period of Art and Building in India

Akbar and many of the Mogul rulers who followed him encouraged the work of artists. Many of these artists made beautiful colored pictures for books that are called **illuminated manuscripts.** The Mogul rulers also built many palaces, forts, mosques, or Muslim temples. The most famous Mogul building is the **Taj Mahal** (TAHJH muh-HAHL), a beautiful tomb built by a Mogul ruler for his wife. The Taj Mahal, like many other buildings of the Mogul period, was surrounded with gardens, fountains, and pools. But as the Mogul Empire began to weaken, the art of the Mogul period began to lose its fine beauty.

The Mogul Empire Weakened and Finally Ended in 1707 A.D.

Unlike Akbar, the later Mogul rulers did not allow religious freedom. Instead, they again made the Muslim religion the official religion of India. Hindu temples were destroyed, Hindu officials were removed from government offices, and Hindus again were forced to pay special taxes.

The later Mogul rulers also fought many costly wars. The taxes to pay for these wars were so high that many farmers in India gave up farming and became bandits. These bandits often attacked traders who

PEOPLE IN HISTORY

Malik Ambar

One of the greatest Muslim heroes of India was Malik Ambar (MAH-lick AHM-bahr), who lived from 1546 A.D. to 1626 A.D. What most people do not know is that Malik Ambar started life as a slave.

Malik Ambar's master was the leader of a small state located in western India. Malik Ambar's master soon gave him freedom, and Malik joined the army. And after a few more years, Malik became prime minister and ruler of the state.

Malik united most of the states in central India, and was able to defeat the attacks of the Mogul armies. Malik Ambar was a great government leader as well as a good general. Malik Ambar treated the Hindus as well as the Muslims. Malik Ambar set up royal courts to treat all people fairly. And most important, Malik began a system of land taxes which were fair to all people. No wonder Malik Ambar is still regarded as a great ruler in India today.

Question: To which religion did Malik Ambar belong?

Paintings showing Shah Jahan (left) and Akbar the Great (right)

traveled from one part of India to another. As a result, trade became too dangerous to carry on.

The Mogul Empire slowly weakened. Finally, about 1707 A.D., the Persians captured and destroyed Delhi, the capital city. The Mogul Empire was then divided into many independent states ruled either by the Muslims or the Hindus.

SUMMING UP

The Mogul Empire's greatest ruler was Akbar. Akbar tried to unite all the people of India. He set up a good system of government in India, and the government ruled India well.

However, the Mogul rulers who followed Akbar helped to weaken the Mogul Empire in India by treating the Hindus badly and by fighting many costly wars. Today, the Mogul Empire is remembered best for its many fine artists and beautiful buildings. In the next chapter, you will read about some of the early kingdoms, including Cush and Aksum, that grew and developed in the lands of Africa.

UNDERSTANDING THE LESSON

Do You Know These Important Terms?

For each sentence below, choose the term that best completes the sentence.

1. People from central Asia who conquered India during the early 1500's A.D. were called **(Mongols/Moguls)**.
2. **(Din Illahi/Buddhism)** was a mixture of all of India's religions.
3. In India, books full of colorful pictures were called **(illuminated manuscripts/ encyclopedias)**.
4. The **(Santa Sophia/Taj Mahal)** was a beautiful building in India.

Do You Remember These People and Events?

1. Tell something about each of the following people.

    Baber   Akbar

2. Explain how each of the following developments took place.

    a. Akbar set up a well-organized system of government in India.
    b. The Mogul Empire was finally divided into many states.
    c. The years of the Mogul Empire were a period of art and building in India.

Can You Locate These Places?

Use the map on page 304 to do the following map work.

1. Locate each of the following places. Tell how each place is related to the developments in this chapter.

    Delhi   India

2. Near what river in India is Delhi located?
3. Name the bodies of water along the coast of India.

Do You Know When It Happened?

Why is the following period of years important in India's history?

1500's A.D. to 1707 A.D.

Do You Remember the Main Idea?

Which one of the following ideas is the MAIN IDEA of this chapter?

1. The greatest contribution made by the Moguls to India was a well-organized system of government.
2. The Mogul rulers were weak and unfair. Soon their empire was broken into many separate states.
3. The Moguls united all the people of India. They set up a well-organized system of government, and they produced skilled artists and builders.

What Do You Think?

From what you have read in this chapter, try to answer the following thought questions.

1. How did Akbar's ideas about government and religion show that he was a great ruler?
2. In what ways were the rulers who came after Akbar weak rulers?
3. Which do you think is more important for a nation—to have a strong, well-organized government or to produce great art and buildings? Give reasons for your answer.

Chapter 46

The Early African Kingdoms

GETTING STARTED

1 In Chapter 1, you read that archeologists recently discovered in East Africa the remains of the earliest people on earth. So far, these clues seem to tell us that the people of Africa may have the oldest history of all the people in the world.

You also have read about many events that happened in northern Africa. This chapter tells about the history of Africa south of the Sahara Desert in eastern and western Africa. Between the years 700 B.C. and 1600 A.D. (see the time line below), many African kingdoms grew up south of the Sahara Desert.

2 Before you begin reading the chapter lesson, survey the lesson. Begin your survey by reading the beginning of the lesson. Then look through the lesson and read the headings. Next, study the pictures and read the picture captions. Then study the map which shows the early African kingdoms on page 310. Finally, read the review section called "Summing Up" at the end of the lesson. This survey of the whole lesson will help you to discover the important ideas in this chapter.

Know the Main Idea

As you read the chapter lesson, try to remember the following important MAIN IDEA of the chapter.

Important Black kingdoms developed in early Africa. These kingdoms had strong governments, traded with other nations, and were rich and powerful.

The following questions will help you to understand the MAIN IDEA. Try to answer these questions as you read the lesson.

1. What were the names of some of the earliest kingdoms that grew up in Africa south of the Sahara Desert?
2. What kingdom in Africa was the largest and most powerful?
3. With whom did the African people of the Swahili city-states trade?

Know These Important Terms

converted   Swahili

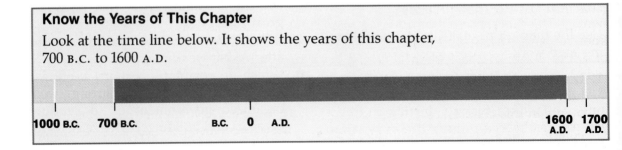

Know the Years of This Chapter

Look at the time line below. It shows the years of this chapter, 700 B.C. to 1600 A.D.

| 1000 B.C. | 700 B.C. | B.C. | 0 A.D. | 1600 A.D. | 1700 A.D. |

Early African brass plaque

EXPLORING THE TIME

Africa used to be called the "dark continent." This meant that very little was known about Africa—particularly that part of Africa south of the Sahara Desert. But today we know much more about Africa. And we have learned that Africa has had a long, remarkable history. In this chapter, you will read about some of the early kingdoms that developed in the lands of Africa.

The Kingdom of Cush Developed South of Egypt

You already studied some African history when you read about Egypt and other lands of northern Africa. From its earliest days, Egypt traded with other parts of Africa. The Egyptians started the colony of Cush (KUSH) along the Nile River, far to the south of Egypt. The Cushites traded with Egypt, and they provided the Egyptians with gold, ivory, ebony (black wood), cattle, animal

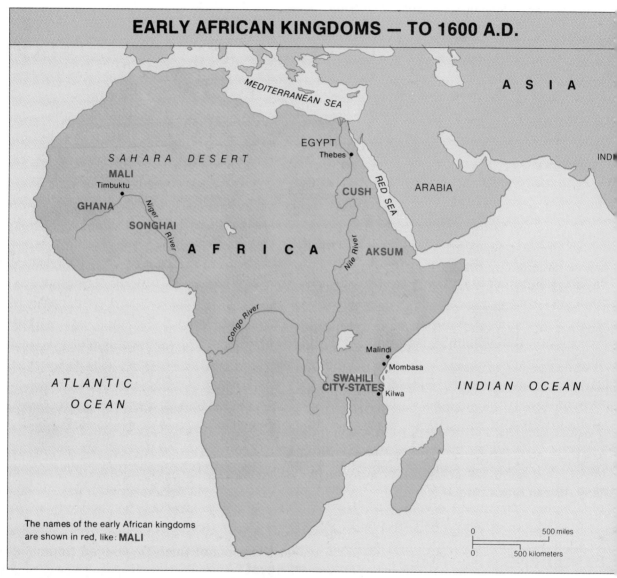

EARLY AFRICAN KINGDOMS — TO 1600 A.D.

MEDITERRANEAN SEA

ASIA

SAHARA DESERT

EGYPT

Thebes

IND

MALI

Timbuktu

CUSH

RED SEA

ARABIA

GHANA

SONGHAI

Niger River

AFRICA

Nile River

AKSUM

Congo River

ATLANTIC

OCEAN

Malindi

Mombasa

SWAHILI
CITY-STATES

Kilwa

INDIAN OCEAN

The names of the early African kingdoms
are shown in red, like: **MALI**

| 0 | 500 miles |
| 0 | 500 kilometers |

Name two early African kingdoms near the Red Sea.

skins, and slaves. The Cushites also traded with Greece and Rome.

During the 700's B.C., Cush split off from Egypt and became an independent nation. In the late 700's B.C., the Cushite ruler became powerful enough to rule all of Egypt. But after about fifty years, the Cushites were forced out of Egypt by the Assyrians. The kingdom of Cush, however, lasted for about a thousand years more.

The Cushites had a well-developed culture. They learned how to make iron weapons and tools. Much of the Cush culture came from Egypt. The Cushites built pyramids and developed a style of writing like Egyptian picture writing.

Cush Was Conquered by Aksum

In the 300's A.D., Cush was conquered by the nearby kingdom of Aksum (ahk-SOOM). The rulers of Aksum were related to the early Egyptians. Today, Aksum is called Ethiopia (EE-thee-OH-pee-UH).

The people of Aksum were **converted,** or changed to, the Christian religion by missionaries from Egypt during the 300's A.D. And most Ethiopians today are still Christians. The Ethiopians traded with many nations. In the Early Middle Ages, their products were traded as far away as India and China.

The Kingdom of Ghana Ruled West Africa

The Cushites were not the only people who used iron for making tools and weapons. A group of people who lived in the West African kingdom of Ghana (GAH-nuh) also knew how to make iron weapons and tools.

By the 700's A.D., Ghana, which was then located northwest of where the nation of Ghana is today, had become an important kingdom. Other African peoples near Ghana did not have such excellent tools and weapons. The use of iron helped Ghana to conquer other peoples and to become a powerful nation.

Ghana traded with northern Africa. It traded gold and slaves in exchange for salt and many other products. Ghana grew rich and powerful from this trade and also from the taxes paid by its people. One of its important kings was Bassi (BAH-see). But in the 1200's A.D., Ghana was destroyed by the empire of Mali (MAH-lee).

GEOGRAPHY AND HISTORY

Mansa Musa (seated)

Mali was one of the strongest and richest kingdoms in Africa. It controlled gold mines and the caravan trade between North Africa and the Sudan. From its main city of Timbuktu, caravan routes headed north and northeast across the Sahara to important trading points in Egypt and along the Mediterranean Sea.

The merchants of Mali traded gold for salt and for products that Arab traders brought from Europe and Asia. The gold was eagerly sought by the Arabs and by Europeans.

News of Mali's wealth spread far and wide. In the early 1400's, the ruler of Mali was Mansa Musa (MAHN-sah MOO-sah). Mali was a Muslim kingdom, and Mansa Musa decided to go to Mecca, the Muslim holy city. On his trip, he took along thousands of slaves and a caravan of gold. He gave away pieces of gold as gifts. An artist in Europe drew a map of Mali about this time. In the center of the map was Mansa Musa offering gold to a man on a camel.

Question: Why was the caravan trade important?

African sculpture from 1500's A.D. Describe the pattern of the headdress.

The Mali Empire Became World Famous

At its greatest, the Mali Empire stretched over a thousand miles from east to west. The Mali Empire lasted for three hundred years. The Mali rulers were Muslims. Several of them made a trip to the holy city of Mecca.

During the late 1200's A.D., Mali was badly ruled. However, in 1307 A.D., Mali's greatest ruler, Mansa Musa (MAHN-sah MOO-sah), became its ruler. Musa encouraged trade, art, and learning in the empire. Under Musa's rule, Mali was the richest empire in Africa.

The huge Mali Empire was divided into provinces, or parts. Each province was ruled by governors who were appointed by the Mali ruler. During the 1300's A.D. and 1400's A.D., Mali had one of the best-organized governments in the world.

Mali had many trading cities, but its main city was Timbuktu (tim-BUCK-too). Timbuktu had many stores, workshops, and large mosques (Muslim temples).

The Songhai Empire Conquered Mali

The Mali Empire—like many other empires —slowly lost its power. By the late 1400's A.D., the kingdom of Songhai (SOWNG-hy) captured Timbuktu, Mali's main city.

The Songhai rulers were Muslims. The most famous Songhai ruler was Askia (AHS-kee-UH) the Great. Askia divided the government into departments that were like the ones formed nearly four hundred years later in the United States government. Then in 1591 A.D., the Songhai Empire was destroyed by Arab invaders.

The Swahili City-States Ruled in Eastern Africa

Between 1100 A.D., the people of the Swahili city-states occupied part of the eastern coast of Africa. The Swahili city-states were a group of trading cities including Mombasa, Kilwa, and Malinda. Muslin traders brought ivory, gold, and slaves from the Swahili city-states, and then shipped them to India, China, and the East Indies. The people of these city-states spoke a language called **Swahili** (swah-HEE-lee), which used both African words and Arabic words. But these cities were conquered in the early 1500's A.D. by the Portuguese, who took over their trade.

SUMMING UP

Among the many great kingdoms of early Africa were Cush, Askum (Ethiopia), Ghana, Songhai, Mali, and the Swahili city-states. Mali was the richest and the most powerful. Many of these African kingdoms had well-organized governments, traded with other nations, and were rich and powerful. In the next chapter, you will read how the Byzantine Empire ended.

UNDERSTANDING THE LESSON

Do You Know These Important Terms?

For each sentence below, choose the term that best completes the sentence.

1. Missionaries (converted/diverted) some African peoples to the Christian religion.
2. A language that used both African and Arabic words was (Swahili/Mongolian).

Do You Remember These People and Events?

1. Tell something about each of the following African rulers.

   Bassi   **Mansa Musa**
   Askia the Great

2. Explain how or why each of the following developments took place.

   a. The people of Aksum became Christians.
   b. Mali became the largest and most famous African kingdom.
   c. The Swahili city-states were conquered.

Can You Locate These Places?

Use the map on page 310 to do the following map work.

1. Locate the following place. Tell how this place is related to developments in this chapter.

   Timbuktu

2. Locate each of the following African kingdoms.

   Cush   **Ghana**
   Songhai   **Mali**
   Aksum

3. Which of the kingdoms in Africa were located in western Africa? Why were the Swahili city-states well located for trade with India, China, and the East Indies?

Do You Know When It Happened?

What are the years of this chapter?

Do You Remember the Main Idea?

Which one of the following ideas is the MAIN IDEA of this chapter?

1. Important kingdoms developed in early Africa. These kingdoms had strong governments, traded with other nations, and were rich and powerful.
2. None of the African kingdoms lasted very long, because they were conquered by the Muslims.
3. All of the African kingdoms traded with Europe and Asia. Mali was the greatest of the African trading kingdoms.

What Do You Think?

From what you have read in this chapter, try to answer the following thought questions.

1. What effect do you think the Sahara Desert had on the trade routes between Mali and northern Africa?
2. Why do you think some of the modern nations in Africa chose their names from the names of the early African kingdoms?
3. Why do you think the Portuguese became interested in the Swahili city-states?

Chapter 47
The End of the Byzantine Empire

GETTING STARTED

1   The Byzantine Empire, you may re-call, developed from the old eastern Roman Empire. The Byzantine Empire lasted for many years, but—like other empires—it finally ended.

The time line below show the years of this chapter—1050 A.D. to 1453 A.D. It was during this period that the Byzantine Empire grew weaker until it finally ended.

2   Before you begin reading the chapter lesson, survey the lesson. Begin your survey by reading the beginning of the lesson. Then look through the lesson and read the headings. Next, study the pictures and read the picture captions. Then study the map showing the end of the Byzantine Empire on page 316. Finally, read the review section called "Summing Up" at the end of the lesson. This survey of the whole lesson will help you to discover the important ideas in this chapter.

Know the Main Idea

As you read the chapter lesson, try to remember the following important MAIN IDEA of the chapter.

The Byzantine Empire helped to spread Greek culture and the Christian religion until the empire was conquered in 1453 A.D.

The following questions will help you to understand the MAIN IDEA. Try to answer these questions as you read the lesson.

1. How did the split between the Byzantine Church and the Roman Catholic Church help to weaken the Byzantine Empire?
2. In which Crusade was the city of Constantinople captured by the Crusaders?
3. Which group of people finally conquered the Byzantine Empire?

Know This Important Term

Ottoman Turks

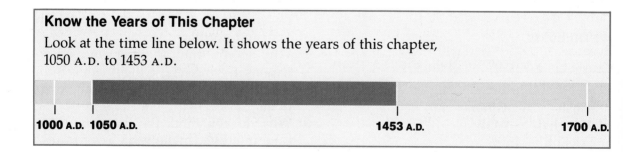

Know the Years of This Chapter

Look at the time line below. It shows the years of this chapter, 1050 A.D. to 1453 A.D.

| 1000 A.D. | 1050 A.D. | | 1453 A.D. | 1700 A.D. |

A Byzantine church in Greece

EXPLORING THE TIME

In earlier chapters, you read how the Byzantine Empire fought to protect itself and that Constantinople, the capital city of the Byzantine Empire, was captured by the Crusaders in 1204 A.D. But until 1453 A.D., the Byzantine Empire continued to make important contributions to European life. In this chapter, you will read about the Byzantine Empire and its history.

The Byzantine Empire Was Attacked by the Turks

During the middle years of the 1000's A.D., the Byzantine Empire was again attacked. This time, its main attackers were the Muslim Turks. The Turks conquered all of Asia Minor from the Byzantine Empire. However, the Byzantine army was able to defend the city of Constantinople from the attackers. But, because of the war, the Byzantine Empire was weakened.

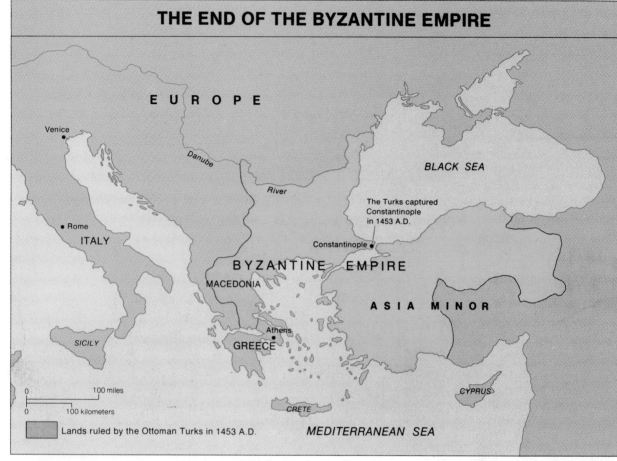

THE END OF THE BYZANTINE EMPIRE

EUROPE

Venice

Danube

River

BLACK SEA

Rome

ITALY

The Turks captured
Constantinople
in 1453 A.D.

Constantinople

BYZANTINE EMPIRE

MACEDONIA

ASIA MINOR

Athens

GREECE

SICILY

CYPRUS

0   100 miles
0   100 kilometers

Lands ruled by the Ottoman Turks in 1453 A.D.

CRETE

MEDITERRANEAN SEA

Which two continents were part of the Byzantine Empire?

The Byzantine Church Split from the Roman Catholic Church

The Byzantine Empire was further weakened because of the growing differences between the Roman Catholic Church in western Europe and the Byzantine Church in eastern Europe. The Patriarch of Constantinople, or leader of the Byzantine Church, did not wish the Pope of the Roman Catholic Church to be more powerful than the Patriarch was. A complete break between the Byzantine Church and the Catholic Church took place in 1054 A.D., when the Greek Orthodox Church split

away from the Roman Catholic Church.

This religious split weakened the Byzantine Empire even more. When the Byzantine Church was no longer a part of the Roman Catholic Church, the rulers of western Europe no longer felt that they must help the Byzantine emperors fight against the Turks. In fact, the European rulers began to think about conquering parts of the Byzantine Empire for themselves.

The Byzantine Empire Recovered Some of Its Power

In the year 1081 A.D., a powerful general

named Alexius Comnenus (uh-LECK-see-us kom-NEE-nus) became the Byzantine emperor. The Comnenus family ruled the Byzantine Empire for the next hundred years.

The Comnenus family forced the rulers of the Balkan kingdoms of Greece and Macedonia to obey them. And they recaptured most of Asia Minor from the Turks. However, the Comnenus rulers failed to win back the parts of the Byzantine Empire captured by the Crusaders.

The Byzantine Empire enjoyed a period of good times under the Comnenus rulers. The Byzantine rulers were rich enough to spend a great deal of money on building many fine palaces and churches. They also encouraged the work of artists, poets, and writers. Byzantine art, polished marble, bronze work, colorful cloth, gold and silver dishes, and fine jewelry were admired by people in western Europe.

The Byzantine Empire Was Weakened

In the 1180's A.D., however, wars broke out again in the Byzantine Empire. The empire

Byzantine emperor's crown (left) and cross (right) made of gold and jewels

became so weakened from these wars that the Crusaders in the Fourth Crusade easily captured Constantinople in 1204 A.D. After that, the Italian city of Venice obtained the right from the Byzantine rulers to trade all over the Byzantine Empire. Many European nobles even set up small kingdoms for themselves in several parts of the Byzantine Empire. And the capture of Constantinople by the Crusaders forced the Byzantine Church again to become a part of the Roman Catholic Church of western Europe.

The European Kingdoms Did Not Last

At last, it seemed as if the Byzantine Empire was ended for good. But the rulers of the small European kingdoms in the Byzantine Empire soon began fighting among themselves, and this weakened their control over the Byzantine Empire. As a result, a Byzantine prince was able to win back western Asia Minor, Greece, and some of the eastern Mediterranean islands from the European rulers.

In 1236 A.D., the Byzantine Empire tried but failed to recapture Constantinople. But twenty-five years later, a Byzantine ruler did capture the city. Within a few years, most of the European kingdoms were destroyed. And the Byzantine Empire was rebuilt again.

The Byzantine Empire Never Became Strong Again

During the next two hundred years, the Byzantine Empire continued, but it was never a strong nation again. Constantinople remained a great trading center, but most of the Byzantine trade was now controlled by Italian merchants. The Byzantine Empire was too poor to have a navy, and often it was not able to pay its army.

The Turks Captured Constantinople in 1453 A.D.

During the middle 1300's A.D., a new enemy, the **Ottoman** (AHT-uh-MUN) **Turks,** began to attack and conquer parts of the Byzantine Empire. By the middle 1400's A.D., all that remained of the Byzantine Empire was Constantinople and the land around it. Finally, in 1453 A.D., a large Turkish army defeated a small Byzantine army that was formed by the Byzantine emperor to defend the city of Constantinople. The capture of Constantinople by the Turks in 1453 A.D. finally ended the Byzantine Empire.

But, as you will read later, Russia and other nations in eastern Europe had already learned a great deal from the spread of Byzantine culture. You will also read later how Byzantine teachers helped people in western Europe again to discover Greek ideas and culture.

SUMMING UP

The Byzantine Empire recovered from many attacks and conquerors before it finally ended in 1453 A.D., when the Turks captured its main city, Constantinople. But during the thousand years that the Byzantine Empire lasted, it helped to spread the Christian religion and Greek culture into many parts of Europe. In the next chapter, which begins Unit 12, you will learn how the European nations' dealings with the Byzantine Empire and Muslim Empire helped trade to grow in western Europe.

UNDERSTANDING THE LESSON

Do You Know This Important Term?

For the sentence below, choose the term that best completes the sentence.

1. The people who were finally able to conquer the Byzantine Empire were the **(Ottoman Turks/Ottoman Persians)**.

Do You Remember These People and Events?

1. Tell something about each of the following subjects.

   Alexius Comnenus
   Comnenus rulers

2. Explain how each of the following developments took place.

   a. The Italian city of Venice obtained the right to trade in all parts of the Byzantine Empire.
   b. The Byzantine Empire was rebuilt after parts of it were controlled by small European kingdoms.
   c. The Byzantine Empire was not able to become strong again.

Can You Locate These Places?

Use the map on page 316 to do the following map work.

1. Locate each of the following places. Tell how each place is related to developments in this chapter.

   Venice   Constantinople
   Greece   Macedonia

2. Why was the city of Constantinople so important in the Byzantine Empire?

Why do you think it was difficult for the Turks to capture Constantinople?

Do You Know When It Happened?

Why is the following year an important year to remember?

   1453 A.D.

Do You Remember the Main Idea?

Which one of the following ideas is the MAIN IDEA of this chapter?

1. The Byzantine Empire was captured by armies from western Europe during the Fourth Crusade.
2. The Byzantine Empire helped to spread Greek culture and the Christian religion until the empire was conquered in 1453 A.D.
3. The Byzantine Empire lasted a thousand years. It grew too weak to protect itself after Venice's merchants were allowed to trade with it.

What Do You Think?

From what you have read in this chapter, try to answer the following thought questions.

1. Do you think the Crusaders and the leaders of western Europe were wise in deciding to conquer parts of the Byzantine Empire instead of helping to defend the Byzantine Empire from attack by the Turks? Explain your answer.
2. How can the loss of trade affect a nation?
3. Why do you think the Turks wanted to conquer the Byzantine Empire?

UNIT 12
Europe During the Later Middle Ages

THE CHAPTERS IN UNIT 12 ARE

Many changes took place in Europe during the Later Middle Ages. Towns grew larger, and trade and business increased. Strong nations with powerful rulers emerged; and important new ideas appeared in writing, science, and building. In this unit, you will find out how and why these important changes took place.

Painting showing a European town in the Later Middle Ages

320

Chapter 48
The Growth of European Trade

GETTING STARTED

1   Today, trade is a very important part of the business life of all the nations in the world. And as you have learned, those nations that traded most with other nations were able to grow and prosper.

During the Early Middle Ages, nations in western Europe grew slowly, because there was little trade. Most people in western Europe did not have the goods or the means to carry on trade. However, about 1000 A.D., trade between western Europe and other lands slowly began to increase. The Crusades and new European products helped to increase trade. This increase in trade brought many changes in Europe, as you will see.

2   Before you begin reading the chapter lesson, survey the lesson. Begin your survey by reading the beginning of the lesson. Then look through the lesson and read the headings. Next, study the pictures and read the picture captions. Then study the map showing European trade routes on page 324. Finally, read the review section called "Summing Up" at the end of the lesson. This survey will help you to discover the important ideas in this chapter.

Know the Main Idea

As you read the chapter lesson, try to remember the following important MAIN IDEA of the chapter.

Trade and business increased in Europe after 1000 A.D. as a result of the Crusades and new European products.

The following questions will help you to understand the MAIN IDEA. Try to answer these questions as you read the lesson.

1. What use did Europeans have for the spices which came from Asia?
2. At first, what kinds of products did Europeans use to trade for the things they needed from other lands?
3. How were the goods for trade carried from place to place in Europe?

Know These Important Terms

Later Middle Ages	merchants
raw materials	fairs
money changers	toll

Know the Years of This Chapter

Look at the time line below. It shows the years of this chapter, 1000 A.D. to 1500 A.D.

800 A.D.	1000 A.D.	1500 A.D.

Increased trade required "money changers" who eventually became the first bankers

EXPLORING THE TIME

When you shop in a store, you often may buy goods made in other countries as well as goods made in the United States. That is because the United States trades with nations all over the world. But during the Early Middle Ages, Europeans were able to buy only goods that were made in and around their own manors, because Europe traded very little with other nations. In this chapter, you will find out how European trade with other nations began to increase in the **Later Middle Ages,** or the years from 1000 A.D. to 1500 A.D.

Europe's Trade Never Completely Ended

Even after the end of the western Roman Empire in 476 A.D., some European trade still went on. During the feudal period, manors sometimes traded with other manors. Some European trade was carried on with the Byzantine Empire. In this important trade, spices and silk from Asia were

EUROPEAN TRADE ROUTES — 1200 A.D. TO 1400 A.D.

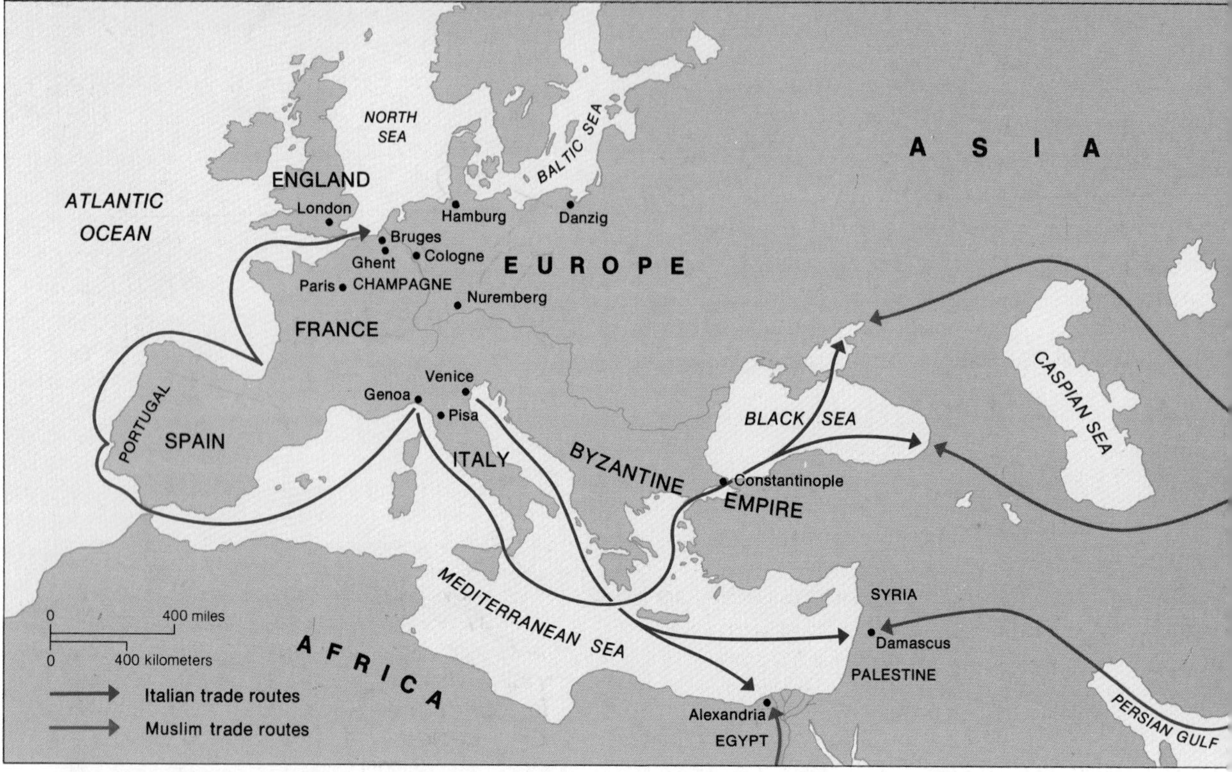

NORTH SEA

BALTIC SEA

ASIA

ATLANTIC OCEAN

ENGLAND

London

Hamburg

Danzig

Bruges

Ghent • Cologne

EUROPE

Paris • CHAMPAGNE

Nuremberg

FRANCE

PORTUGAL

SPAIN

Venice

Genoa

Pisa

ITALY

BYZANTINE

BLACK SEA

CASPIAN SEA

Constantinople

EMPIRE

MEDITERRANEAN SEA

SYRIA

Damascus

PALESTINE

AFRICA

Alexandria

EGYPT

PERSIAN GULF

| 0 | 400 miles |
| 0 | 400 kilometers |

→ Italian trade routes
→ Muslim trade routes

What means of transportation do you think was used by most Italian traders to transport their goods?

exchanged for olive oil and wine from Europe. Europeans particularly wanted spices from Asia in order to keep their food from spoiling and to make it taste better. Even after the Muslims gained control of the Mediterranean Sea, some European traders continued to trade with the Near East.

The Crusades Helped to Increase Trade with Asia

By the 1000's A.D., Europe's trade began to increase again. This happened after some European nations conquered the Mediterranean islands that were controlled by the Muslims. European traders again were able to use the Mediterranean Sea. Then, soon after that happened, the Crusades helped to increase European trade even more.

During the Crusades, men and supplies were carried back and forth between Europe and the Holy Land (Palestine). The Italian cities of Venice, Genoa, and Pisa carried on most of this trade. The Italian ships sailed across the Mediterranean Sea to the Near East and carried back to Italy the goods that came from as far away as India and China. From Italy, these goods were taken by traders to the other nations of Europe.

New European Products Helped to Increase Trade

However, in order to buy products, Europe needed products to sell. At first, Europe had only **raw materials,** or products from nature, to sell—such as hides, lumber, and furs. But later, Europeans learned how to make woolen and silk cloth, metalware, and leather goods. These products were sold by Europe to the Byzantine and Muslim empires.

The Increase in Trade Led to Trade Fairs

By the late 1300's A.D., Italian traders were sending ships through the western Mediterranean Sea around to England and northern European lands. The Italian ships carried to these lands the goods that the Italian traders brought to Europe from the Near East. The Italian ships brought back wood, furs, grain, copper, and fish from England and northern Europe.

Trade increased all over Europe. Much of the trade in Europe took place at **fairs.** The fairs were large trading meetings that lasted for several weeks. **Merchants,** or traders, came to these fairs from all over Europe. Several fairs were held each year in the province of Champagne (sham-PAIN) in northeastern France. Many other fairs took place all over Europe. Some of these fairs are still held today.

The Increased Use of Money Led to Banking

Money is needed before a large trade can be carried on. At first, only a small amount of money was used in Europe. But after trade increased, the amount of money in use also increased. Kings and nobles had coins made that were used as money.

GEOGRAPHY AND HISTORY

A Hanseatic Meeting

In the late Middle Ages, trade was increasing all over Europe and a new group of wealthy merchants appeared. But these merchants were often robbed by kings and nobles who needed money for their armies. To protect themselves, merchants in many towns decided to form the Hanseatic (HAN-see-AT-ik) League. By the 1300's, most of the important towns along the Baltic Sea and the North Sea had joined this league.

The Hanseatic League acted just like a nation. The towns that were members of the League fought wars and signed treaties. The League forced the rulers of Europe to give its merchants fair treatment. In return, the League set standards for its members. Merchants who cheated their customers were fined by the League.

For several hundred years, the merchants who belonged to the Hanseatic League were the most important in Europe. During the 1500's, however, the rise of new nations in Europe and the development of trade routes to the Americas led to the end of the Hanseatic League.

Question: What was the purpose of the Hanseatic League?

European traders often shipped their goods by boat

ers were paid for all their services. Before long, they had very large amounts of money and became bankers.

Bad Travel Conditions Made Trade Difficult

European trade increased in spite of many problems in travel. Roads in Europe were too rough for wagons. Instead, goods were carried over land by horses or mules. And Europe had very few bridges. Therefore, many merchants carried their goods by river rather than by land. Whether they traveled by land or water, merchants had to pay a **toll,** or tax, every time they crossed a noble's land, used a noble's boat, or sold goods at a noble's market. And almost always, merchants faced the danger of having their goods stolen by bandits along the way.

Sea travel was not much safer than land travel. Ships were small, and they had to sail close to land where the sea was safer. But sailing close to land was dangerous, too, because the ships might be wrecked along the shore by a strong wind. Even if merchants escaped shipwreck, they still might be in danger of attack by pirates. But in spite of all these problems, European trade began to increase.

But trading was difficult because some coins were worth more than others. A coin from Venice, for example, sometimes was worth more than four French coins. This problem was partly solved when people called **money changers** set up booths where they decided how much different coins were really worth and exchanged these coins at certain rates.

These money changers kept their money in strong boxes. Some merchants gave their money to the money changers to place in these strong boxes for safekeeping. Other merchants borrowed money from these money changers. The money chang-

SUMMING UP

In the years of the 1000's A.D., trade began to increase in Europe. The Crusades and new European products helped to increase trade. As a result of increased trade, trade fairs were held in Europe and banking developed. In the next chapter, you will find out how the towns of Europe grew as trade increased in the nations of Europe.

UNDERSTANDING THE LESSON

Do You Know These Important Terms?

For each sentence below, choose the term that best completes the sentence.

1. The last part of the Middle Ages, the years from about 1000 A.D. to 1500 A.D., is called the **(Later Middle Ages/Later Ages)**.
2. Products from nature, such as lumber, oil, and furs, are called **(resins/raw materials)**.
3. Large trading meetings which sometimes lasted for weeks were called **(bazaars/fairs)**.
4. Traders were called **(merchants/sellers)**.
5. The people who decided the value of different kinds of coins and who exchanged these coins at certain rates were called **(treasury officials/money changers)**.
6. A **(toll/debt)** was a tax that traders had to pay when they crossed a noble's land.

Do You Remember These People and Events?

1. Tell something about each of the following subjects.

   merchants   **money changers**
   pirates

2. Explain how or why each of the following developments took place.

   a. New European products helped to increase trade.
   b. The increased use of money led to banking.
   c. Travel conditions in Europe made trade difficult.

Can You Locate These Places?

Use the map on page 324 to locate the following places. Tell how each place is related to the developments in this chapter.

Venice   England   Genoa
Pisa   Champagne

Do You Know When It Happened?

What are the years of this chapter?

Do You Remember the Main Idea?

Which one of the following ideas is the MAIN IDEA of this chapter?

1. Trade and business increased in Europe after 1000 A.D. as a result of the Crusades and new European products.
2. European nations wanted to trade during the early years of the Middle Ages, but they did not have any products to offer for trade.
3. Travel conditions in western Europe were so bad that trade was not able to increase until new roads were built.

What Do You Think?

From what you have read in this chapter, try to answer the following thought questions.

1. Describe the things that might have taken place at a fair held in Europe during the 1000's A.D.
2. Why do you think that certain goods from Asia cost so much in Europe?
3. Do you think that the feudal system helped or hurt trade in western Europe? Explain your answer.

Chapter 49
The Growth of European Towns

GETTING STARTED

1 Do you think it is possible for nations to become powerful without having cities? All the great nations that you have studied so far grew up around cities. These cities were the centers of trade, government, and culture in those nations. However, during the early part of the Middle Ages, western Europe had few cities and towns, because most people lived on feudal manors. Then, between 1000 A.D. and 1500 A.D., towns began to develop and grow in western Europe. The growth of these towns, like the increase in trade, led to many important changes in western Europe.

2 Before you begin reading the chapter lesson, survey the lesson. Begin your survey by reading the beginning of the lesson. Then look through the lesson and read the headings. Next, study the pictures and read the picture captions. Finally, read the review section called "Summing Up" at the end of the lesson. This survey of the whole lesson will help you to discover the important ideas in this chapter.

Know the Main Idea

As you read the chapter lesson, try to remember the following important MAIN IDEA of the chapter.

As European trade increased, more towns and cities developed and became important.

The following questions will help you to understand the MAIN IDEA. Try to answer these questions as you read the lesson.

1. What happened to European cities after the western Roman Empire ended?
2. How did merchants' groups help European cities and towns to grow?
3. What city was the largest city in Europe about 1200 A.D.?

Know These Important Terms

civilization	apprentices
charter	journeyman
guilds	master
town council	city middle class

Know the Years of This Chapter

Look at the time line below. It shows the years of this chapter, 1000 A.D. to 1500 A.D.

800 A.D.   1000 A.D.   1500 A.D.

A walled town in Europe

EXPLORING THE TIME

The word **civilization** comes from the Roman word "civitas," or city. In early times, cities such as Athens, Rome, and Alexandria were centers of civilization, or centers of culture. But in the early part of the Middle Ages, Europe had few such centers of culture. In this chapter, you will learn how European cities began to grow and develop in the Later Middle Ages.

Some Towns Remained After the Roman Empire Ended

Cities in Europe did not disappear completely after the end of the western Roman Empire. In Italy, many of the old Roman cities remained, although they became much smaller. Outside Italy, some of the Roman cities became Church centers, where the Church leaders lived and took care of Church duties. These Church centers attracted many settlers and visitors.

Picture showing a European town receiving a charter from its lord. What did the charter provide?

New Towns Grew Up near Castles

If you remember, many castles were built during the Early Middle Ages. The German word for castle is "burg." Many of these burgs, or castles, were located in northern and eastern Europe, which did not have Roman towns. The people living near these burgs were called "burghers" (BURR-gurz), and some of these burgs soon grew larger. Slowly, these burgs became towns.

New Towns Grew Up at Good Trading Locations

When European trade began to increase about the year 1000 A.D., the Church cen-

ters and burgs that were good trading locations grew into towns. Some of these towns grew up along rivers. Some towns grew up near harbors. And some towns grew up where two roads crossed or where two rivers met.

Many Towns Won Their Freedom

However, most of Europe's towns were still ruled by a feudal lord. And the people in the towns paid taxes to the lord and worked for the lord. These duties done for the lord slowed down the growth of the businesses in the towns. To gain more freedom for their towns, some of the richer people in the towns offered their lord some money in exchange for a **charter.** A charter was a document given to a town by the lord that made the burghers, or townspeople, free people. Free people did not have to serve a lord. They were able to govern themselves. The towns that had such charters grew faster.

Some of the town charters were given by the ruler in return for taxes paid by the townspeople. During the years between 1100 A.D. and 1300 A.D., most towns received charters either from a ruler or a feudal lord.

Merchants Helped to Develop the Town Government

The new towns usually were governed by merchant **guilds** (GILDZ). A guild was a group of merchants in the same kind of business. Merchants were the first group to form guilds, starting in the 1000's A.D. Later, guilds of barbers, tailors, lawyers, and other kinds of skilled workers also developed.

The leaders of the guilds also were often the members of the **town council.** The town council made the town's laws and acted as its court. Usually, the town council passed laws that were intended to help the town's guilds.

The Guilds Controlled the Town Businesses

The guilds' main purpose was to protect workers in each kind of business. Only guild members were able to buy or sell goods or do business in town. The guilds set up rules for their own members. All guild members paid their workers the same wages. All guild members worked the same number of hours. All guild members

charged the same prices for the same goods. The guilds also tried to keep the quality of their goods at a high level.

The Guilds Had Their Own System of Training Workers

There were three classes of workers in the guilds. The beginning workers were the **apprentices** (uh-PREN-tiss-suz), or boys who were learning a skill. Apprentices received food, clothing, and shelter, but they did not receive any wages.

When an apprentice was about nineteen years old, he became a **journeyman,** or a day worker. Later, if the journeyman was

Buildings were built by members of town building guilds

skilled enough, he became a **master**—but only after having proved to be skillful enough to the guild by producing a "masterpiece," or a really fine piece of work. When a journeyman became a master, the worker usually opened a shop. In this way, guilds trained very good artisans.

European Towns Were Small and Crowded

Most European towns had small populations. In 1200 A.D. Paris was the largest town in western Europe, and its population was only about 100,000 people. Most towns were small, and they were protected by walls. Town streets were narrow, often about 10 feet wide, and the houses were built of wood. The largest buildings in a town were the church and the guild hall.

As the town's population grew, houses were built closer together, and they were often seven or eight floors high. Towns became crowded with these wooden houses, and fires often destroyed large parts of these towns.

A New Class of People Grew Up in the Towns

A new class soon grew up in the towns. This new class—the **city middle class**—was made up of the merchants of the town. Many of these new middle-class people grew rich through trade and other businesses. As you will read later, the city middle class had an important part in the development of European governments.

A middle-class town merchant's house. What signs of wealth do you see?

SUMMING UP

As European trade increased, towns became more important. The most important groups in the towns were the guilds. The guilds controlled the town governments and organized the workers in each business. Towns in the Later Middle Ages were small and crowded. And a new group, the city middle class, developed in these towns. In the next chapter, you will read about France and England during the Later Middle Ages.

UNDERSTANDING THE LESSON

Do You Know These Important Terms?

For each sentence below, choose the term that best completes the sentence.

1. The word (burg/civilization) comes from the Roman word for city.
2. A (charter/constitution) was a legal document that made townspeople free.
3. The (unions/guilds) were groups of town merchants who were in the same kind of business.
4. The leaders of the guilds were often members of the (town council/town congress), the group which made the town's laws and acted as its court.
5. Beginning workers who were learning a skill were called (apprentices/servants).
6. A (journeyman/traveling person) was a day worker who had completed the beginner's tasks of learning a trade.
7. The most highly skilled workers were called (experts/masters).
8. The merchants of a town formed a new class of people called the (city middle class/city upper class).

Do You Remember These People and Events?

1. Tell something about each of the following subjects.

   guilds   town government

2. Explain how or why each of the following developments took place.

   a. Towns were given their freedom by the feudal lords.
   b. Guilds trained their workers.
   c. Towns were small and crowded.

Can You Locate These Places?

Use the map in Chapter 48 (on page 324) to locate and name the main cities of western Europe during the Later Middle Ages.

Do You Know When It Happened?

During what years did most towns in western Europe obtain charters that gave them the right to govern themselves?

Do You Remember the Main Idea?

Which one of the following ideas is the MAIN IDEA of this chapter?

1. Guilds became important during the Later Middle Ages.
2. The towns and cities were able to grow in western Europe after they were given their freedom by the feudal lords.
3. As European trade increased, more towns and cities developed and became important.

What Do You Think?

From what you have read in this chapter, try to answer the following thought questions.

1. In what ways do you think that life in a city during the Later Middle Ages was different from city life today?
2. Do you think that the guild system of training workers is a good system to use today? Why or why not?
3. Can you think of other ways that cities and towns might be started besides the ways described in this chapter?

Chapter 50
France and England in the Later Middle Ages

GETTING STARTED

1 Did you ever wonder how two great nations in western Europe—France and England—began? They began during the Middle Ages when rulers and nobles in Europe fought each other for power. During the Early Middle Ages, if you remember, most of the rulers of Europe had little power. But by the Later Middle Ages, the rulers of France and England became much more powerful. As this happened, France and England began to develop as nations.

2 Before you begin reading the chapter lesson, survey the lesson. Begin your survey by reading the beginning of the lesson. Then look through the lesson and read the headings. Next, study the pictures and read the picture captions. Then study the map of France and England in 1180 A.D. on page 336. Finally, read the review section called "Summing Up" at the end of the lesson. This survey will help you to discover the important ideas in this chapter.

Know the Main Idea

As you read the chapter lesson, try to remember the following important MAIN IDEA of the chapter.

During the Later Middle Ages, England and France each became larger and united under strong rulers. But in England, the people also gained more rights.

The following questions will help you to understand the MAIN IDEA. Try to answer these questions as you read the lesson.

1. How much land did the ruler of France control in 987 A.D.?
2. What French conqueror increased the power of the English rulers over the feudal nobles?
3. What happened to the English monarchs' power after the Magna Carta?

Know These Important Terms

Anglo-Saxons   common law
Normans   Magna Carta
jury system

Know the Years of This Chapter

Look at the time line below. It shows the years of this chapter, 987 A.D. to 1270 A.D.

800 A.D.	987 A.D.	1270 A.D.	1500 A.D.

Reconstruction of a Late Middle Ages battle

EXPLORING THE TIME

During the years of the Early Middle Ages, many rulers did not have much real power. But by the Later Middle Ages, the rulers of France and England began to have real power. In this chapter, you will read about these rulers.

The French Rulers Began to Unite France

After the Frankish king Charlemagne died, the empire was taken over by feudal nobles. In time, the western part of this empire became known as France.

In the year 987 A.D., the French nobles chose Hugh Capet (kah-PAY) to be ruler of

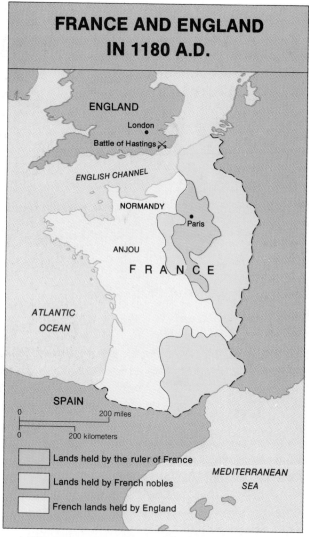

FRANCE AND ENGLAND IN 1180 A.D.

ENGLAND

London

Battle of Hastings ✕

ENGLISH CHANNEL

NORMANDY

Paris

ANJOU

F R A N C E

ATLANTIC OCEAN

SPAIN

0   200 miles

0   200 kilometers

☐ Lands held by the ruler of France

☐ Lands held by French nobles

☐ French lands held by England

MEDITERRANEAN SEA

Where was the Battle of Hastings fought?

the French court system. And Louis sent royal officials to all of the French provinces to check on the work of the local officials. Both Philip Augustus and Louis improved the government of France and helped to build France into one nation.

The Anglo-Saxons Ruled England

England, too, was becoming a nation. From the 40's A.D. to 410 A.D., England was a Roman province. After the Romans left England, tribes of Angles, Saxons, and Jutes took over the country. The Angles and Saxons slowly mixed together and became the **Anglo-Saxons.**

The most famous Anglo-Saxon king was Alfred the Great, who ruled England from 871 A.D. to 899 A.D. Alfred set up schools and encouraged learning. He also formed a code of laws and improved local governments. And a strong army and navy were built up to fight invaders.

England Was Conquered by the Normans of France

After Alfred died, the Danes—a people from northern Europe—began to conquer England. By 1042 A.D., however, the Anglo-Saxons regained power. Then in 1066 A.D., William, the Duke of the French province of Normandy, and an army of **Normans** invaded England. They defeated the Anglo-Saxons at the most famous battle in English history—the Battle of Hastings. William the Conqueror, as he was called, then became the first Norman king of England.

The Normans Increased the Power of the English Monarch

Under the Normans, life in England

France. But Capet controlled only the land around the city of Paris. Most of France was controlled by the French nobles.

When Philip Augustus became the French ruler in 1180 A.D., he was powerful enough to conquer a large part of France held by England. Included in this land were Normandy and Anjou (ahn-JOO).

From 1226 A.D. to 1270 A.D., France was ruled by Louis the Ninth. Louis improved

French, cloth picture of the Norman invasion of England

changed greatly. The most important nobles and Church leaders were Normans. And the English king gained more power over the feudal nobles.

William the Conqueror divided up the large lands owned by the Anglo-Saxons and gave these lands to Norman followers. In return, each Norman lord swore to be loyal only to the crown. As a result, the English king became much more powerful.

The Jury System and Common Law Developed in England

About a hundred years after the Normans conquered England, Henry the Second (who ruled from 1154 A.D. to 1189 A.D.) set up law courts to replace the courts of the nobles and the Church. Serious crimes, such as murder, were now tried only in the royal courts by royal judges.

Henry also developed the **jury system.** A jury was a group of people chosen to report to a royal judge the names of people who might be guilty of crimes. The judge decided if each person was innocent or guilty. Later on, the jury members themselves decided if a person was guilty or innocent. And the judge decided how to punish a guilty person.

When the royal judges decided cases, they wrote down their decisions. After many years, all of these written decisions became known as the English **common law.** The common law was the beginning of the idea of equal justice for all English citizens.

HIGHLIGHTS IN HISTORY

King John Signing the Magna Carta

King John ruled England over seven hundred years ago. He was such an unpopular king that no other English king has used the name John since then. Yet—in spite of himself—John did do one thing that helped bring freedom to millions of people. On June 15, 1215 A.D., John was forced to grant the English nobles the Magna Carta, or Great Charter.

The Magna Carta listed certain rights, which John promised to respect. At first most of these rights were only given to the English nobles. Many years later, however, these rights were slowly granted to all English citizens. And when English citizens settled in America and in other parts of the world, they carried these rights with them.

Many American freedoms, such as the right to have a trial by jury and the right to have a say about the taxes we pay, are based on the Magna Carta. In this way, Americans, too, owe thanks to King John.

Question: In what year was the Magna Carta granted?

The English Nobles Won Rights from the Monarch

Another important development in English government took place under King John, the son of Henry the Second. John was an unpopular ruler because he refused to allow the English nobles to have more power. In 1215 A.D., the nobles revolted against John and forced him to sign the **Magna Carta** (MAG-nuh KART-uh), or "Great Charter." The Magna Carta promised the English nobles certain rights. It also protected some of the rights of the common people.

The Magna Carta forbade the ruler to tax without the approval of the council. It forbade the ruler to put people in prison just because they were not liked. And the Magna Carta also said that English citizens had a right to refuse to obey their ruler if their rights were denied them. The Magna Carta was an important document of freedom. But even after the Magna Carta was signed, the English ruler was still powerful.

SUMMING UP

Under Philip Augustus and Louis the Ninth, France became a larger and stronger nation. Under the Norman kings, England became stronger, but English citizens also gained more rights. In 1215 A.D., the English nobles forced King John to sign the Magna Carta—a great document that protected English citizens' rights and also limited the ruler's power. In the next chapter, you will learn what was happening in other European nations during the Later Middle Ages.

UNDERSTANDING THE LESSON

Do You Know These Important Terms?

For each sentence below, choose the term that best completes the sentence.

1. The people who took over England after the Romans left were called (**Anglo-Saxons/Danes**).
2. People from France who invaded England were called (**Normans/Jutes**).
3. The (**judge system/jury system**) was a group of people who reported to a judge people who might be guilty of a crime.
4. The collection of written decisions by royal judges in England became known as the (**royal charter/common law**).
5. The charter that granted English nobles certain rights and protected some rights of the common people was the (**Royal Charter/Magna Carta**).

Do You Remember These People and Events?

1. Tell something about these persons.

   Hugh Capet   **William the**
   Philip Augustus   **Conqueror**
   Louis the Ninth   **Henry the Second**
   Alfred the Great   **King John**

2. Explain how each of the following developments took place.

   a. The jury system and common law developed in England.
   b. The Magna Carta protected people.

Can You Locate These Places?

Use the map on page 336 to locate the following places. Tell how each place is related to developments in this chapter.

Normandy   Paris
France   England

Do You Know When It Happened?

Why are the following years important in England's history?

   1066 A.D.   1215 A.D.

Do You Remember the Main Idea?

Which one of the following ideas is the MAIN IDEA of this chapter?

1. In both England and France, the ruler was never able to gain enough power to control the country.
2. During the Later Middle Ages, England and France each became larger, and each became united under strong rulers. But in England, the people also gained more rights.
3. The person who wore the crown of England gained great power, but lost it after the Magna Carta was signed.

What Do You Think?

From what you have read in this chapter, try to answer the following thought questions.

1. What kinds of cases do you think might have been tried before the early juries in England?
2. What do you think is meant by the phrase "equal justice for all English citizens"? Do you think that this idea had an effect on our own system of laws in the United States? Explain your answer.
3. How do you think King John felt when he was forced to sign the Magna Carta?

Chapter 51
Other European Nations in the Later Middle Ages

GETTING STARTED

1   Just as England and France were becoming nations, Germany, Italy, Poland, Russia, and Spain also were developing during the Later Middle Ages. What were the beginnings of these nations like?

Between 800 A.D. and 1500 A.D., the rulers of many European lands were trying to gain power and to unite their kingdoms. These developments were taking place about the same years as were many of the developments in England and France described in the last chapter.

2   Before you begin reading the chapter lesson, survey the lesson. Begin your survey by reading the beginning of the lesson. Then look through the lesson and read the headings. Next, study the pictures and read the picture captions. Then study the map of Europe in 1360 A.D. on page 342. Finally, read the review section called "Summing Up." This survey will help you to discover the important ideas in this chapter.

Know the Main Idea

As you read the chapter lesson, try to remember the following important MAIN IDEA of the chapter.

During the Later Middle Ages, many European nations were weak, and their rulers were not able to unite them.

The following questions will help you to understand the MAIN IDEA. Try to answer these questions as you read the lesson.

1. What happened when the German rulers tried to unite Germany?
2. What two groups of people mixed together to form the Russian people?
3. What name was given to the Muslim people who controlled Spain?

Know These Important Terms

Holy Roman Emperor	Magyars
Holy Roman Empire	Lithuanians
Poles	Slavs
Bohemians	Rus

Know the Years of This Chapter

Look at the time line below. It shows the years of this chapter, 800 A.D. to 1500 A.D.

800 A.D.   1500 A.D.

The Alhambra palace in Spain

EXPLORING THE TIME

Not all European rulers were like the monarchs of England and France, who were able to unite their countries in the Later Middle Ages. Some European rulers were not strong enough to unite their countries. And some rulers were too busy fighting wars. In this chapter, you will learn how these other European nations developed.

The German Rulers Tried to Rule Italy

In 800 A.D., Charlemagne, ruler of the Frankish Empire, received the title **Holy Roman Emperor** from the Pope. This title was supposed to mean that the old western Roman Empire still continued and that this empire was ruled by Charlemagne.

After Charlemagne died, a German kingdom developed in the eastern part of the Frankish Empire. The German rulers

THE NATIONS OF EUROPE IN 1360 A.D.

Describe the location of the Holy Roman Empire in Europe.

who ruled this German territory wanted to keep the title of Holy Roman Emperor. This title gave them the right to rule a large part of Italy. But whenever German rulers tried to rule Italy, they were stopped either by the Pope or by the German nobles. One of the few German rulers powerful enough to rule both Germany and a large part of Italy was Otto the Great. Otto the Great ruled from 936 A.D. to 973 A.D. Beginning at this time, the lands of Germany and most of Italy were called the **Holy Roman Empire.**

After Otto's death, however, the German rulers lost Italy. But they increased their own power and made Germany the strongest nation in Europe. In the 1100's A.D., the German ruler Frederick Barbarossa won back a large part of Italy. But in 1268 A.D., the German ruler lost control of most of Italy.

Germany and Italy Split Up Into Many Small States

The German rulers spent so much time trying to conquer Italy that the German nobles were able to split Germany into hundreds of small feudal states. Italy, too, became divided into many independent states. And Italy and Germany were not able to become strong and united nations until seven hundred years later—during the late 1800's A.D.

The Countries of Eastern Europe Were Weak

The German rulers also tried to conquer the peoples who lived east of Germany. These peoples included the **Poles,** the **Bohemians** (boh-HEE-mee-UNZ), the **Magyars** (MAG-yahrz), and the **Lithuanians** (lith-WAY-nee-UNZ). These people accepted the Roman Catholic religion and developed into important new nations.

Many Germans settled in these nations, and German ideas became very important in their development. However, the rulers of Lithuania, Poland, Hungary (the Magyar kingdom), and Bohemia were not able to unite their nations because they were too busy fighting their own nobles and foreign enemies.

The Slavs and the Rus Settled Russia

Russia was another country of eastern Europe. Russia was first settled by the **Slavs,** a people who came from Asia long before the Christian religion began. Russia received its name from a group of Swedish people called the **Rus**. During the 800's A.D., the Rus people settled in northwestern Russia. Slowly, the Rus people and the Slavs mixed together and formed the Russian people.

The Russians traded a great deal with the Byzantine Empire. And about 990 A.D., a Russian ruler married the Byzantine emperor's sister and accepted the Greek Orthodox (the Byzantine) religion. After that, the Russian people became members of the

Otto the Great, an emperor of the Holy Roman Empire, ruled both Germany and a large part of Italy

Greek Orthodox Church, too. In the next fifty years, the Russians also took over many Byzantine ideas, including the Greek alphabet, which the Russian nation still uses today.

The Mongols Conquered Russia in the Years of the 1200's A.D.

Russia enjoyed a period of good times until the middle 1200's A.D., when it was attacked and conquered by the Mongols. If you remember, the Mongols ruled a huge empire that reached China across Asia to eastern Europe.

343

Alexander Nevski was the ruler of Novgorod in early Russia. How can you tell the Church had a great influence on Russian royalty?

Under the Mongols, the Russians kept their own laws and religion. However, the Mongols controlled all of Russia's dealings with western Europe. As a result, the Mongol ideas became very strong in Russia during this period.

Russia Grew into a Stronger Nation Under Mongol Rule

The Mongols collected taxes from the Russians. They also forced the local Russian rulers to visit the Great Khan, or Mongol ruler, to show that the Mongol ruler con-trolled Russia. The most important of the local Russian rulers was Alexander Nevski (NEV-skee). Under Nevski's son, Moscow became the most important Russian city.

During the 1300's A.D., Moscow became the strongest city in Russia, and it tried to win independence from the Mongols. However, Russia remained a part of the Mongol Empire until the 1400's A.D.

Spain Threw Off Muslim Rule

As you may recall, Spain was conquered by the Muslims in the 700's A.D. The Moors—as the Muslims in Spain were called—built up a strong kingdom. But the small Christian kingdoms in northern Spain hoped to reconquer Spain from the Muslims.

In 1031 A.D., the Moorish kingdom split into several small kingdoms. This split gave the Christian kingdoms a chance to defeat the Moors. By the early 1200's A.D., they had won back most of Spain.

Now Spain was controlled by the Christian kingdoms of Castile (kah-STEEL), Aragon, Leon (lay-OHN), and Navarre (nuh-VAHR). In Chapter 58, you will learn how these kingdoms became one nation.

SUMMING UP

During the Later Middle Ages, neither Germany nor Italy was able to unite as a nation. In eastern Europe, Poland, Bohemia, Hungary, and Lithuania also failed to unite. Russia was conquered by the Mongols, but it grew stronger under the Mongol rule. In southwestern Europe, Spain won back most of its land from the Moors, but Spain became divided into several kingdoms. In the next chapter, you will read about a new interest in learning that spread in Europe.

UNDERSTANDING THE LESSON

Do You Know These Important Terms?

For each sentence below, choose the term or terms that best complete the sentence.

1. The title given by the Pope to the German ruler who ruled the old western Roman Empire was (**Holy Roman Emperor/Rex Emperor**).
2. The lands of Germany and most of Italy were called the (**Holy Roman Empire/ Holy Rex Empire**).
3. Which of the following peoples lived in eastern Europe: (**Poles/Saxons/ Bohemians/Jutes/Magyars/ Lithuanians**)?
4. The first people who settled Russia were (**Mongols/Slavs**) from Asia.
5. The (**Rus/Slavs**) were people from Sweden who settled in northwestern Russia.

Do You Remember These People and Events?

1. Tell something about each of the following persons.

   Otto the Great   Frederick Barbarossa

2. Explain how or why each of the following developments took place.

   a. Germany and Italy were divided into many small states.
   b. Russia developed into a stronger nation under the rule of the Mongols.
   c. Spain drove out the Moors.

Can You Locate These Places?

Use the map on page 342 to locate the following places. Tell how each place is related to the developments in this chapter.

German states	Russia	Bohemia
Lithuania	Italy	Castile
Hungary	Poland	Aragon
Moscow	Navarre	

Do You Know When It Happened?

What are the years of this chapter?

Do You Remember the Main Idea?

Which one of the following ideas is the MAIN IDEA of this chapter?

1. Germany grew into a strong nation during the Later Middle Ages, and it ruled Italy and many lands in eastern Europe.
2. During the Later Middle Ages, many European nations were weak, and their rulers were not able to unite them.
3. During the Later Middle Ages, most European nations united under monarchs, just as England and France were doing.

What Do You Think?

From what you have read in this chapter, try to answer the following thought questions.

1. How did Germany's and Italy's division into many small states affect the people in these lands?
2. Suppose that Russia had not been conquered by the Mongols and that it was able to use more ideas from the Byzantine Empire and western Europe. What changes do you think might have taken place in Russia as a result?
3. Why did the rulers of Europe want to unite their countries?

Chapter 52

Education and Learning in the Later Middle Ages

GETTING STARTED

1   The chapters in this unit have described developments in Europe during the Later Middle Ages. You have read in these chapters how England and France began to develop as nations, while many of the peoples of other European lands were not able to form strong nations.

During the Later Middle Ages, other important developments also were taking place in western Europe. As trade increased and people traveled farther, more and more ideas were exchanged. One result of this exchange of ideas was a new interest in learning and education.

2   Before you begin reading the chapter lesson, survey the lesson. Begin your survey by reading the beginning of the lesson. Then look through the lesson and read the headings. Next, study the pictures and read the picture captions. Finally, read the review section called "Summing Up." This survey will help you to discover the important ideas in this chapter.

Know the Main Idea

As you read the chapter lesson, try to remember the following important MAIN IDEA of the chapter.

During the Later Middle Ages, European nations began to develop a greater interest in learning and education.

The following questions will help you to understand the MAIN IDEA. Try to answer these questions as you read the lesson.

1. How did European scholars learn about the writings of the Greek philosophers?
2. Who were two important leaders in education and learning during the Later Middle Ages?
3. Where did schools of higher learning grow up in Europe?

Know These Important Terms

revival of learning	academic freedom
scholars	bachelor's degree
scholasticism	master's degree
universities	doctor's degree

Know the Years of This Chapter

Look at the time line below. It shows the years of this chapter, 1100 A.D. to 1500 A.D.

| 800 A.D. | 1100 A.D. | 1500 A.D. |

Wall painting showing a teacher with students in the Late Middle Ages

EXPLORING THE TIME

With the increase in trade, the rise of towns, and the growth of strong nations in western Europe, learning also became more important. A new interest in Greek and Roman ideas led to a **revival of learning,** or a new and greater interest in learning. In this chapter, you will read about the causes and the results of the revival of learning in Europe during the Later Middle Ages.

European Scholars Began the Revival of Learning

People who study certain subjects very carefully are called **scholars.** Scholars had an important role in the Later Middle Ages. In the 1100's A.D., scholars began to study the Christian religion in a new way. They tried to show that religious faith and scientific thinking agreed with each other. This study was called **scholasticism** (skuh-LASS-tuh-SIZZ-um).

Thomas Aquinas

Thomas Aquinas (uh-KWY-nus) was a great scholar of the Middle Ages. He studied in Cologne under Albert the Great, one of the leading scholars and teachers in Europe.

Because Thomas rarely spoke in class, other students called him "the Dumb Ox." His teacher knew they were wrong. He told them, "the Dumb Ox will bellow so loud that his bellowings will fill the world." Albert was right. Thomas Aquinas' great work, *Summa Theologica*, was read by popes, rulers, scholars, and teachers all over the world.

Aquinas was greatly influenced by the writings of Aristotle. He tried to apply scientific thinking as well as religious faith to a number of philosophical questions. One subject he discussed in *Summa Theologica* was law. Aquinas explained how divine law, natural law, and human laws were related:

> All law proceeds from the reason and will of the lawgiver; the Divine and natural laws from the reasonable Will of God; the human law from the will of man, regulated by reason.

Question: Whose writings influenced Aquinas?

One of the most famous scholars who helped to develop scholasticism was Peter Abelard (AB-uh-LAHRD), who taught at the University of Paris. Abelard helped to make scholasticism an important method in European learning.

European Scholars Studied Greek and Arabic Writings

During the late 1100's A.D., European scholars began to study the early Greek writings. Europeans were very interested in the writings of the two great Greek philosophers, Plato and Aristotle. These philosophers' writings were brought to Europe in Greek, Arabic, and Hebrew books. European scholars translated, or wrote, these books into Latin. They also translated into Latin many Arabic books on mathematics and science. European scholars learned a great deal from these Greek and Arabic writings.

European Scholars Took Over Aristotle's Ideas

At first, many scholars felt that Aristotle's beliefs did not agree with Christian ideas. However, Thomas Aquinas (uh-KWY-nus), a great Roman Catholic philosopher, wrote a book that explained how Aristotle's teachings really supported the beliefs of the Roman Catholic Church. As a result of Aquinas' book, scholars began to accept many of the ideas of Aristotle.

Scholasticism Became Less Important

But after the death of Thomas Aquinas in 1275 A.D., scholasticism became less important to European scholars. Some scholars took over Aristotle's ideas without even trying to "prove" that they agreed with the Christian religion. Instead, these scholars spent a great deal of time arguing about less important matters. As a result, scholasticism became less important than it was before. However, later on scholasticism became important again, and scholasticism is still used by Catholic leaders today.

Schools of Higher Learning Grew Up in Europe

During the years of the 1100's A.D., many **universities** and colleges were started in Europe. Universities were schools of higher learning where the most outstanding teachers taught. The first universities began as guilds, or organized groups of students and teachers.

Some universities, such as the University of Bologna (buh-LOH-nyuh) in Italy, were controlled by the students. But most universities followed the examples of the University of Paris. In Paris, the teachers set up the rules for the university, and the students took their orders from the teachers. This system is followed in most universities today.

The Universities Had Great Freedom

Most universities received charters from either a monarch or the Pope. These charters gave the universities many rights and freedoms, including the power to run their own affairs. For example, students and teachers were not forced to pay taxes or serve in the army. The universities even had their own laws and law courts. Today, this idea of freedom of the universities is still very strong and very important all over the world. This freedom of universities to rule their own affairs is called **academic freedom.**

Universities of the Later Middle Ages did not have libraries or labs. They merely had places where the teachers and students lived and a few large lecture halls. If some teachers and students did not like the town in which their university was located, they simply moved the university to another town. Many new universities developed in this way.

A classroom at the University of Paris

A library of a European university during the Later Middle Ages. What subjects can you identify?

The Universities Increased Learning

The main power of the university was its right to give teaching degrees. After about four years of study, a student received a **bachelor's degree.** He or she was then ready to become a beginning teacher. Many students continued to study another two or three years until they received a **master's degree.** As masters, these students were well trained to be teachers.

The highest degree given by the university was the **doctor's degree.** The doctor's degree was given to advanced students in law, medicine, or religion. Many years of study were needed for the doctor's degree. To earn this degree, the student had to spend a whole day answering questions from teachers and other scholars. If the student passed this test, he or she was given a doctor's degree. The student was now able to be a scholar.

The universities of the Later Middle Ages helped to make learning more important. They trained students to become teachers, doctors, lawyers, government leaders, and Church leaders. Today's colleges and universities are carrying on the work started by the universities of the Later Middle Ages.

SUMMING UP

During the Later Middle Ages, European nations began to take a greater interest in learning. Very important in this revival of learning were the new study of Greek philosophy and Arabic science and mathematics, the rise of universities, and scholasticism. In the next chapter, you will read about Europe's progress in science, building, and writing.

UNDERSTANDING THE LESSON

Do You Know These Important Terms?

For each sentence below, choose the term that best completes the sentence.

1. The new interest in learning and education during the Later Middle Ages is called the **(renewal of learning/revival of learning)**.
2. **(Pupils/Scholars)** were people who studied certain subjects very carefully.
3. The method of study that tried to show that religious faith and scientific thinking agreed with each other was called **(scholasticism/scientific proof)**.
4. Schools of higher learning where outstanding teachers taught were called **(seminars/universities)**.
5. The freedom by schools of higher learning to rule their own affairs was called **(learning freedom/academic freedom)**.
6. After about four years of study, a student received a **(college degree/bachelor's degree)**.
7. After about seven years of study, a student received a **(second degree/master's degree)**.
8. The highest degree granted to students was the **(doctor's degree/scholar's degree)**.

Do You Remember These People and Events?

1. Tell something about each of the following persons.

Peter Abelard	Plato
Thomas Aquinas	Aristotle

2. Explain how each of the following developments took place.

   a. European scholars began to study Greek and Arabic writings.
   b. Universities grew up and gained great freedom.
   c. Universities made learning more important.

Do You Know When It Happened?

What are the years of this chapter?

Do You Remember the Main Idea?

Which one of the following ideas is the MAIN IDEA of this chapter?

1. During the Later Middle Ages, European nations began to develop a greater interest in learning and education.
2. The revival of learning helped England and France to become great nations.
3. The Catholic Church disliked the revival of learning, because it was difficult to prove that religious faith and scientific thinking agreed with each other.

What Do You Think?

From what you have read in this chapter, try to answer the following thought questions.

1. Do you think there would have been a revival of learning in Europe if scholars had not had the writings of Plato and Aristotle to study? Explain your answer.
2. Do you think it was more difficult to earn a university degree in the Later Middle Ages than it is today? Why or why not?
3. Is it important for universities to be free to govern themselves? Explain your answer.

Chapter 53

Science, Building, and Writing in the Later Middle Ages

GETTING STARTED

1   The revival of learning in western Europe during the Later Middle Ages had many important results. During the years from 1100 A.D. to 1500 A.D., great advances were made in European science, building, and writing. As you will learn, these great advances were a part of the revival of learning described in the last chapter.

2   Before you begin reading the chapter lesson, survey the lesson. Begin your survey by reading the beginning of the lesson. Then look through the lesson and read the headings. Next, study the pictures and read the picture captions. Finally, read the review section called "Summing Up" at the end of the lesson. This survey of the whole lesson will help you to discover the important ideas in this chapter.

Know the Main Idea

As you read the chapter lesson, try to remember the following important MAIN IDEA of the chapter.

During the Later Middle Ages, many new ideas and inventions helped to change life in Europe.

The following questions will help you to understand the MAIN IDEA. Try to answer these questions as you read the lesson.

1. Who was one of the first persons to use the scientific method and to make famous this method of study of experimenting and observing carefully?
2. What two inventions helped nations to begin to depend on mechanical power rather than on human power?
3. How long did it take to build some of the churches built during the Middle Ages?

Know These Important Terms

scientific method	Romanesque
magnetic compass	Gothic
rudder	stained glass
water power	epics
windmill	

Know the Years of This Chapter

Look at the time line below. It shows the years of this chapter, 1100 A.D. to 1500 A.D.

800 A.D.	1100 A.D.	1500 A.D.

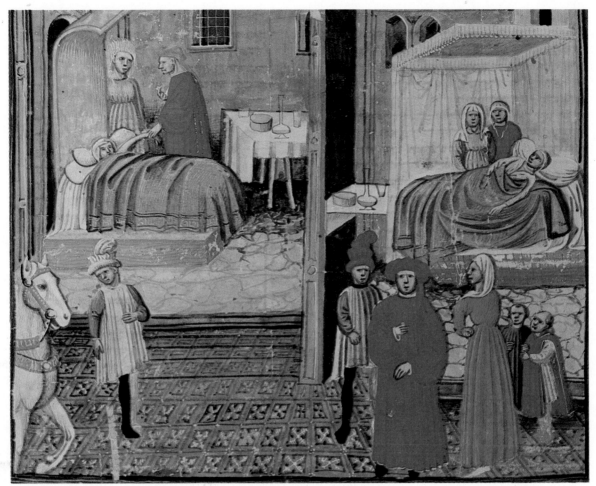

Painting showing a medical doctor visiting a patient. What do you think the doctor is doing?

EXPLORING THE TIME

If you have ever seen a snowball roll down a hill, you know that it moves faster as it grows larger. The same thing happened in Europe as learning spread in the Later Middle Ages. In this chapter, you will learn how the revival of learning in Europe soon led to new ideas in science, building, and writing in the years of the Later Middle Ages.

Europeans Made Progress in Mathematics and Science

About 1100 A.D., European scholars began to study Arabic and Greek ideas in science and mathematics. Europeans began to use Arabic numerals and the zero in mathematics. They studied and improved Arabic and Greek ideas in algebra, geometry, and trigonometry (TRIG-uh-NAHM-uh-TREE). They also studied Arabic ideas in astronomy, medicine, and chemistry.

HIGHLIGHTS IN HISTORY

Alchemists at Work

Chemistry is one of the oldest sciences. But until three hundred years ago, chemistry was called alchemy. Chemistry, or alchemy, was first studied in Mesopotamia, Egypt, India, and China. From there, alchemy spread all over the world.

The main goal of the alchemists, or those who studied alchemy, was to turn common metals, such as tin and lead, into valuable metals, such as gold or silver. Alchemists were always searching for a powder or liquid to do this. In their search for this magic powder or liquid, alchemists made many discoveries that are still important today.

Alchemists discovered many drugs that we still use to cure diseases. They taught us about the strengths and weaknesses of most metals. And alchemists' ideas and discoveries helped to prepare the way for many of the modern theories that are part of the chemistry courses students now study in school.

Question: What was the main goal of the alchemists?

Roger Bacon was the best-known European scientist of the Middle Ages. Today we remember Bacon best for his use of the **scientific method.** This method of study tries to find the truth by making experiments and by carefully observing things. Roger Bacon accepted only facts that were proved by the scientific method. However, the scientific method did not become popular until long after the Middle Ages ended.

The Later Middle Ages Was a Period of New Inventions

Several new inventions became important after 1100 A.D. One invention, which came from China, was the **magnetic compass** for sailing. The compass was a small instrument with a magnetic needle that always pointed north. Sailors used the magnetic compass to find their direction at sea. Another invention that improved sailing was the **rudder**, or steering lever, which made it easier to steer ships. The use of better sails also speeded up sailing.

During these years, Europeans also were helped by the invention of the spinning wheel, the mechanical clock, the button, and better ways of making iron. And gunpowder (from China) also became important in warfare.

Machine Power Began to Be Used

The most important change in daily life during the later years of the Middle Ages was the use of new kinds of power to do many jobs. European farmers now learned to use **water power** for turning machinery to grind grain and also to saw wood. And the invention of the **windmill** made it possible for farmers to use wind as power, too. The windmill was mainly used to pump water from the ground. By the Later Middle

Ages, the nations of Europe used more machine power and depended less on human power than nations ever had done before in the world's history.

Many Famous Churches Were Built During the Middle Ages

Today, visitors in Europe still are able to see the beautiful churches that were built during the Middle Ages. The churches of the early years of the Middle Ages were built in the **Romanesque** (ROH-muhn-ESK) style, which was based on the kind of buildings that were built by the Romans. The Romanesque churches had thick walls, round arches, and narrow windows.

Beginning in the late 1100's A.D., the **Gothic** (GAHTH-ik) style began to be widely used. Gothic churches were built higher and had thinner walls and larger windows than did Romanesque churches. Gothic church windows were made with beautiful designs in **stained glass**, or colored glass. Gothic churches also were decorated with many religious statues.

During the Middle Ages, all the people of the town helped to build a church. Each town tried to build a bigger and more beautiful church than the other towns. Some of these churches took hundreds of years to build!

Important Poems and Stories Were Written in the Middle Ages

Many of the books in the Middle Ages were written in Latin, the official Church language. These Latin writings included many works in religion, history, and poetry. Many works of Church music also were written during this period.

But other writers during the Middle Ages began to use the language of their

Gothic church windows were made with beautiful designs in stained glass, or colored glass

own nation. The earliest of these writings were long poems called **epics**. They included the Anglo-Saxon *Beowulf* (BAY-uh-WOOLF), the Spanish *El Cid* (SID), and the French *Song of Roland*. No one knows who really wrote these epic poems. Probably they were written down by many different persons.

Dante and Chaucer Were Famous Writers of the Later Middle Ages

Two great writers of the Later Middle Ages were Dante (DAHN-tay), an Italian, and Geoffrey Chaucer (CHAW-sur), an Englishman. Dante was born in Florence, Italy, and

Chaucer wrote stories about a group of people on a trip to Canterbury

he wrote in Italian. His most famous poem was the *Divine Comedy*. In this beautiful poem, Dante described a trip to heaven and hell as he pictured them to be. The *Divine Comedy* is one of the greatest of all poems.

Chaucer was born in London, England, and he wrote in English. His most famous work was the *Canterbury Tales*. These stories about a group of people who made a trip to Canterbury, England, in the 1300's A.D. tell a great deal about English life of that period. In this way Chaucer, like Dante, helped to shape his nation's written language.

SUMMING UP

In the later years of the Middle Ages, many new ideas and inventions helped to change life in Europe. Sailing improved, and new kinds of power began to replace human power. Beautiful Romanesque and Gothic churches were built. Many important poems and stories were written, including those of Dante and Chaucer, two of the world's greatest writers. In the next chapter, you will learn more about the Roman Catholic Church during the Later Middle Ages.

UNDERSTANDING THE LESSON

Do You Know These Important Terms?

For each sentence below, choose the term that best completes the sentence.

1. A method of study that tries to find the truth through experiments and observations is called the **(Bacon method/ scientific method)**.
2. A device with a needle that always points to the north is called the **(magnetic compass/astro)**.
3. The **(helm/rudder)** is the steering lever on a ship.
4. The use of water to turn machinery is called **(water motor/water power)**.
5. The invention of the **(windlass/ windmill)** made it possible to use wind power.
6. A style of architecture with thick walls, round arches, and narrow windows is called **(feudalistic/Romanesque)**.
7. **(Gothic/Spanish)** architecture made use of high thin walls and large stained glass windows.
8. Colored glass used in the windows of churches was called **(painted glass/ stained glass)**.
9. Long poems written during the Middle Ages were called **(operas/epics)**.

Do You Remember These People and Events?

1. Tell something about each of the following subjects.

Roger Bacon	*El Cid*
Beowulf	**Dante**
Song of Roland	**Geoffrey Chaucer**

2. Explain how each of the following developments took place.

   a. Mechanical power began to replace human power.
   b. Most towns built beautiful churches.
   c. Writers like Dante and Chaucer helped to develop their nation's written language.

Do You Know When It Happened?

What are the years of this chapter?

Do You Remember the Main Idea?

Which one of the following ideas is the MAIN IDEA of this chapter?

1. During the Later Middle Ages, many new ideas and inventions helped to change life in Europe.
2. Science, building, and writing developed during the Later Middle Ages. But these developments had little effect upon the people.
3. Most of the great buildings and writings of the Later Middle Ages are still used today.

What Do You Think?

From what you have read in this chapter, try to answer the following thought questions.

1. Is the scientific method used by Roger Bacon still important today? Explain your answer.
2. Why do you think mechanical power soon became more important than human power?
3. Do you think it was important that epics and the works of Dante and Chaucer were written in other European languages, not Latin?

Chapter 54

The Roman Catholic Church in the Later Middle Ages

GETTING STARTED

1 The Roman Catholic Church was the most powerful force in Europe during the Early Middle Ages. In this unit, you have been reading about the important changes that took place in Europe during the Later Middle Ages. The Church played an important part in these changes. But as you will learn, during the period from 1000 A.D. to 1500 A.D., the Church was changing, too.

2 Before you begin reading the chapter lesson, survey the lesson. Begin your survey by reading the beginning of the lesson. Then look through the lesson and read the headings. Next, study the pictures and read the picture captions. Finally, read the review section called "Summing Up." This survey will help you to discover the important ideas in this chapter.

Know the Main Idea

As you read the chapter lesson, try to remember the following important MAIN IDEA of the chapter.

The Roman Catholic Church played an important part in the changes that took place in Europe during the Later Middle Ages.

The following questions will help you to understand the MAIN IDEA. Try to answer these questions as you read the lesson.

1. How did the Roman Catholic Church regard the development of guilds and the increase in trade?
2. Why was the Roman Catholic Church interested in education?
3. What new groups of religious people were formed in the Roman Catholic Church, and what new duties did they have?

Know These Important Terms

patron saint	Dominicans
interest	Franciscans
friars	

Know the Years of This Chapter

Look at the time line below. It shows the years of this chapter, 1000 A.D. to 1500 A.D.

800 A.D.	1000 A.D.	1500 A.D.

Painting by Giotto showing St. Francis kneeling with a group of Franciscan monks

EXPLORING THE TIME

What was happening to the Roman Catholic Church as changes were taking place in Europe in the later years of the Middle Ages? How did the growth of trade and the rise of towns affect the role of the Church? How was the Church affected by the growing power of European nations? In this chapter, you will find the answers to these questions.

The Church Encouraged Trade and Guilds

The Roman Catholic Church favored the growing trade in Europe, because trade provided some of the goods that people needed to improve their lives. The Catholic Church helped trade to grow by helping in the building and in the repair of roads. One Catholic religious group, known as the Order of Bridge Brothers, worked at building bridges.

Plays about religion were popular in the Later Middle Ages

price that allowed the merchant or artisan to pay the expenses and still have a small profit left. The Church believed that it was a sin to charge more than a fair price.

The Church Began to Approve of Money Lending

As you may recall, the growth of trade helped the money changers and money lenders to become bankers. However, the Roman Catholic Church did not allow its members to charge **interest,** or a fee for lending money. Therefore, many of the early bankers were Jews. However, as the need for money increased, the Church began to allow bankers to charge interest, if this interest was kept low.

Not long after the Church approved of charging interest, Catholic merchants—mostly Italians—took over the banking business. Soon, large banks were found in all the larger towns of Europe. Even the Church used these banks to take care of its money.

The Church Helped to Encourage Education

Almost all of the teachers in European universities were Roman Catholic priests or members of Roman Catholic groups. The Church was interested in education, because it wished to train people to become Church leaders. The Church also was interested in training students to become scholars of Church law.

The leading scholars of the Middle Ages, such as Abelard and Aquinas, and most of the important scientists, such as Roger Bacon, were religious people. In fact, the main reason for studying science during the Middle Ages was in order to aid people to understand God.

The Church also encouraged the town guilds, and the guilds worked with the Church. Each guild had its own **patron saint,** or saint who was supposed to aid it and protect it. Guild members put on plays and attended Church services as a group. And all guilds gave money and labor to help build churches in their towns.

The Church Also Protected Buyers of Goods

The Church also tried to keep the guilds from cheating their customers. The Church required that merchants and artisans charge a "fair price." A fair price was a

Pope Innocent the Third Increased the Power of the Church

As changes took place in European life, the Roman Catholic Church also began to change. Mainly, it tried to make itself more powerful in the affairs of Europe. One of the important leaders of this new plan for the Church was Pope Innocent the Third.

Pope Innocent the Third was leader of the Church from 1198 A.D. to 1216 A.D. It was during this same period that the rulers of England and France were becoming more powerful. Pope Innocent wished to form a league of Christian nations with the Pope as its head. Under this league, the nations were to live together peacefully and to fight only against the Muslims.

But the Pope never was able to form such a league. However, the Pope did become powerful enough to make the rulers of England, Portugal, Hungary, Poland, and other nations become vassals. The Pope was also strong enough to choose the Holy Roman Emperor (or the German emperor). And under Pope Innocent the Third, Church leaders were better trained, and the Church's control became stronger.

Pope Innocent the Third (standing) called for soldiers to fight in the Third Crusade

Monks helped the Church to spread religion throughout Europe

New Religious Groups Made the Church Stronger

Pope Innocent encouraged members of the monasteries to leave the monasteries and work among people outside. Those who did were called **friars** (FRY-urz), a word that means "brothers." A friar was both a monk and a priest. Friars were not allowed to own any property or to receive wages. They supported themselves by receiving food, clothing, and shelter from the people they served.

The two most famous groups of friars were the **Dominicans** (duh-MIN-ih-KUNZ) and the **Franciscans** (fran-SISS-kunz). The Dominicans were started by St. Dominic, and they became famous as teachers. Many of the Dominicans taught in European universities. The Franciscans were started by St. Francis. They carried on missionary work, or the work of spreading the Christian religion. Some Franciscans also became teachers. Both the Dominicans and the Franciscans encouraged other friars to follow their example and to spread a new interest in the Christian religion all over Europe.

SUMMING UP

The Roman Catholic Church played an important part in the changes that took place in Europe in the Later Middle Ages. The Church favored a growing trade, helped the guilds, and encouraged the new universities. The Church also worked to spread the Christian religion all over Europe. In the next chapter, which begins Unit 13, you will learn about the exciting years in Europe that were the beginning of modern history.

UNDERSTANDING THE LESSON

Do You Know These Important Terms?

For each sentence below, choose the term that best completes the sentence.

1. Saints who were supposed to aid and protect guild members were called (**holy saints/patron saints**).
2. (**Sales tax/Interest**) is a fee charged for lending money.
3. Members who left the monasteries to work among the people of Europe were called (**friars/fathers**).
4. The (**Dominicans/prophets**) were friars who became famous as teachers.
5. The (**hermits/Franciscans**) were friars who did missionary work.

Do You Remember These People and Events?

1. Tell something about each subject.

Peter Abelard	**Roger Bacon**
Thomas Aquinas	**Dominicans**
Pope Innocent the Third	**Franciscans**

2. Explain how each of the following developments took place.

   a. The Church began to allow bankers to charge interest on loans.
   b. Pope Innocent tried to increase the Church's power in government.
   c. New groups of friars spread a new interest in the Christian religion.

Can You Locate These Places?

Use the map of Europe in Chapter 51 (page 342) to locate the following places. Tell how each place is related to the developments in this chapter.

England	**Hungary**
Portugal	**Poland**
Holy Roman Empire	

Do You Know When It Happened?

In what years was Pope Innocent the Third the leader of the Church?

Do You Remember the Main Idea?

Which one of the following ideas is the MAIN IDEA of this chapter?

1. The Roman Catholic Church continued to grow strong during the Later Middle Ages, but it was against most changes taking place in Europe.
2. The Roman Catholic Church was successful in forming a league of Christian nations with the Pope as its head.
3. The Roman Catholic Church played an important part in the changes that took place in Europe during the Later Middle Ages.

What Do You Think?

From what you have read in this chapter, try to answer the following thought questions.

1. What do you think was the most important contribution of the Church during the Later Middle Ages?
2. Do you think that a league of Christian nations formed under the Pope might have helped European nations to live peacefully? Explain your answer.
3. Why might friars have had more difficult lives than the monks who lived in a monastery?

Unit 13
The Beginning of Modern Europe

THE CHAPTERS IN UNIT 13 ARE

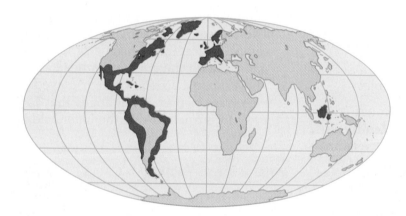

During the later years of the Middle Ages, many developments took place which greatly changed European life. As a result, these years from about 1300 to 1600 mark the beginning of modern history. In this unit, you will find out about these developments.

As Queen of France, Catherine de Medici actively participated in French government

Chapter 55
The Renaissance in Europe

GETTING STARTED

1 Usually, before a really important change takes place in history, many small changes take place that lead up to it. The many changes that were taking place in western Europe during the later part of the Middle Ages led to many more rapid and important changes that took place during the next few hundred years. As a result, between 1300 and 1600, a great new period developed in Europe. As you will see, this new period ended the Middle Ages.

2 Before you begin reading the chapter lesson, survey the lesson. Begin your survey by reading the beginning of the lesson. Then look through the lesson and read the headings. Next, study the pictures and read the picture captions. Finally, read the review section called "Summing Up" at the end of the lesson. This survey of the whole lesson will help you to discover the important ideas in this chapter.

Know the Main Idea

As you read the chapter lesson, try to remember the following important MAIN IDEA of the chapter.

The humanists and the printing press helped to develop a new period in Europe called the "Renaissance."

The following questions will help you to understand the MAIN IDEA. Try to answer these questions as you read the lesson.

1. Where did the Renaissance begin in Europe?
2. Who was called the "founder of humanism"?
3. What changes were brought about in Europe by the use of the printing press?

Know These Important Terms

Renaissance	humanists
patrons	printing press

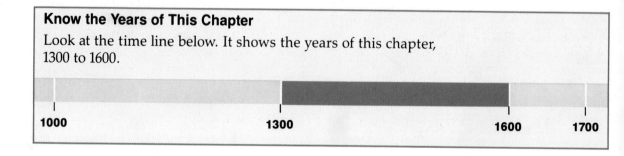

Know the Years of This Chapter

Look at the time line below. It shows the years of this chapter, 1300 to 1600.

1000　　　　1300　　　　1600　　1700

Religious procession in St. Mark's Square in Venice, Italy

EXPLORING THE TIME

The cultures of Greece and of Rome continued long after these great nations ended. You have learned how the Byzantine Empire and the Muslim Empire preserved Greek and Roman ideas after these ideas almost disappeared in western Europe. And you have also learned how the scholars of western Europe began to study Greek and Roman ideas during the Middle Ages. In this chapter, you will learn how this study led to a great period—the period of the beginning of modern history in Europe.

The Middle Ages Slowly Ended

During the years between 1300 and 1600, the nations of Europe passed from the Middle Ages into modern history. The name that historians use for this great period of change is the **Renaissance** (REN-uh-SAHNS). The word "Renaissance" means "rebirth." Historians call this period the Renaissance because the cultures of Greece and Rome were reborn, or discovered again, at this time.

Actually, the cultures of Greece and Rome were studied by European scholars in the Early Middle Ages. But the Renaissance scholars became much more interested in the Roman and Greek cultures than the scholars of the Middle Ages.

The Renaissance Began in Italy

The Renaissance took place at different times in different parts of Europe, but most historians agree that it began in Italy during the 1300's. The cultures of Greece and Rome always had been stronger in Italy than in other parts of Europe. And Italy also knew about the Byzantine and Muslim cultures because it traded with those lands.

After the Crusades, some Italian merchants and nobles built up great fortunes from trade. Many of them wished to make their cities more beautiful and made them great centers of culture. Therefore, these Italians became **patrons** of culture—the people who supported the work of the artists, writers, builders, musicians, and philosophers who started the Renaissance.

The Humanists Helped the Renaissance to Develop

Beginning in the 1300's, many more scholars began to study the writings of the great Greek and Roman writers. These scholars were called **humanists,** because they were interested in everything that concerned human beings. Petrarch (PEE-trahrk) was the "founder of humanism." It was Petrarch who gave the name "Renaissance" to this period of years. During the 1400's, the

Petrarch (left) and Erasmus (right) were humanists who helped to begin the Renaissance

humanists built up fine libraries of books for the Pope and for the rulers of many Italian cities.

The Humanists Were Interested in People

The humanists' ideas were very different from the ideas of the scholars of the Middle Ages. The scholars of the Middle Ages were interested mainly in religion. But the humanists were more interested in people and their ability to think and use ideas. The scholars of the Middle Ages were interested in groups of people, not in persons. The humanists were interested in each individual as a person. The scholars of the Middle Ages had little interest in nature or beauty. But the humanists loved both nature and beauty. The humanist ideas were the basis of the Renaissance. And the rich Italian patrons of culture helped to support the work of many humanists.

Humanist Ideas Spread to Northern Europe

The humanist ideas spread from Italy northward into France, the German states, the Netherlands (Holland), and England. The most famous of the northern humanists was Erasmus (ih-RAZZ-mus). Erasmus was a great humanist, but he was also interested in religion. He translated, or wrote, the New Testament books of the Bible from Greek into Latin. In doing so, he corrected many mistakes in the old Bible that was used before. Erasmus tried to bring out the truth about many matters. And many later European thinkers built upon Erasmus' ideas.

A page from the Bible printed by Johann Gutenberg on an early printing press. Why is the printing press considered the greatest invention of the Renaissance?

Printed Books Helped Knowledge to Spread in Europe

The greatest invention of the Renaissance was the **printing press** to print books. The printing press was based on movable type. In the old block printing method, blocks of wood with carved pictures and words were pressed onto a page of a book. But the carving of each block took a long time. With movable type, the letters were cut out of metal and were used over and over again to make up new words. The printer arranged the letters into words and put them onto a printing press. The first European to use the printing press was probably Johann Gutenberg (GOOT-un-BURG), about the year 1450.

Johann Gutenberg's printing press. The invention of the printing press helped to spread knowledge.

Before the invention of the printing press, it often took a whole year or more to copy a book by hand. After the invention of the printing press, thousands of copies of a book were printed at one time. As a result, books became much cheaper, and they were read by many more people. Now things that had been known before only by a few scholars became known by thousands of people. Many of the events that you will read about in later chapters were a result of this great invention that spread knowledge.

SUMMING UP

The Renaissance began in Italy and spread to northern Europe. Many Renaissance ideas were based on the ideas of the humanists. The humanists were scholars who were interested in everything that concerned human beings. Both the humanists and the printing press helped to spread knowledge among Europeans. In the next chapter, you will read about the painting, sculpture, and music of the Renaissance.

UNDERSTANDING THE LESSON

Do You Know These Important Terms?

For each sentence below, choose the term that best completes the sentence.

1. The great period of change which began in Italy about 1300 is called the **(Revolution/Renaissance)**, a word that means "rebirth."
2. Rich Italian nobles who supported the works of artists, writers, builders, musicians, and philosophers were called **(founders/patrons)** of culture.
3. **(Humanists/Scholastics)** were scholars who were interested in everything that concerned human beings.
4. The **(printing press/block printing)** was a machine with movable type used to print books.

Do You Remember These People and Events?

1. Tell something about each of the following persons.

   **Petrarch   Johann Gutenberg
   Erasmus**

2. Explain how or why each of the following developments took place.

   a. The Renaissance began in Italy sooner than in other parts of Europe.
   b. The humanists were more interested in man than in religion.
   c. The humanists and the printing press spread the new ideas of the Renaissance throughout Europe.

Can You Locate These Places?

Use the map of Europe in Chapter 51 (page 342) to locate each of the following places. Tell how each place is related to developments in this chapter.

Italy	France
German states	England

Do You Know When It Happened?

Why are the following years important in European history?
   1300 to 1600

Do You Remember the Main Idea?

Which one of the following ideas is the MAIN IDEA of this chapter?

1. The Renaissance began in Italy, but it took a long time for it to spread to other parts of Europe.
2. The humanists and the printing press helped to develop a new period in Europe called the "Renaissance."
3. The Renaissance was a period of great change in western Europe.

What Do You Think?

From what you have read in this chapter, try to answer the following thought questions.

1. Compare the ideas of the humanists with the ideas of the scholars of the Middle Ages. With whose ideas do you most agree? Why?
2. Do you think that the humanists were interested in the common people? Explain your answer.
3. Do you think that the Renaissance would have developed if the printing press had not been invented?

Chapter 56
Renaissance Art, Buildings, and Music

GETTING STARTED

1   Do you think that good ideas always lead to other good things? During the years of the Renaissance, the ideas of the humanists led to remarkable developments in art, architecture, and music. And many of the great paintings, statues, and buildings of the Renaissance years are still important to us today. Just as a reminder, the years of the Renaissance were about 1300 to 1600. Check these years on the time line at the bottom of this page.

2   Before you begin reading the chapter lesson, survey the lesson. Begin your survey by reading the beginning of the lesson. Then look through the lesson and read the headings. Next, study the pictures and read the picture captions. Finally, read the review section called "Summing Up" at the end of the lesson. This survey of the whole lesson will help you to discover the important ideas in this chapter.

Know the Main Idea

As you read the chapter lesson, try to remember the following important MAIN IDEA of the chapter.

The great people of the Renaissance produced some of the most important works of art in all of the world's history.

The following questions will help you to understand the MAIN IDEA. Try to answer these questions as you read the lesson.

1. Why did Italian painters begin to use new ideas in art, and what were some of these new ideas?
2. Who was the greatest sculptor of the Renaissance?
3. What new musical instruments were developed in Europe during the years of the Renaissance?

Know These Important Terms

architecture
Medici family

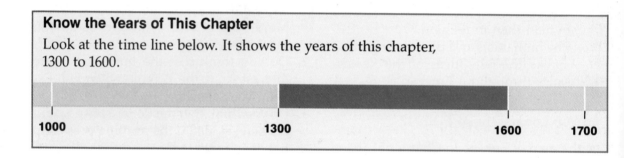

Know the Years of This Chapter

Look at the time line below. It shows the years of this chapter, 1300 to 1600.

| 1000 | 1300 | 1600 | 1700 |

St. Peter's Cathedral in Vatican City (Italy) is the center of the Roman Catholic Church

EXPLORING THE TIME

The humanists' interest in the civilizations, or cultures, of Greece and Rome led to a new interest in Greek and Roman painting and **architecture,** or the art of building. This new interest in painting and architecture began in Italy. A new interest in sculpture and in music also developed. In this chapter, you will read about painting, sculpture, architecture, and music during the Renaissance.

The Italians Helped to Develop Painting

By about the year 1300, Italian painters, sculptors, and architects began to study the Roman statues, paintings, and buildings that they saw around them in Italy. And soon they began to form new ideas about art.

The Italian painters felt free to begin to use new ideas, because very few paintings were preserved from Roman times. The first Italian painter to develop a truly new painting style was Giotto (JAWT-toh), who

373

Leonardo da Vinci

Today, when we talk about a "Renaissance person," we mean someone who does many different things very well. In history, Leonardo da Vinci was probably the best example of a Renaissance person. He not only did many things very well—he did them brilliantly!

You already know about Leonardo's great work as a painter. But did you know that Leonardo was also a great architect? Leonardo also made great statues and did fine sketches of the human body, based on his study of anatomy. And Leonardo also was a fine musician.

But this is only the artistic side of Leonardo's life. Leonardo designed roads, bridges, and canals. His plans for a submarine and a helicopter look very practical even today. And for a hobby, Leonardo collected rocks and plants!

Question: In what ways was Leonardo da Vinci a "Renaissance person"?

was born in Florence, Italy, about 1276. Giotto painted simple figures which seemed full of life and movement. Another painter of Florence was Masaccio (muh-ZAHCH-ee-OH), who lived from 1401 to 1428. Masaccio improved on Giotto's use of color, and the people who were painted in Masaccio's pictures also seemed more real.

Later Italian Painters Were the Greatest of the Renaissance

The greatest Renaissance painters appeared during the late 1400's and 1500's. By that time, artists were using oil paints, or paints with an oil base. These paints were more colorful and lasted longer than the paints used before.

Probably the most famous Italian painter of the Renaissance was Leonardo da Vinci (LEE-uh-NAHR-doh duh VINN-chee), who was born near Florence in 1452. Two of his works—the "Mona Lisa" and "The Last Supper"—are among the best-known paintings in the world. Leonardo da Vinci was also a fine sculptor, architect, musician, engineer, and inventor. With his understanding of so many different subjects, Leonardo da Vinci came to be the perfect example of the "Renaissance person."

Another famous Italian painter was Raphael (RAHF-ee-UL), who lived from 1483 to 1520. Raphael painted many pictures of the "Madonna and Child" (Mary with the Infant Jesus).

Italian painters from Venice also produced great art. Among the most important of these painters were Titian (TISH-un), born in 1477, and Tintoretto (TIN-tuh-RET-toh), born in 1518. Titian painted many pictures of rich patrons. Tintoretto painted stories from the Bible and stories of the Greek gods.

Leonardo da Vinci—painter, sculptor, architect, musician, writer, engineer, and inventor—painted this painting, "The Annunciation of Mary"

Italians Produced Great Works of Sculpture

Two of the most famous sculptors of the Renaissance were Donatello (DAHN-uh-TELL-oh) and Verrocchio (vuh-RAWK-ee-OH). Donatello, who lived from 1386 to 1466, was the first Renaissance sculptor to show the human body as it really is. Verrocchio was a pupil of Donatello. These two sculptors were the first sculptors since Roman times to make statues of soldiers on horseback. They also were the first sculptors to make their statues out of bronze.

Michelangelo Was the Greatest Renaissance Sculptor

The great Renaissance sculptor, Michelangelo (MY-kuhl-ANN-juh-LOH) of Florence (1475 to 1564), carved some of the most beautiful statues of all time. His statues of David, of Moses, and of Mary and Jesus —the "Pietà" (PEE-ay-TAH)—are among the most famous statues in the world. Michelangelo's statues look so real and powerful that they almost seem to be alive.

Michelangelo was also a great painter and architect. Thousands of people visit

Michelangelo's statue of Moses is one of the most famous sculptures in the world

Rome each year to see his paintings on the ceiling of the Sistine Chapel. They also visit St. Peter's Church in Rome, whose famous dome was planned by Michelangelo.

Great Churches and Palaces Were Built During the Renaissance

Many new churches and palaces were built during the Renaissance. The architects of these buildings based many of their designs on Greek and Roman buildings. They used the Roman dome, arch, and columns.

Patrons Made the Renaissance Possible

Who paid for all the paintings, statues, and buildings of the Renaissance? If you remember, it was the patrons—or rich merchants, bankers, nobles, rulers of cities, and high church officials.

In Italy, it was a great honor to sponsor, or support, famous artists. During the 1400's, members of the **Medici** (MED-uh-CHEE) **family,** who ruled the city of Florence, sponsored many famous artists. In the 1500's, the Popes of Rome were the great patrons of painters, sculptors, and architects. The patrons who sponsored art made it possible for artists to live comfortably and to spend their lives at their work.

Northern Europe Also Had Fine Painters

The German states and the Netherlands also had fine artists. Among the most famous of these artists were Van Eyck (van EYK), Dürer (DYOOR-ur), Holbein (HOHL-byn) the Younger, and Brueghel (BROY-gul). These artists also had patrons.

Music Developed During the Renaissance

Music also made progress during the Renaissance. The violin, the flute, the organ, and the first type of piano were developed in these years. And a great deal of new music was written for orchestras, choirs, and Church singing groups. The most famous Renaissance composer, or writer of music, was Palestrina (PAL-uh-STREE-nuh), an Italian who lived from 1526 to 1594.

SUMMING UP

The Renaissance was an important period of great painters, sculptors, architects, and composers. The great artists of the Renaissance produced some of the most important works of art in all the world's history. These artists were supported by rich patrons who encouraged all forms of art. In the next chapter, you will read about the rise of strong monarchs in Europe during the Renaissance years.

UNDERSTANDING THE LESSON

Do You Know These Important Terms?

For each sentence below, choose the term that best completes the sentence.

1. The art of building is called (construction/architecture).
2. Rulers of the city of Florence who supported many famous artists were members of the (Papal family/Medici family).

Do You Remember These People and Events?

1. Tell something about each of the following persons.

Giotto	Verrocchio
Masaccio	Michelangelo
Van Eyck	Leonardo da Vinci
Raphael	Dürer
Titian	Holbein the Younger
Tintoretto	Brueghel
Donatello	Palestrina

2. In the following exercise, match each subject in Column A with the correct person in Column B.

Column A	Column B
1. "Mona Lisa"	a. Titian
2. "Pietà"	b. Leonardo da Vinci
3. "Madonna and Child"	c. Michelangelo
4. pictures of patrons	d. Palestrina
5. music	e. Raphael

3. Explain how each of the following developments took place.

   a. Paintings of the Renaissance were more colorful than were most paintings before.
   b. Michelangelo was the greatest sculptor of the Renaissance.
   c. Greek and Roman ideas were used in the architecture of the Renaissance.

Do You Know When It Happened?

During what years did the Medici family sponsor many famous artists? When did the Popes of Rome become the patrons of painters, sculptors, and architects?

Do You Remember the Main Idea?

Which one of the following ideas is the MAIN IDEA of this chapter?

1. A new interest in painting, sculpture, architecture, and music began during the Renaissance in Italy.
2. The great people of the Renaissance produced some of the most important works of art in all the world's history.
3. New buildings, based on Roman and Greek architecture, were constructed during the Renaissance.

What Do You Think?

From what you have read in this chapter, try to answer the following thought questions.

1. Which great works of the Renaissance period do you like best—the paintings, the sculpture, the buildings, or the music? Explain your answer.
2. Why do you think that the art of the Renaissance was so different from the art of the Middle Ages?
3. Do you think that artists, sculptors, and musicians should be supported by rich patrons? Explain your answer.

Chapter 57

The Growing Power of European Monarchs

GETTING STARTED

1 During the Later Middle Ages, you will recall, the rulers of England and France were strong enough to unite their countries. But in other lands of western Europe, monarchs were not yet powerful enough to unite their peoples. Feudalism still remained very strong in these lands, and the feudal nobles still held great power.

However, during the period from 1200 to 1500, more monarchs of western Europe were able to gain enough power to become the real rulers of their nations. They gained power by taxing the town merchants and the Church. They also bought new weapons and hired soldiers. As a result, feudalism slowly ended in western Europe.

2 Before you begin reading the chapter lesson, survey the lesson. Begin your survey by reading the beginning of the lesson. Then look through the lesson and read the headings. Next, study the pictures and read the picture captions. Finally, read the review section called "Summing Up" at the end of the lesson. This survey of the whole lesson will help you to discover the important ideas in this chapter.

Know the Main Idea

As you read the chapter lesson, try to remember the following important MAIN IDEA of the chapter.

During the years between 1200 and 1500, many monarchs in western Europe grew powerful enough to become the real rulers of their nations.

The following questions will help you to understand the MAIN IDEA. Try to answer these questions as you read the lesson.

1. What new weapons helped to destroy feudalism?
2. How did European rulers obtain money to hire soldiers and to build up armies?
3. How did the life of the serfs change in western Europe?

Know These Important Terms

foot soldiers   hired soldiers

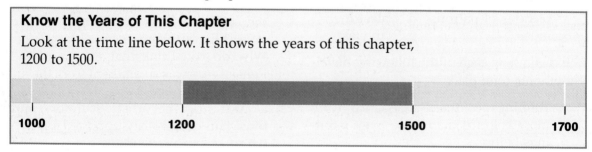

Know the Years of This Chapter

Look at the time line below. It shows the years of this chapter, 1200 to 1500.

| 1000 | 1200 | 1500 | 1700 |

European nobles and knights wore elaborate armor into battle

EXPLORING THE TIME

During the Renaissance years, important changes were taking place in the nations of western Europe. If you remember, during the Later Middle Ages, many European nations grew stronger and their monarchs became more powerful. In this chapter, you will read how these monarchs finally gained enough power in the years between 1200 and 1500 to become the real rulers of their nations.

New Weapons Helped to Destroy Feudalism

Perhaps you recall that the feudal system grew up in Europe partly because rulers were too weak to protect their nobles. Instead, nobles had their own armies of knights on horseback. By the years of the 1200's, however, knights were no longer as powerful in battle as they had been before. Now **foot soldiers,** or ordinary fighting soldiers, had powerful arrows that pierced, or cut through, a knight's covering of armor. When armor was made stronger to protect the knight, the stronger armor was much heavier. Therefore, if a knight fell off his horse in battle, he often was not able to keep on fighting.

But it was the use of gunpowder, beginning in the early 1400's, that really ended the power of the knights. With gunpowder, weapons now shot through armor and also broke down castle walls. Therefore, castles no longer protected the nobles from attack.

Hired Soldiers Helped Monarchs to Become More Powerful

In order to increase their own power, monarchs began to build up large armies. They did this by hiring paid soldiers. The monarchs learned that **hired soldiers** were more dependable than knights. For one thing, the feudal knights did not always obey a monarch's request to fight. Also, the knights were required to fight only for forty days. After that time, they were free to ride away to their own castles. The hired soldiers often proved to be more loyal than knights. Hired soldiers expected to win money and glory by fighting for the monarch.

Towns and Trade Helped Monarchs to Grow Powerful

Where did the monarchs get the money to hire soldiers and build up armies? They got it from taxes paid by the merchants in the growing towns. As you read earlier, the town merchants wished to trade with other places. But it was very difficult for merchants to carry on trade if they had to pay a

Italian painting showing a hired soldier between a castle (right) and a town (left)

Farmers bringing crops to sell in town had to pay a tax to the ruling monarch's official (left). Church leaders also had to pay Church taxes to the Crown (right).

tax every time they crossed a noble's land. If a country was united under a strong ruler, the merchants did not have to pay so many different taxes. Therefore, the town merchants usually supported the monarch against the nobles.

The towns supported the monarch by supplying fighting men and tax money. And the monarch repaid the towns by giving them charters. These charters gave the towns the right to govern themselves. The tax money paid to the monarch made the Crown much richer than any of the nobles. The monarch then used this money to hire soldiers and supply the army.

Rulers Gained More Power by Taxing the Church

As the monarchs grew more powerful, they also tried to tax Roman Catholic groups. However, the Popes at first were against these taxes. One of the French monarchs even tried to have Church leaders judged by France's royal courts, but he did not succeed in doing so. However, later Popes did allow monarchs to help choose Church leaders and to tax the Church. These taxes on the Church made the rulers richer and helped them to increase their power in their nations even more.

Any person who lived in a town for about a year became free by law. Once a person became free, neither taxes nor work were due to the old feudal manor. Many serfs ran away to a town or a city in order to be free.

Meanwhile, many of the serfs who remained on the manors began to be treated better. Their taxes were lowered, and they were allowed to rent the land that they farmed instead of working for the lord. The lord had to give these rights to his serfs, or the serfs might run away. By the end of the Middle Ages, most of the serfs in western Europe were becoming free farmers.

The Nobles Lost Power as Monarchs Grew Stronger

The nobles might have kept the monarchs from becoming so powerful if they had united against them. But the nobles kept on fighting among themselves. And the monarchs encouraged this fighting by pretending to support one group of nobles against another group. As a result, the nobles became weak as the monarchs in western Europe grew stronger.

As the serfs gained more freedom, they became farmers who rented their own land. What led to the serfs' freedom?

Feudalism Slowly Ended in Western Europe

As the monarchs became stronger, the nobles became weaker. The growing weakness of the nobles was partly a result of the fewer number of serfs on feudal manors. The serfs, if you remember, were forced to stay on the land and work for their lord, because they had no other way of living. But after towns grew, the serfs no longer had to stay on the feudal manors.

SUMMING UP

During the years between 1200 and 1500, many monarchs in western Europe grew powerful enough to become the real rulers of their nations. They gained power by taxing the town merchants and the Church. Fighting among the nobles, new weapons, and new armies of hired soldiers also helped the monarchs to grow more powerful. In the next chapter, you will learn how these new rulers in western Europe ruled their nations.

UNDERSTANDING THE LESSON

Do You Know These Important Terms?

For each sentence below, choose the term that best completes the sentence.

1. Ordinary soldiers who fought on foot and used bows and arrows were called **(artillery soldiers/foot soldiers)**.
2. Soldiers who were not knights and who were paid by a monarch to fight in the army were **(spies/hired soldiers)**.

Do You Remember These People and Events?

1. Which groups of people might have wished the feudal system to end?

   monarchs   **town merchants**
   nobles   **serfs**

2. Explain how each of the following developments took place.

   a. New weapons helped to destroy the feudal system.
   b. Towns and trade helped monarchs to grow more powerful.
   c. As feudalism ended, the life of the serfs improved.
   d. The monarchs were able to keep the nobles from uniting.

Do You Know When It Happened?

During what years were the kings in western Europe able slowly to end feudalism?

Do You Remember the Main Idea?

Which one of the following ideas is the MAIN IDEA of this chapter?

1. During the years between 1200 and 1500, many monarchs in western Europe grew powerful enough to become the real rulers of their nations.
2. The use of gunpowder brought an end to feudalism because castles were no longer able to hold off an attack.
3. The Church brought about an end to feudalism and helped monarchs to gain control of their nations.

What Do You Think?

From what you have read in this chapter, try to answer the following thought questions.

1. You have read how new weapons helped to bring an end to a way of life. Can you think of some modern examples of new inventions or discoveries that have brought about the end of an older way of doing something?
2. Do you think that monarchs had a right to tax the Church? Give reasons for your answer.
3. If you were a serf during the later years of the Middle Ages, would you have run away to a town or would you have stayed on the manor? Give reasons to explain your answer.

Chapter 58

The Growth of European Governments

GETTING STARTED

1 Strong nations usually have strong governments. During the years from 1200 to 1500, European monarchs gained more power. And the countries ruled by these monarchs were developing into large "nation-states," or modern nations.

A modern nation occupies a large territory and its government controls the people who are citizens. Often the strength of a nation-state is based on the loyalty of its citizens. Before the Renaissance period, no European country was really a modern nation, because most of western Europe was divided up into many small kingdoms. And in most of the kingdoms of western Europe the peoples' loyalties were divided between the monarch and the nobles. But as modern nations developed, the people gave their loyalty only to the monarch.

2 Before you begin reading the chapter lesson, survey the lesson. Begin your survey by reading the beginning of the lesson. Then look through the lesson and read the headings. Next, study the pictures and read the picture captions. Finally, read the review section called "Summing Up" at the end of the lesson. This survey of the whole lesson will help you to discover the important ideas in this chapter.

Know the Main Idea

As you read the chapter lesson, try to remember the following important MAIN IDEA of the chapter.

By the 1400's, the monarchs of England, France, and Spain became powerful rulers. But only in England did the monarch share power with a council.

The following questions will help you to understand the MAIN IDEA. Try to answer these questions as you read the lesson.

1. Who was the ruler of England when the Parliament was formed?
2. Why was France's council weak?
3. Which nation was the most powerful nation in Europe in the 1400's?

Know These Important Terms

Hundred Years' War	Estates-General
House of Commons	clergy
House of Lords	Parliament
Lancaster monarchs	cortes

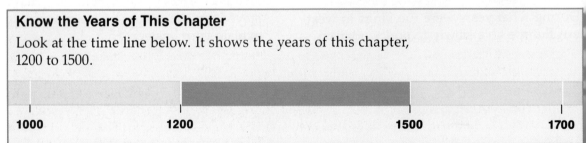

Know the Years of This Chapter

Look at the time line below. It shows the years of this chapter, 1200 to 1500.

1000	1200	1500	1700

Gold coin showing Isabella, ruler of Castile, and Ferdinand, ruler of Aragon, who, together united the kingdoms of Spain

EXPLORING THE TIME

What kinds of governments were formed in England, France, and Spain as their rulers became stronger? Did the rulers allow the people of their nations to take part in governing the nation? In this chapter, you will read about the growth of the governments in England, in France, and in Spain.

The English Council Developed into Parliament

When you last read about England, King John had been forced to sign the Magna Carta in 1215 A.D. This famous charter limited the ruler's power and gave English citizens certain rights. After John, Henry the Third became king. During the reign of Henry the Third, two members from each

English county (or district) and town began to meet with the council of nobles who advised the king. This meeting became known as **Parliament,** a name that came from the French word that means "to talk things over."

The English Parliament was called together whenever the king needed money. Henry the Third called many Parliaments together, and they became a regular part of the English government. Later, Parliament divided into two parts. The members chosen by the counties and towns formed the **House of Commons.** The members who were nobles formed the **House of Lords.** The House of Lords also served as England's highest court.

Parliament Grew Stronger and Gained More Power

Before voting to give money to the Crown, the House of Commons asked the monarch to pass certain laws. If passed, the Crown usually received more money from Parliament than if they were not passed. In time, Parliament itself began to pass the laws. And the monarchs accepted most of these laws in order to gain Parliament's support.

Parliament also won the right to approve all new taxes the monarch wanted from the people. And later, Parliament became powerful enough to hold trials to judge royal officials accused of wrong actions. Some English monarchs tried to rule without Parliament, but most monarchs found it easier to rule if they had Parliament's support.

The English Crown Also Gained More Power

During the early 1400's, when the **Lancaster monarchs** ruled England, Parliament won more power to help choose the Crown's officials and to decide what new tax laws were to be passed.

But the English Crown grew more powerful, too, because many English nobles were killed in the wars that took place in England under the Lancaster rulers. The remaining nobles were too weak to ever win power again over any English monarch.

Parliament helped the monarch to rule England

The Hundred Years' War made the French Crown stronger

The French Council Was Weak

The French monarch also had a council of advisers, called the **Estates-General.** The three groups, or "estates," that made up this council were the **clergy,** or church leaders, the nobles, and the common people. However, the Estates-General never became as powerful as the English Parliament.

The **Hundred Years' War** between England and France from 1337 to 1453 weakened the Estates-General. France fought this war mainly to recapture some French land held by England. And France did win back all of its territory from England except for the seaport town of Calais (ka-LAY).

However, the French victory hurt the Estates-General for the following reason.

During the war, the French people were so afraid of defeat that they paid taxes to the Crown without demanding any rights for their Estates-General. As a result, the French monarch gained more and more power. When King Louis the Eleventh died in 1483, he completely controlled the French nation. And the Estates-General had little power.

Spain's Rulers Became Very Powerful

In Spain, the Crown also gained complete power to rule. When you last read about Spain, it was made up of four Christian kingdoms. These kingdoms controlled most of Spain. Only one kingdom, Granada, in

PEOPLE IN HISTORY

Joan of Arc

In the year 1429, the English soldiers in France faced a French army led by a seventeen-year-old girl, Joan of Arc.

Joan of Arc was a deeply religious person. She believed that God had chosen her to free France from the English conquerors. Joan of Arc went to the French king, Charles the Seventh, and told him her ideas. He decided to give Joan of Arc a small army and some weapons. Soon Joan won victory after victory leading this French army.

In 1430, however, Joan was captured and became a prisoner of the English. She was sentenced and put to death. But soon after, the English army was forced out of France. Joan of Arc became one of France's greatest heroes. In 1922, Joan of Arc was made the national saint of France.

Question: Who was Joan of Arc?

southern Spain, was still held by the Moors, or Muslims.

However, the recapture of most of Spain from the Moors left the Spanish monarchs weak and the nobles strong. Many Spanish towns formed leagues, or groups, to protect themselves from the nobles. These leagues helped the ruler against the nobles. The Spanish monarchs had a council called the **cortes** (KORR-tezz), which included townspeople as well as nobles and church leaders. But the cortes never became as powerful as the English Parliament.

In 1469, Isabella, who later became ruler of the Spanish kingdom of Castile, married Ferdinand, later the ruler of the Spanish kingdom of Aragon. Their marriage united most of Spain. In 1492, these rulers took over the rest of Spain, except for Navarre. To make Spain even more united, King Ferdinand and Queen Isabella ordered all Muslims and Jews in Spain to leave Spain or become Christians. Later, Spain was hurt by the loss of these people, who were mainly merchants, bankers, skilled artisans, and scholars. However, in the 1400's, Spain was the most powerful nation in Europe.

SUMMING UP

The monarchs of England, France, and Spain became powerful rulers by the 1400's. In England, the monarch shared some power with the Parliament. In France, the monarchs gained full power to rule their nation. And after Spain became united in 1492, the Spanish king and queen had more power than any other European rulers. In the next chapter, you will read about the search for new trade routes to Asia by European nations.

UNDERSTANDING THE LESSON

Do You Know These Important Terms?

For each sentence below, choose the term that best completes the sentence.

1. The meeting of members from English counties and towns with the monarch's council of nobles was called (**Parliament/ the King's Court**).
2. Members from the English counties and towns formed the (**House of Commons/ House of Lords**).
3. The English nobles formed the (**House of Commons/House of Lords**).
4. During the early 1400's, Parliament won more power from the (**Lancaster monarchs/Stewart monarchs**).
5. The (**Estates-General/States Major**) was a council of advisers to the French monarch.
6. The (**clergy/Fourth Estate**) were the French church leaders in the Estates-General.
7. The war between England and France which lasted from 1337 to 1453 was called the (**French and English War/ Hundred Years' War**).
8. The council of advisers to the Spanish monarchs was called the (**Granada/ cortes**).

Do You Remember These People and Events?

1. Tell something about each of the following persons.

   Henry the Third   **Ferdinand**
   Louis the Eleventh   **Isabella**

2. Explain how or why each of the following developments took place.

   a. Parliament grew stronger and gained more power.
   b. The Estates-General in France never became as powerful as the English Parliament.
   c. The Christian kingdoms of Spain were united into one nation.

Do You Know When It Happened?

Why is the following year important in Spain's history?

1492

Do You Remember the Main Idea?

Which one of the following ideas is the MAIN IDEA of this chapter?

1. Spain became the most powerful nation in Europe when it was united under Queen Isabella and King Ferdinand.
2. By the 1400's, the monarchs of England, France, and Spain became powerful rulers. But only in England did the monarch share power with a council.
3. France and England both developed a government controlled by a council that gave advice to the Crown.

What Do You Think?

From what you have read in this chapter, try to answer the following thought questions.

1. If you were the ruler of England in the 1400's, how might you have felt about Parliament?
2. Why did the countries of Europe not become modern nations until the period from 1200 to 1500?

389

Chapter 59
Europe's Discovery of the New World

GETTING STARTED

1   You have already read that the first people to discover the Americas were people from Asia. You also read that these people probably reached North America by crossing over the Bering Strait. These people became the American Indians.

Europeans, however, did not learn about the Americas until thousands of years after the people from Asia settled in North America. Europe's first discovery of North America took place about 1000 A.D. Europe's second discovery took place in 1492. You will learn about these discoveries and the important effect they had on Europe in this chapter.

2   Before you begin reading the chapter lesson, survey the lesson. Begin your survey by reading the beginning of the lesson. Then look through the lesson and read the headings. Next, study the pictures and read the picture captions. Then study the map that shows Europe's search for new trade routes to Asia on page 392. Finally, read the review section called "Summing Up" at the end of the lesson. This survey of the whole lesson will help you to discover the important ideas in this chapter.

Know the Main Idea

As you read the chapter lesson, try to remember the following important MAIN IDEA of the chapter.

The search for new trade routes to Asia led to Columbus' discovery of North America in 1492.

The following questions will help you to understand the MAIN IDEA. Try to answer these questions as you read the lesson.

1. Who were the first Europeans to discover North America?
2. Which four European nations were most interested in increasing their trade with Asia so that they might become wealthy?
3. Who finally proved that it was possible to reach Asia by sailing westward from Europe?

Know These Important Terms

    Norse sailors   New World

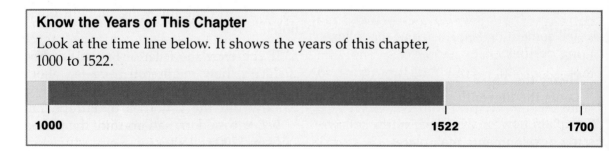

Know the Years of This Chapter

Look at the time line below. It shows the years of this chapter, 1000 to 1522.

| 1000 | 1522 | 1700 |

Numerous exploratory voyages in search of the New World left from the coasts of Europe. Describe some of the activities on this dock.

EXPLORING THE TIME

Did you ever taste a piece of fruit that was not ripe? If you did, perhaps you did not want to finish eating it. In the same way, Europe's first discovery of North America took place before the time was "ripe"— before Europe became interested in other lands. In this chapter, you will learn how Europe slowly began to become more interested in exploring other parts of the world.

The Norse Sailors' Discovery of North America Was Forgotten

The first Europeans to discover North America were the **Norse sailors,** a group of adventurous sailors from northern Europe. About the year 1000 A.D., a group of Norse sailors landed on the eastern coast of North America. They called this new land Vinland.

But the Norse sailors did not stay in Vinland. Shortly after this, they returned to

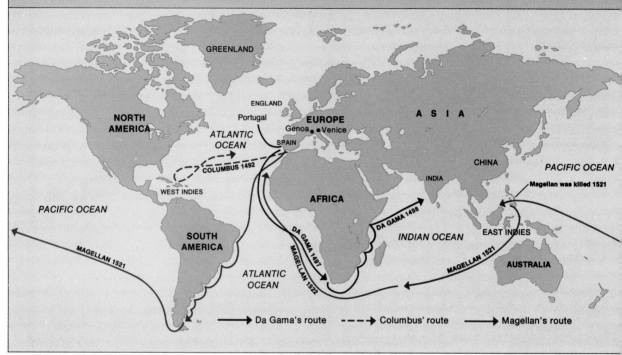

THE SEARCH FOR NEW ROUTES TO ASIA — 1490 TO 1522

What oceans did Magellan's ships cross?

Europe, where they told stories about their adventures in North America. However, the Norse sailors' discovery soon was forgotten in Europe.

Europe Was Not Prepared to Explore New Lands

Why was the Norse sailors' discovery of North America soon forgotten? Do you remember what Europe was like in the year 1000 A.D.?

In 1000 A.D., Europe was divided into many small, weak kingdoms. Most Europeans lived on feudal manors, and their lives were difficult. They knew little about other places in the world, because Europe traded very little with other lands. It is not surprising that Europeans showed little interest in the Norse sailors' discovery.

The Crusades Increased European Trade with Asia

But life in Europe slowly began to change after 1000 A.D. Trade increased and towns and cities grew. The Crusades helped to speed up this change, because they helped Europeans to learn about many products from Asia, such as spices and fine cloth.

Spices were very important to Europeans. They needed spices to keep their food from spoiling and to make it taste better. Many Europeans became interested in trading with Asia in order to get spices, cloth, and other new products from Asia.

The Italian Cities Controlled the Trade with Asia

However, the powerful Italian cities of Venice and Genoa controlled the trade with Asia. The goods from Asia were carried along trade routes, or trade paths, from China and India to the eastern Mediterranean ports. From these ports, ships from Venice and Genoa carried the goods to Italy.

If a European nation wished to buy products from Asia, it had to buy them from an Italian city. The Italian cities grew rich from trading with Asia. And the rulers of European nations grew jealous of the Italian cities.

Europe's Rising Nations Wanted New Sea Routes to Asia

By the years of the 1400's, Spain, Portugal, England, and France were becoming powerful nations ruled by strong rulers. These rulers wished to increase their trade with Asia in order to increase their own wealth and power. But this meant that they had to find new trade routes to Asia, because the Italian cities controlled the old trade routes.

Europe Became Interested in Exploring

By the 1400's, bigger and better ships were being built in Europe. Maps became more accurate, and compasses were improved. As a result, longer sea trips were now possible.

Many Europeans grew interested in reading about other lands. One popular book of that time was the story of Marco Polo, an Italian trader who had visited China in the 1200's. Marco Polo described China as a land of great wealth and beauty.

Many Europeans wished to find out more about China and the other lands of Asia.

Portugal Led the Way in Exploring

During the early 1400's, Prince Henry the Navigator (NAV-uh-GAY-tur), the brother of the ruler of Portugal, sent many ships along the western coast of Africa to search for a new sea route to India. By 1498, Vasco da Gama (VASS-koh duh GAH-muh), a Portuguese sea captain, sailed around Africa and reached India.

After da Gama, other Portuguese ships sailed around Africa to India and returned with many products to sell to Europe. Portugal became one of the richest nations in Europe.

Columbus Discovered North America While Sailing Westward

Spain also wished to find a new sea route to Asia. In 1492, the rulers of Spain sent Christopher Columbus of Genoa, Italy, to find a sea route to Asia. Columbus believed that Asia was directly west of Europe. He set out for Asia by sailing westward across the Atlantic Ocean.

On October 12, 1492, Columbus landed in the West Indies, a group of islands south of Florida. Columbus believed that he had reached islands south of India. He did not know that he had discovered North America, a huge continent between Europe and Asia.

Columbus never reached Asia. However, his discovery of North America was the discovery of a **New World** by Europeans. The New World—North America, Central America, and South America—was later named "America" in honor of another explorer, Amerigo Vespucci (uh-MER-ih-GOH vess-PEW-chee).

Christopher Columbus (center) discovered many islands of the West Indies for Spain

Magellan's Ship Finally Reached Asia

After Columbus' discovery, other Europeans tried to reach Asia by sailing westward. In 1519, Ferdinand Magellan (muh-JELL-un), a sea captain, left Spain with five Spanish ships. Magellan sailed around South America into the Pacific Ocean. Magellan died during the trip, but one of his ships reached the East Indies of Asia and returned to Spain in 1522. Magellan's trip proved that it was possible to reach Asia by sailing westward. It also proved that it was possible for a ship to sail completely around the world.

SUMMING UP

Europeans were not ready to follow up the Norse sailors' discovery of North America in 1000 A.D. But by the years of the 1400's, conditions in Europe had changed a great deal. Strong nations grew up, and Europe's rulers now wished to increase their nations' wealth by trading with Asia. This search for new trade routes to Asia led to Columbus' discovery of the New World. In the next chapter, you will read about the first colonies and settlements that were started by Europeans in the New World.

UNDERSTANDING THE LESSON

Do You Know These Important Terms?

For each sentence below, choose the term that best completes the sentence.

1. A group of sailors from northern Europe who discovered North America around the year 1000 A.D. were the (Norwegians/Norse sailors).
2. The (New World/Vinland) was another name for North and South America.

Do You Remember These People and Events?

1. Tell something about each of the following persons.

   Marco Polo   Christopher Columbus
   Prince Henry   Amerigo Vespucci
   Vasco da Gama   Ferdinand Magellan

2. Explain how or why each of the following developments took place.

   a. The Norse sailors' discovery of North America was forgotten.
   b. European nations wanted to find new sea routes to Asia.
   c. The search for new trading routes led to the discovery of a New World.

Can You Locate These Places?

Use the map on page 392 to do the following map work.

1. Locate each of the following places. Tell how each place is related to the developments in this chapter.

   Venice   India   England
   Spain   Genoa   Africa
   West Indies   Portugal   East Indies

2. Trace the route of Vasco da Gama. Also trace the route of Magellan. Which explorer found the shortest route to Asia?

Do You Know When It Happened?

Why are the following years important in this chapter?

   1000 A.D.   1498
   1492   1522

Do You Remember the Main Idea?

Which one of the following ideas is the MAIN IDEA of this chapter?

1. The search for new trade routes to Asia led to Columbus' discovery of North America in 1492.
2. In 1000 A.D., Europe was not interested in new lands or faraway places.
3. Portugal was the first nation to become wealthy because it discovered a new trade route to Asia.

What Do You Think?

From what you have read in this chapter, answer the following thought questions.

1. Why do you think the Norse sailors sailed so far away from their homes when most people in Europe were not interested in faraway lands?
2. Do you think the New World should have been named "Columbia" in honor of Columbus rather than called "America"? Give reasons for your answer.
3. Do you think that Columbus would have sailed westward to reach Asia if he had known that North America lay between Europe and Asia?

Chapter 60

European Settlements in the New World

GETTING STARTED

1   At first, the New World did not interest European nations. To Europe, the New World seemed to be only a huge land that blocked the way to Asia. The problem for European nations was to find a way to sail through or around the New World to reach Asia. Between 1492 and 1700 (see the time line below), this search for a water passage through North America led several European nations to explore and to begin settlements in the New World.

2   Before you begin reading the chapter lesson, survey the lesson. Begin your survey by reading the beginning of the lesson. Then look through the lesson and read the headings. Next, study the pictures and read the picture captions. Then study the maps showing the European explorers of North America on page 400 and Spain's New World empire on page 398. Finally, read the review section called "Summing Up" at the end of the lesson. This survey of the whole lesson will help you to discover the important ideas in this chapter.

Know the Main Idea

As you read the chapter lesson, try to remember the following important MAIN IDEA of the chapter.

Spain was the first nation to build a powerful empire in the New World. But later, other European nations also started colonies in the Americas.

The following questions will help you to understand the MAIN IDEA. Try to answer these questions as you read the lesson.

1. Who were the two Spanish explorers who had the most success in finding riches in the New World?
2. How did the Spanish settlers in the New World solve their labor problem?
3. What event brought an end to Spain's control of the Atlantic Ocean?

Know These Important Terms

water passage	Spanish Armada
claim	New France
missions	New Netherland

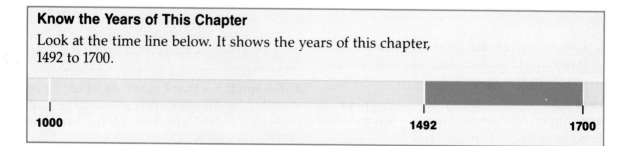

Know the Years of This Chapter
Look at the time line below. It shows the years of this chapter, 1492 to 1700.

1000   1492   1700

guzmã. michv ácã.

Aztec drawing showing the Spanish conquest of part of the New World

EXPLORING THE TIME

After Columbus discovered the New World, other European nations soon sent ships to explore the New World. Soon Spanish, English, French, Portuguese, and Dutch explorers arrived in the New World. In this chapter, you will read about these explorers and about the early colonies started by European nations in the New World.

European Explorers Searched for a Water Passage Through North America

Some European nations tried to reach Asia by searching for a **water passage,** or water route, through North America. In 1497, England sent John Cabot to find this passage. Cabot sailed along the eastern coast of North America, but he found no passage. However, Cabot's search gave England a **claim,** or the right to settle this land.

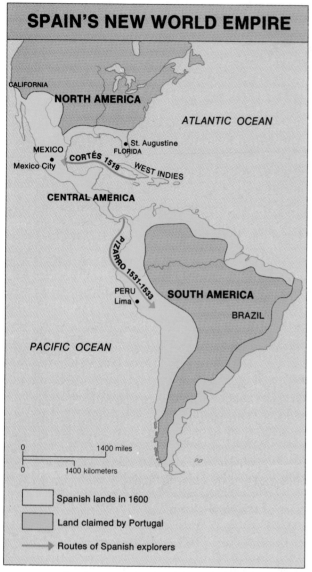

SPAIN'S NEW WORLD EMPIRE

CALIFORNIA

NORTH AMERICA

ATLANTIC OCEAN

MEXICO
Mexico City
St. Augustine
FLORIDA
CORTÉS 1519
WEST INDIES

CENTRAL AMERICA

PIZARRO 1531-1533

PERU
Lima
SOUTH AMERICA

BRAZIL

PACIFIC OCEAN

0   1400 miles
0   1400 kilometers

Spanish lands in 1600

Land claimed by Portugal

Routes of Spanish explorers

In which country did Portugal develop settlements?

From 1524 to 1536, Giovanni da Verrazano (GEE-oh-VAH-nee duh VAIR-uh-ZAHN-oh) and Jacques Cartier (ZHOCK KAR-tee-AY) explored the eastern coast of North America for France. They did not find a passage, but Cartier discovered the St. Lawrence River.

In 1609, Henry Hudson, exploring for the Netherlands (Holland), believed he had discovered this water passage, but instead he discovered the Hudson River.

The trips of these early explorers gave England, France, and the Netherlands claims to land in North America. But only Spain was strong enough to build colonies in the New World before the 1600's.

Spanish and Portuguese Explorers Searched for Riches

By 1513, Spanish explorers were searching for gold, silver, and jewels in Mexico, Central America, and South America. Two Spanish explorers did find riches. The first was Hernando Cortés (kor-TEZ). Cortés conquered the Aztec Indians of Mexico in 1521 and captured their gold, silver, and jewels. Then, in 1531, Francisco Pizarro (pih-ZAHR-roh) attacked the Inca Indians of Peru and captured even greater riches.

In 1500, a Portuguese explorer named Cabral (kuh-VRALL) reached the coast of Brazil. Portugal claimed this land, and began a colony in Brazil.

Spain Built a Great Empire in the New World

But by the 1560's, Spain's search for riches in the Americas was over. From that time on, Spain became more interested in building strong colonies, or settlements, in the New World. Spanish colonies were started in the West Indies, Mexico, Central America, South America, Florida, California, and the southwestern part of what is now the United States. These colonies sent valuable farm and mining products to Spain. These colonies helped Spain to become the richest and strongest nation in Europe.

Religion Was Important in the Spanish Colonies

The Roman Catholic Church carried on very important work in the Spanish colonies. The Church built many schools and hospitals as well as churches. Spanish priests opened **missions,** or religious centers, where they taught the Indians the Christian religion and many European skills.

The Catholic Church also helped to spread learning and education. Two fine universities were started in the mid-1500's in Mexico City and in Lima (LEE-muh), Peru. And scholars in the Spanish colonies wrote many books during this period.

Slaves Were Brought from Africa to the Spanish Colonies

The Spaniards who came to the New World needed workers to do their hard work for them. At first, the Spaniards tried to force the Indians to work for them. But many Indians either ran away or died. Then the Spaniards brought slaves from Africa to work for them. Beginning in the early 1500's, thousands of people were captured in Africa and shipped to the Spanish colonies in the Americas as slaves.

Spain Lost Control of the Atlantic Ocean

Between 1500 and 1560, the Spanish navy was strong enough to keep other nations away from the New World. But after 1560, the English navy became strong enough to capture many Spanish ships. In 1588, the ruler of Spain sent a large fleet called the **Spanish Armada** (ahr-MAH-duh) to attack England. A great sea battle took place, and England defeated the Spanish Armada. This defeat ended Spain's control of the Atlantic Ocean. Now other European nations were able to start colonies in the New World.

France Formed an Empire in the New World

France began settlements along the St. Lawrence River in Canada in the early 1600's. In the 1670's and 1680's, French explorers traveled as far west as the Mississippi River. Soon the French settlements stretched all the way from the St. Lawrence River to the Mississippi River in Louisiana. These French settlements were called **New France.**

The fur trade was very important in New France. French fur traders gave the Indian knives, guns, tools, blankets and jewelry in return for furs. The furs then were shipped to Europe, where they were sold for high prices.

The Netherlands (Holland) Also Started Colonies in the New World

During the early years of the 1600's, a Dutch trading company started several small colonies called **New Netherland** in what is now the state of New York. But the Dutch trading company was more interested in fur trade than in settling a colony. And in 1664, New Netherland was taken over by England.

As you probably know, England also started colonies in North America. Beginning in 1607, England started colonies along the Atlantic coast from Canada to Florida. You will read more about these English colonies later in Chapter 70.

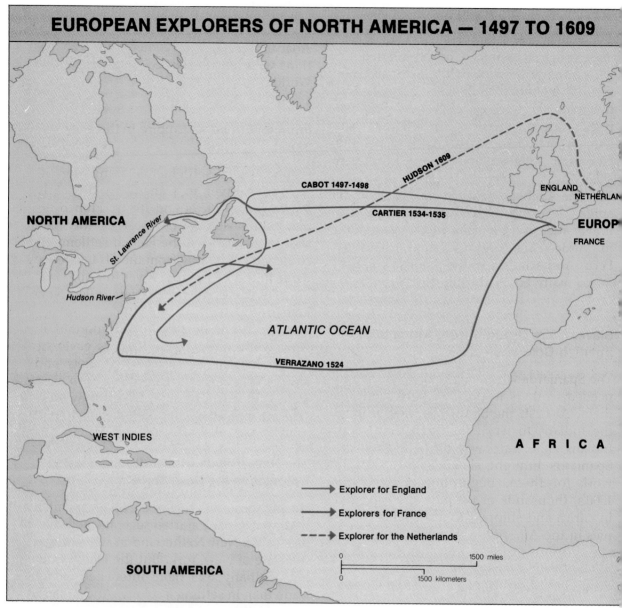

CABOT 1497-1498

HUDSON 1609

ENGLAND

NETHERLAN

CARTIER 1534-1535

NORTH AMERICA

St. Lawrence River

EUROP

FRANCE

Hudson River

ATLANTIC OCEAN

VERRAZANO 1524

WEST INDIES

AFRICA

→ Explorer for England

→ Explorers for France

---→ Explorer for the Netherlands

| 0 | | 1500 miles |
| 0 | | 1500 kilometers |

SOUTH AMERICA

From which country did Cartier and Verrazano sail?

SUMMING UP

During the 1500's and early 1600's, English, French, and Dutch explorers gave their nations claims to land in the New World. But it was not until the later 1600's that these nations were able to start colonies in the New World. In the meantime, Spain built a large empire in Mexico, Central America, and South America. In the next chapter, you will read about an important new religious movement in Europe.

UNDERSTANDING THE LESSON

Do You Know These Important Terms?

For each sentence below, choose the term that best completes the sentence.

1. Early explorers were searching for a **(water passage/water gate)** through North America.
2. The right of a nation to settle new land is called a **(claim/token)**.
3. **(Pueblos/Missions)** were religious centers where Spanish priests taught the Indians the Christian religion.
4. The large Spanish fleet sent to attack England was called the **(Spanish Caravel/Spanish Armada)**.
5. The French settlements in the New World were called **(French Granada/New France)**.
6. The Dutch settlements in what is now New York state were called **(New Netherland/New Holland)**.

Do You Remember These People and Events?

1. Tell something about each person.

   John Cabot   **Hernando Cortés**
   Henry Hudson **Francisco Pizarro**
   Jacques Cartier
   Giovanni da Verrazano

2. Explain how each of the following developments took place.

   a. Spain built a great empire in the New World.
   b. European nations explored the lands of the New World.
   c. Other European nations besides Spain started colonies and settlements in the New World.

Can You Locate These Places?

Use the map on page 398 to do the following map work.

1. Locate the Spanish colonies in the Americas. What Spanish colony was located in South America?

Do You Know When It Happened?

Why is the following year important in the history of the New World?

1588

Do You Remember the Main Idea?

Which one of the following ideas is the MAIN IDEA of this chapter?

1. European nations claimed and settled different parts of the New World.
2. Spain was the only European nation that was interested in the New World. And Spain built a strong empire in the New World.
3. Spain was the first nation to build a powerful empire in the New World. But later, other European nations also started colonies in the Americas.

What Do You Think?

From what you have read in this chapter, try to answer the following questions.

1. Why do you think people in Spain and other European nations left their homelands to settle in the New World?
2. How do you think Spain stopped other European nations from starting colonies in the New World during most of the 1500's?

Chapter 61
Luther and the Protestant Movement

GETTING STARTED

1   In the last chapter, you read about the exploration and settlement of the New World. This development has been called the "beginning of modern times." But while the New World was first being settled, important events were taking place in Europe. And these events also had an important part in the "beginning of modern times."

Between 1300 and 1550 (see the time line at the bottom of this page), problems and disagreements were developing in the Roman Catholic Church in Europe. As a result of these new problems in the Church, an important religious change took place. A Protestant movement began and led to the formation of several new churches, as you will learn in this chapter.

2   Before you begin reading the chapter lesson, survey the lesson. Begin your survey by reading the beginning of the lesson. Then look through the lesson and read the headings. Next, study the pictures and read the picture captions. Finally, read the review section called "Summing Up." This survey will help you to discover the important ideas in this chapter.

Know the Main Idea

As you read the chapter lesson, try to remember the following important MAIN IDEA of the chapter.

The Protestant movement led to the forming of several new churches and caused other important changes in Europe.

The following questions will help you to understand the MAIN IDEA. Try to answer these questions as you read the lesson.

1. What practices caused problems in the Roman Catholic Church during the 1300's and 1400's?
2. Why was Martin Luther against the sale of indulgences by the Catholic Church?
3. What did Protestant churches teach?

Know These Important Terms

indulgences	Calvinism
Protestant Reformation	Jesuits
Lutheran Church	Protestants
Church of England	

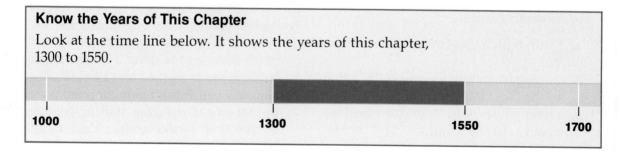

Know the Years of This Chapter

Look at the time line below. It shows the years of this chapter, 1300 to 1550.

| 1000 | 1300 | 1550 | 1700 |

Martin Luther nailed a list of ninety-five statements on the door of the Wittenberg church in October 1517. Against what church was Luther protesting?

EXPLORING THE TIME

People who do not like certain things often protest, or talk against, them. In the 1500's, people in Europe who did not like certain things about the Roman Catholic Church came to be called **Protestants,** a name that meant they were protestors. In this chapter, you will read about the changes that resulted from the Protestant movement.

The Catholic Church Lost Power in the 1300's and 1400's

During the years of the 1300's, the Roman Catholic Church began to lose some of its power. In 1305, the ruler of France forced the Pope to leave Rome and to live in the city of Avignon (AH-veen-YON) in southern France. Then, in 1378, the Italian Church leaders chose an Italian Pope as leader of the Catholic Church.

The sale of indulgences by some unscrupulous Church leaders caused Martin Luther to break with the Catholic Church

From 1378 to 1417, the Catholic Church had two Popes—one in Rome and one in Avignon. Later, the Italian Church leaders refused to accept the two Popes. Instead, the Italian Church leaders elected a new Pope. The Church now had three Popes—Gregory the Twelfth, Benedict the Thirteenth, and John the Twenty-Third. Finally, a council, or meeting, of Church leaders in 1417 removed all three Popes and chose a new Pope. The new Pope, Martin the Fifth, who was elected at the Council of Constance, was accepted by all Roman Catholics. Pope Martin brought peace, but the Church lost some of its power.

Certain Practices Caused Trouble in the Catholic Church

Certain practices that grew up in the Catholic Church during the 1300's and 1400's soon caused trouble. Important jobs in the Church were bought and sold. Some Church leaders did not perform their duties properly. And some Popes were more interested in government and art than in religion. Although some Church leaders wished to improve the Church, they made little progress.

Another practice that many of the Church members disliked was the sale of

indulgences. Indulgences were documents given to Catholics to save them from being punished for their sins. These indulgences were not supposed to be sold, but many persons who received the indulgences gave money to the Church.

Martin Luther Protested Against the Sale of Indulgences

In 1517, a Church leader went to the German state of Saxony to sell indulgences. The money from selling these indulgences was to be used to complete the building of St. Peter's Church in Rome.

The sale of these indulgences greatly troubled a young churchman named Martin Luther, who taught at the University of Wittenberg (WIT-un-BURG). By 1517, Luther believed that selling indulgences was a bad Church practice. He demanded that the Church stop selling indulgences.

Luther was warned by Church leaders to stop his protests or be punished, but he refused to obey. On an October evening in 1517, Luther nailed a list of ninety-five statements on the door of the Wittenberg church. Luther declared in these statements that only God, not the Church, was able to forgive sins. Therefore, the Church had no right to sell indulgences as forgiveness for sin.

Luther Was Successful for Many Reasons

Luther's protest against the Catholic Church came at a time when many Europeans were turning against the Church. Many deeply religious Catholics felt that the Church must be reformed, or changed. Many European rulers hoped that Luther's protests might weaken the Church and help them to take over Church property. Many

DOCUMENTS IN HISTORY

Martin Luther

Martin Luther was a German monk who started a religious revolution. This revolution was called the Protestant Reformation. It was a "protest" against the Catholic Church and a call for "reform."

Luther believed that the Bible should be the guide to the way people worshiped. He said that some Church practices went against ideas in the Bible.

Luther was particularly upset by the wealth of the Church. Part of the wealth came from the sale of indulgences—forgiveness for sins. Luther believed that God alone could forgive sins.

In 1517, Luther drew up a list of his protests against the Church. He nailed the list, called "Ninety-five Theses," to a church door for all to see:

5. The pope has neither the will nor the power to remit [cancel] any penalties except those he has imposed by his own authority....

21. Thus those preachers of indulgences are in error who say that by the indulgences of the pope a man is freed and saved from all punishment.

62. The true treasure of the church is the holy gospel [the Bible]....

Question: Why was Luther against the sale of indulgences?

Ignatius Loyola was the leader of the Jesuits and helped strengthen the Catholic Church

merchants backed Luther because they did not like the Church's ideas about business.

Meanwhile, Luther's ideas were spread rapidly across Europe by the printing press. Luther's movement came to be called the **Protestant Reformation** (REF-ur-MAY-shun), or simply the Reformation. The Reformation was the movement to reform, or change, the Roman Catholic Church.

The Lutheran Church Was Formed

The Pope excommunicated Luther, or cut him off from the Catholic Church, in 1521. Then Luther formed a new church, the **Lutheran Church.** Within twenty-five years, the people of most of the German states, Sweden, and Denmark became Protestants and joined the Lutheran Church.

Other Protestant Churches Were Formed

King Henry the Eighth of England started a Protestant church called the **Church of England.** A French Protestant named John Calvin began a movement called **Calvinism,** which had many followers in Switzerland, England, Scotland, the Netherlands (Holland), and France. Still

other new Churches were formed during the middle 1500's. All these Protestant Churches taught that people must guide their lives according to the teachings of the Bible, not to the Catholic Church's practices.

The Catholic Church Changed Some of Its Practices

The Catholic Church soon changed some of its practices, too. In 1545, an important council, or meeting, of Catholic Church leaders was held at Trent, Italy. This Council of Trent decided that Church jobs must not be sold and that all Church leaders must live a truly religious life. After the Council of Trent, the Catholic Church grew stronger.

One other development helped the Catholic Church. A few years before the Council of Trent, a Catholic group called the **Jesuits** (JEZH-OO-ITZ) was formed by a Spanish soldier named Ignatius Loyola (ig-NAY-shus LOY-oh-LUH). The Jesuits were able to win back many people to the Catholic Church. However, the Protestant movement continued to spread, especially in northern Europe.

SUMMING UP

In the 1300's and 1400's, certain practices caused problems in the Catholic Church. Luther's protests against these practices began the Protestant movement that led to the beginning of several new Churches. The Catholic Church later made itself stronger, but the Protestant movement continued. In the next chapter, which begins Unit 14, you will read about the wars between the Protestant and Catholic nations of Europe.

UNDERSTANDING THE LESSON

Do You Know These Important Terms?

For each sentence below, choose the term that best completes the sentence.

1. People who were against certain practices of the Roman Catholic Church were called **(Protestants/Puritans)**.
2. **(Indulgences/Religious relics)** were documents given to Catholics to help save them from being punished for their sins.
3. The movement to reform or change the Catholic Church was called the **(Protest Revelation/Protestant Reformation)**.
4. The **(Lutheran Church/German Church)** was started by Martin Luther.
5. The Protestant Church started by Henry the Eighth of England was called the **(Westminster Abbey/Church of England)**.
6. **(Trentism/Calvinism)** was a Protestant movement in western Europe.
7. The Catholic group founded by Ignatius Loyola was called the **(Loyolas/Jesuits)**.

Do You Remember These People and Events?

1. Tell something about each of the following persons.

   Martin Luther   **Henry the Eighth**
   John Calvin   **Ignatius Loyola**

2. Explain how or why each of the following developments took place.

   a. The Catholic Church lost a great deal of power in the 1300's and 1400's.
   b. Luther's protest movement was successful.
   c. The Catholic Church changed some of its practices.

Can You Locate These Places?

Use the map of Europe on page 412 to locate the following places. Tell how each place is related to developments in this chapter.

   France   Italy
   German states   England

Do You Know When It Happened?

Why is the following year important in the history of Europe?

   1517

Do You Remember the Main Idea?

Which one of the following ideas is the MAIN IDEA of this chapter?

1. The Roman Catholic Church was not able to stop the Protestant movement.
2. The Catholic Church was weak before the Protestant movement, and it never really recovered from the Reformation.
3. The Protestant movement led to the forming of several new Churches and caused other important changes in Europe.

What Do You Think?

From what you have read in this chapter, try to answer the following questions.

1. In what ways do you think the Reformation was the result of the Renaissance?
2. The Protestant movement also helped the Catholic Church in some ways. Explain this statement.
3. Martin Luther was one of the important people of early modern history. In what way did Luther change history?

Unit 14
The Growth of Europe

THE CHAPTERS IN UNIT 14 ARE

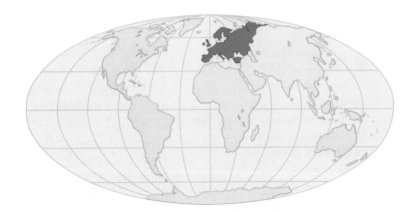

As the nations of Europe grew stronger, the rulers of Europe also became more powerful. And these rulers often led nations to war against each other. But the years from 1500 to 1800 also were a great period in European science and culture. In this unit, you will learn about European culture as well as about the rulers who ruled Europe and fought wars during these years.

Painting showing the French Palace of Versailles

Chapter 62
Europe at War

GETTING STARTED

1   The Protestant movement, started by Martin Luther, spread quickly throughout Europe. Many European rulers became Protestants. As a result, most of the people in their nations also became Protestants. But some nations in Europe remained Roman Catholic. These religious differences between nations soon helped to cause wars in Europe.

During the years between 1500 and 1648, several wars were fought in Europe, partly for religious reasons and partly to keep one nation or group of nations from growing too powerful. The Thirty Years' War was fought for both these reasons. You will read about some of these wars in this chapter.

2   Before you begin reading the chapter lesson, survey the lesson. Begin your survey by reading the beginning of the lesson. Then look through the lesson and read the headings. Next, study the pictures and read the picture captions. Then study the map of Europe in 1648 on page 412. Finally, read the review section called "Summing Up" at the end of the lesson. This survey of the whole lesson will help you to discover the important ideas in this chapter.

Know the Main Idea

As you read, try to remember the following important MAIN IDEA of the chapter.

In the 1500's and 1600's, the nations of Europe fought many wars for religious reasons and also to keep any one nation from becoming too powerful.

The following questions will help you to understand the MAIN IDEA. Try to answer these questions as you read the lesson.

1. What did Spain and Austria do to try to stop the Protestant movement?
2. How were the German states affected by the Protestant movement?
3. Why did France join with the Protestant nations during the Thirty Years' War?

Know These Important Terms

balance of power	Protestant Union
Hapsburg family	Catholic League
Edict of Nantes	Thirty Years' War
Tudor family	

Know the Years of This Chapter

Look at the time line below. It shows the years of this chapter, 1500 to 1648.

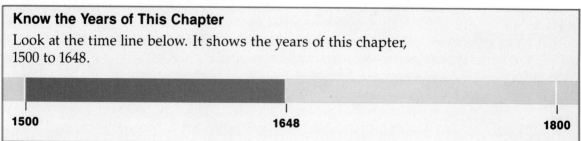

1500   1648   1800

Engraving showing one of the many battles of the Thirty Years' War. Do you think this town would be easy to defend? Why?

EXPLORING THE TIME

Have you ever heard the term **balance of power** used to describe dealings among nations? In Europe, beginning in the 1500's, if one nation became too powerful, the other nations often joined together against it in order to balance, or equal, its power. In this chapter, you will learn about the wars that were fought to keep a balance of power among European nations during the years of the 1500's and 1600's.

Spain Tried to Make the Netherlands Become a Catholic Nation

During the 1500's, Spain was the richest and most powerful nation in Europe. Spain was ruled by Philip the Second, a member of the **Hapsburg family.** Philip was a Roman Catholic. For this reason, he tried to end the Protestant movement in the Netherlands, which belonged to Spain. However, the people of the Netherlands fought back and kept Spain from forcing them to return to the Catholic Church.

THE NATIONS OF EUROPE IN 1648

— Boundary of the Holy Roman Empire

0   500 miles

0   500 kilometers

Describe the location of the German states in relation to the continent of Europe.

Austria Tried to Stop the Protestant Movement

During the 1500's, Austria also was ruled by the Hapsburgs. The ruler of Austria now also held the title of Holy Roman Emperor—or ruler of the German states and Italy. However, the real power of the Hapsburgs came from their control of Austria, Bohemia, and Hungary in central Europe. The Austrian Hapsburgs were Catholics and fought the Protestant movement.

English ships defeated the ships of the Spanish Armada in 1588

France Allowed the Protestants to Have Religious Freedom

France was another important Catholic nation. In 1589, Henry the Fourth, a Protestant, became the ruler of France. However, since most French citizens were Catholics, Henry decided to become a Catholic too. Yet he also tried to help the French Protestants.

In 1598, Henry issued a royal order called the **Edict of Nantes** (EE-dikt of NANTZ), which allowed French Protestants to worship as they wished. This Edict, or order, also allowed French Protestants to serve as officials in the French government.

England Was a Strong Protestant Nation

England was the most powerful Protestant nation in Europe. During the 1500's, England was ruled by the **Tudor family.** As you recall, Henry the Eighth, the second Tudor monarch, started the Church of England.

To keep the balance of power in Europe, England attacked Spanish ships and also helped the Netherlands to fight against Spain. But Spain fought back by sending the great Spanish Armada against England in 1588. However, England proved that it was a powerful nation when England defeated the Spanish Armada.

Germany Was Divided into Protestant States and Catholic States

When the Protestant movement began, Germany was still divided into many states. Some remained Catholic, but some became Protestant. In 1608, the Protestant states joined together to form a **Protestant Union.** A year later, the Catholic states formed a **Catholic League.** While these German groups disagreed on religion, they were agreed on one matter. Both the Catholic League and the Protestant Union disliked the growing power of Austria.

The Thirty Years' War Broke Out in Europe

In 1618, Ferdinand the Second, the ruler of Austria, tried to destroy the growing Protestant religion in Bohemia. This led to the outbreak of war between Bohemia and Austria. The war lasted until 1648, and it was known as the **Thirty Years' War.**

The Catholic nations of Spain and Austria were allies. Denmark and the Protestant Union nations supported Bohemia. By the end of the 1620's, Austria and Spain defeated the Protestant nations.

But in 1630, Gustavus Adolphus (gus-TAY-vus ah-DOLL-fuss), the ruler of Sweden, came to the aid of the Protestants. Under Gustavus Adolphus, the Swedish army won several important victories against the Austrians. And in 1635, Austria made peace with the German Protestant states.

However, the fighting did not end yet, because France suddenly entered the war on the side of the Protestants. Even though France was a Catholic nation, the French leaders feared the power of the Austrians more than they feared the spread of the Protestant religion. Therefore, the fighting

did not end for another thirteen years. Then a peace treaty was finally signed at Westphalia in 1648.

The Thirty Years' War Caused Important Changes in Europe

The Thirty Years' War had important results. Austria's growing power was checked. And the German states suffered so much during the war that they remained weak for many years. Some German territory was given to foreign rulers. The German states gained the right to govern their own affairs, but they still remained a part of the Holy Roman Empire. In this way, Germany remained weak and divided.

The Thirty Years' War had other results, too. France replaced Spain as the most powerful nation of Europe. And the religious wars came to an end. After 1648, European rulers realized that Protestants and Catholics must learn to live in peace with each other.

At the end of the Thirty Years' War, Europe was divided into many independent nations. These nations were no longer united by ties of religion. Instead, rulers now went to war or made peace whenever they felt that it was best for their nations.

SUMMING UP

In the 1500's and 1600's, the nations of Europe fought many wars. Some of these wars were fought for religion. Some of the wars were fought to keep a balance of power among nations. The Thirty Years' War was fought for both these reasons. In the next chapter, you will read about the events that were happening in England during the years from 1485 to 1760.

UNDERSTANDING THE LESSON

Do You Know These Important Terms?

For each sentence below, choose the term that best completes the sentence.

1. The joining together of nations to balance, or equal, the power of another nation is called the (**alliance of power/ balance of power**).
2. The rulers of Spain and the rulers of Austria were members of the (**Bohemian family/Hapsburg family**).
3. The (**Edict of Nantes/Diet of Worms**) allowed French Protestants to worship as they wished.
4. The (**Stuart family/Tudor family**) ruled England during the 1500's.
5. The German Protestant states formed a group called the (**Luther League/ Protestant Union**).
6. The German Catholic states formed a group called the (**Catholic League/ Roman League**).
7. The war that was fought for religious reasons and to keep a balance of power among nations was the (**Religious War/ Thirty Years' War**).

Do You Remember These People and Events?

1. Tell something about each of the following persons.

   Philip the Second   **Henry the Eighth**
   Gustavus Adolphus   **Henry the Fourth**
   Ferdinand the Second

2. Explain how or why each of the following developments took place.

   a. The Hapsburg family fought the Protestant movement.

   b. France, a Catholic nation, fought against Austria, also a Catholic nation, in the Thirty Years' War.
   c. The Thirty Years' War balanced the power of the Protestant nations and the Roman Catholic nations.

Can You Locate These Places?

Use the map on page 412 to locate the following places. Tell how each place is related to the events in this chapter.

Austria   Sweden   Denmark

Do You Know When It Happened?

When was the Thirty Years' War fought?

Do You Remember the Main Idea?

Which one of the following ideas is the MAIN IDEA of this chapter?

1. The Protestant movement spread in Europe and was accepted by many nations.
2. In the 1500's and 1600's, the nations of Europe fought many wars for religious reasons and also to keep any one nation from becoming too powerful.
3. Austria grew to be the strongest nation in Europe.

What Do You Think?

From what you have read in this chapter, try to answer the following thought questions.

1. Can you think of a modern example of nations trying to keep a balance of power?
2. Do you think that the idea of balance of power is good or not good? Explain.

Chapter 63
England and the Growth of Parliament

GETTING STARTED

1 In Chapter 58, you read about the beginning of the English Parliament, or lawmaking body. The beginning of Parliament was one of the first steps in developing a democratic government in England. However, in the beginning the English monarch still had more power than the Parliament did. But, as you will see, between 1485 and 1760, Parliament succeeded in gaining more power than the monarch. Check these years on the time line at the bottom of this page.

2 Before you begin reading the chapter lesson, survey the lesson. Begin your survey by reading the beginning of the lesson. Then look through the lesson and read the headings. Next, study the pictures and read the picture captions. Finally, read the review section called "Summing Up" at the end of the lesson. This survey of the whole lesson will help you to discover the important ideas in the chapter.

Know the Main Idea

As you read the chapter lesson, try to remember the following important MAIN IDEA of the chapter.

Between 1485 and 1760, the English Parliament slowly became the most important part of the English government.

The following questions will help you to understand the MAIN IDEA. Try to answer these questions as you read the lesson.

1. How did the Tudor kings rule?
2. Who ruled England when it first became a republic?
3. What title was given to the leader of the English government after 1689?

Know These Important Terms

Stuart family	Bill of Rights
divine right	petition
Prime Minister	Cabinet
Glorious Revolution	civil war

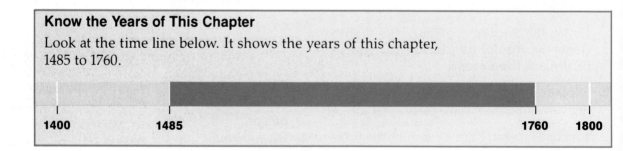

Know the Years of This Chapter

Look at the time line below. It shows the years of this chapter, 1485 to 1760.

| 1400 | 1485 | 1760 | 1800 |

Engraving showing Queen Elizabeth the First presiding over the English Parliament

EXPLORING THE TIME

By the 1600's, the nations of Europe were ruled by strong rulers, but not all the rulers ruled in the same way. Most of the rulers ruled their nations as they wished. However, the English monarch ruled with the help of a group of lawmakers elected by the people. In this chapter, you will learn how Parliament, the elected English lawmaking body, slowly became the real ruler of England.

The Tudors Ruled Without Needing Much Help from Parliament

In England, early monarchs called a meeting of Parliament whenever they wished Parliament to pass a law or to allow them to collect new taxes. But the Tudor kings and queens, who ruled from 1485 to 1603, did not call Parliament together often. The first Tudor king, Henry the Seventh, did not need new taxes, because he did not spend much money. And his son, the famous Henry the Eighth, did not need new taxes,

PEOPLE IN HISTORY

Mary, Queen of Scotland

Queen Elizabeth of England was a great and skillful ruler. Her cousin, Mary, Queen of Scotland, however, made one mistake after another. Finally, Mary was forced to give up her throne. And in 1568, Mary escaped from Scotland to England, where she asked Elizabeth to protect her.

Queen Elizabeth did not know what to do with Mary. Mary was a danger to Elizabeth, because some citizens wanted Mary to become queen of England instead of Elizabeth. Yet Elizabeth did not want to have to get rid of Mary. Therefore, Queen Elizabeth decided to keep Mary in the palace but to guard Mary carefully. And Mary remained there for the next twenty years!

In 1586, Elizabeth discovered that a plan was being made to kill her. Mary was believed to be in on this plan, and so members of Parliament demanded that Mary be killed. Elizabeth finally agreed, and in 1587, Mary was executed for treason. The unhappy Mary, Queen of Scotland, went to her death with dignity and courage.

Question: Mary was the ruler of what nation?

because he raised money by selling Church lands.

The last Tudor ruler, Elizabeth the First, ruled from 1558 to 1603. Elizabeth did not need very much help from Parliament either. During Elizabeth's forty-five years as queen, England enjoyed very good times. And during Elizabeth's rule, England won a great victory against the Spanish Armada in 1588. Elizabeth became so well liked as a ruler that many English citizens were not concerned that Parliament did not meet very often.

A Civil War Broke Out Between the Stuart King and Parliament

The English rulers who came after Elizabeth were not popular rulers. These rulers were members of the **Stuart family.** The first two Stuart monarchs—James the First and his son, Charles the First —believed that they had a **divine right** to rule. The term "divine right" was supposed to mean that the ruler's power to rule came from God and that the people, therefore, must obey the ruler.

The House of Commons in Parliament was against the idea of "divine right." The House of Commons had many members who were landowners and merchants. These members believed that they were important enough to help govern England. But the Stuart monarchs did not agree. To punish these monarchs, Parliament refused to pass the tax laws requested. When Charles the First tried to pass laws without Parliament, a **civil war,** or a war within England, broke out in 1642. This war was fought between the groups that supported the Crown and the groups that supported Parliament.

Oliver Cromwell (standing) ruled England during the years of the Republic

England Became a Republic

In 1649, Parliament's supporters defeated Charles the First's supporters in the civil war. England then became a republic, or a nation that was ruled by a government that was elected by the people. But during this republic, England was really ruled by one person, Oliver Cromwell, who ruled without Parliament. The people of England were not happy under Cromwell's republic. After Cromwell died, the English people elected a new Parliament. The new Parliament asked Charles the Second—the son of Charles the First—to become the king of England.

England Had a Glorious Revolution

Charles the Second became king in 1660, and he ruled until 1685. Then his brother, James the Second, became king. But the English people were not happy about having James as king, because he was a Catholic. They were afraid that James might try to make England into a Catholic nation. However, James' Protestant daughter, Mary, was married to William of Orange, the leader of the Netherlands. William was also a Protestant.

In 1688, Parliament invited William and Mary to become the king and queen of England, and they did so. This was called the **Glorious Revolution** and resulted in new freedoms for English citizens.

Englishmen Gained More Freedom Under the Bill of Rights

After the Glorious Revolution, Parliament passed a very important law in 1689 called

The English Parliament chose William and Mary (seated) as England's rulers in 1688

the **Bill of Rights**. The Bill of Rights protected the rights of Parliament against the Crown. It declared that the monarch was not allowed to pass laws or to take any other action without Parliament's approval. Parliament was to meet often. And the members of Parliament were to be allowed to speak as they wished in Parliament.

The Bill of Rights also gave all citizens the right to **petition**, or ask the government to pass laws that they wanted. And the Bill of Rights protected citizens from being kept in jail too long without a trial and from being given cruel punishment.

After 1689, Parliament Became More Powerful Than the Crown

After 1689, Parliament met more often, and the House of Commons began to pass all tax laws for England. Soon the monarch selected advisers from members of Parliament. The advisers became known as the

Cabinet. By the mid-1700's, the most important member of the Cabinet was the **Prime Minister,** who was the real leader of the government. The Prime Minister and the Cabinet, not the monarch, now made most of the important government decisions in England.

SUMMING UP

The Tudor kings and queens, who ruled England from 1485 to 1603, did not call meetings of Parliament very often, but they got along well with Parliament. However, when the Stuart monarchs tried to rule Parliament, Parliament turned against the Crown. After a civil war, Parliament slowly became the most important part of the English government. In the next chapter, you will read about France and one of its most famous monarchs.

UNDERSTANDING THE LESSON

Do You Know These Important Terms?

For each sentence below, choose the term that best completes the sentence.

1. The (Stuart family/Wellingtons) came after the Tudor family as rulers of England.
2. The belief that a monarch's power to rule came from God was known as (benevolent right/divine right).
3. A war within a nation is called a (revolutionary war/civil war).
4. The time when William and Mary became the rulers of England is called the (Year of the Republic/Glorious Revolution).
5. The (Magna Carta/Bill of Rights) protected the rights of Parliament against the Crown.
6. The right of all citizens to ask the government to pass the laws they wanted was called the right of (request/petition).
7. The (Cabinet/Royal Board) was the group of advisers that the monarch selected from Parliament.
8. The real leader of the government in England is called the (President of Parliament/Prime Minister).

Do You Remember These People and Events?

1. Tell something about each person.

Henry the Seventh	James the Second
Henry the Eighth	Charles the First
Queen Elizabeth	Charles the Second
Oliver Cromwell	William and Mary
James the First	

2. Explain how or why each of the following developments took place.

   a. The supporters of Parliament and the supporters of the Stuart monarchs fought a civil war.
   b. William and Mary became the king and queen of England.
   c. The Parliament slowly became the real ruler of England.

Do You Know When It Happened?

Why are the following years important in England's history?

   1688   1689

Do You Remember the Main Idea?

Which one of the following ideas is the MAIN IDEA of this chapter?

1. After a civil war, Parliament became the real ruler of England.
2. Between 1485 and 1760, the English Parliament slowly became the most important part of the English government.
3. When the rulers of England became weak, Parliament was able to take over and to control the government.

What Do You Think?

From what you have read in this chapter, try to answer the following thought questions.

1. Do you agree or disagree with the idea of the "divine right" of monarchs? Give reasons for your answer.
2. In what ways was the English Parliament like the Congress of the United States? In what ways was it different?
3. Why did some people support strong monarchs rather than Parliament?

Chapter 64
France Under Louis the Fourteenth

GETTING STARTED

1   As you have learned, the rulers of England slowly lost their power to Parliament. But in France, the government developed in a very different way. Between 1500 and 1774, the rulers of France gained more and more power. And the French people—including the nobles—had less and less power in the government.

2   Before you begin reading the chapter lesson, survey the lesson. Begin your survey by reading the beginning of the lesson. Then look through the lesson and read the headings. Next, study the pictures and read the picture captions. Finally, read the review section called "Summing Up" at the end of the lesson. This survey of the whole lesson will help you to discover the important ideas in this chapter.

Know the Main Idea

As you read the chapter lesson, try to remember the following important MAIN IDEA of the chapter.

The Bourbon monarchs made France a strong nation. But they did not allow the French people the right to help make their own laws.

The following questions will help you to understand the MAIN IDEA. Try to answer these questions as you read the lesson.

1. How long was France ruled by the Bourbon monarchs?
2. Where did Louis the Fourteenth build a grand palace?
3. How did French citizens feel about their rulers after Louis the Fifteenth died?

Know These Important Terms

> Bourbon family
> absolute monarchs
> Huguenots
> intendants
> despot

Know the Years of This Chapter

Look at the time line below. It shows the years of this chapter, 1500 to 1774.

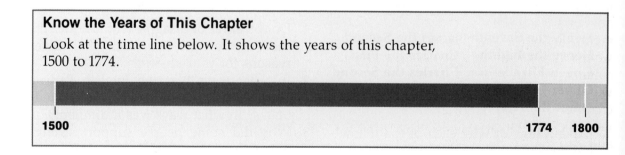

1500   1774   1800

Painting showing Louis the Fourteenth, the French king who believed that he had a "divine right" to rule

EXPLORING THE TIME

King Louis the Fourteenth of France was reported to have said, "I am the nation." Louis meant that he himself had all the government power in France. This statement described the monarchs of France well. While the English monarchs were becoming weaker, the monarchs of France were becoming more powerful. In this chapter, you will learn how the French monarchs were able to build up their power and become strong rulers.

Henry the Fourth Ended the Civil War in France

In the early 1500's, the French monarchs had little power, and often they were forced to agree to the wishes of the French nobles. In the later 1500's, the French Crown lost more power when a civil war broke out in France between the French Catholics and the French Protestants.

In 1589, Henry the Fourth, a member of the **Bourbon** (BOOR-bun) **family**, became ruler of France. Henry was a Protestant, but became a Catholic to please most of the

French people, who were Catholics. Within a few years, Henry united the Catholics and Protestants in France and ended the civil war.

Under the Bourbons, French Nobles Lost Their Power

The Bourbon monarchs ruled France for the next two hundred years. One of the French leaders who helped to build up the Crown's power during this period was Cardinal Richelieu (REE-shuh-LYOO). Richelieu was an important Catholic Church leader. He was also the chief adviser of Henry's son, Louis the Thirteenth.

Cardinal Richelieu wished to make Louis the Thirteenth the most powerful ruler in Europe. This meant that Richelieu had to cut down the power of the nobles. Richelieu took power away from the French nobles by giving more power to local government officials called **intendants.** The intendants took over many duties from the nobles. Richelieu also made the Crown more powerful by not calling meetings of the Estates-General—the monarch's council of advisers.

The French Nobles Rebelled Against the Ruler

After Louis the Thirteenth died in 1643, his four-year-old son, Louis the Fourteenth, became king. Cardinal Mazarin (MAZZ-uh-RAN), another important Catholic Church leader, ruled France for the young Louis. However, the French nobles rebelled against the young monarch. But Mazarin ended this rebellion after five years of fighting. By 1661, when Mazarin died, Louis the Fourteenth had complete power in France, and the nobles were no longer as powerful.

Louis the Fourteenth Ruled as a "Divine Right" Monarch

Louis believed that he had a "divine right" to rule. But he wished to use his powers as ruler to make France a great nation. Therefore, Louis chose government officials from the French middle class. These citizens had been educated in the skills needed for good government. And they helped to govern France well.

Louis also tried to please the French nobles. He appointed some of them to serve in government offices that had little power and did not make them pay many taxes. However, Louis also forced the most important nobles to live in the great palace that was built at Versailles (vur-SY), a village near Paris, where he was able to keep a close watch over them.

Louis also took control of the Catholic Church in France and expected all French citizens to be members of the Catholic Church. In 1685, he ended the Edict of Nantes, the law that had given religious freedom to the **Huguenots** (HYOO-guh-NOTZ), or French Protestants. Thousands of these Huguenots—many of them wealthy merchants—left France.

Louis Encouraged French Artists and Writers

The palace at Versailles was proof of Louis' great power. The palace was surrounded by pools and gardens, and it was filled with beautiful mirrors, carpets, paintings, and statues. Louis entertained many foreign visitors as well as his own nobles at Versailles. Some of France's most famous artists and writers attended gatherings at the palace.

During Louis' rule, some of the greatest French writings were produced. These

French nobles lived and ate well at Versailles

included the comic plays of Molière (mohl-YEHR), the tragic plays of Corneille (korr-NAY) and Racine (rah-SEEN), and the stories of La Fontaine (LAH fon-TAYN). France became the center of culture for all of Europe. French architecture and buildings, French clothing, and French court manners were copied by other rulers of Europe. Even the French language was spoken by the members of the other European rulers' courts.

Louis' Wars Finally Weakened France

However, France did not enjoy good times under Louis the Fourteenth, because he spent too much money. The palace at Versailles cost millions of dollars to build and furnish. Louis spent even more money to fight wars. These wars gained more land for France, but at the same time, they also weakened France.

The Monarchs of France in the 1700's Ruled Badly

Louis the Fourteenth died in 1715, after having ruled France for over seventy years (1643–1715). He had set an extraordinary example of powerful leadership for other European monarchs. These rulers tried to be as powerful as Louis. They wanted to be **absolute monarchs,** or all-powerful rulers.

Painting showing a typical open-air market. How did the vendors display their wares?

Another name for such an absolute monarch was a **despot.** However, though many rulers tried to imitate Louis the Fourteenth, none of them ruled longer or had a more magnificent court.

In France, the monarch who followed Louis the Fourteenth was Louis the Fifteenth. The new monarch ruled France badly. By the time he died in 1774, many citizens hated the rule of a despot. And many citizens wished to end the power of the despot and to change their form of government to something more closely resembling a democracy.

SUMMING UP

The Bourbon monarchs made France a strong nation by controlling the nobles and by using people from the middle class as government officials. The greatest Bourbon monarch was Louis the Fourteenth. Louis the Fourteenth built up French culture and became the absolute ruler of France. But Louis weakened France by spending too much money in fighting wars. In the next chapter, you will read about other absolute monarchs who ruled in Europe.

UNDERSTANDING THE LESSON

Do You Know These Important Terms?

For each sentence below, choose the term that best completes the sentence.

1. The rulers of France between 1589 and 1774 belonged to the **(Bourbon family/Louis dynasty)**.
2. Local government officials in France who took away the power of the French nobles were called **(petty officers/intendants)**.
3. **(Huguenots/Calvinists)** was another name for French Protestants.
4. All-powerful monarchs were called **(absolute monarchs/ablest right rulers)**.
5. An all-powerful monarch was also called a **(dictator/despot)**.

Do You Remember These People and Events?

1. Tell something about each of the following persons.

   Henry the Fourth
   Cardinal Richelieu
   Louis the Thirteenth
   Cardinal Mazarin
   Louis the Fourteenth
   Louis the Fifteenth

   Molière
   Corneille
   Racine
   La Fontaine

2. Explain how or why each of the following developments took place.

   a. The French nobles lost their power to the Bourbon monarchs.
   b. Many French Protestants were forced to leave France.
   c. France became the center of culture of all Europe.
   d. French citizens began to hate the rule of an absolute monarch.

Can You Locate These Places?

Turn back to the map in Chapter 62 (page 412). Locate the following places.

   France   Paris

Do You Know When It Happened?

What are the years of this chapter? What happened to the government of France during these years?

Do You Remember the Main Idea?

Which one of the following ideas is the MAIN IDEA of this chapter?

1. The Bourbon monarchs made France a strong nation. But they did not allow the French people the right to help make their own laws.
2. During the rule of the Bourbon monarchs, France became the center of culture of all Europe.
3. France became a Roman Catholic nation because all of the French Protestants were forced to leave France.

What Do You Think?

From what you have read in this chapter, try to answer the following questions.

1. Do you think that the French colonies in the New World helped France to become a strong nation under the Bourbon monarchs? Explain your answer.
2. What advantages do you think an absolute monarch had? What were the problems that such a ruler had?
3. If you had lived in France during the rule of Louis the Fourteenth, would you have approved or not approved of the ruler?

Chapter 65
The Benevolent Despots of Europe

GETTING STARTED

1 The idea that monarchs were absolute rulers first developed in France, but soon this idea spread to other countries in Europe. Between 1640 and 1795 (see the time line below), rulers in many European nations tried to become absolute monarchs and to gain complete control of their government. Some of these rulers, as you will see, also tried to help improve conditions in their nations. But often they were not able to improve the lives of their people.

2 Before you begin reading the chapter lesson, survey the lesson. Begin your survey by reading the beginning of the lesson. Then look through the lesson and read the headings. Next, study the pictures and read the picture captions. Then study the map of Austria and Prussia on page 430. Finally, read the review section called "Summing Up" at the end of the lesson. This survey of the whole lesson will help you to discover the important ideas in this chapter.

Know the Main Idea

As you read the chapter lesson, try to remember the following important MAIN IDEA of the chapter.

During the 1700's, benevolent despots ruled Austria, Prussia, and Spain.

The following questions will help you to understand the MAIN IDEA. Try to answer these questions as you read the lesson.

1. What city became the capital of the Austrian Empire?
2. How did Joseph the Second try to help the people of the Austrian Empire?
3. Why did Frederick the Great of Prussia not free the serfs in the country?

Know These Important Terms

benevolent despot
Hohenzollern family

Know the Years of This Chapter

Look at the time line below. It shows the years of this chapter, 1640 to 1795.

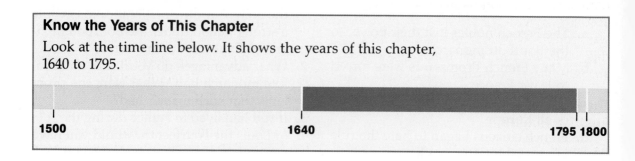

| 1500 | 1640 | 1795 1800 |

Wood sculpture showing the Austrian ruler Maria Theresa

EXPLORING THE TIME

Many European monarchs tried to copy Louis the Fourteenth. They tried to become absolute monarchs of their nations. This was true in Austria, Prussia, and Spain. In this chapter, you will learn about these absolute rulers and their nations.

The Hapsburg Rulers Built Up the Austrian Empire

As you have read, the Hapsburg rulers of Austria also were the rulers of the Holy Roman Empire. But after the Thirty Years' War, the Hapsburg rulers became less interested in the Holy Roman Empire (the German states and Italy). Instead, they tried to build up a strong empire by uniting Austria with Hungary and Bohemia.

But building up the Austrian Empire was not easy. In the middle 1600's, the Turks had conquered much of Hungary, which belonged to Austria. It took Austria almost fifty years to conquer Hungary back from the Turks. It took another hundred years for

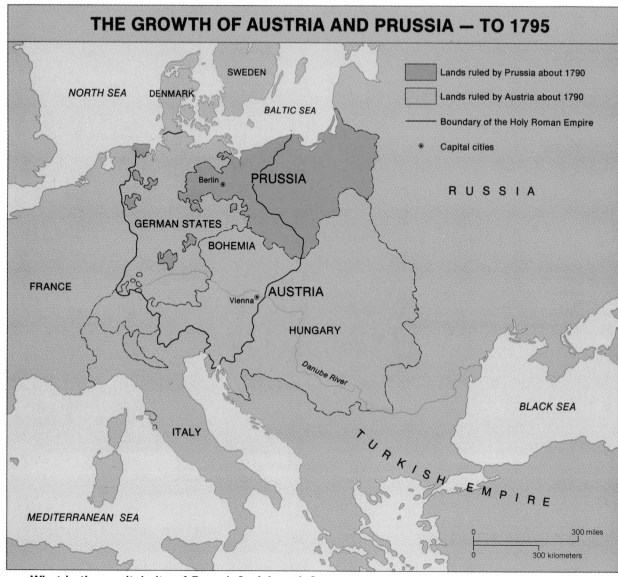

THE GROWTH OF AUSTRIA AND PRUSSIA — TO 1795

Lands ruled by Prussia about 1790

Lands ruled by Austria about 1790

Boundary of the Holy Roman Empire

Capital cities

NORTH SEA

SWEDEN

DENMARK

BALTIC SEA

PRUSSIA

Berlin

RUSSIA

GERMAN STATES

BOHEMIA

FRANCE

Vienna

AUSTRIA

HUNGARY

Danube River

ITALY

BLACK SEA

TURKISH EMPIRE

MEDITERRANEAN SEA

300 miles

300 kilometers

What is the capital city of Prussia? of Austria?

the Hapsburg rulers to add most of northern Italy, part of Poland, and all of Bohemia to the Austrian Empire.

The Hapsburg Emperors Became Strong Rulers

By 1700, Vienna became the capital city of the Austrian Empire. As the Austrian Empire grew stronger, its rulers became more powerful. And the Hapsburg ruler's palace in Vienna was very much like Louis the Fourteenth's palace at Versailles.

One of the greatest Hapsburg rulers was a woman, Maria Theresa (muh-REE-uh tuh-RAY-suh). Maria Theresa, who ruled from 1740 to 1780, helped to make the Austrian Empire more powerful. She tried to unite the many different peoples in the Austrian Empire. By the time that Maria Theresa died in 1780, the Austrian Empire was one of the strongest nations in Europe.

Joseph the Second Tried to Help Austria

Austria's ruler had absolute, or complete, power. Joseph the Second, Maria Theresa's son, tried to use that absolute power to help improve life in the Austrian Empire. An absolute ruler who tried to help people was called a **benevolent despot,** or a kind despot. For example, Joseph gave Protestants and Jews equal rights with Catholics.

Joseph also tried to make the many different peoples in the Austrian Empire all feel that they were a part of one great nation. Therefore, he made German the official language for the whole Austrian Empire. He had a new set of laws written for the whole empire that replaced the old local laws used before.

Joseph also freed the serfs in Austria. He allowed the freed serfs to own their own land and to have the same rights as other Austrians. And Joseph forced the Austrian nobles to pay their share of taxes.

However, the Austrian nobles, the Catholic Church, and many of the people of the Austrian Empire were against many of Emperor Joseph's changes. Before Joseph died in 1790, he was forced to end most of the changes.

Prussia Became a Strong German State

When the Hapsburgs lost interest in Germany, Prussia developed into the most important German state. Prussia was ruled by the **Hohenzollern** (HOH-un-ZOLL-urn) **family.**

Joseph the Second ruled Austria as a benevolent despot

During the 1600's and 1700's the Hohenzollern rulers built up Prussia's power. The first Hohenzollern ruler was Frederick William, who became king in 1640. Frederick William took power away from the Prussian nobles, strengthened the government, and built up a powerful Prussian army. The rulers who followed Frederick William continued the plan, and Prussia became a well-organized nation that was always prepared to fight a war.

Frederick the Great Ruled Prussia as a Benevolent Despot

About one hundred years after Frederick William ruled Prussia, another Frederick became ruler of Prussia—Frederick the Great. Frederick conquered a great deal of land for Prussia.

However, Frederick really earned the title "the Great" by success as a benevolent despot. Frederick improved Prussia in

Frederick the Great

Frederick William I, the ruler of Prussia, always carried a stick. If someone bothered him, he just hit the person with the stick. And no one seemed to bother him more than his quiet son, Frederick.

Young Frederick was kept busy from six o'clock in the morning when he got up until after ten o'clock at night when he went to bed. At the age of thirteen, he was made an officer in the Prussian army. No wonder, then, that at age eighteen, Frederick tried to escape from Prussia. However, his father discovered Frederick's plan and put him in prison.

For a few months, it looked as if Frederick might even be executed, or put to death. Finally, after nearly two years in prison, Frederick was freed and allowed to return to the army. But Frederick had learned his lesson. From that time until Frederick William I died, Frederick never again disagreed with his stubborn father. And later, Frederick became one of Prussia's greatest rulers.

Question: What kind of person was Frederick's father?

many ways. He opened elementary schools for children and set up trade, or craft, schools for older children. He allowed the Prussian people to worship as they wished. And he built canals and encouraged trade and new industries. Frederick ruled well, but he did not free the serfs in Prussia. He did not wish to anger the Prussian nobles.

Spain Was Also Ruled by Benevolent Despots

During the 1600's, Spain lost its place as the most powerful nation in Europe. In the years after 1700, Spain was ruled by members of the Bourbon family—the family that also ruled France. Like the French Bourbon rulers, the Spanish Bourbons tried to make Spain's government stronger by cutting down the power of the nobles and by ruling as absolute monarchs, or despots.

However, the Spanish Bourbon monarchs tried to rule as benevolent despots. They allowed the Protestants who lived in Spain to have religious freedom. They encouraged Spanish trade and industry. And they provided Spain with a set of laws for the whole nation. But the Spanish Bourbons did not succeed in making Spain a powerful nation again.

SUMMING UP

During the years of the 1700's, benevolent despots ruled the nations of Europe. These rulers had great power and controlled the nobles and the Churches. These rulers also tried to use their power to help their nations and their peoples. However, these benevolent despots did not give their peoples more freedom. In the next chapter, you will read about Russia's growth as a great nation.

UNDERSTANDING THE LESSON

Do You Know These Important Terms?

For each sentence below, choose the term that best completes the sentence.

1. An absolute ruler who tried to help his people was called a **(necessary despot/ benevolent despot)**.
2. Prussia was ruled by the **(Wilhelm family/Hohenzollern family)**.

Do You Remember These People and Events?

1. Tell something about each of the following persons.

   Maria Theresa
   Joseph the Second
   Frederick William
   Frederick the Great

2. Explain how or why each of the following developments took place.

   a. The Hapsburg rulers built a large, powerful empire in Europe.
   b. Joseph the Second did not have lasting success when he tried to help the Austrian people.
   c. Frederick the Great was a benevolent despot.

Can You Locate These Places?

Use the map on page 430 to do the following map work.

1. Locate the following places. Tell how each place is related to the developments in this chapter.

Austria	Turkish Empire
Hungary	Bohemia
Vienna	Prussia

2. In what direction did you have to travel from Vienna to reach Italy?
3. What large body of water was located to the north of Prussia?
4. How can you tell the difference on a map between the name of a city and the name of a country? between the name of a country and the name of a water body?

Do You Know When It Happened?

During what years did benevolent despots rule many nations in Europe?

Do You Remember the Main Idea?

Which one of the following ideas is the MAIN IDEA of this chapter?

1. Absolute rulers gained control of most of the countries in Europe during the 1700's.
2. During the 1700's, benevolent despots ruled Austria, Prussia, and Spain.
3. During the 1700's, the Hapsburg rulers of Austria built a large empire.

What Do You Think?

From what you have read in this chapter, try to answer the following thought questions.

1. In which European country would you have liked to live in the 1700's? Explain your answer.
2. Why was it never possible to have complete freedom under the rule of a benevolent despot?
3. If you had been a ruler in a European country during the 1700's, what changes would you have tried to make in your country?

Chapter 66
Russia Becomes a Great Nation

GETTING STARTED

1 One nation in eastern Europe—Russia—was located in Asia as well as Europe. Russia, as you may recall, took over many ideas from the Byzantine Empire. Later, Russia became part of the great Mongol Empire that stretched all the way across Asia into eastern Europe.

During the Mongol period, Russia had few dealings with the nations of Europe. But after the Mongol rule ended in Russia, the rulers of Russia became interested in the progress made by nations in western Europe. Between 1500 and 1796 (the years of this chapter), the Russian rulers tried to bring European ideas into Russia. In this chapter, you will read about their efforts.

2 Before you begin reading the chapter lesson, survey the lesson. Begin your survey by reading the beginning of the lesson. Then look through the lesson and read the headings. Next, study the pictures and read the picture captions. Then study the map showing the growth of Russia on page 437. Finally, read the review section called "Summing Up" at the end of the lesson.

This survey will help you to discover the important ideas in this chapter.

Know the Main Ideas

As you read the chapter lesson, try to remember the following important MAIN IDEA of the chapter.

By the 1500's, Russia became an independent nation ruled by a czar. The czars tried, without much success, to make Russia like the nations of western Europe.

The following questions will help you to understand the MAIN IDEA. Try to answer these questions as you read the lesson.

1. What powers did the Russian rulers have?
2. In what ways were the Russian ways of living in the 1600's more like the peoples' of Asia than of Europe?
3. What effect did the ideas and culture of western Europe have on Russia during the 1700's?

Know These Important Terms

czar   Romanov family   Cossacks

Know the Years of This Chapter

Look at the time line below. It shows the years of this chapter, 1500 to 1796.

1500   **1796 1800**

The Russian czar Ivan the Terrible had the Cathedral of St. Basil built in Moscow. Describe its distinctive features.

EXPLORING THE TIME

In the last chapter, you read about some European rulers who used their powers to help their people. You learned that these rulers were called benevolent despots. However, some of the strongest rulers in Europe were not benevolent despots. In this chapter, you will learn how the Russian emperors ruled Russia.

Russia's Rulers Became Powerful in the 1500's

Russia remained part of the Mongol Empire until the late 1400's. Then, Ivan the Great, the Grand Duke of Moscow, freed most of Russia from the Mongols. In the 1500's, his grandson, Ivan the Terrible, became the first **czar** (ZAHR) of Russia. The word "czar" came from the Latin word "caesar," which meant "emperor."

GEOGRAPHY AND HISTORY

Catherine the Great

Russia became a powerful nation during the reign of Catherine the Great, from 1762 to 1796. Catherine extended Russian territory to the west by conquering a large part of Poland. She extended Russia to the south by gaining control of Turkish territory on the Black Sea.

The Black Sea was a great prize because of its strategic location. A strategic location is a place that has a special economic and military importance. The Black Sea was a strategic location for the Russians because it gave them a direct sea route to the Mediterranean Sea (see the map on page 437).

From the Black Sea, Russian ships could reach the Mediterranean through the Bosporus, a narrow strait dividing Europe and Asia. The old Atlantic route to the Mediterranean was much longer and placed Russia at a disadvantage in world trade. Ports on the Black Sea gave Russia shorter trade routes and naval bases for their military campaigns against the Turks.

Question: What makes a certain location strategic?

The czars, or emperors, of Russia were very powerful. They controlled both the Russian government and the Russian Church. Most of the czars even were able to control the powerful Russian nobles.

The Czars Forced Russian Farmers to Become Serfs

But the czars did not use their great powers to help the Russian people. In fact, during the 1500's and 1600's, the czars passed laws that forced Russian farmers to become serfs who worked on their lords' estates. By the mid-1600's, most Russian farmers were serfs for life. The Russian serfs had difficult lives, and they were completely controlled by their lords.

The Czars Added a Great Deal of Land to Russia

But the czars were not able to force all Russians to become serfs. Some Russians lived on the plains of Russia, where they hunted and traded. These Russian equestrians, or **Cossacks** (KOSS-aks), were able to wander freely from place to place.

During the 1600's and 1700's, Russia took over a great deal of new land in Asia. Many Cossacks moved into these frontier lands, or unsettled lands. Some moved southward toward the Black Sea. Others moved eastward toward Siberia.

Russian Slowly Became Interested in European Culture

As late as the 1600's, the Russian ways of living were still more like those of the peoples of Asia than the peoples of Europe. The Russians belonged to the Greek Orthodox Church of eastern Europe rather than the Roman Catholic Church of western Eu-

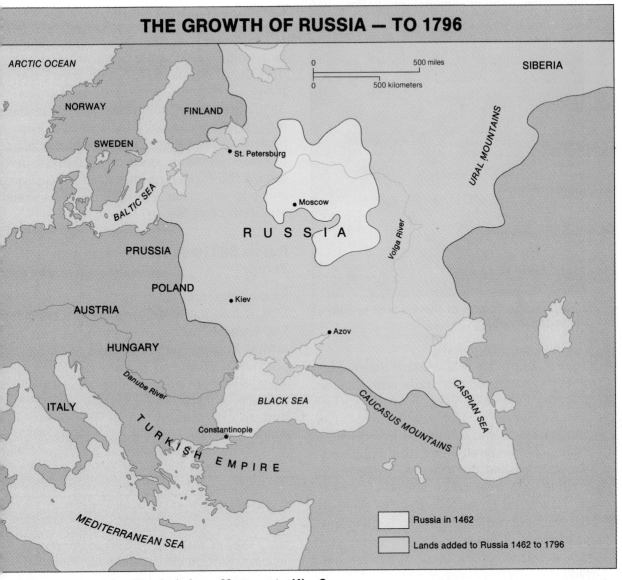

THE GROWTH OF RUSSIA — TO 1796

ARCTIC OCEAN

SIBERIA

NORWAY

FINLAND

SWEDEN

St. Petersburg

BALTIC SEA

URAL MOUNTAINS

Moscow

R U S S I A

Volga River

PRUSSIA

POLAND

Kiev

AUSTRIA

Azov

HUNGARY

Danube River

BLACK SEA

CAUCASUS MOUNTAINS

CASPIAN SEA

ITALY

T U R K I S H   E M P I R E

Constantinople

MEDITERRANEAN SEA

Russia in 1462

Lands added to Russia 1462 to 1796

0   500 miles
0   500 kilometers

About how many miles is it from Moscow to Kiev?

rope. The Russian people, like the peoples of Asia, included mainly a small class of rich nobles and a large class of poor farmers, or serfs. Russia did not have a large middle class of merchants, as did western Europe. And Russia traded more with Asia than with Europe, because Russia did not have many seaports in Europe.

Peter the Great Encouraged Russia's Interest in Europe

In 1689, Peter the Great, a ruler of the **Romanov** (ROH-muh-noff) **family,** became czar. Peter the Great believed that Russia must learn more about western European ways of living if Russia was to develop into

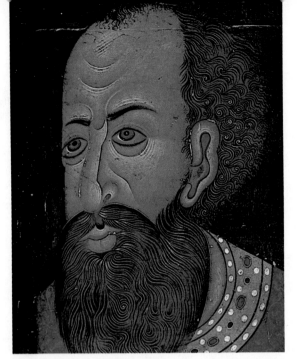

Czar Ivan the Fourth of Russia was known as "Ivan the Terrible"

a great nation. He believed that Russia must begin by increasing its trade with western Europe. Peter took over from the Turkish Empire the seaport of Azov (ah-ZOFF) on the Black Sea, and conquered from Sweden some of the land along the Baltic Sea. Russia now had the seaports it needed for trading with western Europe.

Peter the Great also tried to build up the Russian army and navy to be like those of western European nations. He replaced the Russian nobles in local government with officials like those in western Europe. He encouraged Russians to set up industries like those of western Europe.

Peter the Great opened schools to teach western European science. And he moved the capital of Russia from Moscow to St. Petersburg. But his plan to "westernize" Russia, or to make it more like western Europe, did not please the Russian nobles. After he died in 1725, they regained power.

Catherine the Great Continued Peter's Plans

However, Catherine the Great, who became the ruler of Russia in 1762, carried on Peter's plans. Catherine improved the local governments in Russia, limited the powers of the nobles, and encouraged the spread of European science and learning. Catherine also increased Russian trade with Europe by forcing the Turkish Empire to allow Russian ships to sail from the Black Sea into the Mediterranean Sea.

Russia Still Had Few Contacts with Europe

By the time that Catherine the Great died in 1796, Russia had taken over eastern Poland. The Russian nation now included part of central Europe. But even then, few European ideas spread to Russia. The few Russians who learned anything about life in western Europe were mainly merchant traders and nobles. Most Russians remained serfs on large Russian estates.

SUMMING UP

Until the late 1400's, Russia was a part of the Mongol Empire. By the 1500's, Russia became an independent nation ruled by a czar. Under the czars, Russia grew to become one of the most powerful nations in Europe. Peter the Great and Catherine the Great tried to make Russia more like the western European nations. But by the end of the 1700's, Russia still had few dealings with western Europe. In the next chapter, you will read about new wars that began among the nations of Europe.

UNDERSTANDING THE LESSON

Do You Know These Important Terms?

For each sentence below, choose the term that best completes the sentence.

1. The word (czar/caesar) comes from a Latin word meaning "emperor."
2. Russian equestrians who lived on the plains of Russia, where they hunted and traded, were called (serfs/Cossacks).
3. The (Romanov family/Cossack family) was a ruling family in Russia.

Do You Remember These People and Events?

1. Tell something about each of the following persons.

   Ivan the Great   **Peter the Great**
   Ivan the Terrible
   Catherine the Great

2. Explain how or why each of the following developments took place.

   a. The czars became the absolute rulers of Russia.
   b. Russia slowly became interested in the culture of western Europe.
   c. By the end of the 1700's, Russia still had few dealings with Europe.

Can You Locate These Places?

Use the map on page 437 to do the following map work.

1. Locate each of the following places. Tell how each place is related to developments in this chapter.

   Black Sea   **Siberia**
   Azov   **Baltic Sea**
   Moscow   **St. Petersburg**

2. Notice the narrow water passage between the Black Sea and the Mediterranean Sea. What empire controlled this important water passage? Why do you think that Russia needed to use this water passage for trade?

Do You Know When It Happened?

During what years were laws passed to force Russian farmers to become serfs?

Do You Remember the Main Idea?

Which one of the following ideas is the MAIN IDEA of this chapter?

1. By the 1500's, Russia became an independent nation and developed like the nations of western Europe.
2. By the 1500's, Russia became an independent nation ruled by a czar. The czars tried, without much success, to make Russia like the nations of western Europe.
3. The Russian czars became absolute rulers and did nothing to improve the lives of the Russian people.

What Do You Think?

From what you have read in this chapter, try to answer the following thought questions.

1. How were the absolute rulers of Russia different from the benevolent despots in the nations of western Europe?
2. What do you think that a day in the life of a Russian serf was like?
3. Do you think that Russia might have made more progress if it had fewer serfs? Explain your answer.

Chapter 67
Europe at War Again

GETTING STARTED

1   The "balance of power," you may re-call, became very important in Europe in the 1500's. By the late 1600's, the idea of a balance of power also included the colonies of European nations.

Between 1689 and 1763, the nations of Great Britain (England) and France were often enemies. Each tried to keep the other from becoming too powerful. As you will learn, the desire of many European nations to own colonies, to increase trade, and to keep a balance of power helped to cause several wars during the 1600's and 1700's.

2   Before you begin reading the chapter lesson, survey the lesson. Begin your survey by reading the beginning of the lesson. Then look through the lesson and read the headings. Next, study the pictures and read the picture captions. Then study the map showing Europe in 1763 on page 442. Finally, read the review section called "Summing Up." This survey of the whole lesson will help you to discover the important ideas in this chapter.

Know the Main Idea

As you read the chapter lesson, try to remember the following important MAIN IDEA of the chapter.

From 1689 to 1763, many European nations fought wars to increase their trade, to gain colonies, and to keep a balance of power.

The following questions will help you to understand the MAIN IDEA. Try to answer these questions as you read the lesson.

1. What two nations were enemies during the Second Hundred Years' War?
2. How did Great Britain (England) gain control of a large part of North America and of India?
3. What part did colonies play in the business policies of most European nations?

Know These Important Terms

Second Hundred Years' War
ally
peace treaty
mercantilism

Know the Years of This Chapter

Look at the time line below. It shows the years of this chapter, 1689 to 1763.

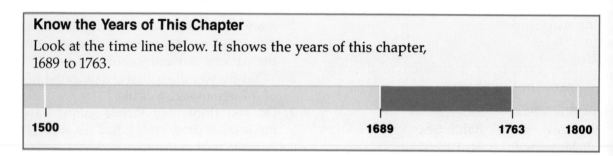

| 1500 | | 1689 | 1763 | 1800 |

Wars were fought over colonies like the Portuguese colony of Macao in China. What were some of the occupations of Macao?

EXPLORING THE TIME

In the years from 1689 to 1763, a **Second Hundred Years' War** was fought in Europe. During this long war, some very important changes took place in Europe and in other parts of the world as well. In this chapter, you will read about the Second Hundred Years' War and its far-reaching results.

The War Began in 1689

Do you recall the Hundred Years' War fought between England and France from 1337 to 1453? In 1689, a Second Hundred Years' War broke out, and again England and France were enemies.

By 1689, both England and France were powerful European nations. Both nations owned colonies in other parts of the world,

NATIONS OF EUROPE IN 1763

NORWAY
SWEDEN
NORTH SEA
DENMARK
BALTIC SEA
RUSSIA
IRELAND
GREAT BRITAIN
NETHERLANDS
London
PRUSSIA
Berlin
POLAND
SILESIA
GERMAN STATES
AUSTRIA
ATLANTIC OCEAN
Paris
Vienna
HUNGARY
FRANCE
SWITZERLAND
TURKISH EMPIRE
PORTUGAL
Madrid
SPAIN
ITALY
CORSICA
SARDINIA
Gibraltar
MEDITERRANEAN SEA
SICILY

—— Boundary of the Holy Roman Empire

0   500 miles
0   500 kilometers

In 1763, which countries bordered the Holy Roman Empire?

especially in North America and in India. Both nations wished to make their colonies more powerful. Therefore, during this long war, England and France fought each other in their colonies as well as in Europe. These years and years of fighting were expensive. To raise money to pay for the war, the government had to raise taxes.

At First the War Had Few Results

The first part of the Second Hundred Years' War was called the War of the League of Augsburg. France fought against England, the Netherlands, Austria, and Spain. France lost the war, which ended in 1697, with only a few changes in territory.

Great Britain Won New Territory in Another War

Four years later, in 1701, the War of the Spanish Succession (suk-SESH-un) began when a grandson of the ruler of France became the ruler of Spain. Many European nations feared that France was becoming too powerful and might upset the European balance of power. Therefore, England, the Netherlands, and Austria again fought against France and its new **ally**, or friend, Spain. (During this war, England and Scotland joined together to become the nation of Great Britain.)

The War of the Spanish Succession was fought in both America and Europe, and it ended in 1713 in a defeat for France. By the **peace treaty,** or peace agreement that ended the war, France agreed that in the future no French monarch was to be the ruler of Spain. But Spain had to give Great Britain (England) the island fortress of Gibraltar (jih-BRAWL-tur), which was located off the southern tip of Spain at the western end of the Mediterranean Sea. And France had to give southeastern Canada, Nova Scotia (NOH-vuh SKOH-shuh), and Newfoundland to Great Britain.

Two More European Wars Were Fought

For twenty years, Europe did not have any wars. Then, in 1733, the War of the Polish Succession broke out. In this war, France and its ally, Spain, fought against Austria and Russia for the control of Poland. Austria and Russia won this war in 1735.

Five years later, the War of the Austrian Succession began when Prussia attacked Austria in 1740. France and Spain became allies of Prussia. And Great Britain and the Netherlands became allies of Austria. This war was fought in Europe, India, North America, and the West Indies. When the war ended in 1748, Austria had to give its territory of Silesia (sy-LEE-zhuh) to Prussia.

Great Britain Gained Control of North America and India

Before long, another European war began in 1756. In Europe, this war was called the Seven Years' War. In North America, it was called the French and Indian War. The war was fought between Great Britain and France for control of colonies in North America and India. It ended in 1763 in a great victory for Great Britain. France had to give up nearly all of its territory in North America and India. These huge lands now became part of the British Empire.

The European Nations Were Interested in Trade and Colonies

What did the European nations expect to gain by fighting the Second Hundred Years' War? They fought each other mainly to conquer more land, to take over each other's trade with other nations, and to win new colonies.

The leaders of these nations believed that having colonies and controlling trade with other nations was the best way to make their nations richer and more powerful. These leaders believed in a policy called **mercantilism** (MUR-kun-til-iz-um). Mercantilism was the business and trading policy followed by the leading nations of western Europe during the 1600's and 1700's. Mercantilism meant that a nation had to sell more goods than it bought in order to bring more money into the nation and make it richer.

Can you name the famous London river labeled here in Latin?

The European Nations Set Up Strict Trading Laws

In order to make mercantilism succeed, a mercantilist nation believed that it must set up strict rules for its own trade and industries. Some of these rules made it unlawful for foreign goods to enter the nation. Other rules made it unlawful to sell the nation's valuable raw materials, or products of nature, to other nations.

If a mercantilist owned colonies, these colonies were expected to buy the goods produced by that nation's industries. These colonies also were expected to supply raw materials, such as wood, metal ore, and furs, which were needed in that nation's industries. In this way, a mercantilist nation expected to become richer.

SUMMING UP

From 1689 to 1763, many of the nations of Europe fought a Second Hundred Years' War to increase their trade and to gain new colonies, as well as to keep the balance of power in Europe. The Seven Years' War was the last war in this long war. When it ended in 1763, Great Britain won vast new territories in North America and India. In the next chapter, you will learn about the beginning of modern science in Europe.

UNDERSTANDING THE LESSON

Do You Know These Terms?

For each sentence below, choose the term that best completes the sentence.

1. The long war in Europe that lasted from 1689 to 1763 was called the **(First Hundred Years' War/Second Hundred Years' War)**.
2. A friendly nation that helps another nation in a war is called an **(ally/aide)**.
3. The agreement that ends a war is called a **(peace treaty/compromise)**.
4. The policy of business and trade that required nations to sell more goods than they bought and to make them richer was called **(reciprocal trade/ mercantilism)**.

Do You Remember These People and Events?

1. Tell something about each war.

   War of the League of Augsburg
   War of the Spanish Succession
   War of the Polish Succession
   War of the Austrian Succession
   Seven Years' War

2. Explain why each of the following developments took place.

   a. Great Britain and France were enemies in the Second Hundred Years' War.
   b. European nations believed in a business trade policy called mercantilism.
   c. Strict trading laws were a part of mercantilism.

Can You Locate These Places?

Use the map on page 442 to locate the following places. Tell how each place is related to the developments in this chapter.

Great Britain	**Russia**	**Austria**
Netherlands	**Silesia**	**Poland**
Spain	**France**	**Prussia**
Gibraltar		

Do You Know When It Happened?

When was the Seven Years' War fought?

Do You Remember the Main Idea?

Which one of the following ideas is the MAIN IDEA of this chapter?

1. From 1689 to 1763, many European nations fought wars to increase their trade, to gain colonies, and to keep a balance of power.
2. Great Britain and France were constantly at war in the 1600's and 1700's. France finally defeated Great Britain.
3. The Second Hundred Years' War was fought because some European nations did not accept mercantilism.

What Do You Think?

From what you have read in this chapter, try to answer the following questions.

1. Do you think that European nations might have increased their trade and gained colonies without fighting a Second Hundred Years' War? Give reasons for your answer.
2. Do you think that the policy of mercantilism was a good way to increase trade?
3. If you had been a colonist in America or India, how would you have felt about the trading laws of Great Britain?

Chapter 68
The Birth of Modern Science

GETTING STARTED

1   Today, science is very important in our lives. In fact, science has supplied so many of our modern ways of living that we sometimes forget that people once knew very little about science.

Before the 1500's, people had learned only a few things about astronomy, the human body, and the forces of nature. It was not until the 1500's that people began to use scientific methods and to make scientific discoveries that were really the beginning of modern science. You will read about some of these discoveries in this chapter.

2   Before you begin reading the chapter lesson, survey the lesson. Begin your survey by reading the beginning of the lesson. Then look through the lesson and read the headings. Next, study the pictures and read the picture captions. Finally, read the review section called "Summing Up" at the end of the lesson. This survey of the whole lesson will help you to discover the important ideas in this chapter.

Know the Main Idea

As you read the chapter lesson, try to remember the following important MAIN IDEA of the chapter.

European scientists made many important discoveries during the years between 1500 and 1800. These discoveries were the beginning of modern science.

The following questions will help you to understand the MAIN IDEA. Try to answer these questions as you read the lesson.

1. Before the time of Copernicus, what did most people believe about the movement of the sun and the planets?
2. What English doctor discovered that the blood circulates, or flows, through the body by means of arteries and veins?
3. Who discovered the law of gravity?

Know These Important Terms

Copernican theory   law of gravity
law of falling bodies   elements

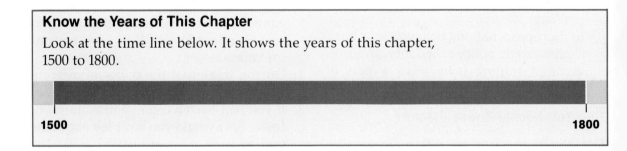

Know the Years of This Chapter
Look at the time line below. It shows the years of this chapter, 1500 to 1800.

1500   1800

Engraving showing early astronomers. What astronomical instruments can you identify?

EXPLORING THE TIME

By 1500, western Europe was divided into many nations, as you know. But ideas were able to spread from one nation to another. During the 1500's, scientists in all the nations of Europe developed many new and important ideas. In this chapter, you will learn about some developments in European science from 1500 to 1800.

European Scientists Made New Discoveries in Astronomy

During the years of the Later Middle Ages, European scientists studied the ideas of Greek and Arabic scientists. By the 1500's, European scientists were beginning to make new discoveries in science.

Some scientists began to find out new things about astronomy, or about the planets and stars. Earlier scientists believed that

447

Galileo Galilei

Today, scientists only believe in theories, or ideas, that can be proved. We call this the scientific method. One of the first scientists to use the scientific method was Galileo Galilei (GAL-uh-LEE-oh GAL-uh-LAY-ee).

In Galileo's day, people believed that a heavy object fell faster than a light object. Galileo used the scientific method to prove that this was not true. Galileo dropped a heavy object and a light object from the Leaning Tower of Pisa and proved that they hit the ground at the same time.

Galileo later built a telescope and made important discoveries in astronomy. Galileo's discoveries proved to him that Copernicus' theory was right—the earth does move around the sun. However, most Church leaders refused to accept this theory.

In 1633, Galileo was forced to sign a statement saying that he did not really believe the earth moves around the sun. But as he signed this statement, Galileo is supposed to have whispered to himself "and yet it does move . . ." Galileo died nine years later. He knew that he had been forced to keep quiet, but he also knew that his ideas were right.

Question: How did Galileo use the scientific method?

the sun and planets circled around the earth. But in the 1540's, a Polish astronomer named Copernicus (koh-PURR-nih-KUSS) discovered that the earth and the planets really circle around the sun. Copernicus' ideas were called the **Copernican theory.**

But scientists were not able to prove the Copernican theory until the telescope was invented in the early 1600's. The telescope made it possible to study the planets and stars by seeing them much closer than they are. As a result, astronomers learned that the Copernican theory was correct. Several famous scientists of the 1600's used the telescope to prove Copernicus' theory and to add important new ideas to astronomy. These astronomers included Galileo (GAL-uh-LEE-oh) of Italy, Brahe (BRAWH) of Denmark, and Kepler (KEP-lur) of Germany.

European Scientists Made New Discoveries in Medicine

European scientists also made important new discoveries in medicine. In 1543, a doctor named Vesalius (vih-SAY-lee-US) wrote a book about anatomy, or the human body. The book corrected many of the earlier ideas about human anatomy. Later, William Harvey, an English doctor, discovered that the blood in the human body flowed through the body by means of arteries and veins. This discovery helped doctors to improve their practice of medicine.

Europeans Made Progress in Mathematics

Europeans also made great progress in mathematics. Before the end of the 1500's, Simon Stevin, a Dutch citizen, invented the decimal system for finding the correct weights and measures of objects. In the

1600's, René Descartes (day-KART), a French citizen, put together algebra and geometry to make a new subject in mathematics called analytic (AN-uh-LIT-ik) geometry. Astronomers used analytic geometry to discover and measure distances between stars and planets.

In the late 1600's, Wilhelm Leibnitz (LYB-nits) of Germany and Isaac Newton of England each developed a mathematical system called calculus (KAL-kyuh-LUSS). Calculus made it possible for modern engineering to develop.

Galileo Discovered the Law of Falling Bodies

Galileo, you recall, was one of the astronomers who used a telescope to prove that the earth and the planets move around the sun. But Galileo also proved another important fact. He proved that if two objects of different weights and sizes are dropped from the same height, they will fall to the ground at the same rate of speed. This discovery was called the **law of falling bodies.** This law became one of the laws, or main ideas, of physics (FIZZ-ikz), the science that deals with matter and energy.

Newton Discovered the Law of Gravity

The greatest scientist of this period probably was Isaac Newton of England. Newton was born in 1642, the year that Galileo died. Newton's great discovery was the **law of gravity.** According to this law, all objects tend to attract, or pull toward, each other.

Some people believe that Newton developed his law of gravity after he saw an apple fall to the ground. He wondered why the apple fell downward instead of moving in some other direction. His answer was that gravity pulled the apple "down."

Isaac Newton discovered the Law of Gravity

Newton's law of gravity helped to explain how the planets and stars move in space. It explained why the earth and other planets move around the sun instead of moving away from each other.

Scientists Made New Discoveries About Electricity

European scientists also learned a great deal about electricity during the 1600's and 1700's. In 1600, an Englishman named William Gilbert helped to discover electricity. Then, in 1752, Benjamin Franklin, an American colonist in Philadelphia, proved that lightning was a form of electricity.

Another great development in electricity was the invention of the battery in the year 1800 by Alessandro Volta (AH-lass-SAHN-droh VOHL-tah) of Italy. The battery

Alessandro Volta (center) explaining his invention of the battery to other scientists in 1800

stored up electricity, and it provided a steady amount of electricity for experiments. The battery made it possible to do many experiments with electricity.

European Scientists Developed Modern Chemistry

Robert Boyle of England, who lived from 1627 to 1691, was the "founder of modern chemistry." Boyle discovered many new facts about chemistry. During the 1700's, scientists discovered some new **elements,** or basic kinds of matter, such as gases in the air. Joseph Priestley of England discovered oxygen—the element in the air that all human beings as well as animals must breathe to stay alive.

Most scientists before the 1700's believed that fire burned because it contained a magic substance. But a French scientist, Antoine Lavoisier (AN-twahn LAH-vwah-ZYAY), proved during the late 1700's that oxygen was needed to make fire burn.

SUMMING UP

European scientists made many great discoveries during the years between 1500 and 1800. Among their important discoveries were Galileo's law of falling bodies, Harvey's discovery that blood flows through the body, Newton's law of gravity, and the new findings in physics, astronomy, mathematics, and chemistry. In the next chapter, you will read about Europe's progress in music, art, architecture, and writing from 1550 to 1800.

UNDERSTANDING THE LESSON

Do You Know These Important Terms?

For each sentence below, choose the term that best completes the sentence.

1. The belief that the earth and the planets circle around the sun is called the **(Copernican theory/Galileo theory).**
2. The **(law of weights/law of falling bodies)** states that if two objects of different weights are dropped from the same height at the same time, they will fall to the ground at the same rate of speed.
3. According to the **(law of propulsion/law of gravity),** all objects tend to attract, or pull toward, each other.
4. **(Chemicals/Elements)** are basic kinds of matter, such as gases in the air.

Do You Remember These People and Events?

1. Tell something about each of the following persons.

Copernicus	Wilhelm Leibnitz
William Harvey	Benjamin Franklin
Vesalius	Alessandro Volta
René Descartes	Robert Boyle
Simon Stevin	Joseph Priestly
Galileo	Antoine Lavoisier
Isaac Newton	

2. Explain how or why each of the following developments took place.

   a. Scientists were not able to prove the Copernican theory until the telescope was invented.
   b. Newton's law of gravity helped explain the movement of the planets.
   c. The battery helped scientists to experiment with electricity.

Do You Know When It Happened?

During what years did European scientists make many important discoveries?

Do You Remember the Main Idea?

Which one of the following ideas is the MAIN IDEA of this chapter?

1. Modern science began in Europe during the 1600's and 1700's, when important discoveries were made about the human body.
2. Scientific discoveries were made slowly because so many different nations in Europe were almost always at war.
3. European scientists made many important discoveries during the years between 1500 and 1800. These discoveries were the beginning of modern science.

What Do You Think?

From what you have read in this chapter, try to answer the following thought questions.

1. Why do you think that the discovery of the circulation, or flow, of blood was an important discovery?
2. Can you think of a way to prove the law of falling bodies by using some other method than Galileo's method?
3. Which of the scientific discoveries of this period do you consider to be the most important? Give reasons for your answer.

Chapter 69
European Culture—1550 to 1800

GETTING STARTED

1   The period between 1550 and 1800 (see the time line below) was a time when new ideas were spreading rapidly across Europe. Among these new ideas were the new scientific discoveries made during these years. As you will learn, during these same years great artists, musicians, writers, and thinkers in many European nations also produced many great ideas and works of art.

2   Before you begin reading the chapter lesson, survey the lesson. Begin your survey by reading the beginning of the lesson. Then look through the lesson and read the headings. Next, study the pictures and read the picture captions. Finally, read the review section called "Summing Up" at the end of the lesson. This survey of the whole lesson will help you to discover the important ideas in this chapter.

Know the Main Idea

As you read the chapter lesson, try to remember the following important MAIN IDEA of the chapter.

From 1550 to 1800, new ideas about life, religion, and government developed in Europe. These years were also a period of great art, architecture, music, and writing.

The following questions will help you to understand the MAIN IDEA. Try to answer these questions as you read the lesson.

1. What new types of art and music became popular in the 1600's and 1700's?
2. What was the title of the first novel?
3. What European writer had a great effect on the Americans who wrote the Declaration of Independence?

Know These Important Terms

baroque	novels
opera	Enlightenment
symphony	deism

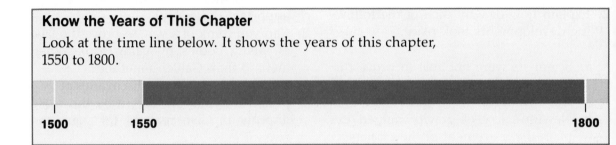

Know the Years of This Chapter

Look at the time line below. It shows the years of this chapter, 1550 to 1800.

1500   1550   1800

Europeans at a theater

EXPLORING THE TIME

If you remember, a great Renaissance in learning and the arts developed in Europe from about 1300 to about 1600. As a result, the years from the late 1500's to about 1800 were a "golden age" in the cultures of most European nations. In this chapter, you will read about the great European culture that developed during these years.

A New Style of Art Developed in Europe

By 1550, the great progress in European painting spread to Spain. Two of the most famous painters in Spain were El Greco (L GREK-oh) and Velásquez (vuh-LASS-kwezz). El Greco painted mainly religious scenes. Velásquez painted portraits of Spanish monarchs and their families.

In northern Europe, Rubens (ROO-benz), a painter who lived in the land that today is Belgium, painted colorful outdoor scenes, pictures of people, and pictures based on stories of the Greek gods. Rembrandt (REHM-brannt), who lived in the Netherlands, painted portraits that showed great skill and deep feeling.

The larger and more colorful style of painting developed by such artists as Velásquez, Rubens, and Rembrandt was called **baroque** (buh-ROHK).

453

The Baroque Style Also Was Used in Architecture

The baroque style was very important in architecture, or buildings. The designs of many important European buildings of the 1600's, including the palace of Versailles, were based on baroque style. By the 1700's, however, many Europeans returned to more simple styles of architecture, such as the Greek and Roman building styles.

New Forms of Music Developed

During the 1600's, a new type of music called **opera** was developed by Monteverdi (MON-tuh-VERR-dee) of Italy. Opera is a music-play that combines singing and acting. In the 1700's, Wolfgang Amadeus Mozart (MOHT-zahrt) of Austria wrote several famous operas.

However, the most famous type of music developed in the 1700's was the symphony. A symphony is a long piece of music written to be played by an orchestra. Both Mozart and Joseph Haydn (HY-dun) of Austria wrote many symphonies that are still played and enjoyed today.

Many Great Books Were Written in Europe

By the late 1500's, more and more writers were writing in the language of their country rather than in Latin. You have already read about the great writers in France at the time of Louis the Fourteenth.

In Spain, Miguel de Cervantes (sur-VAN-teez) wrote a famous book, *Don Quixote* (kee-HOH-tee), which made fun of knights and chivalry.

In England, William Shakespeare, who wrote many poems and plays, became the greatest play writer in the English language. Another famous English writer of

Many European palaces and government buildings of the 1600's were designed in the Baroque style

Painting by the Dutch artist Rembrandt showing a group of merchants

the 1600's was John Milton, who wrote the long poem *Paradise Lost*, which was something like Dante's *Divine Comedy*. In the 1700's, an English writer named Jonathan Swift wrote *Gulliver's Travels*, a story of an imaginary trip to faraway lands. Another Englishman, Henry Fielding, wrote one of the first **novels,** or long made-up stories about interesting persons. This novel was called *Tom Jones*.

A New Belief About Life Developed in Europe

The new ideas and discoveries in learning during the 1500's and 1600's also changed Europe's beliefs and ideas about life. This change during the years of the 1700's is called the **Enlightenment.**

The Enlightenment was based on the following ideas. People can think, and can use their brains to reason, or to find the answers to problems. If people use reason, they can discover the scientific laws that govern all of life. By following these natural scientific laws, people can improve themselves and the world they live in.

The Enlightenment Resulted in New Ideas About Religion

The Enlightenment brought new ideas about religion, and these ideas led to a movement called **deism** (DEE-iz-UM). The people who accepted deism believed in God, but they did not believe in having churches or religious ceremonies. The great French philosopher Voltaire (vohl-TAIR) wrote many books about deism. And Voltaire's writing helped to make deism accepted by many of the educated people of Europe.

455

Wolfgang Amadeus Mozart, with his sister, is shown playing the piano for European nobles

The Enlightenment Resulted in New Ideas About Government

The Enlightenment also resulted in important new ideas about government. One leader of the Enlightenment, John Locke of England, believed that governments were good only if they were formed by the people. Locke wrote that the purpose of all governments was to protect people's lives, freedom, and property. Locke declared that, if a government did not serve this purpose, the people had the right to replace this government with a better government.

Do Locke's ideas remind you of anything? Do you recall the American Declaration of Independence written in 1776? Many of the ideas in the Declaration of Independence came from John Locke, whose ideas were very well known to Americans.

Locke's ideas also were popular in France. Jean Jacques Rousseau (JHAN JHOCK roo-SOH), a famous French philosopher, used many of Locke's ideas in a book called *The Social Contract.* As you will find out in Chapter 73, Rousseau's writing was very important in changing the history of France.

SUMMING UP

From about 1550 to about 1800, a "golden age" of culture developed in most European nations, and it produced great paintings, architecture, music, and writing. In these years, Europe's beliefs and ideas about life also changed. This change, called the Enlightenment, resulted in important new ideas about religion and government during the 1700's. In the next chapter, which begins Unit 15, you will read about the American Revolution—an event that resulted from ideas of the Enlightenment period.

UNDERSTANDING THE LESSON

Do You Know These Important Terms?

For each sentence below, choose the term that best completes the sentence.

1. The style of painting developed by artists such as Velásquez, Rubens, and Rembrandt is called (**Florentine/ baroque**).
2. An (**opera/dialogue**) is a music-play that combines singing and acting.
3. A long musical piece written to be played by an orchestra is called a (**concert/symphony**).
4. (**Dialogues/Novels**) are long made-up stories about interesting persons.
5. Changes in Europe's beliefs and ideas about life during the 1700's is called the (**Enlightenment/Discovery**).
6. The people who accepted (**deism/ Puritanism**) believed in God, but they did not believe in having churches or religious ceremonies.

Do You Remember These People and Events?

1. Tell something about each of the following persons.

El Greco	Shakespeare
Velásquez	John Milton
Rubens	Jonathan Swift
Rembrandt	Henry Fielding
Monteverdi	Miguel Cervantes
Mozart	John Locke
Voltaire	Jean Jacques Rousseau

2. Explain how or why each of the following developments took place.

   a. A new belief about life developed in Europe.

   b. New ideas about government developed.

   c. The period from about 1550 to 1800 was a "golden age" in the cultures of most European nations.

Do You Know When It Happened?

During what years did a great "golden age" of culture develope in Europe?

Do You Remember the Main Idea?

Which one of the following ideas is the MAIN IDEA of this chapter?

1. The writings of the "golden age" of European culture greatly affected the people in the British colonies of North America.
2. From 1550 to 1800, new ideas about life, religion, and government developed in Europe. These years were also a period of great art, architecture, music, and writing.
3. The Enlightenment resulted in important new ideas about religion and government.

What Do You Think?

From what you have read in this chapter, try to answer the following questions.

1. How were John Locke's ideas of government different from the ideas of absolute rulers?
2. Do you agree or disagree with the ideas of the Enlightenment? Give reasons for your answer.
3. What do you consider to be the greatest works in European culture from 1550 to 1800? Explain your answer.

Unit 15
Years of Revolution and Change

THE CHAPTERS IN UNIT 15 ARE

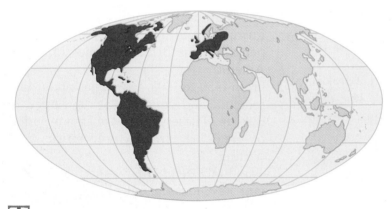

Three great revolutions took place during the last years of the 1700's and the early 1800's—the American Revolution, the French Revolution, and the revolutions in Latin America. The main purpose of all these revolutions was to win freedom and greater rights for the peoples of these nations. In this unit, you will study the three great revolutions and their results.

Painting showing General George Washington crossing the Delaware River during the American Revolution

458

Chapter 70
The American Revolution

GETTING STARTED

1   Today, the United States is a leader among the nations of the world. But during its earliest history, the United States was a small group of thirteen colonies along the Atlantic coast of North America. These colonies were started during the years from 1607 to 1732 by Great Britain.

By 1776, the American colonies were well able to govern themselves, but they were still not a nation. It took the American Revolution, which was fought from 1776 to 1783, to free the American colonies from Great Britain and to make it into the nation called the United States. This chapter tells the background and story of the American Revolution.

2   Before you begin reading the chapter lesson, survey the lesson. Begin your survey by reading the beginning of the lesson. Then look through the lesson and read the headings. Next, study the pictures and read the picture captions. Then study the map of North America in 1783 on page 462. Finally, read the review section called "Summing Up." This survey will help you to discover the important ideas in this chapter.

Know the Main Idea

As you read the chapter lesson, try to remember the following important MAIN IDEA of the chapter.

The thirteen American colonies developed their own ways of living by 1776. During the American Revolution, they won their independence.

The following questions will help you to understand the MAIN IDEA. Try to answer these questions as you read the lesson.

1. Which of the thirteen colonies was started first? started last?
2. Why did the American colonies decide to fight for their independence?
3. What European nations helped the American colonies against Great Britain?

Know These Important Terms

American Revolution	assembly
town meetings	legislature
council	

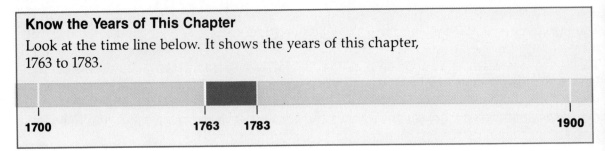

Know the Years of This Chapter

Look at the time line below. It shows the years of this chapter, 1763 to 1783.

1700   1763   1783   1900

Engraving showing the Battle of Lexington, April 19, 1775

EXPLORING THE TIME

All during the world's history, revolutions, or complete changes in a nation's government, have taken place. Many of these revolutions have caused wars and fighting. The revolution that you probably know most about was the **American Revolution.** This great event led to the forming of the United States of America. In this chapter, you will learn how the American people revolted against Great Britain in 1776 and won their independence as a new nation.

Great Britain Formed a Group of Thirteen Colonies in North America

Great Britain's first successful settlement in North America was the Jamestown Colony in Virginia, which was started in the year 1607. And Great Britain started other colonies in the 1600's and 1700's. When Georgia was started in 1732, Great Britain now had thirteen colonies along the Atlantic coast of North America.

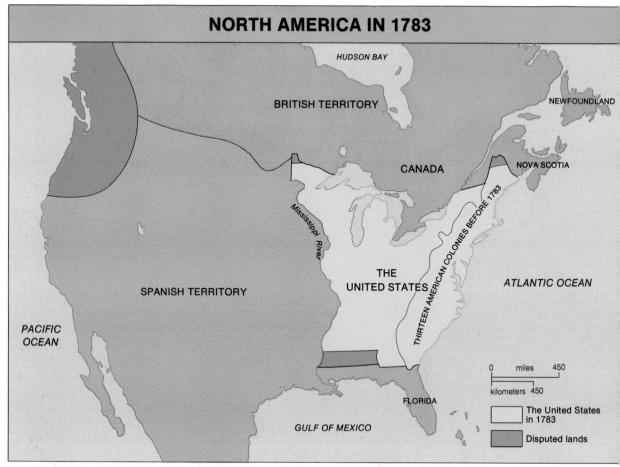

NORTH AMERICA IN 1783

HUDSON BAY

BRITISH TERRITORY

NEWFOUNDLAND

CANADA

NOVA SCOTIA

Mississippi River

THIRTEEN AMERICAN COLONIES BEFORE 1783

SPANISH TERRITORY

THE
UNITED STATES

ATLANTIC OCEAN

PACIFIC
OCEAN

| 0 | miles | 450 |

kilometers 450

The United States
in 1783

Disputed lands

FLORIDA

GULF OF MEXICO

In 1783, which European country held the most territory in
North America?

The American Colonies Were Allowed to Govern Themselves

The people in the American colonies were given more freedom to rule themselves than were colonists of any other European nations at that time. Each American colony had its own **legislature,** or lawmaking body. The colony's legislature usually was divided into a governor's **council** and an **assembly.** Members of the colony's assembly were elected by the voters of the colony and this assembly had a very important power. It had the power to pass most tax laws in the colony.

The American colonies also controlled their own local governments. In towns and counties, the colonists usually chose their own judges, police, and jury members. In the New England colonies (Massachusetts, Connecticut, Rhode Island, and New Hampshire), local matters were talked over in **town meetings** attended by all the people of the town. At these meetings the people made their own decisions about local matters.

The American Colonies Enjoyed Religious Freedom

As time went on, most of the American colonies allowed people to worship as they wished. Many Quakers, Jews, Catholics, and Protestants came to America partly to enjoy religious freedom. These newcomers built their own churches. And people of many different religions in the colonies learned to live together in spite of their different religious beliefs.

The American Colonies Became a Place to Build a Better Life

Many people also came to the American colonies in order to make a better living. In the New England colonies, many settlers became merchants, shipbuilders, and owners of fishing fleets. In the Middle colonies (New York, New Jersey, Pennsylvania, and Delaware), many colonists made a good living from trading, industries, and farming. And in the Southern colonies (Virginia, Maryland, North Carolina, South Carolina, and Georgia), some colonists built up great fortunes by growing tobacco and rice on plantations, or large farms.

Of course, most settlers in the American colonies did not become rich. But most colonists were better off in the American colonies than they had been in Europe, where many people were without jobs and lived hard lives. In the American colonies, it was fairly easy to buy some land, settle down as a farmer, and become a good citizen.

Great Britain Tried to Tax the American Colonies

During the French and Indian War (1754 to 1763), Great Britain spent a lot of money to

DOCUMENTS IN HISTORY

Thomas Paine

In the years leading up to the American Revolution, newspapers and pamphlets played a very important role. They helped to spread the idea of independence throughout the American colonies.

Thomas Paine was one of the leading "propagandists" of the American Revolution. A propagandist is a person who spreads ideas or opinions in order to promote a cause. Paine's goal was to persuade the colonists to cut their ties to Great Britain.

Paine's pamphlet *The Crisis* was published in the winter of 1776. It helped boost the spirit of the cold, tired American troops.

I call not upon a few, but upon all, not on *this* state, or *that* state, but on *every* state.... Let it be told to the future world that in the depth of winter, when nothing but hope and virtue could survive, that the city and the country, alarmed at one common danger, came forth to meet and to repulse it.

Question: What is a propagandist?

463

send troops and supplies to help the American colonists defeat the French forces. After the French forces were defeated, the British government still kept an army in North America to protect the colonists from Indian attacks. To support this British army, Great Britain needed more money.

In the 1760's, the British government tried to raise money by taxing the American colonists. However, the colonists declared that they were able to protect themselves against the Indians. Besides, they said, the British Parliament did not have the right to tax them. Only the colonists' own elected assemblies in the colonial legislatures had that right, and only if the colonists approved!

The American Colonists Revolted Against Great Britain in 1776

Parliament, however, continued to try to tax the colonists. Finally, when Great Britain sent more troops to America to force the colonists to obey Parliament's laws, the American colonists decided to declare their independence from Great Britain. The Declaration of Independence was the great document written by the American colonists in which they declared their freedom from Great Britain. The Declaration was approved on July 4, 1776, and the new American nation—the United States—was born!

The American Colonies Won Their Independence

But winning independence was not easy. It took the Americans eight years to win the American Revolution, or the War for Independence. However, the new American nation received help in fighting the war. France, which was defeated by Great Britain in the French and Indian War, decided

Painting showing some of the leaders who signed the Declaration of Independence

to help the United States against Great Britain. France sent army leaders, ships, and money to help the Americans. And Spain and the Netherlands (Holland) also fought against Great Britain.

By 1783, Great Britain was defeated, and it accepted the United States as an independent nation. The United States now became a democracy—a free nation whose people governed themselves.

SUMMING UP

At first, the American colonies were given much freedom to govern themselves. Great Britain also allowed the colonies to develop their farms, trade, and industries. And the American colonists learned how to take care of their own affairs and to protect themselves. Therefore, when the British government later tried to tax and control the colonies, the colonists revolted and declared their independence. By 1783, the American colonists won their fight for independence. In the next chapter, you will learn how democracy developed in the United States.

UNDERSTANDING THE LESSON

Do You Know These Important Terms?

For each sentence below, choose the term that best completes the sentence.

1. The war that won independence for the United States from Great Britain was the **(Glorious Revolution/American Revolution)**.
2. The **(congress/legislature)** was the lawmaking group in the American colonies.
3. The governor's **(council/committee)** was an important part of most of the colonial legislatures.
4. Members of the colonial **(assembly/board)** were elected by the voters of the colony and were a part of the lawmaking group.
5. In the New England colonies, local matters were decided in the **(colonial assembly/town meetings)**.

Do You Remember These People and Events?

1. Tell something about the ways of life that developed in the following groups of colonies.

   New England colonies
   Middle colonies
   Southern colonies

2. Explain how or why each of the following developments took place.

   a. The American colonies were allowed to govern themselves.
   b. The American colonists began a successful revolution against Great Britain.
   c. The Americans won their fight for independence.

Can You Locate These Places?

Use the map on page 462 to do the following map work.

1. Locate the thirteen American colonies.
2. What river marked the new western boundary of the United States in 1783?

Do You Know When It Happened?

Why are the following years important in the history of the United States?

   1776   1783

Do You Remember the Main Idea?

Which one of the following ideas is the MAIN IDEA of this chapter?

1. European nations helped the United States to win its independence from Great Britain.
2. The thirteen American colonies developed their own ways of living by 1776. During the American Revolution, they won their independence.
3. The American Revolution was a war fought about the right of taxation.

What Do You Think?

From what you have read in this chapter, try to answer the following thought questions.

1. Why do you think people in the three groups of American colonies developed somewhat different ways of making a living?
2. In what ways do you think that life in American colonies was different from life in Europe?

Chapter 71
The Growth of American Democracy

GETTING STARTED

1   When you think of the word "democracy," you usually think of the United States and its democratic form of government. But people sometimes forget that this democratic form of government was not easy to establish. At the time when the United States became a new nation, nearly all the nations in the world were ruled by monarchs. The idea of setting up a democratic government in a large modern nation was a new idea. As you will see, this new idea proved to be successful in the United States.

2   Before you begin reading the chapter lesson, survey the lesson. Begin your survey by reading the beginning of the lesson. Then look through the lesson and read the headings. Next, study the pictures and read the picture captions. Finally, read the review section called "Summing Up" at the end of the lesson. This survey of the whole lesson will help you to discover the important ideas in this chapter.

Know the Main Idea

As you read the chapter lesson, try to remember the following important MAIN IDEA of the chapter.

The new American nation set up a democratic government, which gradually allowed more and more people to have the right to vote.

The following questions will help you to understand the MAIN IDEA. Try to answer these questions as you read the lesson.

1. What part of the Constitution promised Americans many freedoms and rights?
2. How was democracy spread during President Andrew Jackson's time?
3. When did most Blacks become citizens and voters?

Know These Important Terms

constitutions   political parties
republic   abolitionists
Bill of Rights
Emancipation Proclamation

Know the Years of This Chapter

Look at the time line below. It shows the years of this chapter, 1783 to 1870.

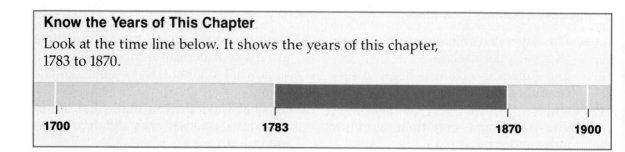

1700   1783   1870   1900

Benjamin Franklin—American patriot, politician, diplomat, scholar, writer, publisher, scientist, and inventor

EXPLORING THE TIME

The first government of the American nation began in 1783. But this new American government was a weak one, and it lacked strong powers. This American government was not able to solve many problems faced by the new nation. As a result, the American people formed a new government in 1789. Under this government, the United States grew strong, and it became one of the greatest nations of the world.

The American People Set Up a New Government

During the American Revolution, most of the American states wrote new **constitutions,** or plans of government. Almost all these state constitutions had a bill of rights, or a list of freedoms, for all Americans. Each bill of rights promised the people the right to speak or write as they wished, to worship as they wished, to meet together, and the right to be tried by a jury if they were accused of a crime.

President Andrew Jackson (left) helped to bring more democracy to the American people. Describe Jackson's audience.

In 1789, the people of the United States formed a new government under the Constitution of the United States. This new government was a **republic,** or a government whose officials were elected by the people.

The new American government was led by a President and a Congress elected by the people. George Washington was elected the first President of the United States. The new Constitution also set up a court system for the whole nation. The Constitution soon included a **Bill of Rights,** or a list of many freedoms and rights that were promised to all Americans by their nation's laws.

Political Parties Were Formed in the New Nation

Two **political parties,** or political groups, were started during the early years of the United States. The members of one of these parties were called Federalists. The members of the other party were called Republicans. Federalists mainly favored a strong national government that was led by wealthy people. The Republicans favored a national government in which the common people also took part.

At first, the Federalists controlled the national government. But in 1800, the Republicans took control when Thomas Jefferson became President. By 1815, the Republicans were the strongest party and the Federalists lost most of their power as a party.

Democracy Grew Stronger in the United States

By the 1820's, most of the states gave voting rights to more and more people in America, especially the farmers and the city workers. These new voters wanted government leaders who understood their problems. In 1828, these new voters supported Andrew Jackson, an army hero from Tennessee.

Andrew Jackson was elected President of the United States in 1828 and again in 1832. Jackson was leader of a new political party, the Democratic Party. Under President Jackson, many important changes took place that led to more democracy. Free public schools were opened in many states to educate more Americans. People who were not able to pay their debts were no longer sent to prison. And working conditions in many factories were improved.

But American Democracy Did Not Include the Slaves

One group of Americans did not share in the growing democracy in the United States —the slaves. Blacks were first brought to America as workers in 1619. Later, most Blacks came to the colonies as slaves from Africa and the West Indies.

By the end of the American Revolution, slavery had almost disappeared in the Northern states. But the number of slaves in the Southern states continued to grow, mainly because of the increase in cotton growing in the South after the 1790's. Cotton growing required a great many workers. And Southern plantation owners used

more and more slaves for growing cotton.

By the 1830's, however, many Americans were beginning to feel that slavery was wrong. These Americans were called **abolitionists** (AB-uh-LISH-uh-NISTS), because they wanted to abolish, or end, slavery.

A Civil War Ended Slavery

The abolitionist movement slowly grew. In 1854, a new Republican Party was formed. The Republican Party wished to stop slavery from spreading into the new territories and states of the United States. In 1860, Abraham Lincoln of the Republican Party was elected President of the United States. After Lincoln was elected, eleven Southern states left the Union, or the United States, and formed a new nation called the Confederacy. In April of 1861, war began between

Black Americans gained the right to vote after the Civil War

President Abraham Lincoln visited this military camp in Maryland during the Civil War

the Union and the Confederacy. This war was called the Civil War, or the War Between the North and South.

During the war, President Lincoln signed the **Emancipation Proclamation,** an order that freed all slaves in the Southern states. After the Union won the war in 1865, the Congress of the United States tried to guarantee free Black people the rights of citizenship.

Blacks Became Citizens and Voters

By 1870, three important amendments, or changes, were made in the Constitution of the United States. The Thirteenth Amendment ended slavery. The Fourteenth Amendment made Black Americans citizens of the United States. And the Fifteenth Amendment gave Blacks the right to vote.

SUMMING UP

After the American Revolution, the new American nation set up a democracy under the Constitution of the United States. America's democracy grew stronger by the 1820's as most states gave more and more people the right to vote. After the Civil War ended, slavery was abolished, and by 1870 Black men and women became citizens and Black men gained the right to vote. In the next chapter, you will learn how freedom spread to other nations in the Americas.

UNDERSTANDING THE LESSON

Do You Know These Important Terms?

For each sentence below, choose the term that best completes the sentence.

1. Plans of government are called **(contracts/constitutions)**.
2. A **(republic/federation)** is a government whose officials are elected by the people.
3. The list of freedoms and rights in the Constitution of the United States is called the **(Amendments/Bill of Rights)**.
4. Political groups who support certain ideas about government are called **(political parties/politicians)**.
5. People who wanted to end slavery in the United States were called **(Republicans/abolitionists)**.
6. The **(Emancipation Proclamation/Freedom order)** was an order from the President that freed all the slaves in the Southern states.

Do You Remember These People and Events?

1. Tell something about each of the following American Presidents.

   George Washington   **Andrew Jackson**
   Thomas Jefferson   **Abraham Lincoln**

2. Explain how each of the following developments took place.

   a. During Andrew Jackson's time, democratic ideas were spread.
   b. At first, American democracy did not include slaves.
   c. Slaves were freed and became citizens.

Do You Know When It Happened?

Why are the following years important in United States history?

   1789   1865   1820's

Do You Remember the Main Idea?

Which one of the following ideas is the MAIN IDEA of this chapter?

1. The new American nation set up a democratic government, which gradually allowed more and more people to have the right to vote.
2. The United States became a republic, but slaves were not included as citizens.
3. The plan of government of the United States needed to be changed before it became successful.

What Do You Think?

From what you have read in this chapter, answer the following thought questions.

1. How have ideas about democracy in government changed through the years? How are they changing today?
2. Which President mentioned in this chapter is your favorite? Give reasons for your answer.
3. What might have happened if the United States had decided to have a monarch instead of a President?

Chapter 72
Revolution in Latin America

GETTING STARTED

1 The idea of democracy, or the right of a people to govern themselves, spread quickly after the American Revolution. People in other parts of the world began to think that the right to govern themselves was an idea worth fighting for.

In the early 1800's, many nations in Latin America fought for and won their independence. But winning independence did not always lead to democracy, as you will learn.

2 Before you begin reading the chapter lesson, survey the lesson. Begin your survey by reading the beginning of the lesson. Then look through the lesson and read the headings. Next, study the pictures and read the picture captions. Then study the map showing the new independent nations of Latin America on page 474. Finally, read the review section called "Summing Up" at the end of the lesson. This survey of the whole lesson will help you to discover the important ideas in this chapter.

Know the Main Idea

As you read the chapter lesson, try to remember the following important MAIN IDEA of the chapter.

Many Latin American nations won their independence in the early 1800's. But many of these nations were not able to set up democratic governments.

The following questions will help you to understand the MAIN IDEA. Try to answer these questions as you read the lesson.

1. In what ways was the government in the Spanish colonies different from the government in the thirteen American colonies?
2. Which island colonies did not revolt against Spain?
3. How did the United States try to make European nations stay out of the affairs of Latin America during the 1800's?

Know These Important Terms

viceroys   manufactured goods

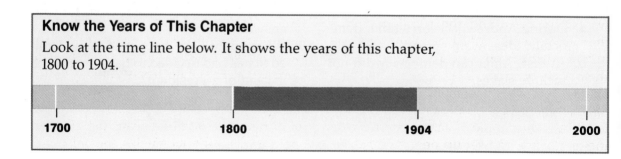

Know the Years of This Chapter
Look at the time line below. It shows the years of this chapter, 1800 to 1904.

| 1700 | 1800 | 1904 | 2000 |

Engraving showing a revolt by the people in the colony of St. Dominique (Haiti)

EXPLORING THE TIME

The people in Latin America (Mexico, Central America, and South America) were greatly encouraged by the American Revolution. These people of Latin America also wanted freedom and the right to govern themselves. After the United States won its independence from Great Britain in 1783, the people of Latin America began to think about winning their independence from Spain and Portugal. In this chapter, you will learn how the people of Latin America won independence and set up new nations.

Spain Gave Its Colonists Little Freedom

In Chapter 60, you read how the Spanish colonies developed in the New World. The settlers in these colonies were not allowed to govern themselves. Instead, they were governed mainly by Spanish officials. The highest government officials in the colonies were the **viceroys** (VICE-royz), who were chosen by the ruler of Spain. The viceroys took their orders either from the ruler of Spain or from the monarch's council.

NEW INDEPENDENT NATIONS OF LATIN AMERICA IN 1825

MEXICO

WEST INDIES
CUBA
SANTO DOMINGO
HAITI
PUERTO RICO

ATLANTIC OCEAN

CENTRAL AMERICA

VENEZUELA
COLOMBIA
BOLIVAR
GUIANAS

ECUADOR

PACIFIC OCEAN

BOLIVAR

PERU
SOUTH AMERICA
BRAZIL

BOLIVIA

SAN MARTIN

PARAGUAY

ARGENTINA URUGUAY
CHILE
SAN MARTIN

Independent nations

Colonies of European nations

Routes of the leaders for independence

0   1000 miles

0   1000 kilometers

Trace the routes of the leaders of Latin American independence.

Spain Controlled Its Colonies' Trade

Spain kept a strict control over the trade of its Latin American colonies. Spain expected its colonies to send gold, silver, and farm products to Spain. The Spanish colonies also were expected to buy from Spain most **manufactured goods,** or machine-made products, such as tools and furniture that they needed. Spain did not allow its colonies to set up their own industries. These strict trading rules helped Spain to become a rich nation, but they also held back the growth of the colonies that Spain held.

Spain's Colonies Wanted Independence

For many years, the Spanish colonies were forced to accept Spain's strict government and trading rules. But when the thirteen American colonies won their independence from Great Britain in 1783, the Spanish colonies, too, began to work for their freedom.

In 1808, Napoleon Bonaparte (nuh-POH-lee-UN BOH-nuh-PART), the French ruler, conquered most of Spain. Spain was now too weak to control its colonies. Within the next few years, most of the Spanish colonies in Latin America declared their independence from Spain.

The Latin American Nations Won Their Independence

One of the early wars for independence in Latin America broke out in 1810 in Venezuela (VENN-uh-zu-WAY-luh), in northern South America. Led by Francisco Miranda (muh-RAN-duh), the Venezuelans tried to set up their own government. But Spain was able to defeat this revolt. However, by 1826, Simón Bolívar (see-MOHN boh-LEE-varr), another leader in the independence movement, helped to win independence for Venezuela, Colombia, Bolivia (boh-LIV-ee-UH), and Ecuador (EK-wuh-DOR).

Meanwhile, Argentina, Chile, and Peru in southern and western South America won their freedom from Spain under the leadership of José de San Martín (hoh-ZAY day SAN mar-TEEN) and Bernardo O'Higgins. By 1822, Brazil, which belonged to Portugal, also won its independence.

Mexico won its independence from Spain in the year 1821. Even before this event, the slaves on the French island of Haiti (HAY-tee) in the West Indies won their independence in 1804 by revolting against

PEOPLE IN HISTORY

Simón Bolívar

Simón Bolívar (boh-LEE-varr) is known in Latin America as "El Libertador." In Spanish, this means "giver of freedom." And Bolívar did help to give freedom to the nations of Venezuela, Colombia, Bolivia, and Ecuador. Bolívar's birthday now is celebrated as a national holiday in Latin America.

Bolívar's family was rich and respected. In 1807, Bolívar took a trip to the United States, and perhaps the things he saw there caused him to want free government in Latin American nations. In any case, in 1810, Bolívar began the fight to win independence for Latin America. Bolívar led the army and fought many battles against the Spanish troops.

By the 1820's, Bolívar's army won victory. Bolívar was chosen as president of Colombia, Peru, and Bolivia. As president, he ruled honestly and well. Under his leadership, the new nations of Latin America made a good start. No wonder that today a statue of Bolívar is found in every capital city of Latin America.

Question: Name some nations that Bolívar helped to become independent.

475

José de San Martín was one of the leaders of the Latin American revolutions

France. But Spain's islands in the West Indies, Cuba, and Puerto Rico (PWEHR-toh REE-koh), did not revolt against Spain.

Latin America Lacked Democracy

Latin America won its freedom, but it was not able to develop democratic governments right away. Spain and Portugal had not allowed the Latin American people to have any practice in governing themselves. Latin America's trade and industry had been held back under the rule of Spain and Portugal. As a result, most of the people were poor and had too little education to understand how to set up democratic governments and keep them going. For these and other reasons, many Latin American nations accepted the rule of strong leaders or army generals during most of the 1800's.

The United States Protected Latin America

Spain wanted to win back its colonies. But both the United States and Great Britain warned Spain to keep out of the affairs of the Americas. Therefore, Spain did not try to reconquer its old colonies.

But during the late 1800's and early 1900's, some European nations loaned a great deal of money to Latin American nations. Sometimes, the Latin American nations were not able to pay back this money. Often when this happened, the European nations sent warships to Latin America to try to force nations to pay the money they owed.

Many Latin Americans Began to Dislike the United States

In 1904, President Theodore Roosevelt of the United States decided to prevent foreign nations from taking over Latin American nations. To do this, he sent United States' troops to protect some of these nations. Many Latin Americans were against Roosevelt's actions. In fact, many Latin Americans were already angry at the United States because it took control of the Panama Canal Zone in 1903. But the United States continued to send troops to several nations in Latin America in order to protect American business interests.

SUMMING UP

In the early 1800's, most of the Latin American nations won their independence. However, these nations were not able to set up democratic governments. When Spain became interested in reconquering Latin America, the United States and Great Britain warned Spain to keep out of the Americas. In the early 1900's, the United States sent troops into Latin America in order to protect the Panama Canal and American business interests in the nations of Latin America. In the next chapter, you will read how a great revolution broke out in France.

UNDERSTANDING THE LESSON

Do You Know These Important Terms?

For each sentence below, choose the term that best completes the sentence.

1. The highest government officials in the Spanish colonies were called (viceroys/royal governors).
2. Machine-made products such as tools and furniture are called (mercantile goods/manufactured goods).

Do You Remember These People and Events?

1. Tell something about each person.

   Napoleon Bonaparte
   Simón Bolívar
   Bernardo O'Higgins
   Francisco Miranda
   José de San Martín
   Theodore Roosevelt

2. Explain how or why each of the following developments took place.

   a. The government in the Spanish colonies was different from the one in the thirteen American colonies.
   b. Most Latin American nations were not able to form democratic governments.
   c. Many Latin American nations began to dislike the United States.

Can You Locate These Places?

Use the map on page 474 to do the following work.

1. Locate each of the following places. Tell how each place is related to the developments in this chapter.

Venezuela	Chile	Argentina
Ecuador	Mexico	Puerto Rico
Cuba	Brazil	
Colombia	Haiti	

2. Which countries in the list above are located in South America? Which of these countries are located in the West Indies?
3. Which country is located farther east, Mexico or Brazil? Argentina or Chile?
4. Which country is located farther north, Peru or Venezuela? Mexico or Brazil?

Do You Know When It Happened?

During what years did many Latin American nations fight for independence?

Do You Remember the Main Idea?

Which one of the following ideas is the MAIN IDEA of this chapter?

1. Many Latin American nations won their independence in the 1800's, but were soon controlled by European nations.
2. The United States and Great Britain helped the nations in Latin America to win their independence from Spain.
3. Many Latin American nations won their independence in the early 1800's. But many of these nations were not able to set up democratic governments.

What Do You Think?

From what you have read in this chapter, answer the following thought question.

   How might Latin America's history have been different if democratic governments had been set up? Explain.

Chapter 73

The Beginning of the Revolution in France

GETTING STARTED

1   The idea of democracy also spread to France after the American Revolution. By this time many French citizens hated their ruler and the harsh, undemocratic government. Therefore, by 1789—the year when George Washington became the first President of the United States—France was ready for a change. From about 1774 to 1789, the French people were preparing for this great change, or revolution, which also affected all the nations of Europe within a few years. In this chapter, you will read about the French Revolution.

2   Before you begin reading the chapter lesson, survey the lesson. Begin your survey by reading the beginning of the lesson. Then look through the lesson and read the headings. Next, study the pictures and read the picture captions. Finally, read the review section called "Summing Up." This survey of the whole lesson will help you to discover the important ideas in this chapter.

Know the Main Idea

As you read the chapter lesson, try to remember the following important MAIN IDEA of the chapter.

The French Revolution began in 1789 when the people of the Third Estate formed the National Assembly and promised to write a new constitution for France.

The following questions will help you to understand the MAIN IDEA. Try to answer these questions as you read the lesson.

1. What group of French citizens made up the First Estate? the Second Estate? the Third Estate?
2. What beliefs did writers like John Locke and Jean Jacques Rousseau have about government?
3. Who was the ruler of France during the years just before the French Revolution?

Know These Important Terms

French Revolution	bourgeoisie
National Assembly	Estates

Know the Years of This Chapter

Look at the time line below. It shows the years of this chapter, 1774 to 1789.

| 1700 | 1774 | 1789 | 1900 |

Engraving showing the active part taken by women to win the French Revolution

EXPLORING THE TIME

In the year 1789, a great revolt broke out in France against the French monarch and his government. This great revolt was the **French Revolution.** The French Revolution led to many changes in France and in the rest of Europe. In this chapter, you will learn how the French Revolution began.

The French Government Faced Trouble

As you read in Chapter 64, France was ruled by an absolute monarch, or a ruler who had complete power to rule. The French monarch had the power to pass all laws, to put people into prison, and to collect taxes.

Louis the Sixteenth, who became king in 1774, was a weak ruler. And Louis began

Louis the Sixteenth of France (right) met with the Third Estate but refused to agree to their demands. Describe the mood of the bourgeoisie.

to lose the support of the French people. The government owed much money, and the people of France were suffering from hard times.

The People of France Were Divided into Three Groups

The French people were divided into three **Estates,** or groups. The First Estate was made up of Roman Catholic Church leaders. The First Estate was less than 1 per cent of the French population, but it owned more than 20 per cent of all the land in France.

The Second Estate was made up of the French nobles. The nobles were only 1 per cent of the population, but they, too, owned nearly 20 per cent of the land.

The Third Estate was the largest group in France, and it included all the rest of the French people. The Third Estate included the peasants (small farmers), city workers, servants, and shopkeepers. The Third Estate also included the doctors, lawyers, writers, and merchants in the cities and towns. This group of people was called the **bourgeoisie** (BOOR-zhwa-ZEE). The bourgeoisie soon became the leaders of the Third Estate.

The French Peasants Hated the Old Feudal Laws

The peasants in the Third Estate hated the French government for many reasons. They did not like being forced to pay rent to their feudal lords. They also did not like having to pay for the use of the lords' flour grinding mill, whether they used it or not. In addition, the peasants did not like the lords to hunt foxes on the peasants' farmland, because the lords' horses often destroyed the peasants' crops.

The Bourgeoisie Hated the High Taxes

The bourgeoisie and all other members of the Third Estate had to pay several high taxes, including an income tax, to the government. They also had to pay a tax to the Church. But the First Estate and the Second Estate did not have to pay many taxes. The bourgeoisie felt this tax system was not fair to the Third Estate.

Writers Attacked the French Government

Many members of the French bourgeoisie were well educated. They read the writings of such philosophers as John Locke, Voltaire, Montesquieu (MON-tus-KYEW), and Jean Jacques Rousseau.

These writers believed that the people had the right to rule themselves and that the ruler's power must be limited. The ideas of these writers became very popular among the bourgeoisie.

Louis the Sixteenth Called a Meeting of the Three Estates

By the late 1780's, the French government needed money badly in order to pay its debts. In 1789, therefore, King Louis the Sixteenth called a meeting of the Estates-General. The Estates-General was a group of advisers to the Crown with members from all three Estates. The Estates-General had not been called together for many, many years.

When the Estates-General last met in the year 1614, each Estate was allowed one vote. This meant that the Church leaders (the First Estate) and the nobles (the Second Estate) always were able to vote against the Third Estate by two to one. But in 1789, the Third Estate refused to allow this to happen

HIGHLIGHTS IN HISTORY

French Citizens Attacking the Bastille

The day of July 14 is a holiday in France. This day marks the capture of the Bastille (bah-STEEL) prison in the year 1789. The Bastille in Paris was the royal prison, where French citizens who dared to speak against the ruler or the government often were locked up for years without a trial.

The Bastille was a large, well-built prison. Its walls were 90 feet high and 9 feet thick. But it was defended by only a small group of the ruler's soldiers. When thousands of French citizens began to attack the Bastille on July 14, 1789, the commander of the Bastille surrendered after just a few hours of fighting.

The people of Paris freed the prisoners in the Bastille—there were only seven of them. When the ruler of France heard the news, he was angry and declared, "It is a revolt!" The ruler's advisers knew better, for they corrected him, saying, "It is not a revolt, sir; it is a revolution!"

Question: On what date did the Bastille fall?

On June 20, 1789, the National Assembly met on the Tennis Court at Versailles and decided to write a new constitution

again. The Third Estate had as many members as both the First Estate and Second Estate together. The Third Estate now demanded that all members in all three Estates vote together as one group on all matters. The Third Estate also demanded that all decisions be made by the majority vote of all the members in the three Estates.

The French Revolution Began in 1789

However, the French nobles and Church leaders were against this idea. The First Estate and the Second Estate still wanted each Estate to meet separately and have one vote. As a result, the members of the Third Estate decided to take action. They declared themselves the **National Assembly** of France.

As the National Assembly, the Third Estate intended to act as a lawmaking body for all the people of France. On June 20, 1789, the members of the National Assembly met, and they promised not to end their meeting until they wrote a constitution for France. This promise by the National Assembly to make a new government plan for France was the beginning of the French Revolution.

SUMMING UP

The French people were divided into three Estates, or groups. The First Estate and Second Estate—the Church leaders and the nobles—made up only 2 per cent of the population, but they paid few taxes and owned much of the land. The rest of the French people belonged to the Third Estate, which paid high taxes and had few rights.

The French Revolution began when the Third Estate formed itself into the National Assembly and promised to write a constitution for France. In the next chapter, you will learn what happened during the years of the French Revolution.

UNDERSTANDING THE LESSON

Do You Know These Important Terms?

For each sentence below, choose the term that best completes the sentence.

1. The revolt in France against the French king and the government was called the **(French Revolution/French War for Independence)**.
2. The three groups, or classes, of people in France were called **(Estates/Assemblies)**.
3. The doctors, lawyers, merchants, and writers were called the **(elite/ bourgeoisie)**.
4. In 1789, the **(Estates-General/National Assembly)** began to act as the law-making body of France.

Do You Remember These People and Events?

1. Tell something about each of the following subjects.

First Estate	John Locke
Second Estate	Voltaire
Jean Jacques Rousseau	Third Estate
Louis the Sixteenth	bourgeoisie

2. Explain why each of the following developments took place.

   a. The French peasants hated the old feudal laws.
   b. The ruler called a meeting of the Estates-General.
   c. The Third Estate did not like the way that the Estates-General voted.

Can You Locate These Places?

On the map of Europe in Chapter 74 (page 486), locate the following places.

France	Paris
Atlantic Ocean	Mediterranean Sea

What nations on the map have a border that touches France?

Do You Know When It Happened?

Why is the following year important in French history?

1789

Do You Remember the Main Idea?

Which one of the following ideas is the MAIN IDEA of this chapter?

1. The three Estates were equally important in the government of France, and most of the French people supported this law-making body.
2. The French Revolution began in 1789 when the people of the Third Estate formed the National Assembly and promised to write a new constitution.
3. The French Revolution was started by the bourgeoisie, a group that wanted to gain control of the French government.

What Do You Think?

From what you have read in this chapter, try to answer the following thought questions.

1. Do you think that the Third Estate was right to want to change the government of France? Explain your answer.
2. Do you think that the bourgeoisie were good leaders of the Third Estate? Why or why not?

Chapter 74
The Years of the French Revolution

GETTING STARTED

1 As you read in the last chapter, the French Revolution began when leaders of the Third Estate, which included most of the French people, formed the National Assembly. The members of the National Assembly now began to control the government of France.

The French Revolution lasted from 1789 to 1799 (see the time line below). It began as a peaceful revolt. But it soon turned into one of the greatest revolutions in history. And it brought important changes to France and to the French people.

2 Before you being reading the chapter lesson, survey the lesson. Begin your survey by reading the beginning of the lesson. Then look through the lesson and read the headings. Next, study the pictures and read the picture captions. Then study the map showing Europe in 1789 on page 486. Finally, read the review section called "Summing Up." This survey will help you to discover the important ideas in this chapter.

Know the Main Idea

As you read the chapter lesson, try to remember the following important MAIN IDEA of the chapter.

Three different governments ruled France during the French Revolution. Then, in 1799, Napoleon Bonaparte set up a new, strong government for France.

The following questions will help you to understand the MAIN IDEA. Try to answer these questions as you read the lesson.

1. During the first period of the Revolution, what group controlled France?
2. What political party ruled France in the second period of the French Revolution?
3. Who ruled France during the third period of the French Revolution?

Know These Important Terms

Declaration of the Rights of Man
National Convention
Jacobin Party
Committee of Public Safety
Reign of Terror
Directory

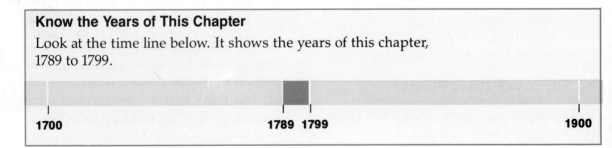

Know the Years of This Chapter
Look at the time line below. It shows the years of this chapter, 1789 to 1799.

| 1700 | 1789 1799 | 1900 |

New and unusual rules, requirements, and certifications added
to the chaos of the revolution

EXPLORING THE TIME

In the last chapter, you read that the National Assembly in 1789 promised to write a new constitution for France. The National Assembly kept its promise, and it wrote a new constitution. However, before the French Revolution ended, France had several more changes in government. In this chapter, you will learn how three different governments ruled France during the Revolution.

The National Assembly Ended the Old Feudal System

The French Revolution may be divided into three periods. The first period lasted from 1789 to 1792. During these years, the National Assembly, or the new law-making body, made many important changes in France. These changes were favored by mobs of armed French citizens who supported the Revolution.

The National Assembly began by ending all the old feudal rights of the nobles

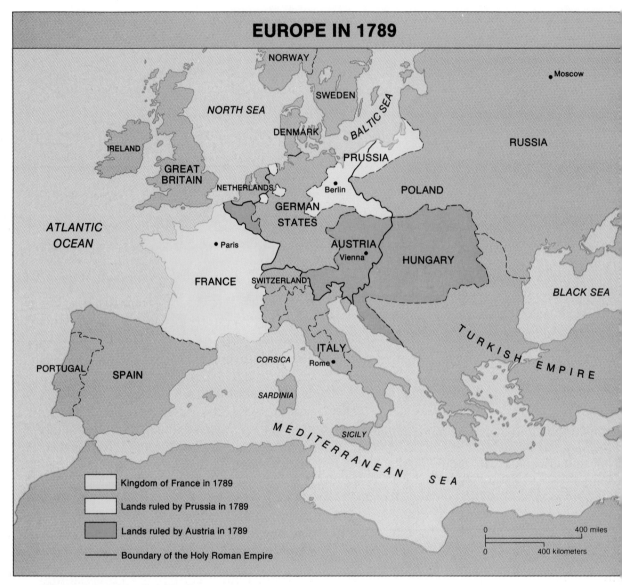

EUROPE IN 1789

NORWAY

Moscow

SWEDEN

NORTH SEA

BALTIC SEA

DENMARK

RUSSIA

IRELAND

PRUSSIA

GREAT
BRITAIN

NETHERLANDS

Berlin

POLAND

GERMAN
STATES

ATLANTIC
OCEAN

Paris

AUSTRIA

HUNGARY

Vienna

FRANCE

SWITZERLAND

BLACK SEA

T U R K I S H   E M P I R E

ITALY

CORSICA

Rome

PORTUGAL

SPAIN

SARDINIA

M E D I T E R R A N E A N   S E A

SICILY

	Kingdom of France in 1789
	Lands ruled by Prussia in 1789
	Lands ruled by Austria in 1789
——	Boundary of the Holy Roman Empire

0   400 miles

0   400 kilometers

Which island in the Mediterranean was part of the Kingdom of France in 1789?

and the Church. The peasants no longer had to serve their feudal lords or to pay taxes to them. And the nobles and the Church leaders were forced to give up many of their rights and to pay their share of taxes. These changes weakened the power of the nobles and the Church.

The French People Won New Rights and Freedoms

But weakening the power of the nobles and Church leaders was only the beginning of the French Revolution. In late 1789, the National Assembly wrote the **Declaration** of the **Rights of Man.** This document promised all French citizens freedom and the rights of property, as well as the right to change their government. It also promised citizens freedom of speech, freedom of religion, freedom to write as they wished, and the right to have a fair trial.

The National Assembly Ended the Church's Power

The National Assembly also took over all the land that belonged to the Roman Catholic Church. The National Assembly then sold these lands in order to help pay the government's debts.

In return for these Church lands, the government agreed to pay the salaries of all Church leaders. However, these Church leaders were to be elected by voters in the same way that government officials were elected.

A New Constitution Was Written for France

By the end of 1791, the National Assembly completed the new constitution for France. The new constitution set up a national legislature, or law-making body. It forbade the monarch to pass laws, collect taxes, or declare war without the approval of the legislature.

France Became a Republic in 1792

The second period of the French Revolution lasted from 1792 to 1795. In the spring of 1792, France declared war on Austria and Prussia. The French government feared that these nations were planning to invade France and stop the French Revolution. In the beginning of the war, the French armies were badly beaten. The French people blamed King Louis the Sixteenth and his Austrian wife, Marie Antoinette (muh-REE AN-twa-NET), for the defeats of the French armies.

In 1792, the leaders of the French Revolution took away the Crown's power and called a **National Convention** to write another constitution to set up a French Republic. The following year, the king and queen were put to death as traitors to France. France now became a Republic under a new constitution.

A "Reign of Terror" Took Place in France

The new leaders of the French Republic were Jean Paul Marat (mah-RAH), Georges Jacques Danton, and Maximilien de Robespierre (ROHBZ-pee-AIR). These leaders belonged to the **Jacobin** (JACK-uh-BINN) **Party,** which supported the French Republic.

The new leaders of the Revolution faced many problems. Austria and Prussia were attacking France. And many French citizens were turning against the Revolution because the king and queen had been killed. The Jacobin leaders decided that they must defend the Revolution from all of its enemies. They organized a **Committee of Public Safety** to find out which citizens were against the Revolution. Many citizens who were suspected of being against the Revolution were put to death.

Between 1793 and 1794, so many French citizens were put to death that this period is called the **Reign of Terror,** or the "rule of terror." Before the Reign of Terror was over, thousands of citizens (including Marat, Danton, and Robespierre themselves!) were killed.

Engraving showing Louis the Sixteenth of France just before his execution on January 21, 1793. Why was the king executed?

Many Improvements Took Place During the Republic

However, during the period of the Republic, France improved in many ways. Slavery was ended in all the French colonies. The lands that were taken away from the Church and the nobles were given to many French peasants. And the armies of the French Republic defeated Austria and Prussia. This victory gave all French citizens a feeling of great pride in their nation.

The Government of the Directory Replaced the Republic

By 1795, many French citizens hated the rule of the Jacobin leaders because of the Reign of Terror. As a result, the Jacobin government was overthrown. The third period of the Revolution now began in 1795. During this third period, France was ruled by a group of five people called the Directory.

However, the Directory did not govern well and it became disliked. In 1799, the Directory was overthrown by a young general, Napoleon Bonaparte, who set up a strong, new government for France.

SUMMING UP

The French Revolution had three main periods. During the first period, France was ruled by the monarch and a legislature. During the second period, the ruler of France was put to death, and France became a Republic. During the third period, the Directory governed France. Then in 1799, a young general, Napoleon Bonaparte, overthrew the Directory. In the next chapter, you will learn how Napoleon ruled France.

UNDERSTANDING THE LESSON

Do You Know These Important Terms?

For each sentence below, choose the term that best completes the sentence.

1. The document that promised all French citizens freedom, as well as the right to change their government, was called the **(French Bill of Rights/Declaration of the Rights of Man)**.
2. A group called together to write a second constitution to set up a French Republic was the **(National Assembly/National Convention)**.
3. The leaders during the period of the French Republic belonged to the **(Bourbon Party/Jacobin Party)**.
4. The **(Committee of Public Safety/Watchdog Committee)** was a group set up by the Jacobins to find out which citizens were against the Revolution.
5. The period when thousands of French citizens were put to death was called the **(Death March/Reign of Terror)**.
6. The group of five people who ruled France during the third period of the Revolution was called the **(Directory/Consulate)**.

Do You Remember These People and Events?

1. Tell something about each person.

   Louis the Sixteenth   **Marat**
   Marie Antoinette   **Danton**
   Napoleon Bonaparte   **Robespierre**

2. Explain how or why each of the following developments took place.

   a. The Church lost most of its power in France during the French Revolution.
   b. France became a Republic.
   c. Thousands of French citizens died during the Reign of Terror.

Can You Locate These Places?

Use the map on page 486 to locate the following places. Tell how each place is related to developments in this chapter.

   France   **Prussia**   **Austria**

Do You Know When It Happened?

What were the years of the French Revolution?

Do You Remember the Main Idea?

Which one of the following ideas is the MAIN IDEA of this chapter?

1. Three different governments ruled France during the French Revolution. Then, in 1799, Napoleon Bonaparte set up a new, strong government for France.
2. The French Revolution was a revolt against the Crown, and all the nobles in France were put to death.
3. The French people gained few freedoms, but they had a strong government as a result of the French Revolution.

What Do You Think?

From what you have read in this chapter, try to answer the following questions.

1. How was the French Revolution different from the American Revolution?
2. Do you think that it is important for people to be loyal to their country? Explain.

Chapter 75

France Under Napoleon and Later Rulers

GETTING STARTED

1   Napoleon Bonaparte was one of the most interesting and important leaders in history. Napoleon showed great skill as an army leader, and won the support of the troops and the people of France.

As you will see, Napoleon Bonaparte built a great empire for France. Under Napoleon and the rulers who followed, many changes took place in France. This period of years in France's history included the years from 1799 to 1870 (see the time line at the bottom of this page).

2   Before you begin reading the chapter lesson, survey the lesson. Begin your survey by reading the beginning of the lesson. Then look through the lesson and read the headings. Next, study the pictures and read the picture captions. Then study the map of Napoleon's empire on page 492. Finally, read the review section called "Summing Up" at the end of the lesson. This survey of the whole lesson will help you to discover the important ideas in this chapter.

Know the Main Idea

As you read the chapter lesson, try to remember the following important MAIN IDEA of the chapter.

Napoleon Bonaparte built a great empire in Europe. Long after this empire ended, French citizens continued to remember the years of Napoleon.

The following questions will help you to understand the MAIN IDEA. Try to answer these questions as you read the lesson.

1. When did Napoleon first prove his great skill as an army leader?
2. How did Napoleon try to defeat Great Britain by ruining British trade?
3. At what famous battle were Napoleon's armies finally defeated?

Know These Important Terms

departments   Code Napoleon

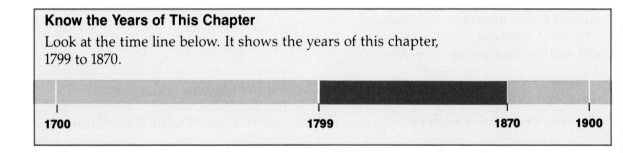

Know the Years of This Chapter
Look at the time line below. It shows the years of this chapter, 1799 to 1870.

| 1700 | 1799 | 1870 | 1900 |

Painting showing Napoleon Bonaparte retreating from Russia in the harsh winter of 1812–1813

EXPLORING THE TIME

By 1799, the French Revolution was over. France had been changed in many important ways during the Revolution. And now Napoleon Bonaparte was the ruler of France. As you will learn in this chapter, Napoleon continued many of the changes and ideas of the French Revolution.

Napoleon Became the Ruler of France

Napoleon Bonaparte was born in 1769 on the island of Corsica. Napoleon attended a French army school, and he became an officer of the French army shortly before the Revolution. During the French Revolution, Napoleon proved his skill as an army leader. The army defeated Austria, France's chief enemy. By 1799, Napoleon was so popular in France that he was able to become the ruler of the French government.

Napoleon Built a Strong Nation

Napoleon wished to set up a well-organized central, or main, government for France. He divided France into **departments,** or sections. Napoleon chose the leaders of

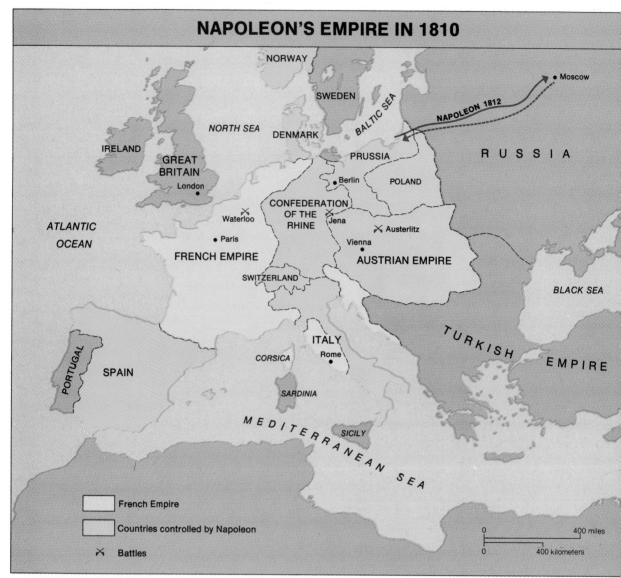

NAPOLEON'S EMPIRE IN 1810

NORWAY

SWEDEN

BALTIC SEA

• Moscow

NAPOLEON 1812

NORTH SEA

DENMARK

RUSSIA

IRELAND

GREAT BRITAIN

London •

PRUSSIA

• Berlin

POLAND

CONFEDERATION OF THE RHINE

ⵝ Jena

ⵝ Austerlitz

ATLANTIC OCEAN

ⵝ Waterloo

• Paris

Vienna •

FRENCH EMPIRE

AUSTRIAN EMPIRE

SWITZERLAND

BLACK SEA

TURKISH

ITALY

Rome •

EMPIRE

CORSICA

SPAIN

PORTUGAL

SARDINIA

MEDITERRANEAN SEA

SICILY

☐ French Empire

☐ Countries controlled by Napoleon

ⵝ Battles

| 0 | | 400 miles |
| 0 | | 400 kilometers |

Name three places where Napoleon fought battles.

these departments. And the government became much stronger.

To solve France's money problems, Napoleon set up the Bank of France. And he set up a new tax system for collecting taxes. Napoleon also improved education in France by starting public elementary schools, high schools, and new colleges.

Napoleon also developed a new set of laws called the **Code Napoleon.** This set of laws protected the rights, property, and religious freedom of all the citizens of France. The code worked so well that many of its laws soon were used by many other nations in Europe and throughout the world.

Napoleon Became Emperor of France

By 1804, Napoleon was so popular that he made himself emperor of France. Soon Napoleon set out to conquer a great empire for France. By 1810, Napoleon's armies had conquered most of Spain, Switzerland, and Poland. He ended the old Holy Roman Empire by conquering almost all of the German states and Italy. Napoleon formed the German states into the Confederation of the Rhine. He forced Austria, Prussia, and Denmark to sign peace treaties with France. He also forced Russia to become France's ally. Napoleon's empire now covered most of central Europe and western Europe.

Napoleon Tried to Defeat Great Britain

Great Britain was determined to stop Napoleon from conquering all of Europe. In return, Napoleon tried to fight Great Britain by cutting off British trade. He set up a plan to keep British goods from entering European ports. But most European nations needed British manufactured goods, and they refused to support Napoleon.

Napoleon then attacked Russia in order to force that nation to support his plan against Great Britain. In 1812, French armies marched into Russia. But Napoleon failed to conquer Russia, and many French soldiers lost their lives.

Napoleon's Rule Came to an End

The French defeat in Russia showed other nations that it was possible to defeat Napoleon. Soon, Austria, Prussia, Great Britain, and Russia joined in attacking Napoleon. By 1814, Napoleon was defeated. He was taken prisoner and forced to live on Elba, a small island off the coast of Spain.

GEOGRAPHY AND HISTORY

Napoleon Bonaparte

Napoleon Bonaparte wanted all of Europe to be part of France's empire. By 1812, he controlled most of Europe and had forced other countries, including Russia, to become his allies. Conquering Great Britain was his final goal.

To force his "allies" to help him to conquer Great Britain, Napoleon attacked Russia. His invasion led to one of history's great tragedies. He did not take into account the harshness of the Russian winter.

Napoleon invaded with an army of more than 600,000 troops. The Russians drew back eastward, taking their livestock with them and burning their crops. When Napoleon's troops reached Moscow, the Russians set fire to the city. The French were forced to withdraw.

Napoleon's troops started for home just as winter began. Their route of more than 800 miles led across a vast open plain. Winter winds brought deep snow to the plain and temperatures as low as 40°F below zero.

Fewer than 40,000 of the French soldiers reached home. Napoleon's defeat by the Russian winter led to his downfall, as the nations of Europe united against him.

Question: How did the Russians contribute to Napoleon's defeat?

Napoleon the Third (right) was emperor of France during the Second Empire

But in 1815, Napoleon escaped and returned to France, and again became emperor. But the European armies, led by the Duke of Wellington, the commander of the British army, joined together to defeat Napoleon. In June of 1815, at the Battle of Waterloo in Belgium, the Duke of Wellington's armies defeated Napoleon for good.

French Monarchs Again Ruled France

In 1814, Louis the Eighteenth became ruler of France. Louis the Eighteenth kept Napoleon's law code and the French government as it was set up under Napoleon. And he allowed French citizens to keep many of the freedoms that they had won during the Revolution.

But Louis died in 1824, and his brother Charles the Tenth became the ruler. Charles ruled badly. He tried to take away some of the French people's freedoms. As a result, the French citizens again revolted against their government in 1830. Charles was forced to give up the throne, and he was replaced by Louis Philippe (LOO-ee fuh-LEEP).

Louis Philippe was supported mainly by the French middle class, or bourgeoisie, which was enjoying good times. However, the French workers and peasants (small farmers) did not share in these good times. Therefore, in 1848 another revolution broke out in France. As a result of this revolution, Louis Philippe was overthrown, and France again became a republic.

The Second Republic Led to the Second French Empire

The new president of the French Republic was Louis Napoleon, the nephew of Napoleon Bonaparte. Louis Napoleon soon had the French people make him emperor. He became Emperor Napoleon the Third, and ruled France from 1852 to 1870. These years in France's history are called the Second French Empire. The Second Empire was a period of progress and good times for France.

SUMMING UP

From 1799 to 1814, Napoleon Bonaparte built a great French empire in Europe, but this empire was finally ended in 1815. However, Napoleon brought some lasting improvements to France. These included a strong French government, a good system of schools and colleges, and Napoleon's code of laws. After Napoleon's defeat, France again was ruled by French monarchs. In 1852, Napoleon the Third became emperor of France. In the next chapter, which begins Unit 16, you will learn what happened in other parts of Europe after Napoleon's defeat in 1815.

UNDERSTANDING THE LESSON

Do You Know These Important Terms?

For each sentence below, choose the term that best completes the sentence.

1. The parts of France which were similar to the states of the United States were called (estates/departments).
2. Napoleon developed a new set of laws for France called the (Napoleonic Laws/ Code Napoleon).

Do You Remember These People and Events?

1. Tell something about each person.

   Napoleon Bonaparte
   Duke of Wellington
   Louis the Eighteenth
   Louis Philippe
   Napoleon the Third

2. Explain how each of the following developments took place.

   a. Napoleon Bonaparte built up a strong French nation.
   b. Napoleon made many lasting improvements in France.
   c. The Second French Republic was set up.

Can You Locate These Places?

Use the map on page 492 to do the following map work.

1. Locate each of the following places. Tell how each place is related to events in this chapter.

Spain	Prussia
Poland	Great Britain
Italy	Switzerland
Austrian Empire	Russia
Denmark	Waterloo

2. With your finger, trace the boundaries of the French Empire on the map. What color symbol shows the French Empire?
3. Name the countries that were not part of the French Empire but which were controlled by Napoleon. What color symbol is used to show these countries on the map?

Do You Know When It Happened?

Why did French citizens revolt against their government in the following years?

   1830   1848

Do You Remember the Main Idea?

Which one of the following ideas is the MAIN IDEA of this chapter?

1. Napoleon Bonaparte built a great empire in Europe that lasted for fifty years.
2. All the changes of the French Revolution were quickly lost when Napoleon Bonaparte became the emperor of France.
3. Napoleon Bonaparte built a great empire in Europe. Long after this empire ended, French citizens continued to remember the years of Napoleon.

What Do You Think?

From what you have read in this chapter, try to answer the following questions.

1. What do you consider Napoleon's greatest contribution to the French people? Explain your answer.
2. Why was Napoleon not able to keep his great empire in Europe?

Unit 16
The Shaping of Modern Europe

THE CHAPTERS IN UNIT 16 ARE

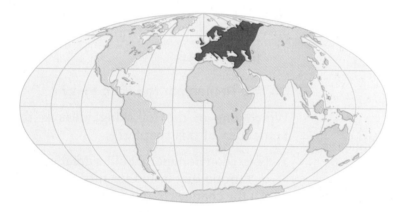

Modern Europe was shaped during the years between 1815 and 1914. Despite some wars, most of these years were peaceful ones. And two great new nations were formed in these years —Germany and Italy. But the older European nations also made important progress. In this unit, you will find out about European life during the hundred years after 1815.

1912 European city scene in a painting by Pierre Bonnard

Chapter 76
Europe After the Congress of Vienna

GETTING STARTED

1   The year 1815 was an important year in Europe. In that year, Napoleon was finally defeated, and Europe began a new period in its history.

In 1815, European leaders were meeting at Vienna, Austria. These leaders did not like the changes caused by the French Revolution and by Napoleon Bonaparte. They wanted conditions in Europe to be what they were before the French Revolution. As you will see, their actions to "turn back the clock" only led to more revolutions in Europe between 1815 and 1870. See these years on the time line below.

2   Before you begin reading the chapter lesson, survey the lesson. Begin your survey by reading the beginning of the lesson. Then look through the lesson and read the headings. Next, study the pictures and read the picture captions. Then study the map showing Europe in 1815 on page 500. Finally, read the review section called "Summing Up." This survey will help you to discover the important ideas in this chapter.

Know the Main Idea

As you read the chapter lesson, try to remember the following important MAIN IDEA of the chapter.

In 1815, European leaders tried to return Europe to the way it was before the French Revolution. Soon, many revolutions broke out in Europe, but most were not successful.

The following questions will help you to understand the MAIN IDEA. Try to answer these questions as you read the lesson.

1. On what idea did all the nations agree at the Congress of Vienna?
2. What two revolutions after the Congress of Vienna were the most successful?
3. Although the revolution in Austria failed, what important improvement resulted from this revolt?

Know These Important Terms

Congress of Vienna	compensation
Quadruple Alliance	alliance
Reform Bill of 1832	
Frankfurt Assembly	

Know the Years of This Chapter

Look at the time line below. It shows the years of this chapter, 1815 to 1870.

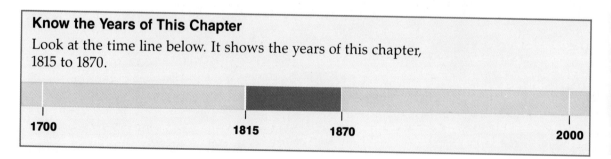

| 1700 | 1815 | 1870 | 2000 |

In 1848, the Frankfurt Assembly met. Its members tried, unsuccessfully, to unite the German states under the Prussian king.

EXPLORING THE TIME

After Napoleon finally was defeated at Waterloo in 1815, Europe's leaders tried to return Europe to the way it had been before the French Revolution. In this chapter, you will learn what happened in Europe as a result of the actions taken at the Congress of Vienna.

The Congress of Vienna Restored the Monarchs to Power

Even before Napoleon was defeated, many important European leaders met at Vienna, Austria, to plan the peace terms. This meeting, called the **Congress of Vienna,** lasted until June of 1815.

One of the leaders of the Congress of Vienna was Prince Metternich (MET-ur-NICK)

EUROPE IN 1815

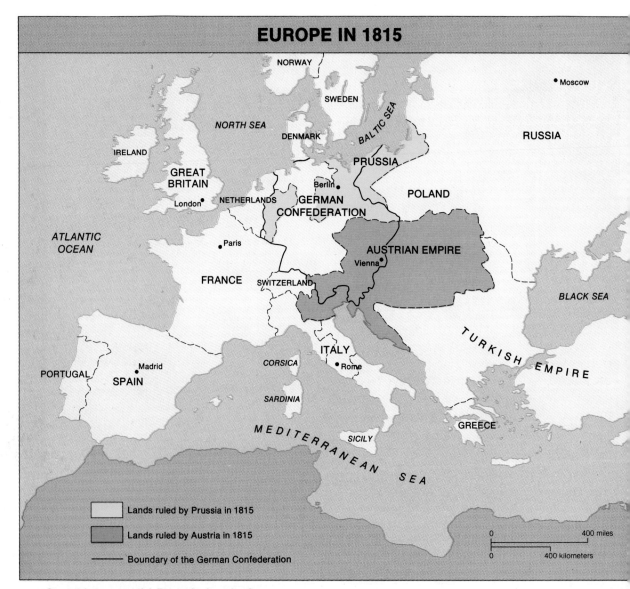

Lands ruled by Prussia in 1815

Lands ruled by Austria in 1815

Boundary of the German Confederation

On which sea did Prussia border?

of Austria. Metternich wished to have European nations ruled as they were in the years before the French Revolution. Another leader was Lord Castlereagh (KASS-ul-RAY) of Great Britain. Castlereagh was interested in helping Great Britain to carry on and increase its trade among nations peacefully. Two other leaders were Czar Alexander the First of Russia and Prince Talleyrand (TAL-ee-RAHN) of France.

All these leaders were from different European nations, but they all agreed on one very important idea. They wished to restore, or bring back, all of the monarchs who had ruled the European nations before the French Revolution.

Some European Nations Gained New Territory

The leaders of the Congress of Vienna also believed that France must give their nations **compensation,** or payment, for the damages they suffered in fighting Napoleon. Most of this compensation was to be paid in the form of land. As compensation, Prussia and Russia gained new land in Europe from other nations, and Great Britain gained new colonies in other parts of the world.

The Leaders of the Congress of Vienna Formed the Quadruple Alliance

The Congress of Vienna leaders also formed an **alliance,** or a group of allied nations, to make sure that the peace terms made at the Congress were obeyed. This group of nations was called the **Quadruple Alliance.** It included Austria, Prussia, Russia, and Great Britain. Later France was also allowed to join. The Quadruple Alliance was soon busy trying to stop revolutions in Italy and Spain during the 1820's.

Europe Soon Had Many Revolutions

But the Congress of Vienna peace settlement began to fall apart by 1830. If you recall, a revolution broke out in France in 1830 when the ruler tried to take away some of the French people's freedoms. As a result of this revolution, Louis Philippe became the new French ruler and the French constitution was changed.

The Revolution of 1830 in France led to other revolutions all over Europe. But only a few of these revolutions were successful. Belgium revolted and became an independent nation. Earlier, in 1829, Greece won its independence from the Turkish Empire.

HIGHLIGHTS IN HISTORY

Clarkson (left) and Wilberforce

Most people try to forget about many of the things they do not like about the world. But this was not true of William Wilberforce and Thomas Clarkson. They became the leaders of the fight to end the British slave trade. And they finally were able to get the British government to stop the British slave trade in 1807.

Wilberforce and Clarkson were still not satisfied. They wanted all the nations of Europe to end their trade in slaves. Therefore, they decided to have Great Britain demand this at the Congress of Vienna. The British government finally promised to try to get all the nations of Europe to agree to stop their slave trade.

At the Congress of Vienna in 1815, the British government failed to get its way on many other things. But it kept its promise about the slave trade. Within a few years after the Congress of Vienna, all European nations stopped the slave trade. In this way, Wilberforce and Clarkson had helped to end the terrible practice of trading human beings as slaves.

Question: Who were Wilberforce and Clarkson?

Great Britain Became More Democratic Without a Revolution

During the early 1830's, Great Britain almost had a revolution, too. Many British people were unhappy because only a small number of British citizens—mainly wealthy land-owners—were allowed to vote.

By 1830, many middle-class British merchants and British workers were de-manding the right to vote for members of Parliament. Many riots broke out in Great Britain. To prevent a revolution, Parliament passed the **Reform Bill of 1832**. The Reform Bill gave more middle-class people in Great Britain the right to vote. And in 1867 and 1884, Parliament passed other reform bills that gave city workers and farm workers the right to vote.

The Austrian Revolution Failed

If you remember, France had another revo-lution in 1848. After this revolution, other revolutions took place in other European nations. In the Austrian Empire, a revolu-tion forced the emperor to promise more freedom to the Austrian people and to give independence to Hungary. But then other parts of the Austrian Empire also revolted and demanded independence. The Aus-trian government was able to put down these revolts, but it also took away the freedoms that were promised to the Aus-trian people by the emperor. However, one important improvement resulted from this revolution. All of the serfs in the Austrian Empire were given their freedom.

The German Revolutions Also Failed

Revolutions broke out in the German states in 1848. As a result, most German rulers promised to give their people more free-dom. But the German people also wished to unite all the German states into one great nation. Therefore, the German leaders met at Frankfurt to talk about this problem.

The members at the meeting, which was called the **Frankfurt Assembly**, wished to unite Germany by electing the Prussian monarch to be the ruler of all Germany. But the Prussian monarch refused this offer. The meeting at Frankfurt ended in failure. And afterwards, most German rulers did not keep their promises to allow their peo-ple more freedom.

The Italian Revolutions Failed, Too

Many of the Italian states also revolted in 1848. A republic was set up in Rome, and other Italian states declared their indepen-dence from the Austrian Empire. However, as soon as the Austrian Empire stopped its own revolution of 1848, Austria ended these revolutions in northern Italy and in Rome.

SUMMING UP

In 1815, the Congress of Vienna tried to return Europe to the way Europe was be-fore the French Revolution. However, by 1830, the peace settlement of the Congress of Vienna fell apart. In Great Britain, more people gained the right to vote, without a revolution. But in other parts of Europe, the people revolted against their governments to try to gain more rights. Most of these revolutions failed, however. In the next chapter, you will find out how the German states became united into one great nation.

UNDERSTANDING THE LESSON

Do You Know These Important Terms?

For each sentence below, choose the term that best completes the sentence.

1. The meeting to decide peace terms after the defeat of Napoleon was called the (Metternich Convention/Congress of Vienna).
2. Payment for damages is called (insurance/compensation).
3. An (alliance/alluvium) is a group of nations allied together.
4. Austria, Prussia, Russia, and Great Britain joined together to form the (Quadruple Alliance/Great Alliance).
5. The (Reform Bill of 1832/Referendum Bill) gave the middle-class people in Great Britain the right to vote.
6. At the (Rhine Assembly/Frankfurt Assembly) an attempt was made to unite the German states.

Do You Remember These People and Events?

1. Tell something about each of the following persons.

   Prince Metternich
   Alexander the First
   Lord Castlereagh
   Prince Talleyrand

2. Explain how or why each of the following developments took place.

   a. The Congress of Vienna leaders formed the Quadruple Alliance.
   b. Great Britain became more democratic without a revolution.
   c. Most revolutions in 1830 and in 1848 failed.

Can You Locate These Places?

Use the map on page 500 to locate the following places. Tell how each place is related to developments in this chapter.

Vienna	Austrian Empire
Russia	Prussia
Great Britain	France
Greece	

Do You Know When It Happened?

In what year was the Reform Bill passed?

Do You Remember the Main Idea?

Which one of the following ideas is the MAIN IDEA of this chapter?

1. In 1815, European leaders tried to return Europe to the way it was before the French Revolution. Soon, many revolutions broke out in Europe, but most were not successful.
2. In 1815, Europe returned to the way it was before the French Revolution. Most European nations gained more freedoms.
3. After 1815, the people in Europe demanded and won many of the same freedoms that the American people enjoyed.

What Do You Think?

From what you have read in this chapter, try to answer the following questions.

1. Do people ever gain anything from revolutions that do not succeed? Explain.
2. Do you think the changes in European boundaries made at the Congress of Vienna were wise ones? Explain.

Chapter 77
Uniting Germany into One Nation

GETTING STARTED

1   The peoples of France, Great Britain, Spain, and Russia became united into strong nations much earlier than did the peoples of Italy and Germany. Italy and Germany did not become united until the late 1800's. However, the German Empire of 1871 became the strongest nation of Europe. In this chapter, you will read about the developments from 1789 to 1871 that united the German states into one strong nation.

2   Before you begin reading the chapter lesson, survey the lesson. Begin your survey by reading the beginning of the lesson. Then look through the lesson and read the headings. Next, study the pictures and read the picture captions. Then study the map of the uniting of Germany on page 506. Finally, read the review section called "Summing Up" at the end of the lesson. This survey will help you to discover the important ideas in this chapter.

Know the Main Idea

As you read the chapter lesson, try to remember the following important MAIN IDEA of the chapter.

Led by Bismarck, Germany became united as a strong nation by 1871.

The following questions will help you to understand the MAIN IDEA. Try to answer these questions as you read the lesson.

1. How many German states were there in Germany at the time of the French Revolution?
2. What changes took place in the German states during Napoleon's control?
3. What important event finally brought the German people together as one nation?

Know These Important Terms

Confederation of the Rhine
German Confederation
Carlsbad Decrees
North German Confederation

Know the Years of This Chapter

Look at the time line below. It shows the years of this chapter, 1789 to 1871.

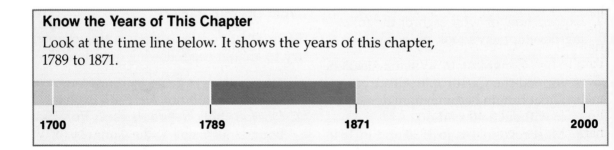

| 1700 | 1789 | 1871 | 2000 |

On January 18, 1871, the Proclamation of the German Empire at Versailles made the Prussian king emperor of a united Germany

EXPLORING THE TIME

In the year 1849, the ruler of Prussia refused to let the Frankfurt Assembly elect him the ruler of Germany. The Prussian ruler believed that only the rulers of the German states, not the Frankfurt Assembly, had the right to elect anyone the ruler of Germany. Finally, in 1871 the Prussian ruler was made German emperor by the rulers of the German states. In this chapter, you will find out how Germany became united as one great nation under one ruler.

Germany Was Partly United by Napoleon Bonaparte

At the time of the French Revolution, Germany was divided into more than three hundred independent states. Austria and Prussia were the two most important German states. Starting in 1792, Austria and Prussia fought several wars against France.

But both Austria and Prussia were defeated by Napoleon and forced to become allies of France. Napoleon then took over nearly all the German states between

THE UNITING OF GERMANY — 1866 TO 1871

300 miles
300 kilometers

DENMARK SWEDEN

BALTIC SEA

NORTH SEA

SCHLESWIG

HOLSTEIN

MECKLENBURG

PRUSSIA

ENGLAND

HANOVER

NETHERLANDS

• Berlin

RUSSIA

G E R M A N

BELGIUM

E M P I R E SAXONY

Frankfurt •

AUSTRIA

• Paris

French lands
added in 1871

Rhine River

BAVARIA

WURTTEMBERG

Danube River

FRANCE

BADEN

	Prussia and states added to Prussia in 1866
	States that joined Prussia to form the North German Confederation, 1867
	States that joined Prussia to form the German Empire, 1871
——	Boundary of the German Empire

SWITZERLAND

When did Bavaria join Prussia to become part of the German Empire?

France and Austria and Prussia. Napoleon united these German states and formed them into the **Confederation of the Rhine.**

The German States Changed Under the Control of France

Many changes took place in the German states under the control of France. The Code Napoleon became the new set of laws used in these states. German nobles lost much of their power. And the German serfs were set free. These changes helped people in the German states to enjoy better lives.

The rulers of Prussia and the other German states not ruled by France decided that they, too, must improve conditions for their people to prevent revolts. Therefore, Prussia freed its serfs and gave its people more freedom. These improvements helped to make the people of the German states feel proud to be Germans.

Prussia Became the Leading German State After 1815

After Napoleon's final defeat in 1815, the leaders of the Congress of Vienna tried to make Germany stronger. They divided Germany into only thirty-nine states and united them into a group called the **German Confederation**. The purpose of this Confederation was to make the German states strong enough to stop France from ever conquering Europe again.

The leaders at the Congress of Vienna also made Prussia stronger by giving it some German territory west of the Rhine River that had been controlled by France. Prussia now became the strongest German state in the German Confederation. Austria was the other strong state in the German Confederation.

Germany Changed Very Slowly Between 1815 and 1862

But after 1815, Germany did not become more united, because most German rulers still wished to rule their states as they had ruled them before the French Revolution. These rulers tried to keep the German people from gaining more freedom. In Prussia, the Prussian people failed to get a new constitution that they were promised earlier by the Prussian ruler. And when many German college students began to talk about uniting Germany into one great nation, the German Confederation passed the **Carlsbad Decrees**. These decrees were laws that forbade college students and teachers to speak and write their ideas about freedom.

In the revolutions of 1848, Germany almost became united as one nation under an emperor. But the ruler of Prussia refused to become the German emperor.

PEOPLE IN HISTORY

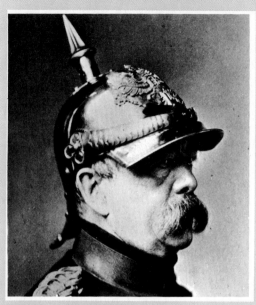

Otto von Bismarck

When Otto von Bismarck (BIZZ-mark) was born in 1815, Germany was weak and not united. When Bismarck died in 1898, Germany was a powerful and united nation. Bismarck built this German Empire by using "blood and iron," or war and weapons. After 1871, however, Bismarck turned to peace.

Bismarck kept Germany out of European wars. He built up a German empire in Africa. He worked to help build strong German industries. And to keep the workers loyal to the empire, Bismarck developed a plan of health insurance, old-age pensions, and low-rent housing.

But when William the Second became emperor in 1890, he forced Bismarck to resign. Bismarck's job had been only half completed. Bismarck had made Germany strong, but had not prepared the German people for democracy.

Question: What nation did Bismarck help build?

507

French prisoners of war in the war between France and Prussia in 1870

However, by 1862 Prussia had a new constitution and a parliament headed by Otto von Bismarck (BIZZ-mark) as the chancellor, or prime minister. Chancellor Bismarck's greatest wish was to have Prussia unite all of Germany.

Bismarck Helped to Unite Germany by Fighting Wars

Bismarck planned to unite Germany by fighting wars against other nations. This "blood and iron" policy gave Bismarck the nickname "Iron Chancellor."

Bismarck built up a powerful Prussian army in order to defeat Austria. Bismarck believed that Austria must be defeated in order to unite Germany. By 1866, Prussia was at war with Austria and other German states.

The strong Prussian army was well prepared for this war. Within seven weeks, Austria was defeated, and Prussia took over the northern German states that supported Austria in the war. Prussia now ended the German Confederation and replaced it with an association called the **North German Confederation.** Prussia became the leader of the Confederation.

Germany Became an Empire in 1871

The North German Confederation was formed in 1867, and it united most of Germany. But the southern German states still were independent. It took another war to unite these states with the rest of Germany.

In 1870, war broke out between France and Prussia. After this war started, the southern German states joined Prussia against France, and France was defeated. This victory against France made most Germans so proud that they now wished to be united under one great nation. In 1871, the North German Confederation became the German Empire. And the Prussian ruler became the German emperor.

The German Empire of 1871 became the strongest nation of Europe. But Germany did not become a democracy. The emperor controlled the army, the navy, and foreign affairs. The prime minister and the other leading officials were chosen by the emperor, not elected. The German parliament, or lawmaking body, was elected, but it had few powers. However, Germany was now strong and united.

SUMMING UP

Between 1789 and 1871, Germany developed from a weak group of many small states into one strong, united nation. Prussia took the lead in uniting Germany after defeating Austria. Bismarck was the Prussian leader who did most to build up a strong German Empire. In the next chapter, you will learn how Italy became united as a nation.

UNDERSTANDING THE LESSON

Do You Know These Important Terms?

For each sentence below, choose the term that best completes the sentence.

1. The **(Confederation of the Rhine/ Confederation of the Baltic)** was the group of German states united by Napoleon.
2. The **(Vienna Confederation/German Confederation)** was the group of German states organized by the Congress of Vienna.
3. The **(South German Confederation/ North German Confederation)** was formed after Prussia defeated Austria in a war.

Do You Remember These People and Events?

1. Tell how Bismarck was able to unite the German states.
2. Explain how each of the following developments took place.

   a. Germany was partly united by Napoleon Bonaparte, and this resulted in important changes.
   b. Prussia became the leading German state after 1815.
   c. The German states were able to unite as one nation.

Can You Locate These Places?

Use the map on page 506 to do the following map work.

1. Locate the following places. Tell how each place is related to this chapter.
   Prussia   Austria

2. What nation was located east of the German Empire? What river flowed through the western part of the German Empire? What river flowed through the southern part of the German Empire?

Do You Know When It Happened?

Why is the following year important in Germany's history?

   1871

Do You Remember the Main Idea?

Which one of the following ideas is the MAIN IDEA of this chapter?

1. Shortly after 1815, the German states were able to unite and to form the German Empire.
2. Changes brought about by Napoleon helped the German states to form a single nation and to give many freedoms to the German people.
3. Led by Bismarck, Germany became united as a strong nation by 1871.

What Do You Think?

From what you have read in this chapter, try to answer the following questions.

1. Why was a united Germany stronger than the German states in a confederation?
2. The Carlsbad Decrees were laws to prevent college students and teachers from speaking or writing about freedom. Were these laws needed? Explain.
3. Do you think that Bismarck's policy of "blood and iron" was a good way to unite a nation? Why or why not?

Chapter 78
Uniting Italy into One Nation

GETTING STARTED

1   As you learned in the last chapter, many German states joined together in 1871 to form a united German nation. During the same years when the German nation was being formed, Italy also was trying to unite. As you will learn, between 1789 and 1870, Italy, too, slowly changed from a country of many states into a united nation. Notice these years in the time line below.

2   Before you begin reading the chapter lesson, survey the lesson. Begin your survey by reading the beginning of the lesson. Then look through the lesson and read the headings. Next, study the pictures and read the picture captions. Then study the map on the uniting of Italy on page 512. Finally, read the review section called "Summing Up" at the end of the lesson. This survey of the whole lesson will help you to discover the important ideas in this chapter.

Know the Main Idea

As you read the chapter lesson, try to remember the following important MAIN IDEA of the chapter.

Led by Count Cavour and Garibaldi, Italy became united as a nation by 1870.

The following questions will help you to understand the MAIN IDEA. Try to answer these questions as you read the lesson.

1. Who conquered most of Italy by 1801?
2. Which state in Italy governed itself and was strong enough to unite northern Italy?
3. Which city became the capital of Italy when Italy was united?

Know These Important Terms

   Carbonari   Young Italy

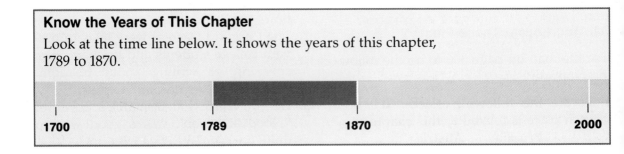

Know the Years of This Chapter
Look at the time line below. It shows the years of this chapter, 1789 to 1870.

| 1700 | 1789 | 1870 | 2000 |

Garibaldi presented the lands his army had conquered to King Victor Emmanuel. What lands did Garibaldi conquer?

EXPLORING THE TIME

What was happening to Italy while Germany was becoming united? You may recall that much earlier in Europe's history, Italy was the center of the Roman Empire. Then after the western Roman Empire ended, Italy became divided into many states, or parts. In this chapter, you will find out how Italy became united as a new nation between 1789 and 1870.

Italy Was Conquered by Napoleon

In 1789, when the French Revolution began, Italy was divided into many states. By 1793, France was at war with most of Europe. And by 1801, Napoleon Bonaparte had conquered most of Italy. All of Italy was now either owned or controlled by France.

Under Napoleon, the serfs in Italy became free. The Italian nobles and the Roman Catholic Church lost some of their powers. And the Code Napoleon became the official laws for all of Italy.

Italy Was Divided by the Congress of Vienna

However, after Napoleon's defeat in 1815, Italy again was divided into many states by the Congress of Vienna. Southern Italy was ruled by the Bourbon family, the family that

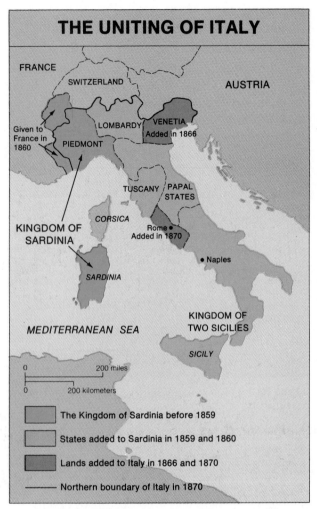

THE UNITING OF ITALY

FRANCE

SWITZERLAND

AUSTRIA

Given to France in 1860

LOMBARDY

VENETIA
Added in 1866

PIEDMONT

TUSCANY

PAPAL STATES

CORSICA

KINGDOM OF SARDINIA

Rome
Added in 1870

Naples

SARDINIA

MEDITERRANEAN SEA

KINGDOM OF TWO SICILIES

SICILY

0   200 miles

0   200 kilometers

The Kingdom of Sardinia before 1859

States added to Sardinia in 1859 and 1860

Lands added to Italy in 1866 and 1870

Northern boundary of Italy in 1870

In what year was Venetia added to Italy?

again ruled France after 1815. Central Italy was given back to the Pope at Rome, who again ruled the Papal States. And the states of northern Italy were again ruled by Austria. The only Italian state that had its own ruler was the Kingdom of Sardinia (sahr-DIN-ee-UH), which included land in Italy and the island of Sardinia.

Many Italians Wished to Unite Italy

Between 1815 and 1848, the Italian rulers tried to govern their states as they were governed before the French Revolution. But many Italians refused to give up the freedoms gained under Napoleon. Soon, many Italians revolted against their rulers.

Some of these revolts were led by a secret group called the **Carbonari** (KAHR-boh-NAH-ree). Other revolutions in Italy were led by Joseph Mazzini (maht-TSEE-nee), the leader of a group called **Young Italy**. These groups wished to overthrow the foreign rulers in Italy and to set up a strong, united Italian nation.

In 1848, revolutions led by these new groups broke out all over Italy. These revolutions forced the ruler of Sardinia, the Pope, and the Bourbon ruler of southern Italy to give their people new constitutions, or plans of government, with more freedoms. Then, all the northern Italian states declared their independence from Austria and joined the Kingdom of Sardinia.

But within a few months, Austria defeated Sardinia and rewon all of the territory that it had lost in northern Italy. Austria and the Pope ended the new constitutions of 1848. But King Victor Emmanuel the Second of Sardinia kept the constitution given to the Sardinian people in 1848.

Count Cavour Built Up Sardinia

Many Italians came to believe that Sardinia was the only state in Italy that was strong enough to unite all of Italy into an independent nation. Under Sardinia's prime minister, Count Cavour (kah-VOOR), Sardinia's farming and trade improved greatly, and Sardinia became a prosperous state. Cavour also made the Sardinian government stronger by cutting down the power of the Sardinian nobles. Cavour also cut down the power of the Roman Catholic Church.

Sardinia Defeated Austria with France's Help

But before Sardinia was able to unite Italy, Austria had to be forced out of northern Italy. Count Cavour tried to obtain help from other European nations in order to defeat Austria. In 1858, Napoleon the Third, the emperor of France, agreed to help Sardinia if Sardinia was attacked by Austria.

In 1859, Austria did attack Sardinia. France kept its promise. It sent an army to help Sardinia, and the French and Sardinian armies defeated Austria in 1859. All of northern Italy except the state of Venetia (vehn-EE-she-uh) was now taken over by Sardinia.

Garibaldi Helped Unite Southern and Northern Italy

Meanwhile, the Italian people in southern Italy hoped to overthrow their Bourbon ruler. The person who led southern Italy to freedom was a bold Italian leader named Garibaldi (GAIR-uh-BALL-dee). Garibaldi fought in the revolutions of the 1830's and of 1848. In 1860, Garibaldi's army of a thousand soldiers conquered the island of Sicily and the mainland of southern Italy. Garibaldi then presented these lands to King Victor Emmanuel of Sardinia.

The King of Sardinia Became Ruler of Italy

In 1861, Victor Emmanuel became the ruler of the new Kingdom of Italy. All of Italy was now united except for Venetia and the region around Rome. Venetia became part of Italy in 1866. But Italy still did not have Rome.

GEOGRAPHY AND HISTORY

Giuseppe Garibaldi

In 1848, the people of Italy wanted independence from the foreigners who ruled much of the Italian peninsula. The Austrians ruled the north, the Pope ruled the area around Rome, and the Bourbon family of France ruled the south. Only Sardinia and the Piedmont were independent of foreign rule (see the map on page 512).

Giuseppe Garibaldi was an important leader in the struggle to unite Italy. In 1848, he and a group of volunteers helped the people of northern Italy fight the Austrians. He also helped the Papal States in their struggle for freedom from the Pope. But these victories were soon overturned, and Garibaldi left Italy for several years.

By 1859, Garibaldi was back, and his army had grown to one thousand men. Called "redshirts," they began fighting against the Bourbons in the south. Within a year, Garibaldi had captured all of Sicily and southern Italy. In 1861, Garibaldi gave these lands to Victor Emmanuel, ruler of Sardinia. The united lands became the new nation of Italy.

Question: Who were the redshirts?

Members of the Carbonari worked to help the Italian states to win their freedom

Rome was controlled by the Pope, who was protected by an army of French soldiers. But during France's war against Prussia in 1870, the French army returned to France. Rome was left unprotected, and the Italian army was able to take it over. In 1870, Rome became the capital city of a united Italy.

SUMMING UP

The movement to unite all of Italy into an independent nation lasted from 1815 to 1870. Two Italian leaders who helped to unite Italy were Count Cavour and Garibaldi. Under Cavour, the Kingdom of Sardinia became strong enough to force Austria out of northern Italy. Garibaldi drove the Bourbon ruler out of southern Italy. Then the Kingdom of Sardinia united most of Italy into one nation in 1861. In 1870, Rome became the capital of Italy. In the next chapter, you will find out about other important developments in the nations of western Europe between 1848 and 1914.

UNDERSTANDING THE LESSON

Do You Know These Important Terms?

For each sentence below, choose the term that best completes the sentence.

1. One of the secret groups in Italy that planned revolts against their rulers was called the **(Carbonari/Garibaldi)**.
2. **(Via Italia/Young Italy)** was another group that worked to overthrow the foreign rulers in Italy and to set up a united Italian nation.

Do You Remember These People and Events?

1. Tell something about each of the following persons.

   Napoleon Bonaparte   **Joseph Mazzini**
   Joseph Garibaldi   **Count Cavour**
   Victor Emmanuel

2. Explain how each of the following developments took place.

   a. Italy was divided again by the Congress of Vienna after Napoleon was defeated in 1815.
   b. Sardinia became the strongest state in northern Italy.
   c. Garibaldi helped to unite northern and southern Italy.

Can You Locate These Places?

Use the map on page 512 to do the following map work.

1. Locate each of the following Italian states.

   Kingdom of Two Sicilies   Venetia

   Kingdom of Sardinia   Tuscany
   Lombardy   Papal States

2. Study the map legend. Name two large regions that were part of the Kingdom of Sardinia before 1859.
3. Locate the city of Rome. Do you think that Rome was well located to be the capital of Italy? Give reasons for your answer.

Do You Know When It Happened?

Why are the following years important in Italy's history?

   1861   1870

Do You Remember the Main Idea?

Which one of the following ideas is the MAIN IDEA of this chapter?

1. After Napoleon united Italy, the Italian people formed their own nation.
2. Led by Count Cavour and Garibaldi, Italy became united as a nation by 1870.
3. Italy took a long time to become united because so many Italian states were controlled by foreign nations.

What Do You Think?

From what you have read in this chapter, try to answer the following thought questions.

1. In what ways do you think that Napoleon Bonaparte's conquest of Italy may have helped the uniting of Italy?
2. Do you think that Italy might have become united without Garibaldi and Count Cavour? Why or why not?

Chapter 79

Western Europe from 1848 to 1914

GETTING STARTED

1 During the years when Germany and Italy were each becoming united, other important changes were taking place in Europe. Many of these changes, especially the changes in Great Britain and France, made democracy stronger and improved ways of living for many people. This chapter tells about these developments in western Europe between 1848 and 1914. See these years on the time line below.

2 Before you begin reading the chapter lesson, survey the lesson. Begin your survey by reading the beginning of the lesson. Then look through the lesson and read the headings. Next, study the pictures and read the picture captions. Finally, read the review section called "Summing Up" at the end of the lesson. This survey of the whole lesson will help you to discover the important ideas in this chapter.

Know the Main Idea

As you read the chapter lesson, try to remember the following important MAIN IDEA of the chapter.

From 1848 to 1914, industries grew rapidly in Great Britain, France, and Germany, and their governments helped to improve working conditions.

The following questions will help you to understand the MAIN IDEA. Try to answer these questions as you read the lesson.

1. What war was fought to keep Russia from taking territory away from the Turkish Empire?
2. What part of the French government was like the House of Commons in the British Parliament?
3. Who was emperor of Germany during the late 1800's and early 1900's?

Know These Important Terms

Franco-Prussian War	Crimean War
Chamber of Deputies	veto
social welfare laws	

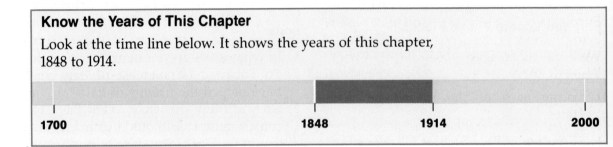

Know the Years of This Chapter

Look at the time line below. It shows the years of this chapter, 1848 to 1914.

| 1700 | 1848 | 1914 | 2000 |

Queen Victoria ruled Great Britain from 1837 to 1901

EXPLORING THE TIME

What was happening in the other nations of Europe while Germany and Italy were being formed into new, united nations? Were the other nations also fighting wars? Were they having revolutions? Were their people winning more rights and freedoms? In this chapter, you will find out what was happening in the nations of western Europe between the years 1848 and 1914.

Great Britain and France Fought Russia in the Crimean War

Between 1848 and 1914, Great Britain enjoyed a peaceful period. But it fought one important war, the **Crimean** (cry-MEE-un) **War**. In the Crimean War (1854 to 1856), Great Britain and France fought to prevent Russia from taking away land from the Turkish Empire. The war was fought in the Crimea, a peninsula of land in the northern part of the Black Sea. Great Britain and

PEOPLE IN HISTORY

Alfred Dreyfus

The word **prejudice** means to prejudge, or to have an opinion before knowing the facts. Prejudice has often led to tragedy.

Alfred Dreyfus (DRAY-fuss) was a captain in the French army, and he was a Jew. When the French army discovered that Germany knew France's army plans, who was to blame? Why Dreyfus, of course! Many people in France were prejudiced against Jews, and they were glad to blame Captain Dreyfus for this crime. In 1894, Dreyfus was arrested and sent to the French prison colony of Devil's Island.

As time went on, it became clear that Dreyfus was not guilty. But the French army refused to admit its mistake. Finally, Émile Zola, a famous French writer, declared that Dreyfus was innocent and accused the army of framing Dreyfus. The army was forced to give Dreyfus a new trial, but Dreyfus was again found guilty!

The whole world was now shocked by the French army's hatred of Dreyfus. As a result, Dreyfus soon was pardoned by the president of France. However, Dreyfus was not finally declared innocent until 1906. The Dreyfus case showed how terrible prejudice can be.

Question: Who was Alfred Dreyfus?

France finally defeated Russia, but the war caused a heavy loss of lives on both sides.

Victoria Was Monarch, But Parliament Ruled Great Britain

From 1837 to 1901, Queen Victoria was the British ruler. She was a very popular queen. But the real ruler of Great Britain was Parliament, the law-making body of the British nation.

The leader of Parliament was the prime minister, who headed the main political party in the House of Commons. The House of Commons passed all the laws of the nation. The House of Lords was part of Parliament, but it had few powers. Its most important power was its power to **veto**, or turn down, certain laws passed by the House of Commons. Usually this power of veto was used to prevent higher taxes from being passed by the House of Commons.

Parliament Passed Important New Laws

The two greatest leaders of the British government during these years were Prime Minister Benjamin Disraeli (dizz-RAY-lee) and Prime Minister William Gladstone. Under their leadership, Parliament passed many important laws. Some of these laws gave more British people the right to vote and set up a public school system.

By the early 1900's, Parliament also passed several **social welfare laws**, or "social security laws." These social welfare laws provided health insurance, unemployment insurance, and old-age pensions for all British workers. The money to pay for this program was to come from higher taxes. But the House of Lords was against paying higher taxes, and its members tried to veto, or turn down, this program. In order to pass these laws, therefore, the

Florence Nightingale helped sick and wounded soldiers during the Crimean War. How does the artist show the foreign location of the war?

House of Commons in 1911 passed a new law that took away the House of Lords' power to veto any laws. The House of Lords remained a part of Parliament, but it no longer had any real power.

In France, the Third Republic Followed the Second Empire

In Chapter 75, you read that Napoleon the Third became emperor of France after the revolution of 1848. Under Napoleon the Third, France fought the Crimean War. Then in 1870, France fought against Prussia in the **Franco-Prussian War**. The Franco-Prussian War was one of the wars that helped Germany to become united. In this war, the powerful Prussian army defeated the weaker French army and Napoleon the Third was captured. As a result, the Second French Empire ended in 1870 and the Third French Republic was set up.

France Grew Stronger Under the Third Republic

In 1875, the French Republic received a new constitution. The new French government had a two-house legislature. All French citizens voted for members of the lower house, or **Chamber of Deputies**, which was like the House of Commons in Great Britain. The French legislature elected a president, but the president had little power. The real leader of the French government was the French premier (prih-MEER), or prime minister, who was elected by the people.

During the years of the Third Republic, French factory workers demanded many improvements in their working conditions. And the French government passed new laws that cut down working hours, provided medical care, and set up old-age pensions.

519

Berlin, the capital city of Germany, about the year 1900. How can you tell that this is a wealthy city?

Bismarck Built Up a Powerful Germany

If you remember, Germany had a constitution and an elected legislature. But the real power of the German government was held by the German chancellor (prime minister) and the German emperor. After Germany became united in 1871, Chancellor Otto von Bismarck helped to build up German industries. Bismarck was so successful that, by 1914, Germany's industries were almost as well developed as those in Great Britain.

The German factory workers also demanded better working conditions and social welfare laws. To gain the support of these factory workers for the government, Bismarck agreed to have social welfare laws passed in the late 1800's that helped the workers. These German laws were so successful that the British and French governments copied Bismarck's program about twenty years later.

However, the German emperor, William the Second, was against these social welfare laws. And the emperor forced Bismarck to leave the government. But the laws supported by Bismarck were so successful that they were continued.

SUMMING UP

During the years from 1848 to 1914, industries in Great Britain, France, and Germany grew rapidly and times were good. In all three nations, new laws improved conditions for factory workers. In Great Britain and France, the governments also became more democratic. But Germany was ruled by the German emperor and the chancellor. And Germany did not become democratic. In the next chapter, you will read about the older European empires during the late 1800's and the early 1900's.

UNDERSTANDING THE LESSON

Do You Know These Important Terms?

For each sentence below, choose the term that best completes the sentence.

1. The **(Crimean War/Black Sea War)** was fought to keep Russia from taking territory away from the Turkish Empire.
2. The power of the House of Lords to turn down certain laws passed by the House of Commons was the power to **(veto/approve)** these laws.
3. Laws which provided health insurance, unemployment insurance, and old-age pensions for British workers were called **(reform laws/social welfare laws)**.
4. The war fought in 1870 between France and Prussia was the **(Six Weeks' Prussian War/Franco-Prussian War)**.
5. The **(Chamber of Deputies/First Estate)** was the lower house of the French legislature.

Do You Remember These People and Events?

1. Tell something about each of the following persons.

   Queen Victoria
   William Gladstone
   Benjamin Disraeli
   Napoleon the Third
   Otto von Bismarck
   William the Second

2. Explain how or why each of the following developments took place.

   a. Working conditions improved for British workers.
   b. The House of Commons became the most important part of Parliament.
   c. France became more democratic during the Third Republic.
   d. German industries grew, but the government was not democratic.

Can You Locate These Places?

Use the map in Chapter 80 (page 524) to locate the following places. Tell how each place is related to this chapter.

   Turkish Empire   **Black Sea**
   Russia

Do You Know When It Happened?

What are the years of this chapter?

Do You Remember the Main Idea?

Which one of the following ideas is the MAIN IDEA of this chapter?

1. From 1848 to 1914, industries grew rapidly in Great Britain, France, and Germany, and their governments helped to improve working conditions.
2. Great changes took place in Great Britain, France, and Germany in the 1800's.
3. Great Britain, France, and Germany fought a war to prevent Russia from gaining control of the Black Sea.

What Do You Think?

From what you have read in this chapter, try to answer the following questions.

1. Do you think that social welfare laws were needed in Western Europe? Explain.
2. Why do you think the House of Lords continued to be part of Parliament even after it lost most of its power?

Chapter 80
The Old Empires of Europe

GETTING STARTED

1   From 1848 to 1914, Great Britain, France, and Germany were building up their industries and improving the lives of their peoples. During this same period, the governments in Great Britain and France also became more democratic.

Meanwhile, what was happening in other parts of Europe in the years from 1848 to 1914? Three large empires—Austria-Hungary, Russia, and the Turkish Empire—controlled most of southeastern Europe at this time. They faced many problems within their empires. Different groups of people wanted to form separate nations. You will find out what happened to these empires as you read this chapter.

2   Before you begin reading the chapter lesson, survey the lesson. Begin your survey by reading the beginning of the lesson. Then look through the lesson and read the headings. Next, study the pictures and read the picture captions. Then study the map of the nations of southeastern Europe in 1914 on page 524. Finally, read the review section called "Summing Up." This survey of the whole lesson will help you to discover the important ideas in this chapter.

Know the Main Idea

As you read the chapter lesson, try to remember the following important MAIN IDEA of the chapter.

Between 1848 and 1914, Austria-Hungary, Russia, and the Turkish Empire became weaker.

The following questions will help you to understand the MAIN IDEA. Try to answer these questions as you read the lesson.

1. Into what two parts was the Austrian Empire divided? What was the new name given to this empire?
2. When were the serfs set free in Russia?
3. What countries won their independence from the Turkish Empire in the 1800's and early 1900's?

Know These Important Terms

nationalities	Duma
mir	Young Turks
Russify	

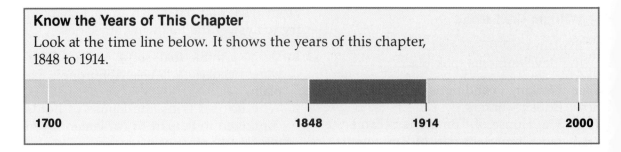

Know the Years of This Chapter
Look at the time line below. It shows the years of this chapter, 1848 to 1914.

1700   1848   1914   2000

Painting showing Emperor Francis Joseph (left) being congratulated by the German emperor William the Second (right, holding paper), on his fiftieth anniversary as emperor of Austria.

EXPLORING THE TIME

Have you heard the saying, "Old soldiers never die; they just fade away"? In much the same way, the older empires of Europe did not end suddenly. They grew weaker over time. In this chapter, you will learn how Austria-Hungary, Russia, and the Turkish Empire grew weaker and began to "fade away" from 1848 to 1914.

The Austrian Empire Became Austria-Hungary in 1867

Emperor Francis Joseph of the Hapsburg family became ruler of the Austrian Empire in 1848. The Austrian Empire had many different **nationalities**, or national groups. Each nationality wanted to form its own nation. They wanted the Austrian Empire to be divided to form a separate nation for each nationality.

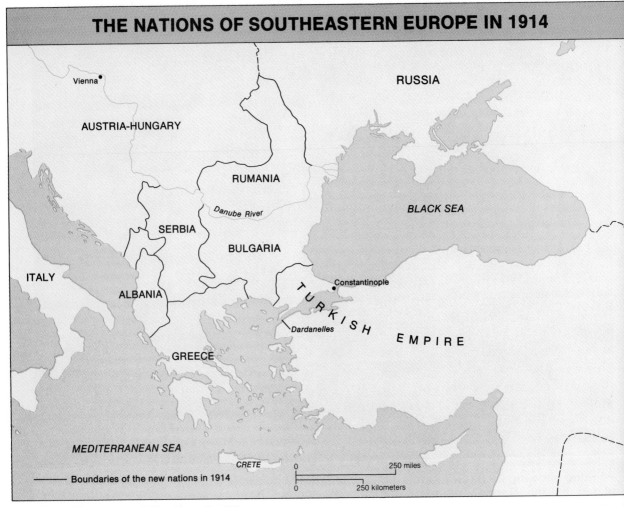

THE NATIONS OF SOUTHEASTERN EUROPE IN 1914

Vienna

AUSTRIA-HUNGARY

RUSSIA

RUMANIA

Danube River

SERBIA

BLACK SEA

ITALY

BULGARIA

Constantinople

ALBANIA

T U R K I S H   E M P I R E

Dardanelles

GREECE

MEDITERRANEAN SEA

CRETE

Boundaries of the new nations in 1914

0   250 miles

0   250 kilometers

Trace the route of the Danube River.

Francis Joseph agreed to divide the empire, but only into two parts. In 1867, therefore, the Austrian Empire was divided in two, and it became known as Austria-Hungary. But all of the nationalities in the empire still were ruled by either the Austrians or the Hungarians. And Emperor Francis Joseph of Austria-Hungary was still the emperor of all of the nationalities who lived in the Austrian Empire. The pressures to divide the Austria-Hungary Empire into smaller nations did not stop.

Austria-Hungary Remained a Weak Empire

Austria-Hungary lasted from 1867 until 1918, but it had one great weakness. The Poles, Croats (KROH-atz), Serbs, Czechs (CHECKS), Slovaks (SLOH-vahks), and other nationalities in its lands did not like being ruled by the Austrians or the Hungarians. These nationalities continued to want to form their own nations. Therefore, they did not support Austria-Hungary.

Most Russians Still Lacked Freedom

By the middle 1800's, Russia still was ruled in nearly the same way that it was ruled during the 1700's. The czar was the leader of the Russian government and the Russian Church. The Russian nobles held all the important government positions. And the Russian serfs had no freedom.

Russia Suffered a Great Defeat in the Crimean War

In 1853, Czar Nicholas the First sent a Russian army into Turkish territory. Great Britain and France feared that Russia intended to take over the Dardanelles (DAHR-duh-NELZ), the water passage between the Black Sea and the Mediterranean Sea. Therefore, Great Britain and France supported the Turkish Empire and declared war on Russia in 1854. As you have read, this war was called the Crimean War.

The Russian army was so poorly trained and badly equipped that Russia lost the Crimean War. This defeat made Czar Alexander the Second realize that changes were needed in Russia if Russia was to become a more powerful nation.

Alexander the Second Freed the Serfs

Czar Alexander knew that Russia was "backward," or slow in developing the skills of its people. In 1861, the czar passed a law that freed the Russian serfs so that they no longer had to work for their lords. The government then gave land to each **mir** (MEAR), or village, in Russia. And the mir then sold this land to the freed serfs.

However, land prices were so high that many of the freed serfs were not able to buy land. Some of the freed serfs were forced to become farm workers at low pay on other farmers' lands. Other freed serfs moved to Russian cities to take jobs as workers.

Alexander Made Other Changes in Russia

Alexander the Second also improved the Russian court system. He allowed the Russian people to have more control over their own local governments. And he opened many new schools. However, when the Poles revolted against Russia in 1863, Alexander changed his policy. He no longer gave more freedom to the Russian people.

The Czars Tried to Make Everyone in the Empire a "Russian"

Trouble soon broke out in Russia again, and Alexander the Second was killed in 1881 by a bomb. The new czar, Alexander the Third, believed that his father's policy of giving the Russian people more freedom was a mistake. Instead, Alexander and his son, Nicholas the Second, tried to **Russify** (RUSS-uh-FY) all the nationalities and religious groups ruled by Russia. That is, these czars tried to force the Poles, Lithuanians, Ukrainians (yew-KRAY-nee-UNS), Finns, and the Jews living in Russia to accept Russian ways, to speak the Russian language, and to join the Russian Orthodox Church. But most of these peoples refused to be Russified, and they continued to want independence.

A Russian Revolution Failed in 1905

In 1904 and 1905, Russia fought and lost a war against Japan. After this defeat, a revolution broke out in Russia in 1905. This revolution forced the Russian government to promise to give the Russian people a constitution and a more democratic form of

In 1905, Russian citizens, demonstrating against their government, were shot down by the czar's soldiers

government. A **Duma** (DOO-mah), or law-making body, finally was set up. However, Czar Nicholas the Second soon took most of the power away from the Duma. By 1914, Russia still had little freedom. The conditions were being created for a revolution by the Russian citizens.

The Turkish Empire Became Weakened

During the 1800's and early 1900's, Greece, Serbia, Bulgaria, Albania, and Rumania won their independence from the Turkish Empire. Meanwhile, other European nations took over parts of the Turks' territory.

The people of the Turkish Empire also were ready to revolt. Finally, in 1908, some new leaders called the **Young Turks** took over the Turkish government, and they made important changes to help build Turkey into a stronger nation.

SUMMING UP

Austria-Hungary, Russia, and the Turkish Empire faced many problems in the years from 1848 to 1914. Their peoples had little freedom, and their governments were not democratic. Many of the nationalities, or national groups, that lived in Austria-Hungary, Russia, and the Turkish Empire wanted to form their own nations. As a result, these empires slowly were weakened. In the next chapter, which begins Unit 17, you will read about a revolution that brought great changes without war or fighting.

UNDERSTANDING THE LESSON

Do You Know These Important Terms?

For each sentence below, choose the term that best completes the sentence.

1. National groups are called (**nationalities/cultures**).
2. A (**mir/volga**) was a word meaning "village" in Russia.
3. To (**Russify/indoctrinate**) meant to force all national groups and religious groups ruled by Russia to accept Russian ways of life.
4. The law-making group set up in Russia was called the (**Council/Duma**).
5. The new leaders who took over the government of the Turkish Empire in 1908 were called the (**New Guard/Young Turks**).

Do You Remember These People and Events?

1. Tell something about each of the following persons.

   Francis Joseph
   Czar Alexander the Second
   Czar Nicholas the First
   Czar Nicholas the Second

2. Explain how each of the following developments took place.

   a. Austria-Hungary became weaker between 1867 and 1914.
   b. The Russian serfs were set free and allowed to buy land.

Can You Locate These Places?

On the map on page 524, locate the following places. Tell how each place is related to the events in this chapter.

Austria-Hungary	**Russia**
Dardanelles	**Black Sea**
Greece	**Turkish Empire**

Do You Know When It Happened?

Why are the following years important in eastern Europe's history?

1861   1905

Do You Remember the Main Idea?

Which one of the following ideas is the MAIN IDEA of this chapter?

1. Between 1848 and 1914, the empires in eastern Europe grew stronger as they became more democratic.
2. Many changes took place in the empires in eastern Europe as different national groups set up their own new nations.
3. Between 1848 and 1914, Austria-Hungary, Russia, and the Turkish Empire became weaker.

What Do You Think?

From what you have read in this chapter, try to answer the following thought questions.

1. How might you have felt if you were a Russian serf who was freed in 1861?
2. If you were a member of one of the nationalities ruled by the Russians, how might you have felt about Russia's attempt to Russify you?
3. Why is the Dardanelles an important location in eastern Europe?

Unit 17
The Rise of Modern Industry

THE CHAPTERS IN UNIT 17 ARE

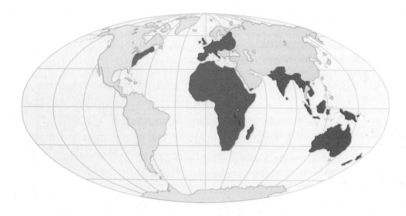

Many great changes that helped to shape the modern world were caused by the Industrial Revolution. The Industrial Revolution changed the ways in which people made their living. But it also changed the ways in which people lived, thought, and acted. In this unit, you will study this great development—the Industrial Revolution.

A steel-works in Europe, 1885

Chapter 81
Machines and the Industrial Revolution

GETTING STARTED

1   You have probably heard the term "industrial nation" used many times. An industrial nation, as compared to an agricultural nation, is a nation that has many factories and industries. Have you ever wondered how the factories and industries in these industrial nations were started?

The development of modern factories began about 1750 as a result of important changes that took place in the ways that products were made, the ways products were transported, and the ways they were sold. All of these important changes brought on a new kind of revolution—the Industrial Revolution. As you will see, the Industrial Revolution spread rapidly and continued to grow. And it is still going on even today.

2   Before you begin reading the chapter lesson, survey the lesson. Begin your survey by reading the beginning of the lesson. Then look through the lesson and read the headings. Next, study the pictures and read the picture captions. Finally, read the review section called "Summing Up." This survey will help you to discover the important ideas in this chapter.

Know the Main Idea

As you read the chapter lesson, try to remember the following important MAIN IDEA of the chapter.

The Industrial Revolution began in Great Britain, and it soon spread to other nations. And it is still going on today.

The following questions will help you to understand the MAIN IDEA. Try to answer these questions as you read the lesson.

1. How was power for machines supplied during the earliest period of the Industrial Revolution?
2. What invention made it possible to build factories almost anywhere?
3. In what nations did an Industrial Revolution begin during the late 1800's?

Know These Important Terms

Industrial Revolution	capitalists
factory system	steam engine

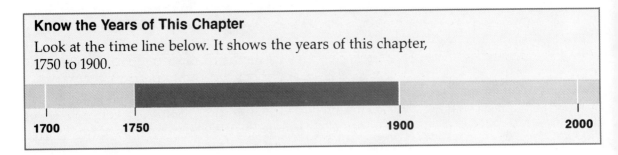

Know the Years of This Chapter

Look at the time line below. It shows the years of this chapter, 1750 to 1900.

| 1700 | 1750 | | 1900 | 2000 |

Cloth being printed in a cotton mill in Europe, 1834

EXPLORING THE TIME

In earlier chapters, you read about the French Revolution, the American Revolution, and other revolutions. However, one revolution that began over two hundred years ago is still going on today. That revolution was the Industrial Revolution. In this chapter, you will read about the Industrial Revolution.

Machines Began to Replace Human Power

By 1750, more and more machines were being invented and being used to make new products in Europe. This greatly increased use of machine power to replace human power was called the **Industrial Revolution.** During the early years of the Industrial Revolution, machines were driven by water power supplied by flowing rivers.

Later, machines were driven by steam power supplied by coal and oil fuel. Today, machines are driven by electric power, atomic power, and solar power.

The increased use of power-driven machines resulted in many important changes. One change was that the production of factory goods was greatly increased. For example, a new machine for spinning yarn invented in the 1770's was able to make as much yarn as sixteen workers made using an older-type spinning wheel.

Factories Were Used to Make Goods

Another important change was that the **factory system** developed. The new machines were too large to be kept in the workers' homes. The machines had to be set up in a large building located near a river that supplied water power. These buildings became known as factories.

Workers making iron

Another important change was the rise of **capitalists,** or people who invested in businesses and industries in hope of making a profit. Before the Industrial Revolution, some workers were able to save money and to start their own businesses. But as the Industrial Revolution developed, large amounts of money were needed to start new businesses. Few workers had this much money. Only a limited number of people had the large amount of capital, or money, to invest in building new factories.

Great Britain Started the Industrial Revolution

The Industrial Revolution began about 1750 in Great Britain. This nation led in the Industrial Revolution for many reasons. It had important natural resources—such as iron ore and coal fuel—and water power to operate machines. It had many skilled workers. It had people with money to invest in factories. It had a government that encouraged manufacturing, or the making of goods by using machines. And its colonies were good customers for the products manufactured in Great Britain.

Steam Power Replaced Water Power in the Industrial Revolution

One of the most important inventions of the Industrial Revolution was the **steam engine**. As early as 1712, Thomas Newcomen (NOO-koh-MEN) invented a steam engine to pump water out of British coal mines. Newcomen's steam engine was improved in the late 1700's by James Watt, a Scot. Watt's steam engine was used to provide power for large factory machines. As a result, factories no longer had to depend on water power. Now factories were built everywhere, not only along rivers.

George Stephenson and his son, Robert, built an early steam locomotive and railroad

The Steam Engine Speeded Up Transportation

Before 1800, many new roads and canals were built in Great Britain. But 10 miles an hour was still about as fast as anybody was able to travel in a horse-drawn coach or canalboat. By 1830, however, George Stephenson, an engineer, built a railroad that connected the cities of Manchester and Liverpool—a distance of more than 40 miles. A steam-powered locomotive train built by Stephenson's son, Robert Stephenson, traveled between the two cities at over 25 miles an hour. The railroad age now was beginning!

Steam power was also used to speed up ships. The first successful steamboat was built by an American, Robert Fulton. In 1807, Fulton sailed a steamboat up the Hudson River from New York City to Albany at a speed of 5 miles an hour. Soon steamships were used on many rivers and lakes. And in 1838, steamships began to cross the Atlantic Ocean.

A Second Industrial Revolution Soon Began

In the early 1800's, the Industrial Revolution spread to other nations in western Europe and to the United States. The nations of

McCormick's reaper, an American invention, helped farmers everywhere to grow larger crops. Note the similarities between this machine and a small, modern-day tractor-mower.

central, eastern, and southern Europe—such as Germany, Italy, Austria-Hungary, Spain, and Russia—did not have an Industrial Revolution until the late 1800's. By this time, western Europe was beginning a second Industrial Revolution.

The second Industrial Revolution was different from the first Industrial Revolution. In the second Industrial Revolution, steel was used more than iron. Electricity, gas, and oil replaced coal to supply power to operate machines. The automobile and the airplane became more important than the railroad. Modern machines became more automatic, and they slowly replaced many workers. And factories and businesses became much larger and needed much more capital, or money, to keep going.

The Second Industrial Revolution Improved Farming Methods and Communication

The second Industrial Revolution produced better farm machinery. Such machines as Cyrus McCormick's reaper increased the amount of farm crops that could be grown. Larger crops helped to feed Europe's growing population in the late 1800's. Communication, or exchanging ideas, also greatly improved. The invention of the telegraph, telephone, and radio helped to greatly improve communication in all the nations of the world.

SUMMING UP

The Industrial Revolution, which resulted in more and more machines replacing human power, began in Great Britain about 1750. And it spread to other nations soon after. The Industrial Revolution greatly changed and improved industry, transportation, communication, and farming. In the next chapter, you will learn how the Industrial Revolution also changed people's lives.

UNDERSTANDING THE LESSON

Do You Know These Important Terms?

For each sentence below, choose the term that best completes the sentence.

1. The greatly increased use of machine power to replace human power was called the **(Commercial Revolution/ Industrial Revolution)**.
2. Setting up machines in large buildings instead of in the workers' homes was called the **(mass production system/ factory system)**.
3. **(Capitalists/Mechanics)** were the wealthy people who built factories and hired workers to run factory machines.
4. The **(steam engine/waterwheel)** was one of the most important inventions of the Industrial Revolution.

Do You Remember These People and Events?

1. Tell something about each of the following persons.

   Thomas Newcomen   James Watt
   Robert Stephenson   Robert Fulton
   George Stephenson
   Cyrus McCormick

2. Explain why each of the following developments took place.

   a. Factories replaced workers' homes as the place where manufacturing was done.
   b. The Industrial Revolution started in Great Britain.
   c. The steam engine was one of the most important inventions of the Industrial Revolution.

Do You Know When It Happened?

About what year did the Industrial Revolution begin?

Do You Remember the Main Idea?

Which one of the following ideas is the MAIN IDEA of this chapter?

1. The Industrial Revolution began in the United States, and it soon spread to the nations in Europe.
2. The Industrial Revolution began with the invention of the steam engine, and it greatly changed transportation and manufacturing.
3. The Industrial Revolution began in Great Britain, and it soon spread to other nations. And it is still going on today.

What Do You Think?

From what you have read in this chapter, try to answer the following thought questions.

1. Can you think of any changes brought about by the Industrial Revolution that are not described in this chapter?
2. What do you think was the most important result of the Industrial Revolution? Give reasons for your answer.
3. What invention of the second Industrial Revolution do you think was the most important? Explain.

Chapter 82
People and the Industrial Revolution

GETTING STARTED

1   In the last chapter, you read that the Industrial Revolution began about 1750 and is still going on today. You read that the Industrial Revolution changed the ways that products were made and transported. And you read how the power used in manufacturing goods changed from human power to machine power.

These changes in the ways that goods were produced and transported brought many changes in the ways that people lived. As you will see, some of these changes helped people to live better. But other changes did not improve the way people lived. In this chapter you will read about those changes.

2   Before you begin reading the chapter lesson, survey the lesson. Begin your survey by reading the beginning of the lesson. Then look through the lesson and read the headings. Next, study the pictures and read the picture captions. Finally, read the review section called "Summing Up." This survey will help you to discover the important ideas in this chapter.

Know the Main Idea

As you read the chapter lesson, try to remember the following important MAIN IDEA of the chapter.

The Industrial Revolution changed European life in important ways. Some of the changes helped to improve people's lives, but other changes did not.

The following questions will help you to understand the MAIN IDEA. Try to answer these questions as you read the lesson.

1. What happened to Europe's population as a result of the Industrial Revolution?
2. How did workers' lives change under the factory system?
3. What effect did corporations have on small factories?

Know These Important Terms

domestic system   corporations

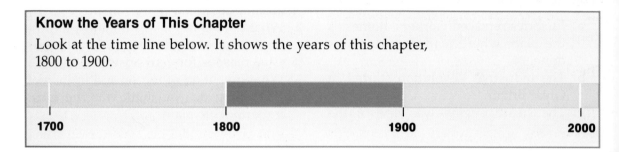

Know the Years of This Chapter
Look at the time line below. It shows the years of this chapter, 1800 to 1900.

| 1700 | 1800 | 1900 | 2000 |

An early gun factory

EXPLORING THE TIME

How did the Industrial Revolution change life in Europe? What happened to people as a result of the Industrial Revolution? Did it make people richer or poorer? In this chapter, you will find out how the Industrial Revolution changed life in Europe.

The Industrial Revolution Led to a Large Growth in Population

The Industrial Revolution helped to make possible the great growth in population during the years of the 1800's. In Great Britain, for example, the population grew from almost 9 million in 1800 to over 18 million in 1850. This meant that the British population doubled its size in these years.

The population growth was a result of changes that came during the years of the Industrial Revolution. Improvements in farm machinery and the discovery of better farming methods increased the food supply. And improvements in medicine and medical practices resulted in better health care for people. As a result, fewer babies died at birth and people lived longer.

HIGHLIGHTS IN HISTORY

Child Workers in a Factory

The Earl of Shaftesbury, a British noble, visited factories and mines in Great Britain during the 1830's. He was shocked to find many children as young as six or seven years old working in the factories. Sometimes these children worked at their machines for 12 or 14 hours without rest!

However, Shaftesbury found that the children who worked in factories were lucky compared to the children who worked in mines. In the mines, children worked at temperatures that were hot enough to melt the candles they used for light. The children often were crowded into openings too low for them to stand up straight. And often they had to work standing knee deep in water. It is surprising that even a few of these children lived through such terrible conditions.

The facts which the Earl of Shaftesbury discovered shocked the British people. As a result, in the 1840's, important laws were passed to improve working conditions in British factories and mines.

Question: Where did British children sometimes have to work?

The Industrial Revolution Helped Cities to Grow

Europe's cities also grew rapidly during the 1800's. Before the Industrial Revolution, nearly nine out of ten people in Europe lived on farms or in small villages. After the Industrial Revolution began, more people began to move into towns and cities. People moved into the cities because they were no longer able to earn their living on farms. As the use of machinery on farms increased, fewer farm workers were needed. At the same time, the growing number of factories in the cities provided many new jobs for workers. Therefore, people moved to the cities to find jobs.

Although cities provided jobs for workers, many of these workers lived under poor conditions in the cities. Many factory workers were paid low wages for their jobs. As a result, most workers lived in crowded buildings or badly built houses that grew up in every factory town.

Workers' Lives Were Changed by the Factory System

Before the Industrial Revolution, a cloth maker with a small amount of money was able to buy yarn and hire a few workers to weave the yarn into cloth in their homes. This was called the **domestic system** of making products. Under the domestic system, workers often had the time to be farmers, too. In this way, these workers sometimes were able to save some money and to open their own businesses. But under the factory system, few workers were able to do this.

A large amount of money, or capital, was needed to build a factory. Few workers were able to save enough money to start

Large factories were built in British cities during the Industrial Revolution

factories. The workers in a factory had to depend on the wages paid to them by the factory owner. They were not able to farm or earn their living in some other way. If workers did not like their jobs, they had to keep on working at them anyway, because plenty of other workers who needed jobs were ready to take their jobs if they left.

Working Conditions Were Difficult for Factory Workers

During the 1800's, working hours in the factories were long and hard. Workers started their jobs early in the morning when the factory whistle blew. And except for time off for meals, they continued working for the next 12 or 14 hours at the same task in the factory. And factories often were crowded, dirty, and not well lighted.

Not only men but women and children also worked these long hours in factories. In fact, many factory owners liked to hire women and children because they were able to pay them less money than men were paid for the same work.

The Industrial Revolution Brought Wealth to Some People

Some people in Europe became richer as a result of the Industrial Revolution. But most of this wealth went to a small group of people who owned most of the large businesses. The workers, who were the largest group of the population, received only a small part of this new wealth. However, the wages of workers increased during the later 1800's, and their living conditions improved.

As corporations grew, the people who ran them gained greater influence in their nations' daily activities

Large Corporations Were Set up During the Late 1800's

During the years of the first Industrial Revolution, one or two people were able to build a factory and keep it going. But by the later years of the 1800's, larger amounts of capital, or money, were needed to open a factory. To supply these large amounts of money, **corporations** were formed. Corporations were large business companies started by people who invested their money together in the company. By the end of the 1800's, many smaller European factories were forced out of business, and some of them were taken over by the large corporations.

SUMMING UP

The Industrial Revolution changed European life in some important ways. It improved farming methods and increased the food supply. It speeded up the growth of cities. It greatly increased jobs for factory workers whose wages gradually increased.

However, the Industrial Revolution also brought difficult conditions for most European factory workers. Factory workers received low wages for long hours of work in crowded, dirty factories. In the next chapter you will read about new ideas that developed about business during the years of the Industrial Revolution.

UNDERSTANDING THE LESSON

Do You Know These Important Terms?

For each sentence below, choose the term that best completes the sentence.

1. The system by which workers made products in their own homes was called the **(feudal system/domestic system).**
2. **(Corporations/Industries)** were large business companies started by people who invested their money together in the company.

Do You Remember These People and Events?

1. Tell about some of the changes that happened to the following groups of people as a result of the Industrial Revolution.

   farmers   women
   workers   children

2. Explain why each of the following developments took place.

   a. The Industrial Revolution helped cities to grow larger.
   b. Factory workers often suffered from poor working conditions.
   c. The factory system changed during the late 1800's.

Can You Locate These Places?

On a map of modern Europe, locate and name some of the main cities of western Europe.

1. In what country is each city located?
2. How many of the cities you named are located on rivers?

3. How do you think goods and products are transported to and from cities located on rivers?
4. How many of these cities are seaports located on the coast of an ocean or sea?

Do You Know When It Happened?

What are the years of this chapter?

Do You Remember the Main Idea?

Which one of the following ideas is the MAIN IDEA of this chapter?

1. The Industrial Revolution changed European life in important ways. Some of the changes helped to improve people's lives, but other changes did not.
2. As a result of the Industrial Revolution, the domestic system of manufacturing was replaced by the factory system.
3. The Industrial Revolution forced workers to work long hours for low wages and to live in run-down parts of cities.

What Do You Think?

From what you have read in this chapter, try to answer the following thought questions.

1. What do you think a working day was like in a British factory during the 1800's?
2. What change in Europe do you think helped workers the most? Give reasons for your answer.
3. Why do you think that people were better off after the Industrial Revolution took place? Explain your answer.

Chapter 83

New Beliefs About the Business System

GETTING STARTED

1   During the Middle Ages, the growth of trade and businesses in European nations helped these nations to become more powerful in many ways.

In the 1600's, the governments of some European nations began to control trade and businesses in their nation according to the ideas of mercantilism. They allowed trade to be carried on only with their colonies or with certain other nations. By the 1800's, however, many European merchants began to dislike mercantilism. They wanted to carry on their businesses without controls by the government. As you will see, these business owners' ideas led to new beliefs about the business system in the 1800's and 1900's.

2   Before you begin reading the chapter lesson, survey the lesson. Begin your survey by reading the beginning of the lesson. Then look through the lesson and read the headings. Next, study the pictures and read the picture captions. Finally, read the review section called "Summing Up" at the end of the lesson. This survey of the whole lesson will help you to discover the important ideas in this chapter.

Know the Main Idea

As you read the chapter lesson, try to remember the following important MAIN IDEA of the chapter.

During the 1800's, business owners gained more freedom to carry on their businesses without government controls. At the same time, workers were able to improve their working conditions.

The following questions will help you to understand the MAIN IDEA. Try to answer these questions as you read the lesson.

1. Why were the merchants of the early 1800's against the ideas of mercantilism?
2. Why were labor unions not successful during the early 1800's?
3. Who was the "founder of Communism"?

Know These Important Terms

laissez faire	profit
freedom of contract	socialism
labor unions	Communists
capitalism	

Know the Years of This Chapter

Look at the time line below. It shows the years of this chapter, 1800 to 1900.

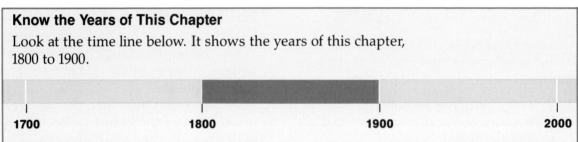

| 1700 | 1800 | 1900 | 2000 |

Casting pig-iron at an iron-works, 1899. What do you think would be the most dangerous aspect of working here?

EXPLORING THE TIME

As you have read, the Industrial Revolution changed life in Europe in many ways. It also changed Europe's ideas and beliefs about many things. In this chapter, you will study some new ideas about the business system that developed in Europe as a result of the Industrial Revolution.

Owners Wanted Businesses to Develop Without Government Controls

During the 1600's and the early 1700's, most European nations believed in a trade and business policy called mercantilism. Under mercantilism, the government carefully controlled the nation's trade and businesses. But as the Industrial Revolution spread, many European business owners came to

Adam Smith, a British writer, helped to spread the new business ideas of capitalism

believe that these government controls were harmful to the growth of their businesses. Business owners now wanted to run their factories and businesses freely, without any government controls. These ideas about business were call **laissez faire** (LES-ay FAIR). "Laissez faire" means to let people do as they wish.

Workers Tried to Get Better Working Conditions

By the 1800's, many business owners believed that **freedom of contract** was important for free business operations. Freedom of contract gave each worker the right to make an agreement with an employer about wages, hours, and working conditions. But in most cases, the worker had to agree to the low wages and long hours fixed by the employer if the worker wanted a job.

Labor Unions Were Formed to Help Workers

Some workers tried to force employers to deal with them more fairly by forming **labor unions.** The labor unions were groups of workers who tried to get better wages and working conditions for themselves. The labor unions tried to make the workers more powerful in dealing with employers.

In the early 1800's, many laws were passed to forbid labor unions. Later, however, unions became lawful. And by the late 1800's and early 1900's, labor unions in western European nations helped to get better wages and working conditions for many workers.

Socialists Wanted to Change the Economic System of Capitalism

The economic system that developed in Europe and most parts of the world by the 1800's was called **capitalism.** Under capitalism, most factories and industries were owned by people who ran these businesses in order to make a **profit,** or money for themselves. But these businesses also provided many jobs for workers and also produced the many goods needed by people to live comfortably in a modern nation.

But during the 1800's, some people felt that workers were not receiving enough benefits from capitalism. Some of these people wanted to end capitalism and replace it with a system called **socialism.** Under socialism, the government was supposed to own all of the important

Many of the European business owners who became wealthy had new townhouses built in cities like Paris

industries and businesses of the nation, and all the people were to receive an equal share of the profits and goods produced in the nation. The people who believed in socialism wanted to set up socialism by peaceful methods. They wanted to form political parties and to win control of their nation's government in free elections.

Karl Marx Began the Ideas of Communism

However, some socialists felt that capitalism was too strong to be changed by peaceful means. These people wanted to bring about an extreme form of socialism by revolution and by taking over the government.

These socialists were called **Communists**. The "founder of Communism" was Karl Marx of Germany.

Marx believed that capitalism was the enemy of all workers. He believed that capitalism allowed workers to earn only enough money to keep alive. Marx and his followers encouraged workers everywhere to revolt against their nations' governments and set up their own "dictatorship of workers."

In a workers' dictatorship, a Communist government was to be set up to control everything in the nation. Then slowly, as more people became trained to live under Communism, the government itself was to disappear, and the people were to control

Factory towns sprang up and grew larger and larger. Unfortunately, many of them became crowded and polluted

everything in the nation for themselves. All the people were to receive enough money, food, and products to live good lives.

History Proved That Marx Was Wrong

Was Marx right? Was a revolution against capitalism the only way to improve workers' lives? At the time that Marx lived (1818 to 1883), many workers lived and worked under difficult conditions. Marx believed that it was not possible to improve these conditions under capitalism. But today we know that Marx was wrong. In modern capitalist nations, such as the United States, wages and working conditions have improved steadily. These nations also have the highest living standards in the world. And the people of these nations enjoy many freedoms and a democratic government.

Therefore, Marx was wrong, but his ideas later helped to cause a revolution in Russia in 1917. (In Chapter 95, you will find out what happened when a Communist government was set up in Russia as a result of this revolution.)

SUMMING UP

By the early 1800's, capitalism was the business system of Europe and most parts of the world. Capitalism was based on the idea of "laissez faire," or the freedom of business owners to carry on their businesses without government controls. However, under laissez faire, most workers were forced to accept low wages and poor working conditions. Slowly, workers formed labor unions to try to improve working conditions.

Some people believed that capitalism itself caused the workers' problems. These people wanted to replace capitalism with another business system called socialism. Karl Marx later developed an extreme form of socialism called Communism. In the next chapter, you will read about the new European empires in other lands in the late 1800's.

UNDERSTANDING THE LESSON

Do You Know These Important Terms?

For each sentence below, choose the term that best completes the sentence.

1. The system of allowing business owners to run their factories and businesses without government controls was called **(free enterprise/laissez faire)**.
2. **(Freedom of contract/Freedom of creed)** gave each worker the right to make an agreement with an employer about wages, hours, and working conditions.
3. Groups of workers who joined together to try to get better wages and working conditions for themselves were called **(front men/labor unions)**.
4. **(Capitalism/Imperialism)** is a business system in which business owners operate industries and factories to make money for themselves.
5. The money made by business owners from operating businesses is called their **(gross/profit)**.
6. The business system in which the government was supposed to own all of the nation's important industries and the people were to share equally in the profits and the goods is called **(totalitarianism/socialism)**.
7. People who wanted to bring about an extreme form of socialism by revolution were called **(Communists/strikers)**.

Do You Remember These People and Events?

1. Tell something about Marx's ideas.
2. Explain how each took place.

   a. Labor unions were formed to help workers.

   b. Socialism and Communism were different from each other.
   c. History proved that Karl Marx was wrong.

Do You Know When It Happened?

What are the years of this chapter?

Do You Remember the Main Idea?

Which one of the following ideas is the MAIN IDEA of this chapter?

1. During the 1800's, most of the workers in Europe became socialists in order to try to improve their working conditions.
2. Communism began in Europe during the 1800's because many people believed that Communism was the only way to improve conditions for workers.
3. During the 1800's, business owners gained more freedom to carry on their businesses without government controls. At the same time, workers were able to improve working conditions.

What Do You Think?

From what you have read in this chapter, answer the following thought questions.

1. If you were a business owner in the 1800's, would you have liked or disliked labor unions? Explain your answer.
2. Do you think that it is possible for a government to "disappear" completely, as the Communists claimed was to happen under Communism? Give reasons.
3. Do you think that the government should have some control over businesses, or should it follow a laissez-faire policy? Explain your answer.

GETTING STARTED

1 There once was a saying, "The sun never sets on the British Empire." By the late 1800's, Great Britain had colonies in all parts of the world. But Great Britain was not the only nation that controlled a colonial empire in the late 1800's. The Netherlands, Spain, France, Germany, Belgium, Italy, and Russia also built colonial empires in the period from 1850 to 1900. Why did all these European nations want empires? Where did these nations find new lands as colonies? And how did these countries go about acquiring new colonies? You will learn the answers to these questions in this chapter.

2 Before you begin reading the chapter lesson, survey the lesson. Begin your survey by reading the beginning of the lesson. Then, look through the lesson and read the headings. Next, study the pictures and read the picture captions. Then, study the map showing European empires in Asia and Africa in 1900 on page 550. Finally, read the review section called "Summing Up." This survey will help you to discover the important ideas in this chapter.

Know the Main Idea

As you read the chapter lesson, try to remember the following important MAIN IDEA of the chapter.

During the late 1800's, European nations built colonial empires in Asia and Africa.

 The following questions will help you to understand the MAIN IDEA. Try to answer these questions as you read the lesson.

1. Why did Europe's empire building stop in the early 1800's?
2. What reasons did European nations have for a new interest in empire building in the late 1800's?
3. What great industrial nations were trade rivals in world markets in the late 1800's?

Know These Important Terms

imperialism	over-populated
markets	national pride
competitors	

Know the Years of This Chapter

Look at the time line below. It shows the years of this chapter, 1850 to 1900.

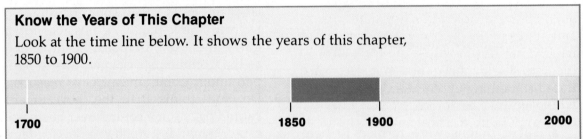

| 1700 | 1850 | 1900 | 2000 |

The Suez Canal, connecting the Red Sea with the Mediterranean Sea, helped increase trade

EXPLORING THE TIME

Did you ever hear the name "empire builder" used to describe someone? Empire builders are people who try to gain more and more power for themselves. Sometimes nations have been empire builders, too. In the late 1800's, empire building was called **imperialism**. In this chapter, you will learn why imperialism, or empire building, became important to many nations of Europe in the late 1800's.

European Nations Lost Interest in Empire Building

You have already read about the colonial empires built by Great Britain, France, Spain, the Netherlands, and Portugal in the Americas and other lands in the 1500's, 1600's, and 1700's. But after the American Revolution and the revolutions in Latin America took place, these nations lost many colonies. These nations then lost interest in empire building. They felt that colonies cost more than they were worth.

549

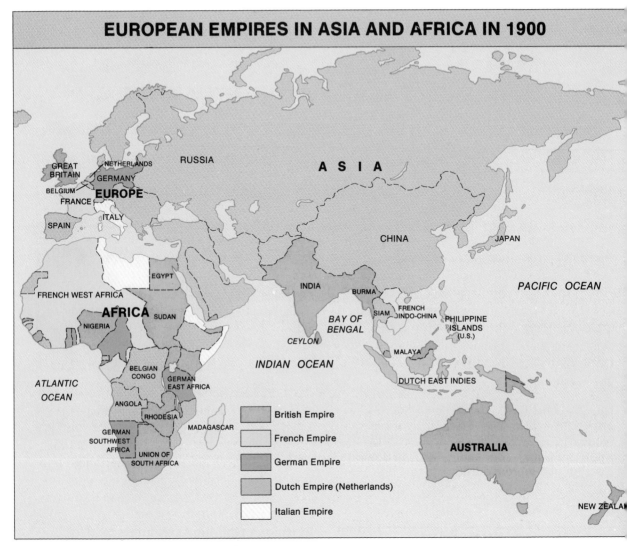

EUROPEAN EMPIRES IN ASIA AND AFRICA IN 1900

British Empire

French Empire

German Empire

Dutch Empire (Netherlands)

Italian Empire

Which nations were part of the Dutch Empire in 1900?

In addition, in the early 1800's, many European nations were too busy at home to worry about colonies. Between 1789 and 1815, most European nations were at war. And after 1815, many of them were busy building new industries and factories.

But by the late 1800's, empire building, or imperialism, again became important to many nations of the world. What were the reasons for this new interest in colonies?

A Need for New Markets Encouraged Imperialism

One of the most important reasons for the new interest in imperialism in the late 1800's was the need of industrial nations to have new **markets,** or places to sell their manufactured goods. During the 1800's, the Industrial Revolution greatly increased the production of factory goods in industrial nations. By the late 1800's, Great Britain, the United States, France, Germany, and other nations were producing more and more factory goods. And these nations now became **competitors,** or rivals, for world markets. With increased competition came the urge to find new markets.

The problem of all these competitor nations was to find buyers for their manufactured goods. They now believed that the answer to their problem was to acquire new colonies in some of the lands in Asia or Africa. The people of these faraway lands did not have factories. If these lands were taken over as colonies, their peoples might become good customers for manufactured goods. In this way, the need for colonies as markets became one of the main reasons for imperialism.

Capitalists' Need to Invest Encouraged Imperialism

As you know, an important and wealthy group of capitalists, or rich people, developed during the Industrial Revolution. Many of these capitalists wished to invest, or spend, their money in order to make even more money. And these capitalists wanted their nations to acquire colonies.

Colonies were good places to invest money in new projects, such as mining, railroad building, or plantation farming. And from these investments in colonies, these wealthy capitalists expected to make large profits, or large amounts of money.

But investing in businesses in faraway lands often was dangerous. Sometimes the peoples of these lands revolted against foreign business owners. Therefore, the wealthy capitalists who wished to invest their money in other lands wanted their nations to take over and to control these lands as colonies. In this way, they hoped to have their nations protect their investments.

Over-Population Encouraged Imperialism

Some nations also wanted to build empires because they felt that they were **over-populated,** or had too many people. But these over-populated nations did not want large numbers of their people to move to foreign countries. Instead, these over-populated nations wanted to acquire colonies where some of their people might settle. In this way, the people who left their nation to settle in colonies still felt they belonged to their nation, and they remained loyal citizens of their nation.

National Pride Encouraged Imperialism

By the late 1800's, many nations also wanted colonies because of **national pride**—a people's need to feel proud of their nation. These nations were jealous of other nations, such as Great Britain, the Netherlands, and Spain, which already had large empires. The nations without colonies felt that these other nations were strong and powerful because these other nations owned empires, or colonies.

By the 1870's, France, Belgium, Germany, Italy, and Russia began to think about catching up to the nations that already had empires. But as soon as one of these nations took over a new colony, all the other nations felt they had to acquire more new colonies, too. As a result, these European nations soon divided up most of Asia and Africa. (In Chapters 85 to 88, you will learn how European imperialism affected the nations of Asia and Africa.)

By 1818, Great Britain controlled most of India. This painting shows English officers in India in the mid-1800's.

SUMMING UP

By the late 1800's, the industrial nations of Europe—Great Britain, The Netherlands, Spain, France, Germany, Belgium, Italy, and Russia—were beginning to develop a new interest in imperialism, or in acquiring colonies. These nations wanted colonies for many reasons. One of the most important was that they needed new markets, or new places where they were able to sell their manufactured goods. They also needed colonies to supply raw materials for their industries. And wealthy capitalists in these industrial nations wanted colonies as places to invest their money in order to make even more money. Other reasons for imperialism were the over-population of some nations and national pride. In the next chapter, which begins Unit 18, you will study European imperialism in China and its effect on this large but weak nation.

UNDERSTANDING THE LESSON

Do You Know These Important Terms?

For each sentence below, choose the term that best completes the sentence.

1. Empire building by nations is called (**socialism/imperialism**).
2. Places where goods and products are sold are called (**markets/plantations**).
3. (**Competitors/Customers**) are rivals.
4. A nation that has more people than it can support is (**underdeveloped/over-populated**).
5. A people's need to feel proud of their country is called (**liberty/national pride**).

Do You Remember These People and Events?

1. Explain how or why each of the following developments took place.

   a. European nations were not interested in imperialism during the early 1800's.
   b. New markets and a need to protect investments encouraged imperialism in the late 1800's.
   c. Over-population encouraged imperialism in the late 1800's.
   d. National pride encouraged imperialism in the late 1800's.

Can You Locate These Places?

Use the map on page 550 to do the following map work.

1. Locate and name some of the lands that were part of the British Empire in 1900.
2. What islands did the Netherlands claim as colonies? Where did Italy have colonies?
3. On what continent did Germany have its largest number of colonies? Name some of these colonies.
4. Locate the French Empire. What color symbol is used to show these lands?

Do You Know When It Happened?

What are the years of this chapter?

Do You Remember the Main Idea?

Which one of the following ideas is the MAIN IDEA of this chapter?

1. Great Britain was so far ahead in building an empire that other European nations were never able to catch up and build empires as large.
2. During the late 1800's, European nations built colonial empires in Asia and Africa.
3. Imperialism was a result of the French Revolution, and all European industrial nations tried to build large empires.

What Do You Think?

From what you have read in this chapter, try to answer the following thought questions.

1. Suppose you were a citizen of one of the European colonies in Asia or Africa. How would you have felt about being ruled by a European nation?
2. What problems can result from too much national pride?
3. What problems might a nation have in governing an empire that includes lands in all parts of the world?

Unit 18
European Imperialism in Asia and Africa

THE CHAPTERS IN UNIT 18 ARE

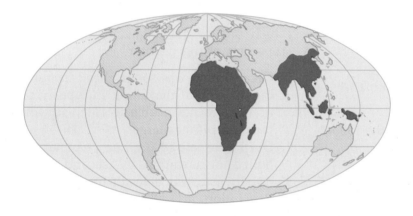

Imperialism, or empire-building, was one of the important results of the Industrial Revolution. The nations of Europe now became more interested than ever before in trading with Asia and Africa. Soon the European nations took control of many nations in Asia and Africa. In this unit, you will read about European imperialism in these nations.

Foreign steamships in a Japanese harbor

554

異邦蒸
トス

Chapter 85

China and the European Nations

GETTING STARTED

1 As you read in the last chapter, the industrial nations of Europe became interested in building colonial empires in the late 1800's. Sometimes these nations carried out their imperialistic ideas by getting new colonies. And sometimes these nations carried out their imperialistic ideas by taking control of the trade of a weaker nation. As you will learn, Great Britain and other European nations soon tried to bring their ideas of imperialism to China—a large, but weak, nation.

2 Before you begin reading the chapter lesson, survey the lesson. Begin your survey by reading the beginning of the lesson. Then look through the lesson and read the headings. Next, study the pictures and read the picture captions. Then study the map showing China in 1900 on page 559. Finally, read the review section called "Summing Up." This survey will help you to discover the important ideas in this chapter.

Know the Main Idea

As you read the chapter lesson, try to remember the following important MAIN IDEA of the chapter.

During the 1800's, Great Britain and other European nations forced the Manchu dynasty to open Chinese ports to European traders.

The following questions will help you to understand the MAIN IDEA. Try to answer these questions as you read the lesson.

1. How did the Manchu dynasty treat European traders?
2. What Chinese port was the first to be opened to foreign traders?
3. What part of China was given to Great Britain as a result of a war?

Know These Important Terms

Manchu dynasty   Opium War

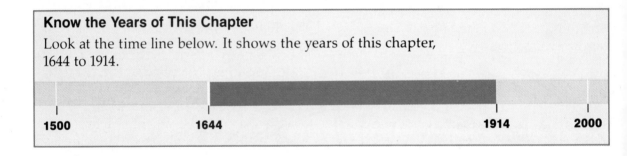

Know the Years of This Chapter
Look at the time line below. It shows the years of this chapter,
1644 to 1914.

| 1500 | 1644 | 1914 | 2000 |

Boats in the port of Guangzhou

EXPLORING THE TIME

When you last read about China in Chapter 44, the Ming dynasty ruled China. Perhaps you remember that the Ming dynasty began to rule China in the year 1368. And perhaps you also remember that the Ming rulers tried to keep Europeans out of China. In this chapter, you will find out what happened to China after the Ming dynasty was overthrown in 1644.

The Manchu Dynasty Overthrew the Mings

The Ming dynasty lasted nearly three hundred years. But by the 1600's, the Mings were much weaker as a result of a Japanese invasion. In addition, China suffered hard times under the Mings because of high taxes and poor government. In 1644, the Mings were overthrown by a new ruling family, the **Manchu dynasty,** which came from the province of Manchuria (man-CHUR-ee-UH).

The Manchus Carried on Ming Practices

The Manchus ruled China from 1644 to 1911. Like other conquerors, the Manchus accepted the teachings of Confucius. And during their long rule, the Manchus followed the same government practices used by earlier Chinese dynasties. The Ming law code was formed. The exam system for government jobs based on Confucius' teachings was continued. And Manchus continued to try to keep foreigners out of China.

China's Trade Grew During the Manchu Period

However, during the Manchu period, China greatly increased its trade with other nations. Japan, India, the Philippine Islands, the European nations, and the United States became customers for China's goods. Chinese silk, tea, cotton goods, chinaware, pottery, jewelry, and furniture became well known all over the world.

The Manchus Strictly Controlled Foreign Traders

The Manchu rulers were very strict with European traders. The Manchus allowed Europeans to trade only at the port city of Guangzhou. And the Manchus taxed the European traders heavily. If the traders refused to pay these taxes or to obey Chinese trading rules, the Manchus stopped trading with them. And as long as the Manchu government remained strong, the European nations did little to help their traders in China.

The Manchu Government Began to Weaken

For about one hundred and fifty years, China enjoyed peace and good times under the Manchus. Taxes were low. Roads and canals were kept in good repair. And the Chinese Empire and the Chinese population grew larger.

But during the late 1700's and the 1800's China suffered from hard times. Many rev-olutions broke out. Although the Manchu government was able to stop these revolutions, many Chinese people were killed and many millions of acres of farmland were destroyed. In addition, these uprisings greatly weakened the Manchu government. European nations now were able to force the Manchus to let European traders enter China.

The Industrial Revolution Increased European Interest in China

During the early 1800's in Europe, the growing production of factory goods gave European nations strong reasons for becoming more interested in China. As you have read, the new steam-powered factory machines in Europe turned out large amounts of many new manufactured products. European nations were not able to sell all these goods in Europe. And some European nations did not have all the raw materials they needed for their industries. As a result, many European nations wished to increase their trade with China in order to sell their factory goods and to obtain raw materials from China.

Great Britain Tried to Open China to European Trade

As you recall, the Industrial Revolution began in Great Britain. And it was Great Britain that was most interested in trading with China.

About 1834, the British government demanded that China open more of its ports to foreign traders. The British government also demanded that China end some of its strict controls on European traders. However, the Manchu government refused to agree to these British demands.

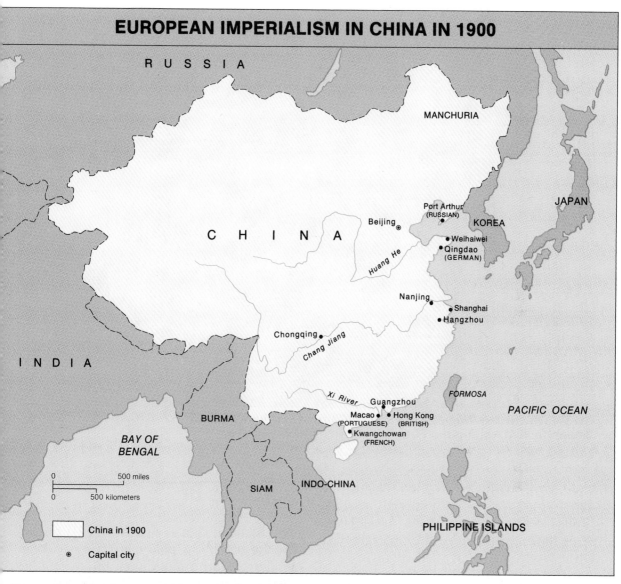

EUROPEAN IMPERIALISM IN CHINA IN 1900

Name the cities in which the following countries had special trading rights: Great Britain, Portugal, Russia.

The "Opium War" Opened China to British Trade

At about this time, the Chinese government was trying to stop European traders from bringing opium (OH-pee-UM) drugs into China to sell to the Chinese. In 1839, the Chinese government destroyed all the opium in the warehouses of European traders. When British traders asked their government to protect them, Great Britain decided to declare war against China.

By 1842, Great Britain defeated China in the **Opium War.** A peace treaty was signed,

The British steamer *Nemesis* destroying Chinese war junks on January 7, 1841, during the First Opium War. Which country won the war?

and China was forced to open Guangzhou and four other ports to foreign traders. China also gave the important port of Hong Kong to Great Britain. And China agreed to lower taxes on foreign products.

Other European Nations Soon Won Trading Rights in China

Soon, other European nations also gained trading rights in China, and China was forced to open more ports to foreign trade. China also was forced to allow foreigners accused of crimes to be judged by courts of their own nation.

SUMMING UP

The Manchu dynasty (1644 to 1911) carried on the old Ming policy of trying to keep foreign traders out of China. But during the 1800's, many European nations wanted to trade with China in order to sell their factory goods to China and to buy raw materials from China for their factories. These nations soon were able to force the Manchus to open China to European traders. Great Britain and other European nations were given ports and special trading rights in China. In the next chapter, you will read about European imperialism in India.

UNDERSTANDING THE LESSON

Do You Know These Important Terms?

For each sentence below, choose the term that best completes the sentence.

1. The family that ruled China from 1644 until 1911 was called the **(Manchu dynasty/Ming dynasty)**.
2. The **(Opium War/Trade War)** was a war fought by Great Britain to protect British traders in China.

Do You Remember These People and Events?

1. Tell something about each of the following groups of rulers.

   Mings   Manchus

2. Explain how each of the following developments took place.

   a. The Manchus strictly controlled foreign trade.
   b. The Industrial Revolution helped to increase Europe's interest in trading with China.
   c. Great Britain and other European nations gained trading rights in China.

Can You Locate These Places?

Use the map on page 559 to do the following map work.

1. Locate the following places. Tell how each place is related to the events in this chapter.

China	Manchuria
Japan	Philippine Islands
Guangzhou	Hong Kong

2. In what part of China is Manchuria located?
3. Name and locate some of the Chinese seaports. What European nations controlled some of these seaports?
4. What city was the capital of China in the 1800's?

Do You Know When It Happened?

Why is the following year important in China's history?

1842

Do You Remember the Main Idea?

Which one of the following ideas is the MAIN IDEA of this chapter?

1. During the 1800's, Great Britain and other European nations forced the Manchu dynasty to open Chinese ports to European traders.
2. Great Britain forced China to open its ports to trade and succeeded in setting up large colonies in China.
3. China had many raw materials needed by the industrial nations in Europe, and trade increased between these nations.

What Do You Think?

From what you have read in this chapter, try to answer the following thought questions.

1. Do you think European nations had a right to force China to open its ports to foreign trade? Give reasons for your answer.
2. How did Great Britain's actions in China show how imperialism worked?

Chapter 86

India and the European Nations

GETTING STARTED

1 In the last chapter, you read how Great Britain and other European nations forced China to open its ports for trade. The European nations also became interested in trading with India. Between 1500 and 1858 (see the time line below), some European nations established trading posts in India. These nations also fought with each other to try to gain complete control of the trade with India. As you will see, Great Britain finally won control of all of India.

2 Before you begin reading the chapter lesson, survey the lesson. Begin your survey by reading the beginning of the lesson. Then look through the lesson and read the headings. Next, study the pictures and read the picture captions. Then study the map of India on page 564. Finally, read the review section call "Summing Up" at the end of the lesson. This survey of the whole lesson will help you to discover the important ideas in this chapter.

Know the Main Idea

As you read the chapter lesson, try to remember the following important MAIN IDEA of the chapter.

From the 1500's to 1763, European nations fought for control of India. Great Britain finally took over complete rule of India.

The following questions will help you to understand the MAIN IDEA. Try to answer these questions as you read the lesson.

1. What European nation was the first to set up trading posts in India?
2. Who was the official of the British East India Company who helped force the French traders to leave India?
3. When did the British government take complete control of India?

Know These Important Terms

India Act of 1784   sepoys
suttee   Sepoy Rebellion

Know the Years of This Chapter

Look at the time line below. It shows the years of this chapter, 1500 to 1858.

| 1500 | 1858 | 2000 |

Painting showing a British officer riding an elephant in an Indian procession

EXPLORING THE TIME

When Vasco da Gama sailed into the harbor of Calicut (CAL-ih-KUT), India, in the year 1498, a new period opened in the history of India. Not many people of India knew it at the time, but the Europeans were in India to stay. In this chapter, you will learn how certain nations of Europe slowly took control of India.

Portugal Built Up Trading Posts in India

In the early years of the 1500's, Portuguese traders built up a series of trading posts, or trading settlements, along the coast of India. The most important of these settlements was the city of Goa, on the west coast of India. At these trading posts, the Portuguese traders exchanged European products for the spices of the East Indies and Asia.

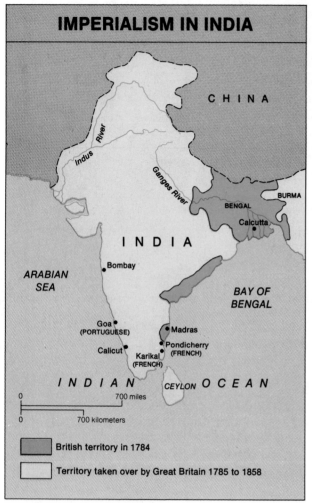

IMPERIALISM IN INDIA

CHINA

Indus River

Ganges River

BURMA

BENGAL

Calcutta

INDIA

Bombay

ARABIAN
SEA

BAY OF
BENGAL

Goa
(PORTUGUESE)

Madras

Calicut

Pondicherry
(FRENCH)

Karikal
(FRENCH)

INDIAN   CEYLON OCEAN

0   700 miles

0   700 kilometers

■ British territory in 1784

☐ Territory taken over by Great Britain 1785 to 1858

Which two major Indian cities were in British territory in 1784?

The Netherlands and England Took Over the Trade with India

The rulers of India did not like to have the Portuguese traders set up trading posts in India. But the Portuguese traders had guns, and the rulers of India did not. As a result, the Portuguese took control of the spice trade in India during the 1500's.

But by 1600, the Netherlands (Holland) and England were strong enough to try to end Portugal's control of this trade. And after some fighting, England and the Netherlands succeeded. These two nations took over the East Indies, and England set up its trading posts in India.

The East India Company Controlled England's Trade with India

The English trading posts in India were not started by the English government. They were started by a group of English traders, or merchants, called the East India Company. The English government gave only the East India Company the right to trade with India. And the East India Company soon made a great deal of money selling India's cotton goods, silk, spices, and sugar to European nations.

Great Britain Defeated France in India

After the Mogul Empire ended in the early 1700's, India was divided into many warring states. By this time, the two most important European nations in India were Great Britain (England) and France.

France, too, now had a group of French traders in India called the French East India Company. And Joseph Dupleix (duh-PLEKS) was its leader. Dupleix believed that France must send French soldiers and weapons to help the rulers of India's states. In return, Dupleix wanted the rulers of India's states to help him force the British traders to leave India. However, the British East India Company used the same plan. Led by Robert Clive, an official of the British East India Company, the rulers of India's states finally forced the French traders to leave India in 1763.

Robert Clive (center) worked with the rulers of India's states to force the French traders to leave India

The British East India Company Ruled India at First

The British East India Company became the real ruler of India. The Company chose the governor, the tax collectors, the judges, and the army officers of India. Most of these officials were British citizens. But, in time, the British government decided that the Company needed help in governing India. By the **India Act of 1784,** the British government began to share the rule of India with the British East India Company.

The British Government Took Over More Territory in India

In 1784, the only large state in India that was completely ruled by Great Britain was Bengal in northeastern India. The India Act of 1784 had declared that the British East India Company was not to take over any more territory in India. Yet by 1818, Great Britain controlled most of India!

Great Britain took over more land in India for two reasons. First, Great Britain feared that Napoleon planned to build a French colony in India. Second, the British government wished to protect British trade with India.

Great Britain Tried to Bring British Ideas to India

As soon as Great Britain gained control of India, many British officials began to introduce British customs and ideas to the people of India. British laws were used in India's courts. British subjects were taught in India's schools. The English language became the official government language of India.

HIGHLIGHTS IN HISTORY

Sepoy Soldiers

The sepoys (SEE-poize) were the native soldiers who served in the British army in India. Some sepoys were Hindus, and some were Muslims. Like most other people of India, they were troubled by the European ideas and customs that the British were bringing to India.

Early in 1857, the sepoys heard a story that the gunpowder for their rifles was packed in paper oiled with the fat of pigs and cows. No Hindu was allowed to touch the fat of a cow. And no Muslim was allowed to touch the fat of a pig. Therefore, the sepoys believed that using these rifles was against their religion.

In May 1857, the sepoys rebelled, or revolted. The sepoys attacked the British soldiers and British settlers in India. The British army fought back to end the Sepoy Rebellion. But the revolt lasted for almost a year. The Sepoy Rebellion showed the weakness of the East India Company. As a result, in 1858, the British government took over the control of India.

Question: Who were the sepoys?

The British officials also tried to put an end to certain practices in India, such as the Hindu custom of **suttee** (suh-TEE). In suttee, a Hindu wife was burned in the fire that burned the body of her dead husband. But it took many years before the Hindus agreed to end this custom.

The British Government Took Complete Control of India in 1858

Many people in India did not like the changes brought by the British officials, and they disliked being ruled by the British. In 1857, soldiers called **sepoys** (SEE-poize) rebelled, or revolted, and tried to force the British settlers to leave India. This revolt was called the **Sepoy Rebellion.** The sepoys rebelled because they felt that Great Britain was not respecting India's religious customs. Great Britain managed to end this rebellion, but the British government now realized that the British East India Company was not able to govern India. Therefore, in 1858, the British government took over control of India from the East India Company.

SUMMING UP

From the 1500's on, European nations fought for control of India. The final winner was Great Britain. By the 1800's, the British East India Company ruled most of India. Many people in India did not like this British rule. In the Sepoy Rebellion of 1857, India revolted against the rule of the British East India Company. As a result, the British government took over complete rule of India. In the next chapter, you will read about European imperialism in Japan and in the lands of Southeast Asia.

UNDERSTANDING THE LESSON

Do You Know These Important Terms?

For each sentence below, choose the term that best completes the sentence.

1. The (**India Act of 1784/Proclamation of 1764**) gave the British government the right to share the rule of India with the British East India Company.
2. The Hindu practice of a wife burning herself in the same fire that burned the body of her dead husband was called (**sacrifice/suttee**).
3. India's soldiers who tried to force the British settlers to leave India were called (**sepoys/rebels**).
4. The rebellion in India against the rule of the East India Company was called the (**Indian Revolution/Sepoy Rebellion**).

Do You Remember These People and Events?

1. Tell something about each of the following persons.

   **Vasco da Gama   Robert Clive
   Joseph Dupleix**

2. Explain how each of the following developments took place.

   a. The British East India Company gained complete control of India.
   b. Great Britain tried to bring British ways of living to India.
   c. The British government took complete control of India in 1858.

Can You Locate These Places?

Use the map on page 564 to do the following map work.

1. Locate the following places. Tell how each place is related to the events in this chapter.

   Calicut   Goa   Bengal   India

2. What clues on this map show that other European nations still were interested in India?

Do You Know When It Happened?

Why is the following year important in the history of India?

   1858

Do You Remember the Main Idea?

Which one of the following ideas is the MAIN IDEA of this chapter?

1. France, Portugal, the Netherlands, and Great Britain gained control of India, and they split the country into several parts.
2. Portugal became the greatest trading nation in India because of the early voyages of Portuguese explorers.
3. From the 1500's to 1763, European nations fought for control of India. Great Britain finally took over complete rule of India.

What Do You Think?

From what you have read in this chapter, answer the following thought questions.

1. How do you think the people of India felt when they saw Vasco da Gama's ship sail into the harbor of Calicut?
2. Can you think of some ways that British rule helped the people of India?

Chapter 87
Imperialism in Japan and Southeast Asia

GETTING STARTED

1   European nations became interested in other lands in Asia besides India and China. Japan was one of these lands, but Japan was too strong to be conquered. The lands of Southeast Asia, on the other hand, were weak. These lands were easily taken over by nations that practiced the ideas of imperialism, or empire building. By the late 1800's, foreign nations forced Japan to trade with them, and foreign nations also took over many lands in Southeast Asia.

2   Before you begin reading the chapter lesson, survey the lesson. Begin your survey by reading the beginning of the lesson. Then look through the lesson and read the headings. Next, study the pictures and read the picture captions. Then study the map of Japan and Southeast Asia in 1914 on page 570. Finally, read the review section called "Summing Up" at the end of the lesson. This survey of the whole lesson will help you to discover the important ideas in this chapter.

Know the Main Idea

As you read the chapter lesson, try to remember the following important MAIN IDEA of the chapter.

In the late 1800's, Japan began to trade with other nations. Japan became the most powerful nation in Asia, but most of Southeast Asia was taken over by foreign nations.

The following questions will help you to understand the MAIN IDEA. Try to answer these questions as you read the lesson.

1. What European nation was the only nation allowed to trade with Japan during the 1700's and early 1800's?
2. What nation opened the ports of Japan to trade with other nations?
3. What wars fought by Japan proved that Japan was one of the powerful nations of the world?

Know These Important Terms

westernized   Russo-Japanese War
Zaibatsu

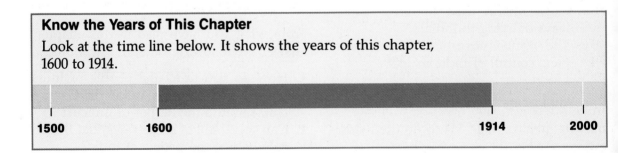

Know the Years of This Chapter
Look at the time line below. It shows the years of this chapter, 1600 to 1914.

1500   1600   1914   2000

Commodore Matthew Perry was successful in getting Japan to open ports to American trade in 1854

EXPLORING THE TIME

Did you know that a model railroad train was important in Japanese history? In the year 1854, a model railroad train was given to the ruler of Japan by Matthew Perry, an American naval officer visiting Japan. The Japanese ruler was so impressed by this model train that he became more willing to allow Japan to trade with the United States. In this chapter, you will learn about the modern history of Japan and of Southeast Asia and about imperialism there.

Japan Ended Dealings with Other Nations in the 1600's

In Chapter 41, you learned that Japan had an emperor, but that the real ruler of Japan was the shogun, or general of the Japanese army. Beginning in the early 1600's, the shoguns began to stop Japan's dealings with other nations. Foreigners were not allowed to enter Japan, and the Japanese people were not allowed to leave Japan. The shoguns set up these strict rules because they wished to prevent European nations from conquering Japan.

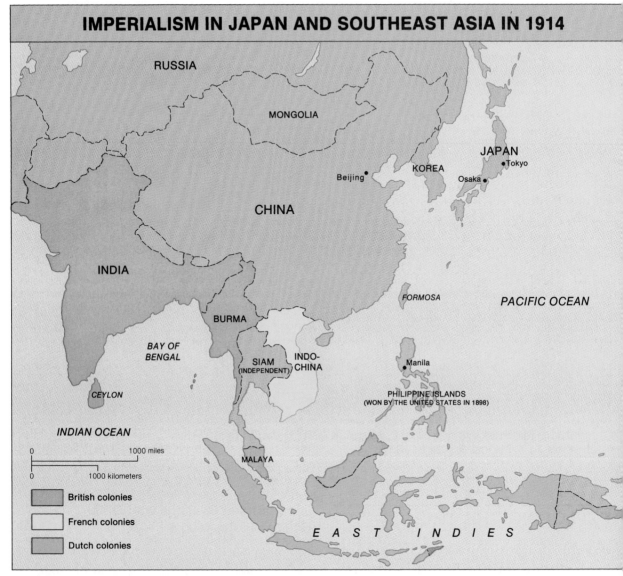

IMPERIALISM IN JAPAN AND SOUTHEAST ASIA IN 1914

RUSSIA

MONGOLIA

JAPAN
•Tokyo

KOREA

Beijing•

Osaka •

CHINA

INDIA

FORMOSA

PACIFIC OCEAN

BURMA

BAY OF
BENGAL

SIAM
(INDEPENDENT)

INDO-
CHINA

•Manila

CEYLON

PHILIPPINE ISLANDS
(WON BY THE UNITED STATES IN 1898)

INDIAN OCEAN

0   1000 miles

0   1000 kilometers

MALAYA

British colonies

French colonies

Dutch colonies

E A S T   I N D I E S

Which country controlled Indo-China in 1914?

As a result, Japan had few dealings with other nations for about two hundred and fifty years. Only one small Dutch trading post was allowed to remain on Japanese territory. However, by the mid-1800's, some Japanese people became interested in the new scientific ideas in Europe and the United States.

The United States Opened Trade with Japan in 1854

Meanwhile, American merchants, or traders, were becoming very interested in trading with the nations of Asia. These merchants wanted the American government to ask Japan to begin trading with the United States.

In 1853, the United States sent four ships to Japan under the command of Matthew Perry. Perry's orders were to sign a treaty, or a written agreement, with Japan to begin trade between the United States and Japan. When Perry arrived in Japan in 1853, however, the Japanese shogun, or army ruler, refused Perry's request to allow Japan to trade with the United States.

In February of 1854, Perry returned to Japan with seven warships. This time, the shogun did not dare to refuse Perry's demands. (It was during this second visit that Perry showed the Japanese ruler the model railroad train made in the United States.) The shogun finally ordered that two Japanese ports be opened to American trade. Within fifteen years, Japan also was trading with European nations as well as with the United States.

The Japanese Emperor Took Over the Rule of Japan

Many people in Japan, especially the merchants, welcomed Japanese trade with other nations. Some of these people felt that the shogun was preventing Japan from becoming a modern industrial nation. These people believed that Japan must be **westernized,** or become more like European nations, if it was to become powerful. These people wanted the emperor, not the shogun, to rule Japan. In 1867, they overthrew the shogun, and for the first time in over six hundred years, the emperor again became the real ruler of Japan.

Emperor Mutsuhito (MOOT-suh-HEE-toh) ruled Japan from 1867 until 1912. During his rule, Japan was westernized, or made more like a European nation, in many ways. Feudalism was ended in Japan. Public schools were opened. A European type

American president Theodore Roosevelt (center) helped Japan and Russia to make peace in 1905

of law code was set up. And in 1889, Japan received a constitution. However, this constitution was not really democratic. The emperor still kept most of the power of the Japanese government.

Japan Became a Modern Industrial Nation

Under Emperor Mutsuhito, Japan became a great industrial nation. By the time the emperor died in 1912, Japan had railroads, steamships, a telegraph system, banks, and thousands of factories that turned out all kinds of machine-made goods.

The Industrial Revolution greatly changed Japan. The Japanese population grew rapidly. And large cities, such as Tokyo (TOH-kee-OH) and Osaka (oh-SAH-kah), grew up. However, all the banking,

The lands of Southeast Asia did not become powerful. Most of them were poor and eventually were taken over by foreign nations. How can you tell that this is a poor village?

manufacturing, and trading of Japan was controlled by a few wealthy families. Four rich and powerful families who were called the **Zaibatsu** (ZY-baht-soo) controlled most large businesses in Japan.

Japan Developed Into a Powerful Nation

By the early 1900's, Japan became the strongest nation in Asia. In 1894 and 1895, Japan fought and defeated China in a war over Korea. Ten years later, in 1904 and 1905, Japan defeat Russia in the **Russo-Japanese War.** These Japanese victories showed the world that Japan was now as powerful as the nations of Europe.

Most of Southeast Asia Was Taken Over

The lands of Southeast Asia did not become powerful. Most of them were sooner or later taken over by foreign nations. The East Indies were ruled mainly by the Nether-lands. The Philippine Islands were ruled by Spain until 1898. In that year, Spain lost a war against the United States, and the Philippines were taken over by the United States. Burma, Ceylon (now called Sri Lanka), and Malaya were controlled by Great Britain. Indo-China became a French colony. Only Siam remained independent.

SUMMING UP

By the 1800's, European nations became interested in Japan and Southeast Asia. In 1854, Japan began to trade with other nations and to develop rapidly. Japan became an industrial nation, and it was the most powerful nation in Asia. But the lands of Southeast Asia were weak, and most of them were soon controlled by foreign nations. In the next chapter, you will read about European imperialism in Africa.

UNDERSTANDING THE LESSON

Do You Know These Important Terms?

For each sentence below, choose the term that best completes the sentence.

1. A (westernized/patronized) nation was a nation that became more like European nations.
2. Four rich and powerful families in Japan were called the (Zaibatsu/Mikomoto).
3. The (Sino-Russo War/Russo-Japanese War) was a war fought between Japan and Russia in 1904 and 1905.

Do You Remember These People and Events?

1. Tell something about each of the following persons.

   shogun of Japan   Mutsuhito
   Matthew Perry

2. Explain how each of the following developments took place.

   a. Japan opened its ports for trade.
   b. Japan became a powerful, industrial nation.
   c. Most of Southeast Asia was controlled by foreign nations.

Can You Locate These Places?

Use the map on page 570 to do the following map work.

1. Locate each of the following places.

   Japan   Tokyo
   Osaka   Korea

2. What nation controlled each of the following lands of Southeast Asia?

East Indies   Indo-China
Burma   Philippine Islands
Ceylon   Malaya

3. What country in Southeast Asia remained independent?

Do You Know When It Happened?

Why is the following year important in Japan's history?

   1854

Do You Remember the Main Idea?

Which one of the following ideas is the MAIN IDEA of this chapter?

1. European nations took over the trade and government of Japan. They also conquered the lands of Southeast Asia, as they had conquered China and India.
2. In the late 1800's, Japan began to trade with other nations. Japan became the most powerful nation in Asia, but most of Southeast Asia was taken over by foreign nations.
3. Japan opened its ports to trade with the United States. By 1900, Japan became a rich and powerful trading nation.

What Do You Think?

From what you have read in this chapter, answer the following thought questions.

1. What important western ideas might have helped Japan to become more democratic?
2. Why do you think India and Southeast Asia were conquered by foreign nations, while Japan was not?

Chapter 88
Africa and the European Nations

GETTING STARTED

1 You have already seen how European nations gained control of many of the lands in Asia. Africa was another continent where European nations began to take over new lands. Africa also was rich in raw materials that European nations needed.

2 Before you begin reading the chapter lesson, survey the lesson. Begin your survey by reading the beginning of the lesson. Then look through the lesson and read the headings. Next, study the pictures and read the picture captions. Then study the map of Africa in 1914 on page 576. Finally, read the section called "Summing Up." This survey will help you to discover the important ideas in this chapter.

Know the Main Idea

As you read the chapter lesson, try to remember the following important MAIN IDEA of the chapter.

By 1914, European nations ruled most of Africa. Some of the changes they made helped the African people, but some of the changes hurt the African people.

The following questions will help you to understand the MAIN IDEA. Try to answer these questions as you read the lesson.

1. What nation first started a colony at the southern tip of Africa?
2. What three European nations divided up the lands of northern Africa?
3. In what ways did European rule help the Africans? In what ways did it hurt the Africans?

Know These Important Terms

Boers
Boer War
International Association of the Congo
Berlin Conference

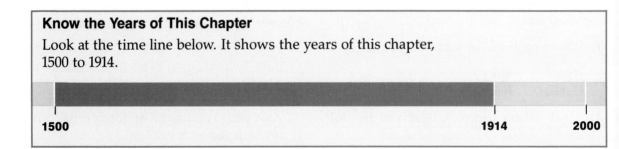

Know the Years of This Chapter
Look at the time line below. It shows the years of this chapter, 1500 to 1914.

1500   1914   2000

Slave market at Zanzibar

EXPLORING THE TIME

In Chapter 46, you read about some of the early kingdoms of Africa. By 1500, Africa was becoming very important to Europe because the European nations now were interested in trading and exploring. In this chapter, you will read how European nations took over most of Africa by the late 1800's.

Portugal Developed a Busy Trade with Africa

Perhaps you recall that Portuguese explorers found a new route to Asia by sailing around Africa and reaching India in 1498. Before long, Portugal built a large number of forts along the African coast to protect this new trade route. These forts grew into busy trading posts where European products were traded for African ivory and gold.

But the most important African trade was in slaves. The African slave trade had been carried on for many years by Arab traders. During the 1400's, the Portuguese traders took over the slave trade from the Arabs. During the 1500's, the slave trade increased because of the demand for slaves in Spain's colonies in the New World.

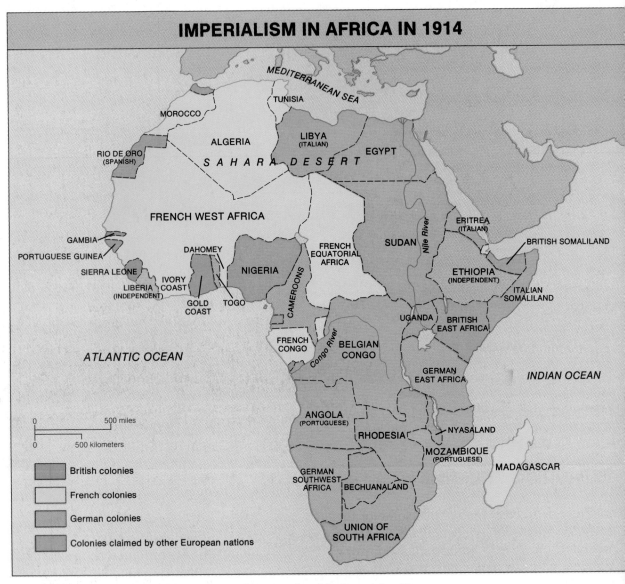

IMPERIALISM IN AFRICA IN 1914

MEDITERRANEAN SEA

TUNISIA

MOROCCO

ALGERIA

LIBYA
(ITALIAN)

EGYPT

RIO DE ORO
(SPANISH)

SAHARA DESERT

FRENCH WEST AFRICA

ERITREA
(ITALIAN)

GAMBIA

PORTUGUESE GUINEA

SIERRA LEONE

LIBERIA
(INDEPENDENT)

IVORY
COAST

GOLD
COAST

TOGO

DAHOMEY

NIGERIA

CAMEROONS

FRENCH
EQUATORIAL
AFRICA

SUDAN

Nile River

BRITISH SOMALILAND

ETHIOPIA
(INDEPENDENT)

ITALIAN
SOMALILAND

ATLANTIC OCEAN

FRENCH
CONGO

Congo River

BELGIAN
CONGO

UGANDA

BRITISH
EAST AFRICA

GERMAN
EAST AFRICA

INDIAN OCEAN

ANGOLA
(PORTUGUESE)

RHODESIA

NYASALAND

MOZAMBIQUE
(PORTUGUESE)

MADAGASCAR

0   500 miles

0   500 kilometers

GERMAN
SOUTHWEST
AFRICA

BECHUANALAND

UNION OF
SOUTH AFRICA

British colonies

French colonies

German colonies

Colonies claimed by other European nations

In 1914, which two African countries remained independent?

A Dutch Colony Was Started at the Southern Tip of Africa

About the mid-1600's, some Dutch traders started a colony at the Cape of Good Hope at the southern tip of Africa. At first, the Cape Colony was just a trading post. But

later, many **Boers** (BOREZ), or Dutch farmers, arrived to settle in the colony.

At the end of the 1700's, the Cape Colony was taken away from the Netherlands (Holland) by Great Britain. But the Boers did not like being ruled by Great Britain. A few years later, many of the Boers moved north of the Cape Colony and set up two new independent Boer nations—Transvaal (tranz-VAHL) and the Orange Free State.

Great Britain Conquered the Boer Nations in Southern Africa

During the late 1800's, gold and diamond mines were discovered in southern Africa. Some of these mines were within the Boer nations of Transvaal and the Orange Free State. However, during the **Boer War** of 1899 to 1902, Great Britain fought the Boers and conquered both the Boer nations. After the Boer War, Great Britain formed all its colonies in southern Africa into one colony, which became part of the British Empire.

Northern Africa Was Divided Among Three European Nations

Long before the Boer War, European nations became interested in other parts of Africa. Most of northern Africa belonged to the Turkish Empire. However, Great Britain took control of Egypt and the Sudan (the land just south of Egypt). France took control of Algeria, Tunisia (too-NEE-zhuh), most of Morocco (muh-ROCK-koh), and most of the Sahara Desert. Italy also tried to conquer Ethiopia (EE-thee-OH-pee-UH) but was defeated. However, Italy later did take control of Libya (LIHB-e-uh).

European Nations Became Interested In Central Africa

Before 1870, most European colonies were near the African coast. But by 1870, European explorers discovered that the lands of central Africa—particularly around the Congo River—were rich in raw materials.

In 1878, King Leopold the Second of Belgium set up an association called the **International Association of the Congo.**

PEOPLE IN HISTORY

Cetewayo

The Zulus were one of the proudest Black peoples of South Africa. During the 1870's, their king was a leader named Cetewayo (SET-eh-WAY-oh). The Zulus did not get along with the Boer settlers, because the Boers were trying to take over the Zulu lands. Great Britain sided with the Boers. In 1879, when the Zulus refused to give up their lands, a British army moved against the Zulus. The British expected a short and easy war. But the British had an unpleasant surprise. Many months of hard fighting took place before the Zulus were defeated and Cetewayo was captured.

Three years later Cetewayo was allowed to visit Great Britain. There he presented his people's case to Queen Victoria and other British leaders. They realized that Cetewayo had been treated unfairly, and they allowed him to return to Zululand. However, most of his powers were taken away from him, and Cetewayo soon died.

Question: What group of people wanted the Zulu lands?

577

Numerous European schools were set up in the African colonies

This Association was supposed to end the slave trade in Africa and teach the Christian religion to Africans in the Congo. But instead, it gave the Congo to King Leopold. The Belgian control of the Congo resulted in cruel treatment of the Congo's people.

Central Africa Was Divided Up

By the 1880's, many European nations were interested in taking over parts of Africa. In 1884, the leaders of these European nations met at the **Berlin Conference** to plan rules for dividing up Africa. The purpose of these rules was to prevent European nations from fighting over African colonies.

The Berlin Conference members agreed that any European nation was allowed to take over any African territory not claimed by another European nation. As soon as a European nation took over an African territory and officially claimed it,

this territory belonged to that nation. This plan was successful. By 1914, European nations had divided up central Africa without going to war.

European Rule Changed African Life

In some ways, the European control of Africa helped the Africans. The European nations ended the slave trade. And the European nations also tried to educate Africans in modern ways of living and to improve health conditions in Africa.

But in other ways, the European control of Africa hurt the Africans. The nations of Europe took over African territory mainly to increase their own wealth from the natural resources of Africa. And many nations took advantage of, or exploited, their colonies, by exporting these natural resources without allowing the colonies to benefit economically.

SUMMING UP

There were both good and bad effects of imperialism on European nations and their colonies. Colonial powers raised living standards in the colonies through the introduction of educational and transportation systems and modern medical techniques. The Europeans themselves benefited from the wealth and power that their colonial investments brought them.

But on the other hand, colonial powers often exploited their colonies economically. Also, many European rulers tried to force their culture on the colonies without being sensitive to local customs and habits. And there were conflicts among the European nations themselves over who would claim specific areas.

UNDERSTANDING THE LESSON

Do You Know These Important Terms?

For each sentence below, choose the term that best completes the sentence.

1. Dutch farmers who settled in southern Africa were called (**Zulus/Boers**).
2. The war fought in southern Africa between the Dutch settlers and Great Britain was called the (**War of the Transvaal/ Boer War**).
3. The (**International Association of the Congo/African Trade Conference**) gave the Congo to the king of Belgium.
4. The (**Berlin Conference/Afro-European Conference**) set up rules for dividing the lands of Africa among European nations.

Do You Remember These People and Events?

1. Tell something about each of the following people.

   Portuguese traders   Boers
   King Leopold

2. Explain how each of the following developments took place.

   a. Great Britain formed its colonies in southern Africa into the Union of South Africa.
   b. Northern Africa was divided among three European nations.
   c. European nations gained control of central Africa.

Can You Locate These Places?

Use the map on page 576 to do the following map work.

1. Which nations controlled lands in northern Africa? Name some of these lands.
2. Which nations controlled lands in central Africa? Name some of these lands.
3. Which nations controlled land in southern Africa? Name some of these lands.
4. Which African nations were able to remain independent?

Do You Know When It Happened?

What are the years of this chapter on Africa?

Do You Remember the Main Idea?

Which one of the following ideas is the MAIN IDEA of this chapter?

1. European nations fought over the lands in Africa. Great Britain and France were able to set up the largest colonies.
2. By 1914, European nations ruled most of Africa. Some of the changes they made helped the African people, but some of the changes hurt the African people.
3. Europeans believed that the African people needed help. Therefore, the Europeans took over the Africans' lands in order to improve African ways of life.

What Do You Think?

From what you have read in this chapter, try to answer the following thought questions.

1. How was the forming of colonies in Africa different from the way colonies were formed in America?
2. If you were living in central Africa in the 1800's, how would you have felt when a European nation took over your land?

579

Unit 19

The Growth of European Culture

THE CHAPTERS IN UNIT 19 ARE

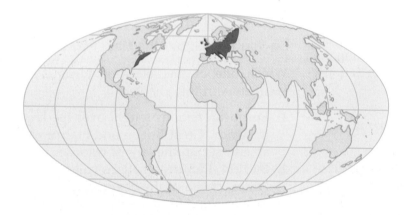

Ideas—what people think—are often as important as people's actions. Great changes took place in European art, music, science, and ways of thinking in the 1800's and early 1900's. Many of the subjects which you are studying in school were first studied during this period. In this unit, you will find out about developments in European culture between 1789 and 1914.

Impressionist painters like Monet tried to give a quick, direct impression, or view, of life without showing many details

Chapter 89
European Art, Music, and Writing

GETTING STARTED

1   During the years from 1789 to 1914, more and more people in Europe became interested in books, paintings, and music. Certain new viewpoints, or ways of thinking about things, began in Europe during this period. As a result, many great works of writing, art, and music which were produced in Europe during these years are still very popular today, as you will learn as you read this chapter.

2   Before you begin reading the chapter lesson, survey the lesson. Begin your survey by reading the beginning of the lesson. Then look through the lesson and read the headings. Next, study the pictures and read the picture captions. Finally, read the review section called "Summing Up." This survey will help you to discover the important ideas in this chapter.

Know the Main Idea

As you read the chapter lesson, try to remember the following important MAIN IDEA of the chapter.

From 1789 to 1914, writing, art, and music were affected by new ideas. Important new writings, paintings, and music were produced in these years.

The following questions will help you to understand the MAIN IDEA. Try to answer these questions as you read the chapter lesson.

1. What event helped to weaken people's belief in rationalism?
2. Who was the most famous romantic composer?
3. What new style of painting developed?

Know These Important Terms

rationalism	realism
romanticism	impressionism

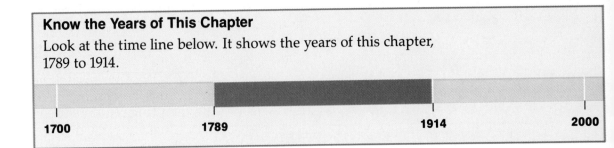

Know the Years of This Chapter

Look at the time line below. It shows the years of this chapter, 1789 to 1914.

1700	1789	1914	2000

Grand Gallery of the Louvre Museum in Paris, France. Why would skylights be important in an art museum?

EXPLORING THE TIME

During the years between 1789 and 1914, Europeans did much more than build industries and empires. They also developed new viewpoints, or ways of thinking, about life. These new viewpoints were shown in the books, paintings, and music that were produced in the European nations during this period. In this chapter, you will read about European writing, art, and music in the years from 1789 to 1914.

European Philosophers Developed a New Viewpoint

During the 1700's, philosophers believed that people could solve their problems by thinking and by planning. This viewpoint was called **rationalism** (RASH-un-ul-IZ-um). Rationalism was popular until the French Revolution began in 1789. Then, wars and suffering caused by this revolution made many people lose their belief in rationalism and the idea that thinking provided the answers to life's problems.

By the early 1800's, many European philosophers believed that feelings and imagination were the best guides to solving problems. The new viewpoint was called **romanticism** (roh-MAN-tuh-SIZZ-um).

Romanticism Guided the Writings of Many Poets

Romanticism helped to shape the ideas of many poets in the early 1800's. Some of the best of the romantic poets were British. They included Lord Byron, John Keats, Samuel Coleridge, William Wordsworth, and Percy Shelley. These men lived exciting, romantic lives, and their poetry was shaped by their lives.

The British romantic poets who came later, such as Robert Browning, Elizabeth Barrett Browning, and Alfred Tennyson, had less adventurous lives. But they were also romantic poets. Elizabeth Browning wrote poems against the use of child labor, or the use of children as factory workers. And Alfred Tennyson used the epic stories of King Arthur and his knights from the Middle Ages as subjects for many of his famous poems.

Romanticism Also Guided Writers of Novels

Writers of novels found many of their ideas in romanticism. The first romantic novel, *The Sorrows of Young Werther*, was written by a great German writer, Goethe (GURR-tuh). *Ivanhoe*, by the Scottish writer Sir Walter Scott, was a romantic novel about knights and chivalry in feudal England. Other romantic novels were Alexandre Dumas' (DOO-mah) *The Three Musketeers* and Victor Hugo's *The Hunchback of Notre Dame*. Both of these writers were French.

Romanticism Shaped the Ideas of Painters and Musicians

Romanticism also affected the work of painters. The French artist Delacroix (DELL-uh-KRWAH) painted very colorful, dramatic pictures. The British painters John Constable and William Turner painted landscapes that showed great feeling for nature.

The great German composer Ludwig van Beethoven (BAY-toh-VUN) was probably the most famous romantic composer. One of Beethoven's symphonies, the "Heroic Symphony," was supposed to be based on Napoleon's army's great victories for France. Other romantic composers were Schubert (SHOO-burt), Mendelssohn (MEN-dul-SUN), and Brahms (BRAHMZ).

Some European composers wrote operas during the years of romanticism. These composers included Wagner (VAHG-nur) in Germany, Rossini (ros-SEE-nee) and Verdi (VER-dee) in Italy, and Bizet (bee-ZAY) in France. These composers' operas are still popular today.

Romanticism Was Replaced by a New Viewpoint

During the late 1800's, romanticism became much less popular. Instead, a new viewpoint called **realism** became popular. If you recall, romanticism was very much concerned with feelings and imagination. Realism was more concerned with things as they really are. Many European writers, painters, and musicians during the late 1800's showed realism in their work.

Realism Shaped the Ideas of Many Writers

Many well-known writers wrote "realistic" novels. Gustave Flaubert (floh-BAIR) of

Libraries became popular in the 1800's. Europeans began to read new "romantic novels" like *Ivanhoe,* *The Three Musketeers,* **and** *The Hunchback of Notre Dame.*

France, for example, wrote a realistic novel called *Madame Bovary,* which described French life as it really was in the mid-1800's. Other realistic French writers were Guy de Maupassant (MOH-pah-SAHN), who wrote short stories about everyday life, and Émile Zola (ZOH-la), who wrote novels.

In Great Britain, George Bernard Shaw wrote plays that were realistic but also amusing. And Thomas Hardy and George Meredith wrote important realistic novels about life in industrial Great Britain. In Russia, two of the important realistic writers were Chekhov (CHECK-off) and Gorki (GOR-kee). Chekhov wrote short stories and plays, and Gorki wrote novels.

Artists Began Impressionist Paintings

During the late 1800's, many realistic artists tried to paint everyday scenes and to show people as they really were. But some of the realistic artists began to paint using a new style of painting called **impressionism.**

The impressionist painters tried to give a quick, direct impression, or view, of life without showing many details. Many of these painters used short brush strokes and light colors to give this realistic and colorful "impression."

At first, impressionist painters, such as Manet (man-NAY), Degas (day-GAH), Monet (mon-NAY), van Gogh (GOH) and Renoir (ren-WAHR), were not popular. But today, the paintings of these impressionists are found in most great museums.

Composers Began to Write Impressionist Music

Musicians of the late 1800's composed music in a new kind of style called impressionist music. Impressionist composers wrote music to describe sounds, to tell a story, or to give their impressions, or viewpoints about life. The most famous of the impressionist musicians was a French citizen, Claude Debussy (duh-BYOO-see).

Vincent van Gogh's famous painting "The Starry Night"

SUMMING UP

During the 1700's, rationalism, or the belief that thinking was the best way to solve problems, shaped many people's ideas. But by the early 1800's, romanticism replaced rationalism. Romanticism was the belief that feelings and imagination were more important than thinking. Romanticism shaped the work of many important artists, writers, and musicians.

But by the late 1800's, realism began to replace romanticism as a guide to life's problems. In painting and music, a new style of realism developed which came to be called impressionism. In the next chapter, you will read about new discoveries in science and in medicine from 1789 to 1914 which helped to improve the lives of peoples everywhere.

UNDERSTANDING THE LESSON

Do You Know These Important Terms?

For each sentence below, choose the term that best completes the sentence.

1. The idea that men are able to solve their problems by thinking and planning is called (**rationalism/realism**).
2. The idea that feelings and imagination are the best guides to solving problems is called (**impressionism/romanticism**).
3. (**Realism/Romanticism**) is an interest in things as they really are.
4. A style of painting that gave a quick view of life without showing many details was called (**impressionism/romanticism**).

Do You Remember These People and Events?

1. Tell how each of the following persons made contributions to romanticism.

Lord Byron	Alexandre Dumas
John Keats	Delacroix
Percy Shelley	John Constable
Alfred Tennyson	Beethoven
Goethe	Verdi
Sir Walter Scott	Bizet

2. Tell how each of the following persons made contributions to realism.

Gustave Flaubert	Émile Zola
Guy de Maupassant	Chekhov
George Meredith	van Gogh
George Bernard Shaw	Renoir
Thomas Hardy	
Claude Debussy	

Do You Know When It Happened?

What are the years of this chapter?

Do You Remember the Main Idea?

Which one of the following ideas is the MAIN IDEA of this chapter?

1. From 1789 to 1914, writing, art, and music were affected by new ideas. Important new writings, paintings, and music were produced in these years.
2. The paintings that were produced in Europe between 1789 and 1914 are still popular today.
3. The French Revolution brought about an increased interest in modern art. Many books, paintings, and works of music were produced between 1789 and 1914 that are still popular today.

What Do You Think?

From what you have read in this chapter, try to answer the following thought questions.

1. Which ideas do you like most—those of the rationalists or the romanticists? Explain your answer.
2. Among the works that you know produced by the romantic writers, artists, and musicians, which work is your favorite? Who do you like best among the realistic writers? Try to explain your choices.
3. Why do you think the impressionist paintings are still so popular today? Explain your answer.

Chapter 90
New Discoveries in Science

GETTING STARTED

1   The Industrial Revolution developed rapidly during the years of the 1800's. Perhaps the Industrial Revolution might have slowed down if scientists had not made new discoveries. But scientists did continue to make new and important discoveries that were useful in industry. As a result, the Industrial Revolution continued to develop. You will learn in this chapter about the many new scientific discoveries that were made from 1789 to 1914.

2   Before you begin reading the chapter lesson, survey the lesson. Begin the survey by reading the beginning of the lesson. Then look through the lesson and read the headings. Next, study the pictures and read the picture captions. Finally, read the review section called "Summing Up" at the end of the lesson. This survey of the whole lesson will help you to discover the important ideas in this chapter.

Know the Main Idea

As you read the chapter lesson, try to remember the following important MAIN IDEA of the chapter.

From 1789 to 1914, new fields of science developed, and great progress was made in science and in medicine.

The following questions will help you to understand the MAIN IDEA. Try to answer these questions as you read the lesson.

1. What important new ideas and discoveries were made in the science of physics?
2. What were some of the new discoveries in medicine?
3. What new theory was developed about plant and animal life?

Know These Important Terms

atomic theory	fossils
theory of relativity	anthropology
theory of evolution	geology

Know the Years of This Chapter

Look at the time line below. It shows the years of this chapter, 1789 to 1914.

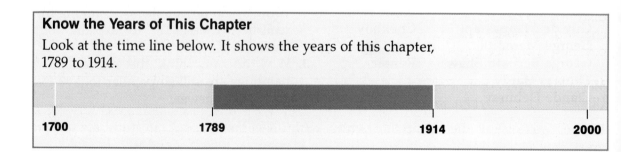

| 1700 | 1789 | 1914 | 2000 |

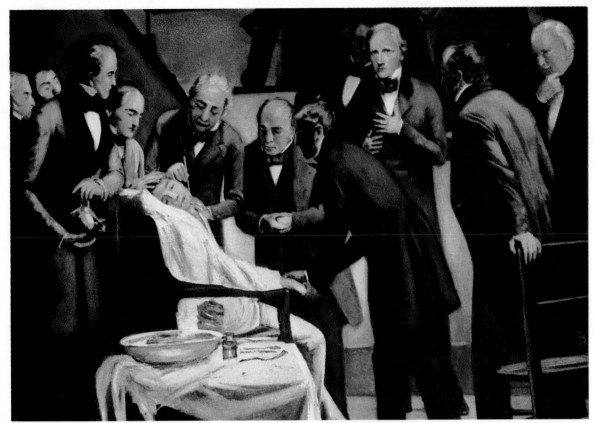

The American doctors William Morton and Crawford Long were the first to use ether during an operation. How might this operation differ from one in a modern hospital?

EXPLORING THE TIME

What was happening in the field of science from 1789 to 1914? Who were the great scientists of this period? How did their discoveries change people's lives? In this chapter, you will read about the new discoveries in science from 1789 to 1914.

Many New Inventions Came from Discoveries in Physics

Physics was one of the sciences in which great progress was made during the years from 1789 to 1914. Scientists in physics developed important new ideas about light, heat, and electricity that led to many useful inventions.

One of the new inventions was the electric generator, which was a device used to supply electric power for factory machines. By the late 1800's, electric generators were used in all industrial nations to provide power for large factory machines. Other important inventions based on the new ideas in physics were the electric light, the telephone, the radio, the camera, and later the automobile and the airplane.

European and American research scientists performed many
experiments and made many important new discoveries. What
instrument is this scientist using?

New Discoveries About Matter Were Made

The **atomic theory,** which is so important
today, was first developed in the early years
of the 1900's. Before that time, scientists
believed that it was not possible to split the
atom—the smallest particle of matter. But in
the early 1900's, Ernest Rutherford of Great
Britain and Niels Bohr of Denmark proved
that the atom was made up of several different parts. This discovery led to another
new discovery that changed people's ideas
about the world.

In 1905, a young scientist from Germany named Albert Einstein presented a
new theory, or idea, about matter called the
theory of relativity. Einstein's main idea in
the theory of relativity was that all matter
exists not only in space but also in time, or

in "space-time." This idea meant that matter is not "fixed" in space. Therefore, the
distances between all bodies in space must
be measured according to their relative, or
constantly changing, positions. This revolutionary idea of space-time was used to
help solve many problems in modern physics and astronomy.

New Discoveries Were Made in Medicine

Medicine also developed rapidly during the
years of the 1800's. Smallpox, a disease that
killed many people, finally was brought
under control by the discovery of vaccination by Edward Jenner of Great Britain.
Ether, as a painkiller, was first used by two
Americans, William Morton and Crawford
Long. Before the discovery of ether, operations were very painful.

Many people died from operations until Joseph Lister, a British doctor, taught other doctors how to use antiseptics, or germ-killing medicines, to prevent infection. Later, Louis Pasteur (pah-STUR) of France and Robert Koch of Germany proved that many serious diseases were caused by germs.

During the late 1800's, scientists learned how to control these diseases by giving people an inoculation, or a small amount of the germs that caused the disease. This small amount of the disease germs was harmless, but it prevented people from getting the disease.

All of these discoveries in the field of medicine were important. They helped to relieve pain and to save lives.

Scientists Began to Study the Earth and Early People

One of the most interesting of the new sciences that developed during the 1800's was **geology.** Geology is the study of the rock forms that make up the earth's crust, or outer layer. The "founder of geology" was a British scientist, Charles Lyell (LY-ul). In the 1830's, Lyell showed that wind, rain, rivers, earthquakes, and volcanoes all help to shape the surface of the earth. He also declared that this shaping had been going on for millions and millions of years!

Other scientists began to study the animal and plant life of past times. These scientists discovered **fossils** (FAHS-uls), which were the hardened remains in rock of very old plants and animals. By the late 1800's, scientists also discovered many skeletons and tools of early people. These discoveries helped to build the new science of **anthropology,** or the study of people and their early development.

PEOPLE IN HISTORY

Louis Pasteur

Every time you drink a glass of milk, you should thank Louis Pasteur (pah-STUR). Pasteur discovered how to keep milk safe and free of germs. In fact, Pasteur was one of the greatest scientists of modern times. He made discoveries which still help to protect our lives today.

Pasteur proved that many diseases are caused by germs. And he spent his life learning how to prevent these diseases. Pasteur learned that heating liquids destroyed the germs in them. This heating process is now called "pasteurization." Pasteur tried his process on wine and beer, and then on milk.

Pasteur also discovered how to prevent other germ-caused diseases. He developed inoculations, or shots, that prevented diseases in cattle and sheep. Finally, Pasteur developed an inoculation that he hoped would cure rabies. The test came in 1885. A nine-year-old boy who was bitten by a dog with rabies was given Pasteur's inoculation. Pasteur's inoculation did work, the boy was saved, and inoculations became widely used to prevent diseases.

Question: What were some of Pasteur's discoveries?

591

The two scientists Madame Curie (left) and Albert Einstein (right) both earned Nobel Prizes

Darwin Developed a New Theory About Plant and Animal Life

The discoveries in geology and anthropology led to the **theory of evolution** (EV-uh-LOO-shun), presented by Charles Darwin in 1859. Charles Darwin was a British scientist who studied plant and animal life for many years.

Darwin believed that modern animals and plants developed over a very long period of time from earlier and simpler forms of animals and plants. These developments resulted mainly from a process that Darwin called "natural selection." Among animals, including humans, natural selection meant that animals that were faster, stronger, or more clever outlived other animals.

Many scientists accepted Darwin's theory. But many other people did not accept it. Some people said that it was against the writings in the Bible. And some people did not like Darwin's theory because they understood it to mean that people's ancestors were animals. But as years passed, more and more people accepted Darwin's theory, and it led to other important discoveries about the development of life on earth.

SUMMING UP

From 1789 to 1914, new fields of science developed. These included geology and anthropology. A new idea that developed from these sciences was Darwin's theory of evolution. Great progress also was made in other sciences and in medicine. In physics, new ideas led to many important modern inventions, such as the electric generator. One of the most important developments in physics was Einstein's theory of relativity. In the next chapter, you will read about developments in the field of the social sciences between 1789 and 1914.

UNDERSTANDING THE LESSON

Do You Know These Important Terms?

For each sentence below, choose the term that best completes the sentence.

1. The idea that the atom was made up of several different parts is called the **(atomic theory/neutron theory)**.
2. The idea that all matter exists not only in space but also in time is the main idea of the **(theory of evolution/theory of relativity)**.
3. **(Geometry/Geology)** is the study of rock forms that make up the earth's crust, or outer layer.
4. The hardened remains in rock of early plants and animals are called **(fossils/federals)**.
5. **(Anthropology/Analogy)** is the study of people and their early development.
6. The belief that modern animals and plants developed over a very long period of time from earlier and simpler forms of animals and plants is called the **(theory of calculation/theory of evolution)**.

Do You Remember These People and Events?

1. Tell something about each of the following persons.

Ernest Rutherford	Joseph Lister
Niels Bohr	Louis Pasteur
Albert Einstein	Robert Koch
Edward Jenner	Charles Lyell
William Morton	Charles Darwin
Crawford Long	

2. Explain how or why each of the following developments took place.

   a. Many new inventions came from discoveries in physics.
   b. Discoveries in medicine helped to control diseases.
   c. Some people did not like Charles Darwin's theory of evolution.

Do You Know When It Happened?

In what year was Einstein's theory of relativity presented?

Do You Remember the Main Idea?

Which one of the following ideas is the MAIN IDEA of this chapter?

1. From 1789 to 1914, new fields of science developed, and great progress was made in science and in medicine.
2. From 1789 to 1914, important new theories were developed that were used to speed up the Industrial Revolution.
3. Discoveries in medicine helped doctors to control and prevent some diseases.

What Do You Think?

From what you have read in this chapter, try to answer the following thought questions.

1. Can you name some present-day inventions that have come from discoveries in physics?
2. What scientific discovery of the 1800's do you consider to be the most important? Give reasons for your answer.
3. Why was the atomic theory important? How did the atomic theory help scientists to shape the modern world? Explain your answer.

GETTING STARTED

1   You probably know what the term "social studies" means. In fact, you probably began to learn about social studies in your early school years. "Social sciences" is another term for social studies. The social sciences teach you how people lived in the past, how they live today, and how they may live in the future. The social sciences include the important study of history. The social sciences also include many other subjects, as you will learn.

During the years from 1789 to 1914, scholars began to use scientific methods to add to their learning in the social sciences. As a result of their efforts, many new subjects such as sociology and psychology developed as part of the social sciences during this period.

2   Before you begin reading the chapter lesson, survey the lesson. Begin your survey by reading the beginning of the lesson. Then look through the lesson and read the headings. Next, study the pictures and read the picture captions. Finally, read the review section called "Summing Up." This survey will help you to discover the important ideas in this chapter.

Know the Main Idea

As you read the chapter lesson, try to remember the following important MAIN IDEA of the chapter.

The social sciences developed during the 1800's, and they helped people to make many improvements in their lives.

The following questions will help you to understand the MAIN IDEA. Try to answer these questions as you read the lesson.

1. In what way did the study of history change during the 1800's?
2. Which social scientists are interested in how people think and behave?
3. What effect did the new social sciences have on religion?

Know These Important Terms

social sciences	psychology
economics	psychiatry
political science	psychoanalysis
sociology	

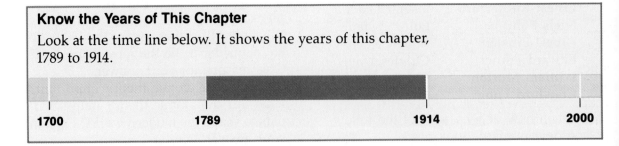

Know the Years of This Chapter
Look at the time line below. It shows the years of this chapter, 1789 to 1914.

| 1700 | 1789 | 1914 | 2000 |

A suffrage parade in Washington, D.C., on March 13, 1913. Can you identify the domed building in the background?

EXPLORING THE TIME

As you know, history is the study of human beings' lives in the past. But history is only one of the subjects about the study of people. We call these subjects about the study of people and their behavior the **social sciences,** or the social studies. In this chapter, you will learn how the social sciences developed during the years between 1789 and 1914.

How the Social Sciences Developed

The social sciences, or social studies, include all those subjects that concern people's life and behavior. History is the oldest of the social sciences. In fact, the writing of history began about 3500 B.C. But the earlier historians usually wrote history in order to tell exciting stories about the past or to develop people's pride in their nation. It was not until the 1800's that historians began to think about history as a science, or

595

Ivan Pavlov (center) was the Russian scientist whose experiments with dogs helped to develop psychology

as a search for the facts about the past. In this way, history developed as a social science.

Another of the older social sciences that made progress during the 1800's was **economics** (EE-ko-NAHM-iks), or the study of the ways that people earn their living and carry on their systems of business. **Political science**, another social science field, also developed during this period. Political science is the study of how people are governed.

Sociology Was a New Social Science

Sociology (SO-see-AHL-uh-JEE), or the study of how people live together in communities and nations, was a new social science that began in the 1800's. Sociology was developed by a Frenchman, Auguste Comte

(KOHNT). Comte believed that social problems, or problems among people, must be studied scientifically, or by finding the facts about them. Some of the ideas of sociology soon were used to try to help people to solve their problems and to lead better lives.

The Study of Human Behavior Was a New Social Science

Psychology (sy-KOLL-uh-JEE), or the study of human behavior and thinking, also was a new social science developed in the 1800's. Perhaps you have read about the famous experiment that was made by the Russian psychologist Ivan Pavlov (PAHV-loff) in the 1890's.

Pavlov believed that people behaved in certain ways because they were trained to do so. He tried to prove this idea in an experiment with a dog. Pavlov rang a bell every time he fed the dog. Soon, the dog's mouth watered (showing that it was hungry) every time the bell rang, even when the dog was not fed. In this way, Pavlov trained the dog to respond in a certain way to the sound of the bell.

The followers of Pavlov believed that it was possible to train anyone to do or learn anything. And this idea is still popular among some psychologists today. But today, most psychologists also believe that people behave in certain ways because of other reasons, too.

Freud Developed a New Way of Treating Mental Problems

The study of psychology led to the beginning of another field of study called **psychiatry** (suh-KY-uh-TREE). Psychiatry is the study of the causes and treatment of mental problems. One of the leading psychiatrists in the late 1800's and early 1900's was Sigmund Freud (FROID) of Vienna, Austria.

Freud believed that many mental problems were caused by unhappy thoughts and feelings that people had but did not realize they had. Freud believed that these unhappy thoughts and feelings were in a part of the mind that he called the "unconscious" or "subconscious" mind.

Freud developed a method of treating his patients called **psychoanalysis** (SY-koh-uh-NAL-uh-SISS). Using this method, patients were able to discover their hidden feelings by revealing everything they were thinking about. Freud's methods helped many people. And many psychiatrists became "Freudians." They used the methods of Freud in treating persons with mental problems.

Sigmund Freud developed a method of treating his patients called psychoanalysis

The Social Sciences Led to Improvements in People's Lives

The new knowledge of the social sciences helped to bring about some important improvements in life during the 1800's. By 1865, the slave trade and slavery itself was ended among European nations and in the United States.

During the 1800's, improvements also were made in the treatment of prisoners and mentally ill people. And during the 1800's, women gained the right to own property, to go to college, and, in some places, even to vote. And in these years, more public schools were opened, and many more students were able to attend school.

Churches continued to play an important part in the lives of people in the 1800's and 1900's

Religion Remained Important in People's Lives

Both the Protestant Church and the Roman Catholic Church faced difficult times during the years between 1789 and 1914. Many people in these years believed that religion was no longer able to solve people's problems and that religion did not fit in with the new discoveries in science.

However, during these years the Churches tried to help people improve their lives. As a result, many people were won back to a belief in religion when they saw that their Church was trying to help people. Many people now began to feel that science and religion both had a place in the modern world. Therefore, religion became important to many people again.

SUMMING UP

During the 1800's, the social sciences, or the social studies, became important to people. The social sciences included the older subjects of history, economics, and political science. The social sciences also included new subjects, such as psychology and sociology. Progress in the social sciences led to many improvements in people's lives during the 1800's. In the next chapter, which begins Unit 20, you will read about the events that led to World War One.

UNDERSTANDING THE LESSON

Do You Know These Important Terms?

For each sentence below, choose the term that best completes the sentence.

1. The subjects that study humans and human behavior are called the (**social thoughts/social sciences**).
2. (**Finances/Economics**) is the study of the ways that people earn their living and carry on their systems of business.
3. (**Political science/Sociology**) is the study of how people are governed.
4. The study of how people live together in communities and nations is called (**community plans/sociology**).
5. (**Psychology/Pharmacy**) is the study of people's ways of behaving and thinking.
6. (**Pediatrics/Psychiatry**) is the study of the causes and treatment of mental illness.
7. The method developed by Sigmund Freud for treating mentally ill patients was called (**psychoanalysis/memorizing**).

Do You Remember These People and Events?

1. Tell something about each of the following persons.

   Auguste Comte   **Sigmund Freud**
   Ivan Pavlov

2. Explain how each of the following developments took place.

   a. The older social sciences developed in the 1800's.
   b. Social sciences led to improvements in people's lives.

c. Religion proved that it was important in the modern world.

Do You Know When It Happened?

The years of this chapter are the years in which the social sciences began to develop. What were these years?

Do You Remember the Main Idea?

Which one of the following ideas is the MAIN IDEA of this chapter?

1. During the 1800's, a new science called "social science" was discovered, and it helped people to solve most of their problems.
2. The developments in the social sciences caused people to turn away from religion and to trust in science.
3. The social sciences developed during the 1800's, and they helped people to make many improvements in their lives.

What Do You Think?

From what you have read in this chapter, answer the following thought questions.

1. The method Pavlov used with his dogs was called "conditioning." Can you think of ways that conditioning is used in school to help you learn your lessons?
2. What other things besides "conditioning" do you think help to determine the way that people behave?
3. Which of the social sciences interests you most? Give reasons for your answer.

Unit 20

World War One and the Years After

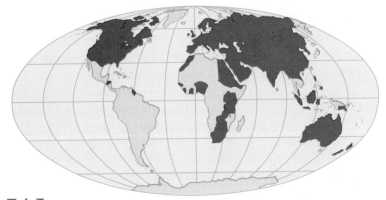

World War One was a long, difficult struggle that led to many great changes in the modern world. While freedom disappeared in several European nations, the peoples of Asia and Africa began their struggle for independence. In this unit, you will find out about these important events.

British planes in a dawn patrol over France

Chapter 92
The Coming of World War One

GETTING STARTED

1 Between the years 1870 and 1914 (see the time line below), events in Europe were leading toward a great war. If you recall, before 1914 many European nations were following a policy of imperialism—the building of great empires. As the Industrial Revolution continued and as factories made more and more products, many industrial nations of Europe wanted to control world trade and world markets. As you will see, this struggle for control of world trade was one of the causes of war in Europe in 1914.

2 Before you begin reading the chapter lesson, survey the lesson. Begin your survey by reading the beginning of the lesson. Then, look through the lesson and read the headings. Next, study the pictures and read the picture captions. Study the map of European nations in 1914 on page 604. Finally, read the review section called "Summing Up" at the end of the lesson. This survey of the whole lesson will help you to discover the important ideas in this chapter.

Know the Main Idea

As you read the chapter lesson, try to remember the following important MAIN IDEA of the chapter.

In 1914, World War One broke out in Europe. Among its causes were extreme nationalism, imperialism, economic rivalry, the building up of armed forces, and alliances.

The following questions will help you to understand the MAIN IDEA. Try to answer these questions as you read the lesson.

1. What European nation felt it had a right to build a strong empire like that of Great Britain and France?
2. Which nations formed the Triple Alliance?
3. What was the most dangerous trouble spot in Europe in 1914?

Know These Important Terms

World War One	Triple Alliance
economic rivalry	Triple Entente
extreme nationalism	

Know the Years of This Chapter
Look at the time line below. It shows the years of this chapter, 1870 to 1914.

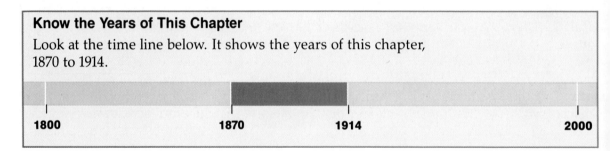

1800   1870   1914   2000

German submarines engaged in unrestricted U-Boat warfare during World War One

EXPLORING THE TIME

On June 28, 1914, Archduke Francis Ferdinand of Austria-Hungary was shot and killed by a Serbian assassin, or murderer. The Archduke was the son of the emperor of Austria-Hungary. On July 28, Austria-Hungary declared war against Serbia. And by the end of August of 1914, many European nations were fighting in this war, called **World War One.** In this chapter, you will learn about the causes of World War One.

Extreme Nationalism Was a Cause of World War One

"My country is better than your country!" This idea became a strong belief in many European nations during the early years of the 1900's. The term used to describe such a belief is **extreme nationalism.** Nationalism is national pride, or love of one's own nation, but extreme nationalism is a nation's belief that it is better than all other nations. The nation also believes that it must win all disputes, or disagreements, that it has with other nations.

ALLIANCES OF EUROPEAN NATIONS IN 1914

NORWAY

SWEDEN

NORTH SEA

DENMARK

BALTIC SEA

RUSSIA

GREAT BRITAIN

NETHERLANDS

GERMANY

BELGIUM

ATLANTIC OCEAN

FRANCE

SWITZERLAND

AUSTRIA-HUNGARY

RUMANIA

BLACK SEA

Sarajevo

SERBIA

BULGARIA

PORTUGAL

SPAIN

ITALY

ALBANIA

TURKISH EMPIRE

GREECE

MEDITERRANEAN SEA

MOROCCO

ALGERIA

TUNISIA

0   400 miles

0   400 kilometers

Members of the Triple Alliance

Members of the Triple Entente

Which countries were members of the Triple Alliance?

The extreme nationalism in many of the European nations soon developed into hatred of other nations. By 1914, this hatred caused many European nations to spend a great deal of time, energy, and money on preparation for war. However, although extreme nationalism was a major cause of World War One, it was not the only cause.

Imperialism Was a Cause of World War One

As you recall, during the late 1800's and early 1900's, some European nations became interested in building large empires. Germany was one of these nations. Great Britain and France already had built up large world empires. Germany did not start to build an empire until late in the 1800's. By then, Germany was able to take over only a few colonies, mainly in Africa. But Germany felt that it had as much right to own a great empire as Britain and France.

Before 1914, a serious quarrel broke out between France and Germany over which nation was to "protect" Morocco, in northern Africa. Most European nations supported France in this quarrel, and Germany had to give up its claim to Morocco. But Germany did not give up its wish to have more colonies. In fact, Germany's wish for more colonies helped to cause World War One.

Economic Rivalry Was a Cause of World War One

The **economic rivalry,** or struggle for trade and business, among the industrial nations of Europe was closely related to imperialism. By the early 1900's, German industries were producing nearly as many manufactured good as Great Britain's industries. Both nations needed new world markets in which to sell their manufactured goods. This need led to economic rivalry between the two nations as each tried to gain control of world markets. This rivalry also helped to cause World War One.

Large Armies and Navies Were a Cause of World War One

The growing feelings of extreme nationalism and rivalry among European nations caused them to build up large armies and navies for defense in case war broke out. Before 1914, these nations spent millions of dollars to build up their armies and navies.

The largest navies belonged to Great Britain and Germany. Great Britain needed its large navy in order to protect its trade

GEOGRAPHY AND HISTORY

Sophie and Francis Ferdinand

In the years before World War One, the Balkan Peninsula was the scene of great rivalry. The Balkans consisted of a number of small nations wedged between three big powers. Each of these big powers—Russia, Austria-Hungary, and the Turkish Empire—wanted to control the Balkans.

Austria-Hungary was a large, loosely connected empire that included peoples of different nationalities. The Serbs, a Slavic group, wanted to be free of Austrian rule and unite with the Balkan nation of Serbia. Serbia became the center of a movement for Slavic independence.

On June 28, 1914, Austrian Archduke Francis Ferdinand and his wife Sophie were shot by a Serbian student. They were on a state visit to the town of Sarajevo (SAHR-uh-yuh-VAW) near Serbia. The murders led Austria-Hungary to declare war on Serbia.

Germany, Austria's ally, joined the fight. Then Russia, which supported Slavic independence, declared war on Germany and Austria-Hungary. Soon, all of Europe was involved in the "Great War."

Question: What role did Serbia play in the fight for Slavic independence?

European gun factories were busy in the early 1900's as nations prepared for war

and to defend the worldwide British Empire. When Germany built up its navy, Great Britain feared that Germany intended to use its navy to cut off British trade. This build-up of armies and navies also was a cause of World War One.

Alliances Were a Cause of World War One

The rivalry and hatred among European nations caused some of them to join together for protection against attack by other nations. As early as 1882, Germany, Austria-Hungary, and Italy joined together in the **Triple Alliance.**

To protect themselves against the Triple Alliance, France and Russia formed their own alliance in 1894. When Germany began to build up its navy, Great Britain then joined France and Russia in 1907 to form the **Triple Entente** (ahn-TAHNT).

These two alliances split Europe into two groups of armed nations. Each of the nations in these groups was ready to go to war because it knew that the other nations in its alliance had promised to give aid. In

this way, these alliances helped to cause World War One.

Problems in the Balkans Were a Cause of World War One

The most dangerous trouble spot in Europe was the Balkan Peninsula. Part of the Balkan Peninsula still belonged to the Turkish Empire. The rest of it was divided among several small nations. Some of these Balkan nations depended on Austria-Hungary for protection. Other Balkan nations depended on Russia for protection. When Austria-Hungary took over two small Balkan nations in 1908, Russia almost went to war against Austria-Hungary. However, Germany supported Austria-Hungary, and Russia backed down. Other small Balkan wars took place in 1912 and 1913, and these wars only made matters worse.

Archduke Francis Ferdinand of Austria-Hungary was visiting the Balkan nation of Serbia when he was murdered on June 28, 1914. This event led to the outbreak of World War One, when Austria-Hungary declared war on Serbia in July of 1914.

SUMMING UP

World War One had many causes. Among these causes were the extreme nationalism among nations, imperialism, economic rivalry for world markets, the build-up of large armies and navies, the forming of two strong alliances, and the fight for control of the Balkan Peninsula. The event that began the war was the murder of Archduke Francis Ferdinand of Austria-Hungary in June of 1914. In the next chapter, you will read about the fighting during World War One.

UNDERSTANDING THE LESSON

Do You Know These Important Terms?

For each sentence below, choose the term that best completes the sentence.

1. The war that broke out in Europe in 1914 was called (**World War One/War of Alliances**).
2. (**Industrialism/Economic rivalry**) was the struggle for trade and business among the industrial nations.
3. An extreme kind of national pride, or love of one's own nation, is called (**extreme rivalry/extreme nationalism**).
4. The (**Triple Alliance/Triple Agreement**) was an agreement made by Germany, Austria-Hungary, and Italy to protect each other against their enemies.
5. The (**Triple Agreement/Triple Entente**) was an alliance made by France, Russia, and Great Britain.

Do You Remember These People and Events?

1. The assassination of Archduke Francis Ferdinand of Austria-Hungary was the event that started World War One. Tell something about this event.
2. Explain how each of the following developments took place.

   a. Germany tried to build an empire like that of Great Britain and France.
   b. European nations began to build large armies and navies.
   c. Problems in the Balkan nations helped to cause World War One.

Can You Locate These Places?

Use the map on page 604 to do the following map work.

1. Locate the Triple Alliance nations.
2. Locate the Triple Entente nations.
3. Locate the following places. Tell how each place is related to the developments in this chapter.

   **Sarajevo   Serbia
   Morocco**

Do You Know When It Happened?

What event took place on this date?

   June 28, 1914

Do You Remember the Main Idea?

Which one of the following ideas is the MAIN IDEA of this chapter?

1. World War One broke out in Europe when Archduke Francis Ferdinand of Austria-Hungary was killed.
2. In 1914, World War One broke out in Europe. Among its causes were extreme nationalism, imperialism, economic rivalry, the building up of armed forces, and alliances.
3. World War One started in Europe because the nations formed strong alliances to preserve the balance of power.

What Do You Think?

From what you have read in this chapter, try to answer the following thought questions.

1. How is the event that starts a war different from the causes of a war?
2. Do you think alliances among nations are good or bad? Give reasons.
3. How do you think extreme nationalism develops in a nation?

Chapter 93
World War One—1914 to 1918

GETTING STARTED

1 Perhaps you wonder why World War One was called a "world war." If you remember, by 1914 many European nations owned colonies and controlled empires in many parts of the world. During World War One, fighting sometimes took place in these colonial empires. But most often, the colonies were expected to send troops and supplies to help the European nations that controlled them. It was the large number of nations fighting in World War One that made it a "world war." The overall scale of the war was enormous. Thirty nations fought in World War One, which lasted from 1914 to 1918. (See the chapter time line at the bottom of the page.)

2 Before you begin reading the chapter lesson, survey the lesson. Begin your survey by reading the beginning of the lesson. Then look through the lesson and read the headings. Next, study the pictures and read the picture captions. Then, study the map of World War One in Europe on page 610. Finally, read the review section called "Summing Up" at the end of the lesson. This survey of the whole lesson will help you to discover the important ideas in this chapter.

Know the Main Idea

As you read the chapter lesson, try to remember the following MAIN IDEA of the chapter.

With the help of the United States, the Allies defeated the Central Powers in World War One.

The following questions will help you to understand the MAIN IDEA. Try to answer these questions as you read the lesson.

1. What plan did German army leaders believe must lead to a quick victory for the Central Powers?
2. Why did Italy join the Allies instead of the Central Powers?
3. What event allowed Germany to send most of its troops to the Western Front?

Know These Important Terms

Central Powers	neutral
Allies	armistice
Western Front	

Know the Years of This Chapter

Look at the time line below. It shows the years of this chapter, 1914 to 1918.

1900	1914 1918	2000

A gun turret near the World War One battle site, Verdun, France

EXPLORING THE TIME

World War One was fought from 1914 to 1918, and it was filled with many long and terrible battles. By 1918, thirty nations and their colonies overseas were fighting in this war. In this chapter, you will read about World War One and some of the battles that were fought during this war.

Germany Attacked Belgium Soon After World War One Began

By August 12, 1914, five of the most powerful nations in Europe were at war. Germany and Austria-Hungary—the **Central Powers**—were at war with Russia, France, and Great Britain—the **Allies**.

The German army leaders believed that a victory for the Central Powers depended

WORLD WAR ONE IN EUROPE — 1914 to 1918

400 miles
400 kilometers

Allies' line of mines across North Sea

NORWAY

SWEDEN

NORTH SEA

DENMARK

BALTIC SEA

RUSSIA

IRELAND

GREAT BRITAIN

London

NETHERLANDS

Berlin

GERMANY

EASTERN FRONT

ATLANTIC OCEAN

Cantigny

BELGIUM

Paris

Chateau-Thierry

WESTERN FRONT

Vienna

FRANCE

SWITZERLAND

AUSTRIA-HUNGARY

RUMANIA

BLACK SEA

PORTUGAL

SPAIN

CORSICA

ITALY

SERBIA

BULGARIA

TURKISH EMPIRE

ALBANIA

SARDINIA

GREECE

MEDITERRANEAN SEA

SICILY

CRETE

Allies

Central Powers

Neutral nations

Allies' victories

Which European nations remained neutral during World War One?

upon conquering France quickly. They decided to attack France through Belgium, a small nation northeast of France. Before the war began, Germany and other European nations had signed an agreement promising never to attack Belgium. Now Germany broke its promise and invaded Belgium. The Belgium army was defeated in a few weeks.

The German Attack on France Slowed Down

Soon German soldiers were marching toward Paris, and it appeared that Germany was going to win the war. But then Germany was forced to move some of its troops fighting in France over to eastern Europe to fight against the Russians. Therefore, the German attack against Paris was slowed down. As a result, the French army now was able to attack the Germans. In September of 1914, the French army stopped the Germans at the Battle of the Marne.

Both France and Germany now realized that the war was not going to end soon. Both armies now dug trenches, or long ditches. They moved into these fortified trenches all along the **Western Front,** or the fighting line in western Europe.

Other Nations Entered the War

As the war continued, the Turkish Empire and Bulgaria joined Germany and Austria-Hungary (the Central Powers). Italy did not join the Central Powers. Italy joined the Allies (Great Britain, France, and Russia) in 1915, because the Allies promised to give Italy new territory after the war. Japan also joined the Allies, because it hoped to take over Germany's colonies in Asia.

The United States Joined the Allies in 1917

When World War One broke out in 1914, President Woodrow Wilson of the United States declared that the United States intended to remain **neutral.** This meant that the United States was not going to favor either side, the Allies or the Central Powers. Americans were allowed to sell supplies—even war supplies—to both the Allies and the Central Powers.

However, by 1916, Germany decided that it must cut off Great Britain's food supply in order to win the war. Therefore, Germany began to sink, without warning, all ships in the waters around Great Britain, whether these ships were carrying war supplies or not. The sinking of several United

PEOPLE IN HISTORY

Edith Cavell

Edith Cavell was an English woman whose quiet courage made her a heroine of World War One. Cavell, a nurse, was running a teaching hospital in Brussels, Belgium when the war broke out. Nurse Cavell took into her hospital wounded soldiers who had been captured by the Germans and had escaped. She became involved in an underground movement to help captured soldiers to escape to freedom in England.

Edith Cavell was arrested by the German secret police and shot. On the night before her execution by a German firing squad, Cavell was visited by an English chaplain. Her words to him were her message to the world. "This I would say, standing as I do in view of God and Eternity. I realize that patriotism is not enough. I have no hatred or bitterness towards anyone."

Prime Minister Asquith of England said of Edith Cavell that, "She has taught the bravest man among us the supreme lesson of courage."

Question: Why was Edith Cavell sentenced to death?

American soldiers arrived in France in 1917 to help the Allies win the war

States ships by Germany in February and March of 1917 helped to cause the United States to declare war against Germany on April 6, 1917.

American Troops Arrived on the Western Front in 1917

The United States entered the war just when the Allies needed help most. Early in 1917, a revolution broke out in Russia. Finally, in November of 1917, a Communist government took control of Russia. In March of 1918, Russia signed a separate peace treaty with Germany. Germany was now able to move its soldiers from the Eastern Front between Russia and Germany to the Western Front between Germany and France. Germany now expected to win the war quickly by defeating the French and British soldiers before American troops arrived to help them.

But American soldiers began to arrive in France as early as June of 1917. And by late spring of 1918, many trained American troops began to fight on the Western Front alongside French and British troops.

The War Finally Ended on November 11, 1918

By the summer of 1918, the war was almost over. With American help, the Allies had beaten the German army. And instead of the German navy's starving out Great Britain, the British navy was starving out Germany. In October of 1918, the German government asked for an **armistice** (AHR-mih-STISS), or an end to the fighting. After the German kaiser, or emperor, gave up the throne, the Allies agreed to accept an armistice. The armistice agreement was signed on November 11, 1918.

World War One was one of the costliest, most terrible wars in history. It destroyed much of Europe's wealth in farms and industries. But its greatest cost was in the loss of lives. Ten million people were killed, and 20 million were wounded. The war also caused millions of deaths among the peoples of Europe from sickness and hunger.

SUMMING UP

At the beginning of World War One, Germany expected to conquer France and to win the war quickly. But this plan failed when Germany was forced to send troops to fight Russia in eastern Europe as well. Germany then tried to win the war by sinking ships carrying supplies to Great Britain. But the sinking of some American ships finally led the United States to enter the war in 1917. With American help, the Allies finally defeated Germany, and World War One ended on November 11, 1918. In the next chapter, you will read about the peace that came after World War One.

UNDERSTANDING THE LESSON

Do You Know These Important Terms?

For each sentence below, choose the term that best completes the sentence.

1. In World War One, Germany and Austria-Hungary were called the **(Central Powers/Triple Alliance)**.
2. Russia, France, and Great Britain were called the **(Triple Threat/Allies)**.
3. The fighting line in western Europe was called the **(Orlando Line/Western Front)**.
4. When a nation remains **(neutral/ neglectful)**, it does not favor either side in a war.
5. An **(amendment/armistice)** is an end to the fighting in a war.

Do You Remember These People and Events?

1. Tell something about each of the following leaders.

   Woodrow Wilson   German kaiser

2. Explain how or why each of the following developments took place.

   a. The German army was not able to win a quick victory over France.
   b. The United States joined the Allies.
   c. The war ended on November 11, 1918.

Can You Locate These Places?

Use the map on page 610 to do the following map work.

1. Locate the Central Powers, the Allies, and Western Front.
2. What European nations remained neutral?

3. Why were Germany and Austria-Hungary called the Central Powers?
4. Along what two fronts did most of the fighting in western Europe in World War One take place?

Do You Know When It Happened?

Why are the following dates important in World War One?

   April 6, 1917   November 11, 1918

Do You Remember the Main Idea?

Which one of the following ideas is the MAIN IDEA of this chapter?

1. With the help of the United States, the Allies defeated the Central Powers in World War One.
2. Germany and Austria-Hungary were not able to continue fighting in World War One after a revolution broke out in Russia.
3. The German army was not able to win a quick victory in World War One and was finally defeated.

What Do You Think?

From what you have read in this chapter, answer the following thought questions.

1. Why do you think it might be difficult for a nation to remain neutral during a world war?
2. Besides sending troops and supplies, in what other ways do you think the United States helped the Allies?
3. What kind of peace terms would you have asked for between the Allies and the Central Powers?

Chapter 94
The Peace After World War One

GETTING STARTED

1   Winning the peace after a war can be more difficult than winning the war. That is what the leaders of the Allies discovered when they met in France in 1919 to make plans for peace after World War One. These leaders discovered that it was not possible to please all nations—even nations that were members of the Allies. However, within a few months, these leaders were able to write a peace treaty. This chapter describes the terms of this peace treaty.

2   Before you begin reading the chapter lesson, survey the lesson. Begin your survey by reading the beginning of the lesson. Then look through the lesson and read the headings. Next, study the pictures and read the picture captions. Then study the map of Europe after World War One on page 616. Finally, read the review section called "Summing Up" at the end of the lesson. This survey of the whole lesson will help you to discover the important ideas in this chapter.

Know the Main Idea

As you read the chapter lesson, try to remember the following important MAIN IDEA of the chapter.

The peace treaties that ended World War One punished the Central Powers and established many new nations in Europe.

The following questions will help you to understand the MAIN IDEA. Try to answer these questions as you read the lesson.

1. Who developed a plan for peace early in 1918?
2. What demands did Great Britain and France make in return for accepting the League of Nations?
3. What nation refused to accept the peace treaty with Germany and made a separate peace treaty of its own?

Know These Important Terms

    Fourteen Points
    League of Nations
    Treaty of Versailles
    reparations

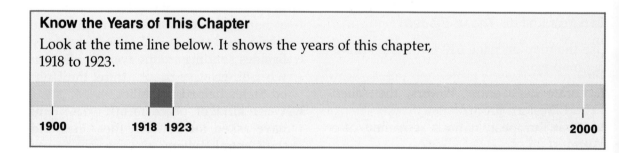

Know the Years of This Chapter

Look at the time line below. It shows the years of this chapter, 1918 to 1923.

| 1900 | 1918 1923 | 2000 |

Peace came at last for the War's survivors on November 11, 1918

EXPLORING THE TIME

In November of 1918, World War One ended in a victory for the Allies. By June of 1919, the Allies finished writing the peace treaty. But this peace treaty was not able to bring lasting peace to the world, as you will learn. In this chapter, you will read about the kind of peace that was planned by the Allies after World War One.

President Wilson Presented a Plan for World Peace

As early as January of 1918, President Woodrow Wilson of the United States developed a plan for peace called the **Fourteen Points.** The most important of these Fourteen Points were the following.

1. No nation in the world was to be ruled by another if it did not want to be. This meant that the nations ruled before the war

615

EUROPE AFTER WORLD WAR ONE — 1923

FINLAND

NORWAY

SWEDEN

ESTONIA

LATVIA

NORTH SEA

DENMARK

LITHUANIA

IRELAND

GREAT BRITAIN

BALTIC SEA

GERMANY

SOVIET UNION
(Called the Soviet Union from 1922 on)

POLAND

NETHERLANDS

GERMANY

BELGIUM

ATLANTIC OCEAN

ALSACE-LORRAINE

CZECHOSLOVAKIA

FRANCE

AUSTRIA

HUNGARY

SWITZERLAND

RUMANIA

BLACK SEA

YUGOSLAVIA

ITALY

BULGARIA

PORTUGAL

CORSICA

ALBANIA

T U R K E Y

SPAIN

SARDINIA

GREECE

M E D I T E R R A N E A N   S E A

SICILY

CYPRUS

CRETE

0   400 miles

0   400 kilometers

New nations after World War One

How many new nations were formed after World War One?

by the Turkish Empire, Russia, and Austria-Hungary would become free nations.

2. The colonies in Asia and Africa ruled by European nations were to be prepared to govern themselves and, in some cases, to become independent nations.

3. A **League of Nations** was to be formed to keep world peace and to settle

disputes, or disagreements, between nations. The main nations of the world were to be members of the League. The chief purpose of the League was to try to prevent war and to settle world problems. The League of Nations was the most important part of President Wilson's peace plan. But many people disagreed with Wilson.

The Allies Did Not Accept Wilson's Plan

In December of 1918 President Wilson went to France to attend the peace conference. The French people greeted Wilson as a great hero. But at the peace conference, the leaders of the Allies did not like many parts of Wilson's plan for peace. The leaders of the Allies who attended the peace conference with President Wilson were Prime Minister David Lloyd George of Great Britain, Prime Minister Georges Clemenceau (KLEM-un-SOH) of France, and Prime Minister Vittorio Orlando of Italy.

The leaders of the Allies were mainly interested in pleasing the people of their own nations by making Germany pay for the hardships and damage they suffered during the war. These leaders were determined to get money and territory from Germany and from the other nations that fought against the Allies. Therefore, these leaders did not accept many parts of President Wilson's peace plan.

The Allies Won Most of Their Demands

Great Britain and France finally accepted Wilson's idea of a League of Nations. But in return, President Wilson was forced to

U.S. President Woodrow Wilson went to Paris and tried to convince Europe's leaders to adopt his peace plan of Fourteen Points

Program for the Peace of the World

By *PRESIDENT WILSON* January 8, 1918

I. Open covenants of peace, openly arrived at, after which there shall be no private international understandings of any kind, but diplomacy shall proceed always frankly and in the public view.

II. Absolute freedom of navigation upon the seas, outside territorial waters, alike in peace and in war, except as the seas may be closed in whole or in part by international action for the enforcement of international covenants.

III. The removal, so far as possible, of all economic barriers and the establishment of an equality of trade conditions among all the nations consenting to the peace and associating themselves for its maintenance.

IV. Adequate guarantees given and taken that national armaments will reduce to the lowest point consistent with domestic safety.

V. Free, open minded, and absolutely impartial adjustment of all colonial claims, based upon a strict observance of the principle that in determining all such questions of sovereignty the interests of the population concerned must have equal weight with the equitable claims of the government whose title is to be determined.

VI. The evacuation of all Russian territory and such a settlement of all questions affecting Russia as will secure the best and freest cooperation of the other nations of the world in obtaining for her an unhampered and unembarrassed opportunity for the independent determination of her own political development and national policy, and assure her of a sincere welcome into the society of free nations under institutions of her own choosing; and, more than a welcome, assistance also of every kind that she may need and may herself desire. The treatment accorded Russia by her sister nations in the months to come will be the acid test of their goodwill, of their comprehension of her needs as distinguished from their own interests, and of their intelligent and unselfish sympathy.

VII. Belgium, the whole world will agree, must be evacuated and restored, without any attempt to limit the sovereignty which she enjoys in common with all other free nations. No other single act will serve as this will serve to restore confidence among the nations in the law which they have themselves set and determined for the government of their relations with one another. Without this healing act the whole structure and validity of international law is forever impaired.

VIII. All French territory should be freed and the invaded portions restored, and the wrong done to France by Prussia in 1871 in the matter of Alsace-Lorraine, which has unsettled the peace of the world for nearly fifty years, should be righted, in order that peace may once more be made secure in the interest of all.

IX. A readjustment of the frontiers of Italy should be effected along clearly recognizable lines of nationality.

X. The people of Austria-Hungary, whose place among the nations we wish to see safeguarded and assured, should be accorded the freest opportunity of autonomous development.

XI. Rumania, Serbia and Montenegro should be evacuated; occupied territories restored; Serbia accorded free and secure access to the sea; and the relations of the several Balkan States to one another determined by friendly counsel along historically established lines of allegiance and nationality; and international guarantees of the political and economic independence and territorial integrity of the several Balkan States should be entered into.

XII. The Turkish portions of the present Ottoman Empire should be assured a secure sovereignty, but the other nationalities which are now under Turkish rule should be assured an undoubted security of life and an absolutely unmolested opportunity of autonomous development, and the Dardanelles should be permanently opened as a free passage to the ships and commerce of all nations under international guarantees.

XIII. An independent Polish State should be erected which should include the territories inhabited by indisputably Polish populations, which should be assured a free and secure access to the sea, and whose political and economic independence and territorial integrity should be guaranteed by international covenant.

XIV. A general association of nations must be formed under specific covenants for the purpose of affording mutual guarantees of political independence and territorial integrity to great and small States alike.

617

agree to many of their demands. The **Treaty of Versailles** (ver-SY)—the peace treaty that ended World War One—was completed by June of 1919.

The Treaty of Versailles forced Germany to pay large amounts of money, called **reparations,** to the Allies. It also forced Germany to return the land of Alsace-Lorraine that it took away from France after the Franco-Prussian War in 1871. And Germany had to give France the use of certain coal mines in western Germany for fifteen years. German colonies in Asia and Africa were to be governed by the League of Nations. (Most of these colonies were later divided up between Great Britain and France.) And Germany's land along the Rhine River was to be ruled by the Allies for fifteen years, and Germany was never to send soldiers into this territory.

The Allies also accepted Wilson's idea that Poland, Yugoslavia, Czechoslovakia, Finland, Estonia, Latvia, and Lithuania were to become free nations. Before World War One, the people of these nations had been ruled by Russia and Austria-Hungary.

The United States Turned Down the Treaty of Versailles

The Treaty of Versailles did not please many peoples. The Germans felt that it was too harsh toward Germany. The British and French people felt that the treaty was not harsh enough toward Germany. And Italians did not like the Treaty of Versailles because it failed to give them all of the territory that was promised to Italy by the Allies during the war.

However, all these nations signed the Treaty of Versailles anyway. But the United States did not sign this treaty. The United States Senate turned down the Treaty of Versailles because the Senate did not approve of many of the treaty's terms. And the United States never joined the League of Nations, although it sent observers to attend League meetings. In fact, the United States signed a separate peace treaty with Germany in 1921.

Many European Nations Gained Independence After the War

The Treaty of Versailles dealt mainly with Germany. The Allies also signed several peace treaties with the other Central Powers. These treaties split the empire of Austria-Hungary into several smaller nations. Austria and Hungary became two separate nations, and Czechoslovakia and Yugoslavia became independent nations. Both Bulgaria and the Turkish Empire lost some territory, too. In loss of territory, the other Central Powers were punished more harshly than Germany itself.

SUMMING UP

The leaders of the Allies did not agree to many parts of President Wilson's plan for peace. The Treaty of Versailles, signed in 1919, and other peace treaties punished Germany and the other Central Powers. The Treaty of Versailles required Germany to pay large sums of money to the Allies and to give up German colonies in Asia and Africa. Austria-Hungary and the Turkish Empire lost much territory to new nations set up in Europe. In the end, the United States Senate refused to accept the Treaty of Versailles or to join the League of Nations. In the next chapter, you will read about the new Communist government that was set up in Russia.

UNDERSTANDING THE LESSON

Do You Know These Important Terms?

For each sentence below, choose the term that best completes the sentence.

1. President Wilson's plan for world peace was called the **(Fourteen Points/ Democratic Blueprint).**
2. The **(United Nations/League of Nations)** was an important part of Wilson's peace plan because it was to prevent war and to settle world problems peacefully.
3. The peace treaty that ended World War One was called the **(Treaty of Versailles/ Peace of Paris).**
4. **(Reparations/Partitions)** are large amounts of money that a nation must pay to other nations for damages it has caused.

Do You Remember These People and Events?

1. Tell something about each of the following leaders.

   **Woodrow Wilson David Lloyd George
   Vittorio Orlando   Georges Clemenceau**

2. Explain why each of the following developments took place.

   a. The Allies' leaders did not accept all of President Wilson's peace plan.
   b. The United States turned down the Treaty of Versailles.
   c. In the loss of territory, Germany was not punished as harshly as were the other Central Powers.

Can You Locate These Places?

Use the map on page 616 to do the following map work.

1. Compare this map with the map in Chapter 92 (page 604). What New European countries do you see? From what older nations were they formed?
2. Locate and name the land that France received from Germany.

Do You Know When It Happened?

In what year was the Treaty of Versailles signed?

Do You Remember the Main Idea?

Which one of the following ideas is the MAIN IDEA of this chapter?

1. The Treaty of Versailles established the League of Nations, which was to settle all future disputes between nations.
2. The peace treaties that ended World War One punished the Central Powers and established new nations in Europe.
3. Austria-Hungary and Bulgaria were the nations most harshly punished after World War One. They lost large parts of their territory.

What Do You Think?

From what you have read in this chapter, try to answer the following questions.

1. Do you think that it is possible for a peace treaty to please all nations at the end of a world war? Explain your answer.
2. Do you think that the terms of the Treaty of Versailles were fair? Give reasons for your answer.
3. If you had been Woodrow Wilson, how would you have felt about the Treaty of Versailles?

Chapter 95
Communism in Russia

GETTING STARTED

1   In Chapter 83, you read how Karl Marx and others developed ideas about Communism during the 1800's as the Industrial Revolution was rapidly spreading. By 1917, Communism was still only an idea about government. No large nation had set up a Communist government.

In 1917, however, the Russian people revolted against their ruler, Czar Nicholas the Second. The government that finally took over Russia after this revolution was a Communist government. How did the Communists succeed in taking over the Russian government? You will learn the answer in this chapter, which describes the development of Communism in Russia in the years between 1917 and 1939.

2   Before you begin reading the chapter lesson, survey the lesson. Begin your survey by reading the beginning of the lesson. Then look through the lesson and read the headings. Next, study the pictures and read the picture captions. Finally, read the review section called "Summing Up." This survey will help you to discover the important ideas in this chapter.

Know the Main Idea

As you read the chapter lesson, try to remember the following important MAIN IDEA of the chapter.

Russia became a strong, industrial nation. But the Communist government of Russia ruled as a dictatorship.

The following questions will help you to understand the MAIN IDEA. Try to answer these questions as you read the lesson.

1. Why did the Russian people revolt against the czar in 1917?
2. Who were the leaders of the Russian Revolution?
3. What Russian leader started the Five-Year Plan for developing farms and industries?

Know These Important Terms

Russian Revolution	commissars
Communist Party	**Bolsheviks**
Central Committee	soviets
New Economic Policy	**Five-Year Plan**

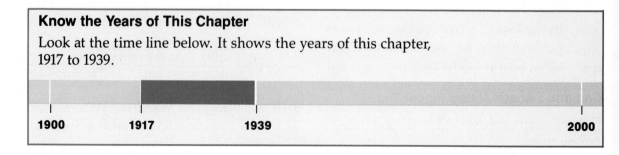

Know the Years of This Chapter

Look at the time line below. It shows the years of this chapter, 1917 to 1939.

1900   1917   1939   2000

Nikolai Lenin returned to Russia when the Revolution began

EXPLORING THE TIME

As you will learn, a revolution broke out in Russia in 1917. This **Russian Revolution** set up a Communist government in Russia. And this Communist government caused many important changes in Russia. In this chapter, you will learn what happened to Russia under its Communist government.

The Russian Czar Was Overthrown

Perhaps you remember that Russia had a revolution in 1905 after it lost a war against Japan. Czar Nicholas the Second ended this revolution. But most of the Russian people remained unhappy because their government did little to improve life in Russia. Then World War One brought many new hardships to the Russian people. As Russia

Photograph taken as the Bolsheviks fought the czar's army in St. Petersburg. Who were the Bolsheviks?

began to lose the war on the Eastern Front, the Russian people blamed Czar Nicholas and the government. As a result, the Russian people began to turn against the czar and the government.

In March of 1917, a great revolution broke out in Russia against Czar Nicholas. Few Russians now supported the czar, and he was forced to give up the throne. Russia set up a new government, and it tried to continue the war against Germany.

The Communists Took Over Russia in November of 1917

However, the Russian Revolution was not yet ended. The **Bolsheviks** (BOHL-shuh-VICKS), or Russian Communists, worked hard to make the Russian people accept Communism. Led by Nikolai Lenin (NEE-koh-LIE LEN-in), the Communists promised to give land to the Russian farmers. They promised to give the ownership of Russian factories to the factory workers. And the Communists promised peace to the soldiers fighting on the Eastern Front.

The main leaders of the Russian Revolution were Lenin and Leon Trotsky (TROT-skee). Lenin was the leader who planned the revolution. Lenin formed **soviets** (SOH-vee-ETZ), or groups of soldiers, workers, and peasants. By November of 1917, the

Bolsheviks were strong enough to start their own revolution. On November 7, 1917, they revolted and took over the Russian government. Russia now became a Communist nation with Lenin as its leader. Then in March of 1918, Russia signed a peace treaty with Germany.

Complete Communism Did Not Work in Russia

At first, Lenin tried to make Russia into a completely Communist nation. All Russian factories, mines, and businesses were controlled by the government and run by Russian workers. All Russian land was owned by the government. And all goods were sold by the government in government-owned stores.

However, Lenin's plan did not work out well. By 1921, much less food and fewer manufactured goods were being produced in Russia than were produced in 1914, before the Russian Revolution began.

Therefore, in 1921, Lenin began a new plan for Russia called the **New Economic Policy** (N.E.P.). Under the N.E.P., the Communist government allowed some small factories to be owned and run by private citizens. It also allowed farmers to sell for their own profit any extra food that they were able to grow. And some private citizens were allowed to run their own small stores and businesses. The N.E.P. lasted until 1928, and it brought some improvements in Russia's farms, businesses, and industries.

Russia Became a Communist Dictatorship

By 1922, Russia became the Union of Soviet Socialist Republics (U.S.S.R.), or the Soviet Union. But, even with this new name, the

DOCUMENTS IN HISTORY

Nikolai Lenin

Nikolai Lenin wrote many books and articles explaining Communism and the Russian Revolution. After he had become the leader of the Soviet Union, Lenin looked back on Russia before the Revolution:

> The old society was based on the oppression of all the workers and peasants by the landlords and capitalists. We had to destroy the society. We had to overthrow these landowners and capitalists.

Lenin also wrote about democracy. It was useful, he said, in bringing about a Communist state:

> Democracy is of great importance for the working class in its struggle for freedom against the capitalists. But democracy is only one of the stages in the course of development from feudalism to capitalism, and from capitalism to communism.

Lenin wrote about democracy and freedom, but he ruled Russia like a dictator. He organized a secret police force to eliminate his political opponents. Lenin's reign of terror continued until he died in 1924.

Question: How did Lenin deal with his political opponents?

Soviet Union was not a republic. It was a dictatorship, or a nation controlled completely by a dictator—an all-powerful ruler—and a small group of government leaders.

The Communists prepared new constitutions for the Soviet Union in 1924 and in 1936. The 1936 constitution, or written plan of government, of the Soviet Union has lasted until today. This constitution provided a legislature, or law-making group, for the Soviet Union. The legislature elected a smaller council, and that council then chose a group of men called **commissars** to rule the Soviet Union.

But the constitution did not give the Russian people freedom. And the Soviet Union was really ruled by the **Communist Party.** The Communist Party was the only political party allowed in the Soviet Union. And only a few Russians were allowed to join the Communist Party. However, this very small party controlled the government of the whole Soviet Union.

Stalin Became the Soviet Dictator

The Communist Party itself was controlled by a small **Central Committee** headed by a Secretary. The Central Committee and its Secretary became the real rulers of the Soviet Union. This was proved in 1924 when Lenin died. Joseph Stalin (STAH-lin), the Secretary of the Communist Party Central Committee, now controlled the Communist Party. And Stalin was able to use his powerful control over the Communist Party to make himself the dictator of the Soviet Union.

Russia Became an Industrial Nation and a "Police State"

In 1928, under Stalin's rule, the Soviet Union began the first **Five-Year Plan.** The Five-Year Plans called for a great increase in production in Russian industries and farms every five years. These Plans also led to greater government control of industry and farming. The first Five-Year Plan ended in 1932.

By the end of the second Five-Year Plan, the Soviet Union had made great progress in its industries. The Soviet Union's production of factory goods now made it one of the leading industrial nations of the world. And the production of Soviet farm goods also greatly increased.

But these Five-Year Plans succeeded mainly because the Soviet government led by Stalin set up a "police state" and used its power to force the Russian people to obey. Russians who did not obey the Communist government were killed or put in prison. In this way, the Communist Party used force to bring Communism to the government of the Soviet Union and set up a police state in the Soviet Union.

SUMMING UP

In 1917, the government of Czar Nicholas the Second was overthrown, and Russia was taken over by the Communists. Under Nikolai Lenin, the Communists set up a dictatorship in Russia, or the Soviet Union. Under Joseph Stalin, the Soviet Union became a strong industrial nation. But Stalin set up a "police state," and the Russian people had no freedom. In the next chapter, you will read about the nations of western Europe in the years after World War One.

UNDERSTANDING THE LESSON

Do You Know These Important Terms?

For each sentence below, choose the term that best completes the sentence.

1. The revolution that set up a Communist government in Russia was called the (**Russian Revolution/Leningrad Revolution**).
2. Another name for the Russian Communists who revolted in 1917 was the (**Anti-Czarists/Bolsheviks**).
3. Groups of soldiers, workers, and peasants were called (**commissars/soviets**).
4. The new plan for Russia started in 1921 was called the (**Private-Government Policy/New Economic Policy**).
5. The group of people who were chosen by the legislature to run the government of the Soviet Union were called (**dictators/commissars**).
6. The (**Communist Party/Leninist Party**) was the only political party allowed in the Soviet Union.
7. The (**Supreme Soviet/Central Committee**), headed by a Secretary, controlled the Communist Party.
8. Under Stalin, the plan to increase factory and farm production in the Soviet Union was called the (**Eight-Year Plan/Five-Year Plan**).

Do You Remember These People and Events?

1. Tell something about each of the following persons.

   **Nikolai Lenin   Joseph Stalin
   Leon Trotsky**

2. Explain how each of the following developments took place.

   a. The Communists took over the government of Russia in 1917.
   b. Complete Communism did not work in Russia.
   c. The Soviet Union became a dictatorship and a "police state."

Do You Know When It Happened?

In what year did Russia become the Soviet Union?

Do You Remember the Main Idea?

Which one of the following ideas is the MAIN IDEA of this chapter?

1. After the Russian Revolution, the Communists took control of the Russian government.
2. The Soviet Union became a dictatorship because the Leninist Party was the only political party allowed in the nation.
3. Russia became a strong industrial nation. But the Communist government ruled Russia as a dictatorship.

What Do You Think?

From what you have read in this chapter, try to answer the following thought questions.

1. What do you consider to be the greatest disadvantages of Communism? Does Communism have any advantages? Explain your answer.
2. Why do you suppose that Joseph Stalin and his followers set up a "police state" in the Soviet Union?
3. Give some reasons why you would not like to live in a "police state."

Chapter 96

Western Europe After World War One

GETTING STARTED

1 Making peace was not the only problem European nations faced after World War One. During the war, many factories and homes were destroyed in Europe. Many nations lacked the money to rebuild because they had spent great amounts of money to carry on the war. And the winning nations faced almost as many problems as the losing nations after the war.

As you will read, the years between 1919 and 1939 (see the time line below) were difficult times for most European nations. This chapter describes western Europe during this difficult period.

2 Before you begin reading the chapter lesson, survey the lesson. Begin your survey by reading the beginning of the lesson. Then look through the lesson and read the headings. Next, study the pictures and read the picture captions. Then study the map showing the British Empire in 1937 on page 628. Finally, read the review section called "Summing Up" at the end of the lesson. This survey of the whole lesson will help

you to discover the important ideas in this chapter.

Know the Main Idea

As you read the chapter lesson, try to remember the following important MAIN IDEA of the chapter.

Great Britain, France, and Germany slowly rebuilt their nations after World War One. But starting in 1929, these nations again suffered hard times.

The following questions will help you to understand the MAIN IDEA. Try to answer these questions as you read the lesson.

1. What parts of the British Empire became self-governing nations by 1937?
2. What events during the 1920's and 1930's proved that the French government was weak?
3. When did Hitler take over Germany?

Know These Important Terms

self-government	depression
Weimar Republic	Nazi Party
British Commonwealth of Nations	

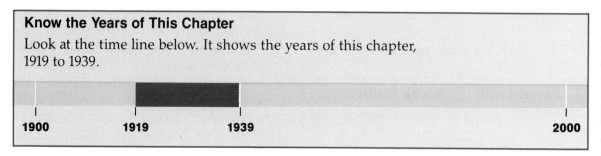

Know the Years of This Chapter

Look at the time line below. It shows the years of this chapter, 1919 to 1939.

| 1900 | 1919 | 1939 | 2000 |

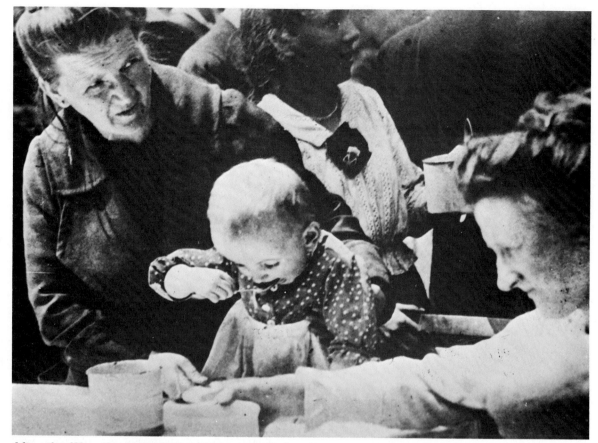

After the War, the United States set up relief stations throughout Europe to help feed, clothe, shelter, and aid the hungry, the sick, and the homeless

EXPLORING THE TIME

"The old gray mare, she ain't what she used to be." This saying seems to describe Europe and its nations in the years after World War One. The war brought great hardships to Europe, and few European nations were as strong after the war as they were before the war. In this chapter, you will read about the nations of western Europe and what happened to them in the years following World War One.

Great Britain Suffered Hard Times After the War

Although Great Britain was on the winning side in the war, it used up much of its money and goods in fighting the war. By the 1920's, the machinery in British factories and mines was old and out of date. Germany, the United States, and Japan had newer and better machinery in their factories. Therefore, these nations were able to produce more goods and to sell them at lower prices than Great Britain.

THE BRITISH EMPIRE IN 1937

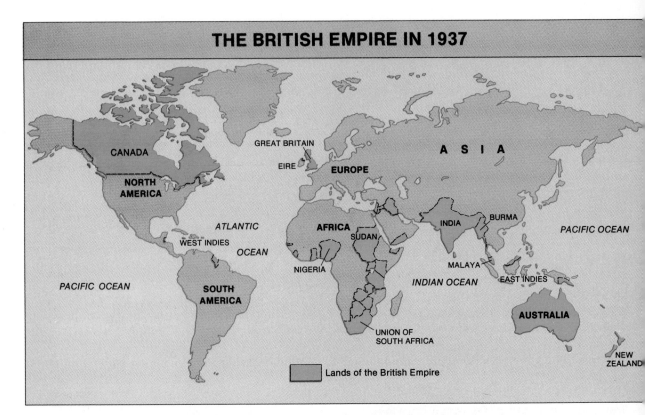

CANADA

NORTH AMERICA

GREAT BRITAIN

EIRE

EUROPE

A S I A

ATLANTIC OCEAN

WEST INDIES

AFRICA

SUDAN

INDIA

BURMA

PACIFIC OCEAN

NIGERIA

MALAYA

EAST INDIES

PACIFIC OCEAN

SOUTH AMERICA

INDIAN OCEAN

AUSTRALIA

UNION OF SOUTH AFRICA

NEW ZEALAND

Lands of the British Empire

Name the only entire continent that was part of the British Empire.

Great Britain lost many customers to other nations. Some British factories had to close, and many workers lost their jobs. In the 1930's, conditions worsened.

Great Britain Set Up a Commonwealth of Nations

After the war, Great Britain continued to allow more freedom to the peoples in the British Empire. As early as 1867, Great Britain gave Canada almost complete **self-government,** or the freedom to govern itself. Later, Australia, New Zealand, and the Union of South Africa became self-governing nations.

In 1931, Parliament passed a law giving complete independence to all the domin-

ions, or self-governing nations, in the British Empire. These dominions now became equal partners with Great Britain in the **British Commonwealth of Nations,** or the nations of the British Empire.

The Irish Free State (Ireland) was one of the British dominions. But, many people in the Irish Free State wanted their nation to be completely free and separate from Great Britain. In 1937, the Irish Free State became an independent nation called Eire (AIR-uh).

France Had a Weak Government

In some ways, France suffered more from World War One than any other nation. Many French factories, farms, and railroads were destroyed. However, France was able

War equipment being destroyed once peace came

to rebuild quickly after the war. Its farms and factories produced many products and sold them in world markets. As a result, the people of France enjoyed good times until the 1930's.

But the French government was not strong during these years. The French Chamber of Deputies—the lower house of the French legislature—had the power to force the prime minister to quit whenever it disagreed with his policies. During the 1920's and 1930's, France often had a new prime minister every few months. These many changes weakened France.

Germany Faced Many Problems

After World War One, the German Empire ended, and Germany became a republic. Germany now was called the **Weimar** (VY-mahr) **Republic** because its constitution was drawn up in the city of Weimar. The new constitution gave freedom to all German citizens, and it gave everyone the right to vote. But the Weimar Republic was forced to accept the Treaty of Versailles, which most Germans hated. As a result, many Germans hated the Weimar Republic because it had accepted the Treaty.

The Weimar Republic faced other problems, too, during the 1920's. Germany was supposed to pay reparations, or money, to the Allies for the damage done to the Allies during World War One. Germany made one payment, and then declared that it was not able to make any more payments. France

Adolf Hitler and the National Socialist Party (Nazi Party) held huge, carefully controlled meetings to gain political support

then tried to force Germany to pay by sending soldiers to the Ruhr (ROOR), which was an important industrial section in western Germany. But after the French soldiers arrived, the Germans in the Ruhr area refused to work. As a result, German industry slowed down.

By 1924, however, conditions in Germany improved when the Allies cut down the amount of the reparations that Germany had to pay. And when France withdrew its troops from the Ruhr, German industries began to recover.

Hitler Set Up a Dictatorship in Germany

But in 1929, a great **depression,** or period of hard times, began all over the world. In Germany, as in other nations, the depression caused businesses and banks to close. Millions of Germans lost their jobs. Many Germans again blamed the Weimar Republic for Germany's problems. Some of these Germans joined the **Nazi** (NAH-tsee) **Party,** or a National Socialist Party, led by Adolf Hitler, an Austrian-born ex-soldier.

Between 1930 and 1933, the Nazi Party grew stronger. The Nazi Party hated the Weimar Republic. Hitler worked to weaken the Republic by blaming it for the depression. In January of 1933, Hitler was made chancellor of Germany. In 1934, Hitler took full control of the German government, and he set up a dictatorship in Germany.

SUMMING UP

Great Britain, France, and Germany slowly rebuilt their nations after World War One. But in 1929 these nations again suffered hard times as a result of a great worldwide depression. In Germany, the German people blamed the new Weimar Republic for the depression. The Weimar Republic ended when Adolf Hitler set up a Nazi dictatorship in Germany. In the next chapter, you will read about the other nations of Europe in the years after World War One.

UNDERSTANDING THE LESSON

Do You Know These Important Terms?

For each sentence below, choose the term that best completes the sentence.

1. A nation's freedom to govern itself is called (**self-government/self-economy**).
2. The self-governing nations of the British Empire were equal members with Great Britain in the (**British Territorial Alliance/British Commonwealth of Nations**).
3. The (**Bonn Republic/Weimar Republic**) was the government set up in Germany after World War One.
4. The period of hard times all over the world after 1929 was called the (**department/depression**).
5. The political party led by Adolf Hitler that took over the government of Germany in the 1930's was the (**Anti-Weimar Party/Nazi Party**).

Do You Remember These People and Events?

1. Tell something about Adolf Hitler in relation to the developments in this chapter.
2. Explain how or why each of the following developments took place.

   a. Great Britain suffered hard times after World War One.
   b. Great Britain set up the British Commonwealth of Nations.
   c. Hitler and the Nazi Party took over the government of Germany.

Can You Locate These Places?

Use the map on page 628 to locate the following places. Tell how each place is related to the developments in this chapter.

Canada   New Zealand
Australia   Union of South Africa
Eire

Do You Know When It Happened?

Why are the following years important in this chapter?

1929   1933

Do You Remember the Main Idea?

Which one of the following ideas is the MAIN IDEA of this chapter?

1. After World War One, the nations of Europe quickly recovered and again started to build new empires.
2. After World War One, all the nations of Europe recovered quickly, except Germany, where the Nazi Party took over the government.
3. Great Britain, France, and Germany slowly rebuilt their nations after World War One. But starting in 1929, these nations again suffered hard times.

What Do You Think?

From what you have read in this chapter, answer the following thought questions.

1. Do you think the British Commonwealth of Nations helped to preserve the British Empire? Give your reasons.
2. Do you think that a nation with a weak government can make real progress? Use the example of France in the 1920's and 1930's, and explain your answer.
3. Why are depressions often followed by periods of great change?

Chapter 97

The Rest of Europe After World War One

GETTING STARTED

1   The nations of eastern and southern Europe, like the nations of western Europe, also faced many problems in the years after World War One. In eastern and southern Europe, many new nations were set up after the war. In both southern and eastern Europe, many nations did not have democratic governments, as you will learn.

2   Before you begin reading the chapter lesson, survey the lesson. Begin your survey by reading the beginning of the lesson. Then look through the lesson and read the headings. Next, study the pictures and read the picture captions. Finally, read the review section called "Summing Up" at the end of the lesson. This survey of the whole lesson will help you to discover the important ideas in this chapter.

Know the Main Idea

As you read the chapter lesson, try to remember the following important MAIN IDEA of this chapter.

After World War One, many nations in eastern and southern Europe set up democratic governments. But these governments did not last long.

The following questions will help you to understand the MAIN IDEA. Try to answer these questions as you read the lesson.

1. What caused the end of the democratic nation of Czechoslovakia?
2. Who became the dictator of Italy?
3. How long did the Spanish Republic last?

Know These Important Terms

Fascist Party   **il Duce**

Know the Years of This Chapter

Look at the time line below. It shows the years of this chapter, 1919 to 1939.

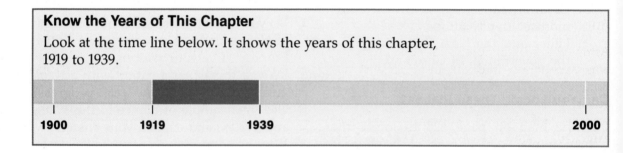

| 1900 | 1919 | 1939 | 2000 |

After the War, impoverished Europeans struggled to rebuild Europe

EXPLORING THE TIME

In the last chapter, you read about Great Britain, France, and Germany after World War One. What was happening in the rest of Europe after World War One? In this chapter, you will read about events in other European nations after World War One.

Austria Became a Weak Republic

After World War One, Austria-Hungary was broken up into the independent nations of Austria, Hungary, and Czechoslovakia. Some land of Austria-Hungary also was given to Poland, Rumania, Italy, and Yugoslavia. And Austria became a republic.

But the Austrian Republic was very much smaller than the old Austria-Hungary. In 1938 (as you will learn later), the weak Austrian Republic was taken over by Germany.

Hungary Was Ruled by a Dictator

After World War One, Hungary became a separate and independent nation. Like Austria, Hungary also became a republic. But in 1919, a Communist government took control of Hungary. Soon afterwards, the Communists were overthrown by Admiral Nicolas Horthy (HOR-tee), who ruled Hungary as a dictator for more than twenty years.

Tomás Masaryk (left) and Eduard Benes were the two great leaders of Czechoslovakia between World War One and World War Two

Czechoslovakia Had a Short But Proud History

After World War One, Czechoslovakia (CHECK-oh-sloh-VAHK-ee-ah) won its independence from Austria-Hungary. Led by two great Presidents, Tomás Masaryk (MAH-sah-RICK) and Eduard Benes (BEH-nesh), Czechoslovakia became one of the most democratic nations of Europe. Czechoslovakia also became one of Europe's leading industrial nations. But as you will read later, this democratic nation of Czechoslovakia was ended when Germany took it over in 1939.

Poland Became a Dictatorship

As you may recall, Poland was divided in 1795 among Russia, Prussia, and Austria. For the next hundred years, the Poles tried but failed to gain their independence. However, after World War One, the Poles' great wish for independence came true. Poland now became a republic with a democratic constitution very much like the French constitution of the Third French Republic.

But Poland was not satisfied with the amount of territory it received in the peace treaty that ended World War One. And the Polish army took territory away from Russia, from Germany, and from Lithuania, a new Baltic nation. In 1926, Joseph Pilsudski (pill-SEWT-skee), an army general, set up a dictatorship in Poland. Poland's dictatorship government continued during the 1930's.

The Balkan Nations Had Many Problems

After World War One, the nations of the Balkan Peninsula all set up new constitutional governments. Rumania and Greece were the most advanced Balkan nations. Yugoslavia and two other small Balkan nations—Bulgaria and Albania—were less developed lands.

All the Balkan nations had many problems. They were slow to build industries, and most of their people were poor farmers who had little education. And most of the Balkan nations remained quite poor during the years after World War One. Soon, dictator governments were set up in most of these nations.

After the War, Italy Was Weak

As you have read, Italy entered World War One after the Allies promised to give Italy more territory when the war ended. After the war, Italy owed many debts. Many people in Italy were unemployed, and living conditions were difficult for many Italians. And Italy received much less territory than it was promised by the Allies. As a result, the Italian people were very unhappy with the leaders of their government.

About this time, a new leader began to gain power in Italy. His name was Benito Mussolini (buh-NEE-toh MOOS-uh-LEE-nee). Mussolini believed that Italy must have a dictator government in order to solve its problems and to make Italy become a more powerful nation.

Mussolini Set Up a Fascist Dictatorship in Italy

In 1919, Mussolini formed his own political party—the **Fascist Party.** The Fascists, or members of the Fascist Party, organized their own army. By 1922, the Fascists were growing stronger, and they were threatening to take over control of Italy. King Victor Emmanuel the Third of Italy was forced to ask Mussolini to become the prime minister of the Italian government.

As soon as Mussolini became prime minister, he began to set up a Fascist dictatorship in Italy. The Fascists soon began to arrest Italians who disagreed with them. By 1926, Mussolini was known as **il Duce** (ILL DOO-chay), the leader, or dictator, of Italy.

PEOPLE IN HISTORY

Benito Mussolini

"Mussolini is always right." All Italians have to do is "obey, believe, and fight." Signs like these were found all over Italy during the 1920's and 1930's. The person who made these signs was the dictator of Italy—Benito Mussolini (buh-NEE-toh MOOS-uh-LEE-nee), who was called "il Duce."

Mussolini always talked about rebuilding the Roman Empire. However, few people in Italy or in Europe believed that he meant it. But Mussolini himself knew that he really meant it. In 1935, he attacked Ethiopia, and a few years later he entered World War Two as an ally of Germany. However, the Italian armies were defeated in the war.

The Italian king arrested Mussolini and planned to turn Mussolini over to the Allies. Then Mussolini was rescued by the German army. However, when the Germans left Italy, Mussolini was captured by Italian patriots. Soon after, Mussolini was killed by these Italians. The man who had led Italy to war was murdered by his own people.

Question: What nation did Mussolini attack in 1935?

After three years of bloody civil war, General Francisco Franco's supporters won control, and in 1939 General Franco became the dictator of Spain

Spain Was Ruled Mainly by Dictators

After World War One, Spain still had a monarch, but the real ruler of Spain was General Primo de Rivera (rih-VERR-uh), who ruled as a dictator. But when Rivera died in 1930, Spain changed its government and became a republic.

But the Spanish Republic did not last long. It lasted only from 1931 to 1936. In 1936, General Francisco Franco (FRAN-koh) led a revolt against the government of the Republic. After three years of bloody civil war, Franco's supporters won control, and in 1939 General Franco became the dictator of Spain. General Franco would continue to rule Spain for the next three decades.

SUMMING UP

After World War One ended, many nations in eastern and southern Europe set up democratic governments. However, none of these governments lasted long. Germany took over Austria in 1938 and Czechoslovakia in 1939. Hungary and Poland set up dictatorships soon after the war. The Balkan nations were too poor to solve their many problems, and they also became dictatorships. Italy also set up a dictatorship government led by Benito Mussolini and the Fascist Party. In Spain, a civil war ended in a dictatorship led by General Franco. In the next chapter, you will read about events in China from 1870 to 1934.

UNDERSTANDING THE LESSON

Do You Know These Important Terms?

For each sentence below, choose the term that best completes the sentence.

1. The political party formed by Benito Mussolini in Italy was called the (Vox Populi/Fascist Party).
2. (Il Duce/Caesar) was a name given to the leader, or dictator, of Italy.

Do You Remember These People and Events?

1. Tell something about each person.

   Nicolas Horthy
   Tomás Masaryk
   Eduard Benes
   Joseph Pilsudski
   Benito Mussolini
   Victor Emmanuel the Third
   General Primo de Rivera
   General Francisco Franco

2. Explain how or why each of the following developments took place.

   a. Austria, Hungary, Czechoslovakia, and Poland set up democratic governments, but these governments did not last.
   b. Dictator governments were set up in most of the Balkan nations.
   c. Dictatorships were set up in Italy and in Spain.

Can You Locate These Places?

Use the map in Chapter 94 (page 616) to locate the following places. Tell how each place is related to the events in this chapter.

Austria	Hungary
Czechoslovakia	Poland
Lithuania	Yugoslavia
Rumania	Italy
Spain	Germany

Do You Know When It Happened?

What important event took place in each of the following years?

1936   1938

Do You Remember the Main Idea?

Which one of the following ideas is the MAIN IDEA of this chapter?

1. After World War One, all the nations of Europe set up democratic governments, but these governments were soon taken over by dictators.
2. After World War One, many nations in eastern and southern Europe set up democratic governments. But these governments did not last long.
3. After World War One, many nations set up democratic governments, but these nations were soon taken over by Germany.

What Do You Think?

From what you have read in this chapter, answer the following thought questions.

1. What conditions in a nation seem to favor a dictator's rise to power?
2. In which nation that you read about in this chapter would you have liked to live after World War One? Give reasons for your answer.

Chapter 98
China in the Modern World

GETTING STARTED

1 In an earlier chapter, you read that European nations in the 1800's had forced China to trade with them. Some European nations, as you remember, even took over parts of China. However, in the late 1800's and early 1900's, the Manchu dynasty was still in control of the government of China. And the Manchu dynasty wished to keep foreign powers and new ideas out of China.

As you can see on the time line at the bottom of this page, the developments in this chapter cover the years between 1870 and 1934. During these years, the Manchu dynasty was overthrown, and China began to develop into a modern nation.

2 Before you begin reading the chapter lesson, survey the lesson. Begin your survey by reading the beginning of the lesson. Then look through the lesson and read the headings. Next, study the pictures and read the picture captions. Finally, read the review section called "Summing Up." This survey will help you to discover the important ideas in this chapter.

Know the Main Idea

As you read the chapter lesson, try to remember the following important MAIN IDEA of the chapter.

During the late 1800's, European nations tried to gain control of China. But in 1912, the Chinese Republic was set up and China began to develop into a modern nation.

The following questions will help you to understand the MAIN IDEA. Try to answer these questions as you read the lesson.

1. Which powerful nations took over territory in China by the late 1800's?
2. Who became the first president of the Chinese Republic?
3. Where did most changes take place in the new Chinese Republic?

Know These Important Terms

Open Door Policy
Boxer Rebellion
Young China
Nationalist People's Party

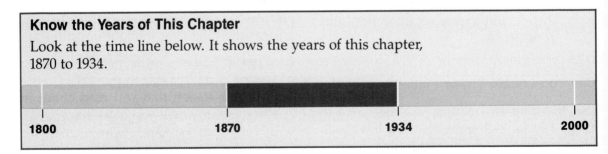

Know the Years of This Chapter
Look at the time line below. It shows the years of this chapter, 1870 to 1934.

| 1800 | 1870 | 1934 | 2000 |

Tz'u-hsi, Empress of China (1835-1908)

EXPLORING THE TIME

By the late 1800's, China was still ruled by the Manchu dynasty. The Manchu dynasty wished to preserve the old Chinese ways of life in China. But many people wanted China to develop some new ways of living and to become a modern nation. In this chapter, you will learn how China developed into a modern nation.

By the Late 1800's, European Nations Partly Controlled China

If you recall, the Manchu dynasty wished to keep all foreigners out of China. But by the late 1800's, many nations of Europe were becoming very interested in China as a source of trade. They wished to sell their manufactured goods to China, and they wished to buy raw materials from China for their factories.

Before long, some nations demanded special trading rights from China. Soon, several European nations tried to control China's trade. After 1870, Russia moved into Manchuria, the northern part of China. And in the 1890's Russia, France, Germany, and Great Britain demanded and won more trading rights, the right to build railroads, and the right to set up naval bases in China.

America's Open Door Policy Helped to Save China's Independence

The government of the United States worried that China might soon lose its independence. In 1899, John Hay, the American Secretary of State, sent official letters to the European nations that controlled Chinese territory. He asked these nations not to take over any more Chinese territory and to protect the independence of China. Hay also requested that all nations be allowed to have equal trading rights in China, whether they controlled any part of China or not. This American plan for China was called the **Open Door Policy.** The Open Door Policy resulted in more nations trading with China.

A Rebellion Against Foreigners in China Failed

By the 1890's, the supporters of the Manchu dynasty were becoming determined to force all Europeans to leave China. Some of these Manchu supporters set up secret societies, or groups, called "Boxers." In 1899, the Boxers attacked and killed some Europeans in China. During this **Boxer Rebellion,** the Boxers destroyed a great deal of property owned by Europeans in China. But the Boxers were soon defeated by an army

of soldiers sent by Japan, the European nations, and the United States.

After the Boxer Rebellion, China was forced to pay a large amount of money to the Europeans who suffered damage in the Boxer Rebellion. China also had to allow Europeans to settle in a part of Beijing, its capital city. And China had to allow foreign soldiers to remain in certain Chinese cities.

China Became a Republic in 1912

After the Boxer Rebellion failed, a group of young Chinese called **Young China** began to demand the overthrow of the Manchu dynasty. The Young China members wanted China to become as modern as the European nations. And they believed that the Manchu dynasty was preventing China from becoming a modern nation.

In 1911, a revolt against the Manchu dynasty broke out. The leader of this revolt was Sun Yat-sen (SOON YAHT-SEN), a Chinese doctor who was supported by the Young China group and other groups that favored modern ideas. The revolt succeeded. The Manchu dynasty was overthrown, and a Chinese Republic was set up in 1912. Sun Yat-sen became the first president of the Chinese Republic.

Chiang Kai-shek Tried to Unite China

Sun Yat-sen was the head of the **Nationalist People's Party** or Nationalist Party. The Nationalist Party favored democracy and freedom for China. But Sun Yat-sen was not able to unite the Chinese Republic. Between 1912 and 1926, one Nationalist Party leader after another led China's government, and the Chinese Republic became weaker. As a result, China was divided up among many

The Chinese Boxers were defeated by an army sent to China by foreign nations. What was this conflict called?

Chinese war lords, or Chinese bandit generals.

However, in 1925, Chiang Kai-shek (CHANG KY-SHEK), an army general, became the leader of the Nationalist Party. By 1927, Chiang Kai-shek was strong enough to reconquer much of China's lands from the Chinese war lords.

During the early 1920's, Communist armies were able to reconquer some territory in southern China. But in 1934, Chiang's armies forced the Chinese Communist armies to give up some of their land and move into the northwestern part of China.

China Became a More Modern Nation After 1912

After China became a republic, it slowly began to develop into a modern nation. The government set up a new money system for all of China. The Chinese system of laws was improved. And the government raised money by charging tariffs, or taxes, on foreign goods, and by making the Chinese people pay an income tax.

Other important changes took place in China, too. In Chinese cities, the family group lost some of its importance, and

President Chiang Kai-shek (center) helped to build China into a modern nation

Chinese women were allowed more freedom. Now books from Europe began to be read and to replace the writings of Confucius. However, most of these changes took place in the large Chinese cities. In the rest of China, most Chinese people continued the old Chinese ways of living.

SUMMING UP

By the late 1800's, China was partly controlled by European nations interested in trading with China. In 1899, the supporters of the Manchu dynasty tried but failed to force all Europeans to leave China. Then in 1911, the Manchu dynasty was overthrown. The Chinese Republic was set up under President Sun Yat-sen. Under Chiang Kai-shek, a Nationalist army leader, China became stronger and more united. By the 1930's, China began to develop into a modern nation. In the next chapter, you will learn how the freedom movement, or an attempt to achieve national independence, developed in Asia and in Africa.

UNDERSTANDING THE LESSON

Do You Know These Important Terms?

For each sentence below, choose the term that best completes the sentence.

1. America's plan to allow all nations to have equal trading rights in China was called the (**John Hay Policy/Open Door Policy**).
2. The attempt by the supporters of the Manchu dynasty to force Europeans out of China was called the (**Manchu Rebellion/Boxer Rebellion**).
3. The (**Chinese Nationalists/Young China**) was a group of young Chinese who wanted to overthrow the Manchu dynasty.
4. The (**Chinese People's Party/Nationalist People's Party**) supported democracy and freedom for China.

Do You Remember These People and Events?

1. Tell something about each of the following persons.

   **John Hay   Chiang Kai-shek
   Sun Yat-sen**

2. Explain how or why each of the following developments took place.

   a. America's Open Door Policy saved China's independence.
   b. China became a republic in 1912.
   c. Chiang Kai-shek tried to unite all of China.

Can You Locate These Places?

Use the map in Chapter 85 (page 559) to locate each of the following places. Tell what each of these places is.

**Manchuria   Beijing
Shanghai   Guangzhou
Hong Kong**

Do You Know When It Happened?

Why is the following year important in China's history?

1912

Do You Remember the Main Idea?

Which one of the following ideas is the MAIN IDEA of this chapter?

1. During the late 1800's, European nations tried to gain control of China. But in 1912, the Chinese Republic was set up, and China began to develop into a modern nation.
2. The United States helped to protect the independence of China and helped to set up a democratic government in China.
3. After the Chinese Republic was formed, China became more modern. But the Chinese who lived outside the cities continued to live as they had lived before.

What Do You Think?

From what you have read in this chapter, answer the following thought questions.

1. Do you think the United States was right to help China keep its independence through the Open Door Policy? Explain.
2. Do you think that the foreign nations had a right to punish China as a result of the Boxer Rebellion? Give your reasons.
3. Why do you think China was slow in becoming a modern nation?

Chapter 99

The Freedom Movement in Asia and Africa

GETTING STARTED

1   In earlier chapters, you read about the large empires formed by Great Britain, France, and other European nations in Asia and Africa during the late 1800's.

After World War One, many peoples in the colonies of these empires hoped to gain more freedom and to set up their own governments. As you will see, some peoples in Asia and Africa did gain a limited freedom in the years between 1885 and 1939. But most of these peoples were not allowed to govern themselves.

2   Before you begin reading the chapter lesson, survey the lesson. Begin your survey by reading the beginning of the lesson. Then look through the lesson and read the headings. Next, study the pictures and read the picture captions. Then study the map of the Middle East in 1939 on page 648. Finally, read the review section called "Summing Up." This survey will help you to discover the important ideas in this chapter.

Know the Main Idea

As you read, try to remember the following important MAIN IDEA of the chapter.

After World War One, many people in Asia and Africa worked to gain their freedom from European control. Although some of the peoples gained more freedom, few gained complete independence.

The following questions will help you to understand the MAIN IDEA. Try to answer these questions as you read the lesson.

1. Who was the leader of India who tried to win more freedom for India?
2. What land in Southeast Asia became self-governing in 1934?
3. What Arab nations won almost complete independence by the 1930's?

Know These Important Terms
  Indian National Congress
  home rule
  passive resistance
  Government of India Act

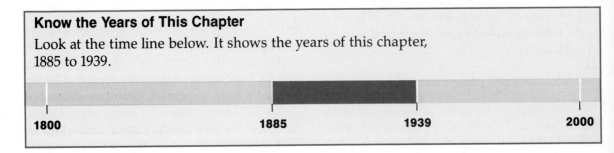

Know the Years of This Chapter

Look at the time line below. It shows the years of this chapter, 1885 to 1939.

| 1800 | 1885 | 1939 | 2000 |

Arabs in Morocco

EXPLORING THE TIME

In planning for the peace after World War One, President Woodrow Wilson of the United States spoke of the "self-determination" of nations—the freedom of each nation to determine, or choose, its own form of government. After World War One ended, the peoples of Asia and Africa hoped to be allowed to choose their own governments. In this chapter, you will find out how the peoples of Asia and Africa worked for self-government and independence.

The People of India Began to Work for Self-Government

For some years after the Sepoy Rebellion of 1857, India was peaceful. But by the 1880's, more and more people in India wanted the right to have a better education and to have a more important part in the government of

DOCUMENTS IN HISTORY

Mohandas Gandhi

For many years, Mohandas Gandhi was editor of a weekly magazine, *Young India.* He often wrote articles about the spinning wheel and how it could help in the Indian struggle for independence.

Gandhi believed that everyone should spin a thread for at least half an hour each day. Those who had no food could sell the thread they made to buy bread. The rich people and the leaders would learn what it felt like to do the work of common people. And if everyone wore clothes made from homespun cloth, India would not need to depend on Britain for fabric.

The following is from an article Gandhi wrote on January 1, 1925.

For me, the spinning wheel is not only a symbol of simplicity and economic freedom, but it is also a symbol of peace. For if we achieve the universalization of the wheel in India, we shall also have the self-confidence and organizing ability which make violence wholly unnecessary for regaining our freedom...

Question: Why was the spinning wheel important to Gandhi?

India. In 1885, these people formed a political party called the **Indian National Congress.**

The Indian National Congress gained some improvements for the people of India. By the early years of the 1900's, Great Britain began to allow the people of India to have a greater part in the government of India. In return, India gave a great deal of aid to Great Britain during World War One.

Mohandas Gandhi Became India's Leader for Independence

During World War One, the Indian National Congress demanded that Great Britain give India **home rule,** or complete self-government, after the war in return for India's aid during the war. In 1919, Great Britain did allow the people of India a greater share in ruling themselves. But it did not allow India to have home rule. The National Congress refused to accept anything but home rule. Its leader, Mohandas Gandhi (moh-HAHN-dus GAHN-dee), demanded home rule for India.

But Gandhi believed that India must not use force or violence to fight for independence. Instead, Gandhi told his followers to use **passive resistance** against Great Britain. Passive resistance meant that the people of India were to use only peaceful means to try to end British rule. These peaceful means included not buying British goods, not voting in British-held elections, and not paying taxes to the government.

India Won Almost Complete Independence

Gandhi's plan of passive resistance slowly succeeded. During the 1920's and 1930's, all of India demanded independence from Great Britain. Finally, in 1935, Great Britain passed a new **Government of India Act.** This law gave the people of India almost complete home rule, or self-government. But most people in India were still not satisfied. And they continued to work for India's complete independence from Great Britain.

The Nations of Southeast Asia Also Worked for Self-Government

After World War One, the nations of Southeast Asia also demanded complete independence. But the only nation in Southeast Asia that gained some independence after World War One was the Philippine Islands.

The Philippine Islands had been taken over by the United States in 1898, after the Spanish-American War. At that time, the American government began to prepare the Philippine people to govern themselves. Then in 1934, the United States gave the Philippine Islands self-government. However, the Philippine Islands did not become completely independent until 1946.

Turkey Kept Its Independence After World War One

After World War One, the Turkish Empire was broken up, and it appeared that the Turkish Empire might be taken over and divided up by the Allies. But in 1923, the Turkish sultan, or ruler, was overthrown, and Turkey became a republic. The leader of this revolution was a general named Mustafa Kemal (keh-MAHL). Kemal became known as Kemal "Ataturk," or "father of the Turks." Kemal was determined to make Turkey become a strong modern nation.

Throughout Turkey, new factories and railroads were built, farming methods were improved, and new schools were opened to teach the Turks modern ideas, including the European alphabet and calendar. By 1938, when Kemal's rule ended, Turkey was becoming a modern nation.

Some Arab Nations Won Almost Complete Independence by the 1930's

Before World War One, the Turkish Empire ruled the Arab states located in the Near East (or Middle East). But when the old Turkish Empire was split up after the war, the Arab states expected to be given their independence. Instead, France took over the Arab state of Syria (including Lebanon), and Great Britain took over Iraq (ih-RACK) and Trans-Jordan, two other Arab states. In addition, Great Britain also took over Palestine, which later was made partly into a homeland for the Jews.

During the 1920's and 1930's, the Arab nations began to fight for their independence. By the mid-1930's, the Arab nations of Egypt, Iraq, Saudi Arabia, and Yemen became almost completely independent from Great Britain.

Many Africans Began to Demand Independence After World War One

In northern Africa, revolts took place against French rule, but they were not successful. However, the movement for African freedom continued. In other parts of Africa, many Africans began to demand self-government. These Africans formed national political groups, or associations, in almost all the African colonies ruled by European nations. The efforts of the strong African national groups helped to prepare the way for the independence of many African colonies in later years.

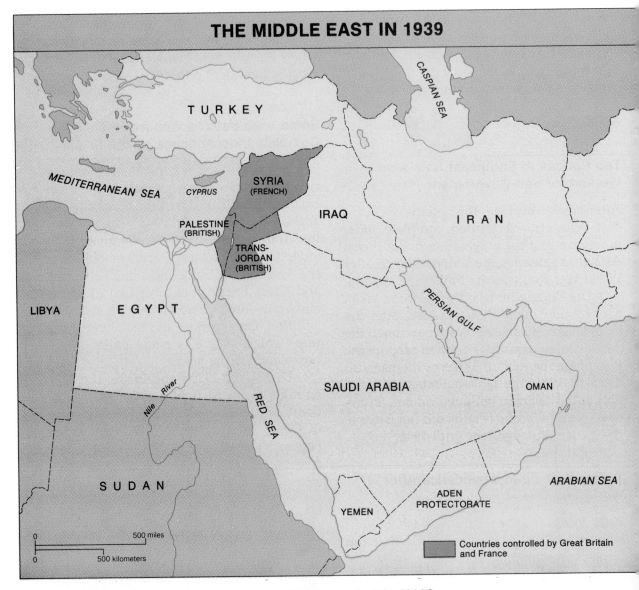

THE MIDDLE EAST IN 1939

MEDITERRANEAN SEA

TURKEY

CYPRUS

CASPIAN SEA

SYRIA
(FRENCH)

IRAQ

IRAN

PALESTINE
(BRITISH)

TRANS-
JORDAN
(BRITISH)

LIBYA

EGYPT

Nile River

RED SEA

PERSIAN GULF

SAUDI ARABIA

OMAN

SUDAN

ARABIAN SEA

YEMEN

ADEN
PROTECTORATE

0   500 miles

0   500 kilometers

Countries controlled by Great Britain
and France

Which Middle Eastern countries were not independent in 1939?

SUMMING UP

After World War One ended, many nations in Asia and Africa demanded independence from European control. India, the Philippine Islands, and some Arab nations gained almost complete independence during the 1930's. But the other nations in Africa and Asia were not able to win their independence. In the next chapter, you will read about the problems that soon led to another great world war.

UNDERSTANDING THE LESSON

Do You Know These Important Terms?

For each sentence below, choose the term that best completes the sentence.

1. The political party that wanted the people of India to have a better education and to have a part in the government of India was the **(Indian National Congress/People's Freedom Party)**.
2. Complete self-government is called **(home rule/auto-government)**.
3. Peaceful methods used by the people of India against British rule were called **(passive resistance/non-violence pact)**.
4. The **(Government of India Act/Indian National Constitution)** gave India almost complete self-government.

Do You Remember These People and Events?

1. Tell something about each of the following persons.

   Mohandas Gandhi   Mustafa Kemal

2. Explain how or why each of the following developments took place.

   a. The nations in Southeast Asia worked for independence, but most of them were not successful.
   b. Turkey developed into a more modern nation.
   c. Some Arab nations won almost complete independence by the 1930's.

Can You Locate These Places?

Use the map on page 648 to locate the following countries. Tell how each country is related to the events in this chapter.

Turkey	Syria
Iran	Iraq
Trans-Jordan	Egypt
Saudi Arabia	Yemen

Do You Know When It Happened?

What are the years of this chapter?

Do You Remember the Main Idea?

Which one of the following ideas is the MAIN IDEA of this chapter?

1. After World War One, many nations in Asia and Africa were given greater freedom because of their part in the war.
2. India was the only new nation in Asia given complete independence after World War One.
3. After World War One, many peoples in Asia and Africa worked to gain their freedom from European control. Although some of the peoples gained more freedom, few gained complete independence.

What Do You Think?

From what you have read in this chapter, try to answer the following thought questions.

1. Do you think passive resistance is better than revolution as a way to bring about change? Explain your answer.
2. Do you think people using passive resistance should break the law? Give reasons for your answer.
3. Why do you think many nations were not ready for self-government after World War One?

Unit 21

World War Two and the Years After

THE CHAPTERS IN UNIT 21 ARE

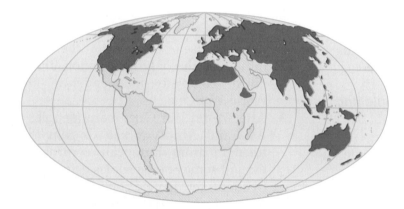

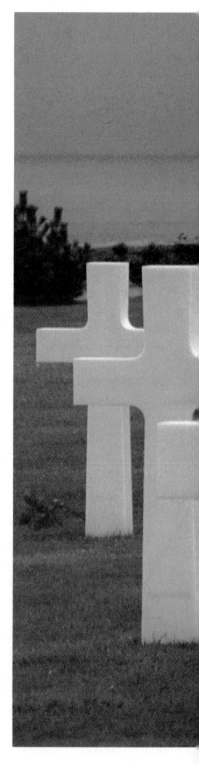

Many new problems developed in the world after World War One. These problems finally led to another worldwide struggle—World War Two. Then when World War Two ended, a new kind of world struggle began—the cold war. In this unit, you will find out about the causes and the results of World War Two and the cold war.

American cemetery at the site of the invasion beaches at Normandy, France

Chapter 100

World Problems in the 1920's and 1930's

GETTING STARTED

1   As you know, keeping peace in the world is a difficult task. The main purpose of the League of Nations, which was set up after World War One, was to try to keep world peace. In the years of the 1920's and 1930's, the League did help to keep peace among nations. But even in these years, problems were developing in the world which the League was not able to solve.

2   Before you begin reading the chapter lesson, survey the lesson. Begin your survey by reading the beginning of the lesson. Then look through the lesson and read the headings. Next, study the pictures and read the picture captions. Finally, read the review section called "Summing Up" at the end of the lesson. This survey of the whole lesson will help you to discover the important ideas in this chapter.

Know the Main Idea

As you read the chapter lesson, try to remember the following important MAIN IDEA of the chapter.

During the 1920's and 1930's, the League of Nations and the nations of the world worked to prevent war. But problems developed among nations and became a danger to peace.

The following questions will help you to understand the MAIN IDEA. Try to answer these questions as you read the lesson.

1. Why was the League of Nations too weak to back up its decisions?
2. Which nations suffered from the high tariffs charged by many other nations?
3. How did the weapons race among nations become a danger to peace?

Know These Important Terms

> tariff
> **Washington Conference**
> **Kellogg-Briand Pact**

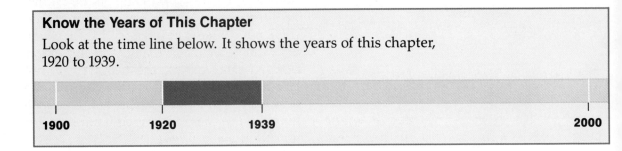

Know the Years of This Chapter
Look at the time line below. It shows the years of this chapter, 1920 to 1939.

| 1900 | 1920 | 1939 | 2000 |

A plenary assembly of the League of Nations in Geneva, Switzerland in 1929

EXPLORING THE TIME

What was the world like after World War One ended? Were the nations of the world able to keep peace? How did the League of Nations try to keep world peace? In this chapter, you will find out about the problems that became dangers to world peace in the 1920's and 1930's.

The League of Nations Had Serious Weaknesses

In an earlier chapter, you read how the League of Nations was set up to prevent war. In the 1920's and 1930's, the League of Nations held many meetings to talk over world problems and to try to solve them.

The League of Nations did settle several disputes between small nations. But the League of Nations was weak. One reason for the League's weakness was that it did not have armies to back up its decisions. Another reason for its weakness was that the United States never joined the League of Nations. Without the powerful support of the United States, the League was not able to succeed. And as you will learn in the next chapter, the weaknesses of the League kept the League from carrying out its main duty of preventing war.

The 1920's were difficult years for most Europeans. Why were these people marching?

War Debts and a High American Tariff Caused World Problems in the 1920's

At the end of World War One, the Allied nations owed the United States 10 billion dollars for the war supplies that they bought from the United States during the war. During the 1920's, these nations were able to pay their war debts by using the money given to them as reparations, or damage payments, by Germany. They also raised money to pay their war debts by selling goods to the United States.

In 1929, the great worldwide depression began. Germany was not able to pay its reparations to the Allies. At the same time, the United States raised its **tariff**, or tax, on foreign goods that came into the United States. This higher tariff on foreign goods made it difficult for European nations to sell their goods to the United States. This loss of American trade added to the hardships many European nations already were suffering from during the depression.

High Tariffs Became a Danger to Peace

The nations of western Europe also raised their tariffs after 1929. These higher tariffs caused serious problems, especially for Italy and Japan. Italy and Japan lacked coal, oil, and other raw materials that they needed for their factories. Therefore, they had to buy these raw materials from other nations.

During the 1920's, Italy and Japan obtained the money to buy raw materials by selling their manufactured goods. But when many nations raised their tariffs on foreign goods after 1929, Italy and Japan were not able to sell enough of their manufactured goods to buy all the raw materials that they needed. In the next chapter, you will learn how Italy and Japan set out to get raw materials by conquering lands that had the raw materials they needed.

The Arms Race Became a Danger to Peace

In 1921, leaders from nine nations met at Washington, D.C. At this **Washington Conference,** Great Britain, Japan, and the United States agreed to stop building large warships. This agreement helped to slow down the navy-building race among nations that began after World War One.

However, none of the larger European nations was willing to cut down the size of its armies or to limit the use of weapons. Many people feared that this arms-building race, or build-up of armies and weapons, was leading to another war.

In 1928, the United States, France, and several other nations signed an agreement called the **Kellogg-Briand Pact.** In this agreement, these nations promised to settle all disputes by peaceful means. As a result, many people in the world believed that the danger of war was ended.

American president Calvin Coolidge (left) signing the Kellogg-Briand Pact for the United States

Workers in German tank factories were required to build tanks as quickly as possible

But in the 1930's, the world learned that Germany, led by Adolf Hitler, was building up its army. Soon the other nations of Europe began to build up the size and strength of their armed forces. The new arms race soon became a danger to world peace in the 1930's.

Boundary Changes in Europe Became a Danger to Peace

By the 1930's, the Treaty of Versailles' boundary changes also became a danger to peace. If you recall, the Treaty of Versailles changed the boundary lines of many European nations. Some of the new boundary lines separated people of the same nationality. For example, many Germans now were part of the new nations of Czechoslovakia and Poland because land was taken away from Germany to set up these nations.

By the 1930's, many of the Germans living in Czechoslovakia and Poland were demanding that their territory be returned to Germany. As you will see, these boundary problems helped to lead to another war.

SUMMING UP

After World War One, the League of Nations, the Washington Conference of 1921, and the Kellogg-Briand Pact of 1928 all tried to prevent new wars. But during the 1920's, many problems arose in the world that were dangers to peace. These problems included unpaid war debts, higher tariffs, the build-up of armies and navies, and nationality problems that resulted from the new European boundary lines set up by the Treaty of Versailles. In this next chapter, you will find out how these problems soon helped to lead nations into another great world war.

UNDERSTANDING THE LESSON

Do You Know These Important Terms?

For each sentence below, choose the term that best completes the sentence.

1. A tax on goods that come into a country from other countries is called a **(tariff/revenue)**.
2. At the **(Tokyo Conference/Washington Conference)**, Great Britain, Japan, and the United States agreed to stop building large warships.
3. The **(Nemann Pact/Kellogg-Briand Pact)** was an agreement by the United States, France, and other nations promising to settle all disputes by peaceful means.

Do You Remember These People and Events?

Explain how or why each of the following developments took place.

a. The League of Nations had serious weaknesses.
b. Japan and Italy suffered most from the high tariffs charged by other nations after 1929.
c. The weapons race became a danger to world peace.
d. Some of the new boundary lines in Europe fixed by the Treaty of Versailles separated people of the same nationality.

Do You Know When It Happened?

In what year did the great worldwide depression begin?

Do You Remember the Main Idea?

Which one of the following ideas is the MAIN IDEA of this chapter?

1. During the 1920's and 1930's, the League of Nations and the nations of the world worked to prevent war. But problems developed among nations and became a danger to peace.
2. The worldwide depression caused hard times in all nations. The League of Nations was not able to solve this problem.
3. The League of Nations kept peace in the world for a while. But soon Italy and Japan left the League and set out to conquer new territory.

What Do You Think?

From what you have read in this chapter, answer the following thought questions.

1. Which of the following things do you think were the greatest danger to world peace—the weakness of the League of Nations? war debts? high tariffs? weapons race? or boundary changes? Explain your answer.
2. Do you think that the nations of the world really tried to prevent war after World War One? Give reasons for your answer.
3. The boundary lines of many new nations of Europe were fixed at the end of World War One. As you have read, some of these boundary lines separated people of the same nationality by placing them in two or three different countries. Do you think boundary lines can be drawn to please all nations? Give reasons for your answer.

GETTING STARTED

1   By the early 1930's, some nations became a danger to world peace because of their actions. The two nations that were the greatest danger were Japan and Italy. And Germany also began to prepare for war. Between 1931 and 1939, these nations gradually ended the peace plan set up by the Treaty of Versailles. And in 1939 another world war began in Europe.

2   Before you begin reading the chapter lesson, survey the lesson. Begin your survey by reading the beginning of the lesson. Then look through the lesson and read the headings. Next, study the pictures and read the picture captions. Then study the map showing the Axis Powers in 1939 on page 660. Finally, read the review section called "Summing Up" at the end of the lesson. This survey will help you to discover the important ideas in this chapter.

Know the Main Idea

As you read the chapter lesson, try to remember the following important MAIN IDEA of the chapter.

The warlike actions of Japan, Italy, and Germany during the 1930's led the way to World War Two.

The following questions will help you to understand the MAIN IDEA. Try to answer these questions as you read the lesson.

1. What part of China did Japan attack and take over in 1931?
2. What was Hitler's plan for Germany?
3. How did World War Two finally begin?

Know These Important Terms

racism	Munich Conference
Axis Powers	Allies

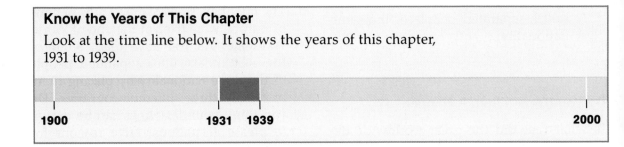

Know the Years of This Chapter
Look at the time line below. It shows the years of this chapter,
1931 to 1939.

| 1900 | 1931 1939 | 2000 |

English children during the bombing of London by the German Air Force

EXPLORING THE TIME

On September 3, 1939, World War Two—the war that everyone feared was coming —finally began. But the first move toward World War Two began earlier. It began in 1931, when Japan attacked China. In this chapter, you will find out how Japan's attack on China started the events that led to World War Two.

Japan Attacked China in 1931

In the last chapter, you learned that high tariffs after 1929 prevented Japan from selling many of its manufactured goods to other nations. As a result, Japan was not able to buy from other nations the many raw materials that it needed for its factories. Soon, Japan decided to conquer the lands that had the raw materials it needed.

In 1931, Japan attacked and took over Manchuria in the northern part of China. China asked the League of Nations for help against Japan, but the League members did not send help. Instead, they only asked Japan to remove its army from China. Japan refused to agree to the League's request. A few years later, Japan conquered more new territory in China.

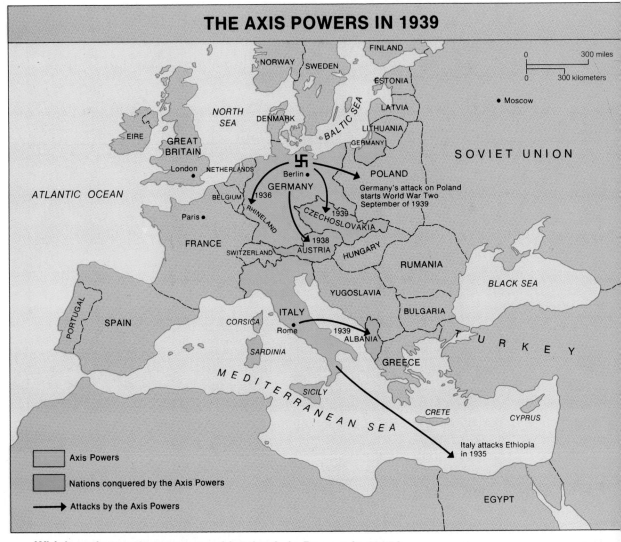

THE AXIS POWERS IN 1939

NORWAY
SWEDEN
FINLAND
ESTONIA
LATVIA
LITHUANIA
GERMANY
SOVIET UNION
Moscow
NORTH SEA
DENMARK
BALTIC SEA
EIRE
GREAT BRITAIN
London
NETHERLANDS
Berlin
GERMANY
POLAND
Germany's attack on Poland starts World War Two September of 1939
ATLANTIC OCEAN
BELGIUM
1936
RHINELAND
1939
CZECHOSLOVAKIA
Paris
1938
AUSTRIA
HUNGARY
FRANCE
SWITZERLAND
RUMANIA
BLACK SEA
YUGOSLAVIA
BULGARIA
PORTUGAL
SPAIN
CORSICA
ITALY
Rome
1939
ALBANIA
GREECE
TURKEY
SARDINIA
MEDITERRANEAN SEA
SICILY
CRETE
CYPRUS
Italy attacks Ethiopia in 1935
EGYPT

0   300 miles
0   300 kilometers

- Axis Powers
- Nations conquered by the Axis Powers
- → Attacks by the Axis Powers

Which nations were conquered by the Axis Powers in 1939?

Italy Attacked Ethiopia in 1935

Italy also became a danger to peace. In the 1890's, Italy had tried but failed to take over the African nation of Ethiopia (EE-thee-OH-pee-UH). Now in 1935, Italy, ruled by dictator Mussolini, attacked Ethiopia again.

Haile Selassie (HY-lee suh-LASS-ee), the emperor of Ethiopia, asked the League of Nations to help. The League ordered its members to stop selling war supplies to Italy. But oil was not included in the list of war supplies not to be sold. This meant that Italy was able to buy the oil it needed for the Italian tanks and planes attacking Ethiopia! By 1936, Ethiopia was conquered.

Hitler Prepared Germany for War

As you have already read, Adolf Hitler set

up a dictatorship in Germany in 1933. Hitler planned to build Germany into a "super state," or a nation that was powerful enough to conquer all of Europe and perhaps the whole world.

Hitler's Nazi government soon took control of all schools, newspapers, and magazines in Germany. It also took over the movie industry and all radio stations. Everyone in Germany was forced to accept the Nazi Party's ideas. Anyone who refused to accept Nazi ideas or who opposed Hitler was arrested.

Hitler Taught Germans to Believe They Were a "Super Race"

One of Hitler's most dangerous ideas was **racism**. Racism is the belief that one race, or group of people, is better than all other races. Although scientists proved that this idea was false, Hitler tried to make the Germans believe that they were members of a "super race," which was called the "Aryan race." Because the Germans were a "super race," Hitler said, the Germans must destroy "weaker" peoples who were not Aryans. The Jews were the main people Hitler wished to destroy. As the world learned later, more than ten million people, including six million Jews, were killed in the Holocaust—Hitler's plan to destroy other races.

Germany Began Its Plan of Conquest

By 1936, Hitler built up the German army, navy, and air force into one of the strongest armed forces in Europe. And in that year, the German army made its first move toward conquering Europe. It moved into the Rhineland, or the territory along the Rhine River in western Germany. As you recall, the Treaty of Versailles forbade the German army from entering the Rhineland.

HIGHLIGHTS IN HISTORY

Neville Chamberlain (left) and Hitler

By 1938, Hitler had decided to take over Czechoslovakia. His first step was to stir up the Germans who lived in the Sudetenland, a part of Czechoslovakia. The Sudeten Germans began to demand that their land be taken away from Czechoslovakia and given to Germany.

Neville Chamberlain, the prime minister of Great Britain, and Edouard Daladier, the prime minister of France, wanted the Czech government to give in to Hitler. However, the Czech government refused, and it prepared to defend its territory. It looked as if war would soon break out.

Then, on September 29, 1938, Chamberlain and Daladier met with Hitler and Mussolini at Munich. No Czech government leader was allowed to attend this meeting, known as the Munich Conference. The Munich Conference lasted only one day. When it was over, the Czechs found out that Chamberlain and Daladier had given in to Hitler. Germany was allowed to take the Sudetenland. War had been prevented —but not for long.

Question: What part of Czechoslovakia did Hitler want?

In 1939, the German army marched into Prague, the capital of Czechoslovakia

The German army's takeover of the Rhineland worried Great Britain and France, but they did nothing to stop Hitler. Then, in 1936, Germany and Italy signed an alliance, or agreement, and called themselves the **Axis Powers.** This agreement gave Germany a strong ally, or friend, in Germany's plan for conquest.

Hitler Soon Took Over Austria and Czechoslovakia

In 1938, Hitler's troops took over Austria. Next, Hitler demanded the Sudetenland (SOO-DAYT-un-LAND), a rich industrial part of Czechoslovakia where many Germans lived. Great Britain and France hoped that if Hitler's demands were satisfied, war might be prevented. In September of 1938, British and French leaders met with Hitler at the **Munich Conference** and agreed to give the Sudetenland to Germany. In return, Hitler promised not to take over any more European territory. But in March of 1939, Hitler broke his promise. He took over not only the Sudetenland, but all of Czechoslovakia! And in April of 1939, Italy—Germany's ally—invaded Albania.

Hitler Attacked Poland, and World War Two Began

Then on August 23, 1939, Germany and the Soviet Union (Russia) signed a treaty to divide up the nations of eastern Europe. On September 1, 1939, German troops marched into Poland. Great Britain and France now knew that Hitler intended to conquer all of Europe. On September 3, 1939, Great Britain and France—called the **Allies**—declared war against Germany. World War Two now began.

SUMMING UP

The first move toward World War Two really began in 1931, when Japan attacked China and took over Manchuria. In 1936, Mussolini's Italy conquered the African nation of Ethiopia. And in 1936, Germany took over the Rhineland. Germany soon took over Austria and Czechoslovakia, too. Then Hitler signed an agreement with the Soviet Union to divide up eastern Europe. World War Two began when Hitler attacked Poland in 1939, and Great Britain and France declared war on Germany. In the next chapter, you will read how the Axis Powers were defeated by the Allies in World War Two.

UNDERSTANDING THE LESSON

Do You Know These Important Terms?

For each sentence below, choose the term that best completes the sentence.

1. **(Racism/Civil Rights)** is the false belief that one race, or group of people, is better than all other races.
2. Germany and Italy became the **(Central Powers/Axis Powers)** when they signed an alliance, or agreement, in 1936.
3. The meeting at which the British and French leaders gave the Sudetenland to Hitler and Hitler promised not to take over any more European territory was called the **(Munich Conference/Rhine Conference)**.
4. Great Britain and France in 1939 were called the **(Allies/Axis)**.

Do You Remember These People and Events?

1. Tell something about each of the following persons.

   **Benito Mussolini   Adolf Hitler
   Haile Selassie**

2. Explain how or why each of the following developments took place.

   a. Japan and Italy took over the territory of other nations.
   b. Adolf Hitler tried to build up a "super nation" and a "super race."
   c. Germany took over Austria and Czechoslovakia, and invaded Poland.

Can You Locate These Places?

Use the map on page 660 to locate the following places. Explain how each place is related to events in this chapter.

Italy   Albania
Austria   Czechoslovakia
Rhineland   Poland
Germany   Soviet Union

Do You Know When It Happened?

Why is the following date important?

   September 3, 1939

Do You Remember the Main Idea?

Which one of the following ideas is the MAIN IDEA of this chapter?

1. World War Two began when Hitler took over Austria and Czechoslovakia, and then invaded Poland.
2. Italy and Japan were forced to invade the territory of other nations because they were not able to obtain all the raw materials they needed.
3. The warlike actions of Japan, Italy, and Germany during the 1930's led the way to World War Two.

What Do You Think?

From what you have read in this chapter, try to answer the following thought questions.

1. Do you think a nation is ever right in taking territory away from another nation? Explain your answer.
2. Why do you think that Hitler's ideas about a "super race" were dangerous? Explain your answer.
3. Why do you think Germany and Italy called themselves the Axis Powers?

Chapter 102

The Allies' Victory in World War Two

GETTING STARTED

1 World War Two started in September of 1939, and it ended in September of 1945. At first, the Axis Powers were well prepared to fight a war and the Allies were not prepared. And it looked as if the Axis Powers were going to succeed in conquering the world. But slowly the Allies' armies were able to push the Axis armies back toward their own territory. Finally, in 1945, the Axis Powers were forced to surrender.

The years from 1939 to 1945 (see the time line below) were war years. You will read about the main events of World War Two in this chapter.

2 Before you begin reading the chapter lesson, survey the lesson. Begin your survey by reading the beginning of the lesson. Then look through the lesson and read the headings. Next, study the pictures and read the picture captions. Then study the maps showing World War Two in Europe and in Asia on pages 666 and 668. Finally, read the review section called "Summing Up" at the end of the lesson. This survey of the whole lesson will help you to discover the important ideas in this chapter.

Know the Main Idea

As you read the chapter lesson, try to remember the following important MAIN IDEA of the chapter.

At first, the Axis Powers were winning World War Two. Then in 1941, the United States entered the war and helped the Allies to win the final victory.

The following questions will help you to understand the MAIN IDEA. Try to answer these questions as you read the lesson.

1. Which nation of the Allies was not invaded and conquered by the German "blitzkrieg"?
2. How did the United States help the Allies before the United States entered the war?
3. What new weapon ended the war in the Pacific Ocean?

Know These Important Terms

blitzkrieg   Operation Overlord
Lend-Lease Act

Know the Years of This Chapter

Look at the time line below. It shows the years of this chapter, 1939 to 1945.

| 1900 | 1939 1945 | 2000 |

British Prime Minister Winston Churchill (left), American President Franklin Roosevelt (center), and Soviet Marshal Joseph Stalin led the Allies to victory over the Axis Powers

EXPLORING THE TIME

Blitzkrieg (BLITS-kreeg) is the German word for "lightning war." Few people knew the word "blitzkrieg" in 1939. But in 1940, after the German army "blitzkrieged" most of Europe, everyone knew that a "blitzkrieg" meant a swift and terrible war. In this chapter, you will learn how the Allies fought and defeated the Axis Powers in World War Two.

Germany Conquered Most of Western Europe

By the end of September of 1939, Germany and the Soviet Union occupied all of Poland. Then, in April of 1940, German troops took over Norway and Denmark. In May of 1940, Germany conquered the Netherlands (Holland), Luxembourg, and Belgium. And by the end of June of 1940, Germany overran France, and France was forced to surrender.

WORLD WAR TWO — VICTORY IN EUROPE

Describe the movement of the Allies' advances.

Great Britain Refused to Surrender

After France fell to Germany, Hitler now planned to conquer Great Britain. The German air force bombed British cities and factories every night for months. British factories were destroyed, and large parts of British cities were badly damaged.

But the British were far from defeated. Led by Prime Minister Winston Churchill, they fought bravely to defend their nation. The British Royal Air Force (R.A.F.) bombed many important targets in Germany and shot down hundreds of German planes. As a result, Hitler was forced to give up his plan to conquer Great Britain.

The Axis Powers Continued to Win in 1941

Meanwhile, the Axis Powers attacked northern Africa and the countries of southeastern Europe. By May of 1941, Greece and Yugoslavia were conquered by the Axis Powers. Then, in June of 1941, Hitler attacked his own ally, the Soviet Union (Russia)! By the end of 1941, the German army had conquered a large part of the Soviet Union.

The United States Helped the Allies

After France fell in 1940, the United States government realized that the United States faced great danger if Germany defeated Great Britain. Therefore, in 1941, the American Congress passed the **Lend-Lease Act** to help Great Britain.

The Lend-Lease Act made it possible for the United States to lend ships, airplanes, and other war supplies to Great Britain (and later to the Soviet Union and other nations fighting Germany). These nations were to pay back the United States at the end of the war.

The United States Entered the War on December 8, 1941

In September of 1940, Japan joined the Axis Powers. In July of 1941, Japan took over French Indo-China. Then Japan decided to attack the United States.

On December 7, 1941, Japanese airplanes suddenly bombed the American navy and air force base at Pearl Harbor, Hawaii. They also attacked American bases on other Pacific islands. On December 8, 1941, the United States declared war on Japan. Three days later, Germany and Italy declared war on the United States.

By 1943, the Allies Began to Win the War

American troops and weapons soon helped the Allies to win the war. In November of 1942, a large army of American, British, and Canadian troops landed in northern Africa. By May of 1943, the German and Italian armies in northern Africa surrendered.

Later in 1943, the Allies' army from northern Africa landed in southern Italy. Within a few months, the Italian government surrendered to the Allies. Earlier, in February of 1943, the German armies in the Soviet Union suffered a great defeat at the city of Stalingrad. Now the Soviet troops, aided by American supplies, began to push back the German armies toward Germany.

Victory in Europe Came on May 8, 1945

On June 6, 1944, **Operation Overlord** began. Operation Overlord was the Allies' long-planned invasion of Axis-controlled Europe. At dawn on June 6, the Allies' invasion army led by General Dwight D. Eisenhower landed in northern France, protected by thousands of bomber planes.

The Allies' invasion of Europe succeeded. By January of 1945, the Allies' army began to push the German army out of France and Belgium. By the spring of 1945, the Allies' army closed in on Germany from the west, while the Soviet army closed in from the east. On May 8, 1945, Germany surrendered, and World War Two ended in Europe.

Victory in Asia Came on August 14, 1945

In the Pacific, by early 1945, the Allies recaptured both the Philippines and the Japanese island of Okinawa (OH-kih-NAH-wah). But Japan still did not give up, and it

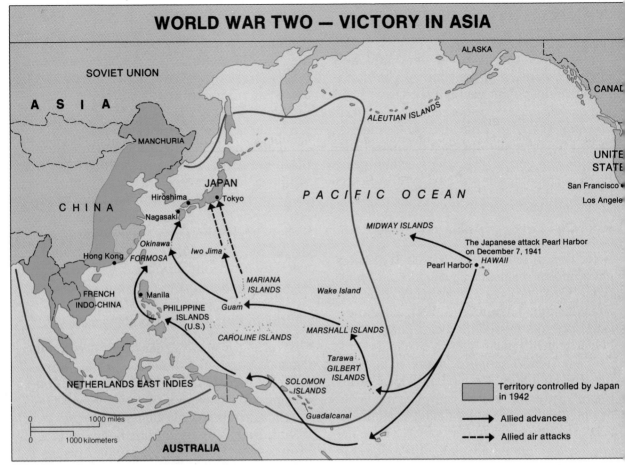

WORLD WAR TWO — VICTORY IN ASIA

ALASKA

SOVIET UNION

CANAD

A S I A

ALEUTIAN ISLANDS

MANCHURIA

UNITE
STATE

JAPAN

PACIFIC OCEAN

San Francisco

CHINA

Hiroshima

Tokyo

Los Angele

Nagasaki

MIDWAY ISLANDS

Okinawa

Iwo Jima

The Japanese attack Pearl Harbor
on December 7, 1941

Hong Kong FORMOSA

Pearl Harbor HAWAII

MARIANA
ISLANDS

Wake Island

FRENCH
INDO-CHINA

Manila

Guam

PHILIPPINE
ISLANDS
(U.S.)

CAROLINE ISLANDS

MARSHALL ISLANDS

Tarawa
GILBERT
ISLANDS

NETHERLANDS EAST INDIES

SOLOMON
ISLANDS

Territory controlled by Japan
in 1942

Guadalcanal

Allied advances

0   1000 miles

0   1000 kilometers

Allied air attacks

AUSTRALIA

Locate the cities of Hiroshima and Nagasaki.

appeared that the war might go on for years.

Therefore, to save the lives of thousands of American soldiers, President Harry S. Truman of the United States ordered that the atomic bomb be used on Japan. The atomic bomb was the most terrible weapon ever developed. On August 6, 1945, an atomic bomb was dropped on Hiroshima (HIR-uh-SHEE-muh). On August 9, a second atomic bomb was dropped on Nagasaki (NAH-gah-SAH-kee). These Japanese cities suffered terrible damage. A few days later, on August 14, 1945, the Japanese

government surrendered. On September 2, 1945, World War Two officially was over.

SUMMING UP

By 1941, France was defeated, and Great Britain was left to fight alone. Then in 1941, Hitler attacked the Soviet Union, and the United States entered the war after Japan attacked Pearl Harbor. The United States helped the Allies to win World War Two in 1945. In the next chapter, you will read about the peace after World War Two.

UNDERSTANDING THE LESSON

Do You Know These Important Terms?

For each sentence below, choose the term that best completes the sentence.

1. The swift and terrible war fought by the German armies was called a (**blitzkrieg/ powder keg**).
2. The (**Cash and Lend Act/Lend-Lease Act**) allowed the United States to lend ships, planes, and war supplies to the Allies.
3. The plan for the Allies' invasion of Axis-controlled Europe was called (**Operation Overlord/Manhattan Project**).

Do You Remember These People and Events?

1. Tell something about each person.

   Winston Churchill   Harry S. Truman

2. Explain how or why each of the following developments took place.

   a. Great Britain was not invaded by the Germans.
   b. The United States entered World War Two on December 8, 1941.
   c. The Germans surrendered when the Allies' army moved into Germany from the west and the Soviet army moved in from the east.

Can You Locate These Places?

Use the maps on pages 666 and 668 to do the following map work.

1. Name and locate the nations conquered by Germany by the end of 1941. What natural feature helped to protect Great Britain from being invaded by Germany?

2. In what part of Italy did the Allies' army land?
3. Locate Pearl Harbor. What islands did the Allies capture in the Pacific Ocean between 1942 and 1945?
4. Notice the Allies' invasion of Europe in 1944. In what country did the Allies' army land? Locate Stalingrad. Trace the Russian army's advance.

Do You Know When It Happened?

When did World War Two officially end?

Do You Remember the Main Idea?

Which one of the following ideas is the MAIN IDEA of this chapter?

1. At first, the Axis Powers were winning World War Two. Then in 1941, the United States entered the war and helped the Allies to win the final victory.
2. The United States entered World War Two after Japan attacked the Hawaiian Islands and other American bases in the Pacific.
3. The war in Europe came to an end after atomic bombs were dropped on two Japanese cities.

What Do You Think?

From what you have read in this chapter, answer the following thought questions.

1. What might have happened if Germany had conquered Great Britain?
2. Why do you think Operation Overlord was such an important plan?
3. How did the atomic bombs dropped on Japan help to end the war more quickly?

Chapter 103
The Peace After World War Two

GETTING STARTED

1   Even before World War Two ended, the leaders of the Allies began to plan for the peace. They remembered the problems after World War One and the weakness of the League of Nations. These leaders wanted to make a better plan to keep world peace. This chapter describes the new plan for peace after World War Two and tells how it was carried out between 1945 and 1947. See the time line below.

2   Before you begin reading the chapter lesson, survey the lesson. Begin your survey by reading the beginning of the lesson. Then look through the lesson and read the headings. Next, study the pictures and read the picture captions. Then study the map of Europe after World War Two on page 672. Finally, read the review section called "Summing Up" at the end of the lesson. This survey of the whole lesson will help you to discover the important ideas in this chapter.

Know the Main Idea

As you read the chapter lesson, try to remember the following important MAIN IDEA of the chapter.

The United Nations was organized to keep world peace. But the Soviet Union threatened peace by setting up Communist governments in many nations in eastern Europe.

The following questions will help you to understand the MAIN IDEA. Try to answer these questions as you read the lesson.

1. Who was leader of the Soviet Union during World War Two?
2. What is the purpose of the General Assembly in the United Nations?
3. What kind of government was set up in Japan after World War Two?

Know These Important Terms

Big Three   concentration camps
United Nations

Know the Years of This Chapter
Look at the time line below. It shows the years of this chapter, 1945 to 1947.

1900	1945 1947	2000

The United Nations was organized to keep world peace after World War Two. In what year was the United Nations founded?

EXPLORING THE TIME

You have already learned that making peace after a war is often harder than winning the war. This was certainly true after World War Two. During the war, the United States, Great Britain, and the Soviet Union worked together to defeat the Axis Powers. But these nations were not able to work together for peace after the war ended. In this chapter, you will find out about the search for peace after World War Two.

The Allied Leaders Began to Plan for Peace During the War

During the war, President Franklin D. Roosevelt of the United States, Prime Minister Winston Churchill of Great Britain, and Prime Minister Joseph Stalin of the Soviet Union met several times to plan for peace. At these meetings, these leaders of the **Big Three** nations—the United States, Great Britain, and the Soviet Union—talked over the problems of making peace once the war was over.

671

EUROPE AFTER WORLD WAR TWO — 1950

FINLAND

NORWAY

SWEDEN

• Moscow

NORTH
SEA

DENMARK

BALTIC SEA

SOVIET UNION

IRELAND

GREAT
BRITAIN

London •

NETHERLANDS

Berlin
•

EAST
GERMANY

• Bonn

Warsaw
•

POLAND

ATLANTIC
OCEAN

BELGIUM

• Paris

WEST
GERMANY

CZECHOSLOVAKIA

FRANCE

SWITZERLAND

AUSTRIA

HUNGARY

RUMANIA

BLACK SEA

PORTUGAL

Madrid
•

SPAIN

ITALY

• Rome

YUGOSLAVIA
(Not controlled by
the Soviet Union)

ALBANIA

BULGARIA

TURKEY

GREECE

•Athens

MEDITERRANEAN SEA

Free nations

Communist nations

Neutral nations

0   400 miles

0   400 kilometers

Compare this map with the map of Europe after World War One (page 616). Describe some differences you find.

Making peace provided a new set of problems: what to do about Germany, how to make new boundaries in Europe and Asia, and how to meet the need of setting up a new world organization to work for peace. But the Big Three leaders did not make final agreements on all these problems.

The United Nations Was Set Up in 1945

In April of 1945, leaders from fifty nations met at San Francisco, California. These leaders set up a new organization of nations to work for world peace. It was called the **United Nations,** or U.N.

The main agency, or part, of the U.N. was the Security Council. The Security Council was made up of five main nations—the United States, Great Britain, the Soviet Union, France, Nationalist China (Formosa)—and six smaller nations. The Security Council was given the power to use armed forces, if necessary, to keep peace among nations. However, each of the five main nations had to agree before the Council took any action. This rule weakened the Security Council because the Soviet Union often did not agree with the other four main nations.

Another agency of the U.N. was the General Assembly, which was made up of all the nations in the U.N. The General Assembly's main duty was to study and talk over world problems. The General Assembly also was to make suggestions to the Security Council about how to settle disputes between nations peacefully.

The U.N. also had an International Court of Justice. This court was set up to help settle legal disputes between nations.

The Soviet Union Began to Spread Communism

After World War Two ended, the United States, Great Britain, and France worked for world peace. But the Soviet Union was mainly interested in increasing its power and in spreading Communism. In eastern Europe, which was controlled by Soviet troops, the Soviet Union set up Communist governments in Poland, Rumania, and several other nations.

Germany Was Divided into West Germany and East Germany

After the peace conference in 1945, Germany became divided into two parts—West

Japanese surrender documents were signed on the American battleship, U.S.S. Missouri, by Foreign Minister Shigeonitsu in the name of the Japanese emperor

Germany and East Germany. The city of Berlin also was divided into two parts—West Berlin and East Berlin. The United States, Great Britain, and France had troops in West Germany. The Soviet Union had troops in East Germany. The Soviet Union also wished to take over West Germany. However, the other nations were determined to prevent the Soviet Union from doing this.

The Allies Worked Together to Punish the Nazi War Leaders

But the Soviet Union did work with the other nations to punish the Nazi war leaders. Toward the end of World War Two, the Allies' armies invading Germany and Poland discovered the terrible German **concentration camps,** or war prisons. The Nazis had used these concentration camps to kill 6 million Jews. The people of the world were shocked to learn of these terrible camps.

Surviving inmates of the Nazi concentration camps were liberated in 1945

When Germany surrendered in 1945, some Nazi leaders were captured. Great Britain, the United States, France, and the Soviet Union held trials to judge whether these Nazi leaders were guilty of war crimes. Several Nazi leaders were found guilty and were punished.

Japan Became a Democratic Nation

From 1945 to 1947, Japan was ruled by the United States Army. General Douglas Mac-Arthur was the leader of the American army in Japan.

The United States helped to set up a democratic government in Japan. In 1947, under a new constitution, the Japanese emperor remained the head of the Japanese government but now had little power. The real power of the Japanese government was given to a two-house legislature. All Japanese citizens were given the right to vote. And a bill of rights was written to protect the rights and freedoms of the Japanese people.

The business life of Japan also improved. Large farmlands were divided and sold to small farmers. The holdings of the few rich families who controlled most of Japan's industry were broken up. Soon Japan's business system began to grow strong again.

SUMMING UP

After World War Two ended, the United Nations was set up to work for world peace. But keeping peace was a difficult problem. After the war, the Soviet Union set up Communist governments in eastern Europe. The Soviet Union also tried to spread Communism to West Germany. In Japan, the American army, led by General Mac-Arthur, helped Japan to become a democratic nation. In the next chapter you will read about the growing worldwide struggle between the Soviet Union and the free nations.

674

UNDERSTANDING THE LESSON

Do You Know These Important Terms?

For each sentence below, choose the term that best completes the sentence.

1. During World War Two, Great Britain, the United States, and the Soviet Union were called the (**Three Giants/Big Three**).
2. The new organization of nations formed in 1945 to work for world peace was called the (**United Nations/Security Council**).
3. The war prisons where 6 million Jews were put to death were called (**concentration camps/occupation camps**).

Do You Remember These People and Events?

1. Tell something about each of the following persons.

   Franklin D. Roosevelt
   Joseph Stalin
   Winston Churchill

2. Explain how each of the following developments took place.

   a. The Security Council of the United Nations was weak.
   b. The Soviet Union spread Communism in eastern Europe.
   c. Japan became a democratic nation.

Can You Locate These Places?

Use the map on page 672 to do the following map work.

1. Locate and name the nations in Europe where Communist governments were set up.

2. Locate East and West Germany. Locate the city of Berlin. In which part of Germany is Berlin located? What problems did Berlin's location cause for Great Britain, France, and the United States?

Do You Know When It Happened?

What two important events took place in 1945?

Do You Remember the Main Idea?

Which one of the following ideas is the MAIN IDEA of this chapter?

1. The Soviet Union set up Communist governments in the countries of eastern Europe, and Germany was divided.
2. The United Nations was organized to keep world peace. But the Soviet Union threatened world peace by setting up Communist governments in many nations in eastern Europe.
3. After World War Two, many Nazi leaders in Germany were given a trial, and many of them were punished.

What Do You Think?

From what you have read in this chapter, answer the following thought questions.

1. Do you think any one nation should be able to stop the Security Council from acting?
2. Do you think a nation has the right to put people in concentration camps? Why or why not?
3. What problems do you think Japan had to solve before it was able to set up a democratic government?

Chapter 104
The Cold War

GETTING STARTED

1 In the last chapter, you read that Communist governments were set up in many nations in eastern Europe at the end of World War Two. The Soviet Union almost completely ruled these governments. These smaller nations ruled by the Soviet Union were called "Soviet satellites" because they were so completely controlled by the Soviet Union. In addition, the Soviet Union soon tried to spread Communism into other nations of Europe between 1945 and 1953. See the time line below.

2 Before you begin reading the chapter lesson, survey the lesson. Begin your survey by reading the beginning of the lesson. Then look through the lesson and read the headings. Next, study the pictures and read the picture captions. Finally, read the review section called "Summing Up" at the end of the lesson. This survey of the whole lesson will help you to discover the important main ideas in this chapter.

Know the Main Idea

As you read the chapter lesson, try to remember the following important MAIN IDEA of the chapter.

After 1945, the free nations of the world, led by the United States, tried to prevent the spread of Communism in Europe and Asia.

The following questions will help you to understand the MAIN IDEA. Try to answer these questions as you read the lesson.

1. How did the Truman Doctrine save Greece and Turkey from Communism?
2. Why did the Chinese government of Chiang Kai-shek move to Formosa?
3. What were the results of the Korean War?

Know These Important Terms

> cold war
> **Truman Doctrine**
> **Marshall Plan**
> **North Atlantic Treaty Organization**
> **Korean War**

Know the Years of This Chapter

Look at the time line below. It shows the years of this chapter, 1945 to 1953.

| 1900 | 1945 | 1953 | 2000 |

British Prime Minister Clement Attlee (left), American President Harry Truman (center), and Soviet Marshal Joseph Stalin attended a conference in Potsdam, East Germany, in July, 1945

EXPLORING THE TIME

During the years just after World War Two, a new kind of war developed—a war without weapons or soldiers. This new kind of war was called the **cold war**. The "cold war" was the name given to the struggle between the free nations of the world and the Communist nations. The cold war began in Europe, and then it spread to other parts of the world.

The Cold War Began in Eastern Europe

In the last chapter, you read that the Soviet Union set up Communist governments in many nations of eastern Europe after World War Two ended. In 1946 and 1947, the Soviet Union also tried to set up a Communist government in Greece, which had been greatly weakened during the war. And the Soviet Union also tried to take control of Turkey's water passage from the Black Sea into the Mediterranean Sea.

Marshall Plan aid helped Greece to rebuild after the War and to defeat Communism

But the United States was determined to stop Communism from spreading farther. In 1947, President Harry S. Truman of the United States promised to give American money and other aid to any European nation that was trying to defend itself against the Soviet Union. This plan was called the **Truman Doctrine**.

Beginning in 1947, the United States gave millions of dollars to Greece and Turkey. As a result, these nations were able to strengthen their governments, build up their armies, and feed their peoples. In this way, they were able to prevent the Communists from taking over these nations.

The United States Helped Build Up Europe

But President Truman and the American government realized that Communism was a serious danger to any nation whose people were poor and hungry. In fact, Commu-

nist leaders were winning many votes in France and Italy by promising these nations food and better times.

Therefore, later in 1947, the United States started the **Marshall Plan**, which was developed by Secretary of State George C. Marshall. The purpose of the Marshall Plan was to help European nations rebuild their cities, factories, and farms so that these free nations were not taken over by the Communists. Under the Marshall Plan, the United States loaned about 12 billion dollars to the governments of European nations to help them build up their farms and factories.

By 1950, the Marshall Plan was a great success. With American aid, many European nations began to recover from the damage of World War Two and began to enjoy good times again. And Communism did not spread to these free nations.

The Free Nations Formed a New Alliance Against Communism

In 1949, the free nations also took another important step to protect themselves against a Soviet attack. Twelve free nations —including Great Britain, France, Italy, the United States, and Canada—formed the **North Atlantic Treaty Organization**, or N.A.T.O. Each N.A.T.O. nation agreed to build up its armed forces and to help defend any other N.A.T.O. nation if it was attacked. The N.A.T.O. nations warned the Soviet Union not to try to spread Communism to the nations of western Europe.

The Communists Took Over China in 1949

However, Communism did spread in Asia. When you last read about the Chinese Communists, they had been pushed into northwestern China in 1934 by the army of

Chinese Communists, led by Mao Zedong (MAU zuh-DUNG), were strong enough to attack the government of Chiang Kai-shek.

The United States tried to bring peace between Chiang Kai-shek's armies and the Communist forces, but American peace efforts failed. By 1949, the Communists controlled nearly all of China, and Chiang Kai-shek was forced to move the Nationalist government and its army to the island of Formosa, off the mainland of China.

In October of 1949, the Communists renamed China the People's Republic of China, and Mao Zedong became its first president. But Communist China was really a dictatorship, and Mao Zedong was its dictator. As in all dictatorships, the people of Communist China had little freedom. During the period from 1949 to 1952, the government seized farmland from landlords against their will. In the process, it is estimated that up to several million landlords were killed.

U.N. Forces Stopped the Communists from Conquering South Korea

At the end of World War Two, the country of Korea was divided into two parts. South Korea was occupied by American troops. North Korea was occupied by Communist troops. The United States held free elections in South Korea. But North Korea was ruled by a Communist government.

In June of 1950, a Communist North Korean army attacked South Korea. The United Nations decided to send an army to help defend South Korea. This United Nations' army was made up largely of American troops. Communist China also sent troops to help North Korea.

The **Korean War,** as the fighting in Korea was called, lasted from 1950 to 1953.

GEOGRAPHY AND HISTORY

Berlin Airlift

After World War Two, Germany was divided into two parts, East Germany and West Germany. The city of Berlin was in East Germany, the part of Germany controlled by the Soviet Union. Berlin was also divided, and each part was controlled by a different nation. The Soviets occupied the central and eastern districts, while soldiers from the United States, France, and Britain occupied districts to the south, north, and west.

In 1948, the Soviet Union closed all roads, railroads, and waterways leading to Berlin. It wanted to force the other nations to leave Berlin. The United States reacted swiftly. American cargo planes from West Germany flew supplies to Berlin. Soon Britain and France joined the "Berlin airlift." More than a thousand flights a day brought food, coal, and other supplies to the people of Berlin.

A year later, the Soviet Union saw that its plans had failed. In 1949, it reopened the roads to Berlin and allowed goods to move freely into the city.

Question: How did the Berlin airlift save Berlin?

American soldiers played an important part in the defense of South Korea from 1950 to 1953

At the end of the war, the Communist forces still held North Korea. But they had been prevented from conquering South Korea.

SUMMING UP

After 1945, the free nations of the world led by the United States prevented the spread of Communism into western Europe. But in Asia, the Communists succeeded in conquering China. In 1949, a Communist government was set up in China led by Mao Zedong.

The Communists also tried to take over South Korea during the Korean War of 1950 to 1953. But United Nations' forces defended South Korea and preserved the independence of that nation. In the next chapter, which begins Unit 22, you will read about the modern nations of Asia.

UNDERSTANDING THE LESSON

Do You Know These Important Terms?

For each sentence below, choose the term that best completes the sentence.

1. The name given to the struggle between the free nations and the Communist nations was the (**N.A.T.O./cold war**).
2. The (**Truman Doctrine/UNESCO Plan**) gave American money and other aid to help the free European nations defend themselves against the Soviet Union.
3. The United States' program to help build up Europe's cities, factories, and farms destroyed by the war was called the (**MacArthur Plan/Marshall Plan**).
4. The (**North Atlantic Treaty Organization/National Alliance**) was an agreement by most of the free nations to help defend themselves against a Communist attack.
5. The fight to keep Communism out of South Korea was called the (**Korean War/War of the United Nations**).

Do You Remember These People and Events?

1. Tell something about each person.

   **Harry S. Truman   Chiang Kai-shek
   George C. Marshall   Mao Zedong**

2. Explain each of the following events.

   a. The nations of western Europe rebuilt after World War Two.
   b. The Chinese Communists took control of China in 1949.
   c. United Nations' forces stopped the Communists from taking over South Korea.

Can You Locate These Places?

Locate the nations listed with each of the following maps. Tell how each nation is related to the events in this chapter.

1. On the map in Chapter 103 (page 672):

   Greece   Turkey

2. On the map in Chapter 105 (page 686):

   **China   Formosa
   North Korea   South Korea**

Do You Know When It Happened?

What important events took place in the following years?

   1947   1949   1950

Do You Remember the Main Idea?

Which one of the following ideas is the MAIN IDEA of this chapter?

1. The Marshall Plan and the Truman Doctrine helped the nations of western Europe to defend themselves against Communism and to rebuild their nations.
2. United Nations' forces halted the spread of Communism into South Korea.
3. After 1945, the free nations of the world, led by the United States, tried to prevent the spread of Communism.

What Do You Think?

From what you have read in this chapter, answer the following thought question.

1. Why do you think that the N.A.T.O. nations were able to stop the spread of Communism in Europe?

Unit 22
The Post-War World

THE CHAPTERS IN UNIT 22 ARE

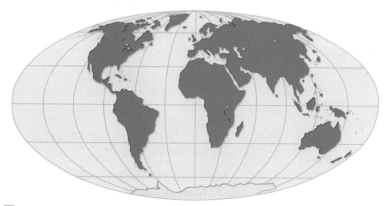

In the years after World War Two great changes took place all over the world. Many new nations of Asia and Africa won their freedom. And the older nations of the world became involved in the cold war struggle between democracy and Communism. In this unit, you will study the events of the cold war and learn about the new nations of the world.

National and international problems are regularly debated by Congress in the Capitol Building in Washington, D.C.

Chapter 105
The Modern Nations of Asia

GETTING STARTED

1   In the last unit, you discovered how a cold war developed between the free nations and the Communist nations after World War Two. This struggle continued in the 1950's and 1960's. In this chapter you will study the modern nations of Asia and learn how the cold war spread to Asia in the years after 1945. Look at the time line at the bottom of this page to see these years of modern history.

2   Before you begin reading the chapter lesson, survey the lesson. Begin your survey by reading the beginning of the lesson. Then look through the lesson and read the headings. Next, study the pictures and read the picture captions. Then study the map showing southern and eastern Asia today on page 686. Finally, read the review section called "Summing Up" at the end of the lesson. This survey will help you to discover the important ideas in this chapter.

Know the Main Idea

As you read the chapter lesson, try to remember the following important MAIN IDEA of the chapter.

The Chinese Communists took over China, but Communism was less successful in other nations of Asia.

The following questions will help you to understand the MAIN IDEA. Try to answer these questions as you read the lesson.

1. Why did the Chinese Communists become less friendly with the Soviet Union?
2. Into what two nations was British India divided?
3. How did the fighting in Vietnam begin?

Know This Important Term

Vietnam War

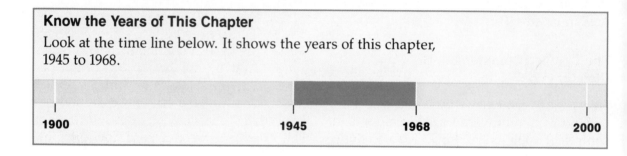

Know the Years of This Chapter
Look at the time line below. It shows the years of this chapter, 1945 to 1968.

| 1900 | 1945 | 1968 | 2000 |

Kuala Lumpur, the modern capital city of Malaysia. What are some signs that this is a modern city?

EXPLORING THE TIME

As you read earlier, the cold war was a struggle between the free nations and the Communist nations. This struggle between freedom and Communism continued, particularly in Asia. In this chapter, you will learn about developments in the nations of Asia in recent years.

The Chinese Communists Set Up a Dictatorship in China

As you may remember, by 1949 a Communist government under Mao Zedong was in control of mainland China. Mao Zedong and his followers set up a Communist dictatorship in China. Like the people of the Soviet Union, the Chinese people had little freedom. All Chinese people were forced to obey the government's orders.

Communist China Fought in Korea

During the Korean War, you recall, Communist China sent troops to fight for North Korea, but the Soviet Union did not send troops. And by the late 1950's, China became much less friendly toward the Soviet Union. The Chinese Communists now believed that the Soviet Communists were not trying hard enough to spread Communism.

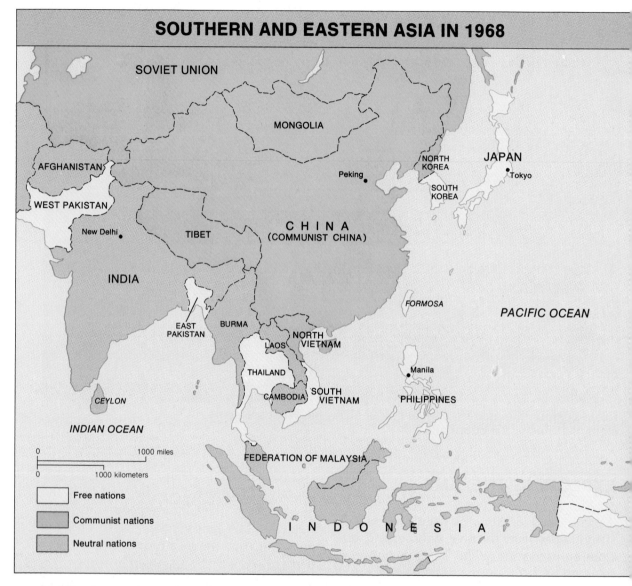

SOUTHERN AND EASTERN ASIA IN 1968

SOVIET UNION

MONGOLIA

AFGHANISTAN

WEST PAKISTAN

New Delhi

TIBET

CHINA
(COMMUNIST CHINA)

Peking

NORTH
KOREA

SOUTH
KOREA

JAPAN

Tokyo

INDIA

EAST
PAKISTAN

BURMA

LAOS

NORTH
VIETNAM

THAILAND

CAMBODIA

SOUTH
VIETNAM

CEYLON

INDIAN OCEAN

FORMOSA

PACIFIC OCEAN

Manila

PHILIPPINES

0   1000 miles

0   1000 kilometers

Free nations

Communist nations

Neutral nations

FEDERATION OF MALAYSIA

I N D O N E S I A

List the free nations of southern and eastern Asia in 1968

Japan Again Became Prosperous

As you read in Chapter 103, Japan developed into a democratic nation after its defeat in World War Two. By April of 1952, when the American army of occupation left Japan, the Japanese people were enjoying prosperity.

In the 1950's and 1960's, Japan was Asia's leading industrial nation. Japanese products, such as transistor radios, steel, and cameras, were traded throughout the world. Democracy in Japan also grew stronger.

In Chapter 117, you will read about Japanese exports in the 1970's and 1980's.

British India Was Split into India and Pakistan

At the end of World War Two, India was still ruled by Great Britain. One reason that India failed to win independence was that the Hindus and Muslims in India refused to be united under the same government.

In 1947, British India split into two independent nations—India and Pakistan (PAH-kih-STAN). India was controlled by the Hindus. Pakistan was controlled by the Muslims. Both nations became republics, and both became members of the British Commonwealth of Nations.

The Prime Minister of India from 1947 to 1962 was Jawaharlal Nehru (juh-WAH-hur-LAHL NAY-roo), a follower of Gandhi. In 1964, two years after Nehru died, Nehru's daughter, Indira Gandhi, became prime minister. The first leader of the Pakistan Republic was Mohammed Ali Jinnah (JIN-uh), a Muslim.

Pakistan and India were not able to settle many of their problems. But they did not go to war, because they both feared Communist China as their main enemy. In 1962, Communist China did attack India and took over some of India's northern territory.

The Nations of Southeast Asia Won Their Independence

After World War Two, many nations of Southeast Asia also became independent. The Philippine Islands received their independence from the United States in 1946 and became the Republic of the Philippines. Burma and Ceylon received their independence from Great Britain in 1948. And Malaya received its independence from Great Britain in 1957, and in 1963 it became known as the Federation of Malaysia.

Jawaharlal Nehru, a follower of Gandhi, became the first prime minister of India

Indonesia, the largest nation in Southeast Asia, won its independence from the Netherlands (Holland) in 1949. The new nation of Indonesia was ruled by President Achmed Sukarno (SOO-KAHR-noh) until 1965. Then Sukarno's government was overthrown, and a strong army government ruled Indonesia to prevent the Communists from gaining control of that nation.

War Broke Out in Vietnam

After World War Two, France gave limited independence to Laos (LAY-os) and Cambodia (kamm-BOH-dee-uh), two parts of French Indo-China. But Vietnam, another part of French Indo-China, demanded complete independence. In 1946, a war broke out between Vietnam and France. The people of Vietnam were led in this war by Ho Chi Minh (HOH CHEE MINN), a Vietnamese Communist leader, who was supported by Communist China.

But by 1954, the French forces in Vietnam were defeated, and Vietnam was

Sophisticated American helicopters were essential in attempts to rescue wounded soldiers in the jungles of Vietnam

divided into two parts—North Vietnam and South Vietnam. North Vietnam was ruled by Ho Chi Minh and the Communists. South Vietnam was ruled by leaders opposed to the Communists.

The United States Sent Troops to South Vietnam

In 1958, North Vietnam organized the Viet Cong, or Vietnamese Communists, to attack South Vietnam. South Vietnam fought this attack, but it failed to defeat the Viet Cong.

When the fighting in Vietnam began, President Eisenhower of the United States sent American army advisers to South Vietnam to help fight the Communists. President John F. Kennedy later sent more American advisers to aid South Vietnam. Then, in 1965, President Lyndon B. Johnson ordered that 200,000 American soldiers be sent to help South Vietnam fight the Communists. The **Vietnam War** now began.

In 1968, President Johnson tried to end this war by offering peace to North Vietnam. By then, 525,000 American soldiers were in South Vietnam. The Vietnam War was a long and terrible war.

SUMMING UP

After World War Two ended, the Communists tried to take over much of Asia. In China, the Communists set up a Communist dictatorship under Mao Zedong. The main trouble spots in Asia were Indo-China, Korea, and Vietnam. In the mid-1960's, the United States sent troops to South Vietnam to help defend that nation against Communist attack. In the next chapter, you will find out about the Middle East.

UNDERSTANDING THE LESSON

Do You Know This Important Term?

For the sentence below, choose the term that best completes the sentence.

1. The war that began in 1965 when American troops fought to defend South Vietnam was called the **(Viet Cong War/ Vietnam War)**.

Do You Remember These People and Events?

1. Tell something about each of the following persons.

   Mao Zedong   Achmed Sukarno
   Ho Chi Minh   Mohandas Gandhi
   Jawaharlal Nehru   President Johnson
   Indira Gandhi
   Mohammed Ali Jinnah

2. Explain how each of the following events took place.

   a. British India split into two nations— India and Pakistan.
   b. The nations of Southeast Asia won their independence.
   c. The United States fought to prevent the Communists from taking over South Vietnam.

Can You Locate These Places?

Use the map on page 686 to do the following map work.

1. Locate Southeast Asia. What new nations can you find there?
2. Name and locate the nations of Asia that have Communist governments. Name and locate the largest Communist nation and the largest free nation.

3. In what ways are Indonesia and Pakistan different from most of the nations in Southeast Asia?

Do You Know When It Happened?

In what year was British India split into India and Pakistan?

Do You Remember the Main Idea?

Which one of the following ideas is the MAIN IDEA of this chapter?

1. Beginning in 1965, the United States fought in Vietnam to keep Communism from spreading in Southeast Asia.
2. The Chinese Communists took over China, but Communism was less successful in other nations of Asia.
3. After World War Two, most of the nations of Southeast Asia gained their independence.

What Do You Think?

From what you have read in this chapter, try to answer the following thought questions.

1. What might be some problems faced by the government of a nation like Pakistan or Indonesia that is divided by geography into two or more parts?
2. Why is it important that Pakistan and India do not go to war against each other even when they disagree about important matters?
3. Why do you think the Chinese Communists were able to take over China?

GETTING STARTED

1 You may remember how the Middle East (or Near East) often has been one of the "trouble spots" of the world. Both in early times and in recent times, the Middle East has been important because of its location. As you know, three continents—Asia, Europe, and Africa—come together in the Middle East. Many land and ocean trade routes pass through the Middle East, especially trade routes that use the Suez Canal.

The Arab nations of the Middle East, like many other nations of the world, wanted to be independent nations. In this chapter, you will read about the new nations that were formed in the Middle East after World War Two. The events covered in this chapter took place from 1945 to 1968.

2 Before you begin reading the chapter lesson, survey the lesson. Begin your survey by reading the beginning of the lesson. Then look through the lesson and read the headings. Next, study the pictures and read the picture captions. Then study the map of the Middle East today on page 692. Finally, read the review section called "Summing Up." This survey will help you to discover the important ideas in the chapter.

Know the Main Idea

As you read the chapter lesson, try to remember the following important MAIN IDEA of the chapter.

The Middle East became a "troubled spot" because the Arab nations faced many problems and they were unwilling to accept the new nation of Israel.

The following questions will help you to understand the MAIN IDEA. Try to answer these questions as you read the lesson.

1. Which Arab nations became independent after World War Two?
2. What land of the Middle East became the homeland of the Jews during the 1920's and 1930's?
3. Why did Great Britain, France, and Israel send troops to attack Egypt in 1956?

Know This Important Term

Suez Canal

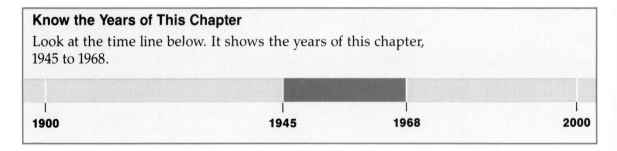

Know the Years of This Chapter

Look at the time line below. It shows the years of this chapter, 1945 to 1968.

| 1900 | 1945 | 1968 | 2000 |

Modern Arab oilfields provide much of the industrial world with the necessary energy to run machinery

EXPLORING THE TIME

What do the names "United Arab Republic" and "Israel" mean to you? Perhaps you remember these two nations better by their old names, Egypt and Palestine. As you know, these nations of the Middle East began long ago. In this chapter, you will learn about these nations and about their neighbors in the Middle East today.

The Arab Nations Developed Slowly

In the years after World War Two, most of the Arab states in the Middle East became independent nations. The Arab nations included the United Arab Republic (Egypt), Iran, Syria, Lebanon, Iraq, Jordan, Yemen, Saudi Arabia, and Kuwait (kuh-WAYT). The Arab nations were still not as well developed as most modern nations, and living conditions were difficult in the Arab nations.

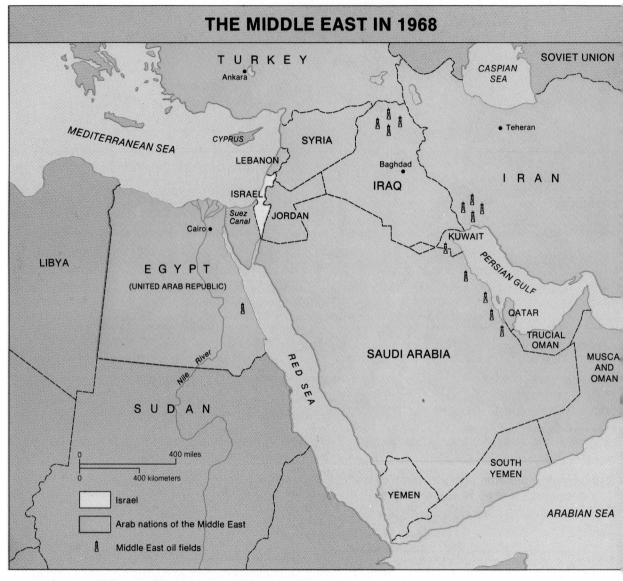

THE MIDDLE EAST IN 1968

Which countries shown on the map have oil fields?

The Middle East Became a Trouble Spot

After the Arab nations in the Middle East became independent, the Middle East was still not a peaceful place. One reason was that the Arab peoples of the Middle East were not prepared to govern themselves. Thus, many Arab governments were weak.

At the same time, a strong rivalry divided many of the Arab nations and leaders. The weakness of the Arab governments and their lack of unity also increased the danger of Communism spreading to these nations.

The rich oil fields, or oil lands, in the Middle East also made it a troubled area. In the years after 1945, the free nations feared that the Soviet Union might try to take over these oil fields. In fact, the Communist nations did encourage the Arab nations to turn against the free nations. As a result, the Middle East became a "trouble spot" in the world.

The Jews Claimed Palestine as Their Nation

One Middle Eastern nation, Palestine, had been settled by Jews as well as by Arabs. After World War One, Palestine was ruled by Great Britain, and Great Britain agreed to allow Palestine to become a Jewish homeland. However, the Arab nations never agreed to this plan because they wanted Palestine to be an Arab nation.

During the 1920's and 1930's, many Jews settled in Palestine. Then, after Hitler became the dictator of Germany, many Jews who escaped from Hitler's Germany went to Palestine to live. And after World War Two, still more European Jews wished to go to Palestine. But the Arab nations forced Great Britain to limit the number of Jews allowed to settle in Palestine.

The Jews Set Up the Nation of Israel in 1948

However, bloody fighting took place between the Arabs and the Jews. Therefore, Great Britain asked the United Nations to solve the Palestine problem.

At the end of 1947, the U.N. voted to partition, or divide, Palestine into two parts —an Arab part and a Jewish part. Great Britain accepted this plan, and Great Britain removed its troops from Palestine in the spring of 1948. The Jews then formed their part of Palestine into the independent nation of Israel.

PEOPLE IN HISTORY

David Ben-Gurion

In 1906, David Ben-Gurion (ben-GHOO-rih-yon) at the age of twenty went to Israel (then called Palestine) to build a Jewish homeland. Ben-Gurion proved to be a great leader. He helped set up the Jewish Legion, which fought on the Allies' side in World War One. He was also one of the founders of Palestine's strongest labor groups. By the 1940's, Ben-Gurion was regarded as the leader of the Jewish people in Palestine.

When the nation of Israel won its independence in 1948, Ben-Gurion became its first prime minister. As prime minister, he successfully defended Israel against Arab attack and built Israel into a strong new nation. After retiring as Israel's leader, the "Old Man," as he was fondly called, continued to lead the nation. He set an example for the young men and women of Israel by settling in the Negev—Israel's southern frontier desert land. In this way, Ben-Gurion showed his faith in the future greatness of Israel.

Question: When did Ben-Gurion become prime minister?

The 1967 Six-Day War between Israel and the Arab nations

also controlled the **Suez Canal,** a water canal joining the Mediterranean Sea and the Red Sea. Nasser wished to end this European control. In 1956, Nasser took over the Suez Canal, which had been controlled by Great Britain and France. Great Britain and France then sent troops into Egypt to try to retake the Suez Canal. Israel also invaded Egypt. But the United Nations ordered these nations to withdraw their troops from Egypt, and Egypt kept control of the Suez Canal.

The Arab Nations and Israel Went to War in 1967

After the 1956 Suez Canal fighting ended, President Nasser of Egypt became the chief leader of the Arab nations. But President Nasser was not able to unite, or bring together, all the Arab nations in the Middle East. And Israel and the Arab nations remained enemies. After many years of trouble, in June of 1967 Israel and the Arab nations went to war. This war lasted only six days, and Israel badly defeated Egypt, Syria, Jordan, and the other Arab nations. But the war settled few problems and the Middle East remained a world "trouble spot."

But the Arab nations refused to accept Israel as a new nation. Fighting began between Israel and the Arab nations in 1948. This fighting ended in a victory for Israel.

Egypt Became a Republic in 1953

The leaders of the army in Egypt blamed the Arabs' defeat by Israel on the dishonest government of Egypt's ruler, King Farouk (fuh-REWK). In 1952, King Farouk was overthrown, and Egypt became a republic the next year. By 1954, Gamal Abdel Nasser (NAHS-ur), a colonel in the Egyptian army, made himself the leader of the Republic of Egypt.

President Nasser tried to improve the lives of the Egyptian people. He broke up large farmlands in Egypt and divided the land among those Arabs who had owned no land. Nasser also tried to build up Egypt's industries, trade, and businesses.

Nasser Took Over the Suez Canal in 1956

However, European business owners controlled many Egyptian businesses. They

SUMMING UP

After World War Two, the Middle East became a "trouble spot" in the world. Some of the causes of trouble in the Middle East were the rivalry among the Arab nations and leaders, the weaknesses of the Arab governments, and the trouble between Israel and the Arab nations. In the next chapter, you will study the modern nations of Africa.

UNDERSTANDING THE LESSON

Do You Know This Important Term?

For the sentence below, choose the term that best completes the sentence.

1. The canal in Egypt that connects the Mediterranean Sea and the Red Sea is called the (Suez Canal/Panama Canal).

Do You Remember These People and Events?

1. Tell something about each of the following persons.

   King Farouk
   Gamal Abdel Nasser

2. Explain how or why each of the following events took place.

   a. The Middle East became a "trouble spot."
   b. The Arabs were opposed to the Jewish nation of Israel.
   c. Nasser was not able to unite the Arab nations.

Can You Locate These Places?

Use the map on page 692 to do the following map work.

1. Locate each of the following places and tell how each is connected to developments in this chapter.

Egypt	Syria
Iran	Lebanon
Jordan	Iraq
Yemen	Saudi Arabia
Kuwait	Israel

2. Locate the Suez Canal. What two large bodies of water does it connect? Why do you think the canal is used by many ships in their voyages between Europe and Southeast Asia?

Do You Know When It Happened?

What important events took place in the Middle East in the following years?

   1948   1956   1967

Do You Remember the Main Idea?

Which one of the follcwing ideas is the MAIN IDEA of this chapter?

1. The Middle East became a "trouble spot" because the Arab nations faced many problems and they were unwilling to accept the new nation of Israel.
2. The Arab nations in the Middle East gained their independence after World War Two, but they were not able to unite as a strong group of nations.
3. The nation of Israel was set up in the Middle East as a homeland for the Jews. But the Arab nations opposed Israel.

What Do You Think?

From what you have read in this chapter, answer the following thought questions.

1. Do you think nations of the Middle East have a right to take over oil companies that were set up there by American and European business owners?
2. Why do you suppose that the new Arab nations found it difficult to work closely together?
3. Why were the Arab nations and Israel not able to settle their problems?

Chapter 107

Nations of Modern Africa

GETTING STARTED

1 In this unit, you are learning about the events that happened in different parts of the world since 1945. In this chapter, you will read about many important developments in the nations of Africa.

The nations of Africa are located mainly south of the Sahara Desert and north of the Republic of South Africa. You will recall that before World War Two, most of these African lands were the colonies of European nations. In the years after the war, most of these African lands tried hard to become independent nations. By the late 1950's and early 1960's, nearly all these lands became free, independent nations.

2 Before you begin reading the chapter lesson, survey the lesson. Begin your survey by reading the beginning of the lesson. Then look through the lesson and read the headings. Next, study the pictures and read the picture captions. Then study the map of Africa today on page 698. Finally, read the review section called "Summing Up." This survey of the whole lesson will help you to discover the important ideas in this chapter.

Know the Main Idea

As you read the chapter lesson, try to remember the following important MAIN IDEA of the chapter.

Many nations of Africa became independent in the late 1950's and 1960's. These nations faced the problems of developing democratic governments and building up strong nations.

The following questions will help you to understand the MAIN IDEA. Try to answer these questions as you read the lesson.

1. Which nation of Africa was the first to gain independence after World War Two?
2. What choice did France give to the French colonies in Africa?
3. Why was the Belgian Congo not prepared to become an independent nation?

Know These Important Terms

Mau Mau
Organization of African Unity

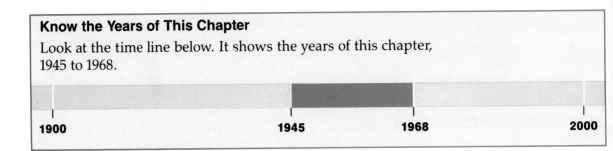

Know the Years of This Chapter

Look at the time line below. It shows the years of this chapter, 1945 to 1968.

| 1900 | 1945 | 1968 | 2000 |

Nairobi, Kenya, is one of the many modern cities of Africa

EXPLORING THE TIME

After 1945, a great independence, or freedom, movement began among the Black peoples of Africa. As this great struggle for freedom spread, nearly every nation of Africa gained its independence. In this chapter, you will learn about the problems faced by the Black peoples of Africa in winning independence for their new nations.

The African Independence Movement Spread After 1945

As early as 1847, the United States government helped to form the independent Black nation of Liberia (LEYE-beer-ee-uh) on the western coast of Africa. Liberia was started for Black Americans who wished to resettle in Africa.

But the modern movement for African independence really began after World War Two. At that time, many African peoples

NEW NATIONS OF AFRICA IN 1968

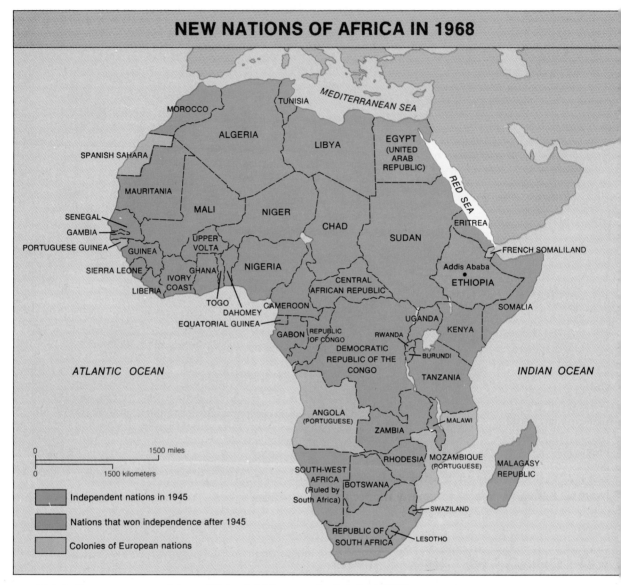

MEDITERRANEAN SEA

MOROCCO
TUNISIA
ALGERIA
LIBYA
EGYPT (UNITED ARAB REPUBLIC)
SPANISH SAHARA
RED SEA
MAURITANIA
SENEGAL
GAMBIA
PORTUGUESE GUINEA
MALI
NIGER
CHAD
SUDAN
ERITREA
FRENCH SOMALILAND
GUINEA
UPPER VOLTA
SIERRA LEONE
GHANA
IVORY COAST
LIBERIA
NIGERIA
CENTRAL AFRICAN REPUBLIC
Addis Ababa
ETHIOPIA
TOGO
DAHOMEY
CAMEROON
SOMALIA
EQUATORIAL GUINEA
GABON
REPUBLIC OF CONGO
UGANDA
RWANDA
KENYA
DEMOCRATIC REPUBLIC OF THE CONGO
BURUNDI
ATLANTIC OCEAN
TANZANIA
INDIAN OCEAN
ANGOLA (PORTUGUESE)
ZAMBIA
MALAWI
RHODESIA
MOZAMBIQUE (PORTUGUESE)
MALAGASY REPUBLIC
SOUTH-WEST AFRICA (Ruled by South Africa)
BOTSWANA
SWAZILAND
REPUBLIC OF SOUTH AFRICA
LESOTHO

0   1500 miles
0   1500 kilometers

Independent nations in 1945

Nations that won independence after 1945

Colonies of European nations

Which European countries still had African colonies in 1968?

began to demand that European nations allow their colonies in Africa to become independent. About ten years later, the first new independent nation in Africa was formed—the nation of Ghana (GAH-nuh).

Other African nations tried to gain their independence, too. Many of these nations succeeded in becoming independent.

Ghana Became the First New Independent African Nation After 1945

On March 6, 1957, Ghana, in western Africa, became the first new independent African nation. Great Britain gave Ghana its independence, and Ghana joined the British Commonwealth of Nations.

Ghana made important progress as a new nation. It set up an elected government headed by a president. Ghana's first president was Kwame Nkrumah (KWAH-may nuh-KROO-muh), a strong, capable leader. But Nkrumah sometimes ruled like a dictator and made many enemies. In 1966, he was overthrown by an army group, which took over the government of Ghana.

Other African Nations Won Their Independence

After World War Two, Great Britain also prepared its other African colonies for independence. In western Africa, Nigeria (NEYE-gheer-ee-uh) became independent in 1960, Sierra Leone (see-ERR-uh lee-OH-nee) became independent in 1961, and Gambia (GAM-bee-uh) became independent in 1965. In eastern Africa, Tanzania became independent in 1964. And the examples of these nations becoming free made other African nations determined to win their independence, too.

Kenya Also Won Its Independence

But the road to independence was much more difficult for Kenya (KEEN-yuh), another British colony in eastern Africa. In the 1950's, fighting broke out between an African group called the **Mau Mau** (MAWO-MAWO) and some British settlers. The Mau Maus were angry because British settlers still owned much of the land in Kenya. The Mau Maus wanted to take over this land, and they also wanted all British settlers to leave Kenya.

Kenya became independent in 1963, and Jomo Kenyatta (YOH-MOH ken-YAHT-tuh), a supporter of the Mau Maus, became Kenya's prime minister. As a result, the British citizens of Kenya feared trouble.

PEOPLE IN HISTORY

Jomo Kenyatta

Jomo Kenyatta (YOH-MOH ken-YAHT-tuh) was one of the great leaders of modern Africa and the founder of Kenya's independence. Kenyatta received a good education in Great Britain and wrote several books. But he became famous as the leader of the African people of Kenya.

In 1946, Kenyatta became the head of the Kenya African Union. When the British government refused to allow the African people their rights, a secret group called the Mau Mau began a civil war. Kenyatta said that he did not support the Mau Mau, but he was arrested by the British anyway.

For the next nine years, Kenyatta was kept in prison. Finally, he was set free, but he was not allowed to serve in the government. By 1963, the British were forced to give Kenya its independence. Kenyatta became Kenya's first prime minister. Kenyatta's wise government made Kenya a good place to live for both Kenya's Black citizens and its white citizens.

Question: What European nation ruled Kenya?

699

However, Prime Minister Kenyatta's government tried, at first, to treat all Kenya citizens fairly and equally.

France's African Colonies Became Independent

After 1945, the French government began to prepare most of its African colonies for self-government. In 1958, Charles de Gaulle (duh GOHL), the President of France, gave all the French colonies in Africa a choice. They were allowed to decide if they wanted to join the French Community—France's "commonwealth of nations." At first, all but one of these French colonies voted to join the French Community. Soon after, however, these colonies asked for independence. By 1960, all of these French colonies became independent African nations, including Chad, Niger, and Mali.

The Africans in the Belgian Congo Also Won Their Independence

Unlike Great Britain and France, Belgium did not prepare its colonies for independence. One of the most important colonies in Africa was the Belgian Congo. Belgium was determined to keep the Belgian Congo because it had many important raw materials. But when other African nations gained their independence, the people of the Congo also demanded their freedom from Belgium. Belgium finally agreed. In 1960, the Democratic Republic of the Congo was formed.

However, the African peoples in the Congo were not united. Two weeks after the Democratic Republic of the Congo was formed, the rich province of Katanga (kuh-TANG-guh) split away. Soon other Congo provinces refused to obey the Congo government, and fighting broke out.

The prime minister of the Congo, Patrice Lumumba (LUH-mum-BAH), was a Communist supporter, and he asked the Soviet Union for help. Many nations now feared that the Communists were taking over the Congo government. Finally, United Nations troops were sent to the Congo, and the danger of a Communist government soon ended. Before long, Katanga was again joined to the Congo. However, the Congo still faced many problems in governing its peoples.

The African Nations Set Up a Plan to Help Each Other

The new African nations began to realize that they needed to work together in order to grow stronger. In 1963, leaders from many independent African nations held a meeting in Addis Ababa (AH-dis AH-buh-BAH), the capital city of Ethiopia. At this meeting, the African leaders formed the **Organization of African Unity** (O.A.U.). The O.A.U. worked to help other African nations to win their independence. It also helped in developing the businesses and trade of African nations and helped to settle disputes, or disagreements, between African nations.

SUMMING UP

After 1945, many nations of Africa won their independence. These new nations faced many problems in governing themselves and in making their nations strong. But all of these nations showed the world that they were determined to try to solve their problems. In the next chapter, you will read about other nations in Africa whose governments were ruled by Europeans.

UNDERSTANDING THE LESSON

Do You Know These Important Terms?

For each sentence below, choose the term that best completes the sentence.

1. The group in Kenya that fought to force British settlers to leave was called the (Masai/**Mau Mau**).
2. The (**Organization of African Unity**/ Organization of Black States) was formed by new nations in Africa to help strengthen all African nations.

Do You Remember These People and Events?

1. Tell something about each of the following persons.

   Kwame Nkrumah   **Jomo Kenyatta**
   Charles de Gaulle **Patrice Lumumba**

2. Explain how or why each of the following developments took place.

   a. Gaining independence was much more difficult for Kenya than for other British colonies.
   b. The French colonies in Africa gained their independence.
   c. The Belgian Congo was not prepared for its independence, and it faced many problems.

Can You Locate These Places?

Use the map on page 698 to do the following map work.

1. Compare this map with the map in Chapter 88 (page 576). Name the nations of Africa that became independent after 1945. What were their names when they were colonies?
2. Locate the city of Addis Ababa in Ethiopia. What part did this city play in the events of this chapter?

Do You Know When It Happened?

In what year did Ghana become an independent nation?

Do You Remember the Main Idea?

Which one of the following ideas is the MAIN IDEA of this chapter?

1. Many nations of Africa became independent in the late 1950's and the 1960's. These nations faced the problems of developing democratic governments and building up strong nations.
2. Most nations in Africa gained their independence. Only the Congo had to fight for its independence.
3. Most of the nations of Africa were able to solve the problems that they faced as independent nations.

What Do You Think?

From what you have read in this chapter, answer the following thought questions.

1. What advantages did certain African nations enjoy if they remained a part of the British Commonwealth of Nations?
2. Why do you think the Communists were interested in the new nations of Africa in the years after World War Two?
3. Do you think a nation should be given its independence if it is not prepared for it?

Chapter 108

Other Nations of Modern Africa

GETTING STARTED

1 In the last chapter you learned about many of the nations of Africa that gained their independence in the late 1950's and the 1960's. This chapter tells about some other independent nations in Africa.

In the early 1950's, most of the northern part of Africa still was controlled by France. Most of the population of North Africa was made up of Arab people. In the southern part of Africa, Europeans controlled the most important nations. These Europeans did not believe that the Black people living in these nations should have rights equal to their own. In addition, a few lands in Africa were still colonies. You will read about all of these places and nations in Africa in this chapter.

2 Before you begin reading the chapter lesson, survey the lesson. Begin your survey by reading the beginning of the lesson. Then look through the lesson and read the headings. Next, study the pictures and read the picture captions. Finally, read the review section called "Summing Up." This survey will help you to discover the important ideas in this chapter.

Know the Main Idea

As you read the chapter lesson, try to remember the following important MAIN IDEA of the chapter.

The Arab nations of northern Africa also became independent nations. In southern Africa, Europeans controlled the governments of important new nations, and they did not give equal rights to Black citizens.

The following questions will help you to understand the MAIN IDEA. Try to answer these questions as you read the lesson.

1. Why did the Republic of South Africa leave the British Commonwealth?
2. What nation refused to free its African colonies?
3. Why did many people in Algeria want their land to remain a part of France?

Know These Important Terms

apartheid   segregation
African National
  Congress

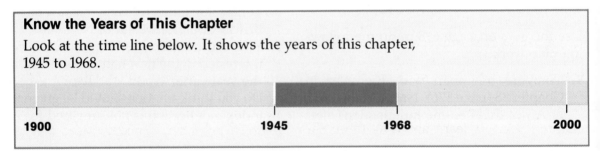

Know the Years of This Chapter

Look at the time line below. It shows the years of this chapter, 1945 to 1968.

| 1900 | 1945 | 1968 | 2000 |

Johannesburg is the largest city in South Africa. What is South Africa's policy of segregation called?

EXPLORING THE TIME

Many nations in Africa won independence in the late 1950's and the 1960's. In northern Africa, the Arab states also won their independence. In fact, only a few African lands did not become independent nations. But the governments of some African nations were controlled by Europeans who did not treat Black African citizens as equals. In this chapter, you will learn about all these nations of Africa.

South Africa Enforced Strict Segregation

The government of the Union of South Africa was controlled by its 3 million European settlers. The rest of the population —14 million people—was mainly Black Africans. In 1948, the European-controlled government of the Union of South Africa began a practice called **apartheid** (uh-PAHRT-hyt). Apartheid means **segregation**, or strict separation of people based on their race. This practice caused problems.

In 1948, the European-controlled government of the Union of South Africa began a practice called apartheid

Apartheid Caused Trouble in the Union of South Africa

The Black citizens of the Union of South Africa did not accept apartheid, or strict segregation. They formed a group called the **African National Congress** to fight against segregation. The African National Congress tried to use peaceful methods to fight against segregation.

The United Nations asked South Africa to end its segregation policy. And several nations within Africa refused to trade with South Africa until it agreed to end segregation. But the government of South Africa still refused to end its policy of segregation.

In 1961, the Union of South Africa became the Republic of South Africa. South Africa also left the British Commonwealth of Nations, because the other Commonwealth nations did not approve the way South Africa treated Black citizens.

Rhodesia Refused to Give Equal Rights to Black Africans

By the 1950's, the British colony of Rhodesia (roh-DEE-shuh) almost completely governed itself. But Black Africans were not allowed to serve in the government of Rhodesia or to have equal rights with the European citizens of Rhodesia. Great Britain was willing to give Rhodesia its complete independence if the Rhodesian government agreed to allow its African citizens equal rights. But the Rhodesian government refused.

In 1965, the Rhodesian government declared Rhodesia's independence from Great Britain. But Great Britain and the United Nations refused to accept Rhodesia as an independent nation, because Rhodesia still refused to allow its African citizens to have equal rights. As a result, Rhodesia's future as an independent nation remained undecided.

Portugal Refused to Free Its Colonies

Portugal did not allow its African colonies of Angola and Mozambique (MOH-zam-BEEK) to become independent. The Portuguese army and secret police worked hard to stop all attempts by the African peoples in these colonies to win independence. But the Black peoples in these colonies still continued to work for independence from Portugal.

Ethiopia Won Back Its Independence

Ethiopia (EE-thee-OH-pee-UH) was the oldest independent nation in Africa. You may remember, however, that in 1935 Italy conquered Ethiopia. The Italian troops remained in Ethiopia until 1941, when they were finally driven out by the British army. At that time, Ethiopia again became an independent nation.

Sudan Also Won Its Independence

As you learned in an earlier chapter, the Arab nation of Egypt won its independence from Great Britain in 1936. Before 1936, both Great Britain and Egypt had ruled

Uganda gained independence from Great Britain in 1962

Sudan, the nation directly south of Egypt. When Egypt became an independent nation, the Egyptians believed that they had the right to take over the complete rule of Sudan. However, Great Britain refused to allow Egypt to rule Sudan.

In 1956, Great Britain gave complete independence to Sudan. The government of Egypt was not pleased that Sudan became independent. But Egypt was forced to accept Sudan as an independent nation.

Morocco and Tunisia Won Their Independence from France

France had ruled most of Morocco since the early 1900's. But most of the population of Morocco were Arabs, who always wanted their independence. But it was not until 1955 that the Arabs of Morocco revolted against the French government. France failed to stop this revolt, and in 1956 Morocco became an independent kingdom.

The people of Algeria fought a civil war before their country won its freedom and independence from France

Tunisia, another of France's Arab colonies in northern Africa, also wanted its independence. Tunisia had been ruled by France since 1881. The people of Tunisia also won their independence from France in 1956.

Algeria Fought a Civil War to Win Its Independence

The fight for independence by Algeria, another French colony in north Africa, was a long and difficult struggle. Algeria had been ruled by France since 1830. Many more French citizens had settled in Algeria than in any other French territory in Africa. These French citizens wanted Algeria to remain a part of France. But the Arabs, who were the majority people of Algeria, wanted Algeria to have its independence.

This fight between the Arabs and the French settlers in Algeria became a bloody civil war in 1954. Finally, in 1960, President Charles de Gaulle of France promised independence to the Algerians. President de Gaulle's promise caused French citizens in Algeria to revolt against the French government. But this revolt ended in 1962, and Algeria became an independent nation.

SUMMING UP

The movement for freedom and independence spread to all parts of Africa. The Arab states of northern Africa that were governed by France won their independence. However, Portugal refused to give its African colonies the independence they wished. And the European-controlled governments of the Republic of South Africa and Rhodesia refused to allow Black citizens equal rights. In the next chapter, you will read about the modern nations of Latin America.

UNDERSTANDING THE LESSON

Do You Know These Important Terms?

For each sentence below, choose the term that best completes the sentence.

1. South Africa's policy of strict separation of people based on their race is called **(Rationalism/Apartheid)**.
2. **(Afrikaans/Segregation)** is a word that means the separation of people based on their race.
3. The organization of South Africa's Black citizens that fought against the separation of races was called the **(Non-Violence Union/African National Congress)**.

Do You Remember These Events?

1. Explain how or why each of the following developments took place.

   a. South Africa adopted a strict segregation policy that caused trouble for the nation.
   b. Rhodesia's future as an independent nation remained undecided.
   c. Algeria fought a war to win its independence.

Can You Locate These Places?

Use the map in Chapter 107 (page 698) to do the following map work.

1. Locate each of the following new African nations.

Republic of South Africa	Rhodesia
Sudan	Morocco
Tunisia	Algeria

2. According to the map, what lands in Africa have not yet gained their independence?

Do You Know When It Happened?

In what year did Algeria become an independent nation?

Do You Remember the Main Idea?

Which one of the following ideas is the MAIN IDEA of this chapter?

1. In the new nations of northern and southern Africa, the governments refused to give equal rights to Black citizens.
2. France and Great Britain granted independence to their African colonies, but the other European nations did not.
3. The Arab nations of northern Africa also became independent nations. In southern Africa, Europeans controlled the governments of important new nations, and they did not give equal rights to Black citizens.

What Do You Think?

From what you have read in this chapter, try to answer the following thought questions.

1. How do you think Black people in South Africa should be treated? Explain.
2. Why do you think Portugal refused to give independence to its African colonies?
3. If you had been a French colonist living in Algeria, would you have wanted Algeria to become an independent nation?

Chapter 109
Latin America in Modern Times

GETTING STARTED

1   Latin America is made up of the American nations located south of the United States. Latin America was settled, you recall, by Spanish and Portuguese settlers. You may also remember that many of the nations of Latin America won their independence shortly after the American Revolution. Unlike the United States, however, most of these nations were not able to set up democratic governments.

In this chapter, you will find out what happened in some of the Latin American nations in the years since 1945. (See the time line at the bottom of this page.)

2   Before you begin reading the chapter lesson, survey the lesson. Begin your survey by reading the beginning of the lesson. Then look through the lesson and read the headings. Next, study the pictures and read the picture captions. Then study the map of Latin America today on page 710. Finally, read the review section called "Summing Up." This survey will help you to discover the important ideas in this chapter.

Know the Main Idea

As you read the chapter lesson, try to remember the following important MAIN IDEA of the chapter.

In the years after 1945, the nations of Latin America developed their businesses, industries, and farms. But their governments were often controlled by dictators, and Communism was a danger.

The following questions will help you to understand the MAIN IDEA. Try to answer these questions as you read the lesson.

1. How did Mexico's new democratic constitution of 1917 help farmers and city workers?
2. Who became dictator of Cuba in 1958?
3. What is the purpose of the Organization of American States and the Alliance for Progress?

Know These Important Terms

    missile bases
    Organization of American States
    Alliance for Progress

Know the Years of This Chapter

Look at the time line below. It shows the years of this chapter, 1945 to 1968.

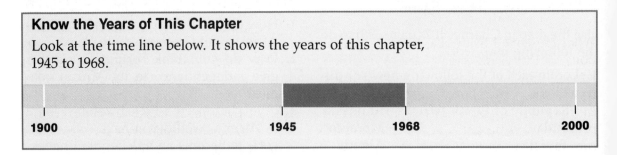

| 1900 | 1945 | 1968 | 2000 |

Once the site of the Aztec capital, Mexico City today is a modern metropolis with a population of over thirteen million people

EXPLORING THE TIME

What happened in the Latin American nations in the years after 1945? What problems did the Latin American nations face in trying to improve the lives of their peoples? In this chapter, you will find out about the problems and progress of the Latin American nations in these years.

Mexico Improved the Lives of Its People

If you remember, Mexico won its independence from Spain in 1821. Then in the early 1860's, Mexico lost its independence for a short time when it was conquered by a French ruler. But the Mexicans revolted against the French ruler in 1867. Then a new Mexican republic was set up, and a new leader gained power.

LATIN AMERICA IN 1968

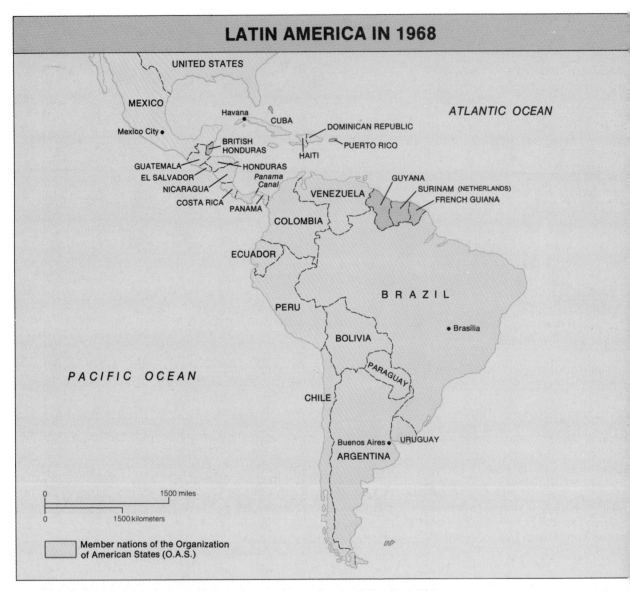

Which South American nations were not members of the O.A.S.?

Mexico's new leader was Benito Juárez (HWAH-rays), a great Mexican patriot. Juárez brought freedom and progress to Mexico. But the leaders who followed him did not govern well. In 1910, the Mexicans again revolted. And in 1917, Mexico received a new, democratic constitution.

Under the constitution, large estates were divided up and given to Mexican farmers who owned no land. Labor unions were formed that helped city workers. By the 1960's, Mexico was one of the leading farming and industrial nations of Latin America, as well as a democratic nation.

Argentina Became a Dictatorship Under Perón

After World War One, Argentina became the richest nation in Latin America as a result of its growing industries. However, most of the people of Argentina remained very poor.

In 1943, Juan Perón (HWAHN pay-ROHN), an army officer, became the leader of the government of Argentina. Many people in Argentina supported Perón because he promised them jobs and higher wages. But Perón used his power to become a dictator. Perón's dictatorship in Argentina lasted until 1955, when Perón was overthrown by a group of army leaders. The army then continued to control the government of Argentina.

Brazil Became a Dictatorship Under Vargas

In the period from 1934 to 1945, Brazil was ruled by Getulio Vargas (zheh-TOO-lyoo VAHR-gus), a dictator who gained power by promising the people a better life.

After 1945, Brazil's government was weak and the army often controlled the government. Even so, Brazil greatly developed its businesses and industries in these years. And it also built a modern new capital city at Brasília.

Castro Became the Dictator of Cuba

In 1898, Cuba became independent, but it remained under the protection of the United States until 1934. Cuba then gained complete independence from the United States. However, a dictator, Fulgencio Batista (fool-HAYN-see-OH bah-TEES-tah), soon took over the Cuban government. Many groups in Cuba tried to overthrow Batista, but none of them was able to do so. Finally, in 1958 Fidel Castro, a new Cuban leader, succeeded in overthrowing Batista.

The American government believed that Castro planned to build a democracy in

Fidel Castro (speaking) set up a Communist government in Cuba

Cuba. At first, the United States supported Castro. But the United States stopped supporting Castro when he set up a dictatorship instead. Castro refused to hold elections or to allow the Cubans freedom. Castro also took over land in Cuba that was owned by American business companies without paying these companies for their land.

In addition, Castro declared that he was a Communist, and that he supported the Communist nations against the democratic nations. In fact, Castro began to receive money and weapons from the Soviet Union.

The Soviet Union Tried to Set Up Missile Bases in Cuba

In 1962, President John F. Kennedy of the United States learned that the Soviet Union was building secret **missile bases,** or rocket-firing bases, in Cuba. These bases were a danger to the United States.

In October of 1962, President Kennedy warned the Soviet Union to remove these missile bases. For a few days war seemed close between the United States and the Soviet Union. But the Soviet Union finally agreed to destroy its Cuban missile bases and the war danger ended.

The Organization of American States Worked for Unity

Long before the 1960's, the United States government realized that as long as most people in Latin America were poor and lacked education, Communism was always a danger there. The United States realized that Communism was a danger in Latin America because the Communists always promised jobs, food, and better lives to people in order to gain control of their governments.

In 1948, the United States helped to organize twenty-one of the American nations into a league called the **Organization of American States** (O.A.S). The main purpose of the O.A.S. was to build unity among the American nations in order to prevent Communist governments from trying to take over these nations.

The Alliance for Progress Was Started to Help Latin America

Then, in 1961, President Kennedy proposed a plan that was called the **Alliance for Progress.** The Alliance for Progress planned to spend 100 billion dollars to improve the businesses and living conditions of the Latin American people. Some of this money came from the United States, and some of it came from Latin America. The Alliance for Progress soon began to have important results in building up Latin America.

SUMMING UP

In the years after 1945, the nations of Latin America developed their businesses, industries, and farms. Then in 1961, the United States tried to help these nations to speed up improvements in their businesses and living conditions by starting a plan called the Alliance for Progress. In the next chapter, you will read about developments and events in the nations of Western Europe in the years after World War Two.

UNDERSTANDING THE LESSON

Do You Know These Important Terms?

For each sentence below, choose the term that best completes the sentence.

1. Rocket-firing bases are called (space stations/missile bases).
2. The league of twenty-one American nations formed to make these nations stronger and to prevent Communists from taking over their governments is called the (Organization of American States/North Atlantic Treaty Organization).
3. The (Alliance for Progress/Pan-American Union) was a plan to improve the businesses and living conditions of the Latin American people.

Do You Remember These People and Events?

1. Tell something about these persons.

   Benito Juárez   Fulgencio Batista
   Juan Perón   Fidel Castro
   Getulio Vargas   John F. Kennedy

2. Explain how or why each of the following developments took place.

a. Mexico improved the lives of its people.
b. Castro became the dictator of Cuba and set up a Communist government.
c. The nations in the Americas began to work together to strengthen themselves.

Can You Locate These Places?

Use the map on page 710 to do the following map work.

1. Locate the following places and tell how each is related to events in this chapter.

   Mexico   Argentina
   Brazil   Brasília
   Cuba   United States

2. Name some Latin American nations that were not discussed in this chapter.
3. Which Latin American nation is located closest to the United States? Which is farthest away?

Do You Know When It Happened?

In what year did the Soviet Union and the United States come close to war over missile bases in Cuba?

Do You Remember the Main Idea?

Which one of the following ideas is the MAIN IDEA of this chapter?

1. Mexico, Argentina, and Brazil are the leading nations in Latin America. They have developed into strong nations and set up democratic governments.
2. The United States has helped the nations of Latin America to develop their farms and their businesses.
3. In the years after 1945, the nations of Latin America developed their businesses, industries, and farms. But their governments were often controlled by dictators, and Communism was a danger.

What Do You Think?

From what you have read in this chapter, answer the following thought question.

1. Why do you think dictatorships often developed in Latin American nations?

Chapter 110
Western Europe After World War Two

GETTING STARTED

1 The nations of Western Europe were able to rebuild themselves in the years after World War Two. But to do so, the nations of Western Europe had to learn how to work together. You will remember that during much of their earlier history, the nations of Western Europe often were at war with each other.

In this chapter, you will read about developments in Western Europe in the years after 1945. And you will find out how these European nations learned to work more closely together, especially in building up their businesses and industries.

2 Before you begin reading the chapter lesson, survey the lesson. Begin your survey by reading the beginning of the lesson. Then look through the lesson and read the headings. Next, study the pictures and read the picture captions. Then study the map on page 716. Finally, read the review section called "Summing Up." This survey will help you to discover the important ideas in this chapter.

Know the Main Idea

As you read the chapter lesson, try to remember the following important MAIN IDEA of the chapter.

After 1945, the nations of Western Europe worked together to become stronger. Some of the nations made agreements that improved business and trade in Western Europe.

The following questions will help you to understand the MAIN IDEA. Try to answer these questions as you read the lesson.

1. What was the purpose of the Common Market?
2. What two political parties controlled the governments of Great Britain after 1945?
3. Who became president of the Fifth Republic of France?

Know These Important Terms

European Coal and Steel Community
Common Market
nationalized

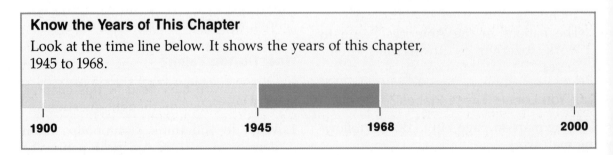

Know the Years of This Chapter
Look at the time line below. It shows the years of this chapter, 1945 to 1968.

1900   1945   1968   2000

Rebuilt factories brought new prosperity to Western Europe after World War Two

EXPLORING THE TIME

"We must build a... United States of Europe." This statement was made in 1946 by Winston Churchill, the wartime prime minister of Great Britain. Churchill believed that all the nations of Western Europe must work together in order to build a lasting peace and to enjoy prosperity. In this chapter, you will learn about the nations of Western Europe after World War Two.

The Nations of Western Europe Formed a Business Alliance

During the early years of the 1950's, the leaders of France, Italy, West Germany, Belgium, Luxembourg, and the Netherlands formed a business alliance called the **European Coal and Steel Community.** This business alliance was a plan to build up the coal and steel industries in these nations.

The European Coal and Steel Community controlled the production of coal

Member nations of the Common Market

Name the member nations of the Common Market in 1968.

and steel in its member nations. It also controlled the shipment of coal and steel by railroad and boat. As a result of this business alliance, the coal and steel industries of these nations became very prosperous.

The Common Market Was Formed to Improve Business and Trade

The success of the European Coal and Steel Community led in 1957 to the development of the European Economic Community, also known as the **Common Market.** The Common Market was formed to help its members to sell their farm products and factory goods.

The nations in the Common Market agreed to lower and then to end their tariffs, or taxes, on goods sold to them by other Common Market nations. But all nations in the Common Market charged the same tax on goods sold to them by nations that were not members of the Common Market.

The Common Market was very successful. It greatly improved the business and trade of the nations that belonged to it.

Great Britain Was Kept Out of the Common Market

However, one important Western European nation, Great Britain, did not join the Common Market at first. Great Britain continued to trade mainly with the British Commonwealth of Nations and the United States. Then in 1961, Great Britain tried to join the Common Market.

However, President Charles de Gaulle of France believed that Great Britain was too closely tied to the British Commonwealth of Nations and to the United States in trade and foreign affairs to make a good member of the Common Market. Therefore, de Gaulle did not allow Great Britain to join the Common Market. In 1967, Great Britain again asked to become a member, but de Gaulle again refused to accept Great Britain in the Common Market.

Great Britain Made Progress After World War Two

During World War Two, the Conservative Party, led by Prime Minister Winston Churchill, controlled the British Parliament. But in 1945, the British voters elected the Labor Party to lead the government.

The leader of the Labor government was Prime Minister Clement Attlee (AT-lee). Led by Attlee, Parliament passed important social welfare laws that provided old-age pensions, unemployment insurance, and complete medical care for the British people. The Labor government also passed an education act that provided free public education for all British students. Under the Labor government, all coal mines, steel mills, railroads, airlines, gas and electric companies, and British banks were **nationalized**—owned and controlled by the government.

The Labor government believed that these changes were needed to help Great Britain rebuild after World War Two. In 1951, the Conservative Party again won control of Parliament. But the Conservative party continued almost all of the Labor government's changes. Then, in 1964, a Labor government again was elected, led by Prime Minister Harold Wilson.

General de Gaulle Became President of the Fifth French Republic

France faced many government problems after World War Two. In 1945, General Charles de Gaulle became President of the Fourth French Republic. But de Gaulle resigned as President in 1946 because the French legislature, or lawmaking body, had more power than he did.

Between 1946 and 1958, many different political parties tried to win control of the French government. These struggles weakened France. In 1958, France received a new and stronger constitution, and the Fifth French Republic was formed. Charles de Gaulle became President, and the new constitution gave him important powers.

GEOGRAPHY AND HISTORY

Forming the Common Market in 1957

After World War Two, the nations of Western Europe realized that they must work together if they were going to grow economically. For this reason, France, West Germany, Italy, Belgium, Luxembourg, and the Netherlands formed the European Economic Community, also known as the Common Market.

These nations were trying to create something like a United States of Europe for trade. Common Market countries could send goods and products to one another without paying any tariffs, or taxes. And all Common Market countries charged the same tariffs on goods shipped to them from nations outside the Common Market.

The system worked well, and the member nations saw their economies grow. By the 1960's, the Common Market was well established. In 1967, the European Economic Community was combined with the European Coal and Steel Community and the European Atomic Energy Community. The new organization, known as the European Community, continued to expand.

Question: Which nations formed the Common Market?

717

Hard work created new affluence for many citizens in the democratic nations of Western Europe

De Gaulle Made France a Stronger Nation

President de Gaulle soon began to rebuild France's government and to strengthen the French army. De Gaulle hoped to make France so strong that it did not need alliances with other nations. For this reason, de Gaulle withdrew France from the N.A.T.O. alliance in 1966. Under de Gaulle, France also developed its own atomic weapons. In these ways, de Gaulle was able to make France a stronger nation.

Italy Rebuilt Rapidly After World War Two

After Italy was defeated as an Axis nation in World War Two, it slowly began to rebuild. In 1946, the Italian people set up a democratic government. Italy received much help from the United States, and, by the 1950's,

Italy's businesses and industries began to grow rapidly.

Italy supported the free nations of Western Europe and became a member of N.A.T.O. By the 1960's, Italy was one of the leading nations of Western Europe.

SUMMING UP

After World War Two, the nations of Western Europe began to build up their strength by working together. Some of these Western European nations formed business alliances to improve their businesses and trade. In Great Britain, France, and Italy, new governments helped these nations to rebuild after the war and to enjoy good times by the 1960's. In the next chapter, you will read about the nations of Eastern Europe in the years after World War Two.

UNDERSTANDING THE LESSON

Do You Know These Important Terms?

For each sentence below, choose the term that best completes the sentence.

1. The business alliance to strengthen the coal and steel industries in the nations of Western Europe is called the (**European Coal and Steel Community/Coal and Steel Market of Western Europe**).
2. The (**European Cooperative/Common Market**) helps the Western European nations to sell their farm products and factory goods.
3. When industries are (**commonized/nationalized**), they are owned and controlled by the government.

Do You Remember These People and Events?

1. Tell something about each of the following persons.

   **Winston Churchill   Harold Wilson
   Charles de Gaulle   Clement Attlee**

2. Explain how or why each of the following developments took place.

   a. Great Britain was kept out of the Common Market.
   b. The Labor government brought about many changes in Great Britain.
   c. President de Gaulle worked to make France a strong nation.

Can You Locate These Places?

Use the map on page 716 to do the following map work.

1. Locate and name the nations that are members of the Common Market.

2. Locate and name the largest nation of the Common Market nations.
3. Name and locate the smallest nation of the Common Market nations.

Do You Know When It Happened?

In what year was the Common Market formed?

Do You Remember the Main Idea?

Which one of the following ideas is the MAIN IDEA of this chapter?

1. The nations of Western Europe joined together in the Common Market to sell their farm products and factory goods.
2. France became a strong nation and withdrew from the North Atlantic Treaty Organization. France refused to allow Great Britain to join the Common Market.
3. After 1945, the nations of Western Europe worked together to become stronger. Some of the nations made agreements that improved business and trade in Western Europe.

What Do You Think?

From what you have read in this chapter, try to answer the following thought questions.

1. Why do you think it was important for nations of Western Europe to work together?
2. Do you think Great Britain should have been allowed to join the Common Market in 1967? Why or why not?
3. Do you think that France acted wisely in leaving N.A.T.O.? Explain your answer.

GETTING STARTED

1   Most nations of Eastern Europe came under the control of the Soviet Union after World War Two. After 1945, Communist governments were set up in these countries, and these governments were controlled by the Soviet Union. You will recall that both Germany and its capital city of Berlin were divided: one half was Communist-controlled, the other half was free. In the same way, the nations of Western Europe were divided from the nations of Eastern Europe. In this chapter, you will read about developments in the nations of Eastern Europe in the years since 1945.

2   Before you begin reading the chapter lesson, survey the lesson. Begin by reading the beginning of the lesson. Then look through the lesson and read the headings. Next, study the pictures and read the picture captions. Then study the map of Europe today on page 722. Finally, read the review section called "Summing Up." This survey will help you to discover the important ideas in this chapter.

Know the Main Idea

As you read the chapter lesson, try to remember the following important MAIN IDEA of the chapter.

The Soviet Union controlled most of the nations of Eastern Europe, but it grew less friendly with two important Communist nations—Yugoslavia and China.

The following questions will help you to understand the MAIN IDEA. Try to answer these questions as you read the lesson.

1. What Communist nation of Eastern Europe was the first to break away from the Soviet Union?
2. In what Eastern European nation did a revolt in 1956 almost succeed in overthrowing the Communist government?
3. Why was Nikita Khrushchev forced to quit as leader of the Soviet Union?

Know These Important Terms

iron curtain
Berlin Wall
Communist propaganda

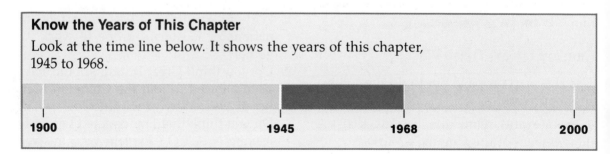

Know the Years of This Chapter

Look at the time line below. It shows the years of this chapter, 1945 to 1968.

| 1900 | 1945 | 1968 | 2000 |

After World War Two, the Soviet Union controlled most of the nations of Eastern Europe

EXPLORING THE TIME

In Chapter 104, you read about the beginning of the cold war in Europe. The cold war began when the Soviet Union took control of Eastern Europe after World War Two. By 1947, all of Eastern Europe from the Baltic Sea in the north to the Adriatic Sea in the south was controlled by the Soviet Union. This line of Soviet control was called the **iron curtain.** In this chapter you will find out how the iron curtain divided Europe after World War Two.

The Iron Curtain Divided West Germany from East Germany

Perhaps you recall that after World War Two, Germany became divided into West Germany and East Germany. The city of Berlin was also divided—into West Berlin and East Berlin. West Germany became a democratic nation led by Chancellor Konrad

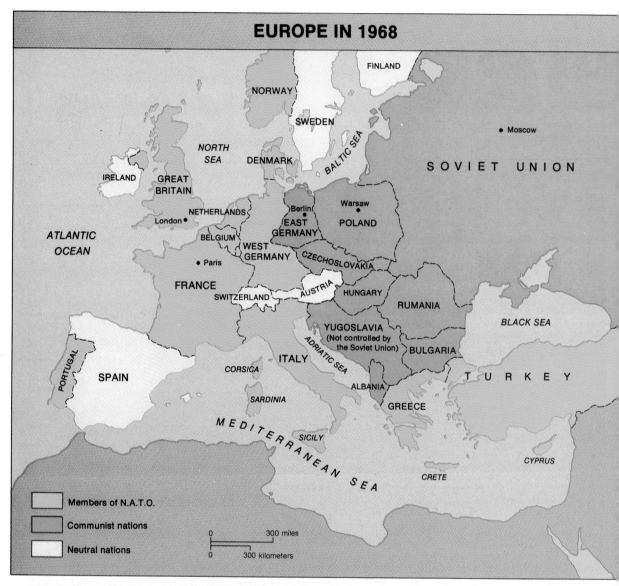

EUROPE IN 1968

FINLAND

NORWAY

SWEDEN

BALTIC SEA

• Moscow

NORTH
SEA

DENMARK

S O V I E T   U N I O N

IRELAND

GREAT
BRITAIN

NETHERLANDS

London •

Berlin

Warsaw
•

ATLANTIC
OCEAN

BELGIUM

EAST
GERMANY

POLAND

WEST
GERMANY

• Paris

CZECHOSLOVAKIA

FRANCE

SWITZERLAND

AUSTRIA

HUNGARY

RUMANIA

BLACK SEA

YUGOSLAVIA
(Not controlled by
the Soviet Union)

BULGARIA

T U R K E Y

ITALY

ADRIATIC SEA

PORTUGAL

CORSICA

SPAIN

ALBANIA

SARDINIA

GREECE

MEDITERRANEAN SEA

SICILY

CYPRUS

CRETE

☐ Members of N.A.T.O.

☐ Communist nations

☐ Neutral nations

0   300 miles

0   300 kilometers

Name five nations that were members of N.A.T.O. in 1968.

Adenauer (AD-un-OW-ur). But East Germany was controlled by the Soviet Union and had a Communist government.

The United States gave a great deal of help to West Germany, which grew strong. But East Germany remained poor. In fact, over 3 million people from East Germany tried to escape and flee into West Germany.

Many of these people tried to escape from East Germany by going from East Berlin into West Berlin. To prevent this, the Communist government of East Germany built the huge **Berlin Wall** between East Berlin and West Berlin. The Berlin Wall also helped the Soviet Union to continue to keep a tight control over East Germany.

Yugoslavia and the Soviet Union Became Less Friendly

One reason that the Soviet Union took over the nations of Eastern Europe after World War Two was that it wanted the raw materials and the factories of these nations. However, the Communist nations of Eastern Europe did not like being controlled by the Soviet Union.

The first nation to turn against the Soviet Union was Yugoslavia. Yugoslavia was ruled by Marshal Tito (TEE-toh), a Communist dictator. Tito wished to keep Yugoslavia's government completely independent from the Soviet Union and refused to follow orders from the Soviet Union.

The Soviet dictator, Joseph Stalin, tried to punish Tito by forcing him out of the Communist Party. But the people of Yugoslavia supported Tito, and Tito remained the leader of Yugoslavia's Communist government.

Eastern Europe Won More Freedom After Stalin Died

In 1953, the Soviet dictator, Joseph Stalin, died. The new leaders of the Soviet Union were not as powerful as Stalin had been. And before long, many riots broke out in

The Communist leaders of East Germany built a huge wall between East and West Berlin that divided the city until 1989

East Germany, Czechoslovakia, and Poland against Soviet control. The most important revolt against Communism took place in Hungary in 1956. In that year, the Hungarian people overthrew the Communist government ruling Hungary. But this revolt failed when Soviet troops were rushed into Hungary. The Communists soon gained control of Hungary's government again.

In 1958, Nikita Khrushchev (kroosh-CHOFF) became the leader of the Soviet Union. In the 1960's, Eastern Europe was still controlled by the Soviet Union. Soviet troops remained in Poland, Hungary, and East Germany to make sure that the governments of these nations remained Communist governments. However, the Soviet Union began to allow these Communist governments to have more control over their own nations. These nations began to trade more with other nations, too.

The Soviet Union and Communist China Became Less Friendly

During the years after World War Two, the Soviet Union began to face trouble from Communist China. The leaders of Communist China felt that the Soviet Union was not doing enough to spread Communism. The Chinese Communists believed that all Communist nations must continue to try to win control of other nations by war and revolution.

However, the Soviet Union now felt that the best way to spread Communism was not by war and revolution, but by spreading **Communist propaganda,** that is, by using peaceful ways to spread Communist ideas into other nations.

This disagreement between the Soviet Union and Communist China divided the two most powerful Communist nations in the world. Together with the Soviet Union's split with Yugoslavia, this quarrel with Communist China helped to weaken the Communist nations.

Khrushchev Was Replaced as Soviet Leader

Meanwhile, the Soviet Union also faced trouble within its own nation. Soviet farms were producing much less food than was needed by the people of the Soviet Union. The Soviet people blamed dictator Nikita Khrushchev for these food shortages. Partly as a result, in 1964 Khrushchev was forced to quit as Soviet leader.

The new leaders of the Soviet Union after Khrushchev were Leonid Brezhnev (BREZH-nef) and Aleksei Kosygin (koh-SEE-gun). Kosygin and Brezhnev turned all their efforts to building up the farms and industries of the Soviet Union. Under these leaders, the Soviet Union continued to spread Communist propaganda to other nations. To this day, the Soviet Union uses covert means to spread Communist aims.

SUMMING UP

After World War Two, the Soviet Union took over most of the nations of Eastern Europe, and it set up Communist governments in these nations. However, by the 1960's, the Soviet Union was forced to allow the nations of Eastern Europe to have more freedom. Meanwhile, the Communist world was weakened by the split between Yugoslavia and the Soviet Union and by the disagreement between Communist China and the Soviet Union. In the next chapter, which begins Unit 23, you will read about the United States and the world today.

UNDERSTANDING THE LESSON

Do You Know These Important Terms?

For each sentence below, choose the term that best completes the sentence.

1. The line of Soviet control between the Communist nations of Eastern Europe and the free nations of Western Europe is called the **(bamboo curtain/iron curtain)**.
2. The **(Berlin Air Lift/Berlin Wall)** was built to keep people from escaping from East Berlin into West Berlin.
3. Spreading Communist ideas into other nations in peaceful ways is called **(Communist propaganda/Communist Fifth Column)**.

Do You Remember These People and Events?

1. Tell something about these persons.

   Aleksei Kosygin   Nikita Khrushchev
   Marshal Tito   Leonid Brezhnev
   Joseph Stalin   Konrad Adenauer

2. Explain how or why each of the following developments took place.

   a. The iron curtain divided Germany.
   b. The nations of Eastern Europe won more freedom after Stalin died.
   c. The Soviet Union and Communist China became less friendly.

Can You Locate These Places?

Use the map on page 722 to locate the following places. Tell how each place is related to the events in this chapter.

   East Germany   Soviet Union
   Berlin   Poland
   West Germany   Hungary
   Yugoslavia   Czechoslovakia

Do You Know When It Happened?

What are the years of this chapter?

Do You Remember the Main Idea?

Which one of the following ideas is the MAIN IDEA of this chapter?

1. The Soviet Union continued to keep control of the nations of Eastern Europe. But the Western European nations forced the Soviet Union to stay behind the iron curtain.
2. The Soviet Union controlled most of the nations of Eastern Europe. But the Soviet Union grew less friendly with two important Communist nations—China and Yugoslavia.
3. The Communist government of the Soviet Union changed in many important ways after the death of Stalin. In the years after 1953, the Russian government lacked strong leaders.

What Do You Think?

From what you have read in this chapter, answer the following thought questions.

1. Why do you think the Soviet Union set up the iron curtain?
2. Why do you think the Communist government of East Germany wanted to keep people from leaving East Germany?
3. The Soviet Union has tried to spread Communism by the use of Communist propaganda. Why do you think the Soviet Union has followed this post-war policy? Explain your answer.

Unit 23
The Nations of the World Today

THE CHAPTERS IN UNIT 23 ARE

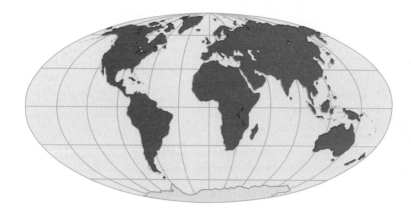

From the late 1960's through the 1980's, the world was a challenging place in which to live. In this unit, you will see how the nations of the world tried to deal with the challenges they faced.

More than one hundred sixty nations participated in the 1988 Summer Olympic Games in Seoul, South Korea

Chapter 112
The United States and the World

GETTING STARTED

1 The depression of 1929 brought serious problems to the United States. But the country found new ways to cope with these challenges. After World War Two, Americans were ready to enjoy a better life.

In the early 1960's, President John F. Kennedy brought a new spirit to America. After his death in 1963, the war in Vietnam grew. A rapid rise in prices and slow economic growth made life difficult for many Americans in the 1970's.

Changes came with the election of Ronald Reagan as President in 1980. Reagan put forward a new concept of a limited role for government.

2 Before you begin reading the chapter lesson, survey the lesson. Begin your survey by reading the beginning of the lesson. Then look through the lesson and read the headings. Next, study the pictures and read the picture captions. Finally, read the review section called "Summing Up." This survey will help you to discover the important ideas in this chapter.

Know the Main Idea

As you read the chapter lesson, try to remember the following important MAIN IDEA of the chapter.

Major changes took place in America after World War Two. Many of these changes became a lasting part of American life.

The following questions will help you to understand the MAIN IDEA. Try to answer these questions as you read the lesson.

1. How did Americans respond to the great depression of the 1930's?

2. How did life in the United States change after World War Two?

3. What problems did Americans face in the 1970's and 1980's?

Know These Important Terms

New Deal	Peace Corps
social security	Watergate
civil rights	inflation
discrimination	trade deficit

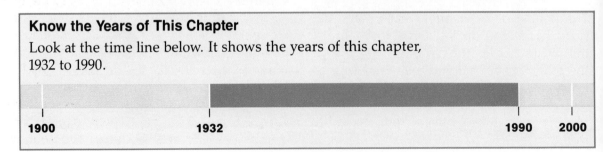

Know the Years of This Chapter

Look at the time line below. It shows the years of this chapter, 1932 to 1990.

1900   1932   1990   2000

On July 4, 1986, Americans celebrated the one-hundredth birthday of the Statue of Liberty. Located in New York Harbor, the statue is a symbol of freedom.

EXPLORING THE TIME

The people of the United States faced serious hardships during the depression of the 1930's. How the country dealt with these hardships changed the nature of government in America. In this chapter, you will read about many changes that took place in the United States from the 1930's through the 1980's.

Americans Fought a Depression

When the depression began in 1929, many Americans thought it would end soon. But it only grew worse. Millions of workers lost their jobs, banks went out of business, and homeless families roamed the country looking for work.

When Franklin Roosevelt was elected President in 1932, he vowed to end the depression. He and Congress worked to

Dr. Martin Luther King, Jr.

The day was August 28, 1963. The place was the Lincoln Memorial in Washington, D.C. Over 200,000 people were listening to one man speak. "I have a dream..." said Martin Luther King, Jr. He explained that his dream was that Blacks would soon be accepted as equal American citizens. This meeting at which Dr. King spoke was called the "March on Washington." The main purpose of the March was to show support for the civil rights bill before Congress.

The March on Washington was successful. Congress soon passed the Civil Rights Law of 1964. But the March also showed that Blacks were insisting upon their full rights of citizenship. In a peaceful but effective way, the March showed that Black Americans were no longer willing to wait for their rights. As President John F. Kennedy said, "Americans... can properly be proud of the demonstration that has occurred here today."

Question: What was the main purpose of the March on Washington?

create many new government programs to help Americans. His plan came to be called the **New Deal.** Under the New Deal, the government created jobs for people and made loans to businesses. It took steps to raise the prices that farmers received for their crops.

One of the most important New Deal programs was the Social Security Act. **Social security** provided weekly payments for workers who lost their jobs. It gave pension payments to workers when they reached the age of sixty-five. These measures helped Americans, but the depression did not fully end until World War Two. Then, because of the war, American factories hummed, and millions of people went back to work.

Americans Enjoyed Post-War Prosperity

After World War Two, many Americans had more money to spend than ever before. Factories stopped making tanks and war planes and began producing consumer goods. These are products people buy for their own use, such as automobiles and refrigerators.

During the post-war years, the birthrate went up sharply. This was known as the "baby boom." Many growing families wanted to have their own homes. To meet the demand, builders put up thousands of houses in areas near cities. New highways connected these suburbs with shopping areas and the cities.

Blacks Won Civil Rights

During this period, most Americans were living better. But many Black Americans did not enjoy the same **civil rights** as whites. In the South, Black children could not go to school with white children. Blacks had to ride at the back of city buses. There were even separate drinking fountains for Blacks. In the North, too, Blacks suffered many forms of **discrimination,** or unequal treatment.

After the war, the status of Blacks began to change. In 1949, President Harry Truman ended segregation, or separation based on race, in the armed forces. The Supreme Court ruled against discrimination in transportation and housing.

The biggest change, however, came in 1954, when the Supreme Court said that segregated schools were illegal. Now Blacks began to demand full equality. In the 1950's, Black leaders such as Martin Luther King, Jr., led demonstrations and protest marches. Blacks held "sit-ins" at segregated lunch counters. Some whites went to the South to help register, or sign up, Blacks so they could vote in elections.

Then Congress took action, passing a series of federal civil rights acts in 1957, 1964, and 1965. These laws protected the right of Blacks to vote. They also made segregation in public places unlawful.

American astronauts were the first people to stand on the moon

Kennedy Brought a New Spirit to the Nation

In 1961, John F. Kennedy became President. At forty-three, he was the youngest person ever elected to the White House. Kennedy brought a spirit of youth and energy to the nation. "Don't ask what your country can do for you," he said. "Ask what you can do for your country."

Kennedy created the **Peace Corps,** a program to send volunteers to work on projects abroad. Thousands of young Americans signed up to help people in Africa, Asia, and Latin America. Kennedy vowed that America would send astronauts to the moon within ten years. In foreign affairs, Kennedy took a strong stand, but at the same time, he worked to promote world peace. In 1963, for example, the United States and the Soviet Union signed the Nuclear Test Ban Treaty. Later that year, Americans were stunned when President Kennedy was killed. Vice-President Lyndon Johnson then became President.

The Vietnam War Divided America

After Lyndon Johnson became President, the number of Americans in Vietnam increased sharply, and American soldiers began fighting in Vietnam. In 1965, there were 184,000 American troops in Vietnam. In 1969, there were more than half a million. But still the South Vietnamese could not win the war.

Many Americans were against the war and believed the United States should bring its troops home. Others wanted America to help South Vietnam win the war. There were marches and demonstrations for and against the war. Some young Americans fled to Canada or Sweden to avoid fighting in a war they thought was wrong. Americans argued bitterly over Vietnam.

Richard Nixon became President in 1969. He announced a new plan for Vietnam. The United States would slowly withdraw its forces, leaving South Vietnam to fight its enemies. Meanwhile, the United States and North Vietnam held peace talks. They finally signed a cease-fire in 1973. The last American troops left Vietnam. Two years later, North Vietnam captured South Vietnam. The long war was over.

President Reagan met with the leaders of many different nations. Here the President is shown with the Prime Minister of Japan.

The United States Weathered a Crisis

President Nixon surprised the world in 1972. He flew to China and met with Chairman Mao Zedong. Nixon's visit opened diplomatic relations between the United States and China after more than twenty years of silence. In 1979, the two nations established full relations.

President Nixon's triumphs were short-lived, however. Nixon ran for President again in 1972. Workers on his campaign team broke into the headquarters of the Democratic Party in the Watergate building in Washington, D.C. They were caught trying to tap telephones and spy on the Democrat's election plans. The crisis that developed came to be known as **Watergate**.

The Watergate burglars went on trial the next year. Several of the President's closest aides were shown to have helped them. Although Nixon said he knew nothing about the robbery, a Congressional investigation revealed that he had indeed known about Watergate. Because he had lied and tried to cover up his involvement, he could have been charged with "obstructing justice," which is a crime. In August 1974, before an impeachment trial could begin, Nixon resigned. Vice-President Gerald Ford then became President. Most Americans felt that their system of government had worked well in this time of crisis. Watergate showed that not even the President was above the law.

Oil Prices Hit the Sky

In 1973, Arab oil-producing nations stopped shipping oil to the United States. They were angry at the United States for helping Israel in its war against Egypt. As a result, oil prices in the United States soared. They stayed high even after oil shipments began in 1974.

To deal with the problem, the new President, Jimmy Carter, drew up an energy plan. It called for the development of new fuels and encouraged people to use less oil. By the early 1980's, however, new sources of oil caused prices to drop. The crisis was over, for the time being.

The United States Had a Celebration— and More Problems

Jimmy Carter was elected President in 1976. It was the nation's two hundredth birthday. Americans celebrated with fireworks, parties, and parades.

Carter worked hard to ease tensions around the world. He helped Israel and Egypt sign a historic peace agreement in 1979, called the Camp David agreement. Carter also urged other nations to protect the rights of their citizens. At home, however, the nation faced serious economic problems. **Inflation,** the rapid rise in prices, was increasing. Americans could not buy as much with the money they had.

During Carter's last year in office, a revolution broke out in Iran. The new Iranian government seized fifty-two Americans working at the U.S. embassy in Iran. Carter's plan to rescue the Americans failed. The hostages were not released until Carter's successor, Ronald Reagan, took office in January 1981.

Reagan Changed American Policies

Ronald Reagan had won the election in 1980 by a large majority. He promised to make many changes. One of his goals was to reduce the role of government in American

George Bush was elected President of the United States in 1988

life. Americans were willing to follow this popular new President.

President Reagan asked Congress to pass a three-year tax cut. He said lower taxes would help the nation's economy and create new jobs for Americans. Inflation went down but unemployment stayed high. The administration cut government spending on environmental protection, job safety, and other programs. At the same time, it spent more on defense.

The Reagan Administration took an active role in Central America. It claimed that the Nicaraguan government planned to spread Communist ideas in Central America. For this reason, the Reagan Administration supported anti-government rebels. In 1984, the Central Intelligence Agency admitted it had mined harbors in Nicaragua to halt the spread of Communism.

With his popularity at an all-time high, President Reagan was re-elected in 1984. During Reagan's second term, inflation continued to drop. Unemployment also fell. Government spending, however, continued to increase, and the national debt reached new heights. At the same time, the United States bought more goods from other countries than it sold. The result was a **trade deficit,** which grew steadily during the Reagan years.

America Continued to Attract Newcomers

During the 1970's and 1980's, thousands of immigrants and refugees flocked to the United States. Most of the newcomers were from Latin America. Many others came from Asia, especially from South Korea and the Philippines. Some fled the governments of Cambodia, Cuba, Haiti, and Vietnam.

Each year, hundreds of thousands of illegal aliens crossed the Mexican-American border

Many people entered the United States illegally. In 1986, the United States passed a new immigration law. The law gave citizenship to thousands of illegal aliens. For many people, America remained the land of opportunity.

SUMMING UP

During the depression, government took on a new role in American life. Americans prospered after World War Two, and Black Americans began to win greater equality. America faced growing economic problems during the 1970's and 1980's. In the next chapter, you will read about Canada and Latin America.

UNDERSTANDING THE LESSON

Do You Know These Important Terms?

For each sentence below, choose the term that best completes the sentence.

1. Roosevelt's plan to help Americans during the depression was called the **(Peace Corps/New Deal).**
2. **(Inflation/Social security)** was one of the most important programs of the New Deal.
3. Black Americans did not always have the same **(civil rights/discrimination)** as whites.
4. President Nixon resigned because he faced impeachment proceedings for his role in **(Vietnam/Watergate).**
5. When a country buys more goods abroad than it sells, the result is a **(trade deficit/tax cut).**

Do You Remember These People and Events?

1. Tell something about each of the following persons.

   Dr. Martin Luther King, Jr.
   John F. Kennedy

2. Explain how or why each of the following developments took place.

   a. After World War Two, many new homes were built in the suburbs.
   b. The American people disagreed about the Vietnam War.
   c. In 1986, many illegal aliens became United States citizens.

Do You Know When It Happened?

In what year did Arab nations stop shipping oil to the United States?

Do You Remember the Main Idea?

Which one of the following ideas is the MAIN IDEA of this chapter?

1. Since 1932, the role of government in American life has been increasing.
2. Major changes took place in America after World War Two. Many of these changes became a lasting part of American life.
3. The United States has fought Communism all over the world.

What Do You Think?

From what you have read in this chapter, answer the following thought questions.

1. John Kennedy said, "Ask what you can do for your country." What do you think you can do for your country?
2. Do you think nuclear weapons should be banned by treaties?
3. What do you think is the greatest challenge faced by the United States today? Explain why.

Chapter 113
Canada and Latin America

GETTING STARTED

1 The years after 1968 were a time of great change in the Americas. Canadians found new prosperity during this period. A new spirit of independence brought changes in Canadian relations with Great Britain and the United States.

The nations of Latin America continued to struggle to overcome poverty. They worked hard to modernize their economies. During the 1970's, rising oil prices made progress difficult for most Latin American nations. However, ten years later, a sudden drop in oil prices hurt oil-producing nations, such as Mexico, which had come to depend on oil earnings.

Latin American countries also struggled politically in the 1970's and 1980's. The "have-nots" fought against the "haves" in bitter civil wars. Often, the conflicts took the form of leftists against dictators.

2 Before you begin reading the chapter lesson, survey the lesson. Begin your survey by reading the beginning of the lesson. Then look through the lesson and read the headings. Next, study the pictures and read the picture captions. Finally, read the review section called "Summing Up." This survey will help you to discover the important ideas in this chapter.

Know the Main Idea

As you read the chapter lesson, try to remember the following important MAIN IDEA of the chapter.

Canada and the nations of Latin America have faced similar problems since 1968. Each nation has found different solutions to its problems.

The following questions will help you to understand the MAIN IDEA. Try to answer these questions as you read the lesson.

1. What problems did the nations of the Americas have in common?
2. How has each nation tried to solve its problems?
3. How well did each nation deal with its problems?

Know These Important Terms

acid rain	Sandinistas
guerrillas	*contras*

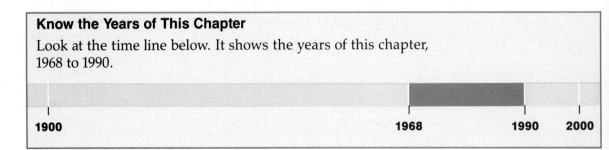

Know the Years of This Chapter

Look at the time line below. It shows the years of this chapter, 1968 to 1990.

1900   1968   1990   2000

A traffic sign, in English and French, in front of a government building in Canada. Why do you think the sign is in both languages?

EXPLORING THE TIME

The 1970's and 1980's were challenging years for the nations of the Americas. Each nation reacted in a different way to its problems and opportunities. In this chapter, you will read about how the nations of the Americas have worked, separately and together, to solve their problems.

Canada Looked to the Future

Canada is part of the British Commonwealth, and most of the people speak English. About 30 per cent of the people,

however, speak French, and during the 1960's, these French-speaking Canadians began to demand their rights. Most of them lived in the province of Quebec (kwee-BEK). Some French-speaking Canadians wanted Quebec to become a separate nation, but this idea was defeated. However, French is now the official language of Quebec.

Canada's biggest trading partner is the United States. Canadians worried that American goods would flood Canada. For this reason, the government taxed many American imports. But in 1988, Canada and the United States reached an agreement that promised to end all taxes on goods

Contra forces in the civil war in Nicaragua. Whom were the *contras* fighting against?

traded between the two nations. Canadians also wanted an agreement limiting air pollution from American factories. They said pollution caused **acid rain.** Acid rain, or rain containing chemicals from factory smoke, destroys forests and lakes. Many Canadians accused the United States of not doing enough to solve the problem.

Mexico Faced Hardships

Mexico's economy has not kept pace with the country's growing population. Vast deposits of oil were found in Mexico during the 1970's. Mexico had a great deal of oil to sell, and it built chemical plants and other factories. For a time, the nation prospered. Then, in the 1980's, the price of oil plunged, and many Mexicans lost their jobs. At the same time, prices of other goods and services rose sharply. Hoping to find better paying jobs, many Mexicans entered the United States illegally.

Mexico had borrowed millions of dollars from the United States and other nations. With the drop in oil prices, Mexico found it impossible to repay its debts.

In Mexico's 1988 presidential elections, Carlos Salinas of the Institutional Revolutionary Party won. The party, known as the PRI, has been in power since 1929. But this time, the PRI almost lost the election. Many Mexicans wanted new policies and new leaders to solve their economic problems.

Strife Divided Central America

In the years after World War Two, many nations in this region were torn by civil war. In Guatemala, leftist **guerrillas,** or rebel soldiers, began fighting army forces in the 1940's. More than 200,000 Guatemalans fled to Mexico, while others entered the United States illegally. A series of leaders ruled Guatemala. Most of them were military officers or were supported by the army. A civilian government again took office in Guatemala in 1986.

To the south of Guatemala is the nation of El Salvador. It, too, was split by violence between opposing groups. Thousands of Salvadorans died in the fighting. In 1979, a military government seized power but could not stop the fighting. Free elections were held in 1984 and still the conflict continued. The Reagan Administration gave military aid to the government of El Salvador to fight the rebels.

In Nicaragua, the leftist rebels called themselves **Sandinistas.** They fought a long war against General Anastasio Somoza (so-MOH-zuh). Somoza had ruled the nation since 1967, with American support. The Sandinistas overthrew Somoza in 1979 and set up a Marxist government. The Soviet Union and Cuba both supported the new government. In turn, Nicaragua sent military aid to guerrilla forces in El Salvador. The United States feared that Nicaragua would try to overthrow other Central American governments.

Civil war broke out in Nicaragua. Those who fought against the government were called *contras.* President Reagan supported the *contras,* and his administration gave money and arms to them secretly. When Congress found out, U.S. government aid to the *contras* was stopped.

In 1987, the President of Costa Rica, Oscar Arias Sánchez, suggested a peace plan for Nicaragua. It was supported by Mexico, Guatemala, and Honduras. For his plan, Arias received the 1987 Nobel Peace Prize. Nicaragua agreed to the plan. Talks between *contra* leaders and the Nicaraguan government took place in 1988.

The United States had controlled the Panama Canal Zone since 1903. In time, the people of Panama wanted to govern the canal themselves. Anti-American riots flared in the region during the 1960's. In 1977, the United States agreed to give up control of the canal slowly. By the year 2000, it will belong to Panama. Panama promised that the canal would remain neutral.

Caribbean Countries Saw Upheaval

Turmoil also marked the Caribbean region during the 1970's and 1980's. In 1983, a Marxist-led coup overthrew the democratic government of Grenada. The United States quickly sent troops. After order was restored, U.S. forces were withdrawn in 1985.

For fourteen years, Haiti was ruled by François Duvalier (dyou-vah-LYAY). Duvalier died in 1971, and his son took power.

In Brazil, large areas of forest have been cleared for mining and for ranching

Haiti is the poorest nation in the Western Hemisphere, but the Duvaliers did nothing to solve the nation's severe economic problems. A bloody civil war took place. Finally, in 1986, the younger Duvalier fled to France. Elections were held and a new constitution was adopted. But in 1988, a military dictator seized power in Haiti. The new leader, General Henri Namphy, tore up the country's constitution.

Tensions continued between the United States and Cuba. In 1977, the two nations agreed to exchange diplomats, but they did not resume full diplomatic relations. In 1978 and 1980, Cuba released hundreds of political prisoners. The United States accepted them, but some turned out to be criminals. Cuba and the United States signed an agreement in 1984. Cuba promised to permit thousands of people who wanted to emigrate to the United States to do so. The agreement went into effect in 1988.

South America Struggled for Progress

Economic problems continued to plague South America. In some countries, such as Colombia, drug dealing became a huge industry. Drug lords grew more powerful than police officials and military leaders.

In Brazil, government leaders tried to improve the economy by tapping the nation's rich natural resources. During the 1970's, Brazil rapidly developed its interior regions. It harnessed its rivers with hydroelectric dams. It opened new areas to mining and cleared vast tracts of land in the Amazon Basin. Environmentalists warned that priceless rain forests were being destroyed. The nation also built new factories.

To pay for these projects, Brazil borrowed heavily from other nations. Although the economy boomed for a time, a series of problems emerged. The gap between rich and poor grew larger, and inflation took away consumers' buying power. The interest on foreign debts soared, and by 1987, Brazil could no longer pay even the interest on its debts. The United States and several other creditor nations worked out new arrangements for the payment of Brazil's debts.

Since 1964, a series of military dictators ruled Brazil. Thousands of political opponents were jailed or murdered. The press was censored, and Brazilians lost many of their civil rights. After more than twenty years, democratic elections were finally held in 1986.

Like Brazil, Argentina is rich in natural resources but has not made full use of them. Many of Argentina's problems have been the result of poor leadership. In 1973, Juan Perón returned from exile and took power. After his death, his wife, Isabella, took his place. The country suffered increasing hardships and violence.

A group of military officers seized power in 1976. The government was very unpopular, and thousands of opponents "disappeared" and were never seen again. As many as five thousand people were killed by the government, and many more were jailed and tortured. Meanwhile, Argentina's economic problems grew worse. Its debts increased, and inflation and unemployment rose sharply.

In April 1982, Argentina invaded the Falkland Islands in the South Atlantic. Although the Falklands belonged to Great Britain, Argentina had long claimed them. When fighting began, British troops quickly took control. Argentina surrendered two months later, and Argentina's President resigned.

The following year, military rule ended in Argentina. After elections, the new government held a trial, and five military leaders were found guilty of murder and other crimes. The Argentine government struggled to pay the nation's huge debt. In 1987, foreign banks set up a new payment plan so that Argentina could pay interest on its debts.

SUMMING UP

The nations of the Western Hemisphere struggled against economic problems and civil strife. Drug traffic increased during the 1970's and 1980's. However, in several Latin American nations, democratic government was restored. Canada faced conflicts with the United States over trade and air pollution. In the next chapter, you will read about the nations of Western Europe.

UNDERSTANDING THE LESSON

Do You Know These Important Terms?

For each sentence below, choose the term that best completes the sentence.

1. Rebel soldiers are called (**army forces/ guerrillas**).
2. The (**Sandinistas**/*contras*) set up a Marxist government in Nicaragua.
3. (**Drought/Acid rain**) is destroying the forests of Canada.

Do You Remember These People and Events?

1. Tell something about each of the following subjects.

   Oscar Arias Sánchez
   François Duvalier
   Falkland Islands

2. Tell how each of the following developments took place.

   a. Brazil borrowed so much money in the 1970's that it could not repay it.
   b. Trade relations between Canada and the United States improved.

Can You Locate These Places?

Use the map on page 710 to locate the following places.

Cuba	Mexico	Guatemala
Panama	Argentina	Nicaragua
Brazil	Haiti	

Do You Know When It Happened?

In what year did the United States agree to give up control of the Panama Canal Zone?

Do You Remember the Main Idea?

Which of the following ideas is the MAIN IDEA of this chapter?

1. Canada and the nations of Latin America have faced similar problems since 1968. Each nation has found different solutions to its problems.
2. Latin American countries have worked together to pay their debts. The richer countries of Latin America have lent money to the poorer countries.
3. Guerrillas have been a serious problem in Canada and Latin America.

What Do You Think?

From what you have read in the chapter, answer the following thought questions.

1. Why do you think many Canadians are opposed to the trade agreement between Canada and the United States?
2. Do you think the United States should be more or less involved in Central America? Explain your answer.
3. How do you think countries such as Mexico and Brazil can solve their economic problems?

Chapter 114
Western Europe

GETTING STARTED

1 Today, the nations of Western Europe are more closely linked than ever before. They depend upon one another economically and for their defense. During the 1970's and 1980's, economic problems faced Europe. Some nations, such as West Germany, were better able to deal with these problems. Others, such as Great Britain, suffered from high unemployment and inflation. Political violence was also a problem during these years.

Three Western European nations, Spain, Portugal, and Greece, were governed by dictators for periods of time. Recently, these nations held free elections and now have democratic governments. In this chapter, you will read about these and other changes that have faced European leaders in the years since 1968.

2 Before you begin reading the chapter lesson, survey the lesson. Begin your survey by reading the beginning of the lesson. Then look through the lesson and read the headings. Next, study the pictures and read the picture captions. Finally, read the review section called "Summing Up." This survey will help you to discover the important ideas in this chapter.

Know the Main Idea

As you read the chapter lesson, try to remember the following important MAIN IDEA of the chapter.

Most of the Western European nations are linked economically. Europe has had to deal with the problems of inflation, slow economic growth, and political violence.

The following questions will help you to understand the MAIN IDEA. Look for the answers to these questions as you read the lesson.

1. Which Western European nation has enjoyed the greatest prosperity?
2. What economic problems faced Western Europe?
3. Which nations gained democratic governments after 1968?

Know These Important Terms

terrorism   duties

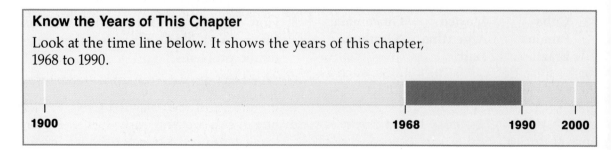

Know the Years of This Chapter

Look at the time line below. It shows the years of this chapter, 1968 to 1990.

| 1900 | 1968 | 1990 | 2000 |

The discovery of oil under the North Sea brought prosperity to Great Britain in the 1970's

EXPLORING THE TIME

Most Western European nations struggled with economic problems during the 1970's and 1980's. Several countries gained democratic governments after many years of dictatorship. Political violence disturbed Western Europe during these years. In this chapter, you will learn about the changes that took place in Western Europe.

Problems Troubled Europe

The years following 1968 were difficult ones for Western Europe. Some nations, such as West Germany, prospered. Others struggled with inflation and slow economic growth. Many Europeans feared the presence of nuclear weapons in their countries.

During the 1970's and 1980's, terrorists struck at targets in Western Europe many times. They hoped that **terrorism,** or random acts of violence, would call attention to their political causes. In 1981, a Turkish terrorist shot and seriously wounded Pope John Paul II. In 1983, members of the Palestinian Liberation Organization (PLO) hijacked an Italian passenger ship and killed one American. In 1986, the Swedish Prime Minister, Olof Palme, was murdered. No group claimed responsibility for the act, and his killer remained unknown.

Great Britain Faced Economic Hardships

Economic difficulties plagued Great Britain during the 1970's and early 1980's. British factories produced fewer goods, and many

PEOPLE IN HISTORY

Margaret Thatcher

When Margaret Thatcher was elected Prime Minister of Great Britain in 1979, she had little experience in foreign affairs.

But she soon proved that she could deal with leaders of other countries. In 1984, she became the first Western leader to meet the new Soviet leader, Mikhail Gorbachev. The two quickly learned to respect each other. Thatcher told Gorbachev that the West wanted good relations with the Soviet Union. But she warned that Europe would always be ready to defend itself. She also said that Britain and Europe would speak out for freedom and human rights. Of Gorbachev, Thatcher said:

> I had to decide whether I thought it was in the Western interest that he succeed. And I think it is.
>
> It is ... both bold and prophetic at this time for the Soviet Union to have a leader who comes right to the top and says, look, for 70 years Communism hasn't produced the hopes and dreams that we had for it ... And we've got to go in the direction of freeing up speech ... freeing up responsibility.

Question: Why did Thatcher think that it was in the Western interest that Gorbachev succeed?

companies went out of business. Thousands of people lost their jobs. Inflation rose steadily. Moreover, Britain could not compete for many of the world markets that once bought its goods. Hoping to expand its markets, Great Britain joined the European Community (Common Market) in 1973. The discovery of vast oil deposits under the North Sea brought prosperity for a time. Then oil prices fell during the early 1980's.

In 1979, the Conservative Party candidate Margaret Thatcher became Prime Minister. She was the first woman to serve in this position. Thatcher took strong steps to deal with economic recession in the 1980's. She also made progress in other areas. Since 1841, the colony of Hong Kong had been part of the British Empire. In 1985, Great Britain and China signed a treaty. It was agreed that Hong Kong would become part of China in 1997 but would remain a free port. In a free port, almost no **duties,** or taxes, are placed on goods brought into the port.

Conflict Shattered Northern Ireland

Britain was also troubled by violence in Northern Ireland. Northern Ireland had been part of Great Britain since 1922, when the southern part of Ireland became independent. Some people in Northern Ireland demanded independence. Extremist groups turned to terrorism to call attention to their demands.

There was also violence between Roman Catholics and Protestants in Northern Ireland. Catholics, who were in the minority, fought for their civil rights. Protestants feared that Catholics would gain too much power. Between 1969 and 1984, more than two thousand people died as a result of the violence. To restore order, Great Britain imposed direct rule over Northern Ireland in 1972. But the fighting continued.

France Underwent Many Changes

Student riots broke out in France in 1968. The students protested against nuclear arms and demanded more rights for young people. President Charles de Gaulle's efforts to reform France proved unpopular, and he was voted out of office in 1969. But his successor continued many of de Gaulle's policies. For example, France tried to develop strong ties with the Arab countries of the Middle East.

A Socialist government came into power in France in 1981. The new government was led by François Mitterand (MEE-teh-ron). Mitterand put many industries under government control and raised taxes for the rich. Under his administration, inflation and unemployment rose sharply. France also suffered a large trade deficit, meaning that it sold less abroad than it imported. The government was forced to take harsh measures to deal with these challenges. Despite the nation's economic problems, Mitterand was re-elected in 1988.

West Germany Prospered

Relations between East and West Germany remained tense throughout the 1960's. But in 1970, West Germany signed a series of treaties with Communist nations. In one of these agreements, West Germany and the Soviet Union promised to respect one another's territory. The two countries also said they would not use force against each other.

Some extreme political groups in Northern Ireland resorted to terrorism to persuade Britain to give up Northern Ireland

The West German government signed similar treaties with Poland, Czechoslovakia, and East Germany. Relations further improved when the East German leader, Erich Honecker (HOH-nuh-kur), visited West Germany in 1987.

After World War Two, American aid helped West Germany become a strong, modern nation. West German prosperity continued during the 1970's and 1980's as the nation's economy thrived. But when the United States placed nuclear missiles on German soil in the 1970's, many West Germans objected. They did not want their nation to become a target in a war between the two superpowers. Some West Germans demanded a "nuclear-free" Europe. Others felt the missiles were necessary to prevent a possible attack by the Soviet Union. The missiles were not removed until the Soviet

Union and the United States signed a disarmament treaty in 1988.

Spain and Portugal Became Democracies

Spain was ruled by a military dictator, General Francisco Franco, from 1936 until 1975. After Franco died, Prince Juan Carlos, the grandson of Spain's last monarch, became the ruler. He promised to reform his nation's government. In 1977, free elections were held in Spain for the first time in forty years.

Two areas of Spain, Catalonia and the Basque region, had long demanded independence. Some of these separatist groups have turned to violence in their struggle. In 1979, Spain granted both regions home rule. In 1981, a group of army officers tried to overthrow the government. Their attempt failed, and Spain remained a democratic republic.

Portugal, too, had been ruled by a dictator for many years. In 1975, Portugal held its first free elections since 1926. The new government granted independence to two Portuguese colonies, Angola and Mozambique. Portugal remained the poorest country in Western Europe. Poverty and economic problems made the future of democracy there uncertain.

Greece Took an Independent Path

A group of military officers seized power in Greece in 1967. Democracy was finally restored in 1974. The nation rejoined N.A.T.O. six years later, and in 1981, it became a member of the European Community. A Socialist government took office in 1985. The new government opposed U.S.

After General Franco's death, Prince Juan Carlos became the ruler of Spain. Within two years, the first free elections in over forty years were held.

military bases in Greece, and it criticized the United States for many of its policies. Relations between the two nations remained strained during the 1980's.

SUMMING UP

Western Europe had to deal with inflation and slow economic growth. It also tried to cope with terrorism. Spain, Portugal, and Greece became democracies after many years under military rule. In the next chapter, you will read about the nations of Eastern Europe.

UNDERSTANDING THE LESSON

Do You Know These Important Terms?

For each sentence below, choose the term that best completes the sentence.

1. The hijacking of a passenger ship is an example of **(terrorism/dictatorship)**.
2. European Community nations send goods to one another without paying **(duties/deficits)**.

Do You Remember These People and Events?

1. Tell something about each of the following persons.

   Margaret Thatcher
   François Mitterand
   Prince Juan Carlos

2. Tell how or why each of the following developments took place.

   a. Violence plagued Northern Ireland.
   b. West Germans objected to nuclear weapons on their soil.

Can You Locate These Places?

Use the Atlas maps on pages 816–817 to do the following map work.

1. Locate the following places.

Great Britain	**Greece**
Portugal	**Spain**
West Germany	**France**

2. Which of these countries has joined the European Community since 1968?

Do You Know When It Happened?

When did Spain hold its first free election in recent years?

Do You Remember the Main Idea?

Which of the following ideas is the MAIN IDEA of this chapter?

1. Everyone wants Western Europe to be nuclear free. In 1988, the nations of Western Europe signed a disarmament treaty with the Soviet Union.
2. Terrorist have ruined the economy of Western Europe.
3. Most of the Western European nations are linked economically. Europe has had to deal with the problems of inflation, slow economic growth, and political violence.

What Do You Think?

From what you have read in this chapter, answer the following thought questions.

1. Why do you think West Germany felt it was necessary to sign treaties with Communist nations?
2. What do you think can be done to end terrorism?
3. Do you think U.S. relations with European countries will change as these countries become more closely linked to one another? In what way?

Chapter 115
Eastern Europe and the Soviet Union

GETTING STARTED

1   In the 1960's and 1970's, most people in Eastern Europe wanted greater independence from the Soviet Union, but the Soviets kept a tight rein on these countries.

The Soviet Union had other problems in foreign affairs. In 1979, it became involved in a long war in Afghanistan that it could not win. The war strained relations with the West. Nevertheless, the Soviet Union and the United States signed important arms treaties during the 1970's and 1980's.

Within the Soviet Union, a number of political changes have occurred since 1968. Mikhail Gorbachev (gawr-buh-CHAWF) took power in 1985 and introduced major economical and political reforms.

2   Before you begin reading the chapter lesson, survey the lesson. Begin your survey by reading the beginning of the lesson. Then look through the lesson and read the headings. Next, study the pictures and read the picture captions. Finally, read the review section called "Summing Up." This survey will help you to discover the important ideas in this chapter.

Know the Main Idea

As you read the chapter lesson, try to remember the following important MAIN IDEA of the chapter.

The Soviet Union tried to keep firm control over the countries of Eastern Europe. At the same time, important changes were taking place in the Soviet economy.

The following questions will help you to understand the MAIN IDEA. Try to answer these questions as you read the lesson.

1. Which Eastern European nations tried to break away from Soviet control? What happened to them?
2. What economic policies did some nations of Eastern Europe adopt?
3. What agreements did the Soviets and the Americans reach during the 1970's and 1980's?

Know These Important Terms

censorship	Solidarity
dissent	SALT treaty
repression	*glasnost*
perestroika	

Know the Years of This Chapter

Look at the time line below. It shows the years of this chapter, 1968 to 1990.

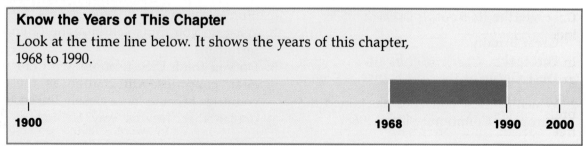

| 1900 | 1968 | 1990 | 2000 |

Pope John Paul the Second, the first Polish Pope, visited Poland after the independent labor movement Solidarity was formed

EXPLORING THE TIME

In the years since 1968, many differences have emerged between the Soviet Union and the Communist nations of Eastern Europe. The Soviets were not entirely able to control events in Eastern Europe. Major changes took place within the Soviet Union, especially after Mikhail Gorbachev became the Soviet leader in 1985.

Czechoslovakia Sought Greater Independence

In the 1960's, Czech leaders tried to gain greater independence from the Soviet Union. Czechoslovakia's new leaders ended press **censorship**, government control of free speech, and promised a democratic

government. The Soviet Union warned Czechoslovakia not to go too far, but Czechoslovakia pressed on. In August 1968, Soviet troops invaded Czechoslovakia and seized its top leaders. Later, the troops were withdrawn, but the Czech government was forced to forget about reform and follow Soviet policy.

But **dissent**, or differences of opinion, continued. In 1977, hundreds of leading Czechs signed a statement demanding greater liberty. Most of those who signed were jailed. The group, called Charter 77, continued to speak out against the Czech government.

Unrest Troubled Poland

The late 1960's was a period of reform in Poland, too. There were student protests, and the government introduced economic reforms. For example, it gave back to individual farmers most of the farms that were owned and run by the government.

During the 1970's, the Polish government had money problems. It had trouble repaying loans from the United States and some Western European nations. To bring in more money, the government raised prices. There were also severe food shortages. Many Poles protested by going on strike and by holding demonstrations. The protests spread quickly in 1980.

One of the most powerful protest groups was a new labor union called **Solidarity**. Solidarity's leaders called for lower prices and the right to organize independent labor unions. The leader of Solidarity, Lech Walesa (va-WENZ-uh), received the 1983 Nobel Peace Prize for his efforts to win freedom for Polish workers.

Under pressure from the Soviet Union, the Polish government quickly put down the protests. In 1981, it declared martial law. It outlawed Solidarity and jailed thousands of protesters. To show its opposition to these measures, the United States cut off trade with Poland and banned air travel between the two nations. This policy remained in effect until Poland ended martial law in 1983. More riots broke out in 1988 when Poland again raised prices.

Economic reforms have made Hungary one of the richest nations in Eastern Europe

Other Communist Nations Took Different Paths

You have already read how Marshal Tito made Yugoslavia an independent Communist nation. After Tito died in 1980, it was feared that Yugoslavia's many national groups would quarrel. A new government was formed with a collective presidency.

The nation's six republics and two provinces took turns choosing a president to head the government. Even so, riots broke out in 1980 among Albanian-speaking Yugoslavs who demanded a separate republic. In 1988, rioting broke out again. This time high inflation and widespread unemployment added to the existing tensions between various national groups.

Rumania also took an independent path. In 1959, it banned the presence of Soviet troops on its soil. In 1965, the Rumanian government declared itself a Socialist rather than a Communist nation. The government, which owns all factories in Rumania, worked hard to industrialize the country.

As you read in Chapter 111, Hungary tried to free itself from Soviet control in

1956. The revolt was crushed by Soviet troops. But the Hungarians continued to seek greater liberty and independence from the Soviet Union. In 1968, the government made major changes in Hungary's economy. The state gave up much of its central economic control. Instead, it allowed consumer demand to influence production and prices. Farmers could grow and sell their own crops, and a limited amount of free enterprise was permitted. State-owned businesses were encouraged to compete with one another. But the state still kept strict control over many other phases of Hungarian life.

These reforms made Hungary one of the most prosperous nations in Eastern Europe. Hungary's successful economic changes inspired many of the reforms introduced by Soviet General Secretary Mikhail Gorbachev after he took power in 1985.

Dissenters Protest Soviet Repression

During the late 1960's and early 1970's, a growing number of Russians dared to speak out against Soviet **repression.** They opposed the harsh treatment of people who disagreed with the government. Writers such as Aleksandr Solzhenitsyn (SOHL-zhuh-NEET-sun) criticized the government for its policies. Solzhenitsyn was forced to leave the Soviet Union and settled in the United States.

Another critic of the Soviet government was the physicist Andrei Sakharov (SAHK-uh-RAWF), a pioneer in the development of Soviet nuclear weapons. Sakharov asked the government to release its political prisoners. In 1980, after criticizing the government for its invasion of Afghanistan, Sakharov was exiled, or sent away, to Gorki, a Soviet city that was closed to foreigners.

DOCUMENTS IN HISTORY

Mikhail Gorbachev

When Mikhail Gorbachev became leader of the Soviet Union in 1985, the Soviet economy was in trouble. Soviet farms and factories, all owned by the government, were not producing enough food and other products. Gorbachev wanted to improve production by changing the way the Soviet economy worked.

For instance, Gorbachev offered farmers a way to control their own farms. The government would rent or lease farms to farmers for long periods of time. Gorbachev felt that if the farmers controlled their farms, they would work harder and produce more food.

Gorbachev explained his new program in a speech in 1988:

> Experience shows that the shortest and most dependable way of achieving the desired output of food is broad introduction everywhere of lease arrangements and other forms of organizing and stimulating labor.... Everything depends on how quickly we can arouse people's interests ... and make them true masters on the farm.

Question: How did Gorbachev encourage farmers to produce more food?

He remained there until 1986, when he was allowed to return to Moscow.

The Soviets Limit Strategic Arms

Soviet relations with the United States were tense during the 1960's. During the Vietnam War, the Soviets sent money and arms to the North Vietnamese while the United States supported the South Vietnamese government. Despite their differences, the Soviet Union and the United States tried to find a way to limit nuclear arms production. At a summit meeting in Moscow in 1972, President Richard Nixon and Soviet leader Leonid Brezhnev agreed to limit the number of intercontinental missiles produced by each nation. This was the first **SALT** (Strategic Arms Limitation Talks) **treaty.**

Five years later, President Jimmy Carter began new arms talks with the Soviets. In 1979, he and Brezhnev agreed on a second SALT treaty in Vienna. But before the U.S. Senate could ratify SALT II, the Soviet Union invaded Afghanistan. In protest, the Senate refused to consider the agreement.

Soviet Troops Fought in Afghanistan

Afghanistan, a nation about the size of the state of Wyoming, borders the Soviet Union and Pakistan. In 1978, a Marxist government took power in Afghanistan. Many Muslims in Afghanistan disliked the new Communist government and fought against it.

The Soviet Union supported the Afghan government by sending troops there in 1979. In protest, the United States refused to take part in the 1980 Olympic Games in Moscow. It also cut off shipments of grain to the Soviet Union. In Afghanistan, thousands of Muslim guerrillas fought against the Soviets and their Afghan allies. Although they had helicopters and superior weapons, the Soviets could not win the war. Some people compared the Soviet position in Afghanistan to America's role in Vietnam. Millions of Afghanis fled to refugee camps in Pakistan. Many Russians wondered why they were fighting in far-off Afghanistan. In 1988, the Soviets began to withdraw their forces, but fighting continued between the rebels and the Afghan government.

The Soviet Economy Lagged

During the 1970's, the rate of growth of the Soviet economy slowed greatly. The government spent enormous sums of money on weapons and heavy industry, the production of goods such as coal and steel that are used to produce other goods. It failed, however, to develop modern technology, and without new industries, such as electronics and computers, the Soviet Union could not compete with other nations. In addition, Soviet planners did not try to improve or increase the supply of consumer goods and services. As a result, the Soviet people suffered shortages of food, clothing, and housing.

After Nikita Khrushchev fell from power in 1964, a series of leaders headed the Soviet Union. None proved able to solve the nation's economic problems. In 1985, Mikhail Gorbachev was chosen General Secretary of the Soviet Union. At fifty-four, he was the youngest man ever to hold this position.

Gorbachev put forward a new plan for the Soviet economy. He called his plan

In 1987, President Reagan and Soviet leader Mikhail Gorbachev signed the INF treaty. What were the terms of this treaty?

perestroika, or restructuring. Soviet restructuring called for cuts in military spending so that Soviet factories could produce consumer goods and high-technology items. Groups of people were allowed to set up cooperative businesses, free of state control. Farmers could raise more of their own produce and sell it in open markets. In the past, central planning decided how much a factory should turn out and what it should charge for its products. Under *perestroika,* factories were expected to make a profit and to compete with one another.

These changes could not take place without increased political freedom, Gorbachev said. For this reason, he called for limited forms of democracy. In 1988, the Communist Party agreed to create a national legislature that would elect a presi-

dent. In addition, it agreed to limit the term of all party officials to five years. In this way, Gorbachev hoped to remove opponents from office.

Many Soviet officials, used to the old system, disliked Gorbachev's reforms. To encourage discussion of his plans, Gorbachev urged a new policy of *glasnost,* or openness. Censorship, control of free speech, was eased, and public criticism of government leaders was permitted. The government freed many political prisoners. But when national groups in Armenia and other regions demanded political rights, they were quickly put down. No leader since Stalin had tried to make such basic changes in the Soviet government. It remained uncertain whether Gorbachev would succeed.

Because of shortages, Soviet people often had to wait in long lines to buy food

In the 1980's Soviet Relations with the West Improved

Relations between the Soviet Union and the United States had been distant since 1980 because of the situation in Afghanistan. In 1985, the two nations resumed arms talks. The United States demanded that cuts be made in the Soviet land forces in Eastern Europe. The Soviets said the United States would have to give up plans for space weapons.

In 1987, President Reagan and Gorbachev signed a treaty limiting Intermediate-Range Nuclear Forces (INF). According to the INF treaty, both nations agreed to destroy all their medium- and short-range missiles.

SUMMING UP

The Soviet Union maintained its control over the Communist nations of Eastern Europe. But several of these nations managed to become at least partly independent of the Soviets. Economic reforms in Hungary gave the Soviets a model for sweeping changes introduced by Mikhail Gorbachev. A long and fruitless war in Afghanistan was a drain on the Soviet economy until 1988, when the Soviet Union began to withdraw its troops. A series of treaties between the Soviet Union and the United States limited nuclear weapons and missile systems. In the next chapter, you will read about the nations of the Middle East and Africa.

UNDERSTANDING THE LESSON

Do You Know These Important Terms?

For each sentence below, choose the term that best completes the sentence.

1. Government control of free speech is called (**dissent/censorship**).
2. (*Perestroika*/**Solidarity**) was a powerful Polish labor union in the 1980's.
3. In the (**SALT treaty/Charter 77**), the United States and the Soviet Union agreed to limit arms.
4. The policy of (*glasnost*/**repression**) allowed more open discussion in the Soviet Union.

Do You Remember These People and Events?

1. Tell something about each of the following persons.

   Lech Walesa   Mikhail Gorbachev

2. Explain how or why each of the following developments took place.

   a. Soviet troops were withdrawn from Afghanistan.
   b. Hungary's economic reforms led to the Soviet policy of *perestroika*.

Can You Locate These Places?

Use the map on page 722 to locate the following Eastern European nations.

Poland	**Yugoslavia**
Hungary	**Czechoslovakia**

Do You Know When It Happened?

In what years did Soviet and American leaders sign the SALT and INF treaties?

Do You Remember the Main Idea?

Which one of the following ideas is the MAIN IDEA of this chapter?

1. The dissent in Eastern Europe died out very quickly. In Poland, the government declared martial law.
2. The Soviet Union tried to keep firm control over the countries of Eastern Europe. At the same time, important changes were taking place in the Soviet economy.
3. The Soviet economy lagged because of a lack of political freedom. Gorbachev introduced a new plan for restructuring the economy.

What Do You Think?

From what you have read in this chapter, answer the following thought questions.

1. Why do you think the countries of Eastern Europe protested Soviet control?
2. How do you think *perestroika* and *glasnost* have changed the Communist system?
3. Do you think the United States and the Soviet Union have become allies? Explain your answer.

GETTING STARTED

1 The Middle East remained a battleground between many different groups. In Lebanon, religious and political sects fought one another. Arabs and Israelis continued their long struggle.

After many years of warfare, Egypt and Israel signed peace agreements in 1979. American President Jimmy Carter helped the two nations settle their major differences. But fighting between Israeli forces and Palestinians living in the West Bank, an area controlled by Israel, grew worse.

In this chapter, you will read about conflicts in Afghanistan, Iran, and Ethiopia. You will also learn more about how racial segregation has affected life in South Africa.

2 Before you begin reading the chapter lesson, survey the lesson. Begin your survey by reading the beginning of the lesson. Then look through the lesson and read the headings. Next, study the pictures and read the picture captions. Finally, read the review section called "Summing Up" at the end of the lesson. This survey of the whole lesson will help you to discover the important ideas in this chapter.

Know the Main Idea

As you read the chapter lesson, try to remember the following important MAIN IDEA of the chapter.

The Middle East was the scene of extensive conflict throughout the 1970's and 1980's. Racial discrimination led to a serious crisis in South Africa.

The following questions will help you to understand the MAIN IDEA. Look for the answers to these questions as you read the lesson.

1. Why did Israel and its Arab neighbors quarrel?
2. Why did an anti-American revolution take place in Iran?
3. What policies caused conflict in South Africa?

Know These Important Terms

drought	Black homelands
famine	sanctions

Know the Years of This Chapter

Look at the time line below. It shows the years of this chapter, 1968 to 1990.

| 1900 | | 1968 | 1990 | 2000 |

In 1982, Beirut, Lebanon, became the center of a war in the Middle East

EXPLORING THE TIME

Violence and change marked the Middle East and Africa during the 1960's and the years that followed. In the nation of South Africa, racial segregation, or Apartheid, brought about violence and caused many world nations to oppose the South African government.

Strife Tore Lebanon Apart

In the years since 1967, Lebanon has been torn apart by war and terrorism. The conflict has involved a number of different religious and political groups. Violence increased after 1967, and by 1975 Lebanon was in the grip of a full-scale civil war. In an effort to restore order, Syria and then Israel sent troops into the war-torn nation.

In 1982, Israel again invaded Lebanon. This time it was to destroy Palestinian settlements in Lebanon. Israel charged that settlements were being used as bases for attacks on Israel. Under the authority of the United Nations, the United States and several other countries sent military forces to restore order. The United States withdrew its forces after a terrorist attack on the U.S. military compound there killed 241 marines. By 1985, Israel had removed most of its troops, but the fighting continued among different groups in Lebanon. Much of Beirut was destroyed, and the Lebanese government had almost no power.

Israel and Its Neighbors Continued to Fight

As you read in Chapter 106, Israel and its Arab neighbors had been enemies ever

Conflicts increased between Israelis and Palestinians in the West Bank

since the nation of Israel was created in 1948. In 1973, Egypt and Syria attacked Israel to regain territory lost in the Six-Day War. The United Nations helped to arrange a cease-fire.

A major step toward peace between Egypt and Israel took place four years later, when the Egyptian leader, Anwar el-Sadat, visited Israel. Later that year, Sadat and Israeli Prime Minister Menachem Begin met at Camp David, near Washington, D.C. With help from President Jimmy Carter, the two leaders signed a peace treaty in 1979.

But fighting continued between Palestinians and Israelis, especially along the West Bank of the Jordan River. Israel had occupied this area since 1967. Palestinians living there protested the Israeli occupation and wanted a land of their own. Many Palestinians were killed in the conflict. Israelis argued bitterly about how much

force to use against the Palestinians, but the fighting continued.

Egypt Sought Peace and Prosperity

During the late 1960's, Egypt received a great deal of military and economic aid from the Soviet Union. After becoming President of Egypt in 1972, Anwar el-Sadat stopped this aid. He felt the Soviets had not done enough to help his country.

Sadat brought many changes to Egypt. You have already read about how he visited Israel in 1977. This move led to a peace treaty between the two nations in 1979. Two years later, Sadat was killed by a group of military officers and was succeeded by his Vice-President, Hosni Mubarak (mu-BAHR-uk). Mubarak faced many serious challenges. Egypt's population was growing rapidly, but the nation could not grow enough food to feed its people. A drop in oil prices during the 1980's made it hard for Egypt to import food and other goods.

Libya Broke with the West

Libya is a desert nation located in North Africa. In 1969, army officers seized control of Libya. A young colonel, Muammar al-Qaddafi (kuh-DAHF-ee), headed the new Socialist government. Qaddafi, a devout Muslim, based many of the nation's laws on Islamic principles. He also put the oil industry under government control.

Libya became rich from its oil earnings. Qaddafi used the nation's oil money to develop its cities and help the poor. He also supported Arab terrorists. His support led the United States to break off relations with Libya in 1981. Five years later, the United States blamed Libya for a terrorist attack in West Berlin that killed one American. In return, President Reagan ordered U.S. warplanes to attack Libyan targets.

Falling oil prices brought economic hardships to Libya during the 1980's. To help the economy, the government returned many businesses to private ownership. Relations with the United States remained tense.

Revolution Swept Iran

For many years, the United States supported the Shah of Iran. The Shah used the nation's oil money to strengthen his hold over the Iranian government and to keep control over his opponents. At the same time, oil made Iran a prosperous nation. The new wealth encouraged many Iranians to take up Western ways of life, including Western music and dress. These changes

PEOPLE IN HISTORY

Anwar el-Sadat

Egyptian President Anwar el-Sadat (sa-DAT) was waiting to review a military parade. He was dressed in his field marshall's gold braided blue uniform. The first part of the parade passed the reviewing stand. Without warning, three uniformed men jumped out of a truck and sprayed the reviewing stand with gunfire. Within seconds, Anwar el-Sadat was dead.

Anwar el-Sadat was born on December 25, 1918, in a small Egyptian village. As a young man, he had fought against the British who were in control of Egypt. Later, he helped to overthrow King Farouk in 1952. When President Gamal Abdel Nasser died in 1970, Sadat assumed the presidency in Egypt. In 1973, he launched an attack against Israel to regain the Sinai Peninsula which was lost in the Six-Day War.

The war made Sadat a hero in the Arab world. The Arabs had regained their pride, lost in early wars with Israel. The war did not, however, win back the Sinai. To do that, Sadat turned to peaceful methods. He risked all to visit Israel in 1977. As he said, "For great aims, we must dare great things."

Question: How did Anwar el-Sadat try to be a peacemaker?

Ayatollah Khomeini leads Iranian soldiers in this painting of the war between Iran and Iraq. What was the main source of conflict in this war?

disturbed those who believed deeply in Islam. Muslims, especially the followers of Islamic leader Ayatollah Ruholla Khomeini (koh-MAY-nee), overthrew the Shah in 1979. The Shah fled to the United States.

The new Islamic government was angry at the United States for supporting the Shah. In November 1979, Iran seized 52 Americans who were working at the U.S. embassy in Iran's capital of Teheran. An American rescue attempt failed, and the following year the United States promised to stay out of Iranian affairs and to release some of the funds belonging to Iran. Iran freed the hostages in January 1981.

In 1980, Iran and Iraq argued over the passageway leading to the Persian Gulf. War broke out between the two nations. Neither side was able to gain an advantage, but still the fighting continued. The conflict spilled into the Persian Gulf. The United States, Great Britain, and the Soviet Union

sent warships to protect oil tankers passing through the gulf from Kuwait and other countries. There were several clashes between the United States and Iran. In 1988, a U.S. naval ship shot down an Iranian passenger plane by mistake. That same year, the Iranians declared that they were ready to hold peace talks with Iraq.

Afghanistan Battled for Freedom

Afghanistan is a rugged mountain nation bordered by the Soviet Union, Iran, Pakistan, and China. A poor country, it was ruled for many years by a king. The king remained head of state even after Afghanistan's first national elections in 1965.

During the 1970's, **drought** (DROWT), a long period without rain, and economic problems caused unrest in Afghanistan. The Afghan army overthrew the king in

1973, and a civil war began. By 1978, a group allied with the Soviet Union had gained power. But many Muslims in Afghanistan opposed a Communist government. Muslim guerrillas fought against the new regime. In Chapter 115, you read about the 1979 invasion of Afghanistan by the Soviet Union. During the long and bloody war that followed, thousands of people were killed. At last, in 1988, the Soviets began to withdraw their troops. But this move did not end the fighting between groups within Afghanistan.

Afghanistan, a rugged mountain nation, suffered through a long civil war

Ethiopia Suffered Famine and Civil War

With a history dating back more than two thousand years, Ethiopia is the oldest nation in Africa. In the early 1970's, drought struck Ethiopia. At least one hundred thousand people died of starvation. Riots broke out in 1974, and that year the emperor, Haile Selassie (HY-lee suh-LAS-ee), was removed from the throne. A military government took power. In 1977, the Soviet Union agreed to provide military and economic aid.

Drought and **famine,** a serious shortage of food, continued in Ethiopia. Fighting between government troops and rebels in the province of Eritrea (ER-uh-TREE-uh) further strained the nation's economy. At the same time, Ethiopia fought against invading troops from Somalia. The fighting blocked international efforts to bring food to starving Ethiopians. The Ethiopian government has been unable to stop the fighting or to rescue the nation from famine.

Apartheid Divided South Africa

In Chapter 108, you read about Apartheid, South Africa's strict policy of racial separa-

tion. Under the system of Apartheid, Blacks hold the lowest position in South Africa's economy and society. In addition, Apartheid keeps Blacks from taking part in government. During the 1970's and 1980's, the government strengthened its Apartheid laws. For example, it began forcing Africans to move to ten so-called **Black homelands.** These barren areas are located hundreds of miles from South African cities, where most Africans work. In 1976, massive protest riots broke out in the township of Soweto (suh-WEE-toh). Government forces killed hundreds of Africans.

Prime minister Pieter W. Botha took office in 1978. Under Botha, South Africa drew up a new constitution. Adopted in 1984, the constitution made Botha President and gave him the right to claim almost unlimited power in emergencies. According to the new constitution, Asians and people of mixed race were allowed to take a limited

Under South Africa's system of apartheid, Blacks are forced to live in barren areas located far from the cities

ing countries of Botswana, Zambia, and Zimbabwe. The purpose of the raids was to destroy bases held by the African National Congress (ANC). The ANC, a Black anti-apartheid group banned by South Africa, had resorted to violence in its struggle against the government.

Many nations criticized South Africa for its racist policies. Archbishop Desmond Tutu, a Black South African anti-apartheid leader, urged other countries to put economic pressure on the South African government. Many Americans called upon their government to protest South Africa's racist policies. In 1986, the U.S. Congress voted to apply economic **sanctions** (measures that punish another nation) against South Africa. President Reagan vetoed the bill, but Congress overrode his veto.

South African Blacks held a nationwide strike in 1986, the tenth anniversary of the Soweto uprising. Violence broke out between the striking workers and South African security forces. Despite worldwide protests, the South African government continued to maintain its policies of Apartheid.

role in government. Black Africans were still excluded, even though about seven out of ten South Africans are black.

Blacks protested the new laws by holding strikes and demonstrations. In 1985, the South African government declared a state of emergency in thirty-six cities. Police had the power to arrest people on sight and to hold them in jail as long as they wished. More rioting took place in 1986. This time, the government placed the entire nation under a state of emergency. The press was severely censored, and thousands of Africans, including many children, were imprisoned. Hundreds of protesters were shot.

It was also in 1986 that the white South African government attacked the neighbor-

SUMMING UP

Many different groups continued to battle one another in the Middle East. Israel and Egypt signed a peace treaty, but tension continued between Arabs and Israelis. Revolutions in Iran and Libya caused a break with the United States. Racial strife in South Africa grew worse. In the next chapter, you will read about the nations of Asia.

UNDERSTANDING THE LESSON

Do You Know These Important Terms?

For each sentence below, choose the term that best completes the sentence.

1. A **(drought/famine)** occurs when a country does not get enough rain.
2. As part of its policy of apartheid, South Africa set up **(sanctions/Black homelands)**.

Do You Remember These People and Events?

1. Tell something about each of the following persons or groups of people.

   Anwar el-Sadat
   Muammar al-Qaddafi
   Ayatollah Khomeini
   Palestinians
   Muslims

2. Lebanon, Afghanistan, and Ethiopia were involved in civil wars in the 1970's and 1980's. Tell something about each of these conflicts.

Can You Locate These Places?

Use the map on page 692 to locate the following places.

Israel	**Iraq**
Egypt	**Lebanon**
Iran	**Syria**

Do You Know When It Happened?

In what year did Israel and Egypt sign a peace treaty?

Do You Remember the Main Idea?

Which one of the following ideas is the MAIN IDEA of this chapter?

1. The Middle East was the scene of extensive conflict throughout the 1970's and 1980's. Racial discrimination led to a serious crisis in South Africa.
2. Drought and famine were the causes of civil war in the Middle East and Africa. Religious differences added to regional tensions.
3. Racial segregation was a problem throughout the Middle East and Africa. South Africa was criticized by many nations for its policy of apartheid.

What Do You Think?

From what you have read in this chapter, try to answer the following thought questions.

1. Why do you think the United States uses economic sanctions against other nations?
2. How has the drop in oil prices affected countries in the Middle East in the 1980's?
3. What do you think South Africa should do about apartheid?

Chapter 117
Asia

1   Political unrest faced many Asian nations after World War Two. China, seeking stability and a way to feed its growing population, experienced many changes and upheavals. India, too, struggled to feed an expanding population while it tried to prevent clashes between religious groups. In 1975, North and South Vietnam were united as the Socialist Republic of Vietnam, and the new nation was faced with rebuilding a land ruined by war.

Both Japan and South Korea built modern industrial economies. Japan remained a democratic nation, but South Korea became increasingly repressive. A dictator took control of the Philippines in 1972 but was replaced with a democratic government in 1987.

2   Before you begin reading the chapter lesson, survey the lesson. Begin your survey by reading the beginning of the lesson. Then look through the lesson and read the headings. Next, study the pictures and read the picture captions. Finally, read the review section called "Summing Up" at the end of the lesson. This survey of the whole lesson will help you to discover the important ideas in this chapter.

Know the Main Idea

As you read the chapter lesson, try to remember the following important MAIN IDEA of the chapter.

Most Asian nations struggled with poverty and political differences. A few nations in this area grew strong economically.

The following questions will help you to understand the MAIN IDEA. Look for the answers to these questions as you read the lesson.

1. Why did Vietnam fight in Cambodia?
2. What problems did China face? How did it try to solve these problems?
3. Which Asian nations developed strong economies?

Know These Important Terms

cultural revolution   gross national
Sikhs   product

Know the Years of This Chapter

Look at the time line below. It shows the years of this chapter, 1960 to 1990.

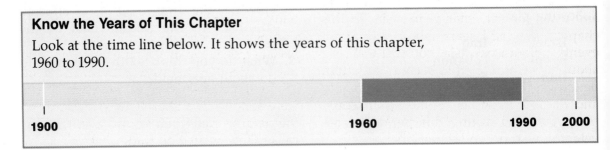

| 1900 | 1960 | 1990 | 2000 |

Traditional and modern elements come together in this city in India

EXPLORING THE TIME

The years after 1960 were a time of great, and often violent, change in Asia. In this chapter, you will learn about important events in Southeast Asia. You will also read about how China tried to become a modern nation and how India dealt with poverty and domestic conflict. Some Asian countries prospered during this period by developing a strong industrial base.

Southeast Asia Struggled for Stability

In Chapter 112, you read about America's role in the Vietnam War and the fall of South Vietnam in 1975. That year, North and South Vietnam were united as the Socialist Republic of Vietnam, with its capital in Hanoi. The land and economy of Vietnam were ruined by the long war. There were serious food shortages. Thousands of Vietnamese fled their country, either because they wanted to find a better way of life or because they did not like Vietnam's new Socialist government.

Vietnam's economy was further strained by its war in Cambodia (now called Kampuchea). Cambodia had been in a state of turmoil since 1970. In 1975, a new government headed by Pol Pot took power in Cambodia. Pol Pot wanted to eliminate all opposition and launched a program of state terror in which millions of Cambodians were killed or died of starvation.

Vietnam sided with the leader of a rebel group. With the help of sixty thousand Vietnamese troops, the rebels forced Pol Pot and his army out of Cambodia in 1979. But the civil war continued, even after leaders of various Cambodian groups held peace talks in 1988.

In 1977, representatives of the United States and the new Vietnamese government met in Paris to discuss several issues. The talks opened the way for Vietnam to join the United Nations. Recent talks between Vietnam and the United States have focused on several thousand Americans listed as missing in action during the Vietnam War.

China Suffered Upheavals

In Chapter 104, you read about how a Communist government seized control of China in 1949. Under Mao Zedong, China tried to modernize its economy and boost farm production, but these efforts failed. The Chinese government was forced to buy food from the Soviet Union and Western nations.

Many Chinese felt dissatisfied with China's lack of progress. They wanted China to return to its basic revolutionary beliefs. A period of internal revolution known as the **cultural revolution** began in

The Chinese leader Deng Xiaoping visited the United States and received a friendly welcome in Texas

China around 1966. Many old Communist leaders lost power, and the Red Guards, young followers of Mao, seemed to take control. During this time of unrest, factory production slowed and farms were producing small crops. By 1969, Mao realized that the cultural revolution had failed, and he brought it to an end.

China Expanded Its World Role

For more than twenty years, the United States refused to recognize, or officially accept, the Communist People's Republic of China. It continued to treat the Nationalist Chinese government of Taiwan as the official government of China. The Nationalist Chinese government of Taiwan also continued to sit in the United Nations. But in 1971, the United Nations removed the Nationalist delegation and seated the People's Republic of China in its place.

In the early 1970's, the United States made attempts to open formal relations with the People's Republic of China. In Chapter 112, you read about President Richard Nixon's visit to China in 1972. After the visit, the two nations agreed to improve their relations with one another. In 1979, President Jimmy Carter established full relations with the Communist Chinese. In the years that followed, the United States and China expanded trade relations, and many Americans began visiting China.

China Made Economic Changes

With more than a billion people, China has the largest population of any nation in the world. Feeding its citizens and modernizing its economy posed serious difficulties for the Chinese. Mao Zedong died in 1976, and new leaders emerged. Those who favored moderate economic policies gained control of the government. They were led by Deng Xiaoping (doong SHAU-ping). Under Deng, China launched new economic reforms in the early 1980's. Many collective farms were broken up and then were turned over to families. Factory managers were given power to make independent decisions. More individual enterprise was permitted in an effort to increase China's productivity.

At the same time, China established economic ties with many non-Communist nations. Chinese leaders were eager to buy high-technology items such as computers, communications equipment, and other electronic goods. The Chinese government

In the early 1980's, the Chinese government introduced economic reforms that allowed some individual enterprise

also welcomed foreign companies that wanted to open businesses in China.

India Struggled for Unity

As you read in Chapter 99, India became an independent nation in 1947. Almost at once, fighting broke out between India's Hindus and its Muslim minority. Many Muslims fled to neighboring Pakistan. In 1971, India and Pakistan went to war. They fought over the future of the Bengalis in East Pakistan who wanted independence. India, which supported the independence movement, invaded East Pakistan and defeated the Pakistani army. The war was settled with the creation of a separate state called Bangladesh.

Further conflict took place during the 1980's when a religious group called the **Sikhs** (SEEKS) began using terrorist tactics. The Sikhs demanded independence from India. Thousands of people were killed in clashes between the Sikhs and government forces. In 1984, Sikh terrorists assassinated India's Prime Minister, Indira Gandhi. Her son and successor, Rajiv Gandhi, held talks with Sikh leaders, but Sikh violence continued.

India Faced Economic Crises

India's population grew steadily, especially in cities such as Calcutta and Bombay. Poverty and starvation spread, but the government could not increase farm production enough to meet the needs of its people. The problem grew worse during the 1970's when drought struck the nation. India had to borrow heavily to buy food from other countries. In the 1980's, India remained a poor nation, with an average yearly income of about $250 per person.

Japan Enjoyed Economic Growth

After World War Two, Japan rebuilt its industry with financial help from the United States. Modern factories turned out steel, machinery, and automobiles. Japan quickly became the world's third largest exporting nation. Only the United States and West Germany sold more goods than Japan.

During the late 1970's and early 1980's, Japan shifted its emphasis from heavy industry to high-technology industry. This included the production of electronics, communications, and data processing equipment. High-technology industries were more profitable and used less energy, an important factor for a nation that had to import almost all its energy resources.

But economic growth strained Japan's relations with the United States. U.S. leaders asked Japan to remove some of its trade barriers so that American businesses could sell more goods to Japan. The Japanese government took steps to open its markets to American exporters. Japan also agreed to open factories in the United States.

In addition, the United States and Japan differed over defense. The United States maintained many military bases in Japan. The U.S. government asked Japan to spend more money to support these bases. In 1987, Japan agreed to increase its defense spending to equal 1 per cent of its **gross national product.** Gross national product is the total value of all goods and services a nation produces in one year.

South Korea Experienced Prosperity and Strife

Like Japan, South Korea experienced rapid economic growth, especially during the 1960's and 1970's. The nation built modern

Workers on an assembly line in a car-manufacturing plant in South Korea

factories that produced steel, textiles, chemicals, and other goods for export. But the South Korean government allowed its people little freedom. Protests broke out, and in 1972, the government declared martial law.

A new South Korean government took office in 1979. The new leader tried to restore order, but anti-government riots continued, especially among students. Although there has been no progress toward reunification with Communist North Korea, the two Koreas did begin economic talks in 1985. South Korea was chosen as the site of the 1988 Olympic Games. Partly to put an end to violence in the country before the games, the government agreed to hold free elections that year. After the Olympic Games, there were more riots in South Korea.

Corazon Aquino was elected President of the Philippines in 1987. Describe some of the problems Aquino faced after becoming President.

dollars from the economy of the Philippines through bribes and corruption.

In 1983, Marcos's chief political opponent, Benigno Aquino (uh-KEE-noh), Jr., returned to the Philippines after living many years in the United States. When he stepped out of the plane in Manila, Aquino was shot and killed. Believing that Marcos had arranged the killing, thousands of people took to the streets in protest.

Hoping to keep U.S. support, Marcos held national elections in 1986. His opponent was Aquino's widow, Corazon (KAWR-uh-ZOHN). Marcos was declared the winner, but there was widespread evidence that it was not an honest election. Army leaders turned against Marcos, and he was forced to leave the country. In 1987, Corazon Aquino was elected President of the Philippines by a large majority.

As President, Aquino faced immediate problems. The Marcos government had drained the nation's economy. Leftist guerrillas and right-wing attack squads fought one another. Many Filipinos were demanding that the United States remove its military bases. But, for the moment, democracy had been restored.

Revolution Occurred in the Philippines

The Philippines became an independent nation after World War Two. A series of democratic administrations governed the island nation until 1972. At that time, President Ferdinand Marcos placed the country under martial law. He claimed that Communists were trying to take over the government. Many Filipinos protested Marcos's rule, and were arrested or killed. Marcos stayed in power by cheating on the election counts and by terrorizing his enemies. He and his family took billions of

SUMMING UP

Political conflict continued in many Asian nations. Japan and South Korea created strong, prosperous economies, while other countries, such as India, Vietnam, and Cambodia, struggled against poverty. Democracy was restored to the Philippines after fifteen years of dictatorship. In the next chapter, which begins Unit 24, you will read about the culture of the modern world.

UNDERSTANDING THE LESSON

Do You Know These Important Terms?

For each sentence below, choose the term that best completes the sentence.

1. In China, the (**cultural revolution/Communist revolution**) began around 1966.
2. The (**Bengalis/Sikhs**) were the religious group that clashed with the Indian government in the 1980's.
3. The total value of all goods and services a nation produces in one year is its (**gross national product/prosperity**).

Do You Remember These People and Events?

1. Tell something about each of the following persons and events.

   **Ferdinand Marcos   Deng Xiaoping
   cultural revolution**

2. Explain how or why each of the following developments took place.
   a. Japan and South Korea developed modern economies.
   b. China and the United States established full relations.

Can You Locate These Places?

Use the map on page 686 to locate the following countries. Describe the wars they fought against each other.

   **Vietnam and Cambodia
   India and Pakistan**

Do You Know When It Happened?

In what year was Corazon Aquino elected President of the Philippines?

Do You Remember the Main Idea?

Which of the following ideas is the MAIN IDEA of this chapter?

1. Most Asian nations struggled with poverty and political differences. A few nations in this area grew strong economically.
2. There was a cultural revolution in all parts of Asia.
3. Asian relations with the United States declined during the 1970's and 1980's.

What Do You Think?

From what you have read in this chapter, try to answer the following thought questions.

1. Do you think that China's new economic policies will lead to closer ties to the United States? Why?
2. What do you think Japan could do to improve relations with the United States?
3. Do you think that the 1988 Olympic games had an effect on South Korea's position in the world? Explain your answer.

Unit 24
Life in the Modern World

THE CHAPTERS IN UNIT 24 ARE

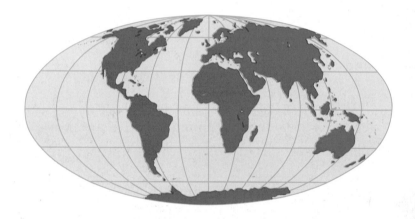

During your lifetime, great advances have been made in areas such as medicine and science. At the same time, violence and poverty have continued to haunt the world. In this unit, you will study how many nations are trying to work together in international organizations to solve these problems.

In the modern world, American technology has extended the traditional boundaries and created new frontiers

772

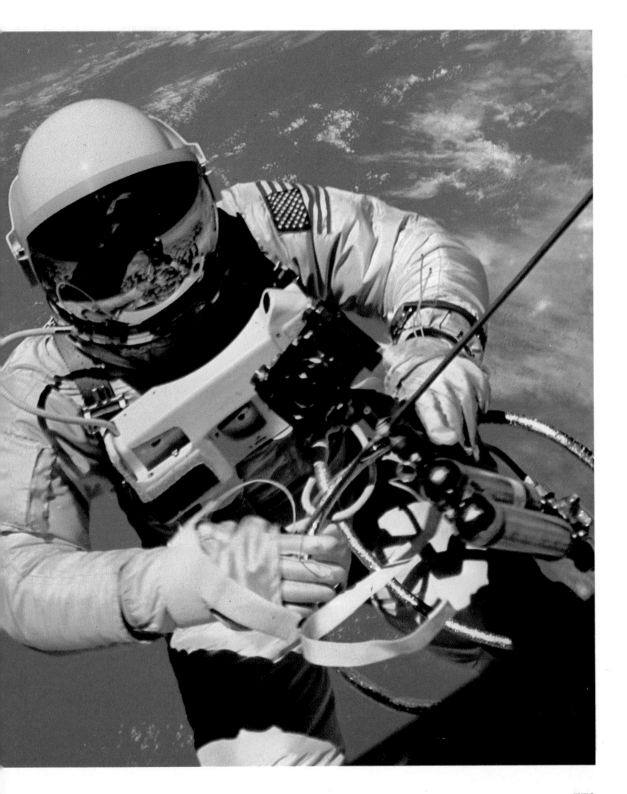

Chapter 118
Culture of the Modern World

GETTING STARTED

1   In the years since 1900, the twentieth century, the nations of the world have faced many challenges. Ten million people died in World War One. A depression followed the war, bringing economic hardship to the industrialized nations of the world. Then there was another terrible world war that lasted six years, from 1939 to 1945. Only a few years later, the cold war struggle between democracy and Communism began.

As you have seen, these problems brought economic and political changes. But art, architecture, music, literature, and technology also changed as people responded to the problems and the challenges of this century. In this chapter, you will learn about the culture of the modern world that developed during these years.

2   Before you begin reading the chapter lesson, survey the lesson. Begin your survey by reading the beginning of the lesson. Then look through the lesson and read the headings. Next, study the pictures and read the picture captions. Finally, read the review section called "Summing Up." This survey will help you to discover the important ideas in this chapter.

Know the Main Idea

As you read the chapter lesson, try to remember the following important MAIN IDEA of the chapter.

In the twentieth century, new developments in art, architecture, music, literature, and technology brought great changes to the culture of the modern world.

The following questions will help you understand the MAIN IDEA. Try to answer these questions as you read the lesson.

1. Who was the founder of modern architecture?
2. How did jazz music develop?
3. What were some concerns of the new writers?

Know These Important Terms

    cubism
    surrealists
    existentialists

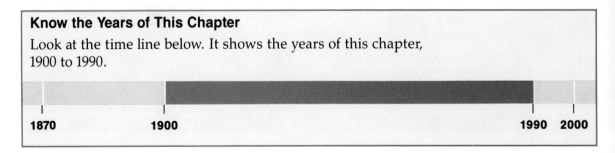

Know the Years of This Chapter

Look at the time line below. It shows the years of this chapter, 1900 to 1990.

| 1870 | 1900 | 1990 | 2000 |

The famous modern artist Pablo Picasso painted an emotional picture of the massacre of Guernica, which took place in Spain during the Spanish civil war

EXPLORING THE TIME

In the twentieth century, new developments in art, architecture, music, literature, and technology changed the culture of the modern world. In this chapter, you will read about these new developments.

Modern Artists Introduced New Forms

Before 1900, artists tried to show in their work the way things looked in the world around them. Since then, many artists have focused more on the thoughts and feelings of the person who looks at the art. For example, some of the paintings of Pablo Picasso (pih-KAH-soh), a Spanish artist who lived in France, show what it would be like to see an object from many different directions at once. This style of art is known as **cubism**.

In the 1920's, other artists, called **surrealists**, began painting images that exist only in dreams and fantasies. Salvador Dali and Max Ernst were leading surrealist painters. In the 1940's, the paintings of artists such as Jackson Pollock and Willem de Kooning had no subject matter at all. These artists would brush or drip paint, sand, and other materials onto large canvases. This kind of painting is known as abstract expressionism.

Architecture Reflected a Changing Culture

Before World War One, a new kind of architecture developed. Louis Sullivan, the founder of modern architecture, designed buildings not to look beautiful, but to serve a special purpose. His famous student, architect Frank Lloyd Wright, believed that

A building, made of steel and glass, designed in the international modern style of architecture

buildings must also fit in well with their surroundings.

A group of European architects, including Walter Gropius (GROH-pee-us) and Le Corbusier (LUH korr-BOO-zee-AY), followed the lead of Sullivan and Wright. Their simple, functional building designs became known as the international modern style. A good example of this style is a house built in Connecticut by Philip Johnson, an American architect. Johnson used steel beams to support the roof of his house. Since the walls were not needed for support, he made them entirely of glass.

New Types of Music Appeared

Musicians joined artists and architects in experimenting with new forms. Russian-born Igor Stravinsky developed bold new rhythms and harmonies. His composition, "The Rite of Spring," was first performed in Paris on May 29, 1913. That event is considered by many to represent the birth of modern music.

Arnold Schönberg (SHOERN-burg) of Austria developed a new twelve-tone scale to use for writing his music. John Cage, one of his American students, invented other new sounds. For one composition, he attached rubber bands and coins to the strings of a piano to change the way the piano sounded.

Another change in the music of modern times was the beginning of jazz music in the early 1900's. Jazz developed from the music of Black Americans. Their spirituals and work songs combined African rhythms

Duke Ellington, a jazz pioneer. Name another great jazz musician.

and European melodies. Among the great jazz pioneers were Louis Armstrong, a trumpet player, and Duke Ellington, a pianist and composer.

In the 1950's, another new kind of music emerged. Called rock and roll, it grew out of the rhythm and blues music played on Black radio stations. A young white singer by the name of Elvis Presley introduced rock and roll to the nation at large. Popular music was never the same again. The Beatles, a British rock group, dominated rock music through the 1960's. The music of both Elvis and the Beatles continues to be popular.

Literature Took New Directions

The many problems of the twentieth century caused writers to ask new questions about the kind of world in which we live. In the 1920's, Ernest Hemingway wrote *A Farewell to Arms*, a novel about the search for meaning in the middle of war. Another American, William Faulkner, wrote *The Sound and the Fury*, in which he shows how the promise of the American dream is not always realized. Both Hemingway and Faulkner won the Nobel Prize in Literature.

John Steinbeck wrote about the great depression in his novel *The Grapes of Wrath*. He tells how the depression hurt western farm workers in the United States.

Other American authors tried to understand the problem of race relations in the United States. *Go Tell It on the Mountain*, by James Baldwin, explores the relationship between Blacks and whites. Toni Morrison's novel *Tar Baby* tells the story of a Black woman who lives in a white world.

European writers also dealt with serious issues. The French writer Marcel Proust (PROOST), in his novel *Remembrance of Things Past*, shows how each day is supremely important, because what is past is gone forever. James Joyce, an Irish writer, describes the events of a single day in Dublin in his novel *Ulysses*.

The French writers Jean-Paul Sartre (SAHR-truh) and Albert Camus (ka-MYOU) were **existentialists**. They believed that life has no real purpose beyond the goals individuals set for themselves.

Many writers in the 1900's have been concerned with political repression. Aleksandr Solzhenitsyn (SOHL-zhuh-NEET-sun),

James Joyce

Ireland is a small island country, but it has produced many great writers. One of the most famous of these writers was James Joyce. He was born in Dublin, Ireland's largest city, in 1882.

James Joyce wrote stories and novels about ordinary Irish people. But he did not want his books to be ordinary. He wanted to use language in new and different ways. Joyce wanted to tell not only what people did, but also what they saw, heard, tasted, smelled, thought, and dreamed.

One of Joyce's novels is titled *A Portrait of the Artist as a Young Man.* The young man in the novel is called Stephen Dedalus, but he is based on Joyce himself. Here Joyce describes Stephen waking up:

The full morning light had come. No sound was to be heard: but he knew that all around him life was about to waken in common noises, hoarse voices, sleepy prayers. Shrinking from that life he turned towards the wall, making a cowl of the blanket and staring at the great over-blown scarlet flowers of the tattered wallpaper.

Question: What did James Joyce write about?

a Russian, spoke out against the Soviet system. His book *One Day in the Life of Ivan Denisovich* describes his punishment in one of Stalin's prison camps. Athol Fugard and Alan Stewart Paton, two South Africans, have written about race relations. Their works deal with the harsh treatment of Blacks by the South African government. Political and social issues have also been important in the works of leading Latin American writers, such as Gabriel García Márquez (MAHR-kes) and Pablo Neruda.

New Technology Changed Art and Entertainment

The development of the television in the 1950's revolutionized modern culture in the Western nations. News programs made the world seem smaller, and national advertising campaigns helped to mold similar tastes within nations. In the 1980's, the video cassette recorder (VCR) expanded the possibilities of home entertainment.

Technological innovations have also affected recorded music. Long-playing records were followed by cassette tapes and then, in the 1980's, by compact discs (CD's). Compact discs provide very high quality sound.

SUMMING UP

In the 1900's, new developments in art, architecture, music, literature, and technology brought great changes to the culture of the modern world. These changes came as people struggled with the problems and challenges of living in the modern world. In the next chapter, you will read about recent efforts toward international cooperation.

UNDERSTANDING THE LESSON

Do You Know These Important Terms?

For each sentence below, choose the term that best completes the sentence.

1. Artists who paint images that exist only in dreams are **(surrealists/cubists)**.

2. **(Expressionists/Existentialists)** believe that life has no real purpose beyond the goals of each individual.

Do You Remember These People and Events?

1. Tell which of these people are artists and which are writers.

Pablo Picasso	**Marcel Proust**
William Faulkner	**Max Ernst**
Salvador Dali	**Toni Morrison**

2. Tell what changes each of these people brought to modern culture.

Louis Sullivan	**Arnold Schönberg**
Igor Stravinsky	**Louis Armstrong**

3. Tell how or why each of the following developments took place.

   a. The development of television revolutionized modern culture.
   b. Jazz developed from Black American music.

Can You Locate These Places?

Use the map on pages 816–817 to locate the following places. Then tell which writers in the chapter are related to these places.

Dublin
South Africa

Do You Know When It Happened?

Tell in what decade (for example, 1920's, 1930's) the following trends developed.

abstract expressionism
Beatles' music
video cassette recorders

Do You Remember the Main Idea?

Which of the following ideas is the MAIN IDEA of this chapter?

1. Modern artists and writers all believe that life has no real purpose. The paintings of abstract expressionist artists had no subject matter.
2. In the twentieth century, new developments in art, architecture, music, literature, and technology brought great changes to the culture of the modern world.
3. Political repression has influenced all of modern culture.

What Do You Think?

From what you have read in this chapter, answer the following thought questions.

1. What serious issues do you think today's writers should deal with?
2. Do you think television has been good or bad for modern culture? Explain your answer.

Chapter 119

Toward International Cooperation

GETTING STARTED

1   In 1945, the leaders of fifty nations signed an agreement to create the United Nations. It was founded to make the world a safer and better place in which to live. Since that time, many other nations have joined this organization. In recent years, the United Nations has focused much attention on the needs of new member nations.

There have been many other international agreements during these years. These have led to more cooperation between nations on trade, economic policy, defense, and disarmament. In addition, scientists from different nations have often worked together to improve world health conditions, to protect the environment, and to explore the oceans and outer space.

2   Before you begin reading the chapter lesson, survey the lesson. Begin your survey by reading the beginning of the lesson. Then look through the lesson and read the headings. Next, study the pictures and read the picture captions. Finally, read the review section called "Summing Up" at the end of the lesson. This survey of the whole lesson will help you discover the important ideas in this chapter.

Know the Main Idea

As you read the chapter lesson, try to remember the following important MAIN IDEA of the chapter.

Since World War Two, the nations of the world have tried to cooperate in making the world a safer and better place in which to live.

The following questions will help you to understand the MAIN IDEA. Try to answer these questions as you read the lesson.

1. How has the United Nations helped new member nations?
2. What are the two weapons treaties signed by the United States and the Soviet Union? Why are they important?
3. How have nations cooperated to protect the environment?

Know These Important Terms

   developing nations
   arms race
   ozone layer

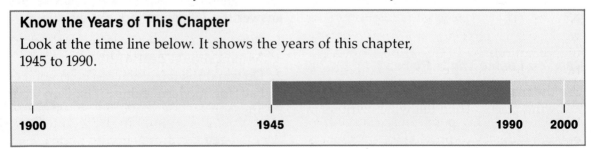

Know the Years of This Chapter
Look at the time line below. It shows the years of this chapter, 1945 to 1990.

| 1900 | 1945 | 1990 | 2000 |

United Nations peace-keeping forces in Lebanon in 1984

EXPLORING THE TIME

Since the end of World War Two, the nations of the world have tried to cooperate in solving the world's problems. In this chapter, you will learn about some of the ways the nations have cooperated.

The United Nations Expanded

As you learned in Chapter 103, in 1945 the leaders of fifty nations formed the United Nations (U.N.), an organization to keep world peace. By 1988, one hundred fifty-nine countries had joined the United Nations. Many of the new members are **developing nations** in Africa, Southeast Asia, and Latin America. Developing nations are generally poor. They do not have enough industry to provide jobs, products,

and services for their people. The United States and other industrialized, or developed, countries of the United Nations have often worked to improve health and living conditions in developing countries.

The United Nations Helped World Peace

Since its founding in 1945, the United Nations has worked to make the world a safer place in which to live. In the 1980's, the United Nations was involved in important peace-keeping missions in the Middle East and Africa.

In Chapter 116, you read about the Soviet invasion of Afghanistan. Fighting continued there for nine years, and neither side was close to a victory. The United Nations helped to work out an agreement to end the fighting. In 1988, the Soviet Union began withdrawing its troops.

Children in developing countries receive vaccinations to help prevent the spread of disease

laria in developing countries. In 1967, W.H.O. began a ten-year program of intensive vaccination that eliminated smallpox throughout the world. In 1978, W.H.O. set another ambitious goal. By the year 2000, it hoped to provide "Health for All." The idea was that every person in the world should be healthy enough to live a productive life. Much of W.H.O.'s effort focused on people living in the poor sections of crowded cities and in developing countries. Millions of children in such areas die each year from diseases carried by impure water. The goal of W.H.O. includes providing safe drinking water and sanitary facilities, immunization for all children, and local health care.

The United Nations also played a role in ending two other conflicts in 1988. In the Middle East, the United Nations was involved in encouraging Iran and Iraq to agree to hold peace talks. In Africa, it helped bring an end to the fighting in Namibia. In 1988, the peace-keeping forces of the United Nations were awarded the Nobel Peace Prize.

Two U.N. agencies help nations cooperate financially. The International Monetary Fund is concerned with the flow of money between nations and the promotion of international trade. The World Bank lends money to developing nations so they can build roads, seaports, and factories.

The United Nations Fought Disease

The World Health Organization (W.H.O.), an agency of the United Nations, has led a worldwide fight against disease. The efforts of W.H.O. have reduced the threat of ma-

Many Nations Cooperated on Trade and Economic Affairs

In Chapter 110, you learned about the Common Market, or European Economic Community, formed by six Western European nations in 1957. This trade association removed taxes on goods sold by one member country to another. By 1986, six more European countries had joined the European Community, as it is now known. The members have recently agreed to become a true community of nations by 1992. This means that there will be no economic barriers between member countries, and people, money, and goods will be able to move freely from one country to another.

The Communist countries of Europe also cooperate in economic and trade affairs. Their organization is called the Council for Mutual Economic Assistance, or COMECON. COMECON and the European Community now have diplomatic relations with one another. In 1988, Hungary, a member of COMECON, signed a trade agreement with the European Community.

A research vessel exploring the continent of Antarctica

Superpowers Agreed to Limit Weapons

In this century, the world has already experienced two terrible world wars and many smaller wars. Nuclear weapons, used for the first time in 1945, destroyed two major cities in Japan. Since that time, people in many nations have been very concerned about the **arms race.** This is the competition between powerful nations to produce bigger and more destructive weapons. People have also been concerned about the danger of destroying a nation or the whole world with nuclear weapons.

In recent years, some progress has been made to control the arms race and to limit nuclear weapons. As you read in Chapter 115, the United States and the Soviet Union have signed two major treaties to limit weapons. The first SALT treaty, signed in 1972, limited the number of intercontinental missiles produced by each nation. The INF treaty, which dealt with Intermediate-Range Nuclear Forces, was signed in 1987. For the first time, the two superpowers agreed to destroy some of their nuclear weapons.

Nations Worked Together on Science and Environmental Issues

In this century, nations have continued to explore and develop the resources of the earth. Since the 1950's, the speed of this development has increased as the number of people living in the world reached 5 billion. Today, it has become very important to control development so that it does not harm the environment. For this reason, cooperation among nations is necessary.

The continent of Antarctica is one of the few regions left on earth that has not been developed. In 1988, thirty-three nations agreed to open all of Antarctica to exploration for oil and minerals. But they also agreed to form a committee to examine the effect of this development on Antarctica's plants and wildlife.

GEOGRAPHY AND HISTORY

Space Shuttle

During the 1960's, the United States and the Soviet Union were involved in a "race in space." Each nation was racing to be the first to send a person to the moon. The United States won that race in 1969. But the two nations continued to develop their separate space programs.

In the late 1980's, American and Soviet officials began to talk about cooperating in space. Soviet leader Mikhail Gorbachev suggested that the two nations work together on a flight to Mars. Some scientists thought that American astronauts and Soviet cosmonauts could go to Mars together by the year 2001.

Many space experts agree that the trip to Mars would be easier if the two nations combined their resources. For example, the mission could use powerful Soviet rockets and advanced American computers. Scientists in the two countries could work together to solve difficult problems. Of course, the success of the project would depend on good political relations between the two countries. Such a project could also help bring the two nations, and the world, closer together.

Question: What two nations were involved in the "race in space" during the 1960's?

International cooperation has also become necessary to protect the world's wildlife. In recent years, for example, the number of whales in the world has been greatly reduced by disease, pollution, and hunting. The International Whaling Commission was established to keep track of the number of whales left in the world's oceans. When the whale population went below a certain level, the commission banned all commercial whaling.

Another problem that requires international cooperation is the thinning of the **ozone layer** of the atmosphere. Ozone is a gas that shields the earth from the harmful rays of the sun. Certain chemicals used in refrigerators and spray cans and other chemicals produced by supersonic planes are damaging the ozone layer. In 1987, thirty-one nations agreed to a plan that gradually reduces production of these chemicals.

Scientific cooperation even extends into outer space. In 1966, the United States, the Soviet Union, and many other nations signed an important treaty. They agreed not to use outer space for purposes of war. In recent years, nations have begun working together in space. In 1975, a U.S. spaceship linked with a Soviet spaceship while both were in orbit around the earth. A Soviet space mission to Mars in 1988 carried experiments from twelve other countries.

SUMMING UP

In the years since World War Two, the nations of the world have tried to solve world problems through cooperation. In the next chapter, you will read about some of the challenges that face the world as we move toward the twenty-first century.

UNDERSTANDING THE LESSON

Do You Know These Important Terms?

For each sentence below, choose the term that best completes the sentence.

1. **Developing nations/Industrialized countries)** are generally poor and cannot provide enough products and services for their people.
2. The competition to produce bigger and more destructive weapons is called the **(arms race/Common Market).**
3. The **(supersonic layer/ozone layer)** protects the earth from the harmful rays of the sun.

Do You Remember These People and Events?

1. Explain how or why each of the following developments took place.

   a. The members of the European Community became more closely linked in the 1980's.
   b. Progress was made in the 1970's and 1980's to control the arms race.
   c. Nations began to work together in space.

2. Tell how the following U.N. agencies have helped nations to cooperate in solving the world's problems.

   International Monetary Fund
   World Bank
   World Health Organization

Can You Locate These Places?

Use the map on pages 816–817 to locate the following places. Tell how each place is related to the events in this chapter.

Namibia
Antarctica

Do You Know When It Happened?

When were the United Nations and the European Economic Community formed?

Do You Remember the Main Idea?

Which one of the following ideas is the MAIN IDEA of this chapter?

1. The United Nations has reduced the need for international cooperation.
2. Environmental issues cannot be solved, even if nations work together.
3. Since World War Two, the nations of the world have tried to cooperate in making the world a safer and better place in which to live.

What Do You Think?

From what you have read in this chapter, answer the following thought questions.

1. What do you think are the most serious health problems facing the world?
2. Why do you think it is important for nations to cooperate in dealing with the world's natural resources?

Chapter 120
Toward the Twenty-first Century

GETTING STARTED

1   In your study of world history, you have learned about the peoples of the world from very early times to the present. In each period, people have had to face many challenges. Often, in trying to meet these challenges, people have been able to improve the way they live.

As you know, people today still face many serious problems in the world. In this chapter, you will read about some of these problems and about the efforts that nations are making to solve them. You will also learn about some challenges that you and young people in all nations will continue to face in the years ahead.

2   Before you begin reading the chapter lesson, survey the lesson. Begin your survey by reading the beginning of the lesson. Then look through the lesson and read the headings. Next, study the pictures and read the picture captions. Finally, read the review section called "Summing Up." This survey will help you to discover the important ideas in this chapter.

Know the Main Idea

As you read the chapter lesson, try to remember the following important MAIN IDEA of the chapter.

The nations of the world face many challenges as they try to provide a good life for a growing population.

The following questions will help you understand the MAIN IDEA. Look for the answers to these questions as you read the lesson.

1. Why is the size of the world's population a problem?
2. How has technology improved the quality of life in the twentieth century?
3. What great challenges remain as the world looks toward the twenty-first century?

Know These Important Terms

    population explosion
    foreign debt

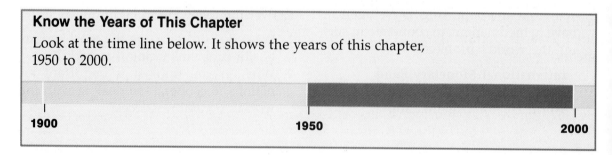

Know the Years of This Chapter

Look at the time line below. It shows the years of this chapter, 1950 to 2000.

| 1900 | 1950 | 2000 |

Increasing populations in modern cities create new challenges

EXPLORING THE TIME

In the twentieth century, the world has seen many changes. Many of these developments have made the world a better place in which to live. Yet, serious problems remain. In this chapter, you will learn about some of the important challenges facing the modern world.

World Population Continues to Increase

By 1987, the world's population had reached 5 billion people. If the birthrate continues at the present level, the world's population will reach 6 billion by the year 2000. Most of the increase in population will occur in developing countries. The population in these less developed regions of the world is now increasing more than three times as fast as in developed regions. This **population explosion** represents a major issue for developing countries and the rest of the world.

Developing countries must provide food, clothing, and shelter for their rapidly growing populations. To do this, they will need to use modern farming methods, build more factories, and develop new industries. They will also need to educate the

A refugee camp, where people who have fled from their homes stay until they can find a place to live

people so that they will have the skills and knowledge required to run a modern nation. Developing nations will need the assistance of industrialized nations to meet this challenge.

The World Still Faces Poverty, Hunger, and Disease

The advances of the twentieth century have failed to eliminate poverty, hunger, and disease in the world. One-third of the world's people live in India and China. Yet those countries produce less than $300 worth of goods and services per year for each person. In contrast, the United States produces more than $15,000 worth of goods and services per year for each person.

Many countries in Africa are even poorer than India and China.

Many developing countries cannot produce enough food to keep up with the growing populations. Weather conditions, soil erosion, and war have also contributed to the problem of hunger. In central Africa, for example, rainfall has been far below average since 1965. Crop failures and soil erosion have made farming almost impossible. In Ethiopia and Sudan, civil war has slowed the flow of food to the hungry. In 1984 and 1985, 2 million people died in Africa because of the famine, or shortage of food.

Hunger and poverty are not easy problems to solve. In addition, many people in the world who are poor and do not have enough to eat are in bad health. As you read in the last chapter, the World Health Organization has worked for many years to eliminate certain diseases and to improve the health of the people in the developing countries.

However, there are health problems that affect both rich and poor nations and rich and poor people. In the 1980's, a disease called Acquired Immune Deficiency Syndrome, or AIDS, appeared in many parts of the world. In 1988, AIDS was present in one hundred thirty-six countries, many of them in Africa. AIDS destroys the body's ability to fight off other diseases. Doctors and researchers around the world are working to find a cure for this deadly disease.

Nations Seek Ways to Pay Debts

In the 1960's and 1970's, many developing countries borrowed huge sums of money from wealthy nations. They needed the

A drought-stricken area in the Sudan. What problems are caused by this lack of rainfall?

money to build factories, roads, bridges, schools, and irrigation systems. With these improvements, the developing countries could provide a better life for their citizens.

By the 1980's, the borrowing countries had spent all the money. But most of their economies had not improved enough so that they could repay the loans from other countries. This problem of **foreign debt** troubles many developing countries today. In 1982, Mexico, Brazil, and several other countries almost went bankrupt, which means they faced financial ruin. The World Bank and the International Monetary Fund have played key roles in working out ways for these countries to repay their foreign debts. These plans have also required the cooperation of the lenders.

People Have Not Achieved Equal Rights

People all over the world have suffered from discrimination. They are not being treated fairly because of their race, religion, or sex.

In the 1950's and 1960's, the civil rights movement in the United States fought for equal treatment for Blacks and other minority groups. In the 1960's and 1970's, the women's movement worked for better conditions for women, such as equal pay for equal work. But full equality for all Americans has not yet been achieved. And, in the rest of the world, there are many people who do not enjoy full rights.

In South Africa, for instance, the government policy of apartheid continues to

Many people worldwide have protested against the use of nuclear weapons

segregate Black people. Blacks are not free to live and work where they choose. And the government has jailed many people who have protested against their policies. Some countries have refused to do business with the South African government until it changes its racist policies.

Wise Use of Technology Improves Our Lives

In the years since World War Two, technology has made most of our lives better in many ways. Medical advances have eliminated the threat of smallpox throughout the world. Operations involving heart and kidney transplants have extended the lives of many people.

In the 1980's, scientists developed powerful computers small enough to put on a desk. These new computers could do in minutes work that once took months or even years to complete. The widespread use of computers began to change the way people lived, worked, and played. In the United States, schools began to use computers for instruction and research.

Although technology has provided the world with many benefits, it has also introduced new challenges. Nuclear power is now used to produce electricity in many countries. However, nuclear energy has not proved to be completely safe. At Three Mile

Island, Pennsylvania, a nuclear reactor almost caused a major radiation accident in 1979. A reactor did explode in 1986 near Chernobyl (cher-noh-BIL) in the Soviet Union. New safeguards and standards are being sought in order to prevent future accidents.

The flight of the U.S. space shuttle *Columbia* in 1981 was the first flight into space of a reusable space plane. It opened a new era of space exploration and research. When the space shuttle *Challenger* exploded in flight in 1986, killing all seven astronauts aboard, the world was reminded that technology is not perfect. But when people use technology carefully and safely, it can make their lives much better.

Protecting the Environment Is a Major Challenge

As technology increased and the population grew, so did all forms of pollution. Factories and sewage disposal were among the sources of air, land, and water pollution. Some cities, states, and countries passed laws to limit the amount of pollutants released into the environment.

New kinds of pollution developed in ways that were not foreseen. Some of the wastes produced by factories and nuclear power plants remain dangerous for hundreds or even thousands of years. In 1978, some residents of Love Canal, New York, had to leave their homes because of danger

Pollution, in many forms, is a major threat to the environment throughout the world

GEOGRAPHY AND HISTORY

Smokestack

The summer of 1988 was the hottest ever recorded in the United States. Other parts of the world also had very hot weather. People began to wonder if the high temperatures were caused by air pollution. One expert on climate change told the Senate that the rise in temperature was not natural. He said that it was caused by a buildup of carbon dioxide gas in the atmosphere.

Carbon dioxide is produced whenever fossil fuels, such as coal and oil, are burned to create energy. Automobile engines, oil-burning furnaces, and coal-burning power plants all give off carbon dioxide. Carbon dioxide in the atmosphere traps the sun's infrared rays around the earth. The effect is the same as when air is warmed in a greenhouse. A buildup of carbon dioxide in the earth's atmosphere can lead to a "greenhouse effect."

Many governments are becoming aware of the ways in which pollution affects our air and our weather. But they have not agreed on the best way to reduce the amount of carbon dioxide in the atmosphere. Because the problem is world-wide, international cooperation will be needed to solve it.

Question: What produces carbon dioxide gas in the earth's atmosphere?

from waste dumped there in the 1940's and 1950's.

In tropical areas, many rain forests are in danger. More than 20 million acres of rain forest are cleared each year for timber or for agriculture. These rain forests play an important part in the fight against air pollution, since they convert carbon dioxide into oxygen. They also provide a home for many of the world's rare animal species.

The world's animals, as well as its forests and minerals, are natural resources. They must all be used wisely, or future generations will inherit an ugly and polluted world.

Nuclear War Remains a Threat

Perhaps the greatest challenge facing the world today is the threat of nuclear war. Ever since atomic bombs were dropped on Japan in 1945, the people of the world have known it is possible to destroy the world.

World leaders have worked to reduce the threat of nuclear war. In Chapter 115, you read about the arms control treaties between the United States and the Soviet Union. By 1990, however, at least ten nations will have nuclear weapons in their arsenals. World leaders must continue to cooperate in responding to the threat of nuclear weapons.

SUMMING UP

The nations of the world face many challenges as they try to provide quality life for a growing population. Advances in science and technology offer hope for the future of the world. The resources of the earth must be used carefully and wisely now and in the future.

UNDERSTANDING THE LESSON

Do You Know These Important Terms?

For each sentence below, choose the term that best completes the sentence.

1. Because developing nations have a rapidly increasing birthrate, they are suffering from a **(population explosion/ population erosion)**.
2. The problem of **(famine/foreign debt)** occurs when nations are unable to pay back their loans.

Do You Remember These Events?

1. Tell something about each of the following world problems and how the world's nations are dealing with them.

   hunger and poverty
   discrimination
   threat of nuclear war
   AIDS
   pollution

2. Tell how the following developments have improved life in the twentieth century.

   medical advances
   computers

Can You Locate These Places?

1. Use the Atlas map on pages 816–817 to locate the following places.

   Ethiopia
   Sudan
   Brazil

2. Name the country in which each of the following places is located.

   Chernobyl
   Three Mile Island

Do You Know When It Happened?

When did the following technological problems take place?

   nuclear accident at Three Mile Island
   nuclear explosion at Chernobyl
   explosion of space shuttle *Challenger*
   evacuation of Love Canal

Do You Remember the Main Idea?

Which one of the following ideas is the MAIN IDEA of this chapter?

1. Advances in technology have solved the world's pollution problems.
2. The nations of the world face many challenges as they try to provide a good life for a growing population.
3. Nuclear power can solve the energy problems of the twenty-first century.

What Do You Think?

From what you have read in this chapter, answer the following thought questions.

1. What do you think are the major environmental issues to be faced in the twenty-first century?
2. More and more countries have nuclear weapons. Why do you think this is dangerous?
3. As the world's population continues to increase, what problems do you think will arise?

APPENDIX

GLOSSARY

This glossary is a list of words and terms—and their meanings—that are important in world history. The glossary will help you to study and review the history terms used in the chapters of your textbook.

abolitionists (AB-uh-LISH-uh-NISTS): people who wanted to end slavery in the United States in the 1800's.

absolute monarchs: monarchs who were all-powerful rulers.

academic freedom: the freedom of universities to rule their own affairs.

acid rain: rain containing chemicals from factory smoke.

Acropolis (uh-KROP-uh-LUS): the hill that was the religious center of the city-state of Athens.

African National Congress: the organization of South Africa's Black citizens that fought against the separation of races.

Ahura Mazda (AH-hoo-rah MAHZ-duh): the Persian god of good and truth in the religious teachings of Zoroaster.

Ainu (AY-noo): the first people who settled in Japan.

alliance: a group of nations allied, or joined together to support each other.

Alliance for Progress: a plan to improve the businesses and living conditions of Latin American people.

Allies: Russia, France, and Great Britain in World War One.

Allies: Great Britain, France, Russia, and the United States in World War Two.

ally: a friendly nation that helps another nation in a war.

alphabet: a system of letters used for writing words and sentences.

American Indians: the early people from Asia who were among the first settlers in the Americas.

American Revolution: the war that won independence for the United States.

ancestor worship: the worship of dead relatives by the Chinese people.

Anglo-Saxons: the people who settled in England and ruled England after the Romans left.

anthropology: the study of people and their early development.

apartheid (uh-PAHRT-hyt): the government of South Africa's policy of segregation, or strict separation of people based on their race.

apostles (uh-POSS-ulz): the twelve followers chosen by Jesus to help spread the new ideas of the Christian religion.

apprentices (uh-PREN-tiss-SUZ): beginning workers in a guild who were learning a skill.

aqueducts (AK-wuh-DUCKTS): huge pipes, supported by arches, used to carry water to Roman cities.

archeologists: people who study archeology.

archeology (ARR-kee-AWL-uh-gee): the study of humanity's past, from the objects people left behind, such as tools, weapons, and pottery.

architecture: the art of building.

arena: a Roman stadium used for sports events.

armistice (AHR-mih-STISS): an end to the fighting in a war.

arms race: the competition between powerful nations to produce bigger and more destructive weapons.

artisans: people who are skilled at making certain products.

Aryans (AIR-ee-UNZ): a group of people from Persia who destroyed the Indus culture about 1500 B.C. and who then developed their own culture in India and started the Hindu religion.

assembly: the part of a legislature in the American colonies made up of members elected by the people of the colony.

atomic theory: the idea that the atom was made up of several different parts, an idea developed in the early 1900's.

Axis Powers: Germany, Italy, and Japan in World War Two.

Aztec (AZ-teck) **Indians:** Indians who developed a great nation in Mexico.

bachelor's degree: a university degree which a student received after about four years of study.

balance of power: the joining together of nations to balance, or equal, the power of one or more other nations in order to keep any nation from becoming too powerful.

baroque (buh-ROHK): the style of European painting and architecture that developed in the 1600's.

Bedouins (BED-oo-INZ): Arab desert wanderers, who moved from place to place in Arabia.

benevolent despot: an all-powerful ruler who tried to help the people.

Berlin Conference: a meeting of European nations in 1884 to set up rules for dividing the land of Africa among the European nations.

Berlin Wall: a wall built by the Communist government of East Germany to prevent people from escaping from East Berlin into West Berlin.

Bible: the religious book of the Christian religion, which includes the Old and New Testaments.

Big Three: Great Britain, the United States, and the Soviet Union—the three Allied nations that fought together and planned for peace during World War Two.

Bill of Rights (American): the list of freedoms and rights promised to all American citizens in the Constitution.

Bill of Rights (English): a great English law of 1689 that protected the rights of Parliament and the people against the ruler.

Black homelands: ten areas in South Africa where many Blacks have been forced to live.

blitzkrieg (BLITS-kreeg)**:** the swift and terrible war waged by the Germans at the beginning of World War Two.

block printing: carving an entire page of a book on wood and then printing it on paper. It began in China during the 800's A.D.

Boers (BOREZ)**:** Dutch farmers who settled in South Africa in the 1800's.

Boer War: the war fought in South Africa between the Dutch settlers (the Boers) and Great Britain from 1899 to 1902.

Bohemians (boh-HEE-mee-unz)**:** a people of eastern Europe.

Bolsheviks (BOHL-shuh-VICKS)**:** the Communist group led by Lenin that revolted in November of 1917 and set up a Communist government in Russia.

Bourbon (BOOR-bun) **family:** the rulers of France between 1589 and 1789.

bourgeoisie (BOOR-zhwa-ZEE)**:** the doctors, lawyers, merchants, and writers in France and other European nations.

Boxer Rebellion: the attempt by supporters of the Manchu dynasty in 1899 to force foreigners to leave China.

British Commonwealth of Nations: the nations of the British Empire, which were equal members with Great Britain in the Empire.

Buddhism (BOO-dizz-um)**:** a religion started by Gautama Buddha in India, which taught that people should "live a good life."

bushi (BOO-shee)**:** the Japanese feudal lords.

Cabinet: a group of advisers that the English king selected from among the members of Parliament.

caliph (KAY-lif)**:** the ruler of the Muslim Empire.

Calvinism: a Protestant movement started by the Frenchman John Calvin, which gained many followers in western Europe.

capitalism: an economic system based on private ownership of businesses and industry.

capitalists: people who invest in businesses and industries in the hopes of making a profit.

Carbonari (KAHR-boh-NAH-ree)**:** one of the secret groups in Italy that planned revolts against their foreign rulers and worked to unite Italy as one nation in the 1800's.

Carlsbad Decrees: laws that forbade German college students and teachers to speak and write their ideas about freedom in the 1800's.

caste (KAST) **system:** a development of the Hindu religion which divided the people of India into four main groups, or castes.

Catholic League: a group of German Catholic states that joined together in an alliance against the German Protestant states in 1609.

cave paintings: paintings made by prehistoric people on cave walls.

censorship: government control of speech.

Central Committee: the small group of people who control the Communist Party in the Soviet Union.

Central Powers: Germany and Austria-Hungary (and the Turkish Empire) in World War One.

Chamber of Deputies: the lower house of the French legislature.

charter: a legal document in the Middle Ages given to a town by a lord that made the burghers, or townspeople, free.

Chin (JIN) **dynasty:** the dynasty that ruled China after the Chou dynasty.

chivalry (SHIV-ul-REE)**:** a special code, or way of life, required of knights in Europe during the Middle Ages.

Chou (JOH) **dynasty:** the dynasty that ruled the Huang He and Chang Jiang valleys of China from about 1000 B.C. until 256 B.C.

Church of England: the Protestant church started by King Henry the Eighth of England.

city middle class: a new class of townspeople made up of merchants and business owners that developed in the Later Middle Ages.

city-states: cities that are like small countries and govern themselves, such as the city-states of Mesopotamia and of early Greece.

civilization: a great "center of culture," coming from the Roman word "civitas," meaning "city."

civil rights: equal rights for Blacks and all other Americans.

civil war: a war within a nation.

claim: the right of a nation to settle new land discovered by its explorers.

classes: the groups of people in a nation, divided according to their importance.

clergy: another name for church rulers, the First Estate in France.

Code Napoleon: a set of French laws drawn up by Napoleon, protecting the rights, property, and religious freedom of all French citizens.

Code of Laws: a collection of laws.

cold war: the world-wide struggle between the free nations and the Communist nations after World War Two.

colonies: settlements that people make in lands away from their own nation.

Colosseum (KOLL-uh-SEE-um)**:** a huge arena that still stands in Rome.

comedies: plays that have a happy ending, such as the Greek comedies that made fun of leading citizens.

commissars: the group of people who were chosen by the Soviet legislature to run the government of the Soviet Union.

Committee of Public Safety: a group set up by the Jacobin Party during the French Revolution to find out which French citizens were against the Revolution.

common law: the collection of written decisions by royal judges in England.

Common Market: a group of six Western European nations that agreed to end or reduce tariffs on all goods traded between these nations.

Communist Party: the only political party allowed in the Soviet Union, and the party which controls the government of the Soviet Union.

Communist propaganda: using peaceful ways to spread Communist ideas into other nations.

Communists: people who want an extreme form of socialism by revolution and by taking over the government.

compensation: payment for damages caused by war.

competitors: rivals for markets among nations.

concentration camps: prisons where 6 million Jews were put to death by Hitler and the Nazi leaders.

Concordat (kon-KORR-dat) **of Worms:** an agreement between the Pope and the German ruler in 1122 A.D. giving the ruler the right to approve the rulers appointed by the Pope as Church leaders.

Confederation of the Rhine: the group of German states united by Napoleon.

Confucianism (kun-FYOO-shun-IZ-um): a set of rules for living developed by the great Chinese thinker Confucius during the Chou dynasty.

Congress of Vienna: the meeting of the leaders of the main European nations in 1814–1815 to plan peace terms for Europe after Napoleon's defeat.

constitutions: written plans of government.

consuls: the two officials who headed the government of the Roman Republic and were elected by the citizens.

contras: a group that fought against the government of the Sandinistas in Nicaragua.

converted: changed.

Copernican theory: the belief that the earth and the planets circle around the sun, an idea put forth by the Polish astronomer Copernicus in the 1540's.

corporations: large business companies started by people who invested their money together in the company.

cortes (KORR-tezz): the council of advisers to the Spanish rulers, which included nobles, clergy, and townspeople.

Cossacks (KOSS-aks): Russian equestrians who lived on the plains of Russia.

council: the part of the legislature in the American colonies that was appointed by the governor.

Council of Clermont: the meeting in France in 1095 A.D. at which the Pope organized the first holy war (Crusade) to try to recapture the Holy Land from the Muslims.

craftspeople: people who are skilled in making a certain product.

Crimean (cry-MEE-un) **War:** a war fought by France and Great Britain in 1854–1856 to prevent Russia from taking land away from Turkey.

Cro-Magnon (kro-MAG-nun) **human:** the first Homo sapiens people, who lived in western Europe.

Crusades: religious wars fought between Christians and Muslims to control the Holy Land.

cubism: a style of art that shows what it would be like to see an object from many different directions at once.

cultural revolution: a period in the late 1960's when China tried to return to its basic revolutionary beliefs.

culture: the ways of living developed by a people, including their way of behaving, their knowledge, their tools, and their beliefs.

cuneiform (kyoo-NEE-uh-FORM): Sumerian writing, which used lines and triangles drawn on clay.

czar (ZAHR): the ruler of Russia, coming from a Latin word meaning "emperor."

Declaration of the Rights of Man: the document of 1789 that promised all French citizens freedom, the rights of property, and the right to change their government.

deism (DEE-iz-UM): the religious movement of the Enlightenment that believed in God, but did not believe in having churches or religious ceremonies.

delta: a triangle of land formed where a river divides into several streams as it flows into a sea.

democracy (duh-MOCK-ruh-SEE): a government that is ruled by the people.

departments: the parts of France set up by Napoleon that are similar to the states of the United States.

depression: a period of hard times all over the world, beginning in 1929, which caused businesses and banks to close in many nations.

despot: another name for an absolute ruler of a nation.

developing nations: nations that are generally poor and do not have enough industry to provide jobs, products, and services for their people.

Din Illahi (DINN uh-LAH-hee): a new religion begun by the Mogul ruler Akbar that was a mixture of all the religions of India.

Directory: the group of five people who ruled France during the third period of the French Revolution, from 1795 to 1799.

discrimination: unequal treatment, often based on race.

dissent: differences of opinion.

divine right: the belief that a monarch's power to rule came from God.

doctor's degree: the highest university degree granted to students, showing the student was now a scholar.

domesticate: to tame animals. In the New Stone Age, people domesticated dogs, sheep, goats, cattle, and pigs.

domestic system: the system by which workers made products in their own homes, before the Industrial Revolution.

Dominicans (duh-MIN-ih-KUNZ): a group of friars who became famous as teachers.

donjon (DUN-jun): the strongest part of a castle, where the lord and his family lived.

drawbridge: a bridge that was lowered from inside a castle wall to allow people to enter the castle.

drought (DROWT): a long period without rain.

Duma (DOO-mah): the lawmaking body set up in Russia after a revolution in 1905.

duties: taxes on imports.

dynasties (DY-nuss-teez): ruling families of a nation, such as the dynasties that ruled China.

Early Middle Ages: the first part of the Middle Ages, lasting from about 476 A.D. to about 1000 A.D.

economic rivalry: the struggle for trade and business among industrial nations.

economics (EE-ko-NAHM-iks): the study of the ways that people earn their living and carry on their systems of business.

Edict (EE-dikt) **of Nantes** (NANTS): an order by the French king in 1598 that allowed French Protestants to worship as they wished.

elements: basic kinds of matter, such as gases in the air.

Emancipation Proclamation: an order by President Lincoln that freed all the slaves in the Southern states during the American Civil War.

emperor: the leader or ruler of an empire.

empire: a strong nation that conquers and rules many lands.

Enlightenment: a change in European beliefs and ideas about life during the 1700's, based upon the idea that if people use their reason they can improve their life.

epics: long poems written during the Middle Ages by writers using the language of their own nations.

Estates: the three groups, or classes, of people in France before the French Revolution.

Estates-General: the council of advisers to the king of France.

Etruscans (ih-TRUSS-kunz): a people from Asia Minor, who settled in western Italy and ruled the city of Rome from 750 B.C. to 500 B.C.

European Coal and Steel Community: a business alliance formed in the early 1950's to strengthen the coal and steel industries in the nations of Western Europe.

excommunicated (EKS-kuh-MYOON-uh-KAY-tud): the Roman Catholic Church's members who were forced to leave the Church.

existentialists: writers who believe that life has no real purpose beyond the goals individuals set for themselves.

extreme nationalism: an extreme kind of national pride or love of one's own nation.

factory system: the use of machines set up in large buildings called factories to make products.

fairs: large trading meetings, sometimes lasting for weeks, held in Europe during the Later Middle Ages.

famine: a serious shortage of food.

Fascist Party: the party led by dictator Benito Mussolini, which controlled the government of Italy from 1922 to 1945.

feudalism (FEWD-ul-IZ-um): the kind of government and the way of life that developed in Europe during the Middle Ages.

fief (FEEF): the land given by a lord to the vassal during the Middle Ages.

Five-Year Plan: the Communist plan to increase factory and farm production in the Soviet Union.

foot soldiers: European soldiers in the 1200's A.D. who fought on foot and used powerful bows and arrows.

foreign debt: inability of a nation to repay loans from other countries.

fossils (FAHS-uls): the hardened remains in rock of very old plants and animals.

Fourteen Points: President Wilson's plan for world peace after World War One.

Franciscans (fran-SISS-kunz): a group of friars who carried on the work of spreading the Christian religion.

Franco-Prussian War: the war fought by Prussia against France in 1870.

Frankfurt Assembly: a meeting of German leaders in 1848–1849 that tried to unite German states but failed.

Franks: the people who formed the most important German kingdom in the Early Middle Ages.

freedom of contract: the right of each worker to make an agreement with an employer about wages, hours, and working conditions.

French Revolution: the revolt that broke out in France in 1789 against the French monarch and the government.

friars (FRY-urz): clergy who were both monks and priests and who left the monasteries to work among the people of Europe.

frontier: the land just beyond the settled part of a country.

geology: the study of rock forms that make up the earth's crust, or outer layer.

German Confederation: a union of German states organized by the Congress of Vienna in 1815.

German tribes: tribes who invaded the Roman Empire in the 300's A.D. and 400's A.D.

glaciers (GLAY-shurz): huge, thick sheets of ice. Glaciers covered the northern parts of North America, northern Europe, and Asia during the "Ice Age."

gladiator (GLAD-ee-AY-tur) **fights:** Roman sports in which slaves fought with one another or with wild animals.

glasnost: Mikhail Gorbachev's policy of openness, or easing of repression in Soviet society.

Glorious Revolution: the time when William and Mary became rulers of England in 1688, replacing the Stuart monarchs.

Golden Age: the greatest period of Greek culture in the 400's B.C., led by the city-state of Athens.

Gothic (GAHTH-ik): a style of architecture, with thin walls and stained-glass windows, used in building churches in the Later Middle Ages.

government: a group of people who make the rules, or laws, that people must obey.

Government of India Act: a law passed by the British Parliament in 1935 that gave India almost complete home rule, or self-government.

Great Pyramid: the largest Egyptian pyramid, built by the Pharaoh Khufu during the Old Kingdom.

Great Wall of China: the wall built by Emperor Cheng to protect the northwestern part of China.

Greek Orthodox Church: another name for the Byzantine Church.

Greek philosophers: the great Greek thinkers, such as Socrates, Plato, and Aristotle.

gross national product: the total value of all goods and services a nation produces in one year.

guerrillas: rebel soldiers.

guilds (GILDZ): groups of town merchants in Europe who worked in the same kind of businesses in the Middle Ages.

Gupta (GOOP-tah) **rulers:** the family that ruled northern and central India during the 300's A.D. and 400's A.D.

gymnasia (jim-NAY-zee-UH): large sports grounds where Greek people spent much of their time practicing sports.

Hammurabi's Code of Laws: a collection of Babylonian laws written down in 1700 B.C. when Hammurabi was ruler of Mesopotamia.

hand ax: a tool that prehistoric people made by chipping stone and probably used for cutting, chopping, and as a weapon.

Han dynasty: the dynasty that ruled China from about 202 B.C. to about 220 A.D.

Hapsburg family: a European family that ruled Spain, Austria, and the Holy Roman Empire during the 1500's and 1600's A.D.

Hegira (hih-JY-ruh): Muhammad's escape from the city of Mecca to Medina in the year 622 A.D.

Hellenistic (HELL-uh-NISS-tick) **culture:** the "world culture" started by Alexander the Great, which was a mixture of ideas from the Greek, Persian, and Hindu cultures.

hermits: religious people who went into wilderness lands in order to worship in peace.

hieroglyphics (HY-ruh-GLIF-iks): Egyptian writing that used pictures to mean words and ideas.

Hinduism: another name for the Hindu religion.

hired soldiers: soldiers who were not knights but who were paid by a ruler to fight in the army during the Later Middle Ages.

Hohenzollern (HOH-un-ZOLL-urn) **family:** the rulers of Prussia in the 1600's and 1700's.

Holy Land: the name given by Europeans to Palestine, the birthplace of the Christian religion.

Holy Roman Emperor: the title given by the Pope to the German ruler who ruled the old western Roman Empire.

Holy Roman Empire: another name for the German states and most of Italy during the Middle Ages until 1806.

home rule: complete self-government, as Gandhi wanted to have in India in the 1930's.

Homo sapiens (HOH-moh SAY-pih-ENZ): the first type of modern human who appeared about 40,000 B.C.

horse-drawn chariots: swift two-wheeled carts pulled by horses that were first used in war by the Hittites.

House of Commons: a part of the English Parliament formed by members from the counties and towns.

House of Lords: a part of the English Parliament whose members were nobles.

Huguenots (HYOO-guh-NOTZ): another name for French Protestants.

humanists: scholars of the Renaissance who were interested in everything that concerned human beings.

Hundred Years' War: the war between England and France which lasted from 1337 A.D. to 1453 A.D.

Hyksos (HICK-sohz): a people from Asia who ruled Egypt from about the 1730's B.C. to about 1580 B.C.

il Duce (ILL DOO-chay): the name given to Mussolini, the dictator of Italy.

illuminated manuscripts: books full of colorful pictures painted by artists.

imperialism: empire-building by nations, for example the nations of Europe in the later 1800's.

impressionism: a style of painting that gave a quick direct impression, or view of life, without showing many details.

Inca (INK-uh) **Indians:** the Indians who developed a great nation in the western part of South America.

India Act of 1784: a law that gave the British government the right to share the rule of India with the British East India Company.

Indian National Congress: the political party of India formed in 1885 that wanted the people of India to have a better education and to have a part in their own government.

indulgences: documents given to Catholics to help save them from being punished for their sins.

Industrial Revolution: the greatly increased use of machine power to replace human power that began in Great Britain about 1750.

inflation: a rapid rise in prices.

intendants: local government officials in France appointed by the king to take over many duties from the nobles.

interest: a fee charged for lending money.

International Association of the Congo: a group that was supposed to end the slave trade in Africa but instead gave the Congo land to the king of Belgium.

iron curtain: the imaginary line between the Communist nations of Eastern Europe and the free nations of Western Europe.

iron weapons: weapons made from iron ore and first used by the Hittites.

irrigation: a means of watering the land.

Islam (is-LAHM): another name for the Muslim religion.

Jacobin (JACK-uh-BINN) **Party:** the party of the leaders of the French Revolution during the French Republic, 1792 to 1795.

Jesuits (JEZH-oo-ITZ): a Catholic group formed by Ignatius Loyola to win back people to the Roman Catholic Church during the Protestant Reformation.

journeyman: a day worker in a guild who had completed the beginner's tasks of learning a trade.

Julian calendar: a calendar started by Julius Caesar and used in Europe for over a thousand years.

jury system: a system that developed in England in the 1100's A.D. in which a group of people were chosen to report to a judge the names of people who might be guilty of a crime.

Justinian's Code of Laws: a collection of Roman laws which later became the basis of laws used by many nations of the world.

Kellogg-Briand Pact: an agreement by the United States, France, and many other nations in 1928, promising to settle all future disputes by peaceful means.

Koran (koh-RAHN): the holy book of the Muslim religion.

Korean War: the fighting in Korea to keep Communism from spreading into South Korea (1950–1953).

labor unions: groups of workers who join together to try to get better wages and working conditions for themselves.

laissez faire (LES-ay FAIR): the system of allowing business owners to run their factories and businesses without government controls.

Lancaster monarchs: rulers of England during the early 1400's A.D.

Later Middle Ages: the last part of the Middle Ages, lasting from about 1000 A.D. to 1500 A.D.

Latins (LAT-unz): the group of people who started the settlement at Rome.

law of falling bodies: if two objects of different weights are dropped from the same height at the same time, they will fall to the ground at the same rate of speed.

law of gravity: all objects tend to attract, or pull toward, each other.

League of Nations: a group of the world's nations whose purpose in the 1920's and 1930's was to prevent war and to settle world problems by peaceful means.

Legalists (LEE-gul-ISTZ): a group of Chinese thinkers during the Chou dynasty who believed that a strong ruler and strict laws were needed to control people.

legislature: a lawmaking body.

Lend-Lease Act: a law passed by the United States Congress in 1941 that made it possible to lend ships, airplanes, and other war supplies to Great Britain and the Allies.

Lithuanians (lith-WAY-nee-UNZ): a people of eastern Europe.

lord: a person who had vassals who were pledged to fight for their lord's defense during the Middle Ages.

Lutheran Church: the Church started by Martin Luther, which gained many members in the German states, Sweden, and Denmark during the Reformation.

Magna Carta (MAG-nuh KART-uh): the charter of 1215 A.D. that granted English nobles certain rights and protected some rights of the common people.

magnetic compass: an instrument with a needle that always points to the north, which helped sailors to find their direction at sea.

Magyars (MAG-yahrz): a people of eastern Europe.

Manchu dynasty: the family that ruled China from 1644 until 1911.

manor: land owned by a noble and farmed by the serfs during the Middle Ages.

manufactured goods: machine-made products such as tools and furniture.

markets: places where manufactured goods and other products are sold.

Marshall Plan: the United States' program to help build up Europe's cities, factories, and farms destroyed during World War Two.

masters: the most highly skilled workers in a guild.

master's degree: a university degree received after about seven years of study, which showed that the student was a well-trained teacher.

Mau Mau (MAWO MAWO): the group in Kenya that fought to force the British settlers to leave Kenya in the 1950's.

Maya (MY-yuh) **Indians:** Indians of Central America who developed the earliest Indian culture.

Medici (MED-uh-CHEE) **family:** rulers of the Italian city of Florence who supported many famous artists during the Renaissance.

mercantilism (MUR-kun-til-IZ-um): the policy of business and trade among European nations in the 1600's and 1700's that required nations to sell more goods than they bought, in order to bring more money into the nation and make it richer.

merchants: traders who bought and sold goods and products.

Messiah (muh-SY-uh): the leader who the Jewish people hoped might someday build a new nation for them.

Middle Ages: the period of years that began in Europe about 476 A.D. and lasted until about 1500 A.D.

Middle Kingdom: the period of Egypt's history from 2000 B.C. to 1780 B.C.

minaret (MIN-uh-RET): the tall, graceful tower found on most Muslim temples.

Ming dynasty: the dynasty that forced out the Mongols and ruled China from 1368 A.D. until 1644 A.D.

Minoan (mih-NOH-un) **culture:** the culture of early Crete, which spread to other Mediterranean islands, Greece, and Asia Minor.

mir (MEAR): a village in the Russian Empire.

missile bases: rocket-firing bases.

missionaries: teachers sent to spread the Christian religion among other people.

missions: religious centers in the New World where Spanish priests taught the Indians the Christian religion.

moat: a ditch filled with water that surrounded a castle and protected it against enemies.

Moguls: people from central Asia who invaded and conquered India during the 1500's A.D.

monasteries (MAHN-uh-STAIR-eez): settlements where groups of Roman Catholic monks live together.

money changers: people who decided the value of different kinds of coins and who exchanged these coins at certain rates.

Mongols: a people from central Asia who conquered China and Russia in the 1200's A.D. and built up a great empire.

monks: clergy who live in groups apart from other people.

monotheism (muh-NAH-thee-IZ-um): the belief in one God.

Moors: a group of Muslims who crossed from northern Africa into Europe and conquered Spain.

mosques (MAHSKS): Muslim temples, or places of worship, in the Muslim religion.

mummies: dead bodies which the Egyptians preserved by using certain chemicals, then wrapping the bodies in linen cloth.

Munich Conference: the meeting in 1938 at which the British and French leaders gave the Sudetenland to Hitler, and Hitler promised not to take over any more European territory.

Muslim religion: the religion started by Muhammad in the 600's A.D.

National Assembly: the French lawmaking body, or legislature, formed by the members of the three Estates in 1789.

National Convention: a group called together in 1792 to write a new constitution, which set up the French Republic during the second period of the French Revolution.

Nationalist People's Party: the party of Sun Yat-sen that supported democracy but failed to unite the Chinese Republic.

nationalities: national groups, which usually want to form their own nation, as in the Austrian Empire, for example, in the 1800's and early 1900's.

nationalized: owned and controlled by the government.

national pride: people's need to feel proud of their nation.

Nazi (NAH-tsee) **Party:** the National Socialist Party of dictator Adolf Hitler, which controlled the government of Germany from 1933 to 1945.

Neanderthal (nee-AN-dur-THAL) **human:** early "cave people" who lived in Europe from about 70,000 B.C. to about 40,000 B.C.

Near East: the lands at the eastern end of the Mediterranean Sea and the lands of southwest Asia.

neutral: a nation that does not favor or support either side in a war.

New Deal: President Franklin Roosevelt's plan to end the depression of the 1930's by creating government programs to help Americans.

New Economic Policy (N.E.P.): Lenin's business plan for Russia in 1921, which lasted until 1928.

New France: the French settlements in the New World.

New Kingdom: the period of Egypt's history from 1580 B.C. to 1085 B.C., when Egypt became an empire.

New Netherland: the Dutch settlements in the land that is now New York State.

New Stone Age: the second part of the Stone Age—the years from about 8000 B.C. to about 4000 B.C.

New World: another name for North America, Central America, and South America.

nobles: large landowners who had their own armies during the Middle Ages in Europe.

Normans: people from the French province of Normandy who invaded England in 1066 A.D.

Norse sailors: the sailors from northern Europe who discovered North America around the year 1000 A.D.

North Atlantic Treaty Organization (N.A.T.O.): an agreement among the free nations, signed in 1949, to defend each other against Communist attack.

North German Confederation: a union of north German states organized by Prussia after Prussia defeated Austria in 1866.

novels: long made-up stories about interesting persons.

Old Kingdom: the period of Egypt's history from 2800 B.C. to 2250 B.C.

Old Stone Age: the first part of the Stone Age—the years from 1 million B.C. to 8000 B.C.

Olympic games: sports contests, held every four years, in which athletes from all Greek city-states took part.

Open Door Policy: a plan proposed by the United States in 1899 to allow all nations to have equal trading rights in China.

opera: a music-play that combines singing and acting, developed in Europe in the 1600's and 1700's.

Operation Overlord: the plan for the Allies' invasion of Axis-controlled Europe in 1944.

Opium War: a war fought by Great Britain against China to protect British traders in China.

ordeal: a test used in the Middle Ages to determine whether a person was guilty or innocent of some crime.

Organization of African Unity (O.A.U.): an organization formed by the new nations of Africa in 1963 to help strengthen all African nations.

Organization of American States (O.A.S.): the league of twenty-one American nations formed to make these nations stronger and to prevent Communism from taking over their governments.

Ottoman (AHT-uh-MUN) **Turks:** the people who attacked and finally conquered the Byzantine Empire.

over-populated: a nation that has more people than it can support.

ozone layer: an atmospheric layer of gas that shields the earth from the harmful rays of the sun.

page: the young son of a noble, who, from age seven to fourteen, was trained to become a knight.

Papal States: the territory in Italy that was ruled by the Pope.

papyrus (puh-PY-rus): a plant used by the Egyptians to make a kind of "paper" to write on.

Parliament: the lawmaking body of England, which began as a council of nobles and members from English towns and counties to advise the monarch.

passive resistance: the peaceful methods used by the people of India against Great Britain in trying to gain India's independence.

Patriarch (PAY-tree-ARK): the leader of the Byzantine Church (the Greek Orthodox Church).

patricians (puh-TRISH-unz): rich landowners who gradually gained power in the government of the Roman Republic.

patrons: rich nobles who supported the works of artists, writers, builders, musicians, and philosophers during the Renaissance.

patron saint: a saint who was supposed to aid and protect a guild or some other group.

Pax Romana (PAKS roh-MAHN-uh): the peaceful years of the Roman Empire, from 14 A.D. to 180 A.D.

Peace Corps: a program created by President John F. Kennedy to send American volunteers to work on projects abroad.

peace treaty: the agreement that ends a war.

peninsula (puh-NIN-suh-LUH): a body of land surrounded by water on all but one side, for example, Greece, Italy, and Spain.

perestroika (pair-uh-STROY-kuh): Mikhail Gorbachev's plan for restructuring the Soviet economy.

petition: the right of the people to ask the government to pass the laws they want.

pharaoh (FAIR-oh): a ruler of Egypt, from a word meaning "the great house" or "great family."

philosophers: thinkers.

plebeians (plih-BEE-unz): the common people of Rome, including soldiers, farmers, workers, and traders.

Poles: a people of eastern Europe.

political parties: political groups who support certain ideas about the government.

political science: the study of how people are governed.

Pope: the bishop of Rome, who became the head of the Roman Catholic Church.

population explosion: the rapid increase in population that is occurring mainly in developing countries.

prehistoric (PREE-hiss-TOR-ik) **people:** the early people who lived before written history.

Prime Minister: the most important member of the British Cabinet by the mid-1700's; the leader of the British government.

printing press: a machine with movable type used to print books, which was invented in Europe during the Renaissance.

profit: the money made by business owners from operating their businesses.

Protestant Reformation (REF-ur-MAY-shun): the movement to reform or change the Roman Catholic Church, which resulted in forming several new churches in the 1500's A.D.

Protestants: people who were against certain practices of the Roman Catholic Church.

Protestant Union: a group of German Protestant states that joined together in an alliance against the German Catholic states in 1608 for mutual protection.

province: a conquered land ruled as part of the Roman Empire.

psychiatry (suh-KY-uh-TREE): the study of the causes and treatment of mental problems.

psychoanalysis (SY-koh-uh-NAL-uh-SISS): a method developed by Freud of treating the mentally ill.

psychology (sy-KOLL-uh-JEE): the study of people's ways of behaving and thinking.

Puranas (poo-RAH-nuz): an important group of Hindu religious books written during the years of the Gupta Empire in India.

pyramids (PEER-uh-MIDZ): huge, four-sided buildings that were built as tombs for the dead pharaohs of Egypt.

Quadruple Alliance: an alliance between Austria, Prussia, Russia, and Great Britain, formed to carry out the peace terms of the Congress of Vienna.

racism: the false belief that one race, or group of people, is better than all other races.

rationalism (RASH-un-ul-IZ-um): the idea that people are able to solve their problems by thinking and planning, an idea held by many Europeans in the 1700's.

raw materials: products from nature, such as hides, lumber, and furs.

realism: an interest in things as they really are, an idea held by many Europeans in the late 1800's.

Reform Bill of 1832: a law passed by Parliament that gave more middle-class people in Great Britain the right to vote.

Reign of Terror: the period of the French Revolution from 1793 to 1794 when thousands of French people were killed.

Renaissance (REN-uh-SAHNS): the name given to the great period of change that began in Italy and spread to most of Europe between 1300 A.D. and 1600 A.D.

reparations: large amounts of money that a nation must pay to other nations for damages it has caused during a war.

repression: harsh treatment of people who disagree with a government.

republic: a form of government in which officials are elected by the citizens.

revival of learning: the new interest in learning and education in Europe during the Later Middle Ages.

Romanesque (ROH-muhn-ESK): a style of architecture with thick walls, round arches, and narrow windows, used in building churches in the Early Middle Ages.

Romanov (ROH-muh-noff) **family:** the rulers of Russia from 1689 until 1917.

romanticism (roh-MAN-tuh-SIZZ-um): the idea that feelings and imagination are the best guides to solving problems, an idea held by many Europeans in the 1800's.

rudder: a steering lever which made it easier to steer ships.

Rus: a group of people from Sweden who settled in northwestern Russia during the 800's A.D..

Russian Revolution: the revolution that began in Russia in 1917 and which soon led to a Communist government in Russia.

Russify (RUSS-uh-FY): a plan by the Russian czars in the 1800's to force all national groups and religious groups ruled by Russia to accept Russian ways of life.

Russo-Japanese War: a war fought in Asia between Japan and Russia in 1904–1905.

sacraments: religious ceremonies of the Roman Catholic Church and other churches.

SALT treaty: agreement to limit the production of nuclear weapons, signed at Strategic Arms Limitation Talks between the United States and the Soviet Union.

sanctions: measures applied by one nation against another to punish it.

Sandinistas: the leftist rebels in Nicaragua.

satrap (SAY-trap): a governor of a district in the Persian Empire.

scholars: people who study certain subjects very carefully.

scholasticism (skuh-LASS-tuh-SIZZ-um): the method of study that tried to show that religious faith and scientific thinking agreed with each other.

scientific method: the method of study that tries to find the truth through experiments and observations.

scribes: people who wrote down official Egyptian records.

Second Hundred Years' War: the long war fought in Europe from 1689 to 1763.

segregation: the strict separation of people based on their race.

self-government: a nation's freedom to govern itself.

Senate: the group of patrician Romans who passed the laws and chose the people who were to be voted on as consuls.

Sepoy Rebellion: the revolt, or rebellion, in India by sepoy soldiers against the rule of the British East India Company in 1857.

sepoys (SEE-poiz): India's soldiers who tried to force the British settlers to leave India.

serfs: the largest group of people on a noble's manor, who farmed the manor land.

Shang dynasty: the dynasty that ruled northern China from about 1500 B.C. to about 1000 B.C.

Shinto (SHIN-toh): the Japanese religion, from a word meaning the "way of the gods."

shogun (SHOH-gun): the Japanese noble who held most of the power to rule and also controlled the Japanese army.

Sikhs (SEEKS): an Indian religious group that has used terrorist tactics.

Slavic languages: languages spoken in the Balkan Peninsula and southeastern Europe.

Slavs: a people from Asia who first settled Russia.

socialism: the business system in which the government is supposed to own all of the nation's important industries and the people are to share equally all goods and profits.

social sciences: the subjects that study people and their behavior, another name for the social studies.

social security: a New Deal program that made weekly payments to workers who had lost their jobs and pension payments to retired workers who had reached the age of sixty-five.

social welfare laws: laws passed by Parliament in the early 1900's that provided health insurance, unemployment insurance, and old-age pensions for British workers.

sociology (SO-see-AHL-uh-JEE): the study of how people live together in communities and nations.

Solidarity: a Polish labor union formed in 1980.

soviets (SOH-vee-ETZ): councils of soldiers, workers, and peasants formed to support the Communists during the Russian Revolution and to make Russia a Communist nation.

Spanish Armada (ahr-MAH-duh): the large Spanish fleet sent to attack England, which England defeated in 1588.

squire: a young noble who at age fourteen began to serve as an assistant to a knight.

stained glass: colored glass that was used in the windows of European churches.

steam engine: an important invention of the Industrial Revolution used to provide power for large factory machines.

Stone Age: the long period of years when prehistoric people lived on earth and used stone tools.

Stuart family: the rulers of England during the 1600's A.D.

Suez Canal: a water canal in Egypt that connects the Mediterranean Sea and the Red Sea.

Sui (SWIH) **dynasty:** the dynasty that united China in 590 A.D. but ended after about thirty years.

Sumerians (soo-MER-ee-unz): a group of people who settled in Mesopotamia about 4000 B.C. and developed skills that later were also learned by all the peoples in the lands of the Near East.

Sung (SOONG) **dynasty:** the dynasty that ruled China from about 960 A.D. for three hundred years.

surrealists: artists who depict images that exist only in dreams and fantasies.

suttee (suh-TEE): the Hindu practice of a wife burning herself in the fire that burned the body of her dead husband.

Swahili (swah-HEE-lee): a language of eastern Africa that combines both African words and Arabic words.

symphony: a long piece of music written to be played by an orchestra, developed in Europe during the 1700's.

tablet houses: schools in Mesopotamia where students learned from clay tablets.

Taj Mahal (TAHZH muh-HAHL): a beautiful building in India built by a Mogul ruler as a tomb for his wife.

Talmud: the religious book that contains the history, ideas, and beliefs of the Hebrew people.

Tang dynasty: the dynasty that ruled China from 618 A.D. to 960 A.D., the years of a "Golden Age" in China.

Taoism (TOW-iz-UM): the religious belief that developed in China during the Chou dynasty and taught that the "pathway" to good life was to live simply and close to nature.

tariff: a tax on goods and products that come into a country from other countries.

temples: places to worship gods. Temples were first built by village people during the New Stone Age.

Ten Commandments: the laws that the Hebrew people believed were given to them by God.

terrorism: random acts of violence.

theory of evolution (EV-uh-LOO-shun): the idea that modern animals and plants developed over a long period of time from earlier and simpler forms of animals and plants, an idea developed by Darwin in the 1850's.

theory of relativity: the idea that all matter exists not only in space but also in time, developed by Einstein in the early 1900's.

Thirty Years' War: a European war that was fought for religious reasons to keep a balance of power among nations from 1618 to 1648.

three-field system: a system of farming during the Middle Ages in which manor land was divided into three parts. Two of the parts were planted with crops and the third field was not planted.

toll: a tax that European traders had to pay when they crossed a noble's land.

tournaments: "battle games" held between knights on horseback during the Middle Ages.

town council: the group which made the European town's laws and acted as its court in the Middle Ages.

town meetings: meetings in the towns of the New England colonies at which colonists decided matters of local importance.

trade deficit: the condition in a nation that buys more goods from other countries than it sells.

tragedies: plays that deal with serious matters, such as the meaning of life and the struggle between good and evil.

Treaty of Versailles (ver-SY): the peace treaty of 1919 that ended World War One.

tribunes (TRIB-yoonz): two officials elected by the common people of Rome to represent them in the government.

Triple Alliance: an agreement between Germany, Austria-Hungary, and Italy made in 1882 to protect each other against their enemies.

Triple Entente (ahn-TAHNT): an alliance agreement made by France, Russia, and Great Britain to protect each other against their enemies.

Truman Doctrine: a plan to give American money and other aid to help European nations defend themselves against the Soviet Union after World War Two.

Tudor family: the rulers of England during the 1500's A.D.

tyrants (TY-runtz): rulers who took control of the government of the Greek city-states.

United Nations: an organization of nations formed in 1945 to work for world peace.

universities: schools of higher learning that were set up in Europe during the Later Middle Ages, and where outstanding teachers taught.

untouchables: the people who were not included in one of the four main Hindu castes in India.

Urdu (OOR-doo): a language developed in India that is a mixture of Hindu and Turkish words.

vandalism: a word meaning to destroy property. The word comes from the Vandals' attack against Rome.

vassals (VASS-ulz): "servants" of a ruler or lord who promised fighting services in return for receiving land and protection during the Middle Ages.

Vedas (VAY-duz): the holy books of the Hindu religion.

veto: the power to turn down laws.

viceroys (VICE-royz): the highest government officials in the Spanish colonies.

Vietnam War: the war that began in 1965 when American troops fought to defend South Vietnam against Communist attack.

villa (VILL-uh): a large farm in the Roman Empire.

war bands: groups of early German fighters, led by strong chiefs, that invaded the Roman Empire.

war lords: bandit leaders who conquered parts of China as the Han dynasty ended.

Washington Conference: a meeting held in 1922 at which Great Britain, Japan, and the United States agreed to stop building large warships.

Watergate: the crisis brought on by a burglary at the Democratic campaign headquarters that resulted in President Richard Nixon's resignation.

water passage: a water route through North America which European explorers searched for but failed to discover.

water power: the use of water for turning machinery to grind grain or to saw wood, for example.

Weimar (VY-mahr) **Republic:** the government set up in Germany after World War One.

Western Front: the fighting line in western Europe in World War One.

westernized: to become more like European nations, as the Japanese under the Emperor Mutsuhito tried to do in the late 1800's.

windmill: the invention that made it possible to use wind power.

World War One: the great war in Europe from 1914 to 1918.

World War Two: the great war in Europe and Asia from 1939 to 1945.

written exam system: the system used in China for choosing government officials during the Tang dynasty and later dynasties.

Yamato (yah-MAH-toh) **tribe:** a Japanese tribe that became the strongest and conquered other Japanese people.

Young China: a group of young Chinese who wanted to overthrow the Manchu goverment in the early 1900's.

Young Italy: a secret group led by Joseph Mazzini that worked to overthrow the foreign rulers of Italy and to unite Italy as one nation in the 1800's.

Young Turks: a group of new leaders who took over the government of Turkey in 1908 and tried to build a strong Turkish nation.

Zaibatsu (ZY-baht-soo): four rich and powerful families that controlled most large businesses in Japan by the early 1900's.

ziggurats (ZIG-uh-ratz): tall temples built by the Sumerians to worship their gods.

Important Years in World History

The Story of Early People

1 million B.C.-8000 B.C.	The years of the Old Stone Age
1 million B.C.	East Africa human-like creatures lived on earth
500,000 B.C.	Java human lived on earth
70,000 B.C.	Neanderthal human lived on earth
40,000 B.C.	Homo sapiens (Cro-Magnon human) lived on earth
8000 B.C.-4000 B.C.	The years of the New Stone Age

The Peoples of Mesopotamia

4000 B.C.	The Sumerians settled in Mesopotamia
1700 B.C.	The Code of Hammurabi was written
538 B.C.	The Persians conquered the Babylonians

The People of Egypt

4000 B.C.	Egyptians settled in the Nile River valley
2900 B.C.	Menes united Egypt
2800 B.C.-2250 B.C.	The years of the Old Kingdom in Egypt
2000 B.C.-1780 B.C.	The years of the Middle Kingdom in Egypt
1580 B.C.-1085 B.C.	The years of the New Kingdom in Egypt
1375 B.C.-1358 B.C.	Ikhnaton was ruler of Egypt
332 B.C.	Alexander the Great conquered Egypt

The Peoples of the Near East

1900 B.C.-1200 B.C.	The years of the Hittite Empire
1275 B.C.	Moses led the Hebrews out of Egypt
1200 B.C.-700 B.C.	The years of the Phoenician trading nation
1025 B.C.-586 B.C.	The years of the Hebrew nation in Palestine
550 B.C.-330 B.C.	The years of the Persian Empire

The Peoples of India and China

3000 B.C.	People of early India settled in the Indus River valley
2000 B.C.	People of early China settled in the Huang He valley
1500 B.C.	The Indus River valley culture was destroyed by the Aryans
1500 B.C.-1028 B.C.	The Shang dynasty ruled in China
1028 B.C.-256 B.C.	The Chou dynasty ruled in China during these years of China's "Classical Age"
551 B.C.	Confucius was born in China

The Development of Greek Culture

3000 B.C.-1400 B.C.	The years of the Minoan culture of Crete
1400 B.C.	Mycenae destroyed Crete's capital city of Knossos
1000 B.C.	The Dorians conquered Greece
620 B.C.	Draco wrote down the laws for the people of Athens
594 B.C.	Solon tried to help the common people of Athens
499 B.C.-479 B.C.	Greek city-states fought a war against the Persians
479 B.C.-404 B.C.	The years of the "Golden Age" of Greece
461 B.C.-429 B.C.	Athens became more democratic, ruled by Pericles
338 B.C.	Philip of Macedonia conquered Greece
334 B.C.-331 B.C.	Alexander the Great ruled Greece and conquered the Persian Empire
323 B.C.-133 B.C.	The years of Hellenistic culture in Greece and the lands of the Near East

The Development of Roman Culture

1000 B.C.	The Latins entered Italy and started a settlement at Rome
750 B.C.-500 B.C.	The Etruscans built up Rome as the strongest Italian city-state
270 B.C.	Rome ruled most of Italy
264 B.C.-202 B.C.	Rome and Carthage were at war
133 B.C.	Rome controlled most of the Mediterranean region
49 B.C.-44 B.C.	Julius Caesar was ruler of the Roman Republic
27 B.C.	Octavian (Augustus) became the first emperor of the Roman Empire
—	Jesus Christ was born
284 A.D.	Diocletian became emperor of the Roman Empire
313 A.D.	Constantine made the Christian religion lawful in the Roman Empire
378 A.D.	The Visigoths defeated the Romans
380 A.D.	Christianity became the official religion of the western Roman Empire
410 A.D.	Alaric, chief of the Visigoths, conquered Rome
455 A.D.	The Vandals captured Rome
476 A.D.	The end of the western Roman Empire

Europe During the Early Middle Ages

476 A.D.-1000 A.D.	The years of the Early Middle Ages
493 A.D.	Theodoric, ruler of the Ostrogoths, began his rule of Italy
751 A.D.	Pepin the Short became ruler of the Frankish Kingdom
768 A.D.-814 A.D.	The years Charlemagne ruled the Frankish Kingdom
800 A.D.	Charlemagne was crowned as "Emperor of the Romans" by the Pope

The Byzantine and Muslim Empires

330 A.D.	Emperor Constantine built Constantinople, which became the capital city of the Byzantine Empire
395 A.D.	Christianity became the official religion of the Byzantine Empire
527 A.D.-565 A.D.	Emperor Justinian ruled the Byzantine Empire
570 A.D.	Muhammad, the founder of the Muslim religion, was born
622 A.D.	Muhammad fled from the city of Mecca to Medina (the Hegira)
early 700's A.D.	The Muslim Empire reached its greatest power, stretching from Spain to India

The Peoples of Asia and the Americas

270 B.C.-230 B.C.	Emperor Asoka ruled the Maurya Empire in India
300's A.D.-400's A.D.	The years of the Gupta Empire in India
221 B.C.-207 B.C.	The years of the Chin dynasty in China
202 B.C.-220 A.D.	The years of the Han dynasty in China
200 B.C.	The chief of the Yamato tribe became emperor of Japan
100 A.D.	The Maya Indians developed a great culture
220 A.D.-590 A.D.	The years of China's "Dark Age"
590 A.D.-618 A.D.	The years of the Sui dynasty in China
618 A.D.-906 A.D.	The years of the Tang dynasty in China
960 A.D.-1279 A.D.	The years of the Sung dynasty in China
1200 A.D.	Yoritomo became shogun of Japan
1200 A.D.	The Aztec Indians built a great empire
1320 A.D.-1500 A.D.	The years of the Turks' rule of India

The Development of the Near East, Asia, and Africa

700 B.C.-300 A.D.	The years of the Kingdom of Cush in Africa
700 A.D.-1200's A.D.	The years of the Kingdom of Ghana in Africa
1054 A.D.	The Byzantine Church split away from the Roman Catholic Church
1081 A.D.	Alexius Comnenus became the ruler of the Byzantine Empire
1095 A.D.	The First Crusade, or war between the Muslims and Christians, began
1099 A.D.	Palestine was conquered by the Crusaders
1100 A.D.-1500 A.D.	The years of the Swahili city-states in Africa
1147 A.D.	The Second Crusade began
1187 A.D.	The Muslims recaptured Jerusalem
1189 A.D.-1192 A.D.	The Third Crusade
1200's A.D.-1400's A.D.	The years of the Mali Empire in Africa
1202 A.D.-1204 A.D.	The years of the Fourth Crusade, ending in the capture of Constantinople
1279 A.D.-1368 A.D.	The years during which the Mongols ruled China
1291 A.D.	The last part of the Holy Land still held by Christians was conquered by the Muslims
1368 A.D.-1644 A.D.	The years of the Ming dynasty in China
1400's A.D.-1591 A.D.	The years of the Songhai Empire in Africa
1453 A.D.	The Byzantine Empire was conquered by the Ottoman Turks
1500 A.D.-1707 A.D.	The years of the Mogul Empire in India
1556 A.D.-1605 A.D.	Akbar the Great was the ruler of the Mogul Empire in India

Europe During the Later Middle Ages

936 A.D.-973 A.D.	Otto the Great ruled Germany and Italy (the Holy Roman Empire)
987 A.D.	Hugh Capet became ruler of France
1066 A.D.	The Normans of France conquered England
1154 A.D.-1189 A.D.	Henry the Second ruled England
1180 A.D.	Philip Augustus became ruler of France
1198 A.D.-1216 A.D.	Pope Innocent the Third was leader of the Roman Catholic Church
1200's A.D.-1400's A.D.	The years during which the Mongols ruled Russia
1215 A.D.	King John signed the Magna Carta in England
1226 A.D.-1270 A.D.	Louis the Ninth ruled France

The Beginning of Modern Europe

1000	Norse sailors discovered North America
1300-1600	The years of the Renaissance in Europe
1337-1453	The years of the Hundred Years' War in Europe
1450	Gutenberg developed the printing press
1452-1519	Leonardo da Vinci lived in Italy
1475-1564	Michelangelo lived in Italy
1492	Ferdinand and Isabella united most of Spain
1492	Columbus discovered the New World
1497	Cabot sailed along the eastern coast of North America
1498	Vasco da Gama reached India by sailing around Africa
1517	Luther began the Protestant Reformation
1519-1522	Magellan's ships sailed around the world
1520	The Lutheran Church, the first of several new Protestant churches, was formed
1521	Cortés conquered the Aztec Indians of Mexico
1524-1536	Verrazano and Cartier explored the east coast of North America
1531	Pizarro conquered the Inca Indians of Peru
1545	The Council of Trent strengthened the Roman Catholic Church
1588	England defeated the Spanish Armada

The Growth of Europe

1485-1603	The Tudor monarchs ruled England
1588	England defeated the Spanish Armada
1589	The Bourbon monarchs became the rulers of France
1603-1642	The Stuart monarchs ruled England
1618-1648	The Thirty Years' War was fought in Europe
1640	The Hohenzollern monarchs became the rulers of Prussia
1642-1649	Civil war broke out in England
1643-1715	Louis the Fourteenth ruled France
1688	William and Mary became the rulers of England (the Glorious Revolution)
1689	The Bill of Rights was passed in England
1689-1725	Peter the Great ruled Russia
1689-1763	The Second Hundred Years' War was fought in Europe
1740-1780	Maria Theresa ruled the Austrian Empire
1756-1763	The Seven Years' War, which ended the Second Hundred Years' War, was fought in Europe and North America
1762-1796	Catherine the Great ruled Russia

Years of Revolution and Change

1607-1732	The years in which Great Britain started the Thirteen Colonies in North America
1776	The Declaration of Independence was signed
1783	The United States won its independence, and the American Revolution ended
1789	The United States set up a new government under the Constitution
1789	The French Revolution began
1799-1814	Napoleon Bonaparte, the ruler of France, tried to conquer Europe
1810-1826	The Latin American nations won their independence

1815	Napoleon's armies were defeated at the Battle of Waterloo
1830	Louis Philippe became ruler of France
1852	Napoleon the Third became emperor of France
1861-1865	The Civil War was fought in the United States
1865-1870	The Thirteenth, Fourteenth, and Fifteenth Amendments were added to the American Constitution

The Shaping of Modern Europe

1814-1815	The Congress of Vienna met to plan peace terms
1829	Greece won its independence from the Turkish Empire
1832	The Reform Bill was passed in England
1848	Revolutions broke out in France, the Austrian Empire, the German states, and Italy
1854-1856	The Crimean War was fought
1861	The Kingdom of Italy was formed
1861	The Russian serfs were freed
1867	The North German Confederation was formed
1867	The Austrian Empire was divided in two and became known as Austria-Hungary
1870	Rome became the capital city of a united Italy
1870	The Franco-Prussian War was fought
1871	The German Empire was formed and Germany was united
1904-1905	The Russo-Japanese War was fought
1905	A revolution broke out in Russia
1908	The Young Turks took over the Turkish government

The Rise of Modern Industry

1750	The Industrial Revolution began in Great Britain
1769	The steam engine was developed by James Watt
1807	The first successful steamboat was built in America
1830	The first railroad was built in England
1838	Steamships began to cross the Atlantic Ocean

European Imperialism in Asia and Africa

1839-1842	The Opium War was fought in China
1853	Perry opened up trade with Japan
1857	The Sepoy Rebellion took place in India
1858	The British government took over control of India
1867	The Japanese emperor overthrew the shogun and became the real ruler
1884	The Berlin Conference met to plan rules for dividing up Africa
1899-1902	The Boer War was fought in South Africa

The Growth of European Culture

| 1859 | Darwin presented the theory of evolution |
| 1905 | Einstein presented the theory of relativity |

World War One and the Years After

1882	The Triple Alliance was formed by Germany, Austria-Hungary, and Italy
1899	The Boxer Rebellion took place in China
1907	The Triple Entente was formed by France, Russia, and Great Britain
1912	China became a republic
1914-1918	World War One was fought
1917	The United States entered the war on the side of the Allies
1917	The Russian Revolution broke out
1919	The Treaty of Versailles was written to plan peace terms
1921	The New Economic Policy began in Russia
1922	Russia became the Union of Soviet Socialist Republics (U.S.S.R.)
1922	Mussolini became the fascist dictator of Italy
1924	Stalin became the Communist dictator of the Soviet Union (Russia)
1929	The great depression began and spread throughout the world
1933	Hitler became the Nazi dictator of Germany
1935	India was given home rule
1936	Franco became dictator of Spain

World War Two and the Years After

1928	The Kellogg-Briand Pact was signed
1931	Japan attacked China in Manchuria
1935	Italy attacked Ethiopia
1936	Germany moved troops into the Rhineland
1936	Germany and Italy formed an alliance
1938	Germany took over Austria and the Sudetenland
1939	Germany took over Czechoslovakia
1939	Germany and the Soviet Union formed an alliance
1939	World War Two began after Germany attacked Poland
1940	Germany conquered Norway, Denmark, the Netherlands, Belgium, Luxembourg, and France
1941	Germany attacked the Soviet Union
1941	The United States entered the war on the side of the Allies
1943	The Allies conquered North Africa and invaded Italy
1944	The Allies invaded France
1945	Germany surrendered, and the war in Europe ended
1945	Japan surrendered, and the war in Asia ended
1945	The United Nations was formed
1947	The Truman Doctrine and the Marshall Plan were developed
1949	N.A.T.O. was formed
1949	The Communists took over mainland China
1950-1953	The Korean War was fought

The Post-War World

1946	The Philippines gained their independence
1947	British India was split into two independent nations—India and Pakistan
1948	Burma and Ceylon received their independence from Great Britain

1948	Israel became an independent nation
1948	The Organization of American States (O.A.S.) was formed
1949	Indonesia won its independence from the Netherlands
1954	Vietnam won its independence from France but split into two parts
1954	Nasser became the ruler of Egypt
1956	Egypt took over the Suez Canal
1957	Ghana won its independence and was the first of the new nations in Africa
1957	The Common Market was formed by nations in Western Europe
1958	Castro became the ruler of Cuba
1958	De Gaulle became the President of France
1958	Khrushchev became dictator of the Soviet Union
1960	The Congo won its freedom
1961	The Alliance for Progress was formed
1962	Algeria won its independence
1962	The Cuban missile crisis occurred
1963	Kenya won its independence
1963	The Organization of African Unity was formed
1965	The United States entered the Vietnam War
1967	The Six-Day War was fought between Israel and the Arab nations

The Nations of the World Today

1933	President Franklin Roosevelt created the New Deal
1954	The U.S. Supreme Court ruled that segregated schools were illegal
1963	The United States and the Soviet Union signed the Nuclear Test Ban Treaty
1972	President Richard Nixon visited China, and the United States and China reopened diplomatic relations
1972	The United States and the Soviet Union signed the first SALT treaty
1973	The United States and North Vietnam agreed to a cease-fire
1974	Democracy was restored in Greece
1975	General Francisco Franco died, and Prince Juan Carlos became ruler of Spain
1975	North Vietnam defeated South Vietnam
1976	Blacks in Soweto, South Africa, rioted to protest the policy of Apartheid
1976	Mao Zedong died and was replaced by the government of Deng Xiaoping
1979	The Soviet Union invaded Afghanistan
1979	Egypt and Israel signed the Camp David Agreement for peace in the Middle East
1979	The Sandinistas set up a Marxist government in Nicaragua
1979	The Shah of Iran was overthrown and replaced by the Ayatollah Khomeini
1980	War broke out between Iran and Iraq
1983	In Argentina, military rule ended and free elections took place
1987	Corazon Aquino was elected President of the Philippines
1988	The United States and Canada signed a trade agreement

Life in the Modern World

1987	The world's population reached 5 billion
1987	The United States and the Soviet Union signed a treaty limiting Intermediate-Range Nuclear Forces (INF)
1988	The Soviet Union began to withdraw troops from Afghanistan

A View of the World About 100 A.D.

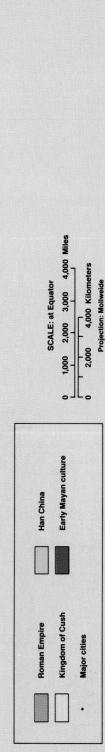

PACIFIC OCEAN

ASIA

Chang'an (Xian)

Mongols

Silk Route (trade route)

EUROPE

German tribes

Rome

AFRICA

Meroë

INDIAN OCEAN

N E S W

ATLANTIC OCEAN

NORTH AMERICA

Eskimo

Great Plains cultures

Eastern Woodland cultures

Teotihuacán

SOUTH AMERICA

Tropic of Cancer

Tropic of Capricorn

PACIFIC OCEAN

80°N

60°N

40°N

20°N

0°

20°S

40°S

160°W 140°W 120°W 100°W 80°W 60°W 40°W 20°W 0° 20°E 40°E 60°E 80°E 100°E 120°E 140°E 160°E

SCALE: at Equator

0   1,000   2,000   3,000   4,000 Miles

0   2,000   4,000 Kilometers

Projection: Mollweide

Roman Empire

Kingdom of Cush

Major cities

Han China

Early Mayan culture

A View of the World About 1000 A.D.

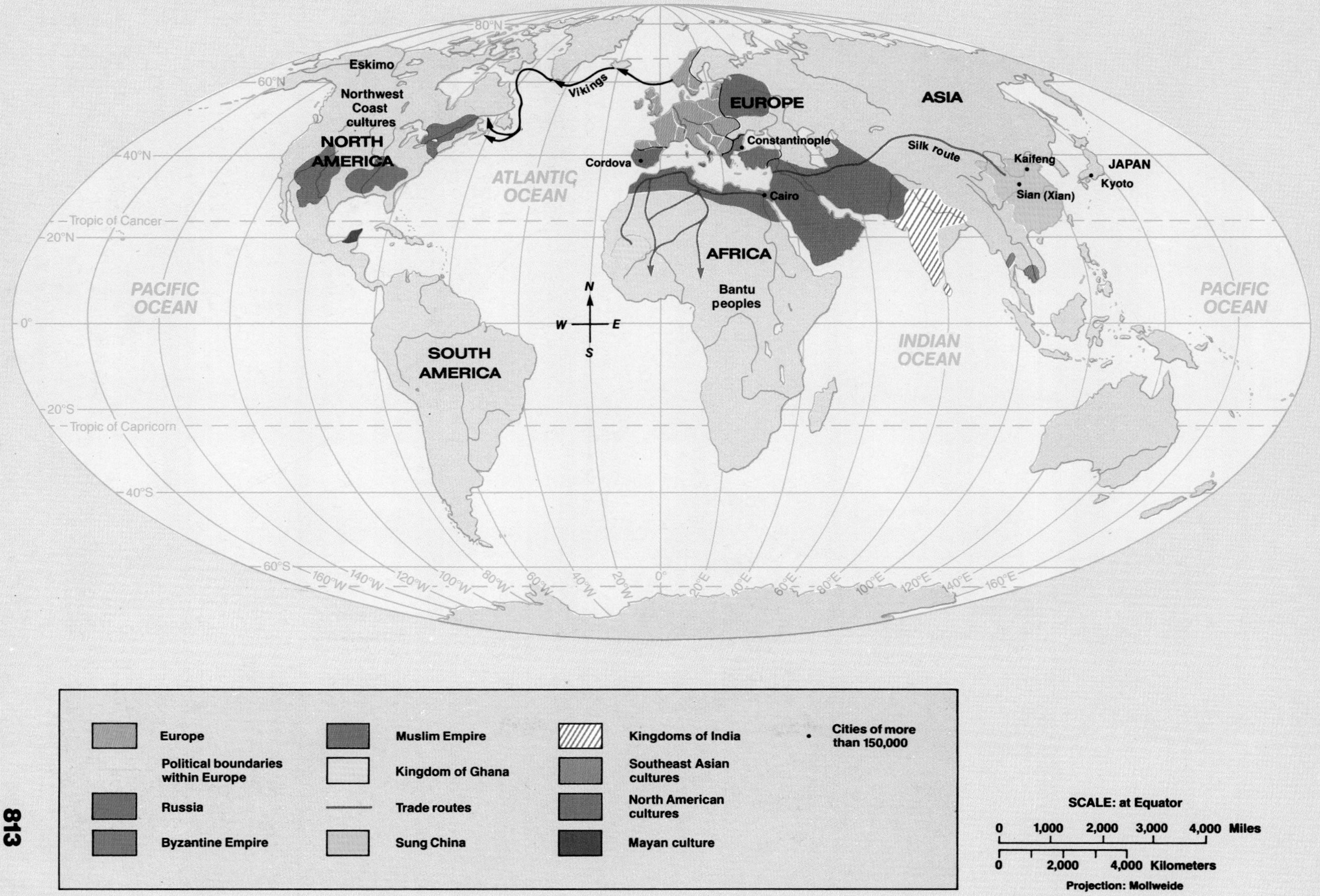

PACIFIC OCEAN

JAPAN
Kyoto

Kaifeng
Sian (Xian)

ASIA

Silk route

INDIAN OCEAN

EUROPE
Constantinople

Cairo

AFRICA

Bantu peoples

Cordova

VIKINGS

ATLANTIC OCEAN

N
E
S
W

SOUTH AMERICA

Eskimo
Northwest Coast cultures
NORTH AMERICA

PACIFIC OCEAN

Tropic of Cancer

Tropic of Capricorn

0°
20°S
40°S
60°S

80°N
60°N
40°N
20°N

20°W
40°W
60°W
80°W
100°W
120°W
140°W
160°W

20°E
40°E
60°E
80°E
100°E
120°E
140°E
160°E

SCALE: at Equator

0   1,000   2,000   3,000   4,000   Miles
0   2,000   4,000   Kilometers
Projection: Mollweide

Cities of more than 150,000

Kingdoms of India
Southeast Asian cultures
North American cultures
Mayan culture

Muslim Empire
Kingdom of Ghana
Trade routes
Sung China

Europe
Political boundaries within Europe
Russia
Byzantine Empire

813

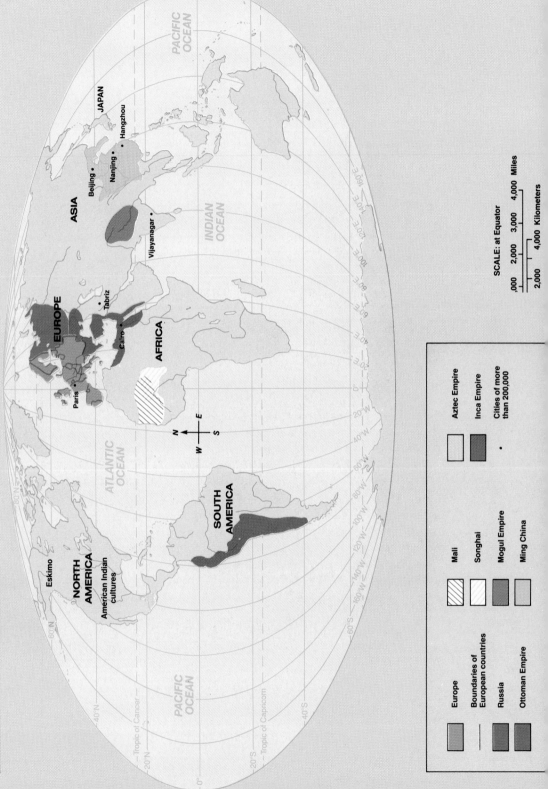

A View of the World About 1500

SCALE: at Equator

PACIFIC OCEAN

ASIA

JAPAN

Beijing
Nanjing
Hangzhou

Tabriz

EUROPE

Vijayanagar

INDIAN OCEAN

Cairo

AFRICA

Paris

ATLANTIC OCEAN

N
W — E
S

NORTH AMERICA

Eskimo

American Indian cultures

SOUTH AMERICA

PACIFIC OCEAN

Tropic of Cancer
20°N
40°N
60°N
80°N

Tropic of Capricorn
40°S
20°S

60°W
80°W
100°W
120°W
140°W
160°W

20°W
20°E
40°E
60°E
80°E
100°E
120°E
140°E
160°E

Europe		Mali
Boundaries of European countries		Songhai
Russia		Mogul Empire
Ottoman Empire		Ming China

Aztec Empire	
Inca Empire	
Cities of more than 200,000	·

2,000   1,000   2,000   3,000   4,000   Kilometers
1,000   2,000   3,000   4,000   Miles

A View of the World About 1850

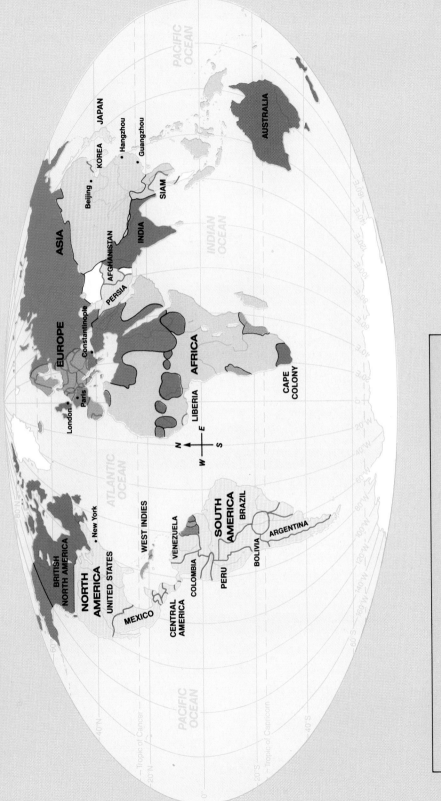

PACIFIC OCEAN

AUSTRALIA

ASIA

JAPAN

KOREA

• Hangzhou

• Guangzhou

Beijing •

SIAM

INDIA

AFGHANISTAN

PERSIA

INDIAN OCEAN

EUROPE

Constantinople

AFRICA

LIBERIA

CAPE COLONY

London •

• Paris

N

W — E

S

NORTH AMERICA

BRITISH NORTH AMERICA

UNITED STATES

• New York

ATLANTIC OCEAN

WEST INDIES

MEXICO

CENTRAL AMERICA

COLOMBIA

VENEZUELA

PERU

BOLIVIA

BRAZIL

SOUTH AMERICA

ARGENTINA

PACIFIC OCEAN

Tropic of Cancer

20°N

60°N

40°N

Tropic of Capricorn

40°S

60°S

20°S

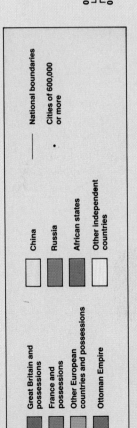

SCALE: at Equator

| 0 | 1,000 | 2,000 | 3,000 | 4,000 Miles |

| 0 | 2,000 | 4,000 Kilometers |

Projection: Mollweide

— National boundaries

• Cities of 600,000 or more

Great Britain and possessions

France and possessions

Other European countries and possessions

Ottoman Empire

China

Russia

African states

Other independent countries

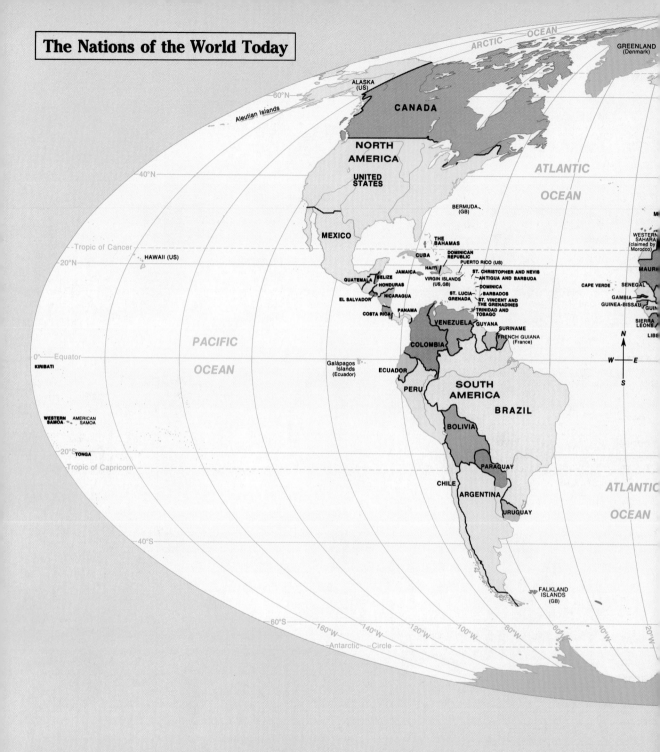

The Nations of the World Today

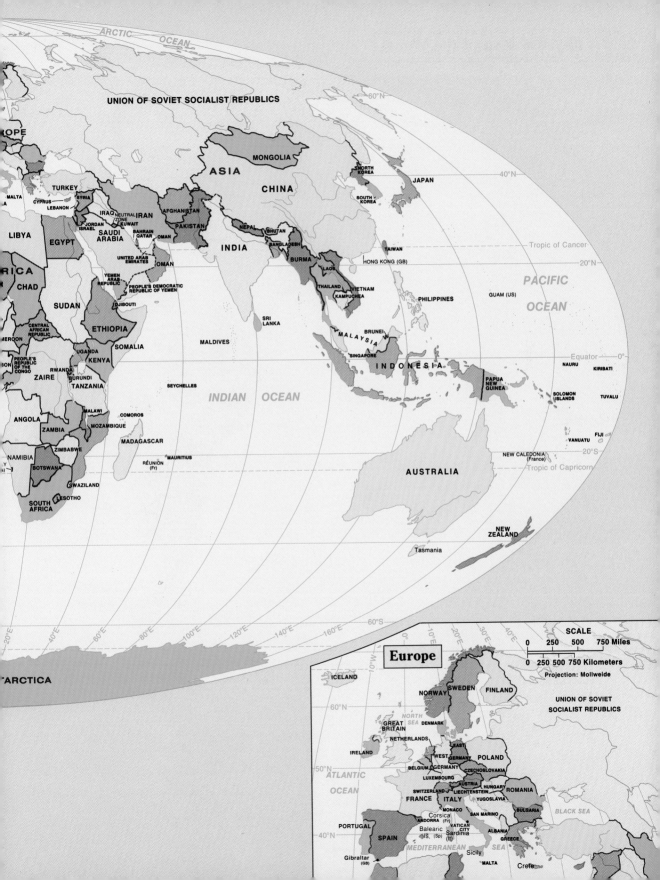

ARCTIC OCEAN

UNION OF SOVIET SOCIALIST REPUBLICS

60°N

ASIA

MONGOLIA

NORTH KOREA

JAPAN

40°N

CHINA

SOUTH KOREA

TURKEY

MALTA

CYPRUS
LEBANON

SYRIA

IRAQ
NEUTRAL ZONE
KUWAIT

AFGHANISTAN

IRAN

PAKISTAN

NEPAL

BHUTAN

LIBYA

JORDAN
ISRAEL

SAUDI ARABIA

BAHRAIN
QATAR

OMAN

TAIWAN

HONG KONG (GB)

Tropic of Cancer

EGYPT

UNITED ARAB EMIRATES

OMAN

INDIA

BANGLADESH

BURMA

20°N

RICA

CHAD

YEMEN ARAB REPUBLIC

PEOPLE'S DEMOCRATIC REPUBLIC OF YEMEN

LAOS

THAILAND

VIETNAM

PHILIPPINES

GUAM (US)

PACIFIC OCEAN

MEROON

SUDAN

DJIBOUTI

KAMPUCHEA

CENTRAL AFRICAN REPUBLIC

ETHIOPIA

SRI LANKA

MALDIVES

BRUNEI

MALAYSIA

ON

PEOPLE'S REPUBLIC OF THE CONGO

UGANDA

SOMALIA

SINGAPORE

Equator 0°

NAURU

KIRIBATI

ZAIRE

RWANDA
BURUNDI

KENYA

INDONESIA

TANZANIA

SEYCHELLES

INDIAN OCEAN

PAPUA NEW GUINEA

SOLOMON ISLANDS

TUVALU

ANGOLA

MALAWI

COMOROS

ZAMBIA

MOZAMBIQUE

MADAGASCAR

FIJI

VANUATU

NAMIBIA

ZIMBABWE

Y

RÉUNION (Fr)

MAURITIUS

NEW CALEDONIA (France)

20°S

BOTSWANA

AUSTRALIA

Tropic of Capricorn

SWAZILAND

SOUTH AFRICA

LESOTHO

NEW ZEALAND

ARCTICA

Tasmania

20°E   40°E   60°E   80°E   100°E   120°E   140°E   160°E   60°S

SCALE

0   250   500   750 Miles

0   250   500   750 Kilometers

Projection: Mollweide

Europe

10°E   20°E   30°E   40°E

ICELAND

NORWAY

SWEDEN

FINLAND

UNION OF SOVIET SOCIALIST REPUBLICS

60°N

NORTH SEA

GREAT BRITAIN

DENMARK

NETHERLANDS

EAST GERMANY

POLAND

IRELAND

WEST GERMANY

BELGIUM

CZECHOSLOVAKIA

50°N

LUXEMBOURG

AUSTRIA

HUNGARY

SWITZERLAND

LIECHTENSTEIN

ROMANIA

ATLANTIC OCEAN

FRANCE

ITALY

YUGOSLAVIA

MONACO

SAN MARINO

BULGARIA

BLACK SEA

Corsica (Fr)

ANDORRA

VATICAN CITY

ALBANIA

PORTUGAL

SPAIN

Balearic Is. (Sp)

Sardinia (It)

GREECE

40°N

Gibraltar (GB)

MEDITERRANEAN SEA

Sicily

MALTA

Crete

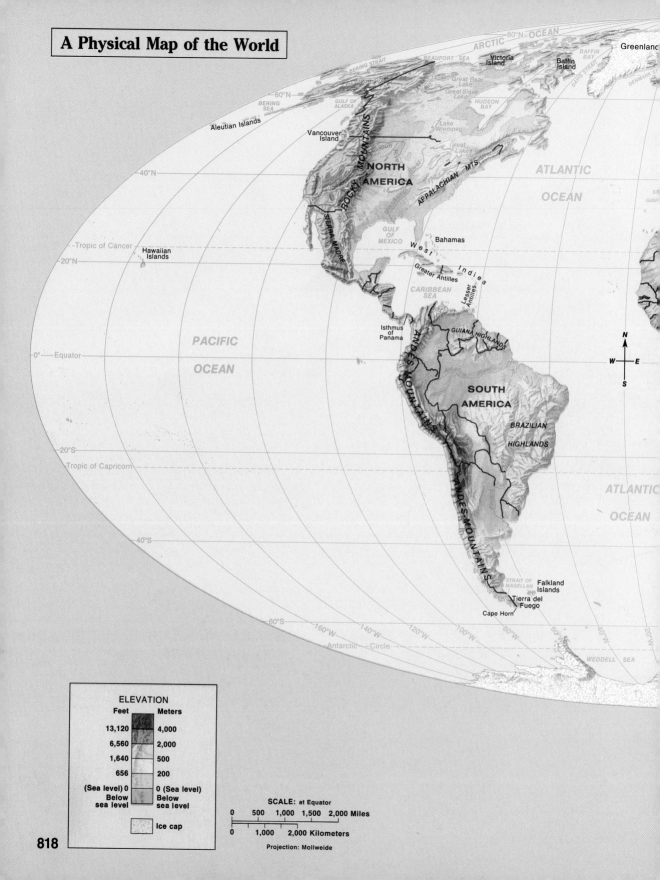

A Physical Map of the World

ARCTIC 80°N OCEAN

Greenland

BEAUFORT SEA

BERING STRAIT

Victoria Island

Baffin Bay

Baffin Island

DAVIS STRAIT

DENMARK STR.

60°N

Great Bear Lake

Great Slave Lake

HUDSON BAY

BERING SEA

GULF OF ALASKA

Aleutian Islands

Lake Winnipeg

ROCKY MOUNTAINS

Vancouver Island

NORTH AMERICA

Great Lakes

APPALACHIAN MTS.

40°N

ATLANTIC

OCEAN

GIBR

SIERRA MADRE

Tropic of Cancer

Hawaiian Islands

20°N

GULF OF MEXICO

Bahamas

West Indies

Greater Antilles

Lesser Antilles

CARIBBEAN SEA

Isthmus of Panama

ANDES MOUNTAINS

GUIANA HIGHLANDS

PACIFIC

OCEAN

0° Equator

N

W   E

S

SOUTH AMERICA

BRAZILIAN HIGHLANDS

20°S

Tropic of Capricorn

ATLANTIC

OCEAN

40°S

ANDES MOUNTAINS

STRAIT OF MAGELLAN

Falkland Islands

Tierra del Fuego

Cape Horn

60°S

160°W   140°W   120°W   100°W   80°W   60°   40°   20°

Antarctic Circle

WEDDELL SEA

ELEVATION

Feet	Meters
13,120	4,000
6,560	2,000
1,640	500
656	200
(Sea level) 0	0 (Sea level)
Below sea level	Below sea level

Ice cap

SCALE: at Equator

0   500   1,000   1,500   2,000 Miles

0   1,000   2,000 Kilometers

Projection: Mollweide

818

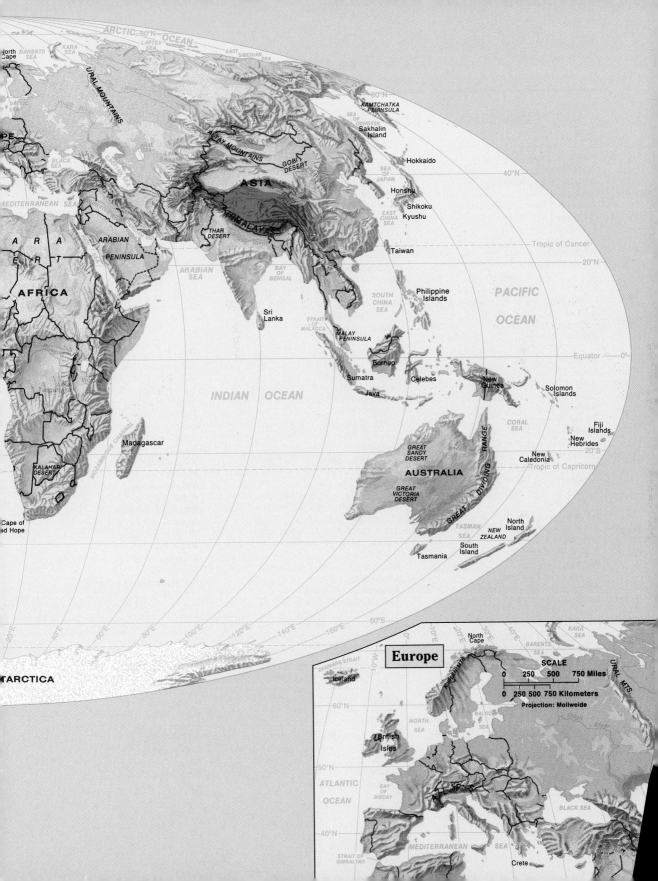

ARCTIC 80°N OCEAN

North
Cape
BARENTS
SEA
KARA
SEA
LAPTEV
SEA
EAST
SIBERIAN
SEA

BALTIC
SEA
URAL MOUNTAINS
60°N
KAMTCHATKA
PENINSULA
SEA OF
OKHOTSK
Sakhalin
Island

VOLGA RIVER
CASPIAN SEA

E

BLACK
SEA

MEDITERRANEAN SEA
ALTAY MOUNTAINS
GOBI
DESERT
ASIA
HIMALAYAS
Hokkaido
SEA
OF
JAPAN
40°N
Honshu
Shikoku
EAST
CHINA
SEA
Kyushu

A
R
A
B
E
R
T
ARABIAN
PENINSULA
THAR
DESERT
Taiwan
Tropic of Cancer
20°N

AFRICA
ARABIAN
SEA
BAY
OF
BENGAL
South
China
Sea
PACIFIC

Sri
Lanka
STRAIT
OF
MALACCA
Philippine
Islands
OCEAN

MALAY
PENINSULA
Borneo
Equator 0°

Sumatra
Celebes
New
Guinea
Solomon
Islands

INDIAN OCEAN
Java

Madagascar
CORAL
SEA
Fiji
Islands
New
Hebrides

KALAHARI
DESERT
MOZAMBIQUE CHANNEL
GREAT
SANDY
DESERT
GREAT DIVIDING RANGE
New
Caledonia
20°S
Tropic of Capricorn

Cape of
Good Hope
AUSTRALIA
GREAT
VICTORIA
DESERT
TASMAN
SEA
North
Island
NEW
ZEALAND

60°S
Tasmania
South
Island

ANTARCTICA

20°E 40°E 60°E 80°E 100°E 120°E 140°E 160°E

North
Cape
KARA
SEA
BARENTS
SEA
URAL MTS.

Europe

Iceland
DENMARK STRAIT
60°N
GULF OF BOTHNIA
BALTIC
SEA

SCALE
0   250   500   750 Miles
0 250 500 750 Kilometers
Projection: Mollweide

NORTH
SEA
British
Isles
50°N

ATLANTIC
OCEAN
BAY
OF
BISCAY
BLACK SEA

40°N

MEDITERRANEAN SEA
STRAIT
OF
GIBRALTAR
Crete

INDEX

Page numbers in *italics* that have *m* written before them refer to maps.

Bill of Rights: English, 420; American, 648

Bismarck, Otto von, 507, 508, 519–520

Black homelands, 761

Blacks: in early African kingdoms, 309–312; and European imperialism, 575–578; in South Africa, 703–704; in Rhodesia, 704–705; and civil rights movement in United States, 730–731; and Apartheid, 761–762, 789–790

Black Sea, m 41, m 80, m 92, m 99, m 138, m 156, m 164, m 170, m 202, m 240, m 246, m 316, m 324, m 412, m 430, 436, m 442, m 457, m 486, m 492, m 500, m 524, m 604

Boer War, 577

Bohemia, 343, 412, 414, 429, m 430

Bohr, Niels, 590

Bolívar, Simón, m 474, 475

Bolivia, m 474, m 710

Bolsheviks, 622

Bombay, 768

Bonn, m 672

Botha, Pieter W., 761–762

Botswana, m 698, 762

Bourbon family, 424, 432, 511

Bourgeoisie, French, 480, 481

Boxer Rebellion, 640

Boyle, Robert, 450

Brahma, 112

Brahms, Johannes, 584

Brasília, m 710

Brazil, 398, m 398, 475, m 710, 711, 740, 789

Brezhnev, Leonid, 724, 752

Britain, m 92, m 182, m 188, m 202, m 203, 209; see also England; Great Britain

British Commonwealth of Nations, 628, m 628, 704

British East Africa, m 576

British East India Company, 564, 565, 566

British Empire, 443, m 550, m 564, m 570, m 576, 628

British Honduras, m 710

British Somaliland, m 576

Brueghel, Peter, 376

Buddha, 114, 260

Buddhism, 114, 260, 268

Bulgaria, m 524, 526, m 672, m 722; and World War One, m 610, 611, m 616, 618, 634

Burghers, 330

Burma, 279, m 550, m 559, m 570, 572, m 628, m 686

Burundi, m 698

Bushi, 279

Byzantine Empire, 239–242, m 240, m 246, m 324, 325, m 342, 368; in

Crusades, 292, m 292, 293, 318; end of, 315–318, m 316; see also Eastern Roman Empire

Byzantium, 240

Cabot, John, 397–398, m 400

Caesar, Julius, 161, 172, 187

Cage, John, 776

Cairo, m 246, m 692

Calcutta, 768

Calicut, 563, m 564

Caliph, 251–252

Calvin, John, 406

Calvinism, 406

Cambodia, 279, m 686, 766

Cambyses, 98

Camp David agreement, 733, 758

Camus, Albert, 777

Canada, 443, m 462, m 628, 667, 737–738

Canterbury Tales, The (Chaucer), 215

Capet, Hugh, 335–336

Capitalists, 532, 544

Carbonari, 512

Carbon dioxide, 792

Caribbean countries, 739

Carlsbad Decrees, 507

Carter, Jimmy, 733, 756, 758, 767

Carthage, m 92, m 164, 166, m 170

Cartier, Jacques, 398, m 400

Caspian Sea, m 41, m 80, m 92, m 99, m 156, m 246, m 298, m 324, m 437, m 648, m 692

Caste system, 113, 114, 261

Castile, m 342, 344, 388

Castlereagh, Lord, 500

Castro, Fidel, 712

Catalonia, 746

Catherine the Great, 436, 438

Catholic Church, see Roman Catholic Church

Catholic League, of Germany, 414

Catholic-Protestant conflict in Northern Ireland, 744–745

Cavalry, in Middle Ages, 215

Cavell, Edith, 611

Cave paintings, 28

Cavour, Count, 512, 513, 514

Censorship, 749

Central Africa, 788

Central African Republic, m 698

Central America, m 284, m 474, 738–739; Indian nations of, m 284, 284–285; Spanish settlements in, 398, m 398; and Reagan administration, 734

Central Intelligence Agency, 734

Central Powers, 609–610, m 610, 611

Cervantes, Miguel de, 455

Cetewayo, Zulu king, 577

Ceylon, m 106, 572, 687

Challenger explosion (1986), 791

Chamberlain, Neville, 661

Chamber of Deputies, French, 519, 629

Champagne, m 324, 325

Chang Jiang, 117, m 118, m 268, m 280, m 298, m 559

Charlemagne, 204, 209–210, 215, 335, 341; empire of, m 203

Charles the First (England), 418, 419

Charles the Second (England), 419

Charles the Tenth (France), 494

Charles Martel, Frankish ruler, 204

Charter 77, 749

Chaucer, Geoffrey, 215, 355, 356

Cheng, Chinese emperor, 265–266

Chernobyl, 791

Chiang Kai-shek, 641, 642, 679

Chile, m 474, 475, m 710

Chin, Chinese state, 120, 265

China, 66, 241, 279, m 280, 393, 659, 764, 766–768, 788; prehistoric people in, 20, m 20; early civilization of, 117–120, m 118; Chou dynasty, m 118, 120, 123–126; Shang dynasty, 119–120; Chin dynasty, 125, 265–266; Han dynasty, 266–267, 268, m 268; "Dark Age" of, 267–268; Sui dynasty, 271–272; Tang dynasty, 272–273; Sung dynasty, 274; under Mongol Empire, 297–299, m 298; Ming dynasty, 299–300, 557; Manchu dynasty, 557–560, m 559, 639; modern, 639–642; Communist, 679–680, 685–686, 724; Nixon's visit to, 732; cultural revolution in, 766–767; economic changes in, 767–768; expansion of, 767

Chin dynasty, 125, 265–266

Chivalry, 215, 220; see also Feudalism

Chou dynasty, m 118, 120

Christian religion: rise of, 193–196; and Byzantine Empire, 240, 424

Churchill, Winston, 666, 671, 716

Church of England, 406

Cicero, 184

Cities: Sumerian, 47; population explosion in, 787

City-states, 42, 137–140, m 144, 164

Civil rights, 730–731; in United States, 730–731, 789

Civil War: English, 418–419; French in later 1500's, 423–424; American, 469–470; Spanish, 636; in Latin America, 736

Clarkson, Thomas, 501

Clemenceau, Georges, 617

Clermont, Council of, 292, m 292

Clive, Robert, 564

Clovis, Frankish king, 203, 215

Code Napoleon, 492, 494, 506, 511

Irish Free State, *see* Eire
Iron curtain, 721
Irrigation: in Tigris-Euphrates valley, 40–41; in Nile River valley, 61; in China, 119, 126
Isabella, queen of Spain, 388
Islam, 246; *see also* Muslim religion
Israel, 733, 756; kingdom of, *m 86, 87*; today, 691, *m 692*, 693–694; conflicts with Arab neighbors, 757–758; invasion of Lebanon, 757; *see also* Palestine
Italian Somaliland, *m 576*
Italy, *m 138, m 170, m 182, m 203, m 240, m 324*, 365, 393, 404, 412, 454, *m 492*, 493, 502, 533, *m 550, m 576*, 577, 705, 718, *m 722*; and early Roman Republic, 163–164, *m 164*; Germanic invasions of, *m 188*, 202; in Middle Ages, 209, 233; and Holy Roman Empire, *m 342*, 342–343, *m 412*; in Renaissance, 368, 373–376; uniting of, 511–514, *m 512*; in World War One, *m 604, m 610*, 611; after World War One, *m 616*, 635–636, 654–655; in World War Two, 660, *m 660*, 662, 667, 715
Ivan the Great (Russia), 435
Ivan the Terrible (Russia), 435
Ivory Coast, *m 576, m 698*
Iwo Jima, *m 668*

Jackson, Andrew, 469
Jacobin Party, 487, 488
James the Second (England), 419
Japan, *m 298, m 550*, 557, 558, *m 559*, 654, 764, 768; early settlement of, 277–278; influence of China, 278–279, *m 280*; imperialism in, 569–572, *m 570*; in World War One, 611; in World War Two, 659, 667–668, *m 668*, 674; today, 686, *m 686*
Java human, 20, *m 20*, 21
Jazz, 776–777
Jefferson, Thomas, 468
Jenner, Edward, 590
Jerusalem, *m 86, 87, m 188, m 292*, 293
Jesuits, 406
Jesus Christ, 194–195
Jews: and the rise of Christianity, 193–195; in Middle Ages, 360; in Israel, 693–694; *see also* Hebrews
Jinnah, Mohammed Ali, 687
Joan of Arc, 388
John (England), 338, 385, 386
John Paul II, Pope, 743
Johnson, Lyndon B., 688, 731
Johnson, Philip, 776
Jordan, 691, *m 692*, 694
Jordan River, West Bank of, 758
Joseph the Second (Austria), 431

Joyce, James, 777, 778
Juan Carlos (Spain), 746
Juárez, Benito, 710
Judah, kingdom of, *m 86*, 87
Julian calendar, 172
Jupiter, 175
Jury system, 337
Justinian, Byzantine emperor, 183, 204–241, *m 240*
Justinian's Code of Laws, 183, 241
Jutes, *m 188, m 202*, 203, 336

Kaaba, 246, 248
Kampuchea, 766
Kellogg-Briand Pact, 655, 656
Kemal, Mustafa "Ataturk," 647
Kennedy, John F., 688, 712, 728, 730, 731
Kenya, *m 698*, 699
Kenyatta, Jomo, 699–700
Khomeini, Ayatollah Ruholla, 760
Khrushchev, Nikita, 724, 752
Khufu, 72
Kiev, 242, *m 437*
King, Martin Luther, Jr., 730, 731
Knights, 215, 216, 219–220, 380
Knossos, *m 132*, 133
Koch, Robert, 591
Koran, 247, 254
Korea, 266, *m 268, m 280, m 298, m 570*, 572, *m 686*
Korean War, 679–680
Kosygin, Aleksei, 724
Kublai Khan, 299
Kuwait, 691, *m 692*

Labor unions, 544
La Fontaine, 425
Laissez faire, 544
Lancaster monarchs, 386
Laos, 279, *m 686*, 687
Later Middle Ages, 323; trade in, 323–326, *m 324*; European towns in, 329–332; France and England in, 335–338, *m 336*; European nations in, 341–344, *m 342*; education and learning in, 347–350; science in, 348, 350, 353–355; writing in, 355–356
Latin America, 736, 738–739; revolution in, 473–476, *m 474*, 549; in modern times, 709–712, *m 710*
Latin language, 183, 208, 209
Latvia, *m 616*, 618
Lavoisier, Antoine, 450
Law of falling bodies, 449
Laws: of Mesopotamia, 42, 46, 54, 99; of Hittites, 81; of Greeks, 139–140; of Romans, 182–183, 208, 241; of German kingdoms, 208–209; of Chinese, 266; of England, 337–338, 386, 419–420; of France, 492

League of Nations, 616, 618, 652–654, 656, 659
Lebanon, 647, 691, *m 692*, 757
Le Corbusier, 776
Leibnitz, Wilhelm, 449
Lend-Lease Act, 667
Lenin, Nikolai, 622, 623, 624
Leonidas (Sparta), 145
Leopold the Second (Belgium), 578
Leo the Third, Pope, 204
Lexington, battle of, 460
Liberia, *m 576*, 697, *m 698*
Libya, *m 576*, 577, *m 698*, 759
Lima, *m 398*, 399
Lister, Joseph, 591
Literature, modern, 777
Lithuania, *m 342*, 343, *m 616*, 618, 634, *m 722*
Lloyd George, David, 617
Locke, John, 456, 481
Lombards, *m 188*, 202–203, *m 203*
Lombardy, *m 512*
London, *m 324, m 336, m 342*
Long, Crawford, 591
Louis the Ninth (France), 336
Louis the Eleventh (France), 387
Louis the Thirteenth (France), 424
Louis the Fourteenth (France), 423, 424–426, 454
Louis the Fifteenth (France), 426
Louis the Sixteenth (France), 480, 481, 487
Louis the Eighteenth (France), 494
Louis Philippe (France), 494, 501
Love Canal, New York, 791–792
Loyola, Ignatius, 406
Lumumba, Patrice, 700
Luther, Martin, 405–406
Lutheran Church, 406
Luxembourg, 715, *m 716*
Lyell, Charles, 591

MacArthur, General Douglas, 674
McCormick, Cyrus, 534
Macedonia, *m 144*, 155–156, *m 156*, 158, *m 170, m 182*, 241, *m 316*
Madagascar, *m 576*
Madras, *m 564*
Madrid, *m 412, m 442*
Magellan, Ferdinand, *m 392*, 394
Magna Carta, 338, 385
Malawi, *m 698*
Malaya, *m 570*, 572, *m 628*
Malaysia, Federation of, 279, 684, *m 686*, 687
Mali, *m 310*, 311, 312, *m 698*
Malik Ambar, 305
Manchu dynasty, 557–560, 639, 640
Manchuria, *m 268*, 557, *m 559*, 640, 659

Photo Credits

Pages 2-3, George Holton/Photo Researchers; 14-15, Joe Monroe/Photo Researchers.
Unit 1: Pages 16-17, George Holton/Photo Researchers. **Chapter 1:** Page 19, George Holton/Photo Researchers; 21, K. Cannon/Anthro-Photo-File; 22, Tom McHugh/Photo Researchers. **Chapter 2:** Page 25, George Holton/Photo Researchers; 27, Courtesy Dept. of Library Services, American Museum of Natural History; 28, U.S. Forest Service. **Chapter 3:** Page 31, Mario Fantin/Photo Researchers; 32, Paolo Koch/Photo Researchers; 33, Courtesy Dept. of Library Services, American Museum of Natural History; 34, George Holton/Photo Researchers.
Unit 2: Pages 36-37, SCALA/Art Resource. **Chapter 4:** Page 39, SCALA/Art Resource; 40, Georg Gerster/Photo Researchers. **Chapter 5:** Page 45, SCALA/Art Resource; 46, The Bettmann Archive; 47, The Granger Collection; 48, Philip Gendreau. **Chapter 6:** Page 51, SCALA/Art Resource; 52(bl), Oriental Institute, University of Chicago; 51(br), The Granger Collection; 53, The Louvre/Rosenthal Art Slides; 54, Georg Gerster/Photo Researchers.
Unit 3: Pages 56-57, Susan McCartney/Photo Researchers. **Chapter 7:** Page 59, Brian Brake/Photo Researchers; 61, Metropolitan Museum of Art, Dodge Fund, 1931; 62, Metropolitan Museum of Art, Egyptian Expedition (15.5.19b). This is a detail. **Chapter 8:** Page 65, Georg Gerster/Photo Researchers; 66, Nelson Gallery/Atkins Museum (Nelson Fund); 67, SCALA/Art Resource; 68, Metropolitan Museum of Art. This is a detail. **Chapter 9:** Page 71, SCALA/Art Resource; 72, George Holton/Photo Researchers; 73, Himler Verlag München; 74, Metropolitan Museum of Art, Gift of Joseph W. Drexel 1889. (89.2.268).
Unit 4: Pages 76-77, Georg Gerster/Photo Researchers. **Chapter 10:** Page 79, The Granger Collection; 81, The Bettmann Archive; 82, Himler Verlag München. **Chapter 11:** Page 85, Erich Lessing/Magnum Photos; 87, SCALA/Art Resource; 88, Photographic Archive of the Theological Seminary of America, New York/Frank J. Darmstaedter. **Chapter 12:** Page 91, Erich Lessing/Magnum Photos; 93, The Louvre/Rosenthal Art Slides; 94, Brown Brothers. **Chapter 13:** Page 97, SCALA/Art Resource; 98, The Bettmann Archive; 100, Alinari/Art Reference Bureau.
Unit 5: Pages 102-103, Paolo Koch/Photo Researchers. **Chapter 14:** Page 105, Larry Burrows/Life Magazine, Time Inc.; 107, Archeological Survey of India, Government of India; 108, SCALA/Art Resource. **Chapter 15:** Page 111, SCALA/Art Resource; 112, Museum of Fine Arts, Boston, Ross Collection; 113, Metropolitan Museum of Art, Eggleston Fund, 1927; 114, Museum of Fine Arts, Boston. **Chapter 16:** Page 117, George Holton/Photo Researchers; 119, From Chiang Yee, *Chinese Calligraphy,* Harvard University Press, fig. 21, p. 55; 120, Lucy Maud Buckingham Collection, 1928.167/The Art Institute of Chicago. **Chapter 17:** Page 123, Metropolitan Museum of Art The Michael C. Rockefeller Memorial Collection, Bequest of Nelson A. Rockefeller, 1979. (79.206.86); 124, Brown Brothers; 125, Metropolitan Museum of Art, Munsey Bequest, 1924; 126, Nelson Gallery/Atkins Museum (Nelson Fund), Kansas City, Mo.
Unit 6: Pages 128-129, Ronnie Jacques/Photo Researchers. **Chapter 18:** Page 131, SCALA/Art Resource; 133, Alison Frantz; 134, The Bettmann Archive. **Chapter 19:** Page 137, The Granger Collection; 139, 140, The Bettmann Archive. **Chapter 20:** Pages 143, 145, SCALA/Art Resource; 146, The British Library. **Chapter 21:** Page 149, SCALA/Art Resource; 150, Staatliche Museum; 151, Metropolitan Museum of Art, Fletcher Fund, 1931. (31.11.10); 152, Alinari/Art Reference Bureau. **Chapter 22:** Page 155, Farrell Grehan/Photo Researchers; 157, R. V. Schoder; 158, SCALA/Art Resource.
Unit 7: Pages 160-161, Larry Mulvehill/Photo Researchers. **Chapter 23:** Pages 163, 165, SCALA/Art Resource; 166, New York Public Library. **Chapter 24:** Page 169, The Granger Collection; 171, The Bettman Archive; 172, Editions Arthaud. **Chapter 25:** Page 175, Nicholas deVore III/Bruce Coleman, Inc.; 176, The Granger Collection; 177, Landesmuseum, Trier; 178, Anderson/Art Reference Bureau. **Chapter 26:** Page 181, SCALA/Art Resource; 184, Angelo Giampiccolo/Photo Researchers. **Chapter 27:** Page 187, Paolo Koch/Photo Researchers; 189, Anderson/Art Reference Bureau; 190, Alinari/Art Reference Bureau. **Chapter 28:** Page 193, SCALA/Art Resource; 194, Zionist Archives and Library; 195, Anderson/Art Reference Bureau; 196, The Mansell Collection.
Unit 8: Pages 198-199, M. Desjardins/Photo Researchers. **Chapter 29:** Page 201, Rosenthal Art Slides; 204, SCALA/Art Resource. **Chapter 30:** Page 207, SCALA/Art Resource; 208, Historical Pictures Service; 209, The Bettmann Archive; 210, SCALA/Art Resource. **Chapter 31:** Page 213, SCALA/Art Resource; 214, The Bettmann Archive; 215, R. J. Ségelat/Bibliothèque Nationale, Paris; 216, The Bettmann Archive. **Chapter 32:** Page 219, SCALA/Art Resource; 220, The Pierpont Morgan Library; 221, 222, The Bettmann Archive. **Chapter 33:** Page 225, SCALA/Art Resource; 226, The British Library; 227, The Granger Collection; 228, Giraudon. **Chapter 34:** Page 231, The Granger Collection; 232, SCALA/Art Resource; 233, The Bettmann Archive; 234, The Granger Collection.
Unit 9: Pages 236-237, Rosenthal Art Slides. **Chapter 35:** Page 239, SCALA/Art Resource; 241, Himler Verlag München; 242, The Granger Collection. **Chapter 36:** Page 245, SCALA/Art Resource; 247, Metropolitan Museum of Art Harris Brisbane Dick Fund, 1939. (39.20); 248, The Granger Collection. **Chapter 37:** Page 251, The Granger Collection; 252, The Bettmann Archive; 253, Metropolitan Museum of Art, Rogers Fund, 1913. (13.152.6); 254, The Bettmann Archive.
Unit 10: Pages 256-257, SCALA/Art Resource. **Chapter 38:** Page 259, George Holton/Photo Researchers; 262, Ronnie Jacques/Photo Researchers. **Chapter 39:** Page 265, Georg Gerster/ Photo Researchers; 266, The Bettmann Archive; 267, O. E. Nelson Photographers. **Chapter 40:** Page 271, Metropolitan Museum of Art, Fletcher Fund, 1940; 272, SCALA/Art Resource; 273, Culver Pictures, Inc.; 274, The Cleveland Museum of Art, Gift of Severance and Greta Millikin, 57.358. **Chapter 41:** Page 277, P. Larsen/Photo Researchers; 278, George Holton/Photo Researchers; 279, The Bettmann Archive. **Chapter 42:** Page 283, George Holton/Photo Researchers; 285, Nicholas deVore III/Bruce Coleman, Inc.; 286, Jack Fields/Photo Researchers.
Unit 11: Pages 288-289, The Granger Collection. **Chapter 43:** Page 291, Van Bucher/Photo Researchers; 293, SCALA/Art Resource; 294, The Bettmann Archive. **Chapter 44:** Page 297, Francis C. Mayer/Photo Researchers; 299, Brown Brothers; 300, The Granger Collection. **Chapter 45:** Page 303, M. Durrance/Photo Researchers; 305, Museum of Fine Arts, Boston, Arthur Mason Knapp Fund; 306(tl), (tr), Metropolitan Museum of Art, Gift of Alexander Smith Cochran, 1913. (13.228.43). **Chapter 46:** Page 309, The Granger Collection; 311, R. B. Fleming/Art Reference Bureau; 312, Metropolitan Museum of Art, Gift of Mrs. John Marriott, Mrs. John Barry Ryan, Gilbert W. Kahn, Roger Wolfe Kahn, 1949 (49.163.3). **Chapter 47:** Page 315, SCALA/Art Resource; 317(bl), Marburg/Art Reference Bureau; 317(br) Alinari/The Mansell Collection.
Unit 12: Pages 320-321, SCALA/Art Resource. **Chapter 48:** Page 323, SCALA/Art Resource; 325, 326, The Bettmann Archive. **Chapter 49:** Page 329, Lawrence L. Smith/Photo Researchers; 330, Bibliothèque Royale Albert Ier, Brussels Royal Library, ms. 9242, fol. 27.4 verso; 331, SCALA/Art Resource; 332, The Pierpont Morgan Library, New York, M. 399 F. 2. **Chapter 50:** Page 335, Erich Lessing/Magnum Photos; 337,

Giraudon; 338, Culver Pictures, Inc. **Chapter 51:** Page 341, Art Resource; 343, SCALA/Art Resource; 344, Culver Pictures, Inc. **Chapter 52:** Page 347, SCALA/Art Resource; 348, The Bettmann Archive; 349, Historical Pictures Service; 350, Culver Pictures, Inc. **Chapter 53:** Page 353, SCALA/Art Resource; 354, Ciba, Ltd.; 355, SCALA/Art Resource; 356, The Bettmann Archive. **Chapter 54:** Page 359, SCALA/Art Resource; 360, Culver Pictures, Inc.; 361, Historical Pictures Service; 362, Fitzwilliam Museum, Cambridge. **Unit 13:** Pages 364-365, SCALA/Art Resource. **Chapter 55:** Page 367, SCALA/Art Resource; 368(bl), Historical Pictures Service, 368(br), Giraudon; 369, 370, The Granger Collection. **Chapter 56:** Page 373, Louis Renault/Photo Researchers; 374, Anderson/Giraudon; 375, SCALA/Art Resource; 376, Marburg/Art Reference Bureau. **Chapter 57:** Page 379, SCALA/Art Resource; 380, American Heritage; 381(tl), Culver Pictures, Inc.; 381(tr), The Bettmann Archive; 382, The Pierpont Morgan Library, New York, M. 399 f. 5v. **Chapter 58:** 385, The Granger Collection; 386, Historical Pictures Service; 387, The Bettmann Archive; 388, Giraudon. **Chapter 59:** Page 391, The Granger Collection; 394, Three Lions, Inc. **Chapter 60:** Page 397, The Granger Collection. **Chapter 61:** Page 403, The Granger Collection; 404, Historical Pictures Service; 405, The Bettmann Archive; 406, Historical Pictures Service.

Unit 14: Pages 408-409, The Granger Collection. **Chapter 62:** Page 411, The Granger Collection; 413, Hulton. **Chapter 63:** Page 417, The Granger Collection; 418, The Bettmann Archive; 419, Brown Brothers; 420, The Bettmann Archive. **Chapter 64:** Page 423, SCALA/Art Resource; 425, The Bettmann Archive; 426, SCALA/Art Resource. **Chapter 65:** Page 429, Erich Lessing/Magnum Photos; 431, 432, Culver Pictures, Inc. **Chapter 66:** Page 435, SOVFOTO; 436, Culver Pictures, Inc.; 438, The Granger Collection. **Chapter 67:** Page 441, The Granger Collection; 444, SCALA/Art Resource. **Chapter 68:** Page 447, 448, The Granger Collection; 449, Culver Pictures, Inc.; 450, The Bettmann Archive. **Chapter 69:** Page 453, SCALA/Art Resource; 454, The Granger Collection; 455, SCALA/Art Resource; 456, Charles Phelps Cushing.

Unit 15: Pages 458-459, Art Resource. **Chapter 70:** Pages 461, 463, The Granger Collection; 464, The Bettmann Archive. **Chapter 71:** Page 467, The Granger Collection; 468, 469, The Bettmann Archive; 470, The Granger Collection. **Chapter 72:** Page 473, 475, 476, The Bettmann Archive. **Chapter 73:** Page 479, The Granger Collection; 480, Harbrace Collection; 481, The Bettmann Archive; 482, The Granger Collection. **Chapter 74:** Page 485, The Granger Collection. **Chapter 75:** Page 491, R. H. Love Galleries, Chicago, Bruce C. Bachman/Rosenthal Art Slides; 493, 494, The Bettmann Archive.

Unit 16: Pages 496-497, The Granger Collection. **Chapter 76:** Page 499, The Granger Collection; 501, Culver Pictures, Inc. **Chapter 77:** Page 505, The Granger Collection; 507, Brown Brothers; 508, Culver Pictures, Inc. **Chapter 78:** Page 511, SCALA/Art Resource; 513, 514, The Bettmann Archive. **Chapter 79:** Page 517, The Granger Collection; 518, Culver Pictures, Inc.; 519, The Granger Collection; 520, Culver Pictures, Inc. **Chapter 80:** Page 523, SCALA/Art Resource; 526, SOVFOTO.

Unit 17: Pages 528-529, The Granger Collection. **Chapter 81:** Page 531, The Granger Collection; 532, The New York Public Library; 533, The Granger Collection; 534, The Bettmann Archive. **Chapter 82:** Page 537, Francis C. Mayer/Photo Researchers; 538, The Granger Collection; 539, The Bettman Archive. **Chapter 83:** Page 543, The Granger Collection; 544, The Bettmann Archive; 546, Hulton. **Chapter 84:** Page 549, Erich Lessing/Magnum Photos; 552, The Granger Collection.

Unit 18: Pages 554-555, The Granger Collection. **Chapter 85:** Page 557, Peabody Museum of Salem; 560, The Granger Collection. **Chapter 86:** Page 563, The Granger Collection; 565, Brown Brothers; 566, Historical Pictures Service. **Chapter 87:** Page 569, The Granger Collection; 571, Brown Brothers; 572, Culver Pictures, Inc. **Chapter 88:** Page 575, The Granger Collection; 577, Culver Pictures, Inc.; 578, Brown Brothers.

Unit 19: Pages 580-581, SCALA/Art Resource. **Chapter 89:** Page 583, SCALA/Art Resource; 585, St. Clair & Price Technical & Medical Photography; 586, The Granger Collection. **Chapter 90:** Pages 589, 590, The Bettmann Archive; 591, Culver Pictures, Inc.; 592(tl), (tr), The Bettmann Archive. **Chapter 91:** Page 595, The Bettmann Archive; 596, Culver Pictures, Inc.; 597, 598, The Bettmann Archive.

Unit 20: Pages 600-601, The Granger Collection. **Chapter 92:** Pages 603, 605, The Bettmann Archive; 606, The National Archive. **Chapter 93:** Page 609, Paolo Koch/Photo Researchers; 611, The Granger Collection, 612, The Bettmann Archive. **Chapter 94:** Page 615, Historical Pictures Service; 617, U.S. Signal Corps. **Chapter 95:** Page 621, SOVFOTO; 622, Brown Brothers; 623, The Bettmann Archive. **Chapter 96:** Pages 627, 629, The Bettmann Archive; 630, UPI. **Chapter 97:** Page 633, The Bettmann Archive; 634, UPI; 635, The Granger Collection; 636, The Bettmann Archive. **Chapter 98:** Page 639, The Granger Collection; 641, 642, Wide World Photos. **Chapter 99:** Page 645, Carl Frank/Photo Researchers; 646, Wide World Photos.

Unit 21: Pages 650-651, Dennis Stock/Magnum Photos.**Chapter 100:** Page 653, Erich Salomon/Magnum Photos; 654, UPI; 655, 656, The Bettmann Archive. **Chapter 101:** Page 659, John Topham/Black Star; 661, Wide World Photos; 662, The Bettmann Archive. **Chapter 102:** Page 665, The Granger Collection. **Chapter 103:** Page 671, George Holton/Photo Researchers; 673, Black Star; 674, The Granger Collection. **Chapter 104:** Page 677, Maurice Prather/Photo Researchers; 678, Wide World Photos; 679, UPI.

Unit 22: Pages 682-683, Tom McHugh/Photo Researchers. **Chapter 105:** Page 685, Bernard W. Wolff/Photo Researchers; 687, Keystone Press; 688, Globe Photos. **Chapter 106:** Page 691, Anthony Howarth/Woodfin Camp & Associates; 693, Wide World Photos; 694, Black Star. **Chapter 107:** Page 697, Bjorn Bolstad/Photo Researchers; 699, Pictorial Parade. **Chapter 108:** Page 703, Georg Gerster/Photo Researchers; 704, Ian Berry/Magnum Photos; 705, Peter Larsen/Photo Researchers; 706, Keystone Press. **Chapter 109:** Page 709, Carl Frank/Photo Researchers; 711, Pictorial Parade. **Chapter 110:** Page 715, Paolo Koch/Photo Researchers; 717, UPI/Bettmann Newsphotos; 718, Jean Gaumy/Magnum Photos. **Chapter 111:** Page 721, Wide World Photos; 723, Jan Molin/Photo Researchers.

Unit 23: Pages 726-727, G. Giansanti/Sygma Press. **Chapter 112:** Page 729, Wesley Bocxe/Photo Researchers; 720, Dan Budnick/ Woodfin Camp & Associates; 731, NASA; 732, Jean Louis Atlan/Sygma Press; 733, Dennis Brack/Black Star; 734, Herman J. Kokojan/Black Star. **Chapter 113:** Page 737, J. P. Laffont/Sygma Press; 738, Sygma Press; 739, Claus Meyer/Black Star. **Chapter 114:** Page 743, Allen Green/Photo Researchers; 744, Jean Louis Atlan/Sygma Press; 745, James Nachtwey/Magnum; 746, Sygma Press. **Chapter 115:** Page 749, Henry Bureau/Sygma Press; 750, C. Wiedenthal/Sygma Press; 751, Peter Turnley/Black Star; 753, J. Langevin/Sygma Press; 754, Peter Turnley/Black Star. **Chapter 116:** Page 757, Robin Moyer/Black Star; 758, A. Tannenbaum/Sygma Press; 759, Henry Bureau/Sygma Press; 760, Richard Hoffman/ Sygma Press; 761, Patrice Franceschi/Sygma Press; 762, A. Tannenbaum/Sygma Press. **Chapter 117:** Page 765, J. P. Laffont/Sygma Press; 66, Arthur Grace/Sygma Press; 767, 769, J. P. Laffont/Sygma Press; 770, Sygma Press.

Unit 24: Pages 772-773, NASA. **Chapter 118:** Page 775, The Museum of Modern Art; 776, Bob Burch/Bruce Coleman, Inc.; 777, Ted Rozumalski/Black Star; 778, The Granger Collection. **Chapter 119:** Page 781, Bill Foley/Woodfin Camp & Associates; 782, John Moss/Photo Researchers; 783, W. Curtsinger/Photo Researchers; 784, NASA. **Chapter 120:** Page 787, Tadanori Saito/Photo Researchers; 788, Lily Solmssen/Photo Researchers; 789, Mike Yamashita/Woodfin Camp & Associates; 790, Rudi Meisel/Woodfin Camp & Associates; 791, Guy LeQuerrec/Magnum Photos; 792, Anne LaBastille/Photo Researchers.